Street by Str

SHEFFIELD

BARNSLEY, CHESTERFIELD, DONCASTER, ROTHERHAM

Bolsover, Chapeltown, Conisbrough, Dronfield, Maltby, Mexborough, Penistone, Royston, Stocksbridge, Thurnscoe, Wombwell

3rd edition December 2007
© Automobile Association Developments Limited
2007

Original edition printed May 2001

 This product includes
map data licensed from
Ordnance Survey® with
the permission of the Controller of Her Majesty's
Stationery Office. © Crown copyright 2007.
All rights reserved. Licence number 100021153.

Published by AA Publishing (a trading name of
Automobile Association Developments Limited, whose
registered office is Fanum House, Basing View,
Basingstoke, Hampshire RG21 4EA. Registered
number 1878835).

Produced by the Mapping Services Department
of The Automobile Association. (A03558)

A CIP Catalogue record for this book is available from
the British Library.

Printed by Oriental Press in Dubai

Ref: ML072y

Key to map pages — ii-iii

Key to map symbols — iv-1

Enlarged map pages — 2-11

Main map pages — 12-197

Index – towns & villages — 198

Index – streets — 199-235

Index – featured places — 236-240

Acknowledgements — 241

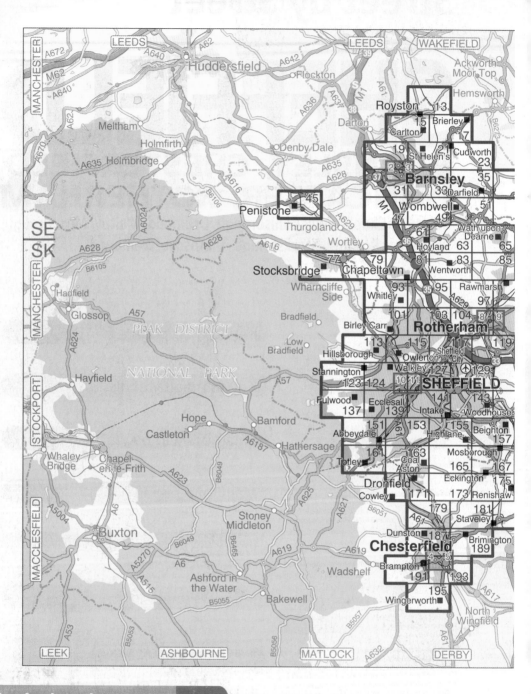

Scale of enlarged map pages 1:10,000 6.3 inches to 1 mile

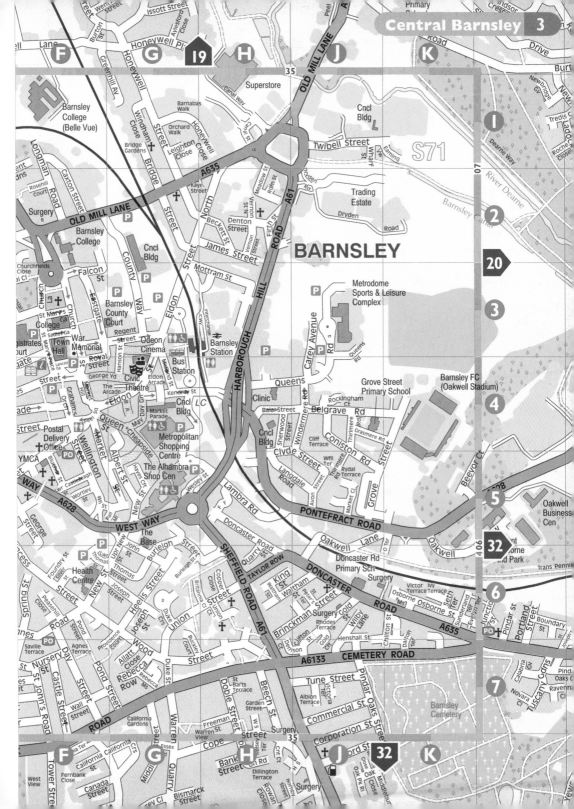

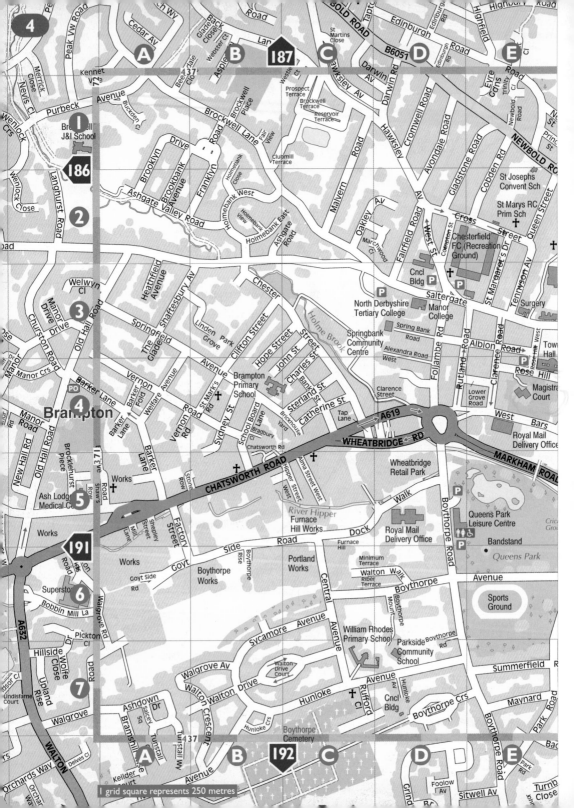

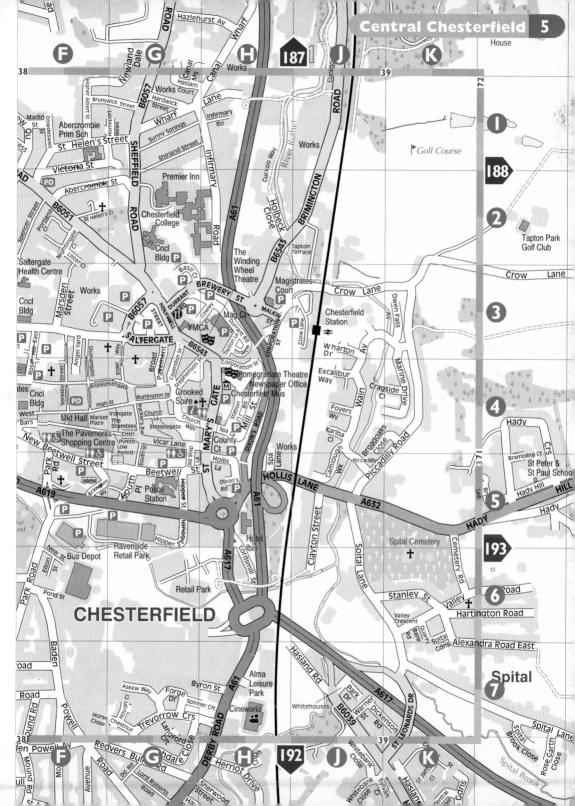

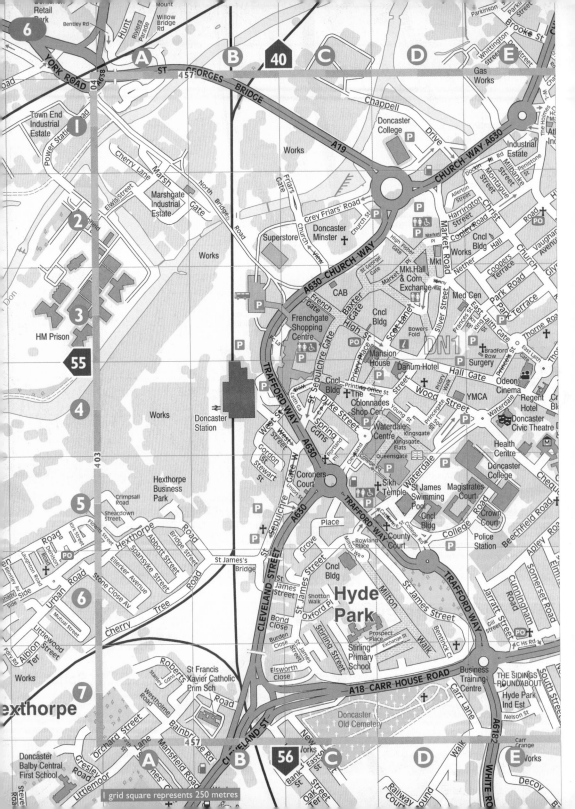

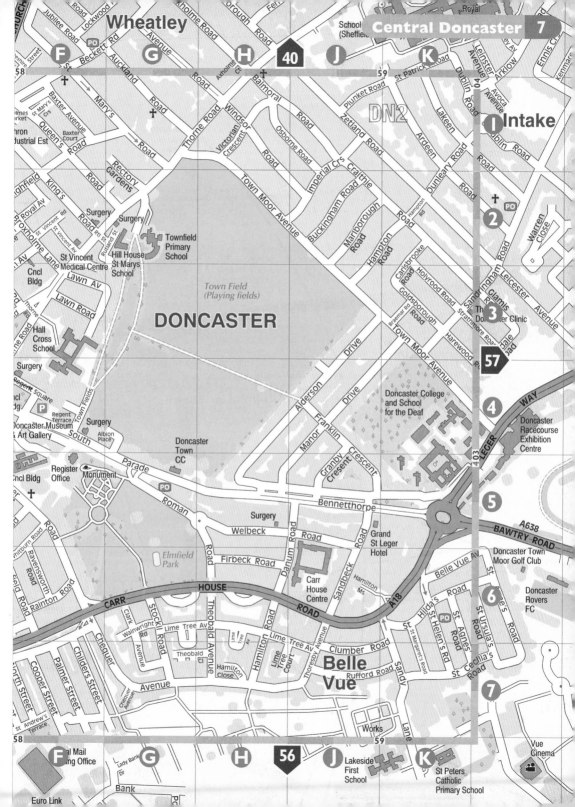

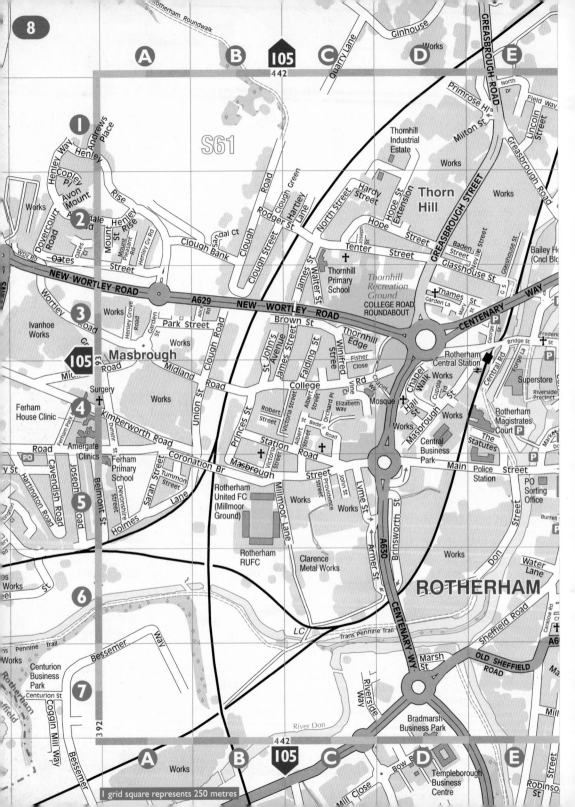

Grid reference labels (top): A B 105 442 C D E

Grid row labels (left): 1 2 3 105 4 5 6 7

Grid reference labels (bottom): A B 105 442 C D E

Map place names and labels:

Rotherham Roundwalk
Ginhouse
Quarry Lane
Works
GREASBROUGH ROAD
North Dr
Primrose Hl
Field Way
Lincoln Street
S61
Thornhill Industrial Estate
Milton St
Greasbrough Road
Works
Andrews Place
Henley Way
Copley Pl
Avon Mount
Rise
Henley Rise
Clough Road
Clough Green
Hartley Lane
Rodger St
North Street
Hardy Street
Hope St Extension
Thorn Hill
Works
Baden Street
Neville Street
Glasshouse St
Bailey Ho (Cncl Blc)
Works
Dovercourt Road
Mount St
Henley
Mount Pleasant Rd
Henley Gv Rd
Clough Bank
Sadal Ct
Clough Street
James St
Walter St
Tenter Street
Hope Street
Glasshouse St
Thames St
Garden La
Mary St
G S
Glasshouse St
Way Rd
Oates Street
NEW WORTLEY ROAD
A629 NEW WORTLEY ROAD
Thornhill Primary School
Thornhill Recreation Ground
COLLEGE ROAD ROUNDABOUT
CENTENARY WAY
P
Wortley Road
Works
Henley Grove Road
Park Street
Garden St
Alice Rd
Brown St
St John's Avenue
James Street
Falding St
Winifred Street
Thornhill Edge
Fisher Close
Vine Rd
Chapel Walk
Rotherham Central Station
George St
Bridge St
St
Frederic
Ivanhoe Works
Masbrough
105
Michael Road
Surgery
Midland Road
Clough Road
Union Street
College
Robert Street
Victoria Street
Albert St
St Bede's
Orchard Pl
Elizabeth Way
Mosque
Hall St
Masbrough
Works
Cupola
Central Rd
Superstore
Riverside Precinct
Ferham House Clinic
Ferham Park
Kimberworth Road
Works
Princes St
Station Road
Victoria St
Albert St
Providence Street
John St
Lyme St
Central Business Park
Rotherham Magistrates Court
The Statutes
Market
PO
P
Road
PO
Cavendish Road
Joseph Road
Belmont St
Amergate Clinics
Dunsil
Ferham Primary School
Devonshire Street
Sarah Street
Tummon Street
Coronation Br
Masbrough
Street
Main Street
Police Station
PO Sorting Office
Burrell
P
Hartington Road
Holmes Lane
Rotherham United FC (Millmoor Ground)
Millmoor Lane
Providence Street
Works
Brinsworth St
Armer St
Works
Don Street
Water Lane
A6
Rotherham RUFC
Clarence Metal Works
A630
Works
ROTHERHAM
Sheffield Road
Cantlow Rd
Works
Pennine Trail
Bessemer Way
LC
Trans Pennine Trail
CENTENARY WY
Marsh St
OLD SHEFFIELD ROAD
Mi
Works
Centurion Business Park
Centurion St
Coggin Mill Way
Bessemer Way
Riverside Way
Bradmarsh Business Park
Rotherham
Sheffield
392
River Don
Works
Bow
Mill Close
Templeborough Business Centre
Robinson St
Street

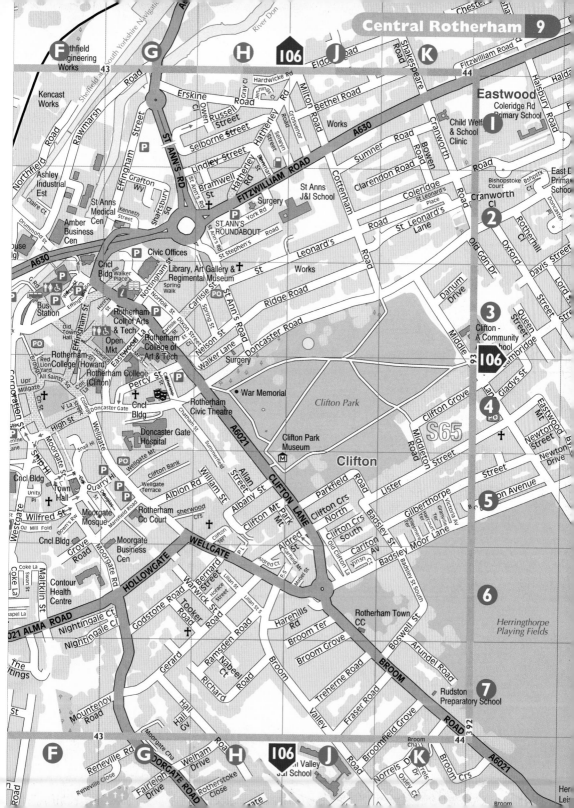

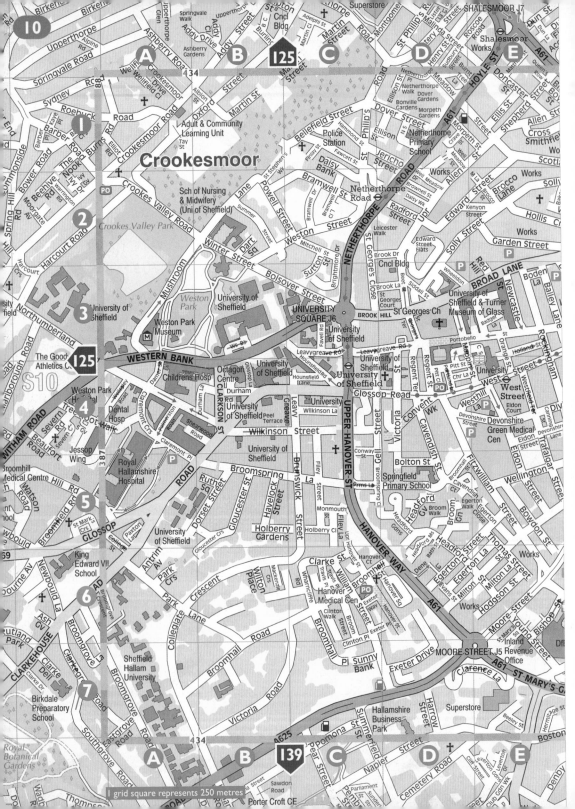

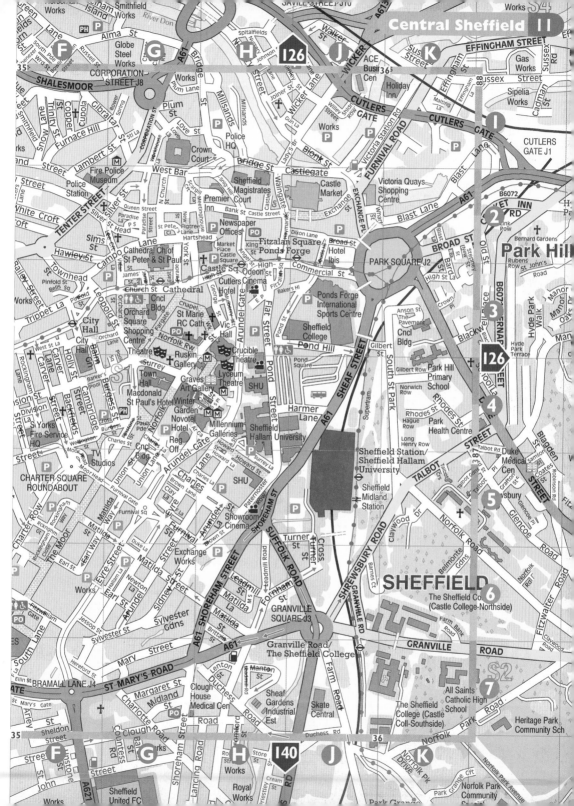

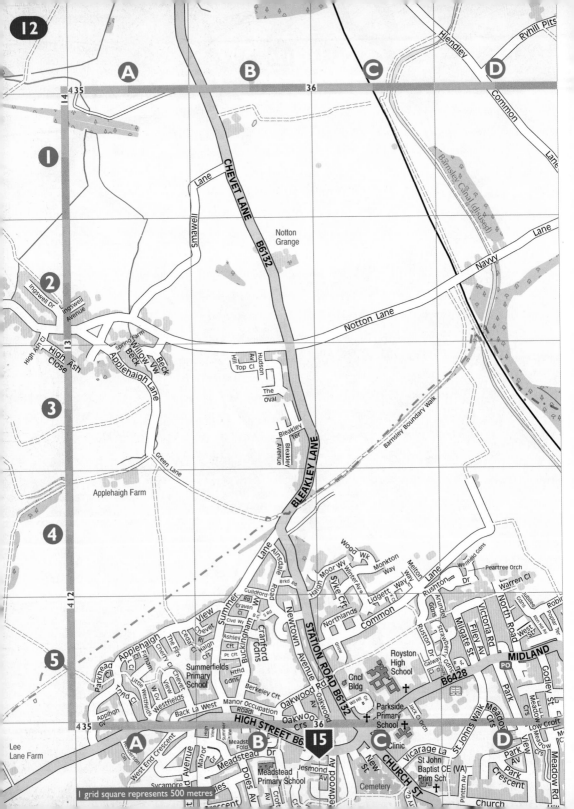

12

A   B   C   D

435   14   36

1

Ryhill Pits

Hiendley

Common

Lane

Barnsley Canal (disused)

CHEVET LANE

Smawell Lane

B6132

Notton Grange

2

Ingswell Dr

Ingswell Avenue

Spring Farm

Willow Vw

Beck

Beck

Applehaigh Lane

High Ash Cl

High Ash Close

13

Notton Lane

Navvy Lane

3

Hill Top Cl

Av

Hudson

The Oval

Bleakley Ter

Bleakley Avenue

BLEAKLEY LANE

Barnsley Boundary Walk

Green Lane

Applehaigh Farm

4

412

Wood Wk

Monkton Way

Winter Av

Peartree Orch

Warren Cl

Melton Lane

Rushton Dr

Wentwell Gdns

Lane

Ainscale Road

Brkd Rd

Haigh Moor Wy

Syke Cft

Lidgett Way

Newtown Avenue

STATION ROAD B6132

Common

Rushton Dr

Arundel Gdns

Strawberry Gdns

Victoria Rd

North Road

Filey Av

Millgate St

West Rd

Godley St

Park Av

Robin

Summer View

Guildford Rd

Craven Cl

Clvd Wy

Ashley Cft

Pt Cft

Cranford Gdns

S Rd

Buckingham

Northlands

Ornsw

Galway Gdns

Jack Cl Orch

B6428

Jubilee

Poplar Ter

MIDLAND

PO

5

Parkhead Cl

Applehaigh

The Firs

Cedar Cl

Cherry Tree

Chevet View

Hfld Gdns

Berkeley Cft

Oakwood

Oakwood Crs

Cncl Bldg

Royston High School

Will Hill

Parkside Primary School

St Johns Walk

Meadow

Park View

Low Croft

Applhgh Gv

Little Westfields

W Cv

Westfields

Summerfields Primary School

Back La West

Manor Occupation Road

Oakwood

HIGH STREET B6

36

15

Clinic

Vicarage La

St John Baptist CE (VA) Prim Sch

Park Crescent

Meadow

Lane Farm

Lee

West End Crescent

Riders La

Manor

Avenue

Meadstead Dr

Meadst Fold

Doles Av

Meadstead Primary School

Jesmond Av

Fedwood Av

CHURCH ST

New St

Cemetery

Pinfth Av

Sycamore

Church

A   B   C   D

1 grid square represents 500 metres

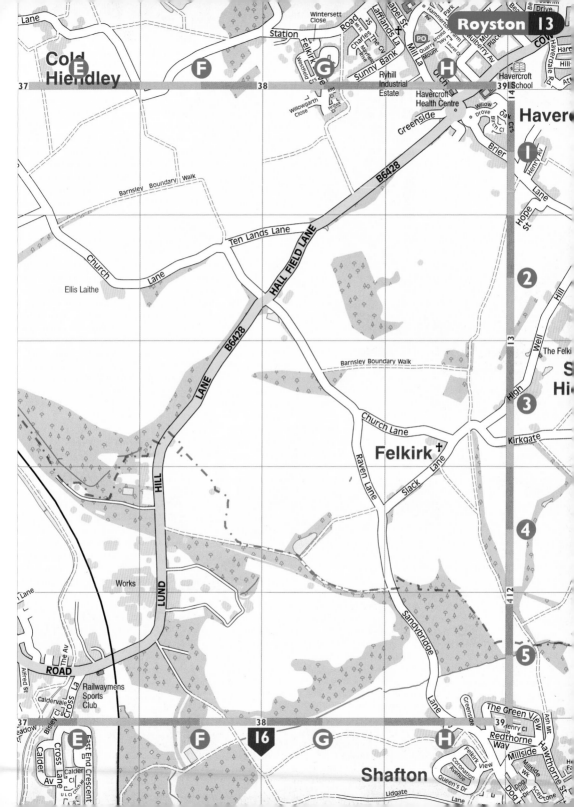

A B C D

I

433 Spring 34

Warren Lane BARNSLEY Notton Park

Barnsley Wakefield

Lee Lane Farm

Golf Course

Limes Close LANE

Bourne Walk The Balk Limes Avenue Fairway Avenue Surgery LEE

2 Common Bourne Ct Barnsley Municipal Golf Club B6428 Wood Lane

Moorland Thorne End Rd Oaklea Cl Orchard Cl New Rd SHAW LA Paddock La Hortles La Park VW Rd Paddock Road Wood Pk VW Wood PK VW Greenset View Grnbn

Road New Rd GREENSIDE B6428 Hall Gv Elliston Av WAKEFIELD ROAD Hill Top AV Warsop Rd Wilford Road Stoney C Ms Crr Thr Rd Royd N Rvds Wood

George St Zion Dr Green Side AV Wood

3 Wellgate Prim School Grnsd Crr St School Mapplewell Prim Sch Raven Royd Beeston Sq N Rvds

Wellgate Crossgate **Staincross** Athersley North Primary School **Athersley**

TOWNGATE PO 10K LA Park Cl Hope St Wentworth Pike Lowe Grove Wollaton Cl Clifton Sheerien Cl Newstead Rd Laxton Road Ollerton Radcliffe Lindl

Mapplewell Health Cen Salcombe BLACKER ROAD Cloverlands Drive Pike Lowe Cloudberry Way Eastfield Crs Eastfield Close Lindhurst Rd Bramcote Forest Rd Forest Road Mansfield Rd

4 Malincroft Mapplewell Drive Beaulieu Bl W Carron Dr Edward Street Wentworth Crs Maple Industrial Estate Wentworth Ms Works Clifton Av Str Rd Upr Bellbank Wy Arnold Avenue Sutton Av

Carr Green Lane Spey Cl Tay Cl Spey Close BAR LANE B6131 WAKEFIELD ROAD Wakefield Road Shortfield Laithes Crs High Croft Dr LAIT

5 Road Hill End **Blacker Hill** **New Lodge** Kirkstall Road K Cl H Cl Icrnc Beverley Rd Langsett Rd Wensley Rd New Carlton Bl Pl Sherburn Wakefield Rd PO Newland Rd B6132 Regent Park AV Wakefield Rd Richard Newman Primary School Athersley S Prim Sch

Standhill Elland Mrdc Pl Ldg Grsbenby Rd Mston Crescent Crescent Stanton Wo

River Dear

A B **19** C D

409 433 34

1 grid square represents 500 metres

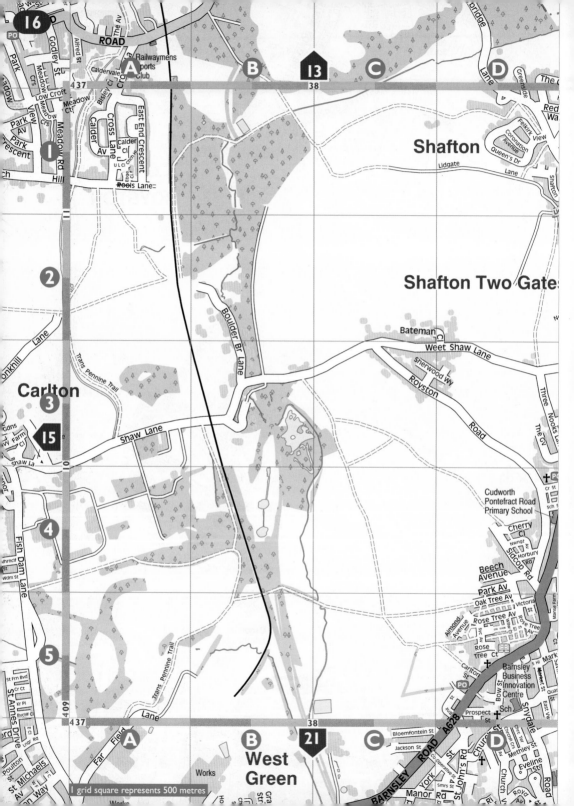

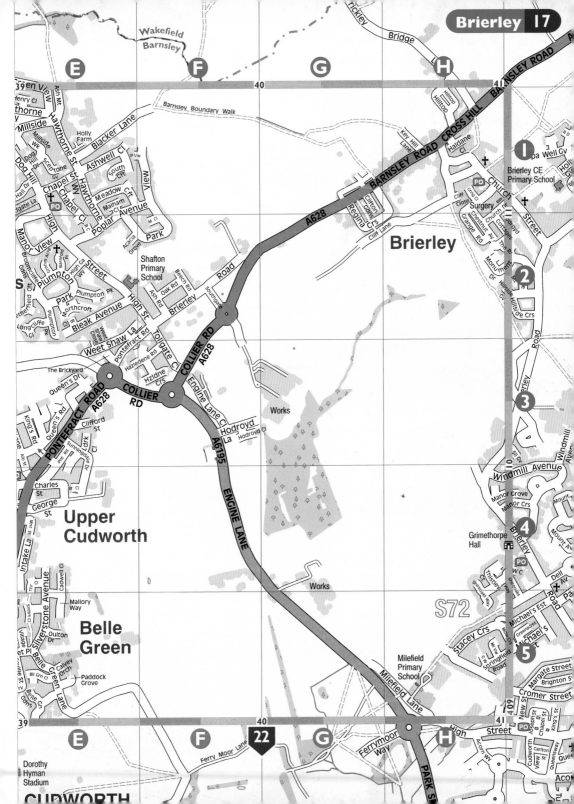

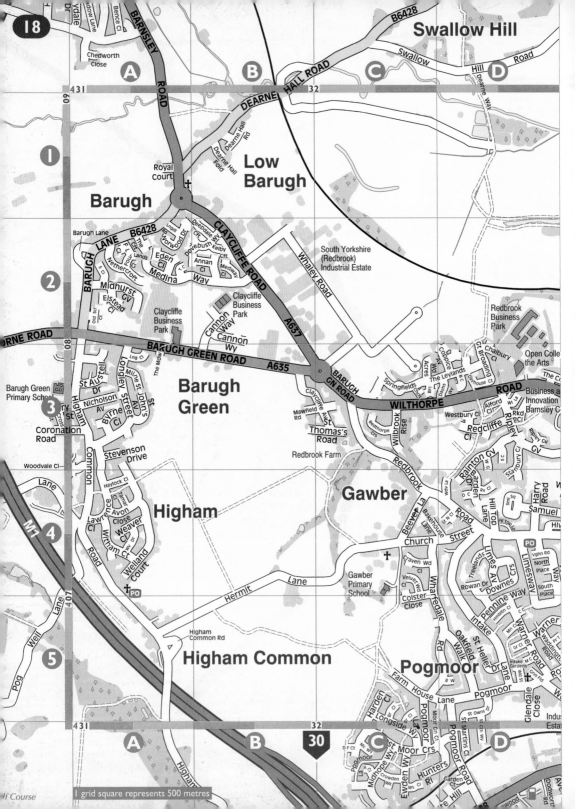

18

Swallow Hill

B6428

Swallow Hill Road

Dearne Way

DEARNE HALL ROAD

431 32

Barnsley Road

Dearne Hall Rd

Dearne Hall Fold

Royal Court

Low Barugh

Barugh

Barugh Lane

B6428

CLAYCLIFFE ROAD

Whaley Road

South Yorkshire (Redbrook) Industrial Estate

Redbrook Business Park

Open College the Arts

Deepdale Cl

Ingot

Norwood Dr

Dovebush

Kelby

Eden Cl

Annan Cl

Medway

Medina

Way

Nethercroft

Midhurst Cv

Elstead Cl

Claycliffe Business Park

Claycliffe Business Park

Cannon Way

Cannon Wy

A657

BARUGH GREEN ROAD

A635

BARUGH GN ROAD

WILTHORPE ROAD

Business a Innovation Barnsley C

The Mdw

Lng Cl

St Austell Dr

Longley Street

St John's Av

St Cross

Higham

Nicholson Av

Byrne Cl

Mawfield Rd

Claycliffe

St Thomas's Road

Springfields

Ct Acres

Copple

Ct Broading

Chalbury Ct

The Leylands

Westbury Cl

Redcliffe Cl

Alford Cl

Ripley

Ripley Gv

DRNE ROAD

Barugh Green Primary School

Coronation Road

Stevenson Drive

Barugh Green

Woodvale Cl

Lane

Common

Haylock Cl

Lawrence Cl

Tarnall

Avon Close

Weaver Cl

Witham Ct

Welland Court

Higham

Redbrook Farm

Redbrook

Gawber

Beevor La

Bakehouse Lane

Church Street

Bainton Gv

Garden Ho

Stanbury Cl

Hill Top

Samuel

Harry Road

M1

Road

PO

Craven Wd Cl

Velvet Wd

Colster Close

Wharfedale Rd

Gawber Primary School

Treelands

Rowan Dr

Limes Av

Downes

Pennine Way

Limesway

Vghn Rd

North Place

South Place

PO

Well Lane

Pog

Hermit Lane

Higham Common Rd

Higham Common

Pogmoor

Intake Lane

St Helier Dr

Oakfield Walk

Warner Road

Waddington

Farm House Lane

Harden Cl

Longside Cl

Pogmoor

Pogmoor

Glendale Close

Indus Estat

431 32 **30**

Hunters Ri

St Martins Cl

Pogmoor Road

1 grid square represents 500 metres

If Course

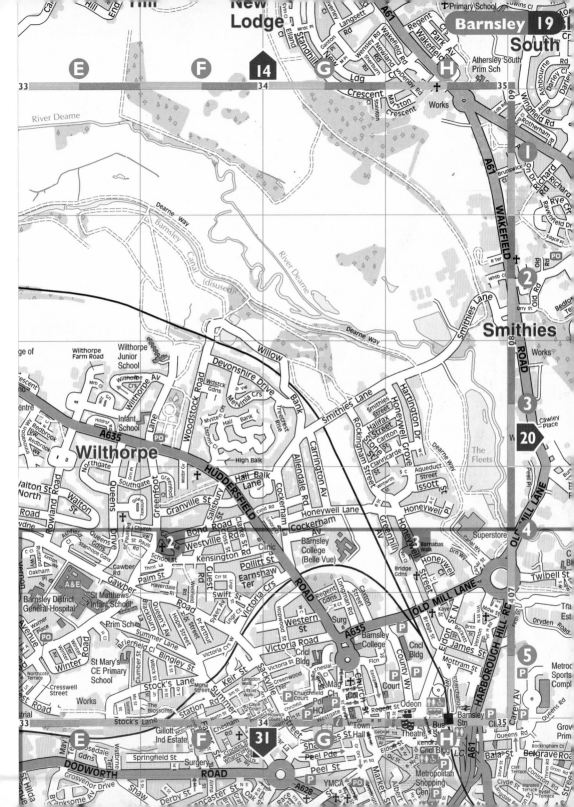

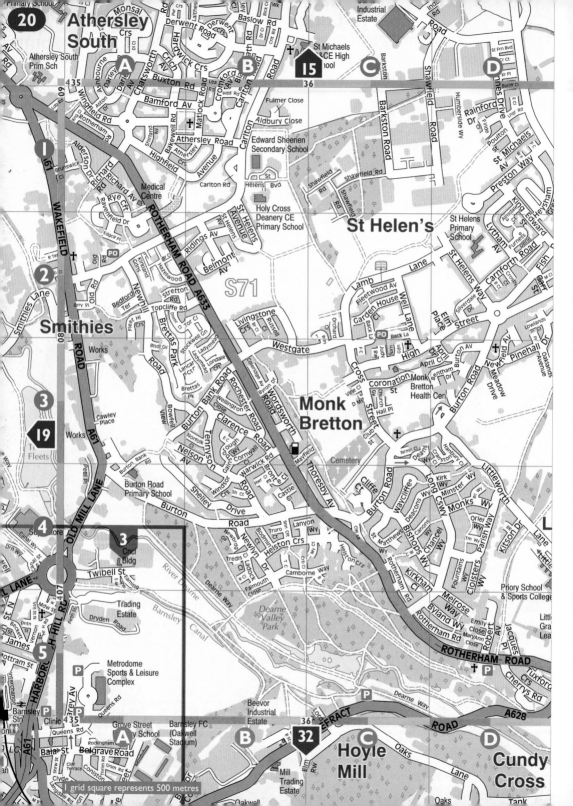

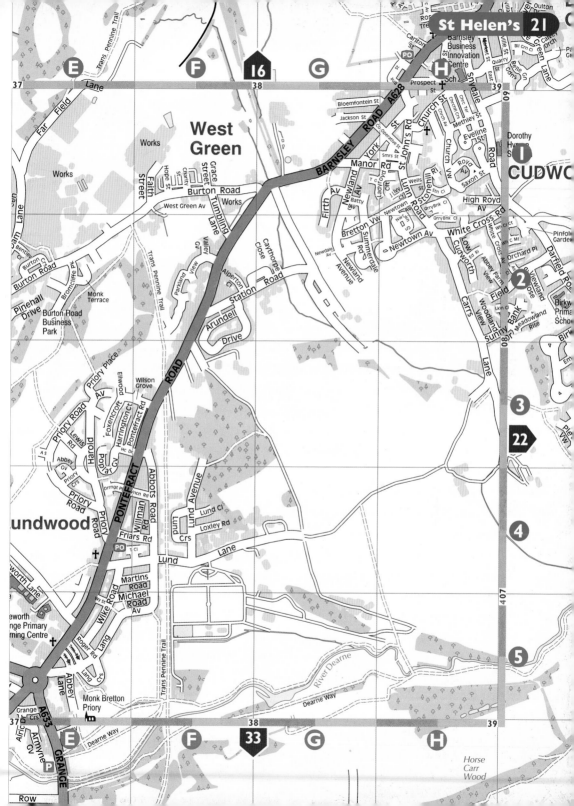

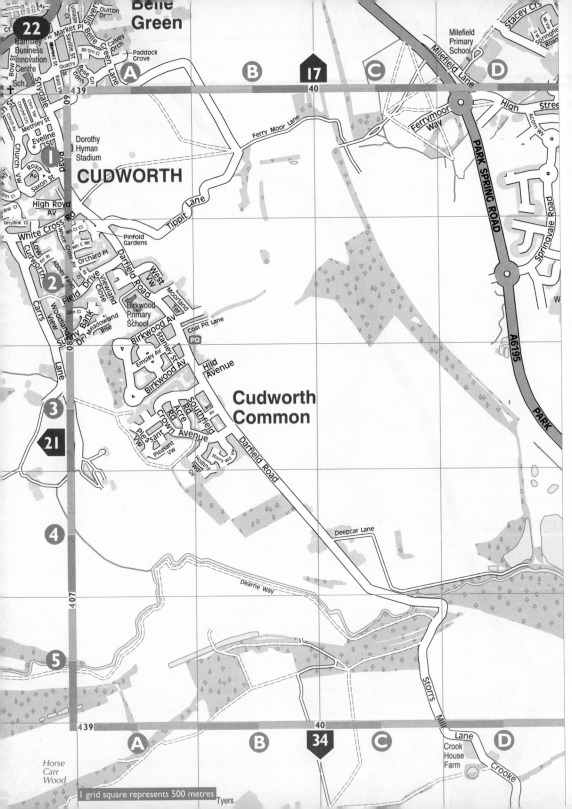

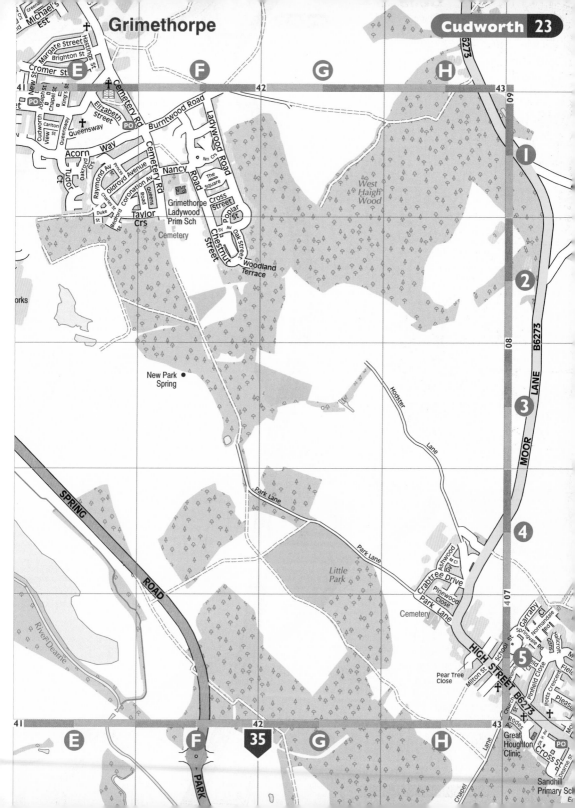

Michael's Est

Greenside
Margate Street
Brighton St
Hastings St
Cromer St
New St

E **F** **G** **H**

41 42 43 60

Joseph St
King's
Chapel St

Cemetery Rd
Burntwood Road
Ladywood Road

Cudworth View
Carlton
Elizabeth street
Queensway
Acorn Way

Charles St
Raymond Av
Prince's
Oldroyd Avenue
Coronation Av
Queens

Rupert
Oakroyd
Nancy
The Square
Nn Crs

Taylor Crs
Bedford St
Duke St

Grimethorpe Ladywood Prim Sch
Cross Street
Poplar St

West Haigh Wood

1

Cemetery

Chestnut Street

Oak Street
Sy Av

Woodland Terrace

2

08

New Park Spring •

B6273

Hooster

3

Lane

...orks

River Dearne

SPRING

ROAD

Park Lane

Park Lane

Little Park

4

Crabtree Drive

Ashwood
M Cl

Park Lane

Pinewood Close

Cemetery

407

Garraby

Normandale

School St

Springvale Rd

Hallcroft

Field

5

Potts Crescent

Pinfield Close

Pear Tree Close

Milton St

HIGH STREET B6273

Rodes Av

Pleas...

Church Lane

E **F** **35** **G** **H**

41 42 43

PARK

Chapel Lane

Great Houghton Clinic

Cross St

PO

Sandhill Primary Sch

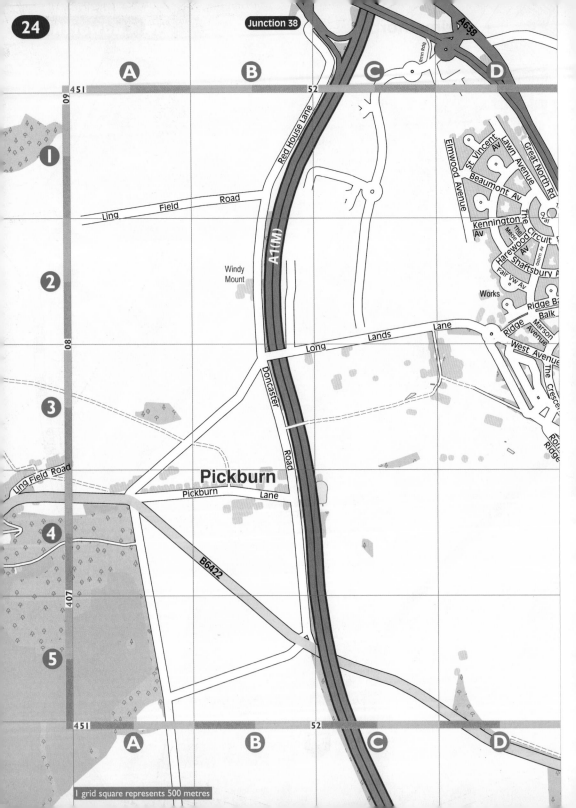

Works

Cemetery

E

F

G

H

53

54

B1220

CHURCH LANE

James Road

Victoria Road

Edward Road

John Street

Alexandra Road

Hangthwaite Road

Holmeroyd Road

55

60

I

Adwick Lane

House

Kingfisher Rd

Kingfisher Close

Kestrel Dr

Osprey Cl

Merlin Cl

Falcon Cl

Whinfell Close

Mill Lane

Fernbank School

Fern Bank

Bosworth Road

Ashburton Close

Cambourne Cl

Drive

Fern Lane

Village Street

Council Bldg

Clarks Ct

Frm Ct

Adwick Station

Lutterworth

Lynden Av

Kingsley Road

Cranleigh Gdns

LP

Shelley Rise

Cheriton Avenue

Balk

Swinburne Avenue

Tenter

Park Way

ADWICK LE STREET

North Doncaster Technology College

PO

Town Hall

Park View

2

80

Washington Road

Grosvenor Road

Wmll Ct

A638

GREAT

Lawn Avenue

Balk Lane

Harrold

Crescent

NORTH

The

Green Lane

Central Avenue

Quarry Lane

Chadwick Rd

Edwin Road

Woodside Rd

Woodlands Primary School

Surgery

WC

Adwick Park Junior School

Balk

Caxton Rd

Windmill

Cemetery

Cemetery Road

Villa Road

Woodlands

Princess

RC Rd

PO

Stafford Street

Staffard Road

Adwick Washington Infant School

Adwick Leisure Centre

B1220 DONCASTER

Road

Second Avenue

First Avenue

Third Av

Welfare

Fourth Avenue

Fifth Avenue

Tudor Rd

Grange Rd

Grange Rd

St Joseph & St Teresas Catholic Primary School

3

26

LANE

ROAD

North Road

Lake Rd

Doncr La

Adwick Grange

Hangthwaite Lane

4

407

5

Langthwaite

Lane

GREAT NORTH ROAD YORK RD A638

Coppice Road

Market Street

Ridge Road

Highfields Primary School

South Street

PO

Highfields

E

F

38

G

H

53

54

55

Long Edge L

Langthwaite Rd

DN5

fields

Tower La

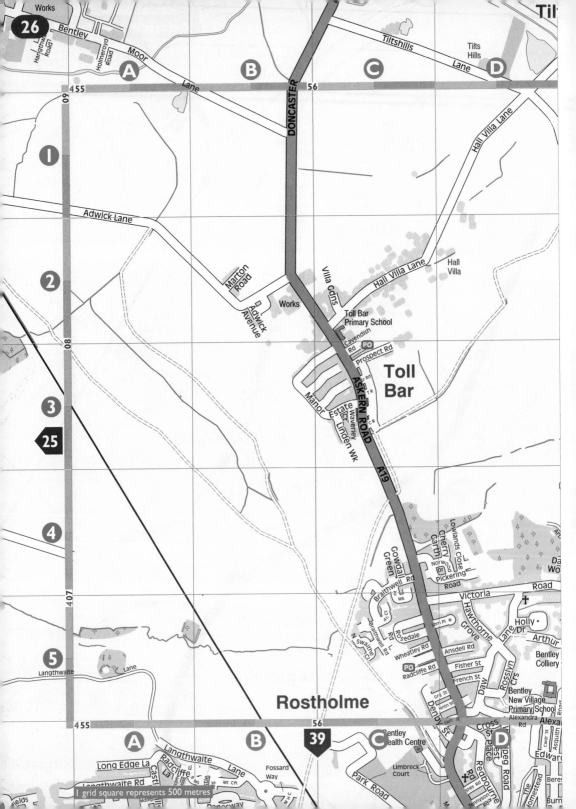

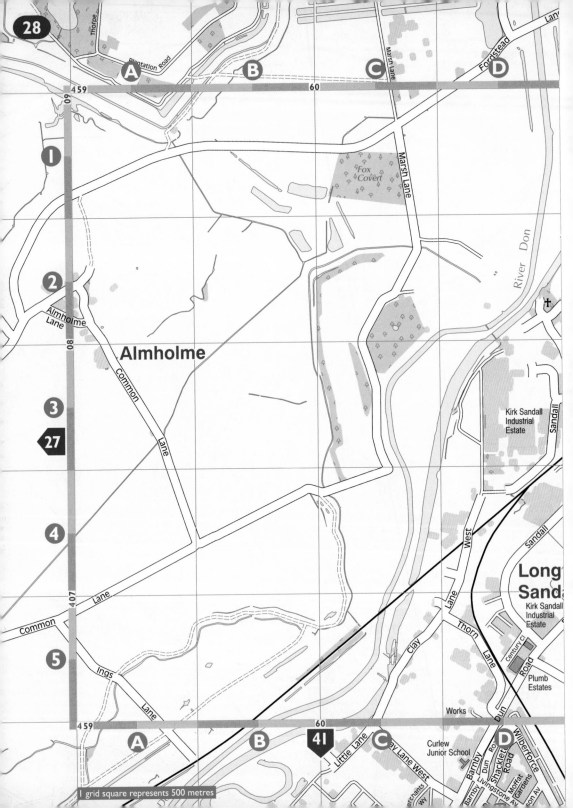

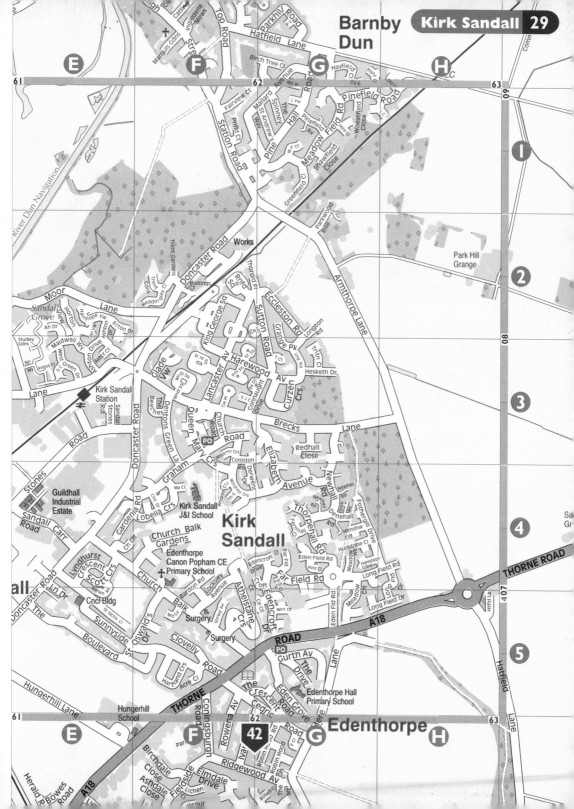

Edenthorpe

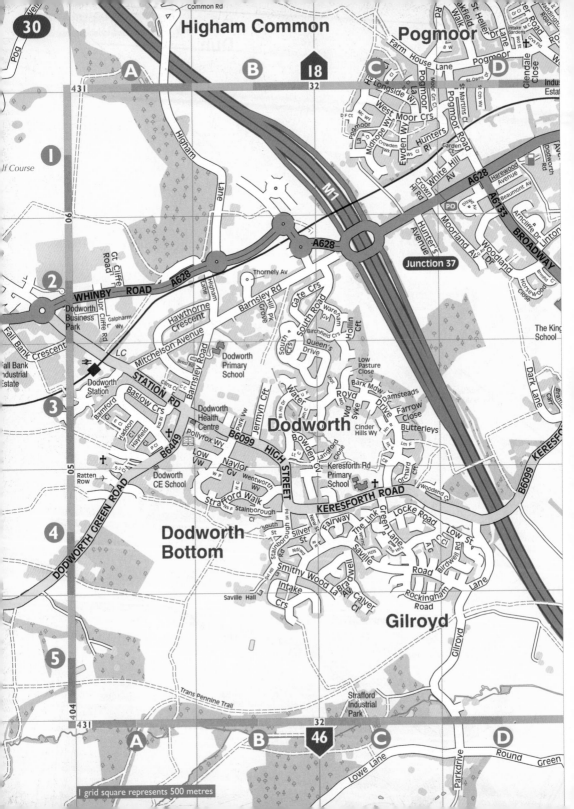

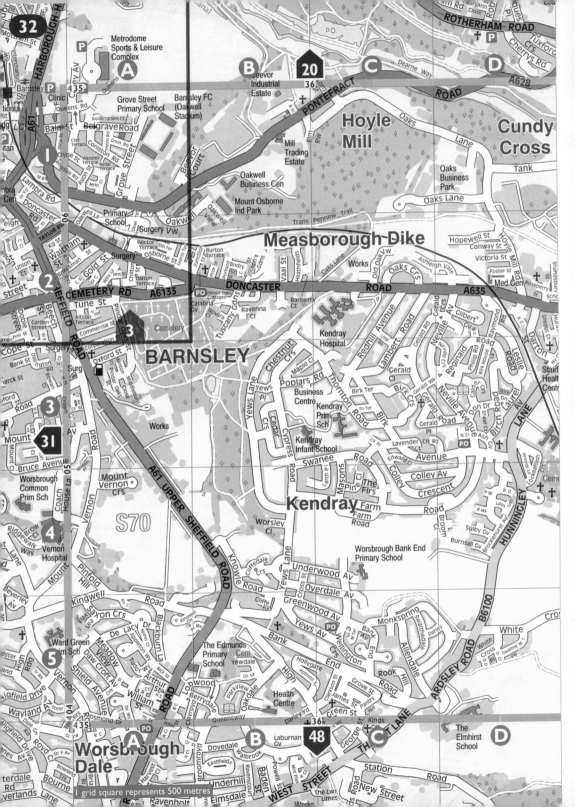

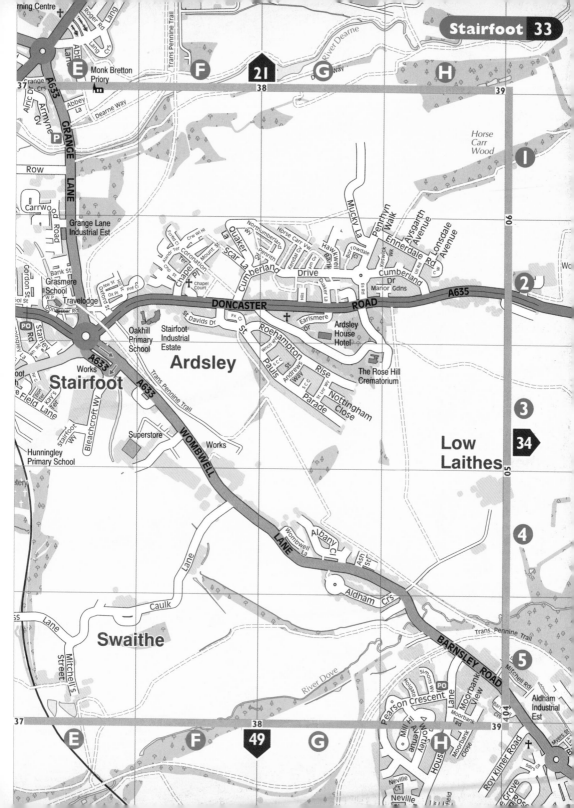

E Monk Bretton Priory

F

21

G

H

I

2

3

34

4

5

E

F

49

G

H

Horse Carr Wood

Abbey La
Dearne Way
Grange Crs
A633

GRANGE LANE
Armyne Gv
Abbey La
Row
Carrwood
Grange Lane Industrial Est

Bank St
Grasmere School
Travelodge
Doncaster Rd
Gordon St

PO
Stanley Rd
Works
A633
Stairfoot
Field Lane
A633
Bleachcroft Wy
Stairfoot Wy
Hunningley Primary School

Oakhill Primary School
Stairfoot Industrial Estate

St Davids Dr

Quaker La
Scar La
Cumberland
Chapel
Chapel Court
Coronation Ter
Mount St

Northumberland
Penrith
Horse Carr Vw
Kendal Gv
Hawkwell Bank
Mucky La
Keswick
Crowdale
Penrhyn Walk
Ennerdale
Aysgarth Avenue
Lonsdale Avenue

Cumberland Dr
Manor Gdns

DONCASTER   **ROAD**   A635

Earismere Dr
Roehampton
Paul
Andrews Way
Rise
Nottingham Close
Parade

Ardsley House Hotel

The Rose Hill Crematorium

Ardsley

Superstore
Works

Low Laithes

Trans Pennine Trail

WOMBWELL

LANE

Albany Cl
Wombwell La
Ash St
Aldham Crs

Lane

Caulk

Lane

Mitchell's Street

Swaithe

River Dove

BARNSLEY ROAD
Trans Pennine Trail

Mitchell Rd
Aldham Industrial Est

PO
Pearson Crescent
Holgate
Simons Wy
Lane
Moorbank View
Moorbank Rd
Moorbank Close
Mill Hill
Wortley Avenue
HOUSE
Roy Kilner Road

Neville Ct
Neville
Grove Ro

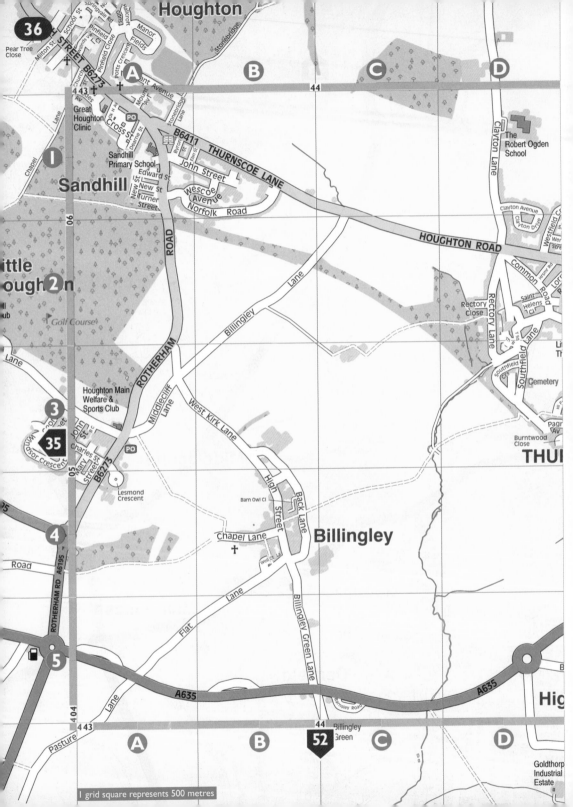

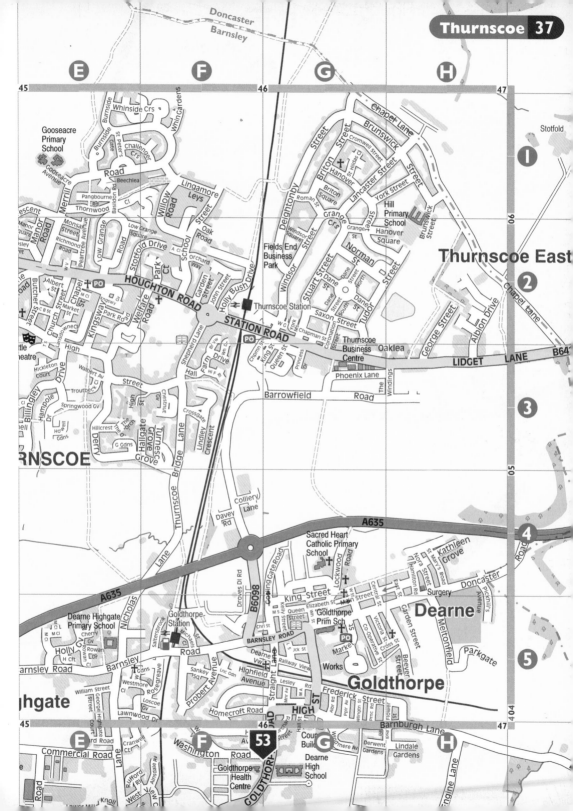

E   F   G   H

Doncaster
Barnsley

Stotfold

1

Gooseacre
Primary
School

Whinside Crs
Whinside Crs

Whingardens

Burnside
Burnside

St Peter's
Gate

Challenger
Crs

Road

Beechlea

Merrill

Gooseacre
Avenue

Lingamore
Leys

Chapel Lane

Brunswick
Street

Briton
Street

Hanover
Street

Cromwell Street

Lancaster Street

York Street

Brunswick
Street

Street

Pangbourne
Rd

Thornwood

Basildon Rd

Willow

Road

Oak
Road

Briton
Square

Roman St

Grange
Crs

Hill
Primary
School

Hanover
Square

Thurnscoe East

Chapel Lane

2

Manor
Road

Butcher Street

Crescent

Monsaal
Street

Richmond

Low Grange
Square

Stotfold Drive

School
Way

Orchard
Way

Windsor
Square

Delginton Dy

Windsor
Street

Stuart Street

Grange
St

St Hildas
Street

Norman
St

Dane
St

Lane

George Street

Albion Drive

HOUGHTON ROAD

Albert
St

PO

Welfare
Road

Park
Ct

Garden
Street

John Street

Holly Bush Drive

STATION ROAD

Thurnscoe Station

W G

Dane
North

Tudor

Saxon Street

Dane
South

Coronation

LIDGET   LANE   B64

Chapel
St

Market
St

Kingsway

Park Road

Shepherd Lane

Farm

Drive

PO

Chapman St

King St

York

Queen St

Princess St

Thurnscoe
Business
Centre

Oaklea

Phoenix Lane

The
Windings

3

Castle
heatre

Hickleton
Court

High

Lansdowne

Hambole
Dr

Troutbeck

Springwood Gv

Derry

High
Street

Chestnut

Hall

Hillcrest

The
Croft

G Gdns

Hallgate

Thurnscoe

Bridge

Lane

Lindley
Crescent

Crossgate

Turnesca
Grove

Barrowfield   Road

RNSCOE

Colliery
Lane

Davey
Rd

A635

Sacred Heart
Catholic Primary
School

Lockwood
Road

Kathleen
Grove

Nora Road

St Mary's Road

Hamilton Rd

Doncaster

4

A635

Nicholas

Droves Dl Rd

B6098

Gooling Gate Road

Saltersbrook

King Street

Queen
Street

Elizabeth St

Central St

East St

Surgery

Meltonfield

Parkgate

5

Dearne Highgate
Primary School

Holly

Cherry
Gv

Rowan
Cdr

Barnsley

Road

Goldthorpe
Station

Michaels

BARNSLEY ROAD

Chri St

M S

Kelly
Street

Goldthorpe
Prim Sch

PO

Market

Co-operative

Victoria St

Cross St

Garden Street

Beever
Street

Dearne

rnsley Road

Westmore

Rosegreave

William Street

George
Street

Loscoe
Gv

Lawnwood Dr

Sankey
sq

Probert Avenue

Highfield
Avenue

Dearne

Lnc Gdn

Railway View

Lesley
Rd

HIGH ST

Works

Frederick   Street

Albr Rd

Pplr Av

Wingtn St

Flower St

Goldthorpe

Barnburgh Lane

hgate

Commercial Road

Washington   Road

53

GOLDTHORPE ROAD

Goldthorpe
Health Centre

Cour
Buil

G

Dearne
High School

Derwent
Gardens

Lindale
Gardens

H

Engine Lane

45   46   47

E   F   G   H

06

05

04

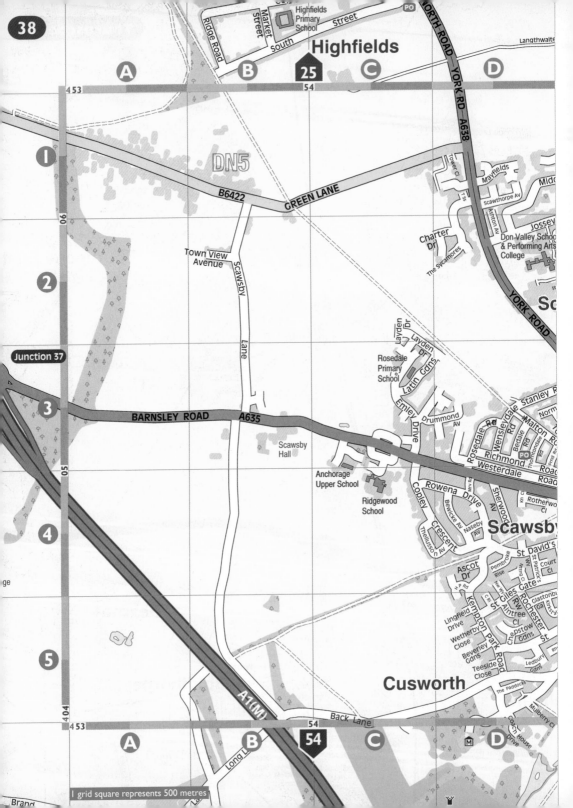

Highfields

Highfields Primary School

Ridge Road

Market Street

South Street

PO

NORTH ROAD

YORK RD A638

Langthwaite

A

B

25

C

D

4 53

54

90

DN5

B6422

GREEN LANE

Tower Cl

Mayfields

Scawthorpe Av

Ashton Av

Jossey

Middle

York Road

So

Town View Avenue

Charter Dr

Don Valley School & Performing Arts College

The Sycamores

Scawsby

1

2

Layden Dr

Layden Dr

Latin Gdns

Rosedale Primary School

Emley Drive

Stanley R

Norm

Junction 37

05

3

BARNSLEY ROAD A635

Lane

Drummond Av

Rosedale Rd

Wensleydale Rd

Bedale Rd

Malton Rd

Richmond

PO

Thorntondale Rd

Fend Rd

Scawsby Hall

Anchorage Upper School

Ridgewood School

Copley

Rowena Drive

Crescent

Bewicke Av

Naseby Av

Westerdale Road

Sherwood Av

Rotherwo Cl

Scawsb

4

Thellusson Av

St David's

Ascot Dr

Pembroke Rise

St Giles Gate

St Patrick's

Court Cl

Rochester

Glastonbu

M P Rd

Lingfield Drive

Wetherby Close

Kempton Park Road

St Patrick's RW

Aintree Cl

Chepstow Gdns

St

5

Beverley Gdns

Teeside Close

Ledbury Gdns

Mulberry Cl

The Paddocks

404

Cusworth

Back Lane

Coach House Drive

A1(M)

Long L

4 53

A

B

54

C

M

D

Brand

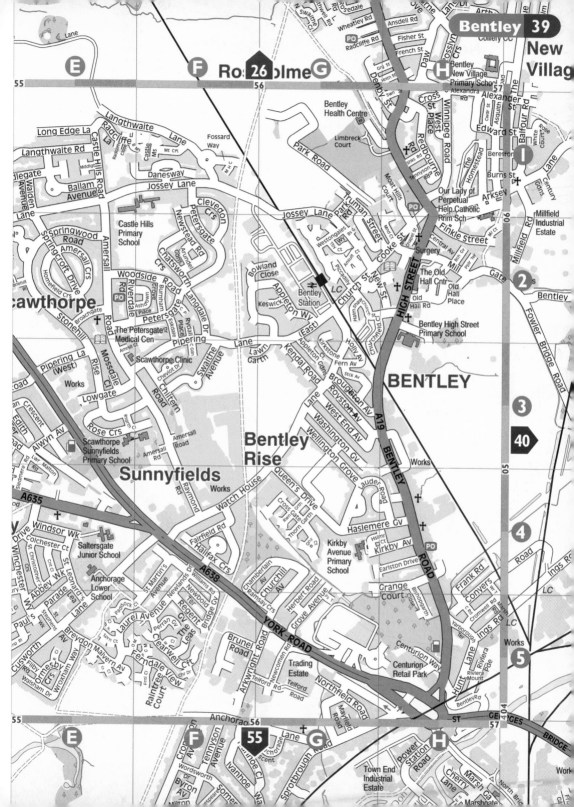

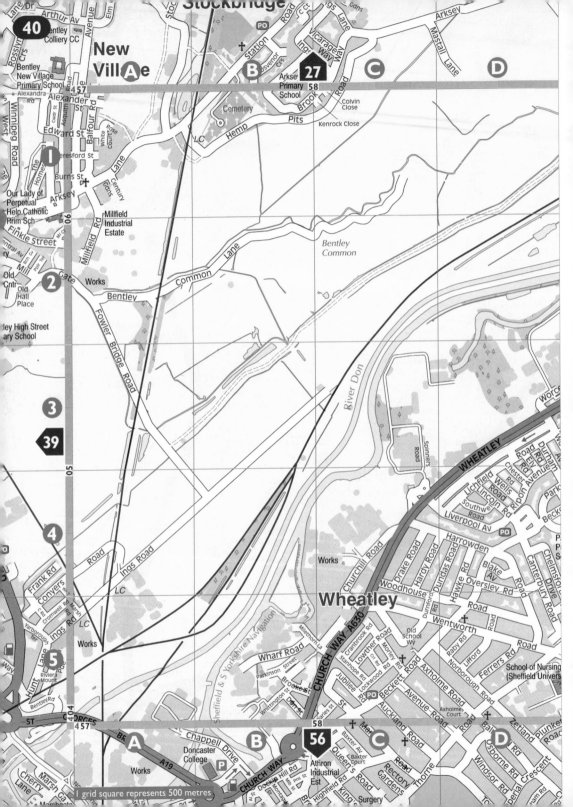

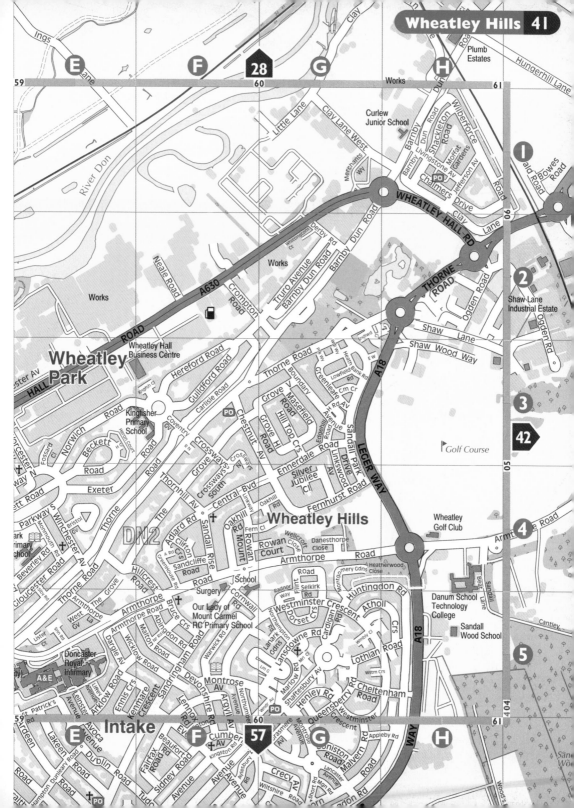

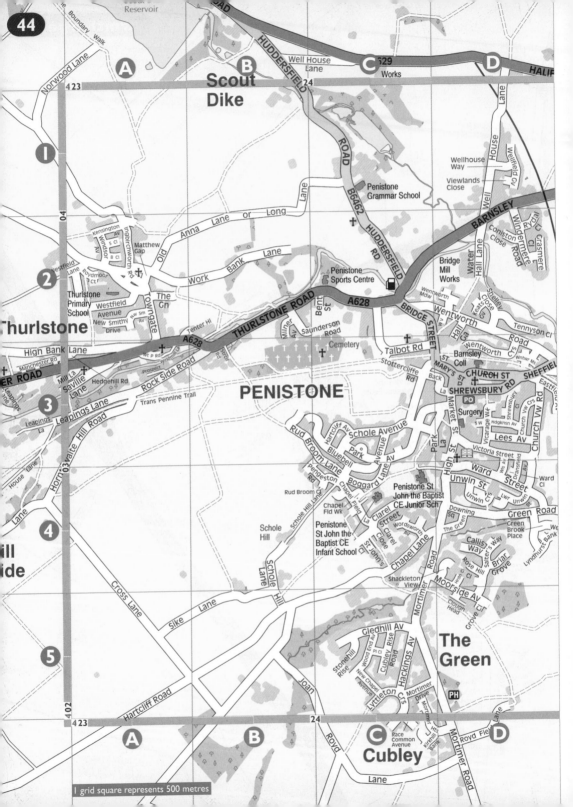

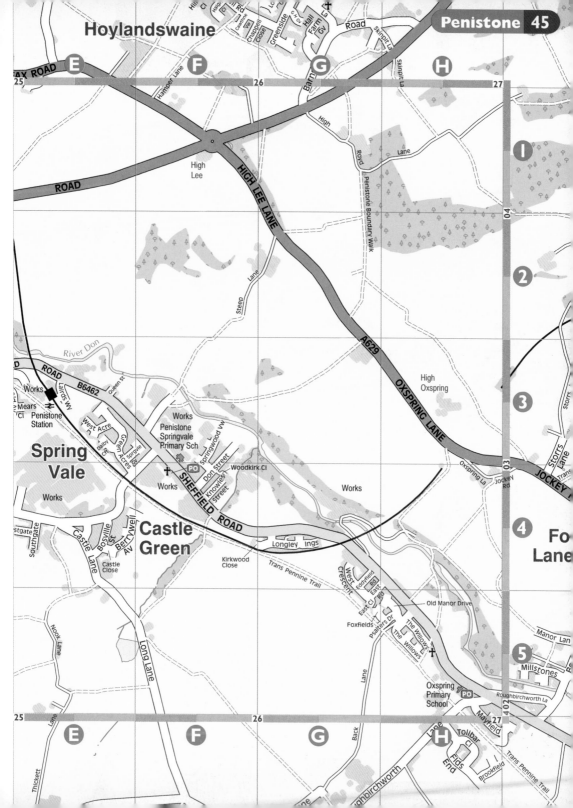

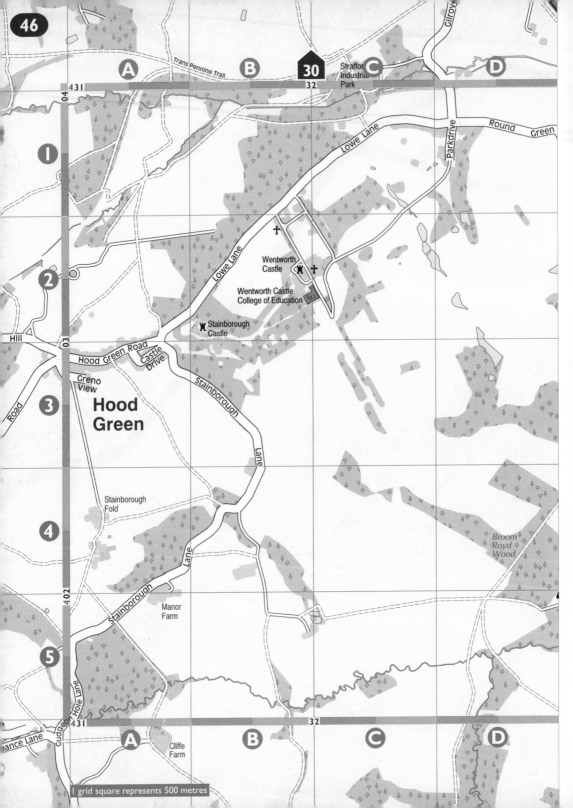

46

431
04
32

Straffor
Industrial
Park

Lowe Lane

Parkdrive

Round   Green

Gilroy

I

Lowe Lane

Wentworth
Castle

Wentworth Castle
College of Education

2

Hill

03

Stainborough
Castle

Hood Green Road

Castle
Drive

Greno
View

**Hood
Green**

Stainborough

Road

3

Lane

Stainborough
Fold

4

402

Lane

Broom
Royd
Wood

Stainborough

Manor
Farm

5

Gudgeon Hole Lane

431

ance Lane

32

Cliffe
Farm

I grid square represents 500 metres

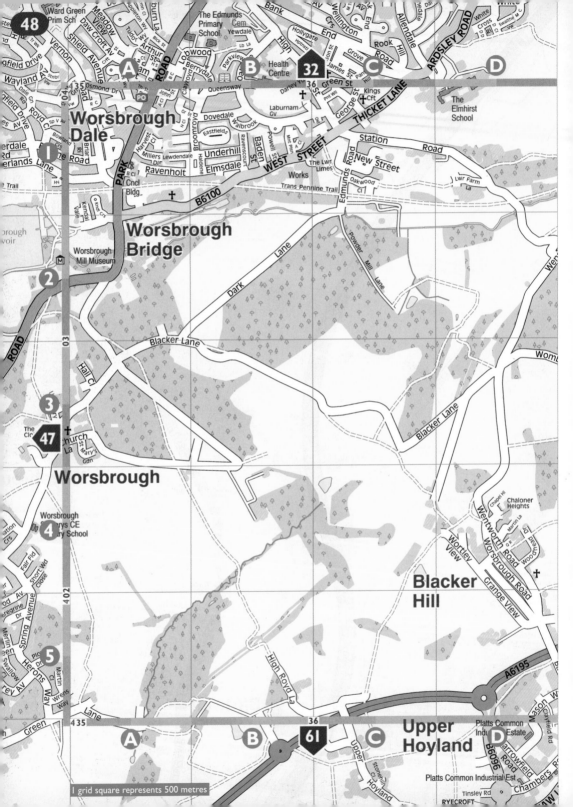

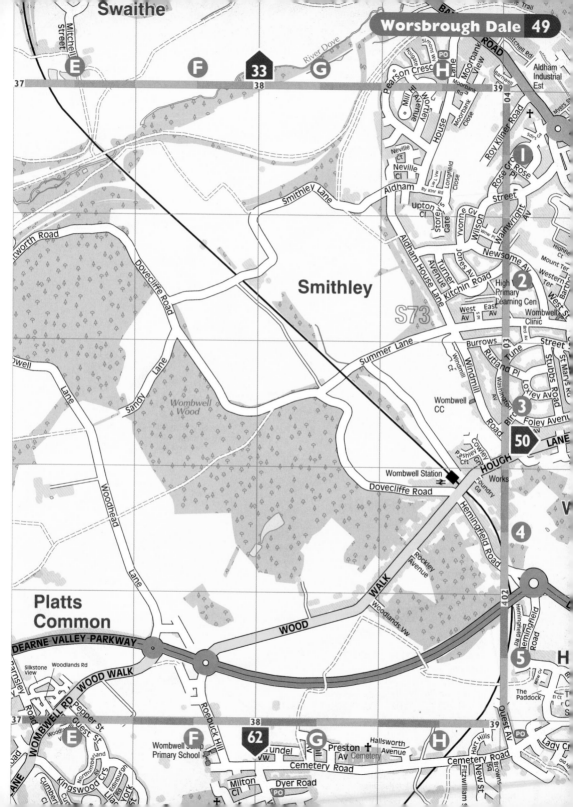

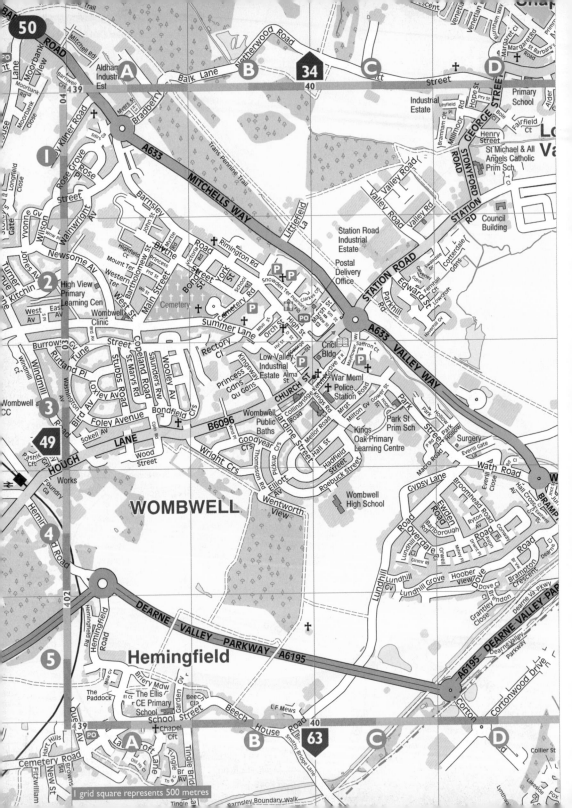

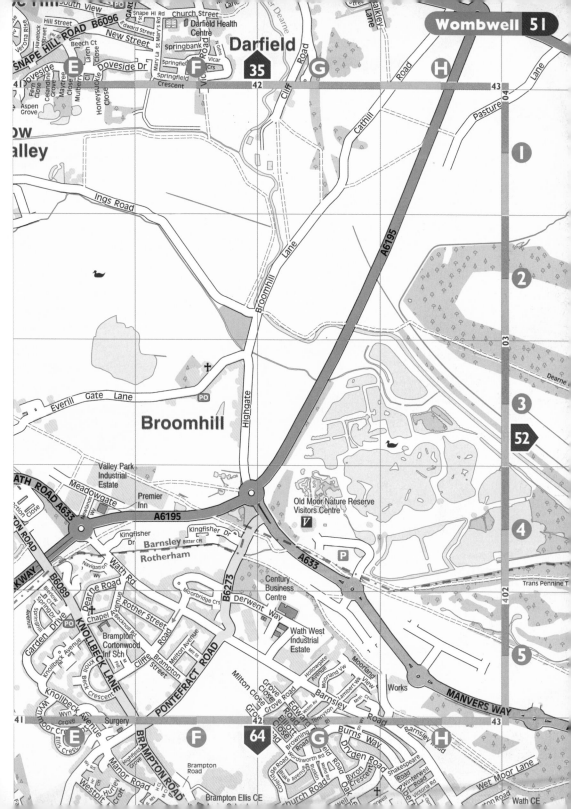

Darfield 35

Broomhill

Old Moor Nature Reserve
Visitors Centre

Barnsley
Rotherham

Valley Park
Industrial
Estate

Premier
Inn

Century
Business
Centre

Wath West
Industrial
Estate

Works

MANVERS WAY

A6195

A633

52

64

E   F   G   H

I
2
3
4
5

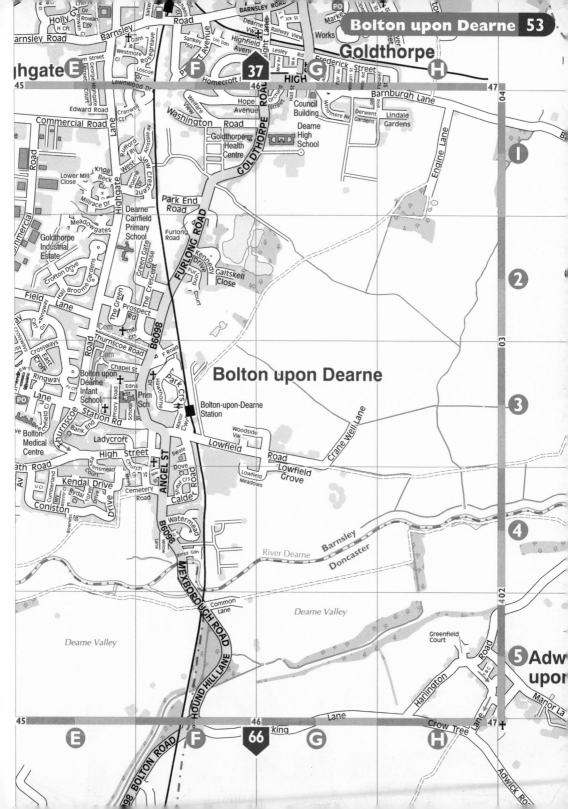

Goldthorpe

Bolton upon Dearne

Dearne Valley

Dearne Valley

River Dearne

Barnsley
Doncaster

GOLDTHORPE ROAD

FURLONG ROAD

B6098

MEXBOROUGH ROAD

HOUND HILL LANE

BOLTON ROAD

Barnburgh Lane

Engine Lane

Crane Well Lane

ANGEL ST

HIGH

Goldthorpe
Health
Centre

Dearne
High
School

Council
Building

Dearne
Carrfield
Primary
School

Goldthorpe
Industrial
Estate

Bolton upon
Dearne
Infant
School

Bolton
Medical
Centre

Bolton-upon-Dearne
Station

E   F   37   G   H

I

2

3

4

5 Adw
upon

E   F   66   G   H

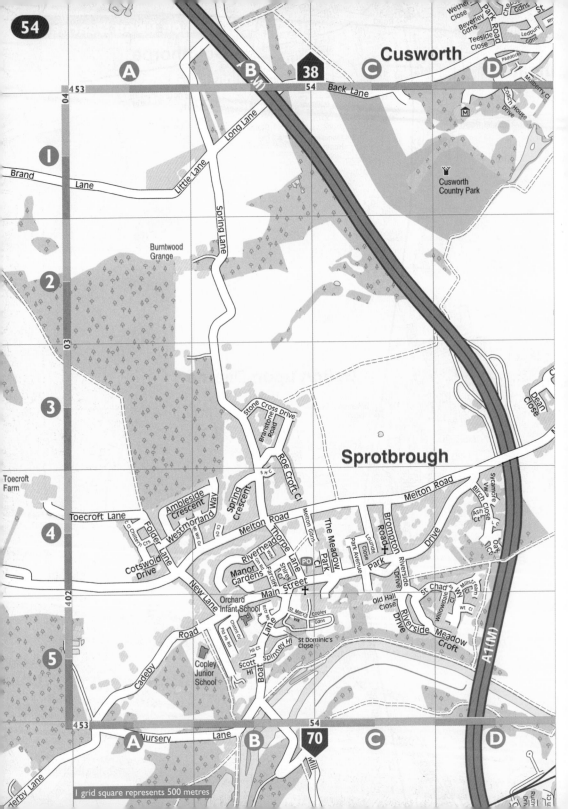

Centurion
Retail Park

Riviera
Mount

Trading
Estate

Telford
Road

Newcomen
Rd

Northfield Road

Brunel
Road

Anchorage Lane

55 56

Anchorage Lane

Crompton Avenue

Tennyson Avenue

Ivanhoe Cl.

Ivanhoe Way

Sprotbrough Road

Wordsworth

Byron
Av

Milton
Av

Kingsley
Av

Shakespeare Av

Somersby Ave

Marlborough Av

Richmond Hill

Mill Hill
Close

Melling Av

Allendale
Gdns

Ashbourne
Gdns

Allendale Road

Montagu Rd

Newton Drive

Newton La

Sprotbrough Road

Cromwell
Drive

Valiant
Gdns

Crusader
Dr

Challenger Drive

Richmond Hill
Primary School

Sprotbrough
Health Centre

Clifton
Drive

Hills Cl.

Castle
Close

Ingle
Grove

Ingleborough Drive

Melton

Ings

Newton
Business Centre

Newton

Town End
Industrial
Estate

River Don

Power
Station
Road

Northfield Road

HM Prison

River Don

Cherry
Lane

Marsh Ga

Marshgate
Industrial
Estate

North Bridge Road

Works

Superst

Doncaster
Station

Hextho
Busine
Park

Coroners
Court

ST GEORGES BRIDGE

TRAFFORD

Wo

I

2 P P P

3 P

56

CLEVELAND STREET

St Sepulchre Gate West

Westerr

Stewart

Burden

Elswort

Works

6

Works

Crimpsall
Road
sheardown
street

Hexthorpe Road

Abbott St

Spansyke St

Ellerker Av

Cherry Tree Road

Roberts Road

Hexthorpe

Eden
Grove

Ramsden Road

Side

Urban
Road

Works

Mutual St

Albion Ter

PO

Works

Travis
Gdns

Shady
Side

Salisbury Rd

Nicholson Rd

Windle Rd

Scarrd Rd

Gladstone Rd

Barnstone St

Langer
St

Glen

Field Av

Hawfield Cl

Bramworth Rd

Dell
Crs

Hexthorpe
Primary
School

Greenfield

River Don

Doncaster
Balby Central
First School

Works

Orchard St

Cresley

St James' Gdns

Mansfield Rd

Littlemoor
Lane

4

Francis Xavier
rimary School

Holly

Westfield Rd

Victoria Rd

Chcl Bldg

Ivor Gv

Evanston
Gdns

Florence Av

St John's Rd

Albany Rd

Alexandra Rd

Earlesmere Av

Lane

Harvest Cl

Burns Wy

Carr Hill

Lister Av

Clarence

Scarth Av

Carr View

Kg Edward Av

PO

Rose Av

Burton Avenue

Sylvester Av

Belmont Av

Queen

St Catherine's Av

Works

Works

5

Church
Cottage

St Peter's
Rd

Waver
La

Anelay Rd

Smith
Sq

Smith St

Dixon Crs

71

Thomson Avenue

West
Av

Sycamore Hall
Preparatory School

A630 HIGH ROAD

Low Sn

BALBY ROAD

A650

Coronation
Rd

Cross
Bank

Lambeth Rd

Balby

Oswin

Furnival

Horse Shoe Ct

E **F** **G** **H**

39 **E** **F** **G** **H**

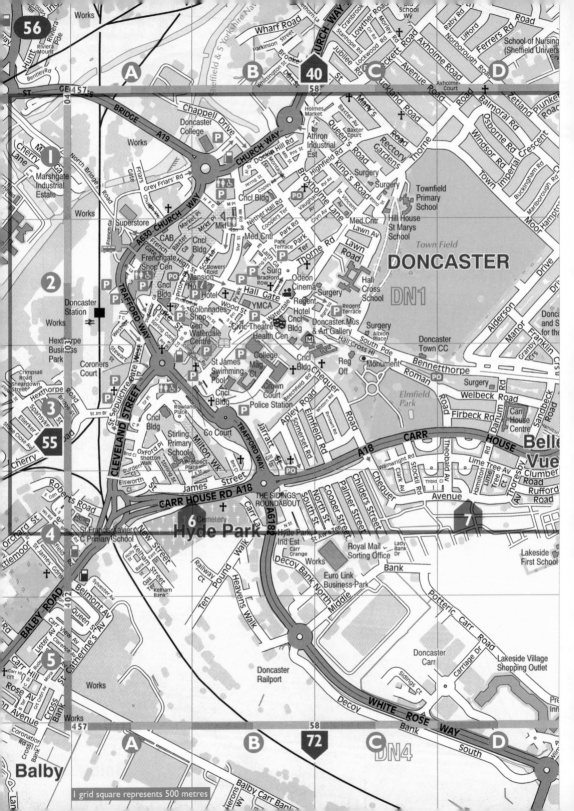

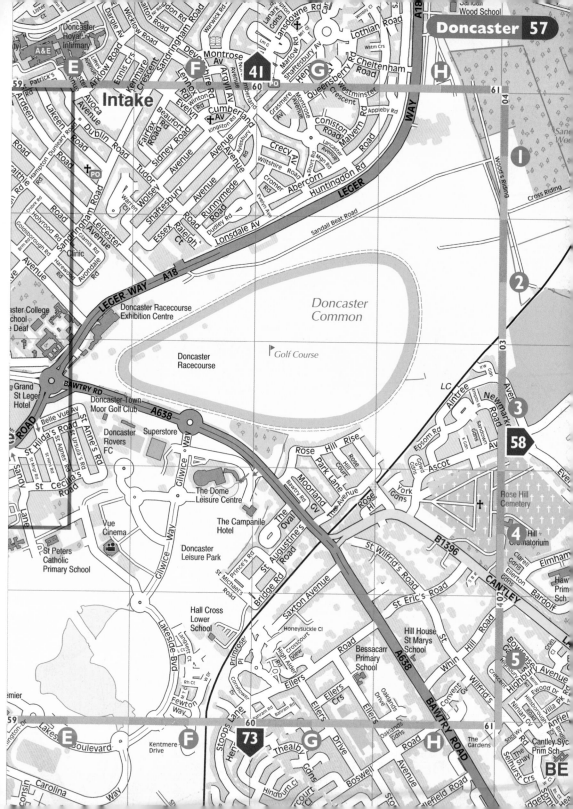

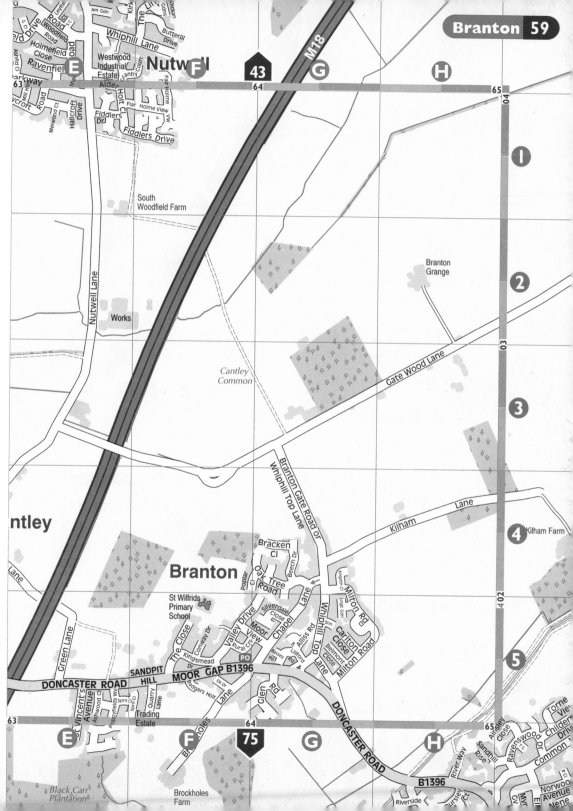

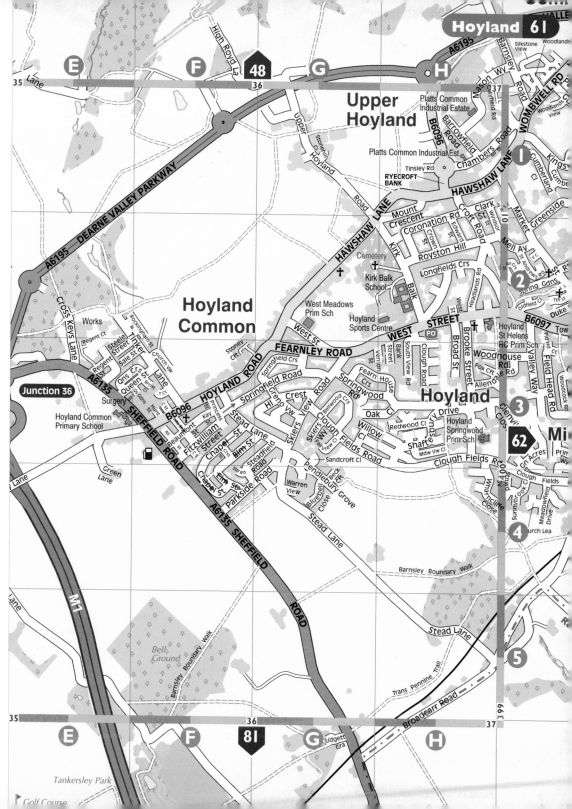

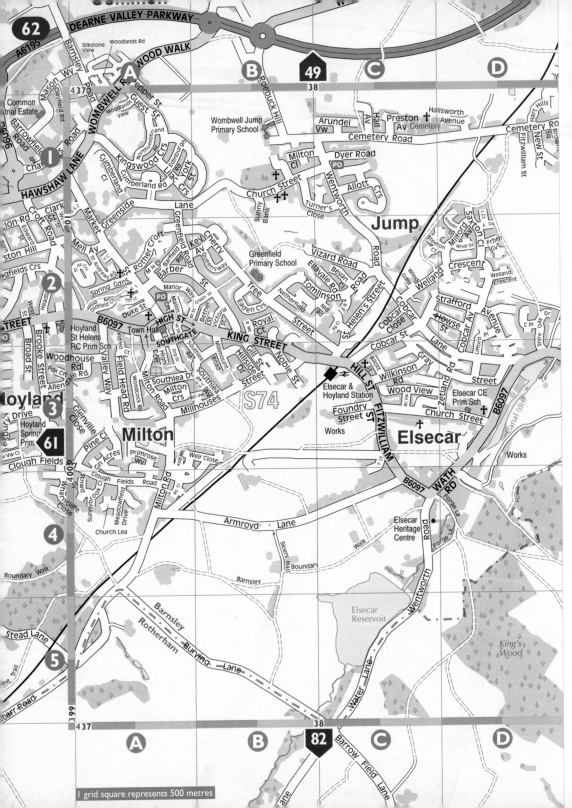

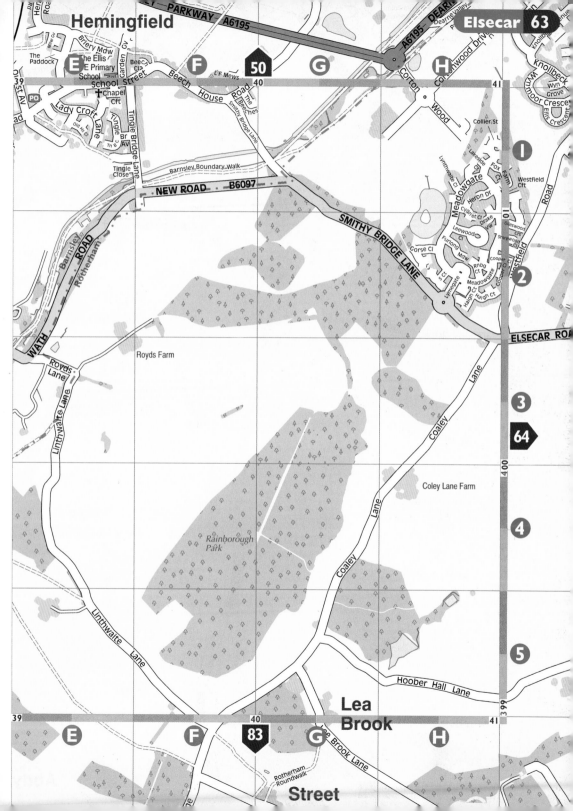

Hemingfield

Elsecar 63

PARKWAY A6195

DEARNE VALLEY

A6195

The Paddock

Briery Mdw

Corton Wood

Cottonwood Drive

Knollbeck

Wynmoor Crescent

Ellis Crescent

E

The Ellis C E Primary School

Garden Cl

Beec Cl

Chapel Cft

School Street

Beech House Road

L F Mews

F

50

G

The Beeches

H

Collier St

Lakeside

Fox Farm

Westfield Cft

I

PO

Lady Croft Lane

Tingle

old Hg

Tingle Bridge Lane

Br AV

Tn B

Tingle Close

Barnsley Boundary Walk

Smithy Bridge Lane

Lynthwaite Cl

Meadowgate

Heron Dr

Cygnet Cl

Drake

Gleswood Cft

Gleswood

shire Wood

2

NEW ROAD B6097

Leewood

WW

Gorse Cl

Furlong

Mdw

Rnbg Ct

cooper

L Cooper

Westfield Road

SMITHY BRIDGE LANE

WATH ROAD

Barnsley Road

Rotherham

Meadowgate

Haigh Ct

Limegate

Haigh Ct

Lynegate

ELSECAR ROAD

Royds Farm

Royds Lane

Linthwaite Lane

3

64

Coaley Lane

Coley Lane Farm

400

4

Rainborough Park

Coaley Lane

5

Hoober Hall Lane

399

Lea Brook

E

F

83

G

Lee Brook Lane

H

Rotherham Roundwalk

Street

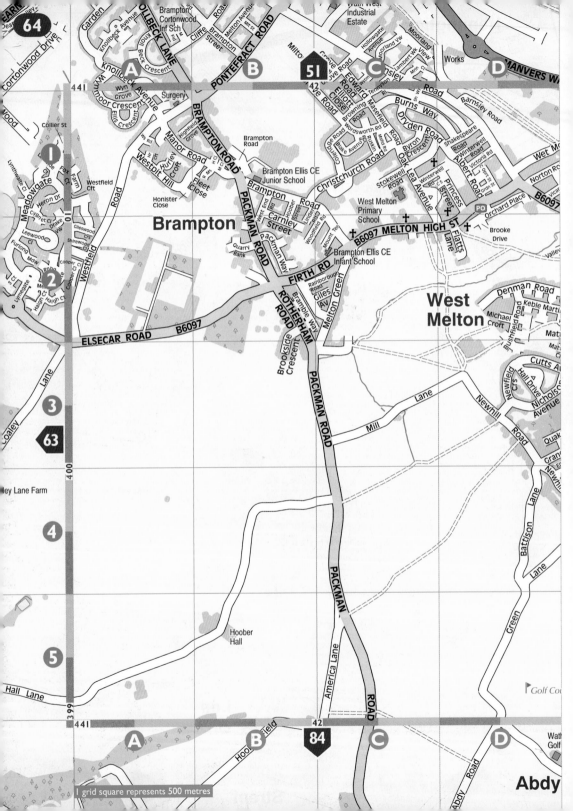

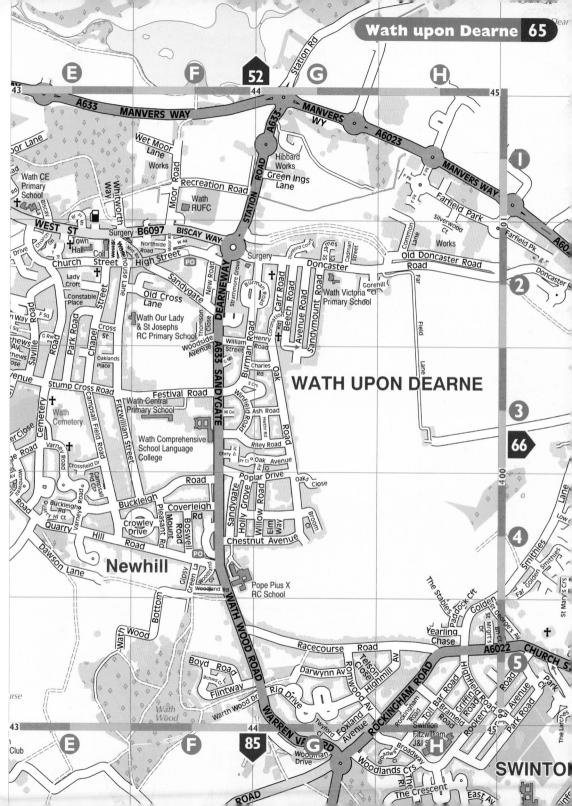

E   F   52   G   H

A633 MANVERS WAY

MANVERS WY

A6023

MANVERS WAY

A60

Wet Moor Lane

Works

Whitworth Way

Moor Road

Hibbard Works

Green Ings Lane

Station Rd

A633

I

Wath CE Primary School

Recreation Road

Wath RUFC

STATION ROAD

Farfield Park

silverwood Ct

Common Lane

Works

Farfield Pk

WEST ST

Surgery B6097

BISCAY WAY

Doncaster Road

Old Doncaster Road

Doncaster R

2

Northside Road

High Street

Surgery

Carr Road

St James St

Cladman Street

Town Hall

Church Street

Coll

PO

New Road

DEARNEWAY

Strathmore Grove

Burman Road

Coronation St

Beech Road

Dunford Court

Wath Victoria Primary School

Gorehill Cl

Far Field Lane

Doncaster R

Lady Croft

Constable Place

Cross St

Old Cross Lane

Wath Our Lady & St Josephs RC Primary School

Woodside Avenue

Thomson Close

A633 SANDYGATE

William Street

Henry Road

Avenue Road

Sandymount Road

Park Road

Chapel Street

Oaklands Place

Charles Rd

WATH UPON DEARNE

Stump Cross Road

Wath Cemetery

Festival Road

Fitzwilliam Street

Campsall Field Road

Wath Central Primary School

Winfield Road

Ash Road

Oak Road

3

66

Wath Comprehensive School Language College

Riley Road

Oak Avenue

Crossfield Dr

Road

Poplar Drive

Oak Close

Buckleigh Rd

Coverleigh Rd

Sandygate

Holly Grove

Willow Road

Elm Way

Broom

4

Buckleigh Road

Crowley Drive

Mount Pleasant Rd

Boswell Road

Chestnut Avenue

Quarry Hill Road

Dawson Lane

Green La

Woodland Rd

PO

Newhill

Pope Pius X RC School

WATH WOOD ROAD

Wath Wood

Bottom

Racecourse Road

A6022 CHURCH S

5

Boyd Road

Flintway

Warth Wood Dr

Rig Drive

Darwynn Av

Telson Close

Highmill

Yearling Chase

Paddock Cft

Golden Smithies

Smithies

St Marys Crs

Wath Wood

WARREN VF RD

Foxland Avenue

ROCKINGHAM ROAD

Swinton Fitzwilliam J&I S

Toll Bar Road

Highfield Road

Bramela Road

Rookery Road

Park Road

E   F   85   G   H

Woodman Drive

Woodlands Crs

Broadway

The Crescent

SWINTON

East Av

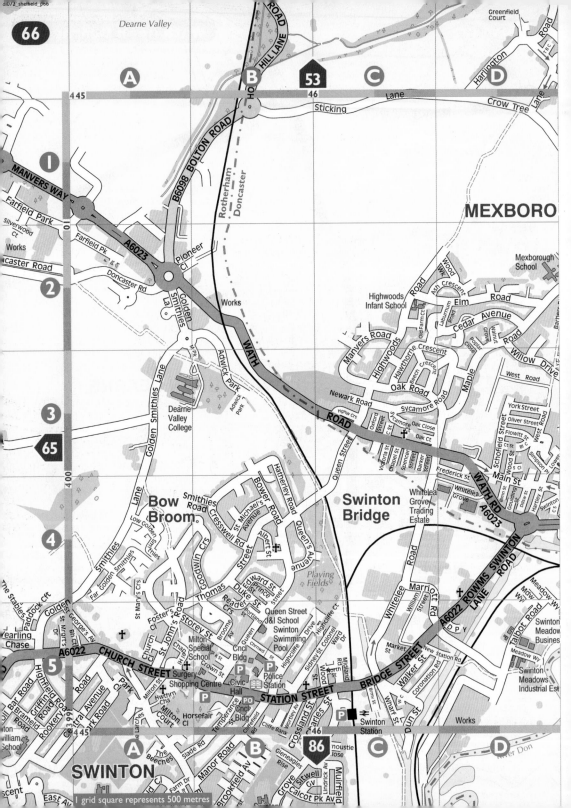

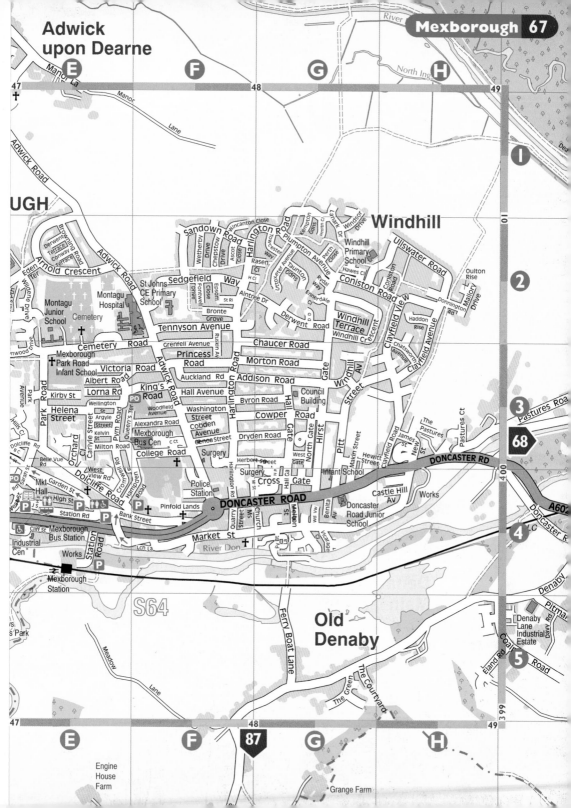

Adwick
upon Dearne

E   F   G   H

47   48   49

UGH

Windhill

Manor La
Manor Lane

River
North Ing

Adwick Road

Eden Ter
Browning Terrace
Conway Terrace
Arnold Crescent
Wilberie Drive
Montagu Junior School
Cemetery
Montagu Hospital
St Johns CE Primary School
Sandown Road
Wetherby Drive
Chepstow Drive
Ascot Close
Fontwell Drive
Epsom Drive
Wincanton Close
Harlington Road
Towcester
Rasen Cl
H Cl
St Rd
Plumpton Avenue
Kempston Gdns
Lanark Dr
Perth
Windsor Drive
Windhill Primary School
Hawes Cl
Ullswater Road
Oulton Rise
Coniston Road
Mallory Drive
Donnington Rd

Sedgefield Way
Bronte Grove
Aintree Dr
Uttoxeter Avenue
Taunton Gdns
Rydal
Ennerdale
Derwent Road
Windhill Terrace
Windhill Crescent
Clayfield View
Haddon Rise
Chatsworth Avenue
Clayfield Avenue

Cemetery Road
Tennyson Avenue
Grenfell Avenue
Princess Road
Ruskin Av
Chaucer Road
Morton Road
Windhill Gate
Windhill Street
Hirst Av
The Pastures
Pastures Ct
Pastures Road

Mexborough Park Road Infant School
Victoria Road
Albert Road
Auckland Rd
Addison Road
Council Building
James St
New St
68

Park Road
Kirby St
Lorna Rd
King's Road
Wellington
St Argyle
Street
Kelvin
Milton Road
Woodfield Avenue
Hall Avenue
Byron Road
Cowper Road
Hall Gate
North Gate
Pitt Street
Makin Street
Hewitt Street
Clayfield Road

Hills Cl
Helena Street
Carlyle Street
Queen's Ter
Alexandra Road
Washington Street
Cobden Avenue
Dryden Road
Genoa Street
West Gate
Herbert Street
Infant School
Doncaster Road

Dolcliffe Rd
Orchard
West View Rd
Mexborough Bus Cen
College Road
C Ct
Surgery
Surgery
Cross Gate
Castle Hill Av
Benita Av
Doncaster Road Junior School
Works

Belle Vue Rd
Dolcliffe Road
Police Station
Pinfold Lands
Bank Street
DONCASTER ROAD
Quarry St
MS
MS
Church St
Vicarage
Meldon
Wd Av
Wd Av

DONCASTER RD
A60

Station Rd
Mkt Hall
High St
Garden St
Cliff St
Mexborough Bus Station
Market St
River Don
Lch La

Works
Industrial Cen
Station Road
Mexborough Station

S64

Old Denaby

Denaby Lane Industrial Estate
Pitman Rd
Eland Rd
Coal Rd
Denaby Road

Meadow Lane
Ferry Boat Lane
The Green
The Courtyard
Grange Farm

47   48   49

E   F   87   G   H

Engine House Farm

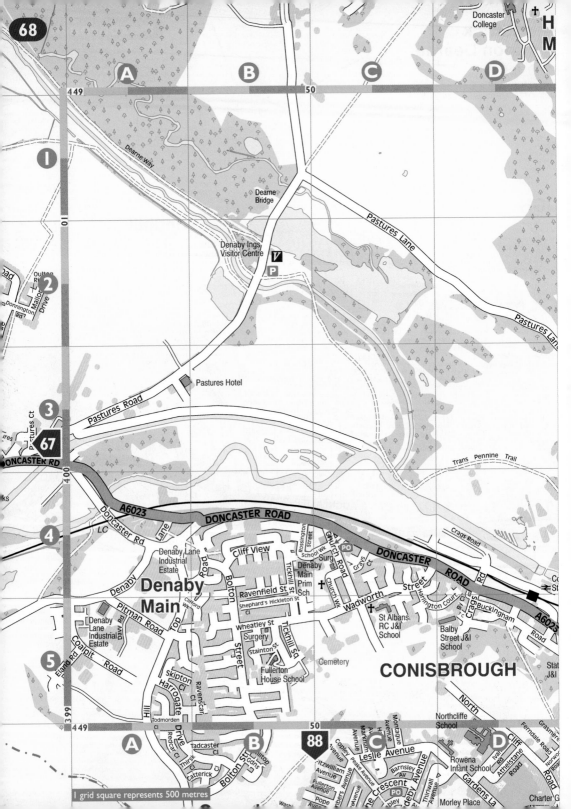

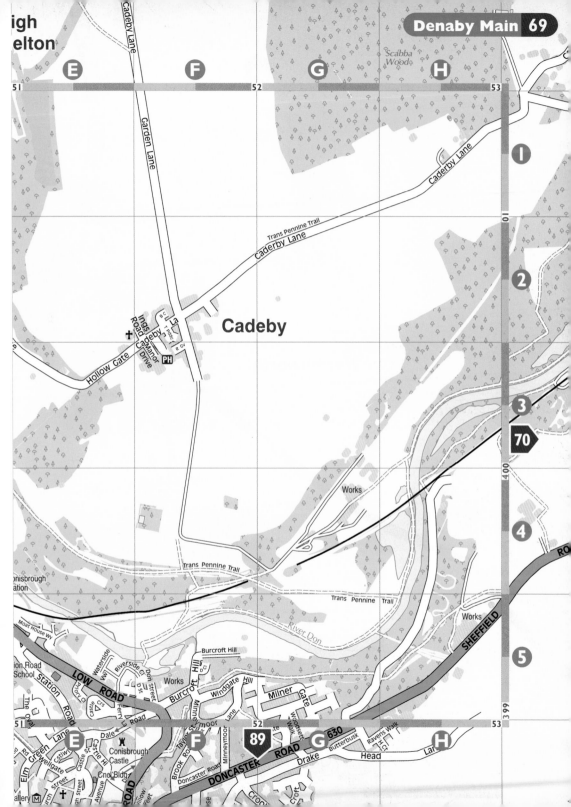

igh
elton

E   F   G   H

Scabba
Wood

51   52   53

Cadeby Lane

Garden Lane

I

Caderby Lane

Trans Pennine Trail
Caderby Lane

2

Ings Road
Cadeby
Cadeby Drive
Manor
Hollow Gate
La
PH

Cadeby

3

70

Works

4

Trans Pennine Trail

onisbrough
ation

Trans Pennine Trail

Works

SHEFFIELD

RO

River Don

5

Burcroft Hill

Moat House Wy

Waterside
Riverside Cl
Don Street
Works

Burcroft Hill

Windgate Hill

Milner Gate
Woosett

Ravens Walk
Walk

LOW ROAD
STATION ROAD

Ferry Road
Minnevmoor Lane

Play Cl
Castle Crs

399

51   52   53

E   F   89   G   630   H

The Oval
School

Green Lane
Elm Rd

Conisbrough
Castle

Castle St
Castle H

Dale

Taylors Field
Brook Rd

Minnevmoor Lane

Doncaster Road

Garte
Walk

Butterbusk

DONCASTER ROAD

Drake Head

Lar

allery
M
Church Street
Avenue
Cnol Bldg
Crook
Croft

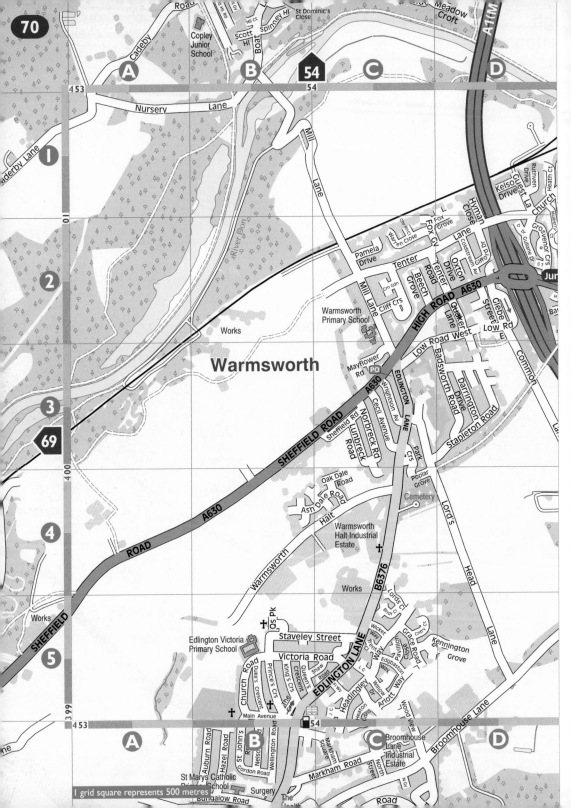

A   B   **54**   C   D

453

Nursery Lane

1

Cadeby Lane

Mill Lane

River Don

2

010

Works

Warmsworth

Warmsworth Primary School

Pamela Drive

Tenter Grove

Beech Grove

Cliff Crs

Crm Gdn

Warren Close

Church Close

Fox Cv

Fox Grove

Coldstream Av

Tenter Drive

Oxton Drive

Hyman Close

Lane

Kelso Drive

Guest La

Ruthven Drive

Church

Grosvenor Crs

A1(M)

Meadow Croft

St Dominic's Close

Copley Junior School

Hill Ct

Scott Hl

Spinney Hl

Boat Lane

3

400

69

SHEFFIELD ROAD

A630

Mill Lane

Mayflower Rd

PO

Wrightson Av

Cecil Avenue

Sheffield Rd

Norbreck Rd

Lumbreck Road

EDLINGTON LANE

A630

HIGH ROAD

Low Road West

Low Rd E

Quaker Lane

Glebe Street

Badsworth Road

Darrington Drive

Stapleton Road

Common

Park Crs

Poplar Grove

Lord's

Jun

4

ROAD

A630

Oak Dale Road

Ash Dale Road

Warmsworth Halt

Warmsworth Halt Industrial Estate

Works

B6376

Lords Cl

Bndt Cl

Cemetery

Head Lane

5

SHEFFIELD

Works

399

Edlington Victoria Primary School

QS Pk

Staveley Street

Victoria Road

Church Road

Duke's Crescent

Prince's Crescent

King's Crs

Queen's Crescent

Shaw

EDLINGTON LANE

Headingley

Wicker Way

Trent Way

Willow

Grace Road

Edgboaston Way

Arlott Way

Kennington Grove

Heaton

Markham Square North

Wood View

Broomhouse Lane

453

A   B   **54**   C   Broomhouse Lane Industrial Estate   D

St Marys Catholic Primary School

Auburn Road

Hazel Road

St John's Rd

Nelson Road

Wellington Road

Cordon Road

Main Avenue

Markham Road

North Street

Surgery

The

Bungalow Road

Road

1 grid square represents 500 metres

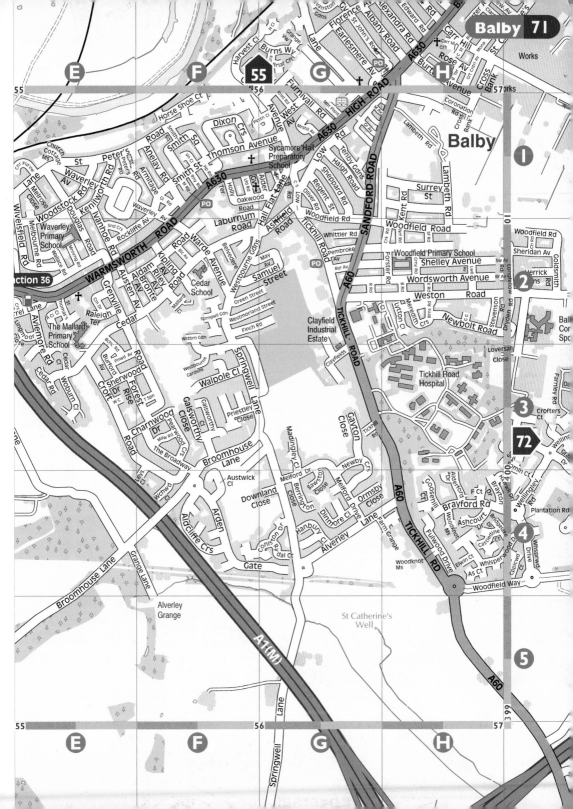

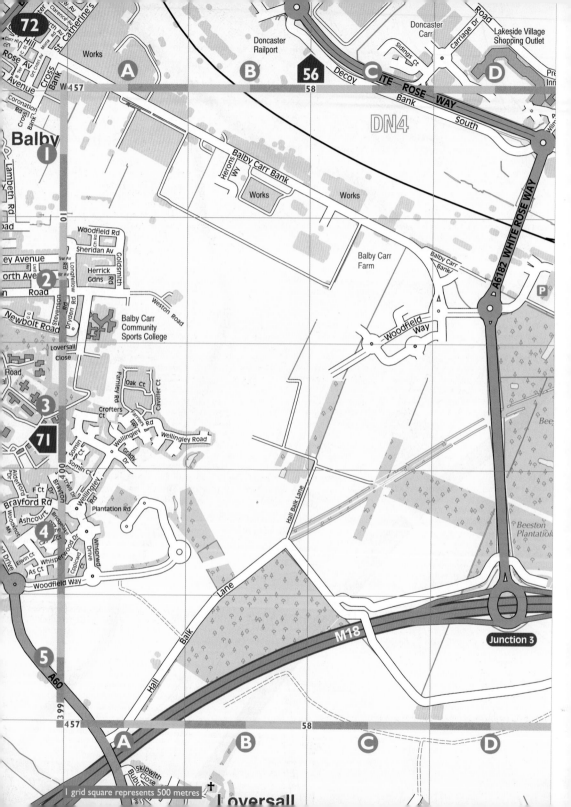

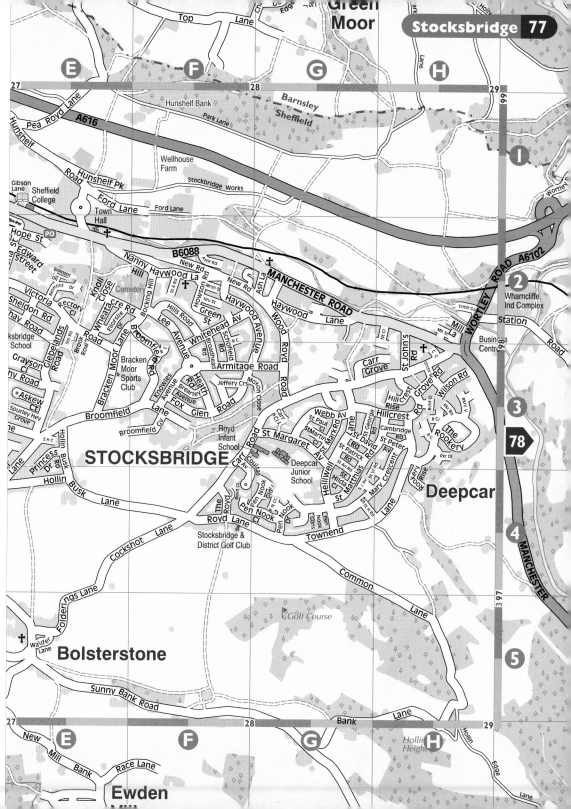

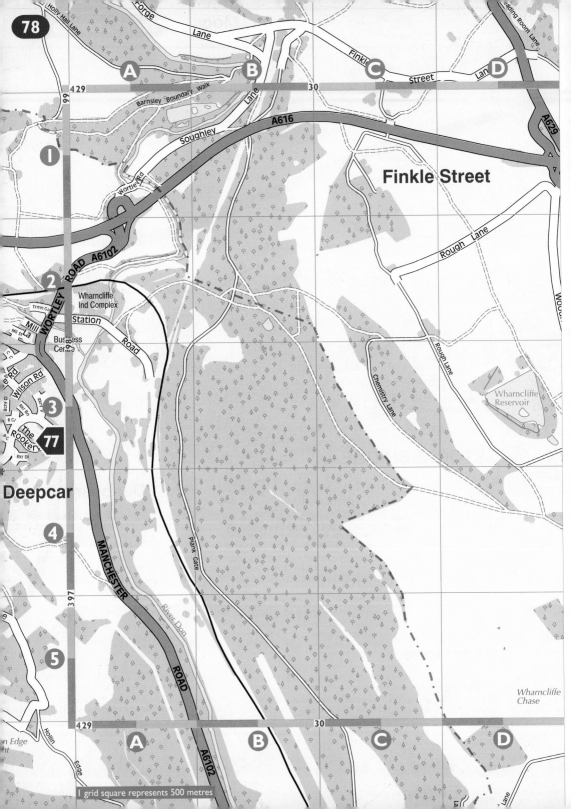

Flats

Trans Pennine Trail

E   **F**   **G**   **H**

31   32   33

A616

Howbrook
Lane

Fields   Lane

Pea   **Bromley**

Howbrook Lane

Cross Lane

Storrs Lane

I

Bromley Carr Road

Carr Head Road

Barnsley Boundary Walk

Howbrook   **2**

Hollinberry Lane

99
86

Ashwood Close

3

NEW

Boswell
Close

Renshawd

Ashwood

80

**Cundy
Houses**

A629

Barnsley Boundary Walk

WESTW

Furness
Road

Booth

Tomps

Hev

Whinmoor Rd

Hague La

Bank Lane

Thompson Hi

**Potter
Hill**

4

Hag

Smithy Fold
Lane

Barnsley Boundary Walk

Hazelshaw Farm

A629

Carlthorpe Grove

ge Road

5

Lodge
Lane

A61

31   32   33

E   **F**   **92**   **G**   **H**

PENISTONE

HALLW

Barnsley

Sheffield

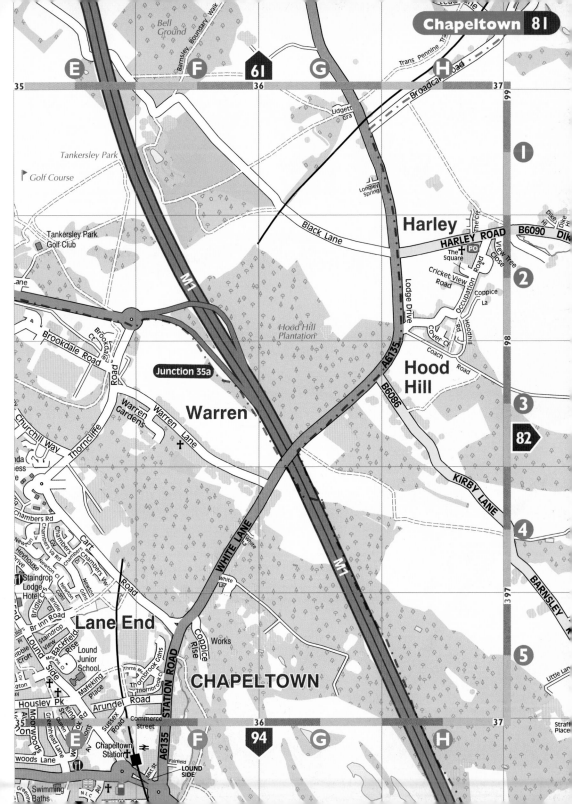

E F 61 G H

35 36 37

Bell Ground

Barnsley Boundary Walk

Trans Pennine Tra

Broadcar

99

Tankersley Park

Golf Course

Lidgett Gra

I

Longley Spring

Tankersley Park Golf Club

Black Lane

Harley

HARLEY ROAD

B6090

Dike Hi Dike

Dik

The Ct

View Tree Close

PO

The Square

2

98

Cricket View Road

Occupation Road

Coppice La

M1

Brookdale Road

Brookdale Ct

Road

Hood Hill Plantation

Lodge Drive

A6135

Cover Cl

Coach Road

Coppice

Hoodhill Road

Hood Hill

3

Junction 35a

B6086

Warren

Warren Gardens

Warren Lane

Thorncliffe

82

KIRBY LANE

Churchill Way

Chambers Rd

Carr

WHITE LANE

White La

4

397

BARNSLEY

Chambers Va Rd

Chambers Vw

Newton Gdns

Newton

Newton Cl

White La

Heyhouse Drive

anda ess

Staindrop Lodge Hotel

Bridle

Br Inn Road

Lane End

STATION ROAD

COPPICE RISE

White Lane

Works

5

Lound Side

Housley Pk

King

Lound Junior School

Staindrop View

Backfield Rise

Mafeking Place

Thornbrook Gdns

Thornbrook Road

Arundel Road

Commerce Street

CHAPELTOWN

Moorwoods

Greenhead Lane

Sussex Road

E F 94 G H

36 37

Straff Place

Swimming Baths

N L C

Chapeltown Station

A6135

Fairfield

LOUND SIDE

Little Lan

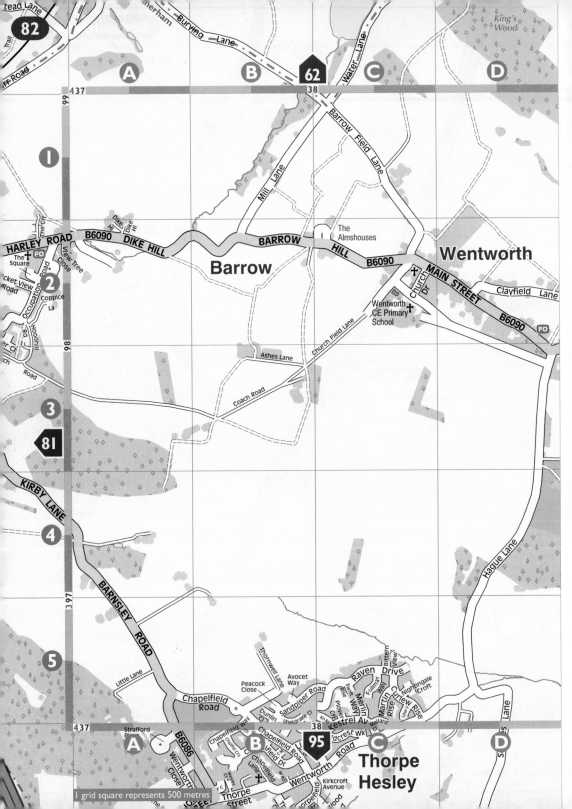

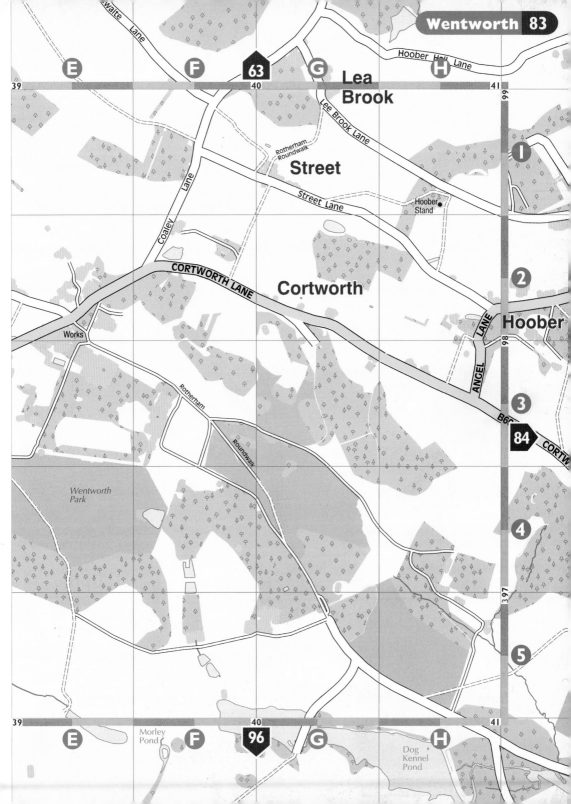

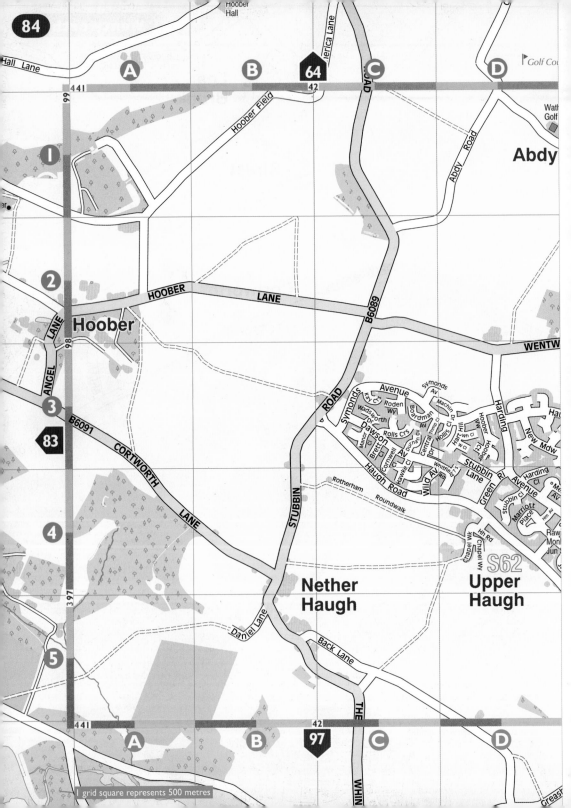

Hall Lane

A B 64 C D

441
99 42

I

Hoober Field

Golf Cou

Watl
Golf

Abdy

Abdy Road

2 HOOBER LANE

B6089

Hoober

98

LANE

ANGEL

WENTW

3 83

B6091

CORTWORTH

LANE

Symonds
Avenue

ROAD

STUBBIN

Symonds

Key Cs

Wadsworth

Roden
Wy

Boardman

Machin
Cr

Hoober
Wy

Harding

New Mdw

Dawson

Manor

Brett

Cornwell
Av

Hawke
Cl

Central
Durnan

Hollis

Hart
Wm Cl

Whitfield

Wild Av

Stubbin
Lane

Green Rd

Harding

Avenue

Rolls Crs

Rotherham

Haugh Road

Roundwalk

Stubbin Cl

Marriott
Place

Raw
Mon
Jun

4

Nether
Haugh

S62

Upper
Haugh

Chapel Wy

Chapel Wk

97

3 97

5

Daniel Lane

Back Lane

441
42

A B 97 C D

THE

WHIN

Greasb

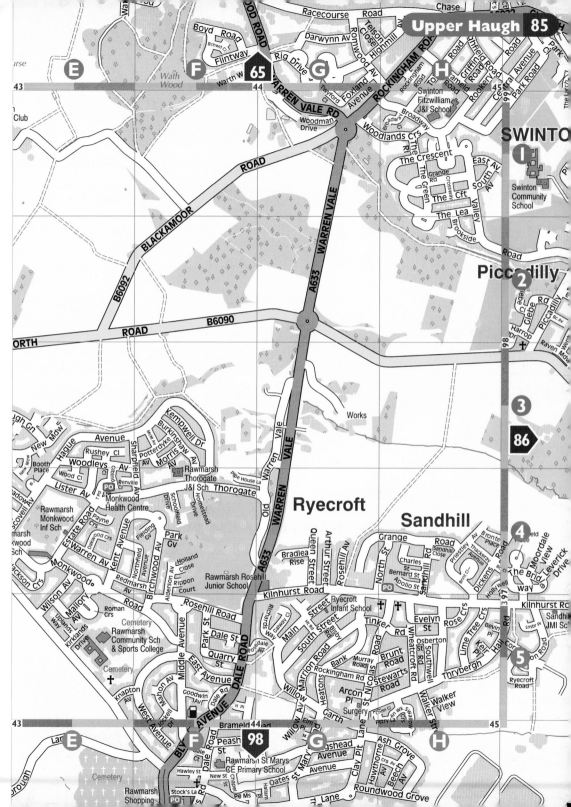

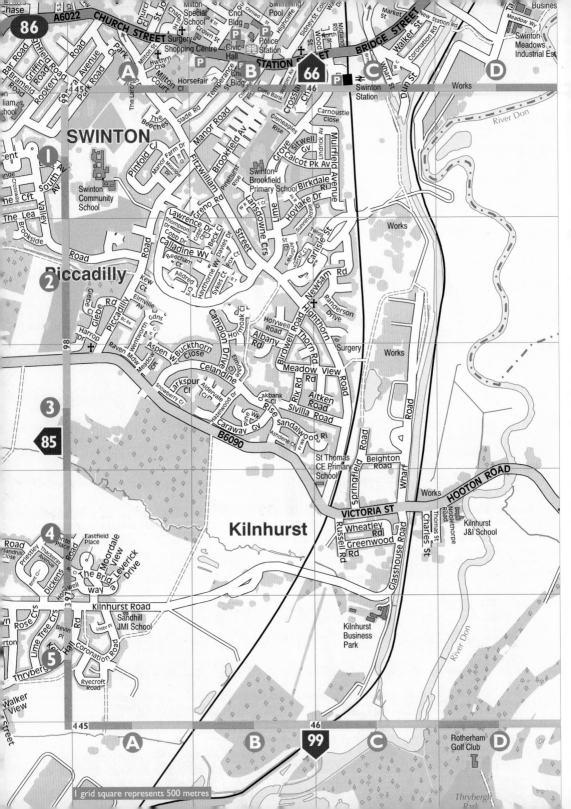

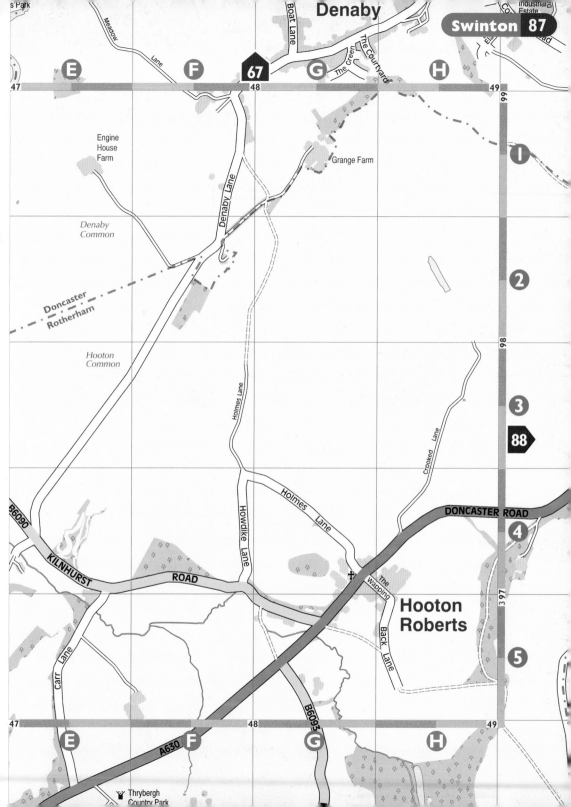

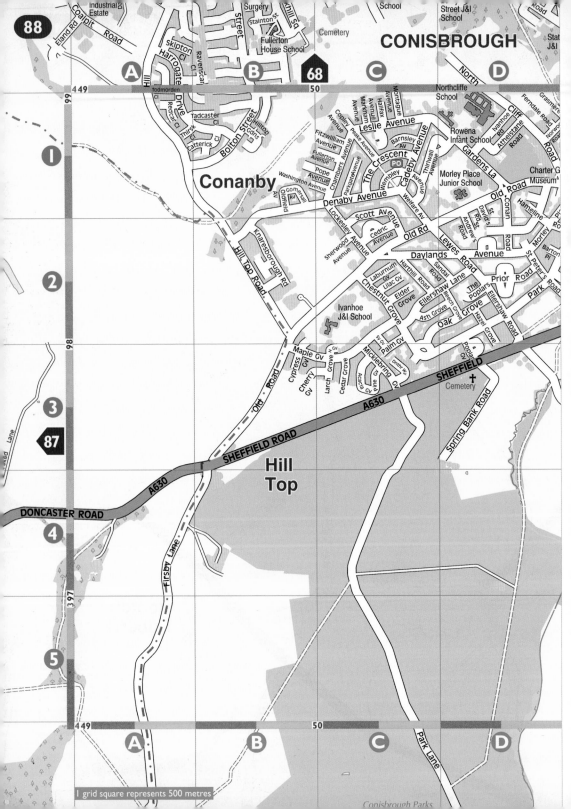

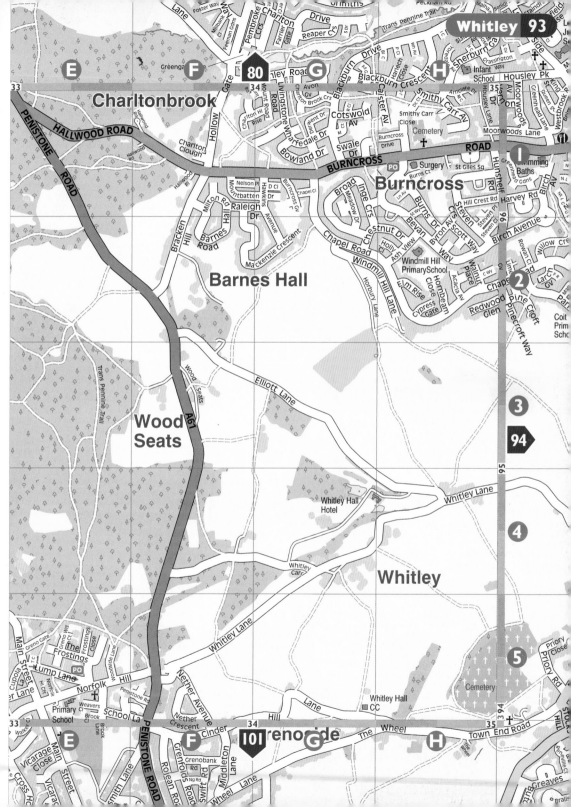

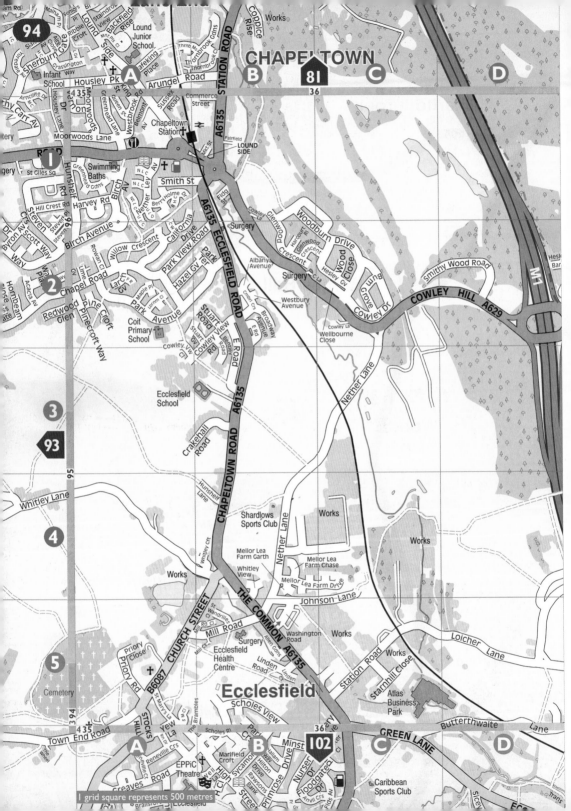

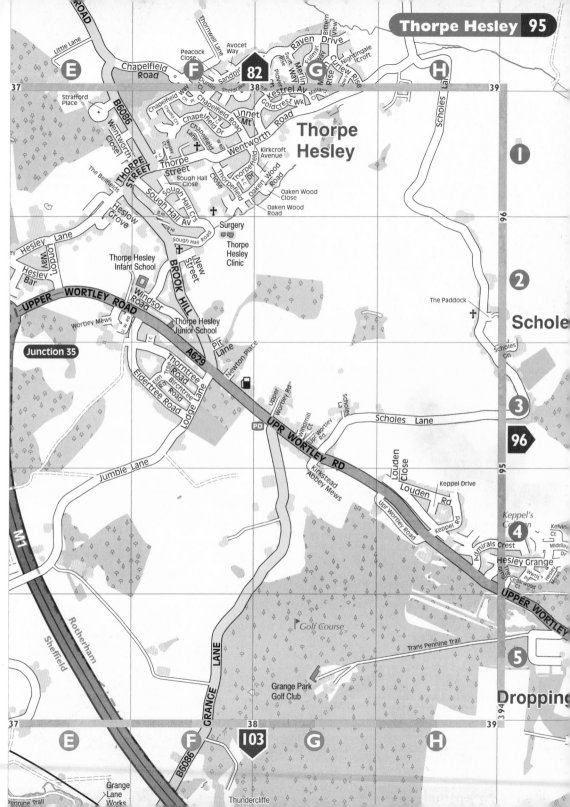

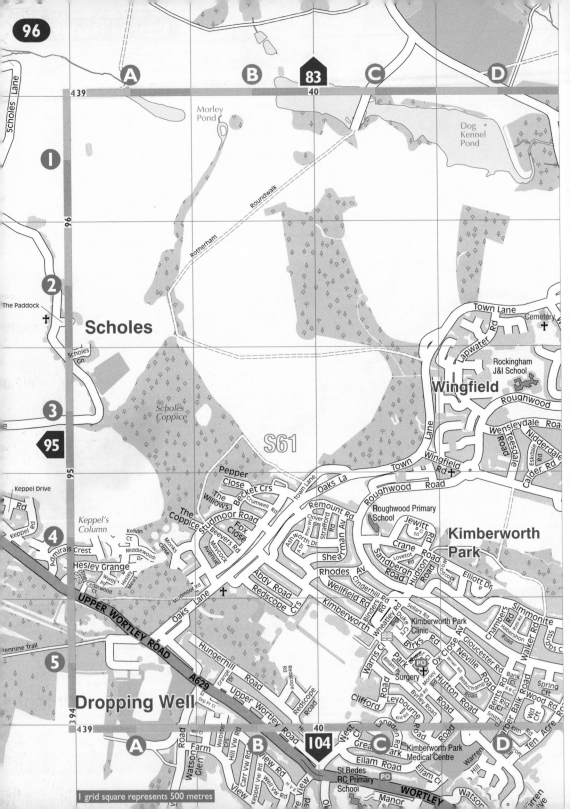

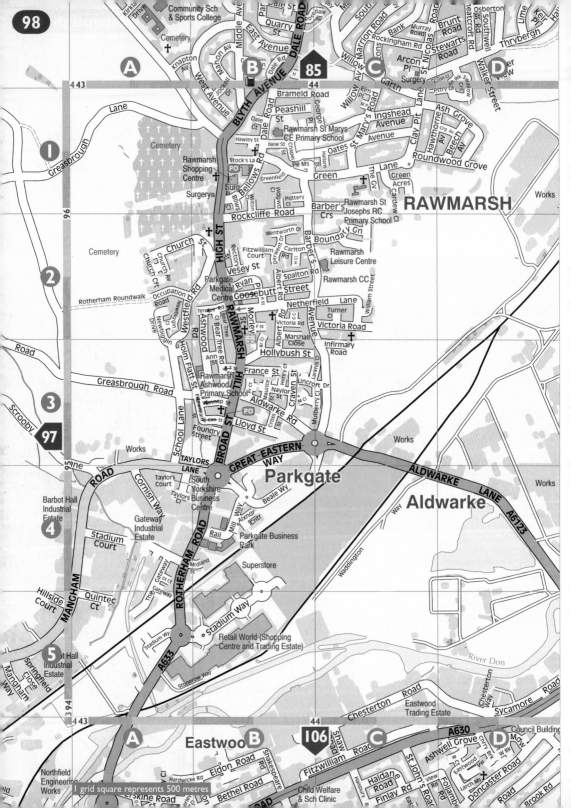

A B 85 C D

I

2

3

97

4

5

A Eastwoo B 106 C D

Community Sch & Sports College

Cemetery

Kirkla Drive

Knapton Av

Majon Av

West Avenue

Middle Ave

East Avenue

Quarry St

Par ale St

Rosedale

South

Dale Rd

DALE ROAD

44

Willow

Marrion Road

Murray Road

Bank

Rockingham Rd

St Nicolas

Brunt Road

Stewarts Road

Arcon Pl

Surgery

Southw

Heatcroft Rd

Thrybergh

Lime

Kel

Osberton Road

Walker Street

er View

BLYTH AVENUE

Bramled Road

Peashill St

George

Willow

Elm

Ash Grove

Clay Pit Lane

Hawthorne Av

Beech Av

Cardew Cl

Roundwood Grove

Rawmarsh St Marys CE Primary School

New St

St Mary's

Ingshead Avenue

Oates St

St Mary's Avenue

Green Acres

Greenfield

Chapel

Hallam St

Lane

The Gv

Green

Works

Cemetery

Rawmarsh Shopping Centre

PO

Surg

Bellows Rd

Stock's La

Pe Ms

Rockcliffe Road

Green

RAWMARSH

Surgery

Barber's Crs

Rawmarsh St Josephs RC Primary School

Y Gn

Church St

Church Av

Church Cft

Cemetery

Fitzwilliam Court

Wentworth Dr

Boundar

Rawmarsh Leisure Centre

Carlton Rd

Spalton Rd

Rawmarsh CC

Vesey St

Barber's

Albert Rd

Rectory

Parkgate Medical Centre

Goosebutt Street

Netherfield Lane

Turner Cl

William Street

Ryan

Westfield Rd

Ashwood Rd

RAWMARSH HILL

Morley St

Victoria Rd

Avenue

Victoria Road

Infirmary Road

Holm Flatt St

Bear Tree Rd

Albert St

Marshall Close

Hollybush St

Occupation Road

Newbiggin

Newbiggin Drive

Terrace Rd

Ann St

France St

Henry St

Lincroft Dr

Rotherham Roundwalk

HIGH ST

BROAD ST

Rawmarsh Ashwood Primary School

Flanwham

Maurice Rd

Naylor St

Craven St

Aldwarke Rd

Mulberry Cl

Works

Lloyd St

PO

Foundry Street

Greasbrough Road

Road

Scrooby Lane

School Lane

TAYLORS LANE

GREAT EASTERN WAY

Parkgate

Beale Wy

ALDWARKE LANE

A6123

Aldwarke

Works

Works

Taylors Court

Taylors Cl

South Yorkshire Business Centre

Mill Way

Alxmor Centr

Rail

ROTHERHAM ROAD

Parkgate Business Park

Waddington

Way

Barbot Hall Industrial Estate

Cornish Way

Gateway Industrial Estate

Stadium Court

Midland St

Superstore

Hillside Court

Quintec Ct

The Gateway

Gateway Ct

Stadium Wy

MANGHAM ROAD

A633

Stadium Way

Retail World (Shopping Centre and Trading Estate)

River Don

ot Hall Industrial Estate

Springfield Close

Mangham Way

Stonerow Way

Chesterton Road

Eastwood Trading Estate

Chesterton Way

Sycamore Road

Northfield Engineering Works

Hardwicke Rd

Eldon Road

Shakespeare Rd

Bethel Road

Fitzwilliam St

Child Welfare & Sch Clinic

Shaw St

St John's Road

Haldane Road

Finlay Rd

A630

Ashwell Grove

Eastwood View

Larch Ms

Doncaster Road

Council Building

Brook Rd

I grid square represents 500 metres

Coronation Road

Ryecroft Road

E **F** **86** **G** **H**

45 46 47

River

Park

Rotherham Golf Club

1

Thrybergh Park

96

2

Golf Course

Manor Ct

Back La

A630

Thrybergh

Cemetery

Chestnut Ct

School La

Church Hill

Arran Hill

Thrybergh Fullerton CE Primary School

3

Lamberts Lane

Bonaroma Training Academy

Beeden Cl

Thrybergh Comprehensive School

95

Top Tree Wy

Park La

St Park Ct

Lane

Dr

Park Nook

Fullerton Crs

Poplar Av

Park Vale Road

Vale Ct

St Leonard's Avenue

Deer Park Rd

Longlands Dr

Deer Leap Dr

Lead through Dr

Reresby Road

Mar

4

Well

Works

Works

Works

Whinney Hill

Thrybergh St Gerards RC M&I School

Carbroads Crs

Royds Cl

Pingle Crs

Bellscroft Av

Park Cl

Park V Dr

Vale Av

East V Dr

West Vale Crs

Brockhurst Way

Warreners Place

Hargrave

Close

Foxcote

Lea

Link Rd

Staples Cl

The Paddocks

Musgrove Rd

Medical Centre

PO

DONCASTER ROAD

Silver St

Oldgate

Glibb

Crs

Townend

Wttn Cl

School

Av

Av

Woodworth

Holling's Lane

S65

5

Superstore

A630

Magna Lane

Arundel Avenue

Foljambe Drive

Chesterhill

Wilson Dr

Meadow Close

Waterhouse Cl

Wadsworth

Mousehole La

Sturton Cft

Brierly Road

394

Osbrin

Saville St

Kewin

Cawdron

Constable

Appleton Cl

Hazlehurst Close

Linkswood

Brookfield

Norwood

Ivy Farm Cft

Dalton Health Centre

Dalton

Dalton Foljambe Primary School

Lrtn Wy

Oak Road

Mowbray Close

Mowbray St

Apln

High Greave Primary School

Bosville St

Laudsdale Road

Fretwell Rd

Dalton Hardwick Lane

Top Fld La

Creswick

E **F** **107** **G** **H**

45 46

Coupland Rd

PO

Mallory R

W Farm La

Vicarage Close

Trinity Croft Prim

The

Far Dalton Lane

Dalton Parva

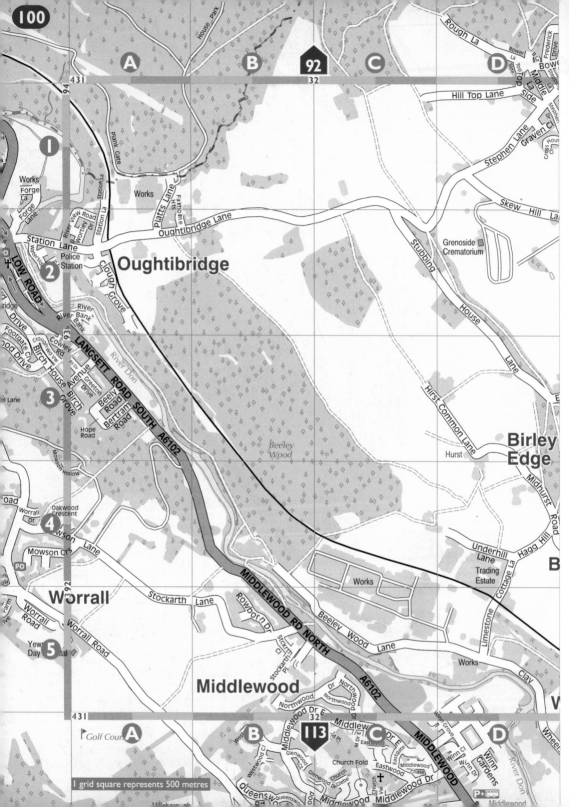

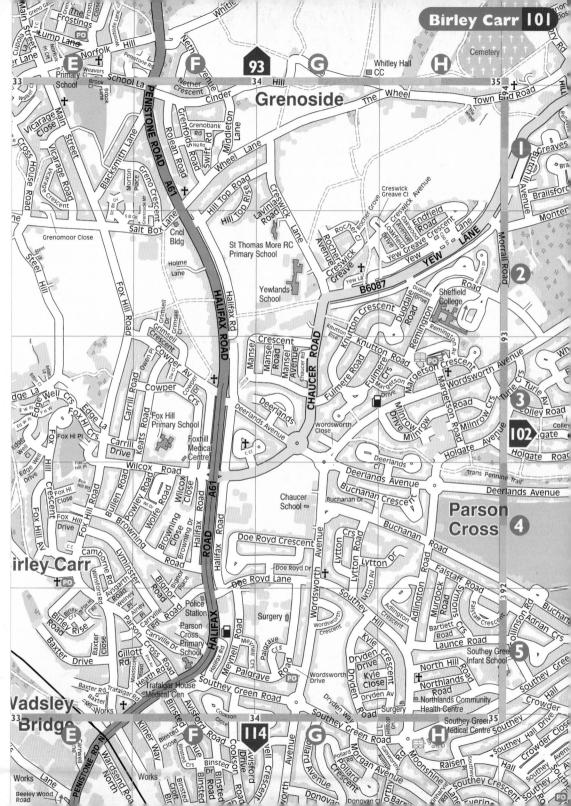

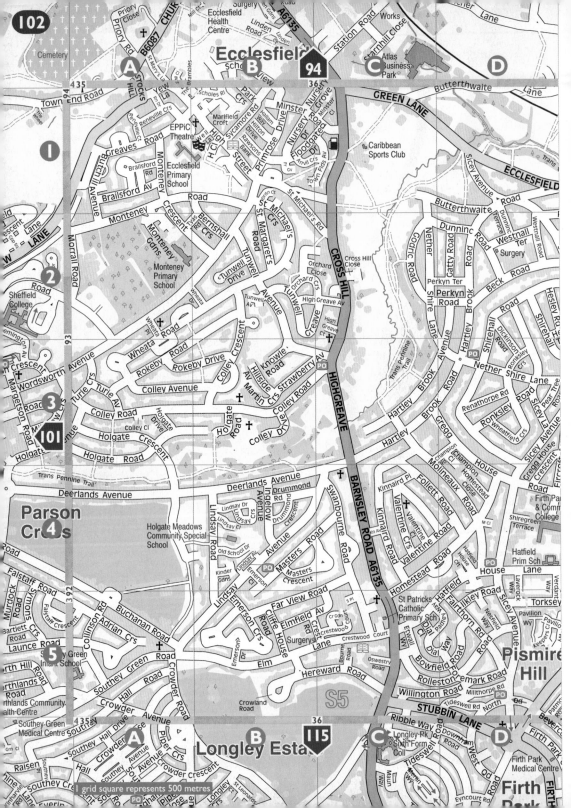

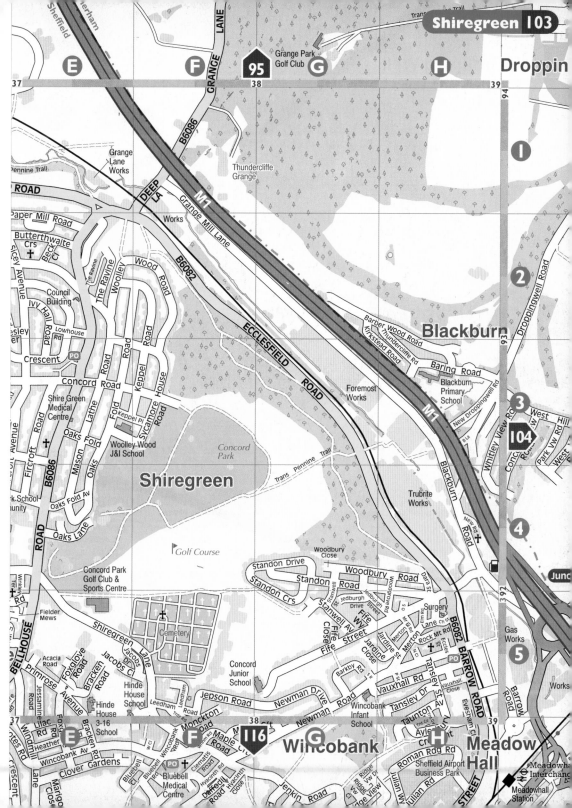

Droppin

Grange Park Golf Club

95

E F G H

I

Sheffield

GRANGE LANE

B6086

M1

Trans Pennine Trail

DEEP LA

Grange Lane Works

Grange Mill Lane

Works

Thundercliffe Grange

ROAD

Paper Mill Road

Butterthwaite Crs

Beck CI

Ivy Hall Road

Lowhouse Rd

Crescent

Council Building

The Ravine

Woolley Wood Road

Concord Road

Keppel Road

Keppel PI

Sycamore House

ECCLESFIELD ROAD

Barber Wood Road

Thundercliffe Rd

Kirkstead Road

New Droppingwell Rd

Droppingwell Road

Blackburn

Baring Road

Blackburn Primary School

Whitley View Rd

West Hill

3

104

Conc Road

Park Vw Rd

West

Fircroft Road

Oaks Fold

Lathe

Fold

Mason

Oaks

Shire Green Medical Centre

Woolley Wood J&I School

Concord Park

Shiregreen

Trans Pennine Trail

Foremost Works

Blackburn Road

New Rd

Trubrite Works

4

B6086

ROAD

Oaks Fold Av

Oaks Lane

Golf Course

Concord Park Golf Club & Sports Centre

Woodbury Close

Standon Drive

Standon Crs

Standon Road

Woodbury Road

Woodgrove Rd

Dara St

Junc

Fielder Mews

Shiregreen Lane

Jacobs CI

Cemetery

Stanwell Av

Fife St

Jedburgh Drive

Jedburgh Street

Jardine St

Merton Rd

Eccles

Rock Mt Rd

Surgery

Lane Ch

BARROW ROAD

B6082

Gas Works

5

BELLHOUSE

Acacia Road

Foxglove Road

Primrose Avenue

Bracken Road

Hinde House School

Hinde House 3-16 School

Concord Junior School

Jepson Road

Monckton Road

Leedham Road

Newman Drive

Newman Road

Barkby Rd

Vauxhall Rd

Tansley Dr

Tansley St

Vauxhall Close

Eccles St

Taunton Av

Evesham CI

Works

E **F** **116** **G** **H**

Lilac Rd

Foxglove Rd

Heather

Windmill

Clover Gardens

Bracken

Wincobank Av

Bluebell

Bluebell Medical Centre

Clematis Road

Maple Road

Daffodil

Hyacinth Road

Hyacinth Road

Jenkin Road

Ridge View

Julian Wy

Wincobank

Wincobank Infant School

Roman Rdg Rd

Sheffield Airport Business Park

Ayle Cr

Aylesham CI

Meadow Hall

Meadowhall Interchange

Meadowhall Station

STREET

Primrose Avenue

Jessamine Rd

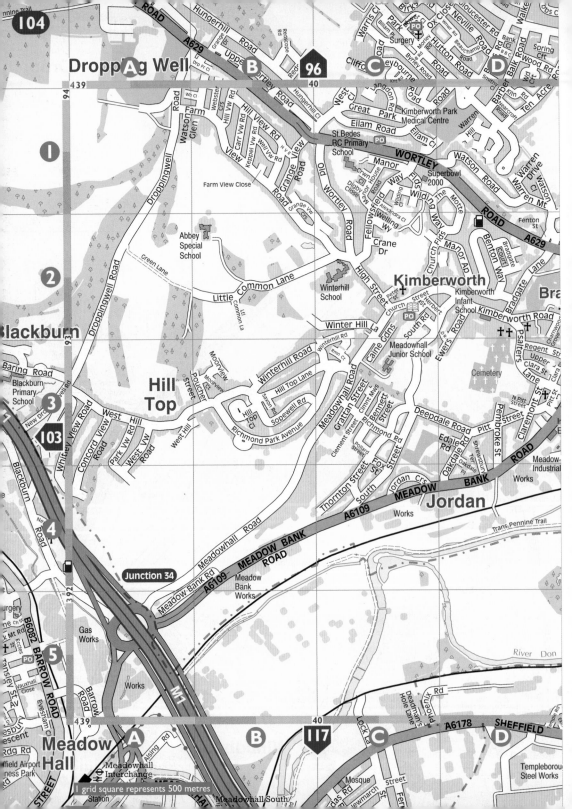

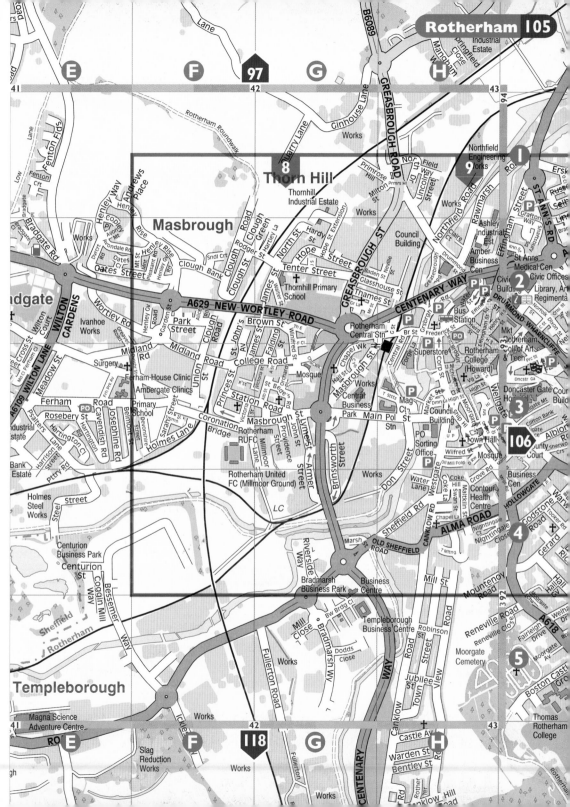

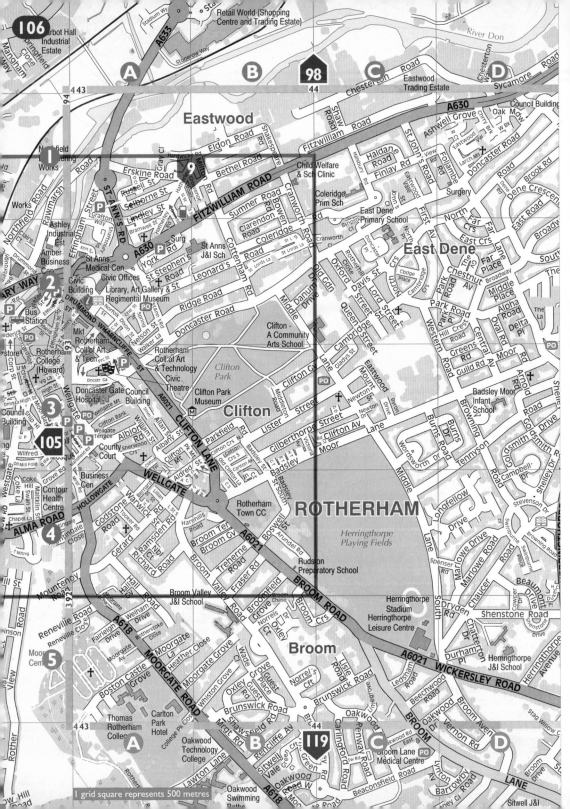

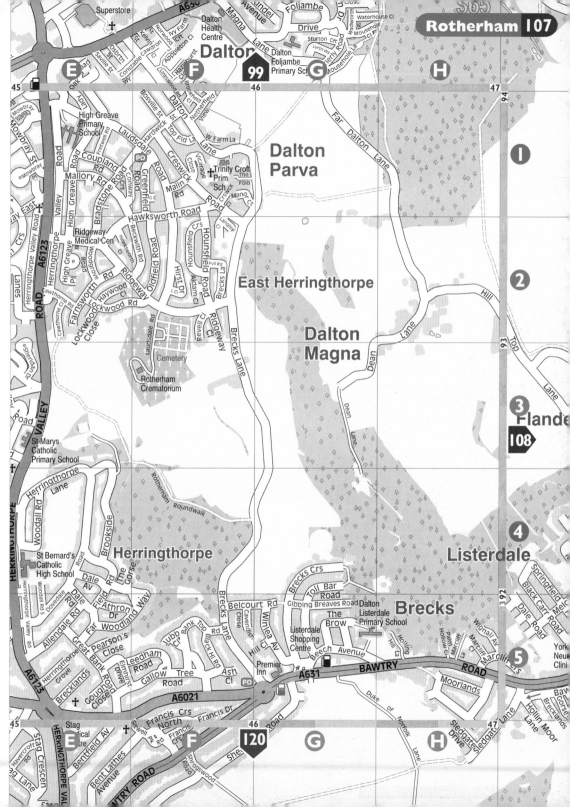

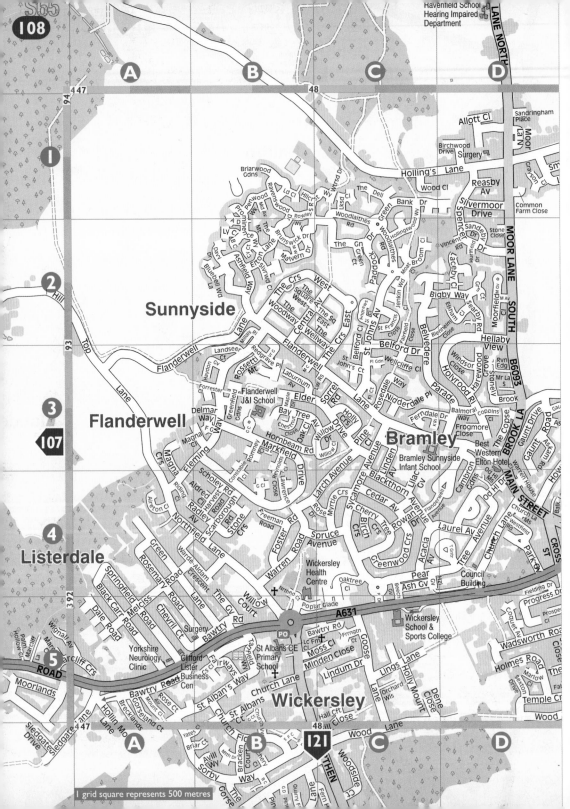

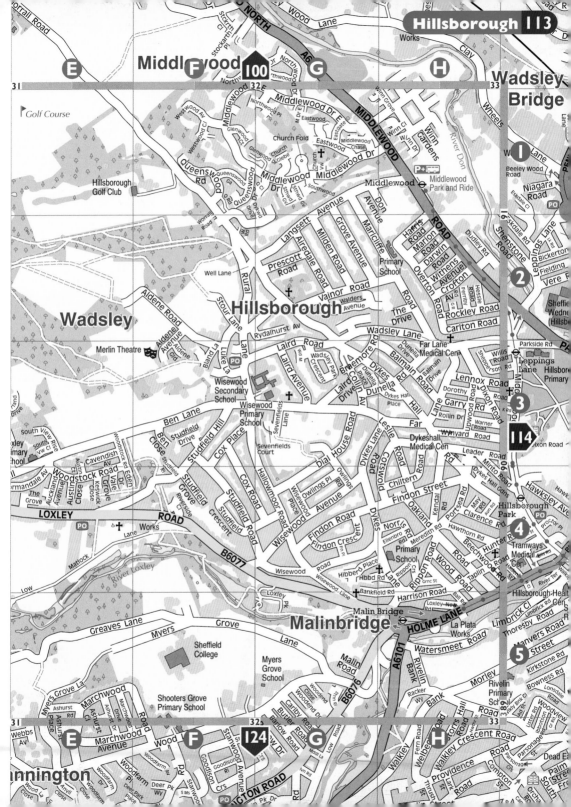

Wadsley
Bridge

Middlewood 100

Wadsley

Hillsborough

Hillsborough Golf Club

Golf Course

Merlin Theatre

Wisewood Secondary School

Wisewood Primary School

Sevenfields Court

Cavendish

Woodstock Road

LOXLEY ROAD
B6077

River Loxley

Greaves Lane

Sheffield College

Myers Grove School

Shooters Grove Primary School

Marchwood

Malinbridge

Myers Grove Lane

La Plata Works

Hillsborough Park

Hillsborough Heal

Tramways Medical Cen

Rivelin Primary Sch

Wadsley Bridge

Beeley Wood Road

Niagara Road

Middlewood Park and Ride

Primary School

The Drive

Leppings Lane Hillsboro Primary

Hillsborough Park

114

HOLME LANE
A6101

Watersmeet Road

124

Hillsborough

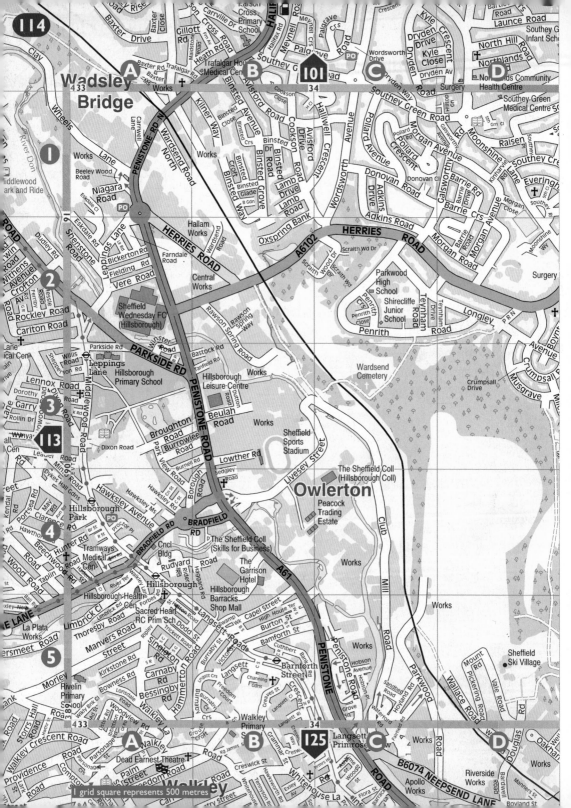

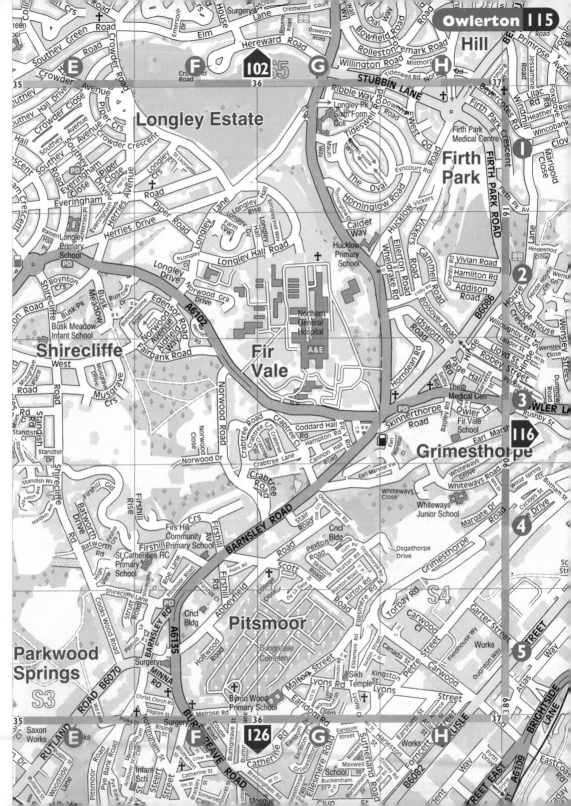

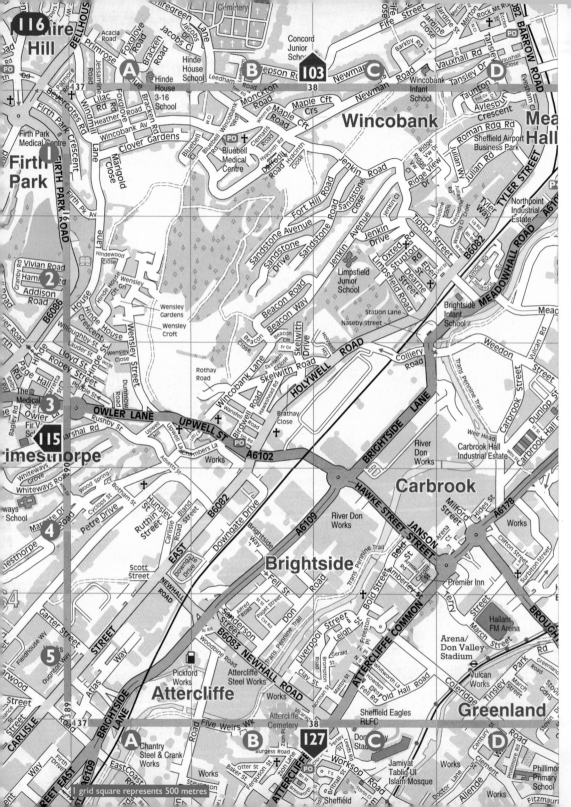

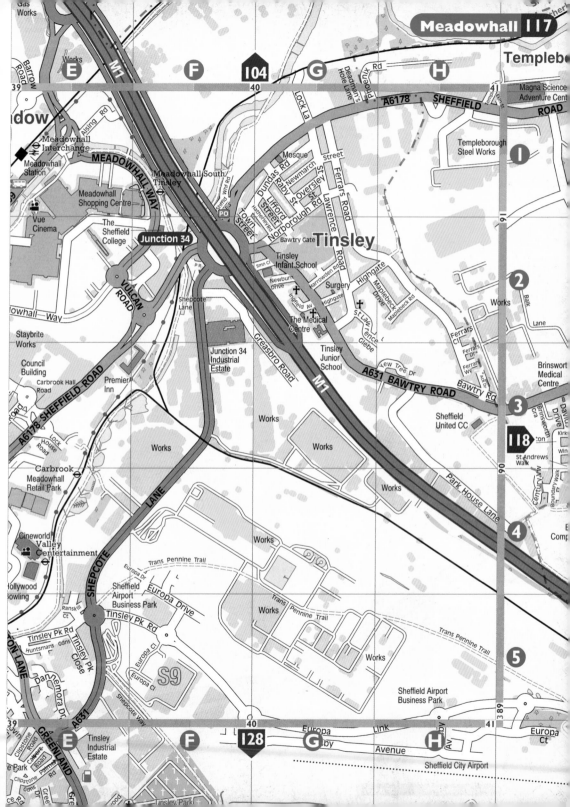

Gas Works

Templebo

Barrow Road

Works **E** **M1** **F** **104** **G** **H**

39 40 41

Deadmans Hole Lane

Phoenix Rd

A6178 **SHEFFIELD** **ROAD**

Magna Science Adventure Cent

Templeborough Steel Works **I**

Meadowhall Interchange

Meadow

Meadowhall Station

Meadowhall South Tinsley

MEADOWHALL WAY

Aisling Rd

Mosque Rd

Dundas Rd

Raby St

Newmarch St

Oversley St

Street

Ferrars Road

Lawrence

Street

Meadowhall Shopping Centre

Vue Cinema

The Sheffield College

Junction 34

Shepcote Lane

Sheffd Whf Rd

PO

Town Street

Lifford Street

Norborough Rd

Hatherley Rd

Bawtry Gate

Tinsley

Tinsley Infant School

smn Cl

Harrowden Rd

Newburn Drive

Lindfield Av

Surgery

Highgate

Highgate

Maplebeck Rd

Maplebeck Drive

Balk Lane

2

Works

Ferrars Rd

Ferrars Cl

Ferrars WY

Ferrars Dr

Brinsworth Medical Centre

VULCAN ROAD

Staybrite Works

Council Building

Carbrook Hall Road

Premier Inn

Junction 34 Industrial Estate

Greasbro Road

M1

The Medical Centre

Tinsley Junior School

St Lawrence Rd

St Lawrence Glebe

L

Yew Tree Dr

A631 BAWTRY ROAD

Bawtry Rd

3

A6178 SHEFFIELD ROAD

Lock House Road

Works

Works

Works

Sheffield United CC

118

Davidson

Brinsworth Cres

St Andrews Walk

Century Wy

Boundary Walk

Carbrook Meadowhall Retail Park

LANE

SHEPCOTE

Works

Works

Park House Lane

4

Comp

Cineworld

Valley Centertainment

Hollywood Bowling

Ranskill Ct

Trans Pennine Trail

Europa Dr

Sheffield Airport Business Park

Europa Drive

L

Works

Works

Works

Trans Pennine Trail

Trans Pennine Trail

Sheffield Airport Business Park

5

39 89 41

Europa Ct

Tinsley Pk Rd

Huntsmans Gdns

Tinsley Pk Close

Danemora Dr

A631

GREENLAND

Clipstone Road

Calvert Road

Palmer Rd

Clipstone Gdns

Tinsley Pk Rd

Shepcote Way

S9

Europa Cl

Europa Cl

E Tinsley Industrial Estate **F** **128** **G** Europa by Link **H** Av Ct

39 40 Europa Avenue 41

Sheffield City Airport

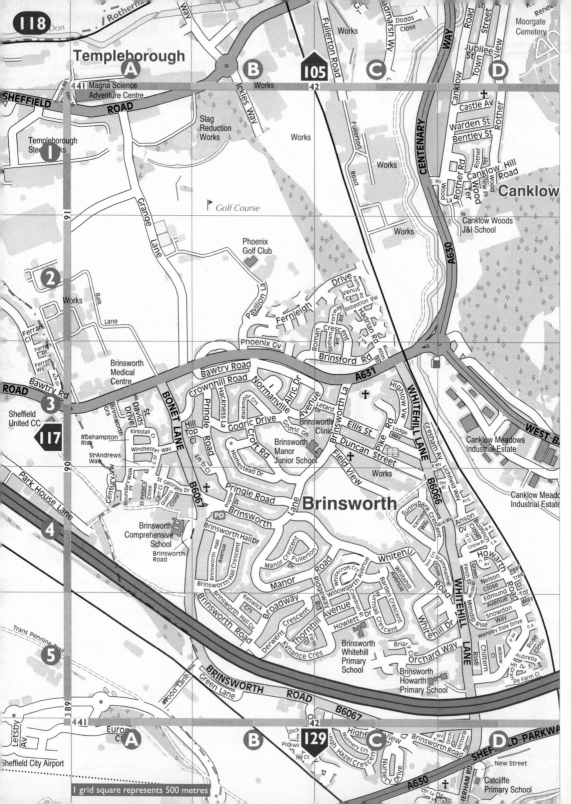

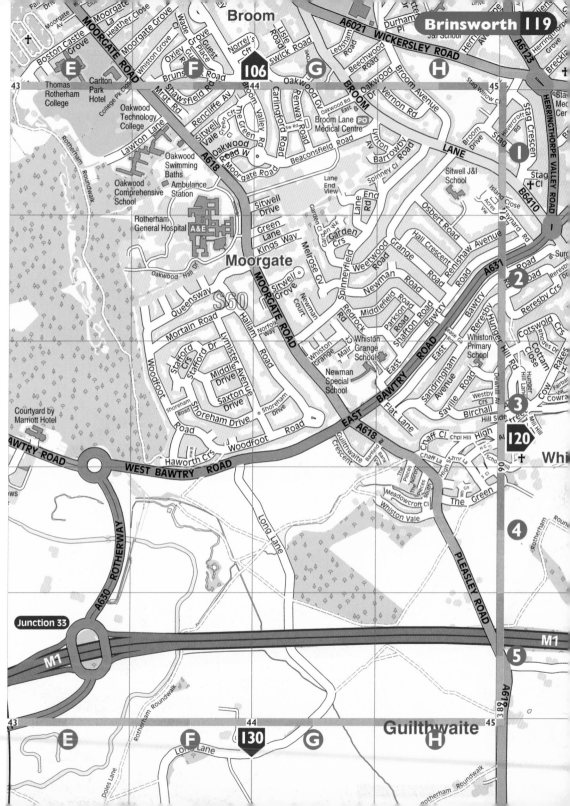

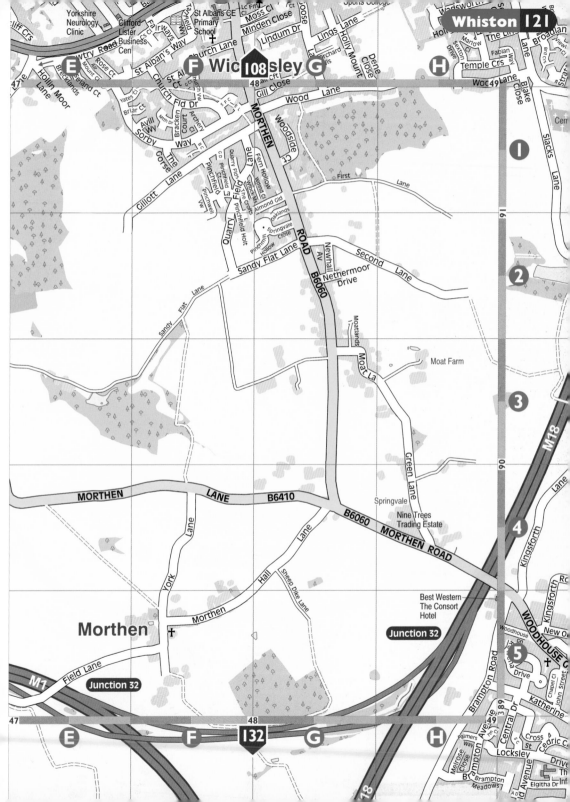

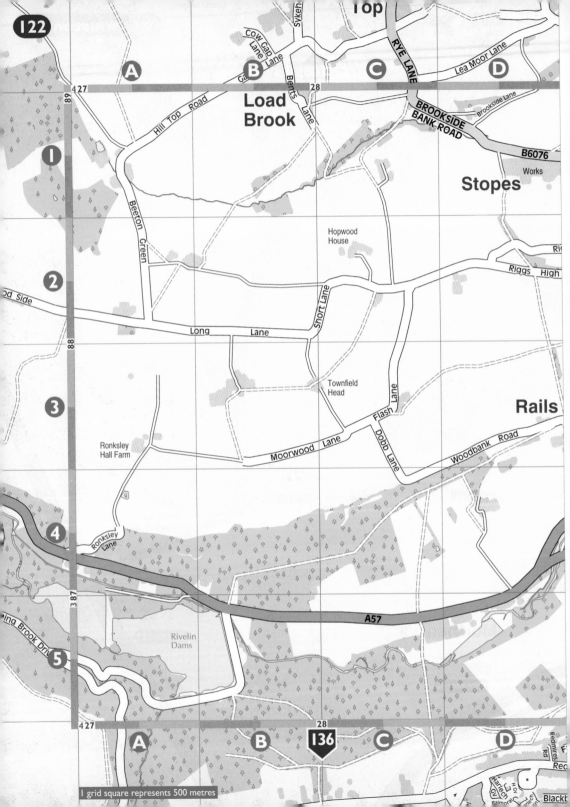

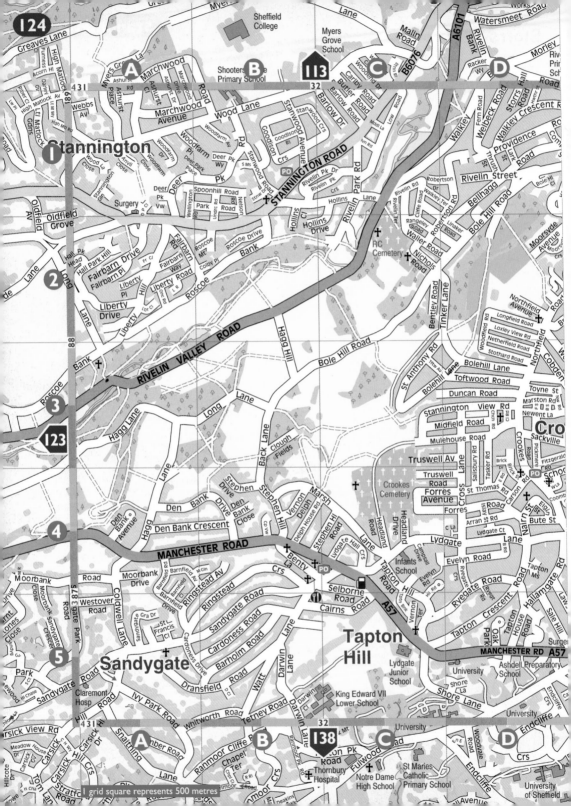

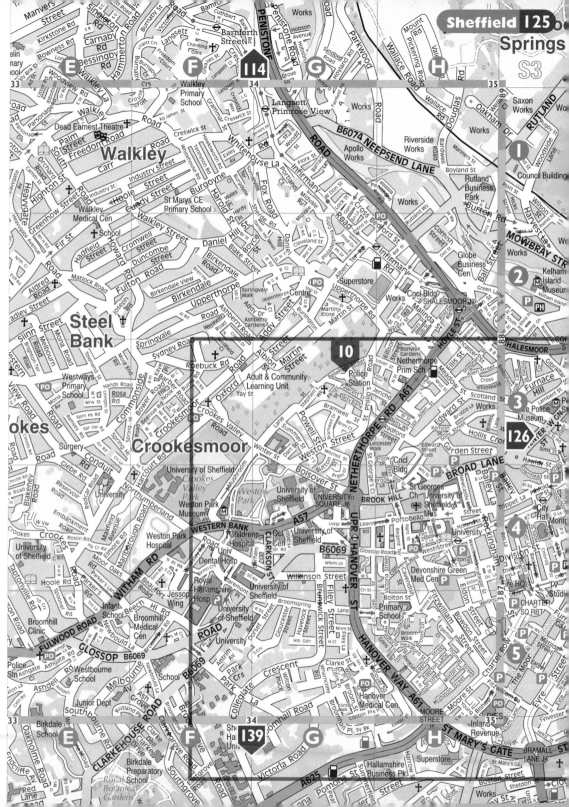

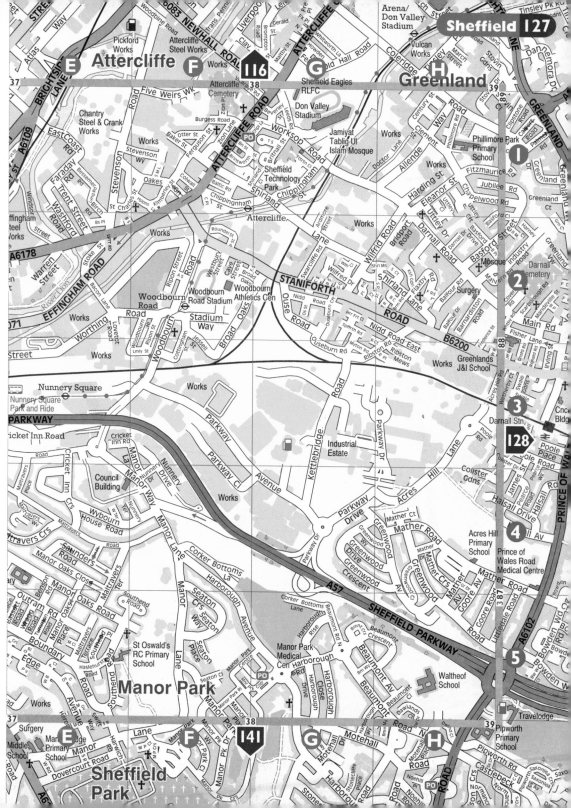

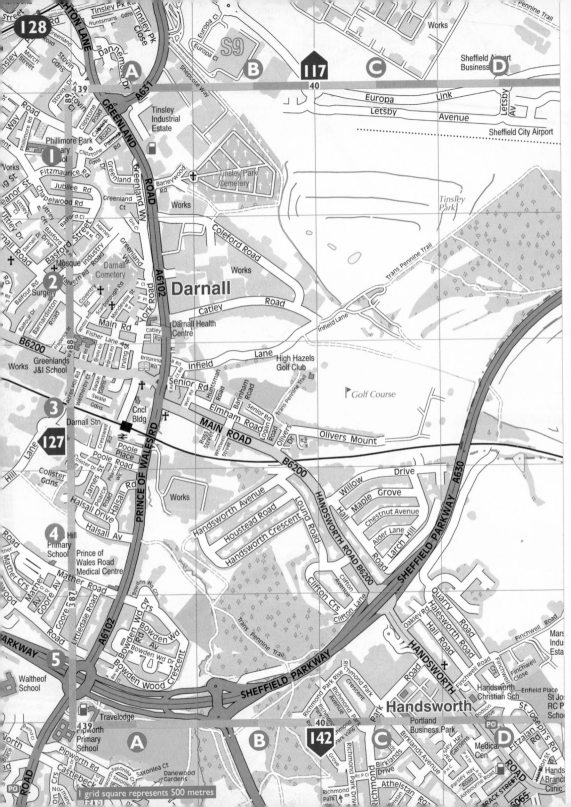

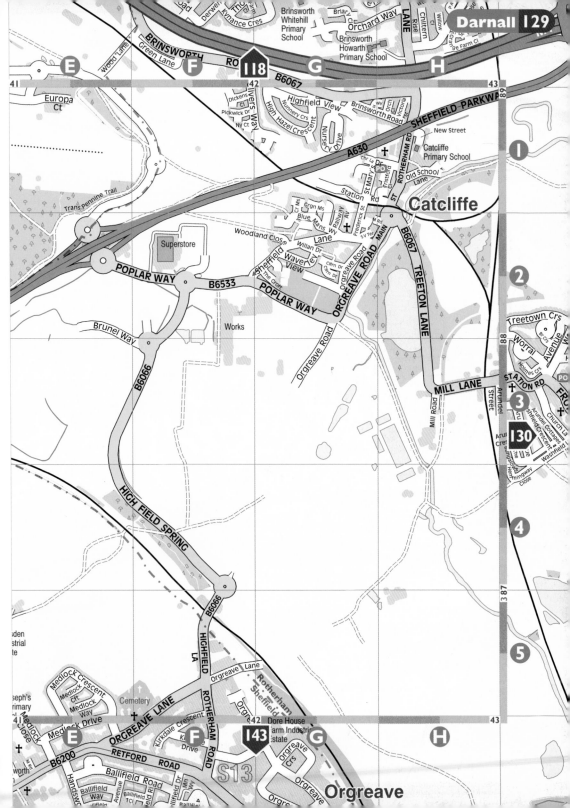

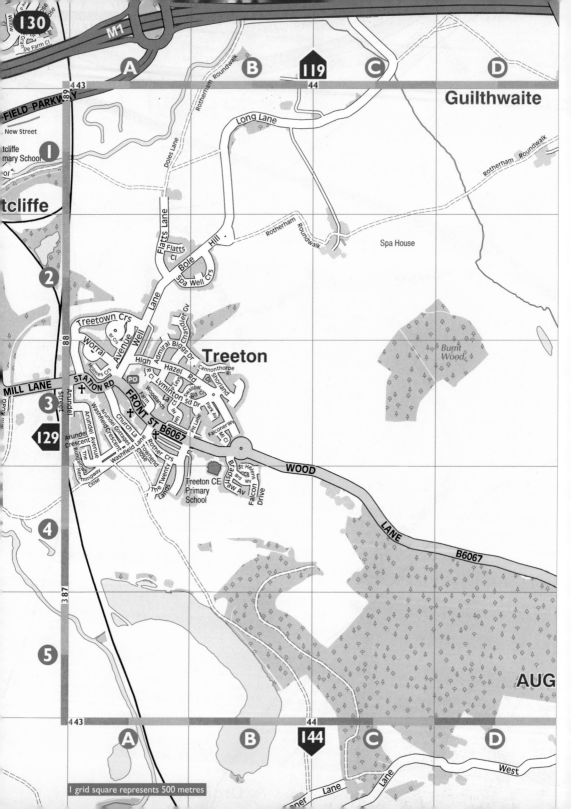

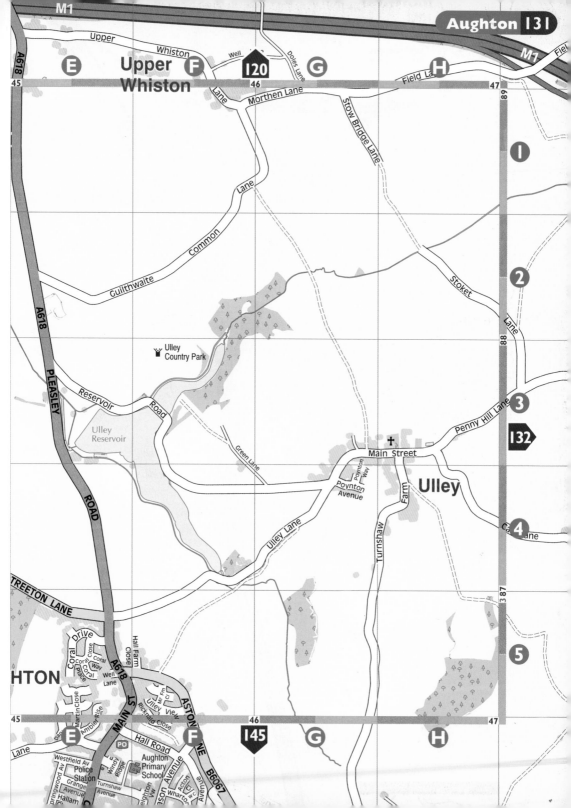

M1

Upper
Whiston

E   Upper   **F**   **120**   **G**
      Whiston   46

Well

Doles Lane

Field Lane   **H**

M1   Fiel

A618

45   89   47

I

Morthen Lane

Stow Bridge Lane

Lane

2

88

Guilthwaite   Common   Lane

Stoke

Lane

Ulley
Country Park

Reservoir   Road

Pleasley

Ulley
Reservoir

Green Lane

Penny Hill Lane   **3**

132

Main Street

Ulley

Poynton
Way

Poynton
Avenue

A618

ROAD

Ulley Lane

Turnshaw Farm

Ca   Lane   **4**

387

5

TREETON LANE

Coral   Drive

Hall Farm Close

Coral Close

HTON

Coral Way
Coral Place
Coral

Well
Lane

A618

MAIN ST.

Ulley
View

Mr Frm
Cl

Rickard Close

ASTON AVE

45   46   47

E   **F**   **145**   **G**   **H**

B6067

Lane

PO

Westfield Av
Av
Police
Station
Grange
Avenue

Windy
Ridge

Turnshaw
Avenue

Hall Road

Aughton
Primary
School

Wharton

Aston
Avenue

Hallam

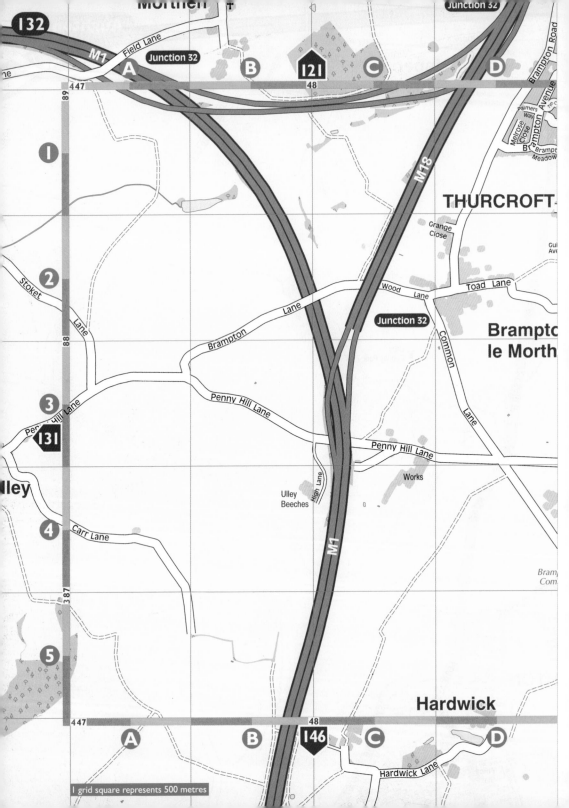

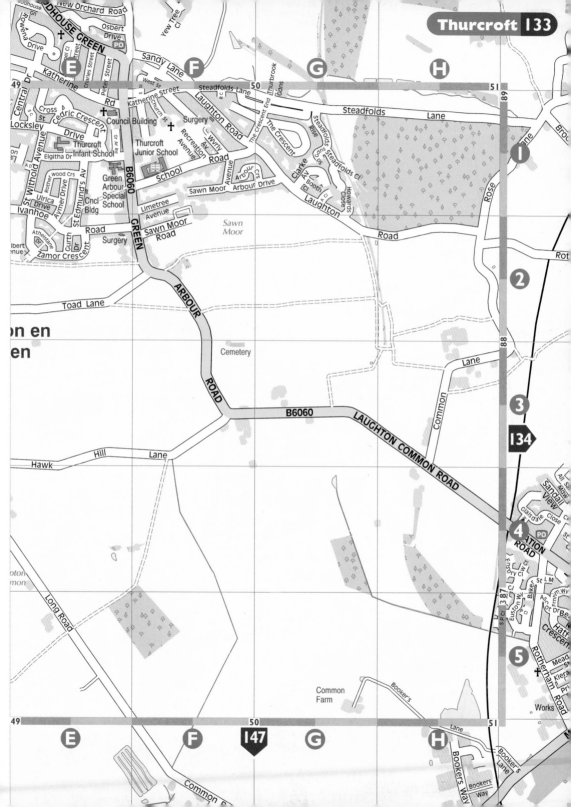

E F G H

WOODHOUSE GREEN
New Orchard Road
Yew Tree Cl
Osbert Drive
PO
Dunhouse Gn
Rowena Drive
Sandy Lane
West St
Steadfolds Lane
Thurbrook Gdns
Katherine Rd
Charles Street
Peter Street
Central Dr
Cross St
Cedric Crescent
Katherine Street
Church St
Laughton Road
Steadfolds Lane
The Crescent End
The Crescent
Council Building
Surgery
Locksley
Elgitha Dr
Drive
Thurcroft Infant School
Recreation Avenue
School Road
Steadfolds Rise
Steadfolds Cl
Withold Avenue
Rother wood Crs
St Edmund's Av
Thurcroft Junior School
Avenue
Wnly Av
Clarke Av
Steadfolds Road
Howards Close
Ivanhoe
Ulrica Drive
Rymer Drive
Cncl Bldg
Green Arbour Special School
Sawn Moor Arbour Drive
Ardsley Crs
Booth Cl
Laughton
Rose Lane
Brook

1

Athelstane Dr
Albert Avenue
Gurth Dr
Zamor Crescent
GREEN
Limetree Avenue
Sawn Moor Road
Surgery
Sawn Moor
Laughton Road
Rot

2

Toad Lane
ARBOUR
Cemetery
Lane
89
88

3

ROAD
Common
134

B6060
LAUGHTON COMMON ROAD

Hawk
Hill
Lane
Sandall View
Glaisdale
St
Close

4
PO
STATION ROAD

on en
en

Long Road

Euston Wy
Spcl Bake
St M
Frm Wy
Dr Be
Hatf Crescent

387

Rotherham Road
Mead
Kiera Pr
St

5

Common Farm
Booker's
Works

E F G H
147

Long
Common

Booker's Lane
Booker's Way
Bookers Way

49
50
51

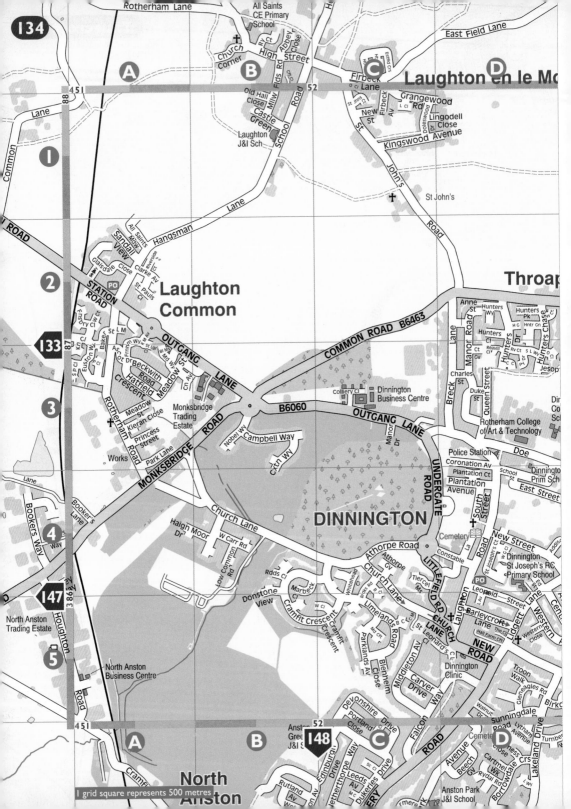

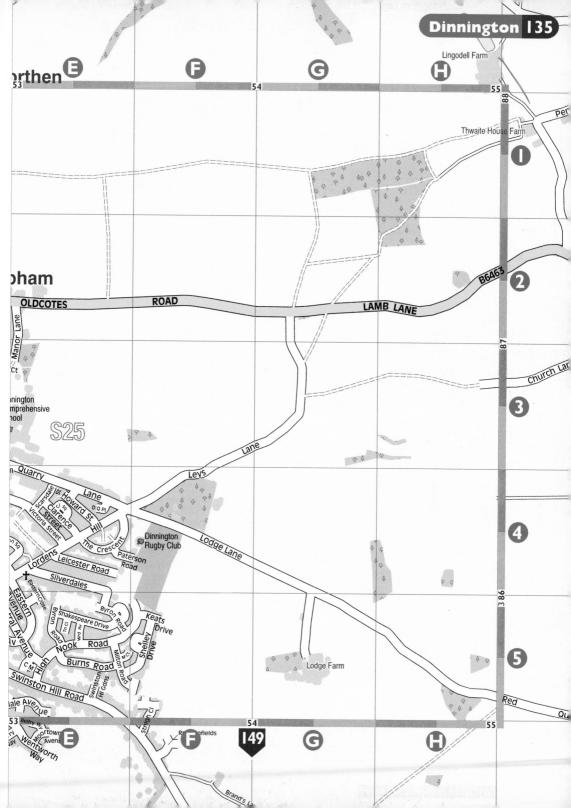

Lingodell Farm

E   F   G   H

54   55

orthen

53

88

Per

Thwaite House Farm

I

B6463

oham

2

OLDCOTES   ROAD   LAMB LANE

87

Church Lar

Manor Lane

Ct

3

nnington
mprehensive
hool

S25

Lane

Leys

4

Quarry

Lane

Scarsdale
Howard St
Clarence
Street
Victoria Street
Hill
D Q Pl

The Crescent

Dinnington
Rugby Club

Lodge Lane

Paterson
Road

Lordens

Leicester Road

Silverdales

386

Eastern

Byron Road

Shakespeare Drive

Keats
Drive

Byron
Road

Nook   Road

Shelley
Drive

Milton Road

Burns Road

Swinston
Hl Gdns

Lodge Farm

5

Red
Qu

SWINSTON HILL ROAD

ale Avenue

53 Belfry W

E   F   149   G   H

54   55

Moortown
Avenu

Strtlgn Cl

Ro   ofields

Wentworth
Way

Brand's La

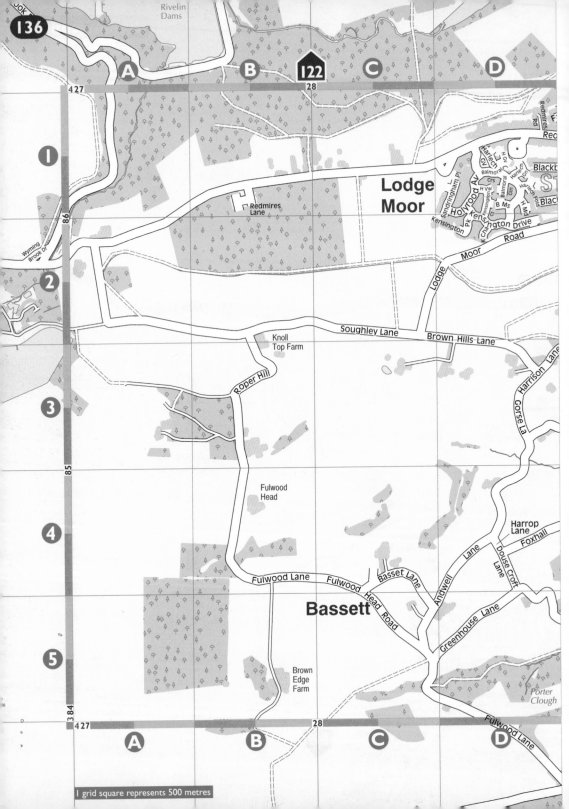

Rivelin Dams

A **B** 122 **C** **D**
28

427

86

I

Redmires
Lane

**Lodge
Moor**

Wyming
Brook Dr

2

Lodge

Moor

Road

Soughley Lane

Brown Hills Lane

Knoll
Top Farm

85

Roper Hill

Harrison Lane

3

Gorse La

Fulwood
Head

4

Harrop
Lane

Foxhall

Andwell

Lane

Douse Croft
Lane

Fulwood Lane

Fulwood Head Road

Basset Lane

Bassett

Greenhouse Lane

5

Brown
Edge
Farm

Porter
Clough

384

427
28

Fulwood Lane

A **B** **C** **D**

Holyrood Av
Sandringham Pl
Harlech Ct
Kensington
Harlech Grn
Harlech Fold
Kensington
Balmoral
Chaddington Drive
Blackb
Blackl

1 grid square represents 500 metres

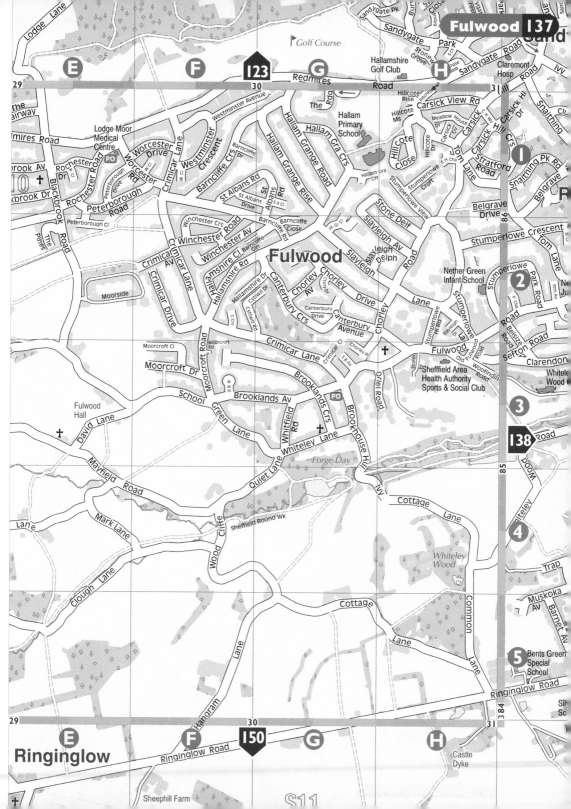

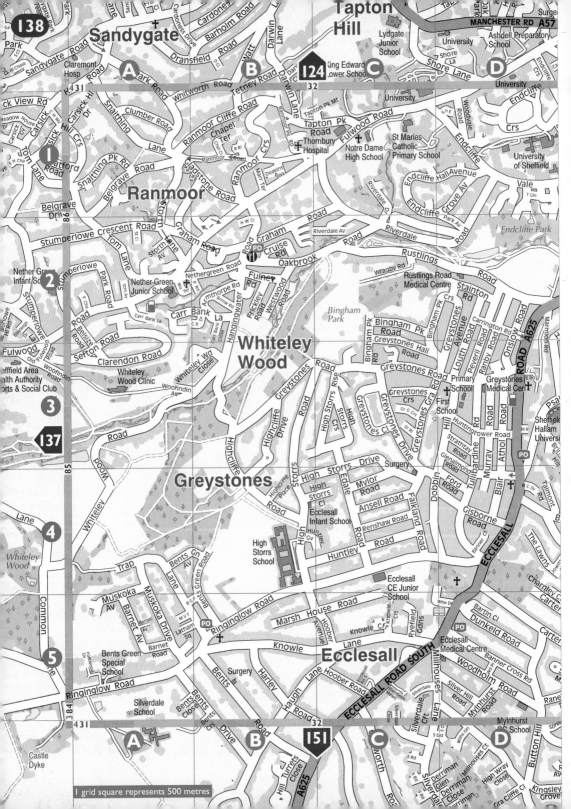

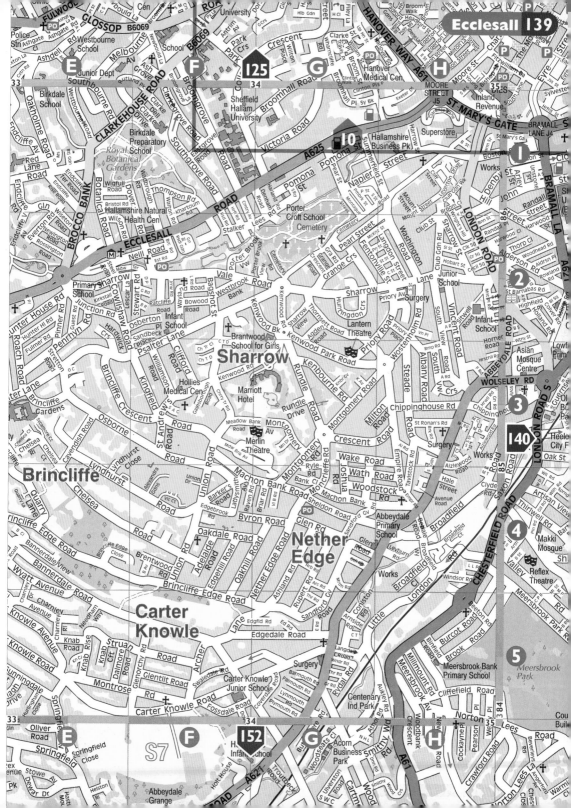

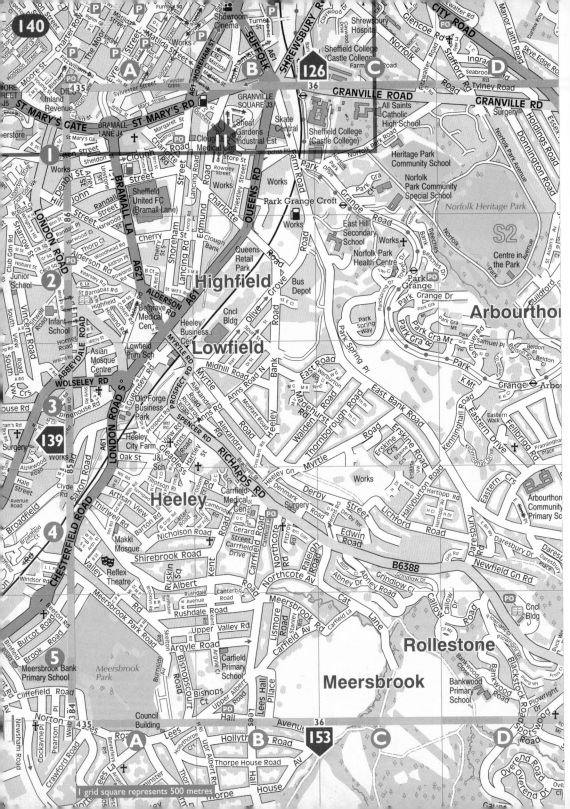

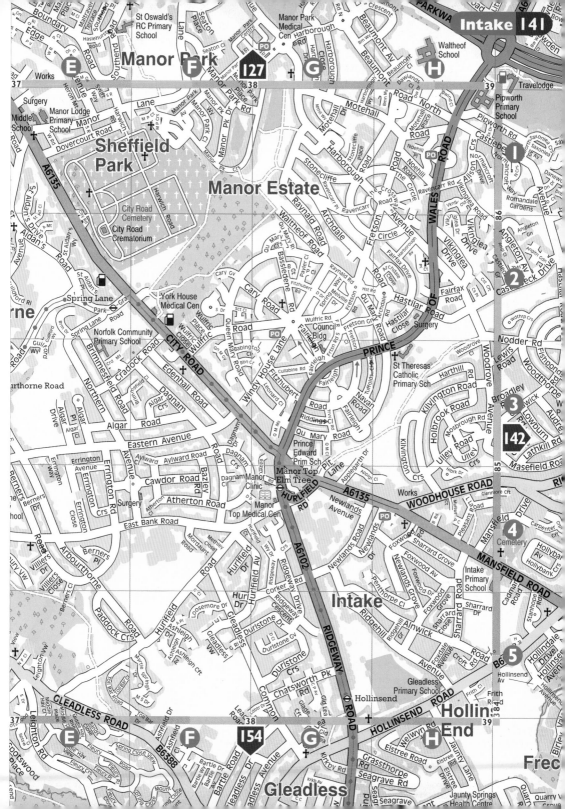

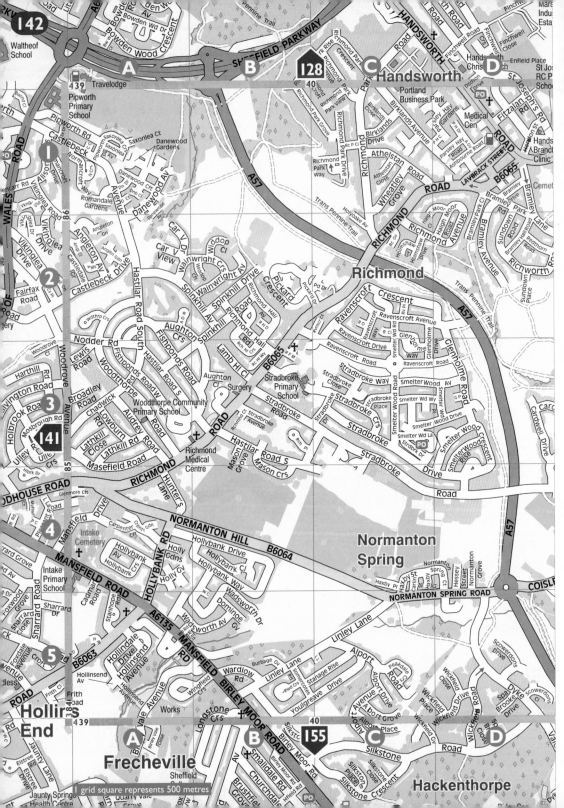

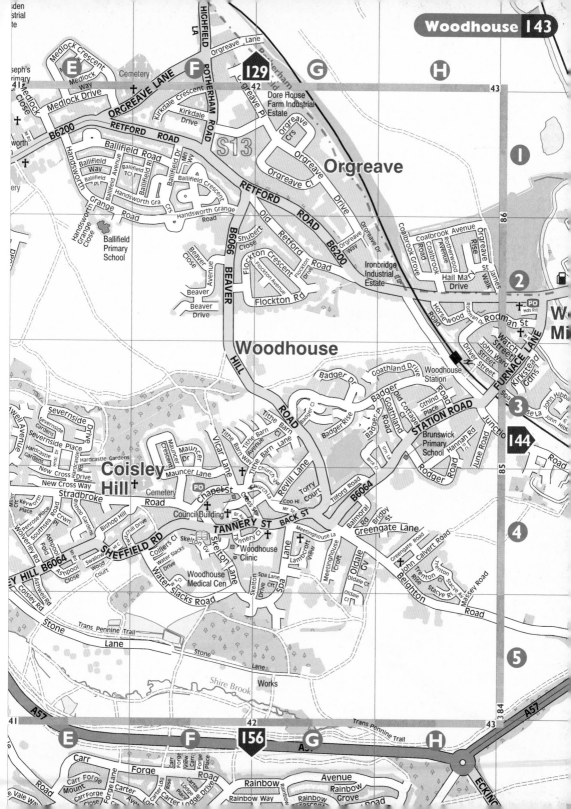

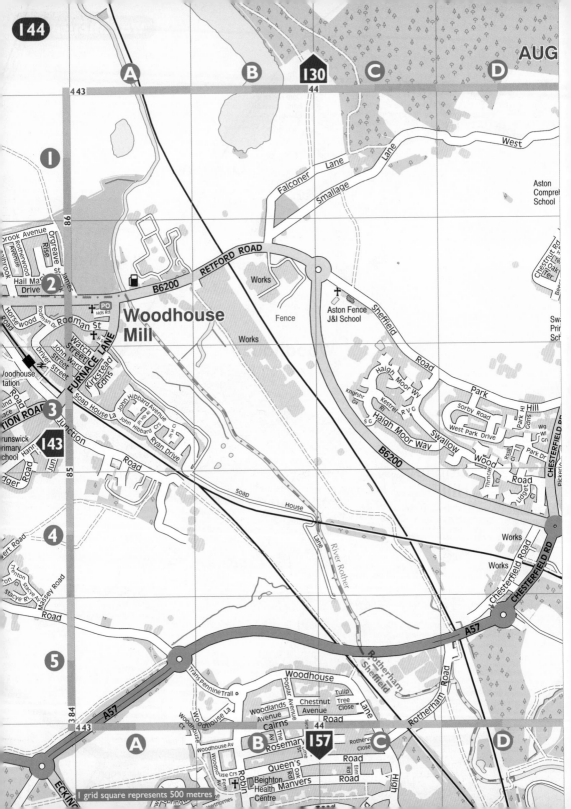

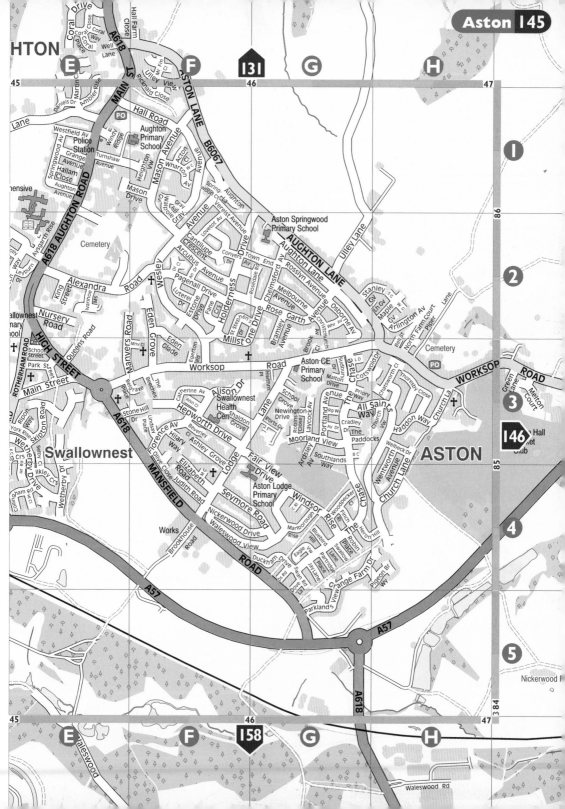

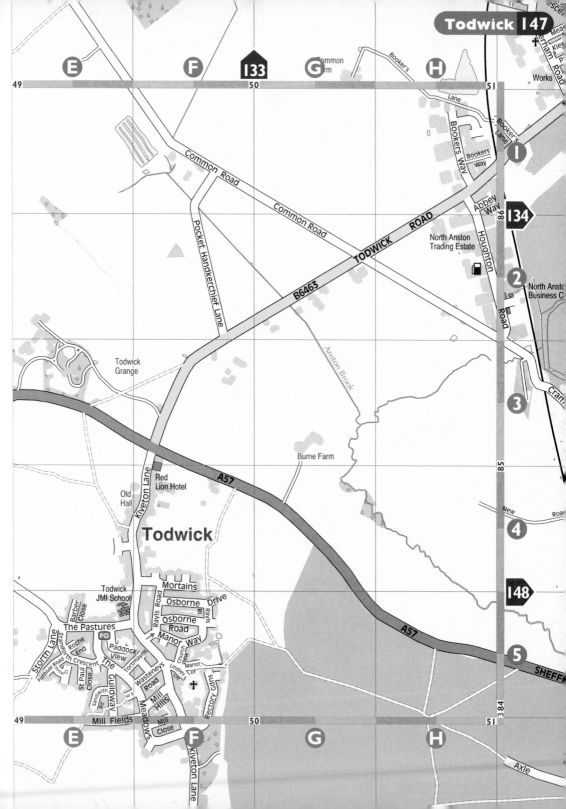

E F **133** G H

49 50 51

Common Road

Common Road

Pocket Handkerchief Lane

TODWICK ROAD

B6463

Bookers Way

Bookers Way

Abbey Way

Houghton

Common Farm

Booker's Lane

Booker's Lane

Works

I

134

North Anston Trading Estate

2

North Anston Business C

Road

Anston Brook

3

Cram

85

Todwick Grange

Burne Farm

Red Lion Hotel

Kiveton Lane

Old Hall

A57

New Road

4

Todwick

148

Todwick JMI School

Mortains

Osborne Road

Osborne Road

Manor Way

Ravis Road

Drive

Ravis

A57

5

SHEFF

Barber Close

The Pastures

PO

Roche End

Paddock View

Storth Lane

Furnival Road

Stanifoorth Crescent

St Paul Close

Sandwith Rd

The Guildway

Portmayns Road

Wasteneys Road

Mill Hills

Church Lane

Manor

Lindley Cft

Rectory Gdns

Mill Meadows

Mill Close

Kiveton Lane

Mill Fields

Axle

49 50 51

E F G H

3 84

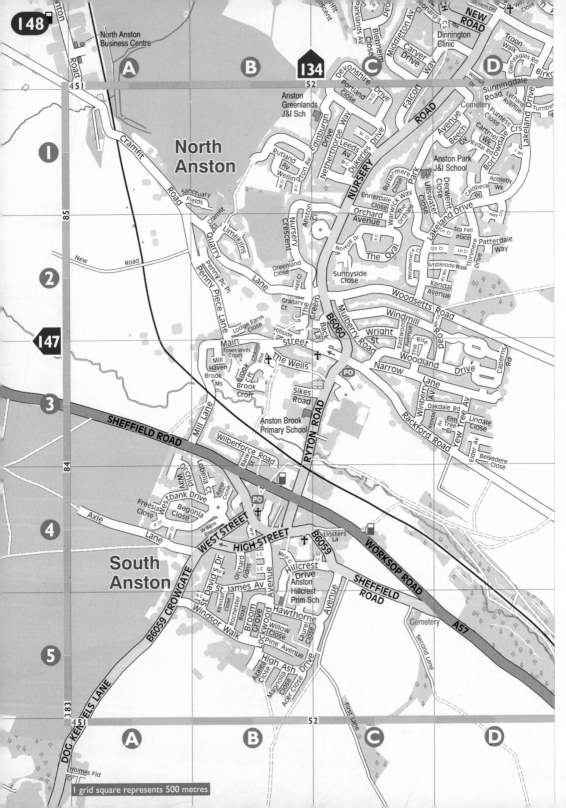

Nook Road
Burns Road
Shelley Drive
High
Mitton Road
Swinston Hill Gdns
Swinston Hill
E
Red Q

dale Avenue
Belfry W
Moortown
Avenue
Wentworth Way

53

Ssnigh Cl

F

135

54

G

H

55

Rowernfields

Lodge Farm

I

85

Brand's Lane

Brand's Lane

2

Works

Brand's Farm

3

84

Swinston Hill Road

Brand's Farm

Bra

Dinnington

Hoads Avenue
Northfiel
Gil

Rackford Farm

Road
Berne Sq
Whitfield
Gdns

4

Wood
J&I S

PO

Wellfield
Crs

Grange
Farm Ct

Anston Stones Wood

5

Lindrick
Road

Taylor
Cres

383

53

54

55

E

F

G

H

Golf Course

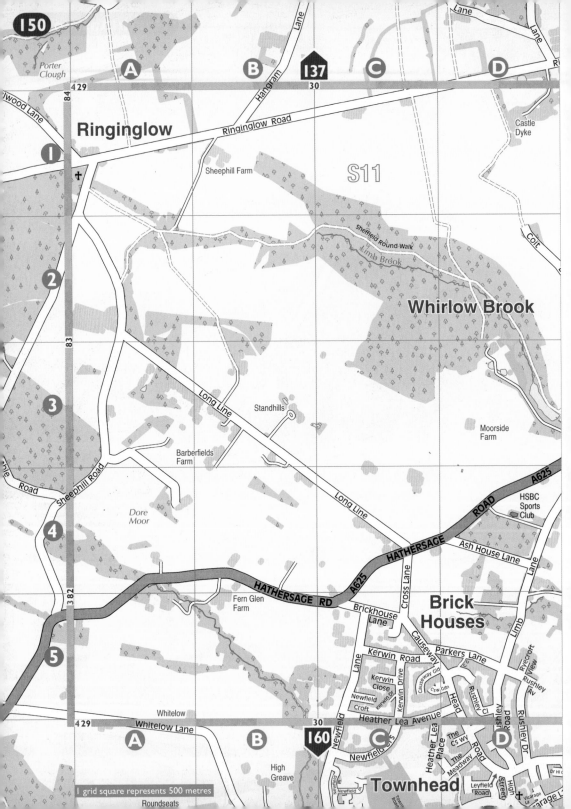

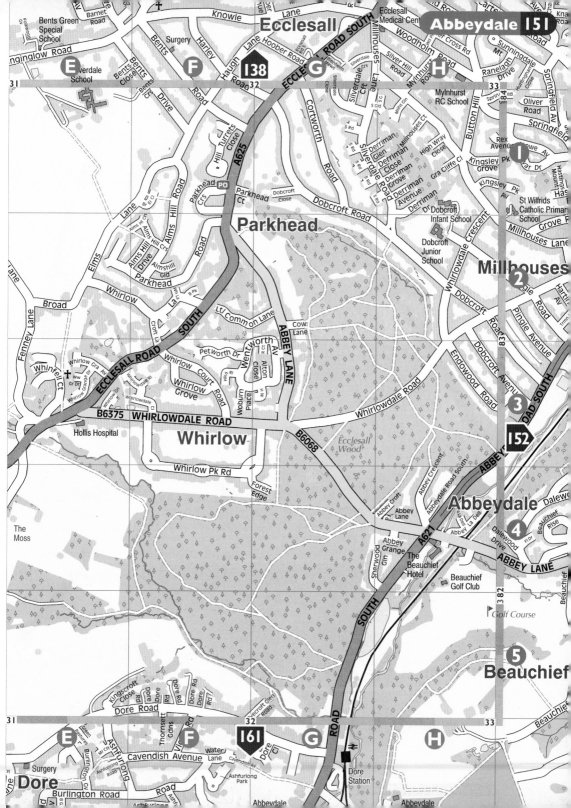

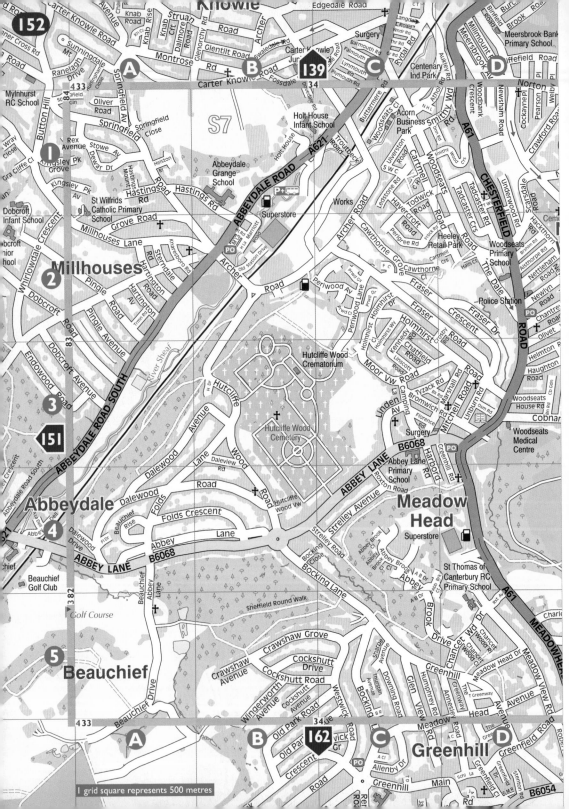

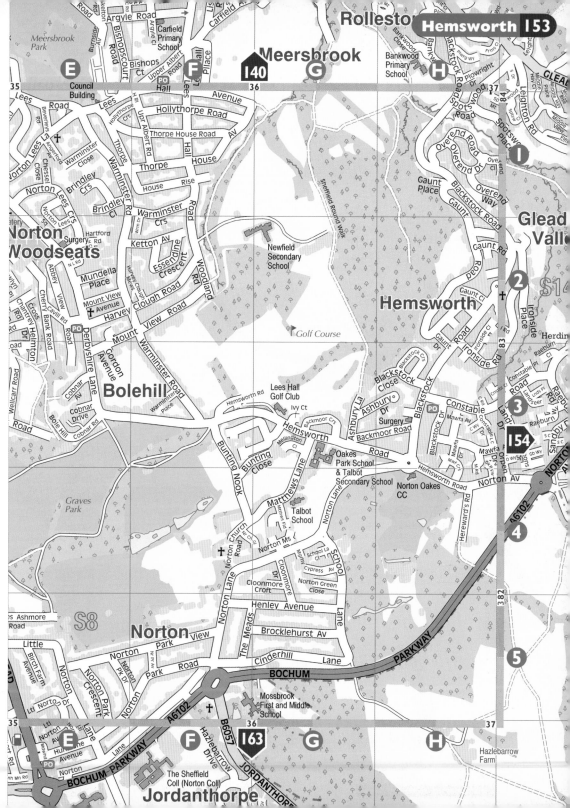

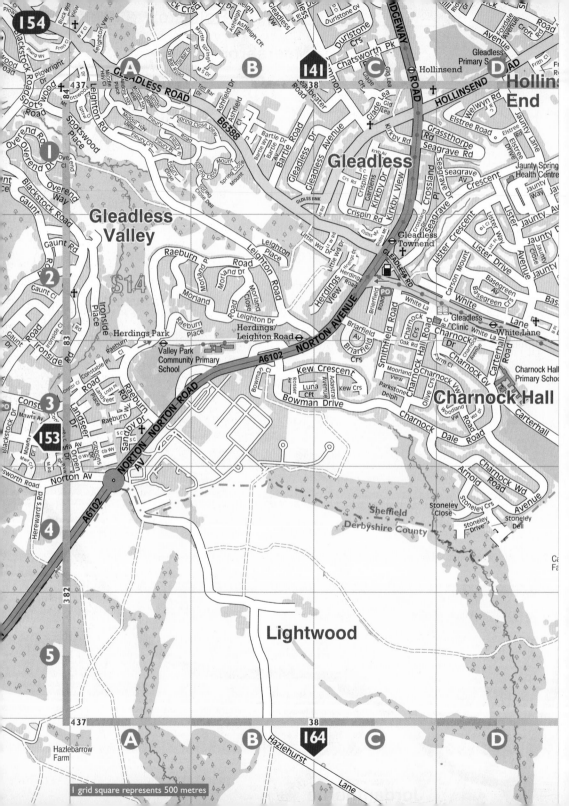

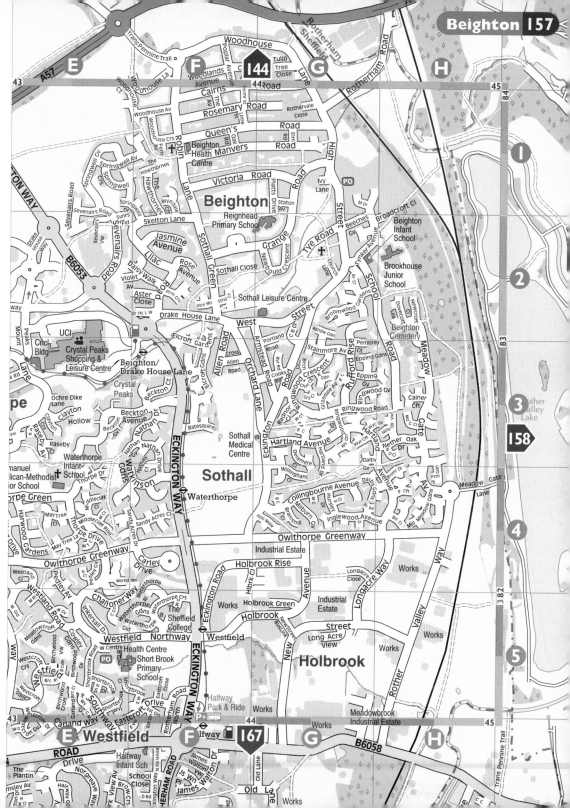

144

E A57 43

F Woodhouse

G Sheffield

H

I

Woodhouse La

Trans Pennine Trail

Popular Avenue

Woodlands Avenue

Tulip Tree Close

Rotherham Road

Cairns Road

Rosemary Road

Rothervale Close

Road

Woodhouse Av

Woomhouse Crs

Queen's Road

Road

Beighton Health Centre

Manvers Road

2

Springwell Gv
Springwell Av
Springwell Cl

The Hawthornes

Victoria Road

High Street

PO

Ivy Lane

Broadcroft Cl

Beighton Infant School

Sevenairs Road

Skelton Lane

Beighton

Platts Drive

Staton AV

Beeches

Winker Avenue

Brookhouse Junior School

B6053

Jasmine Avenue

Reignhead Primary School

Sothall Green

Grange Crescent

Tye Road

School Road

Beighton Cemetery

Lilac Rose Avenue

Daisy Walk

Violet Cl

Sothall Close

Church Lane

Epping

Drake House Lane

Aster Close

West Street

Portland Road

Stainmore Av

Rufford Rise

Ringwood Gv

Calner Cft

Rother Valley Lake

3

UCI

Cncl Bldg

Crystal Peaks Shopping & Leisure Centre

Elcroft Gardens

Allen Road

Orchard Lane

Radnor Crescent

Ringwood Crescent

Ringwood Road

Nether Oak Dr

158

Ochre Dike Lane

Clayton Hollow

Crystal Peaks

Beckton Avenue

Nathan

Batesquire

Sothall Medical Centre

Eckington

Hartland Avenue

Hartland Avenue

Dalby

Raseby Av

Waterthorpe

Thorpe Dr

Watkinson Gdns

Sothall

Willingham

Collingbourne Avenue

Meadow Gate Lane

4

Emmanuel Methodist School

Thorpe Green

Middlecliff Cl

Nathan Drive

Waterthorpe

Milburn Gv

Inglewood Avenue

Mill Meadow Gdns

May Tree Cl

Sandy Acres Dr

Owlthorpe Greenway

Industrial Estate

Longacre Way

Works

5

Harwood Gardens

Thorpe Drive

Carley Drive

Holbrook Rise

Hlbrk Ct

Works

Industrial Estate

Westland Road

Challoner Way

Waterthorpe Gdns

The Sheffield College

Holbrook Green

Holbrook

Long Acre View

Works

Meadowcroft

Cowley

Westfield Northway

Westfield

New Avenue

Street

Rother Way

Works

E **Westfield**

W Centre Health Centre

Short Brook Primary School

PO

Westcroft

Southall

Eastcroft Drive

Rotherham Road North

Halfway Park & Ride

Works

Meadowbrook Industrial Estate

H

Carland Way

ECKINGTON WAY

F Halfway

167

G B6058

ROAD

43 44 45

The Plantin

Halfway Infant Sch

School Close

James Walton Dr

Old Lane

Works

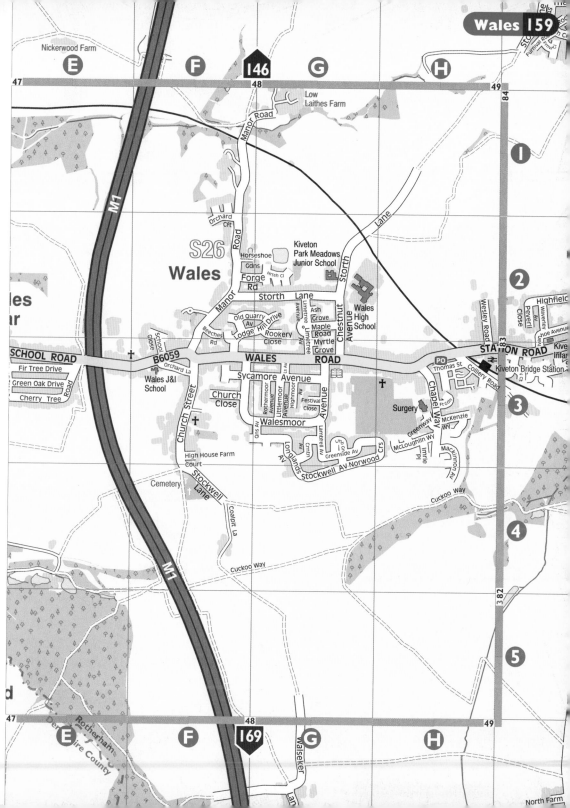

E   F   **146**   G   H

47   48   49   84

Nickerwood Farm

Low
Laithes Farm

M1

I

Orchard
Cft

Manor Road

S26

Wales

Lane

Storth

2

Kiveton
Park Meadows
Junior School

Horseshoe
Gdns

Hrssh Cl

Forge
Rd

Wesley Road

Highfield

Close

Peverl
Av

Waverley
Av

oe Avenue

Kive

Storth Lane

Manor Road

Ash
Grove

Wales
High
School

Avenue

Limetree

Limetree

Chestnut Avenue

Old Quarry
Av

Hill Drive

Lodge

Maple
Road

Myrtle
Grove

Beeches
Rd

Rookery
Close

STATION ROAD

SCHOOL ROAD

B6059

School Close

†

WALES   **ROAD**

PO

Thomas St

Colliery Road

Kiveton Bridge Station

Kiveton Infan

3

Fir Tree Drive

Orchard La

Wales J&I
School

Sycamore Avenue

Ft Grm

McKenzie
Wy

Green Oak Drive

Road

Church
Close

Rothermoor
Avenue

Littlemoor
Avenue

Festival
Close

Highmoor
Av

†

Surgery

Chapel Way

Greenway

McLoughlin Wy

MacKinnon Av

Imrie
Pl

Cherry Tree

Church Street

†

Walesmoor

Sth Av

Av

Lambrell Av

Crtn

Greenside Av

Crs

Stockwell Av

Norwood

McLoughlin Wy

High House Farm
Court

Longlands
Av

Cuckoo Way

4

Cemetery

Stockwell Lane

Coalpit La

3

82

Cuckoo Way

5

M1

E   F   **169**   G   H

47   48   49

Rotherham

Derbyshire County

Walseker
Lane

North Farm

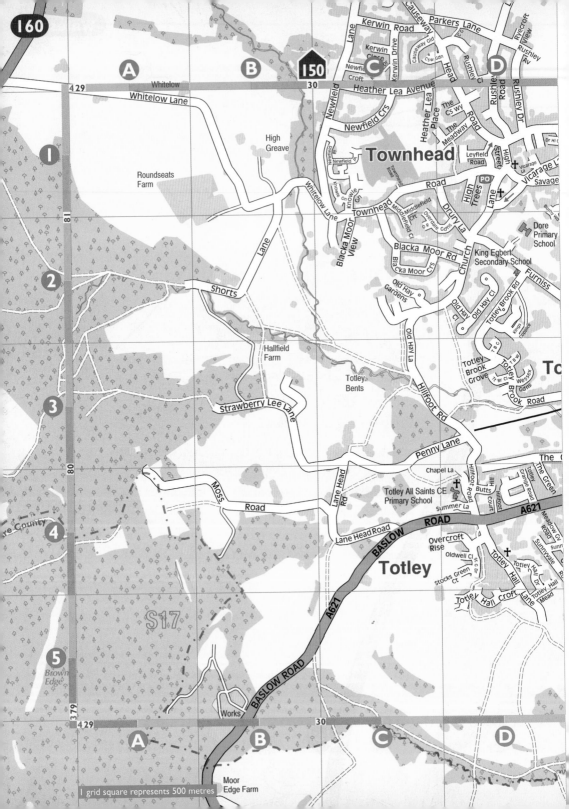

A **B** **C** **D**

4 29
30

Whitelow
Whitelow Lane

High
Greave

Kerwin Road   Parkers Lane
Kerwin Drive   Causeway Cld
Kerwin   Causeway Head
Close   Csw Gdn
Newfld   Rivecroft   Rushley Av
Croft   View   Rushley Dr

Heather Lea Avenue
Newfield Crs

Heather Lea
Place   The   CS Wy
The
Meadway
Leyfield
Road   Vicarage L
Vicarage

Townhead
PO

1

Roundseats
Farm

81

Whitelow Lane
Townhead   Road

High
Trees   High
Lane   Savage

Middlefield
Road   Overdale
Crt   Overdale
Gdns

Blacka Moor Rd

Dr Hl Cl

Dore
Primary
School

Knowle Cft

Blacka Moor View

Blacka Moor Crs

King Egbert
Secondary School

Church
Road

Drury La

Old Hay Cl

Old Hay
Gardens

Old Hay La

Old Hay Cl

Totley Brook Rd

Kings
Copse

Furniss

2

Shorts   Lane

Shorts

To

Totley
Brook
Grove

T B G

Totley
Brook
T B W   Wesset
Gdns
Hillfoot Rd

Brook   Road

80

Hallfield
Farm

Totley
Bents

Strawberry Lee Lane

3

Penny Lane

The Gr

Chapel La
Hillfoot Road   Butts

Hillfoot
Hill
Court

The Green

Crange Road
Meadow Cl   The
Road

Lane Head Rd

Totley All Saints CE
Primary School

Summer La

4

re County

MOSS   Road

Lane Head Road

Overcroft
Rise

BASLOW   ROAD
A621

Totley

Oldwell Cl
Stocks Green
Ct

Totley Hall Dr

Totley Hall Lane

Sunnyvale
Road

Totley
'Mead

3 79

A621

BASLOW ROAD

S17

5

Brown
Edge

Works

4 29   30

A **B** **C** **D**

Moor
Edge Farm

1 grid square represents 500 metres

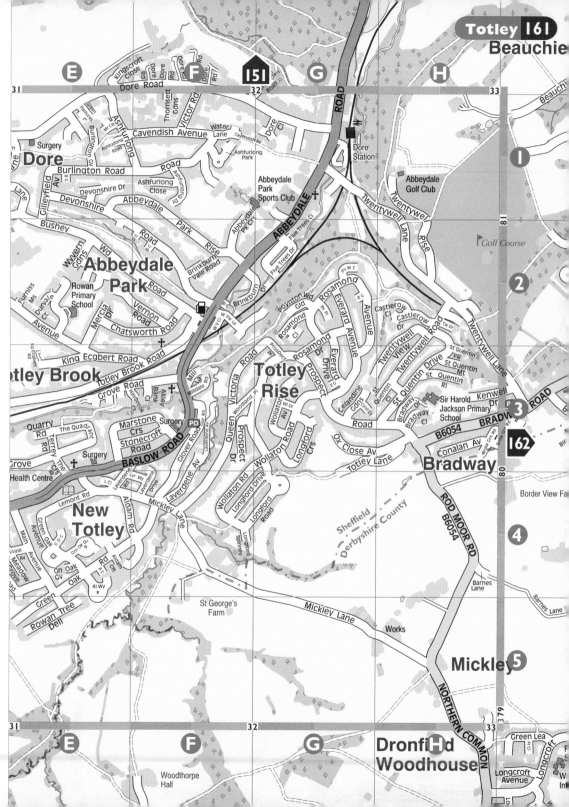

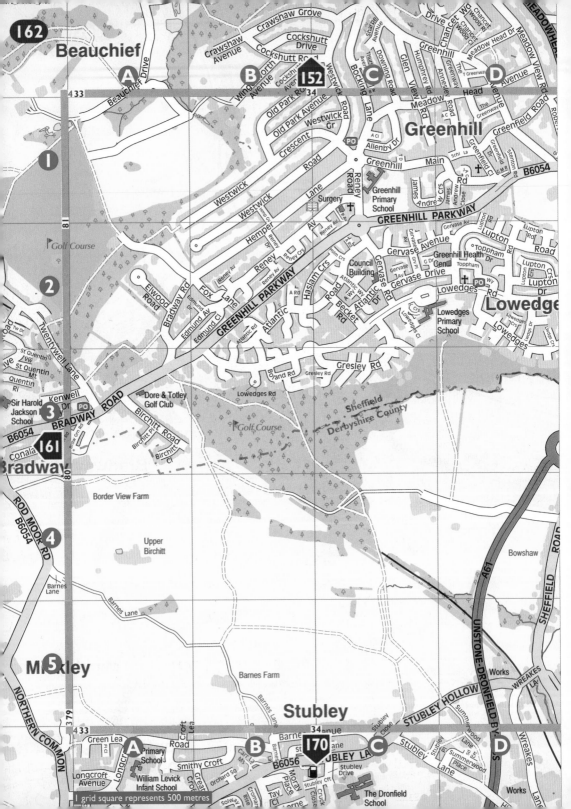

162 Beauchief

A Beauchief Drive

433

I

2

Golf Course

Twentywell Lane

St Quentin
St Quentin
St Quentin
Mt
Quentin
Rl

Sir Harold
Jackson
School

3 Kenwell Dr
PO
BRADWAY ROAD

B6054

Conala **161**
Bradway

ROD MOOR RD
B6054

4

Barnes
Lane

NORTHERN COMMON

5 Mickley

3 79

433

A Green Lea
Longcr
Primary
School
Longcroft
Avenue
William Levick
Infant School
Smithy Croft
Croft
Road
Orchard Sq

Crawshaw Grove
Crawshaw
Avenue
B Wingworth Avenue
Cockshutt Rd
Cockshutt Drive
Cockshutt Rd

Old Park Road
34
Westwick Road
152

Old Park Avenue
Old Park
Crescent
Westwick
Gr

Bocking Lane

Westwick
Road

PO
Allenby Dr
Greenhill
Reney Road
Surgery
Greenhill
Primary
School

Westwick
Lane

Hemper
Lane
Reney
Av
Reney Av
Reney Crs

Reney
Av

Fox
Lane
Edmund Av

Elwood
Road

Bradway Rd

Atlantic
Rd

Atlantic
Road

Edmund Cl
Edmund Av

Atlantic
Road

GREENHILL PARKWAY

Haslam Crs
A Rd

Becket
Rd

Atlantic
Dr

Boyland Rd
Gresley Rd
Gresley Rd

Lowedges Rd

Dore & Totley
Golf Club

Birchitt Road

Birchitt Pit Rd
Birchitt
Cl

Golf Course

Sheffield
Derbyshire County

Border View Farm

Upper
Birchitt

Barnes Lane

Barnes Farm

Barnes
Lane

Stubley

B B6056

Barne
Carr La
Ms

170

STUBLEY LANE
Stubley
Drive

Moral
Place
Tay
Cl

Stubley Crt
The Dronfield
School

Sharpe
Avenue
Drive Wg
Chancet Wood
Chancet
Wood
MEADOWHE

Greenhill
Avenue
Greenway

Meadow Head Dr
Meadow View Rd

D
Avenue

Glen View
Humphrey Rd

Meadow
Road
Annesley
Road

Greenhill
Road

Greenhill

Main

Greenfield Road

Greenhill C

James
Andre

James
Andrew
Crs

Andrew
close

B6054

GREENHILL PARKWAY

Gervase Av

Gervase Avenue
Gervase
Drive

Gervase
Av

Council
Building

Greenhill Health
Cen

Toppham
Toppham
Dr

Lupton
Road

Lupton
Rd

Lupton
Crs

Lowedges

Lowedge

Lowedges Rd

Lowedges
Primary
School

Lowedges

Lowedges
Dr

PO
Wy
Rd
Lupton
Dr

A61

Bowshaw

SHEFFIELD ROAD

UNSTONE-DRONFIELD BY

WREAKES LA

Works

STUBLEY HOLLOW

Summerwood
Lane
Summerwood
Place

C Stubley
Close
Stubley
Lane

D
Works

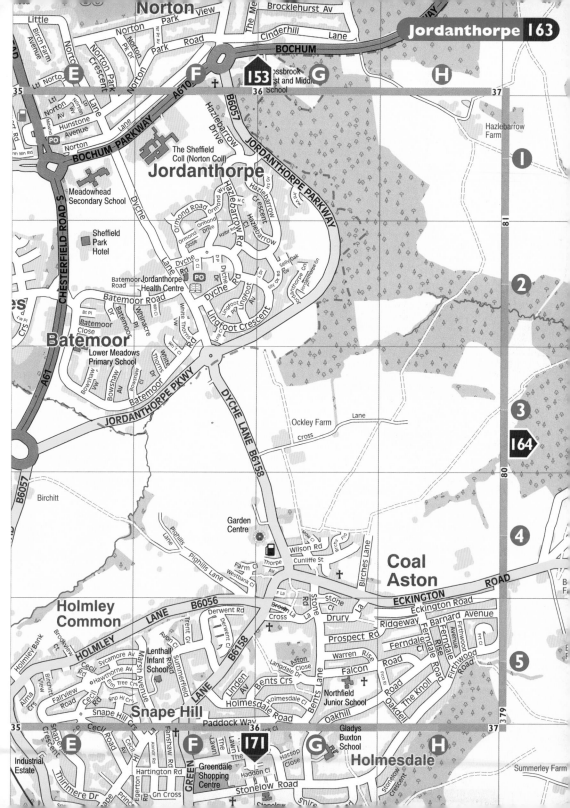

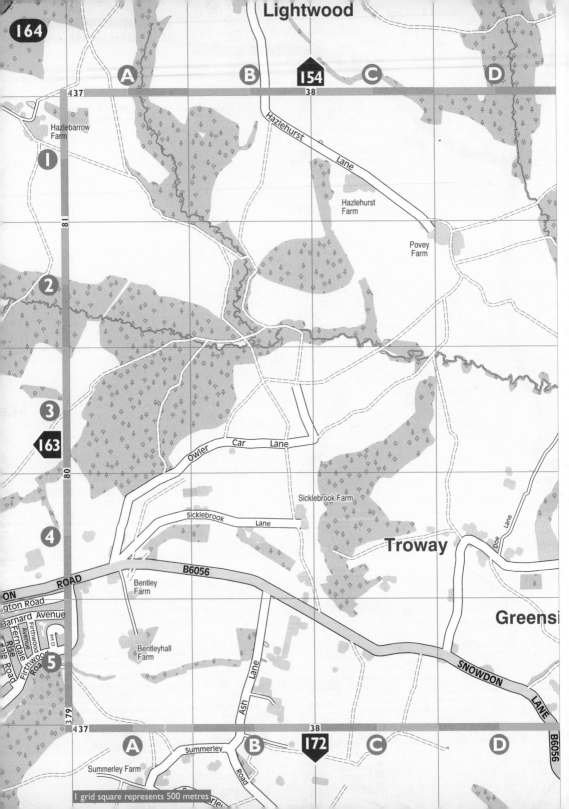

Lightwood

164

A   B   154   C   D

437   38

Hazlebarrow
Farm

1

Hazlehurst Lane

Hazlehurst
Farm

2

Povey
Farm

3

163

Owler Car Lane

4

Sicklebrook Farm

Sicklebrook Lane

Troway

Doe Lane

B6056

Bentley
Farm

ROAD

gton Road

Barnard Avenue

Greensi

Ferndale Rise Road

Firthwood Avenue

Firthwood Road

Bentleyhall
Farm

5

SNOWDON LANE

437   38

A   B   172   C   D

B6056

Summerley

Summerley Farm

Ash Lane

Road

1 grid square represents 500 metres

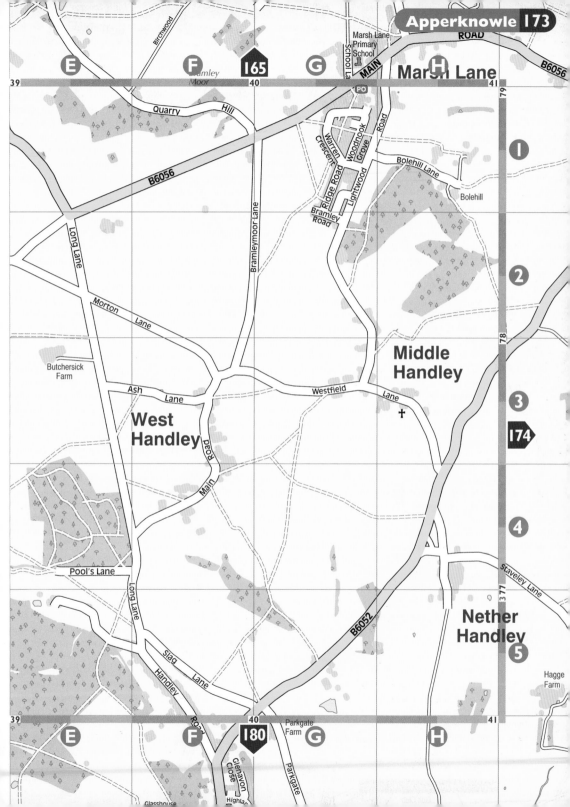

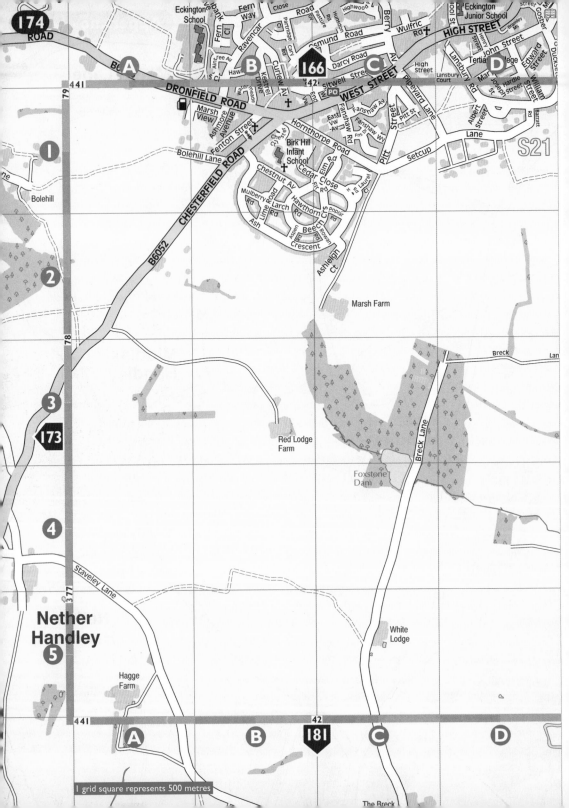

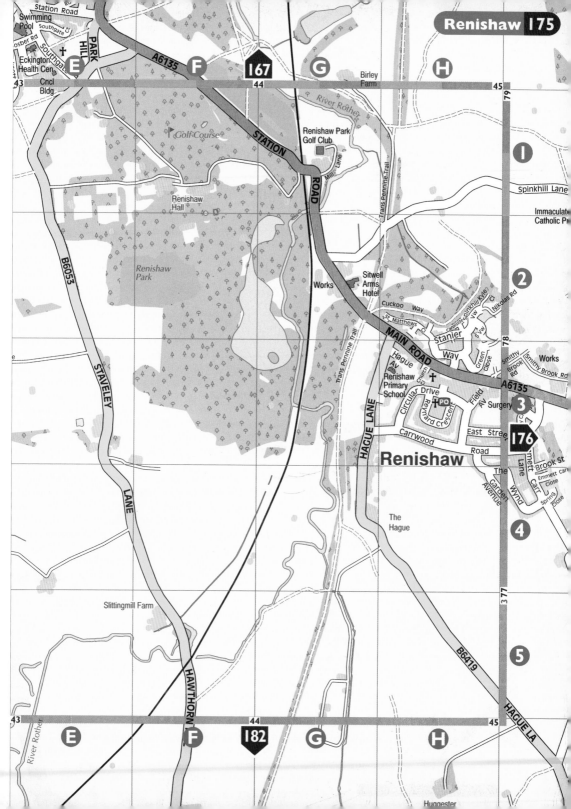

Station Road
Swimming Pool
southgate Cr
Southgate
osber Rd
PARK HILL
Eckington Health Cen
Cncl Bldg
E
43 44
A6135
F
167
G
H
Birley Farm

River Rother

Golf Course
Renishaw Park Golf Club
Mill Lane
I
Spinkhill Lane
Immaculate Catholic P

Renishaw Hall
Renishaw Park

STATION ROAD

Trans Pennine Trail

Sitwell Arms Hotel
Works
Cuckoo Way
2
Nikolas Rd
Spinkhill
Kyle Cl
Stanier Way
Cadeby
VW
VW
Green Close
Smithy Brook Rd
Smithy Brook Rd
Works

St Matthews
MAIN ROAD
A6135

Hague Av
Renishaw Primary School
Circular Drive
Reynard Crescent
PO
Field Av
Surgery
3
176

B6053

STAVELEY LANE

HAGUE LANE

Carrwood
East Street Road
Emmett Carr Lane
The Wynd
Brook St
Emmett Carr Close
Spring Close
Renishaw
The Garden Avenue
4

Slittingmill Farm

The Hague

Trans Pennine Trail

5
B6419

HAWTHORN LANE

River Rother
E
43 44
F
182
G
H
45
HAGUE LA

Huggester

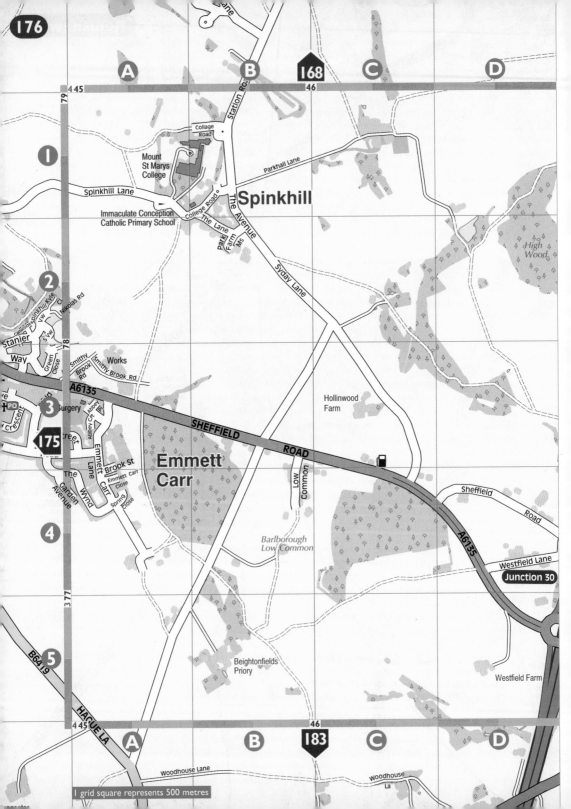

A   **B**   **168**   **C**   **D**

79 4 45   46

Collage Road

Station Road

Parkhall Lane

I

Mount St Marys College

Spinkhill Lane

Spinkhill

The Avenue

College Road

Immaculate Conception Catholic Primary School

The Lane

Park Farm Ms

Srcday Lane

High Wood

2

Spinkhill Kyle

Nikolas Rd

VW

Stanier Way

Green Close

Smithy Brook Rd

Smithy Brook Rd

Works

78

Hollinwood Farm

PO

Surgery

3

A6135

SHEFFIELD

ROAD

Crescent

Abbey Cft Abbey

Emmett Lane

Brook St

Emmett Carr Close

Emmett Carr

Low Common

The Wynd

Spring Close

Garden Avenue

175

Street

Sheffield Road

A6135

Westfield Lane

Junction 30

4

Barlborough Low Common

377

Westfield Farm

5

B6419

Beightonfields Priory

HAGUE LA

4 45

A   **B**   **183**   **C**   **D**

46

Woodhouse Lane

Woodhouse La

I grid square represents 500 metres

178

A   B   **171**   C   D

435   36

I

76

2

Monkwood
Farm

Barlow Brook

Chesterfield
Trading
Estate

Carrwood   Road

Broombank Rd
Industrial
Estate

3

Cobnar Wd
Cl

Carrwood Road

Smeckley
Wood Close

Bridge Wy

Broombank

Road

Broombank Park

Lane

75

4

Dunston Hole
Farm

Sheepb

UNSTONE-DRONFIELD BY-PASS   A61

5

B6050

Newbold
Fields

DUNSTON ROAD

BARLOW ROAD

374

435   36

A   B   **186**   C   D

Dunston

Baines Wood
Close

Kingswood Cl

Nesfield
Cl

Arnside
Cl

Lindale

Dunston

Cobden Drive

Monkwood
Road

Kirkstone
Rd

Hollin

Spring Wd Cl

Cordwell

Coledale

Wd Av

Willow Garth Rd

Sudhall
Close

Kirkstone
Road

Upper
Newbold

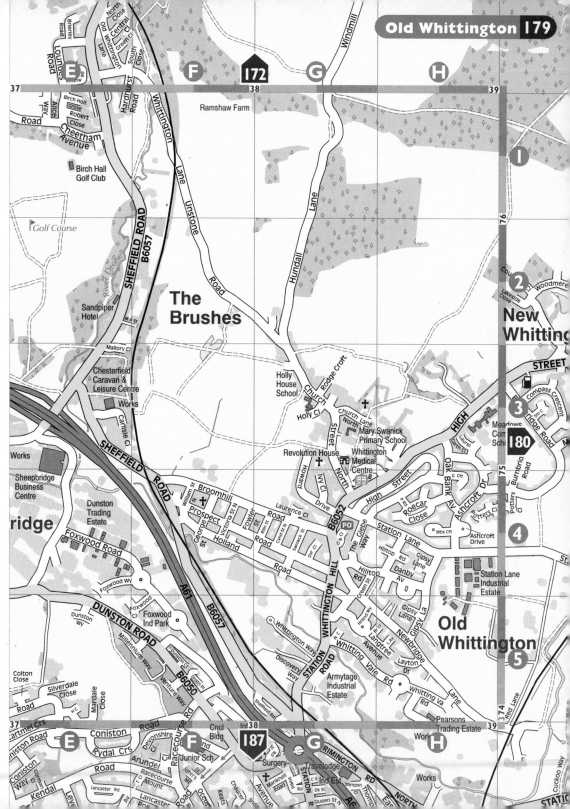

The Brushes

New Whitting

Old Whittington

Ramshaw Farm

Birch Hall Golf Club

Golf Course

Sandpiper Hotel

Chesterfield Caravan & Leisure Centre

Sheepbridge Business Centre

Dunston Trading Estate

Foxwood Ind Park

Holly House School

Revolution House

Mary Swanick Primary School

Whittington Medical Centre

Station Lane Industrial Estate

Armytage Industrial Estate

Pearsons Trading Estate

SHEFFIELD ROAD B6057

SHEFFIELD ROAD

DUNSTON ROAD

A61

B6050

B6057

Whittington Lane

Unstone Road

Hundall Lane

HIGH STREET

STATION ROAD

Ashcroft Dr

Burnbria Road

E F **172** G H I

37 38 39

76

75

374

2 3 **180** 4 5

E Coniston Road F **187** G H

37 38 39

Travelodge

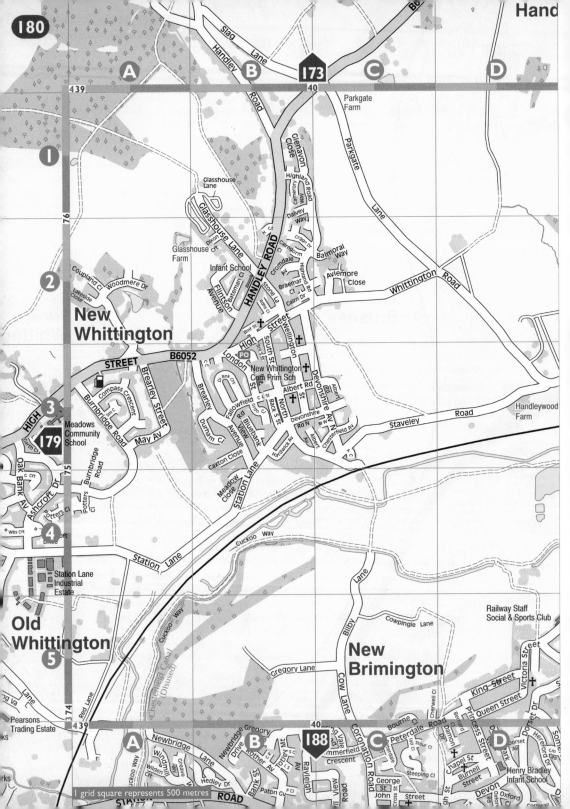

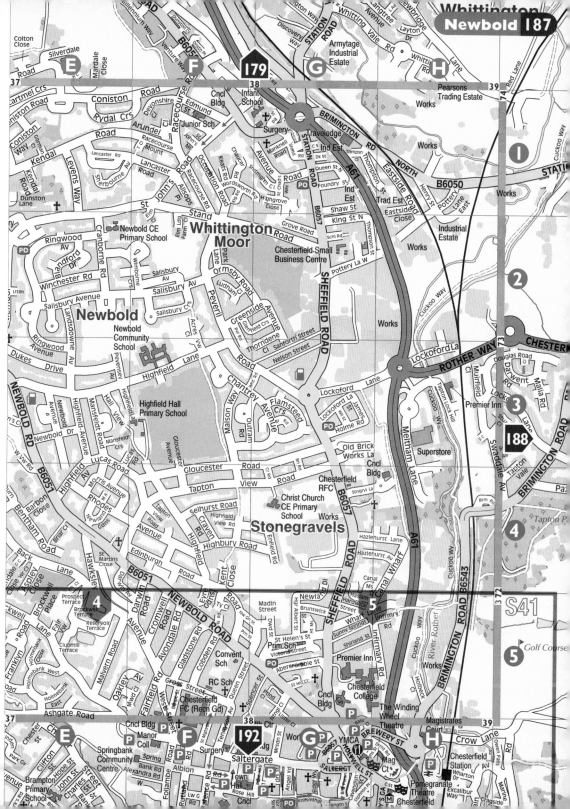

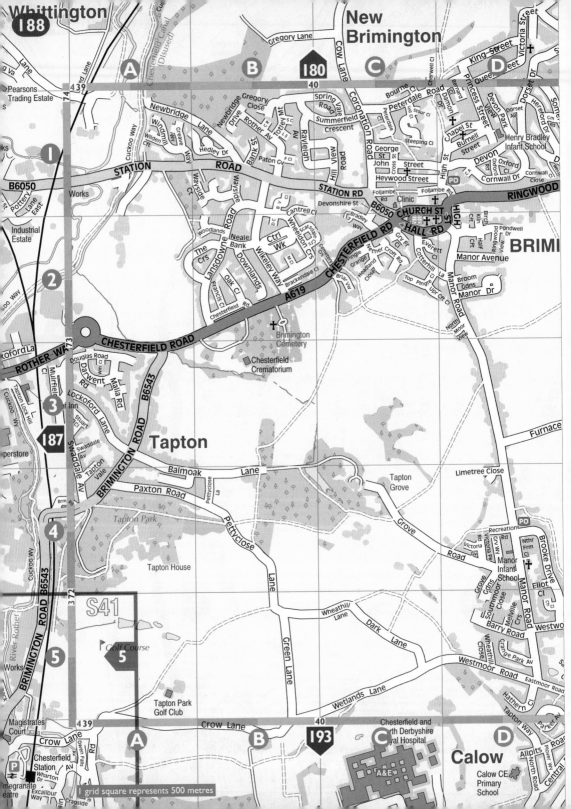

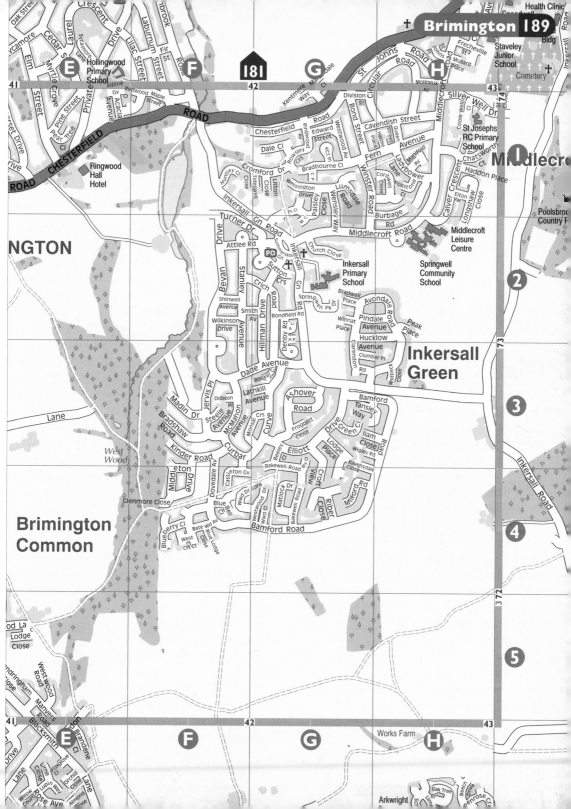

Health Clinic
Speedwell Bldg
Staveley Junior School
Cemetery

E Hollingwood Primary School
Oak Street
Sycamore Street
Cedar St
Laurel Crescent
Laburnum Street
Lilac Street
First St
Myrtle Grove
Elm Street
Pine Street
Peat Tree Cl
Acacia Avenue
Redwood
Maple Street
Alpine
F
181 42
Kentmere Way
Mavendale
G
St Johns Road
St Johns
Circular Road
Frecheville St
Musara
Molineux Av
H
Silver Well Dr
Middlecroft Cl
Coole Well
St Josephs RC Primary School
Chatsworth
Middlecro

I

41 42 43 **74** 43

CHESTERFIELD ROAD

ROAD

Ringwood Hall Hotel

Chesterfield Road
Dale Cl
Cromford Dr
Litton Close
Tideswell
Huntley Cl
Wessington Drive
Rowsley
Edward Street
Ringwood
CFS
Bradbourne Cl
Westwood Av
Paisley Close
Winster Road
Wensley Way
Lumsdale
Fern
Avenue
Queen
Hardie
Ladbower
Cordwell Close
Foxston
Burbage Rd
Matifold
Haddon Place
Calver Crescent
Elton Cl
Longshaw Close

NGTON

Turner Dr
Inkersall Gn Road
Attlee Rd
PO
Sutton Crs
Crich Road
Inkersall Gn Rd
Church Close
Middlecroft Road
Middlecroft Leisure Centre
Springwell Community School

Bevan Drive
Stanley
Shinwell Avenue
Smith Av
Wilkinson Drive
Hillman Drive
Bondfield Rd
Denby Rd
Spring Well PK
Inkersall Primary School
Bradwell Place
Avondale Road
Pindale Avenue
Hucklow Avenue
Clumber Pl
Clarendon Rd
Winnat Place
Peak Place

Inkersall Green

Madin Dr
Jervis Pl
Dobson
Bradshaw Road
Kinder Road
Steele Pl
McMahon Avenue
Avenue
Curbar
Lathkill Avenue
Booker
Dade Avenue
Mondal
Curve
Ashover Road
Froggatt Close
Beeley
Elliott
Lodge Drive
Bamford Tansley Way
Green
William Road
Wigley Rd
Ravensdale Close
Castleton Gv
Bakewell Road
eton Gv
Madlock Dr
Wwd Dr Gdns
Westwood Dr
Bakewell Road
Croft View
Riber Close
Milford Rd

West Wood

eton Drive
Middle Drive
Glenmore Close
Dovedale Av
Blue Bell Cl
Blueberry Cl
Bate Wd Av
Blue Lodge
West Cft Ct
Bamford Road

Brimington Common

Lane

Wd La
Lodge Close

Westwood Road
Manvers Road
Sandringham Road
Blacksmith

41 42 43

E **F** 42 **G** Works Farm **H**

Brandene Cl
eton

Willow Court
Lupin Way
Foxglove Cl
Orchid Close
Almond Av
Lime Close
Penrose Cl
Beech
Oak Tree
Arkwright

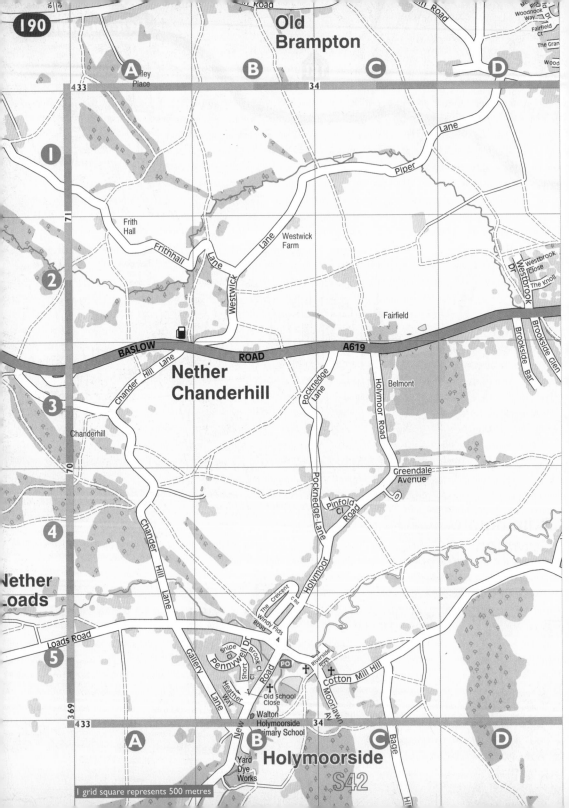

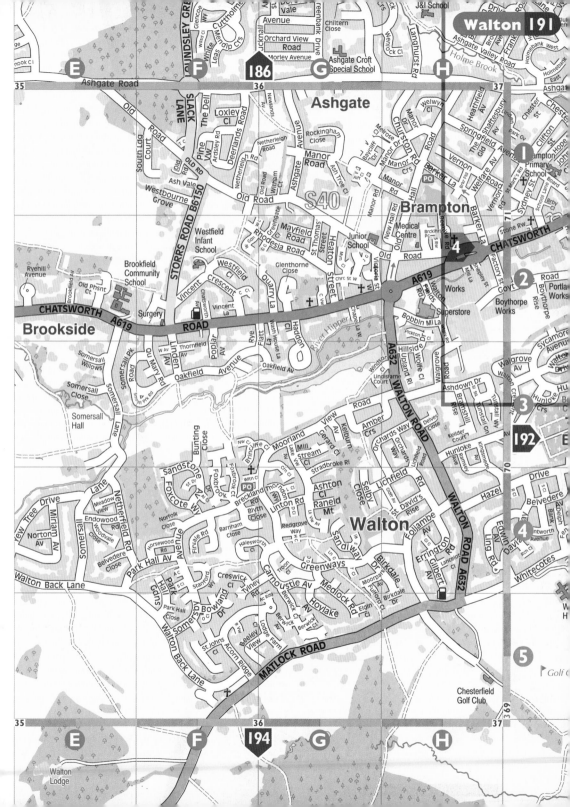

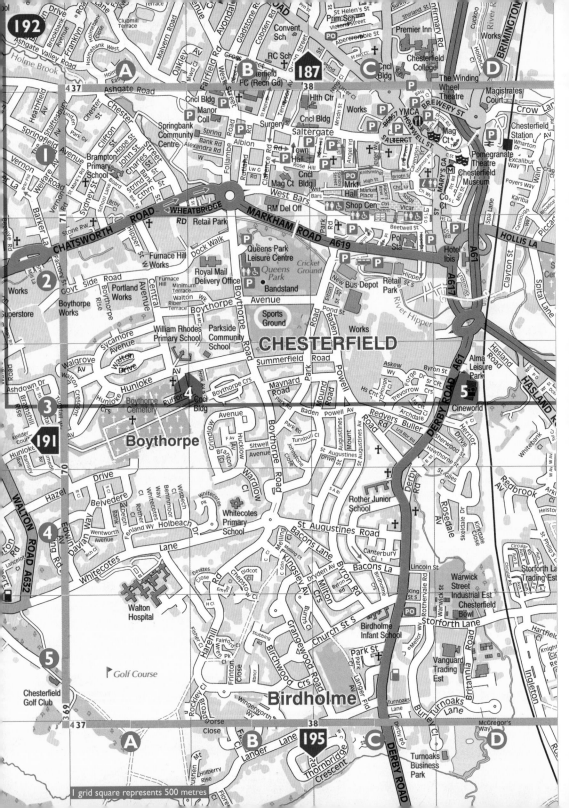

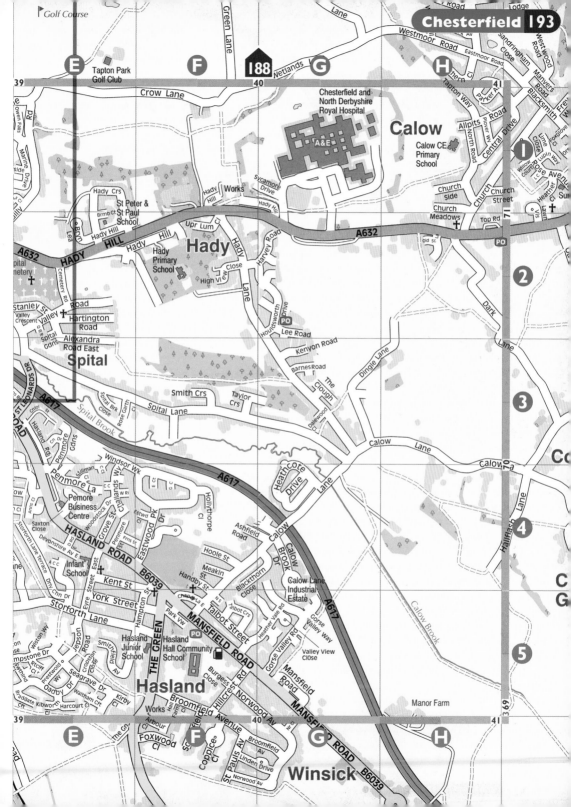

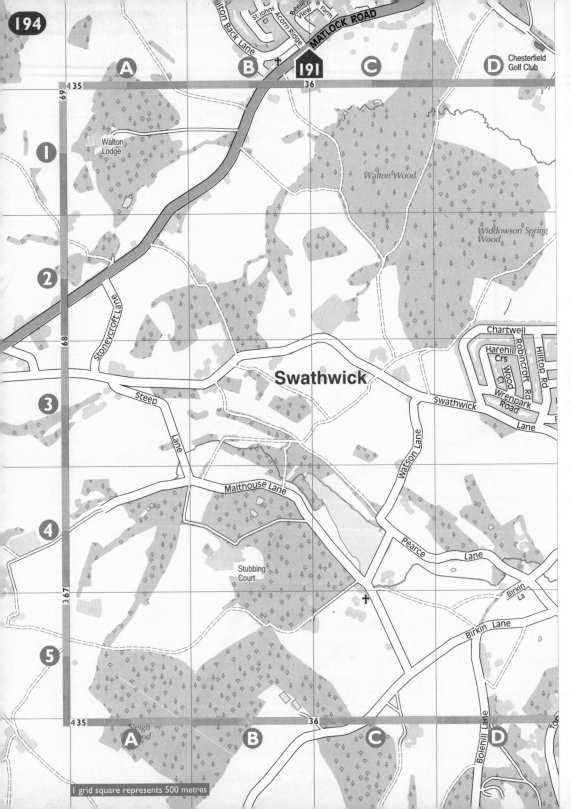

194

Matlock Road
St Johns Ct
Acorn Ridge
Beele... View Farm
Walton Back Lane
MATLOCK ROAD
191
Chesterfield Golf Club

A **B** **C** **D**

435
69
36

Walton Lodge

Walton Wood

Widdowson Spring Wood

1

Stoneycroft Lane

2

68

Chartwell
Harehill Crs
Robincroft Rd
Hilltop Rd
Wood Cl
Swathwick
Swathwick Road
Wrenpark Road
Lane

3

Steep Lane

Watson Lane

Malthouse Lane

4

3 67

Stubbing Court

Pearce Lane

Birkin La

Birkin Lane

5

Bolehill Lane

435
36

Sleigh Wood

A **B** **C** **D**

1 grid square represents 500 metres

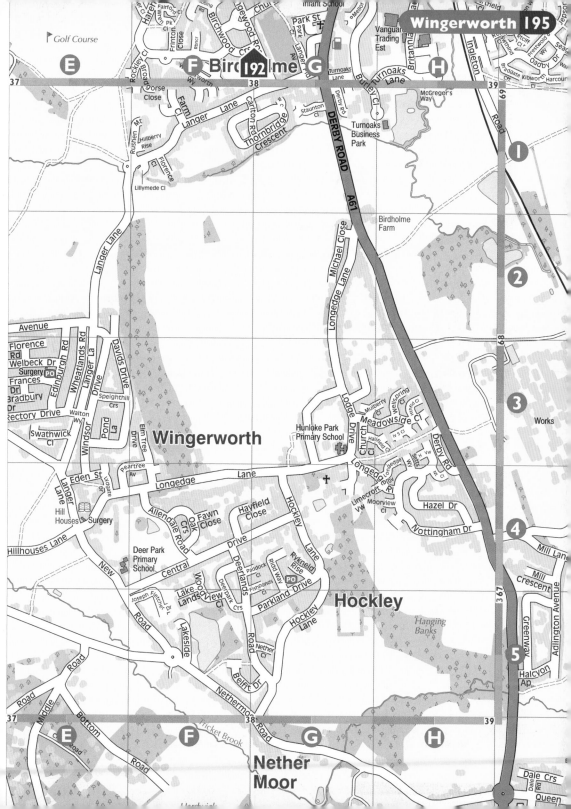

Golf Course

E

F Bird **192** lme **G** **H**

37 38 39 69

Infant School

Park St

Vanguard Trading Est

Britannia

Birchwood Cres

Turnoaks Lane

Burley Cl

Turnoaks Lane

McGregor's Way

Farm Cl

Langer Lane

Carlton Rd

Thornbridge Crescent

Staunton Cl

Derby Rd

Turnoaks Business Park

I

Gorse Close

Hillberry Rise

Florence

Lillymede Cl

Michael Close

Longedge Lane

Birdholme Farm

2

68

Avenue

Florence Rd

Welbeck Dr

Surgery PO

Frances Dr

Bradbury Dr

Rectory Drive

Edinburgh Rd

Wheatlands Rd

Langer La

Davids Drive

Speighthill Crs

Walton Wy

Windsor

Pond La

Elm Tree Drive

Lodge Drive

Hunloke Park Primary School

Church

Meadowside

Mulberry

Wells Spring

Hatfield Cl

Cl

Derby Rd

Works

3

Wingerworth

Swathwick Cl

Langer Lane

Eden St

Lydgate

Peartree Av

Longedge Lane

Longedge

Longedge Rd

Limecroft Vw

Moorview Cl

Hazel Dr

4

Hill Houses

Surgery

Allendale Road

Oak Crs

Fawn Close

Hayfield Close

Hockley Lane

Nottingham Dr

Mill Lane

Hillhouses Lane

Deer Park Primary School

Central

Deerlands

Paddock Cl

Ryknield Rise

PO

Fish Ponds

Mill Crescent

Adlington Avenue

New Road

Lake Lands

Woodview Cl

Joseph Fletcher Dr

Deer Park Crs

Parkland Drive

Hockley

Hanging Banks

Greenway

5

Lakeside

Road

Nether Dr

Belfit Dr

Nethermoor Road

Halcyon Ap

Road

Middle Road

Bottom Road

Ticket Brook

Dale Crs

Dale Rd

Queen

37 38 39

E **F** **G** **H**

Nether Moor

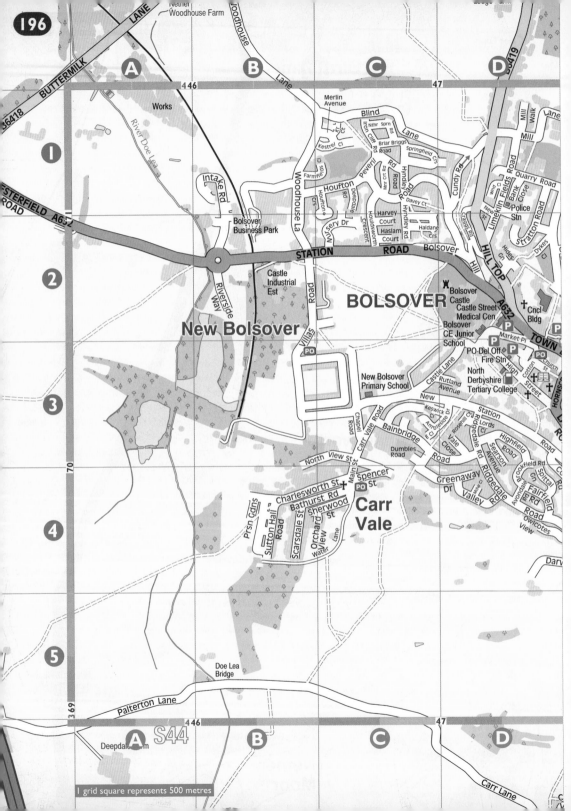

A **B** **C** **D**

BUTTERMILK LANE

Nether
Woodhouse Farm

Woodhouse Lane

4 46 47

SK6419

SK6418

Works

River Doe Lea

CHESTERFIELD ROAD A632

Intake Rd

Bolsover
Business Park

Woodhouse La

Merlin
Avenue

Blind Lane

Nthr Sprn

Nthr Cliff Rd

Kestrel Cl

Briar Briggs
Road

Peveril Rd

Houfton
Crs

Houfton
Rd

Deepdale

Nursery Dr

Farm

Houlds worth
Crescent

Harvey
Court

Haslam
Court

Hyndley Rd

Mrn Crt Rd

Hyndley
Road

Davey Ct

Haldane

Springfield Crs

Cundy Rd

Crs

Deepdale Rd

Crange Rd

New
St

Wld Cl

Merlin Fields Road

Bolsover

Quarry Road

Bank
Close

New St

Police
Stn

Hides

Stratton Road

Dykes Cl

MILL

Mill
Walk Lane

2 STATION ROAD Bolsover HILL TOP A632 TOWN

Riverside
Way

Castle
Industrial
Est

Villas
Road

New Bolsover

PO

BOLSOVER

Bolsover
Castle

Castle Street
Medical Cen

Bolsover
CE Junior
School

Bolsover
Castle

Cnl
Bldg

P

P

Market Pl

PO-Del Off
Fire Stn

P

PO

P

High Street

Cotton Street

Church Street

HORINSLR

3 New Bolsover
Primary School

Chapel Road

Carr Vale Road

Castle Lane

Rutland
Avenue

North
Derbyshire
Tertiary College

Keswick
Cl

Ambleside Cl

Rosehill Cl

Riddedale Rd

Station

Lords

Vale
Close

Station Road

Highfield
Road

New

Bainbridge

Dumbles
Road

North View St

Main St

Bathurst Rd

Sherwood
St

Greenaway
Dr

Searson
Avenue

Ridgedale
Road

Highfield
Road

Avondale

Cookfield Rd

Spittal Rd

Fairfield Rd

Fairfield
Road

Owlcotes
View

4 Charlesworth St

Prsn Gdns

Sutton Hall
Road

Scarsdale St

Orchard
View

Water
Lane

Spencer
St

PO

**Carr
Vale**

Valley

Darw

5

Doe Lea
Bridge

Palterton Lane

A S44 **B** **C** **D**

4 46 47

Deepdale Farm

Carr Lane

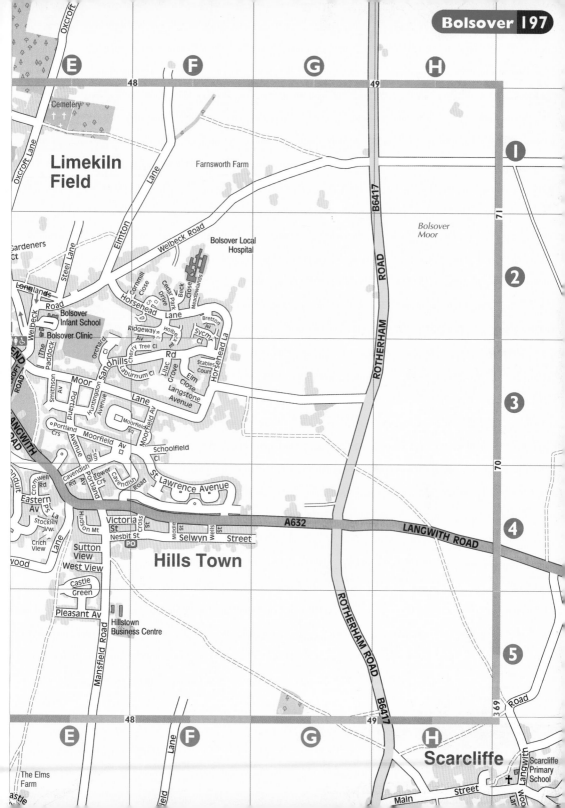

E F G H

48 49

I

Oxcroft Lane

Cemetery

Limekiln Field

71

Farnsworth Farm

Oxcroft Lane

Bolsover Moor

Welbeck Road

Elmton Lane

Steel Lane

Gardeners Ct

Bolsover Local Hospital

ROTHERHAM ROAD

B6417

2

Longlands Road

Welbeck Road

Cornmill Close

Cedar Park Drive

Beck Close

Meadowlands

Bolsover Infant School

Horsehead Lane

Ridgeway Av

Holbeck Av

Bretton Av

Sycamore Cl

Horsehead La

The Paddock

Bolsover Clinic

Orchard Cl

Cherry Tree Cl

Laburnum Cl

Sandhills Rd

Lilac Grove

Elm Close

Stables Court

LANGWITH ROAD

3

Smithson Av

Moor

Lane

Langstone Avenue

Portland Av

Huntingdon Avenue

Moorfield Av

Moorfield Sq

70

Portland Crs

Moorfield Av

Schoolfield Cl

Conduit

Cromwell Rd

Cavendish Rd

Portland Av

Tower Crs

Cavendish Road

St Lawrence Avenue

4

Eastern Av

Stockley Vw

Hudson Mt

Victoria St

Cross St

Middle St

Selwyn Wells St

Street

A632

LANGWITH ROAD

Crich View

Sutton View

Nesbit St

PO

Hills Town

ROTHERHAM ROAD

West View

Mansfield Road

Castle Green

B6417

5

Pleasant Av

Hillstown Business Centre

69

Langwith Road

The Elms Farm

Castle

E F G H

48 49

Scarcliffe

Scarcliffe Primary School

Main Street

Abbeydale 151 H4
Abbeydale Park.........161 E2
Abdy 84 D1
Adwick Le Street........25 F2
Aldwarke 98 C4
Almholme 28 A3
Apperknowle 172 C2
Arbourthorne 140 D2
Ardsley 33 F3
Arksey 27 G5
Armthorpe 42 C4
Ashgate 191 G1
Aston 145 H3
Athersley North 14 D4
Athersley South 15 E5
Attercliffe 116 A5
Aughton 130 D5
Balby 71 H1
Barlborough 177 F3
Barnes Hall 93 F2
Barnsley 3 J2
Barrow 82 B2
Barrow Hill 181 E2
Barugh 18 A1
Barugh Green 18 A3
Bassett 136 B5
Batemoor 163 E3
Beauchief 151 H5
Beighton 157 F1
Belle Green 17 E5
Belle Vue 7 J7
Bentley 39 H3
Bentley Rise 39 F3
Bessacarr 74 A1
Billingley 36 B4
Birdholme 192 B5
Birdwell 47 G5
Birley Carr 100 D4
Birley Edge 100 D3
Birleyhay 165 F3
Blackburn 103 H2
Blacker Hill 14 A5
Blacker Hill 48 C4
Bolehill 153 E3
Bolsover 196 C2
Bolsterstone 77 E5
Bolton upon Dearne ...53 F3
Bow Broom 66 A4
Boythorpe 192 A3
Bradgate 104 D2
Bradway 161 H3
Bramley 108 C3
Bramley 64 A2
Brampton 64 A2
Brampton 191 H1
Brampton en le Morthen .132 D2
Branton 59 F4
Brecks 107 H5
Brick Houses 150 C5
Brierley 17 H2
Brightside 116 B4
Brimington 188 D2
Brimington Common ..189 E4
Brincliffe 139 E4
Brinsworth 118 B4
Bromley 79 G1
Brookside 191 E2
Broom 106 B5
Broomhill 179 F2
The Brushes 179 F2
Burncross 93 G1
Burngreave 126 B1
Cadeby 69 F2
Calow 193 H1
Canklow 118 D1
Cantley 58 D4
Carbrook 116 C4
Carlton 15 H3
Carr Vale 196 C4
Carter Knowle 139 F5
Castle Green 45 F4
Catcliffe 129 H1
Chapeltown 81 F5
Charltonbrook 93 E1
Charnock Hall 154 C3
Chesterfield 5 F6
Clifton 9 J5

Clowne 184 D2
Coal Aston 163 H4
Coisley Hill 143 E4
Conanby 88 B1
Conisbrough 68 C5
Cortworth 83 G2
Cowley 170 B4
Crookes 124 D3
Crookesmoor 10 A1
Cudworth 22 A1
Cudworth Common 22 B3
Cundy Cross 32 D1
Cundy Hos 79 E3
Cusworth 38 C5
Dalton 99 F5
Dalton Magna 107 G2
Dalton Parva 107 G1
Darfield 35 F5
Darnall 128 A2
Dearne 37 H5
Deepcar 77 H4
Denaby Main 68 A4
Dinnington 134 B4
Dodworth 30 B3
Dodworth Bottom 30 A4
Doncaster 7 G3
Dore 161 E1
Drakehouse 156 D2
Dronfield 171 F2
Dropping Well 95 H5
Dunston 186 C1
East Dene 106 C2
East Herringthorpe ..107 F2
Eastwood 106 A1
Ecclesall 138 C5
Ecclesfield 94 B5
Ecklington 166 C4
Edenthorpe 42 C1
Elsecar 62 C3
Emmett Carr 176 A3
Felkirk 13 G3
Finkle Street 78 C1
Firth Park 115 H1
Fir Vale 115 F3
Flanderwell 108 A3
Ford 165 F2
Frecheville 155 E1
Fulwood 137 G2
Garden Village 76 B2
Gawber 18 C4
Gilroyd 30 C5
Gleadless 154 C1
Gleadless Valley 154 A2
Goldthorpe 37 G5
Gosforth Valley 170 B1
Greasbrough 97 G2
Greenhill 162 C1
Greenland 116 D5
Greenside 164 D5
The Green 101 F1
Greystones 138 A4
Grimesthorpe 115 H3
Guilthwaite 130 D1
Hackenthorpe 155 G1
Hady 193 F2
Halfway 167 E1
Hallows 171 G3
Handsworth 128 C5
Hardwick 132 C5
Harlesthorpe 185 E1
Harley 81 H2
Hasland 193 F5
Hay Field 75 G4
Heeley 140 A4
Hellaby 109 H4
Hemingfield 50 A5
Hemsworth 153 H2
Herringthorpe 107 E4
Hexthorpe 55 F5
Higham 18 A4
Higham Common 18 A5
Highfield 140 B2
Highfields 25 G5
Highgate 36 D5
High Green 80 B4
Highlane 155 G5

High Moor 169 E3
Hillsborough 113 F2
Hills Town 197 F4
Hill Top 104 A3
Hill Top 88 B4
Hill Top 171 E4
Hockley 195 G5
Holbrook 157 G5
Hollingwood 181 F5
Hollins End 141 H5
Holmesdale 171 G1
Holmley Common 163 E5
Hoober 84 A2
Hood Green 46 A3
Hood Hill 81 H3
Hooton Levitt 110 C5
Hooton Roberts 87 H5
Howbrook 79 H2
Hoyland 61 H3
Hoyland Common 32 C1
Hoyle Mill 32 C1
Hundall 172 D4
Hyde Park 6 C6
Inkersall Green 189 H3
Intake 57 E1
Intake 141 G5
Jordanthorpe 163 F1
Jordon 104 C4
Jump 62 C2
Kendray 32 B4
Keresforth Hill 31 E4
Killamarsh 168 B2
Kilnhurst 86 B4
Kimberworth 104 C2
Kimberworth Park 96 D4
Kingstone 2 B7
Kirk Sandall 29 F4
Lane End 81 E5
Laughton Common ...134 A2
Lea Brook 63 G5
Lightwood 154 B5
Limekiln Field 197 E1
Listerdale 107 H4
Little Houghton 35 H2
Load Brook 122 B1
Lodge Moor 136 C1
Longley Estate 115 F1
Long Sandall 28 D4
Loundsley Green 186 B5
Low Barugh 18 B1
Lowedges 162 D2
Lowfield 140 A3
Low Laithes 33 H3
Low Valley 50 D1
Loxley 112 C4
Lundwood 20 D4
Malinbridge 113 G5
Maltby 111 E3
Manor Estate 141 F1
Manor Park 127 E5
Marsh Lane 165 H5
Masbrough 8 A3
Mastin Moor 183 F2
Meadow Hall 116 D1
Meadow Head 152 C4
Measborough Dike 32 B2
Meersbrook 140 C5
Mexborough 67 E1
Mickley 161 H5
Middlecliffe 35 G3
Middlecroft 189 H1
Middle Handley 173 H3
Middlewood 100 B5
Millhouses 151 H2
Millhouses 35 H5
Milton 62 A3
Monk Bretton 20 B3
Moorgate 119 F2
Moorhole 156 C5
Mortmen 121 E5
Mortomley 80 C4
Mosborough 156 C5
Nether Chanderhill ..190 A3
Nether Edge 139 G4
Nether Handley 173 H5
Nether Haugh 84 B4
Netherthorpe 182 C4

Newbold 187 E2
New Bolsover 196 A2
New Brimington 180 C5
Newhill 65 E4
New Lodge 14 B5
New Rossington 90 D3
Newton 55 F2
New Totley 161 E4
New Village 27 E5
New Whittington 180 A2
Normanton Spring ...142 C4
North Anston 148 A1
Norton 153 F5
Norton Woodseats ...152 D2
Norwood 158 D5
Nutwell 43 F5
Old Denaby 67 G5
Old Whittington 179 H5
Orgreave 143 G1
Oughtibridge 100 A2
Owlerton 114 B4
Owlthorpe 156 B3
Oxclose 167 G2
Parkgate 98 B2
Parkhead 151 F2
Park Hill 126 D4
Parkwood Springs ...115 E5
Parson Cross 101 H4
Penistone 44 B3
Piccadilly 85 H2
Pickburn 24 B4
Pilley 60 A3
Pismire Hill 102 D5
Pitsmoor 115 F5
Platts Common 49 E5
Plumbley 166 B1
Pogmoor 18 C5
Potter Hill 79 H4
Rails 122 D3
Ranmoor 138 A1
Rawmarsh 98 C1
Renishaw 175 H3
Richmond 142 C2
Ridgeway 155 C5
Ridgeway Moor 165 G1
Ringinglow 150 A1
Rollestone 140 C5
Rossington 91 G2
Rostholme 26 B5
Rotherham 8 D6
Royston 15 H1
Ryecroft 85 G4
St Helen's 20 C2
Sandhill 35 H1
Sandhill 85 H4
Sandygate 124 A5
Scawsby 38 D4
Scawthorpe 38 D2
Scholes 96 A2
Shaftholme 27 E2
Shafton 16 C1
Shafton Two Gates 16 C2
Sharrow 139 F3
Shaw Lands 2 B5
Sheepbridge 178 D4
Sheffield 11 K6
Sheffield Park 141 E1
Shirecliffe 115 E3
Shiregreen 103 F4
Smithies 19 H2
Smithley 49 G2
Snape Hill 34 D5
Snape Hill 163 E5
Sothall 157 F4
South Anston 148 A4
Spital 193 E3
Spinkhill 176 B1
Spring Vale 81 E5
Sprotbrough 54 C3
Staincross 14 A3
Stairfoot 33 E3
Stannington 123 H1
Staveley 182 B5
Steel Bank 125 E2
Stockbridge 27 E5
Stocksbridge 77 E3
Stonegravels 187 F4

Stopes 122 D1
Storrs 112 A5
Street 83 G1
Stubbley 162 B5
Sunnyfields 39 E4
Sunnyside 108 A2
Swaithe 33 E5
Swallownest 145 E3
Swathwick 194 B3
Swinton 85 H1
Swinton Bridge 66 C4
Tankersley 60 C4
Tapton 188 A3
Tapton Hill 124 C5
Templeborough 105 E5
Thorn Hill 8 D2
Thorpe Hesley 95 G1
Throapham 134 D2
Thrybergh 99 G3
Thurcroft 132 D1
Thurnscoe 36 D3
Thurnscoe East 37 H2
Tinsley 117 G2
Todwick 147 F4
Toll Bar 26 C3
Totley 160 C4
Totley Brook 160 D3
Totley Rise 161 F3
Townhead 160 C1
Treeton 130 B3
Troway 164 C4
Ulley 131 H4
Under Tofts 123 G3
Unstone 172 A4
Unstone Green 172 A5
Upper Cudworth 17 E4
Upper Haugh 84 D4
Upper Hoyland 61 G1
Upper Newbold 186 A1
Upper Tankersley 60 A4
Upperthorpe 168 C3
Upper Whiston 120 A5
Wadsley 113 E2
Wadsley Bridge 100 D5
Waldershaigh 76 C5
Wales 159 F2
Wales Bar 158 D2
Walkley 125 E1
Walton 191 G4
Ward Green 31 G5
Warmsworth 70 B3
Warren 81 F3
Waterthorpe 156 D3
Wath upon Dearne 65 G3
Wentworth 82 D2
Westfield 167 E1
West Green 21 F1
West Handley 173 E3
West Melton 64 C2
Westthorpe 168 B4
Wheatley 40 C5
Wheatley Hills 41 G4
Wheatley Park 41 E3
Whinney Hill 99 F4
Whirlow 151 F5
Whirlow Brook 150 C2
Whiston 120 A3
Whiteley Wood 138 B3
Whitley 93 H4
Whittington Moor 187 F2
Wickersley 108 B5
Wilthorpe 19 E3
Wincobank 116 C1
Windhill 67 G2
Wingerworth 195 F5
Wingfield 96 C3
Wombwell 50 A4
Woodall 169 G2
Woodhouse 143 F3
Woodhouse Mill 144 A2
Woodlands 25 F3
Wood Seats 93 F3
Woodthorpe 183 E4
Woodville 47 H4
Worsbrough 48 A2
Worsbrough Bridge ...48 A2
Worsbrough Common .31 F3
Worsbrough Dale 48 A1

USING THE STREET INDEX

Street names are listed alphabetically. Each street name is followed by its postal town or area locality, the Postcode District, the page number, and the reference to the square in which the name is found.

Standard index entries are shown as follows:

Abbey Brook Cl *SHEFS* S8 .....**152** C4

Street names and selected addresses not shown on the map due to scale restrictions are shown in the index with an asterisk:

Adwick Ct *MEX/SWTN* S64 * ...**67** F4

GENERAL ABBREVIATIONS

ACC	ACCESS	CTYD	COURTYARD	HLS	HILLS
ALY	ALLEY	CUTT	CUTTINGS	HO	HOUSE
AP	APPROACH	CV	COVE	HOL	HOLLOW
AR	ARCADE	CVN	CANYON	HOSP	HOSPITAL
ASS	ASSOCIATION	DEPT	DEPARTMENT	HRB	HARBOUR
AV	AVENUE	DL	DALE	HTH	HEATH
BCH	BEACH	DM	DAM	HTS	HEIGHTS
BLDS	BUILDINGS	DR	DRIVE	HVN	HAVEN
BND	BEND	DRO	DROVE	HWY	HIGHWAY
BNK	BANK	DRY	DRIVEWAY	IMP	IMPERIAL
BR	BRIDGE	DWGS	DWELLINGS	IN	INLET
BRK	BROOK	E	EAST	IND EST	INDUSTRIAL ESTATE
BTM	BOTTOM	EMB	EMBANKMENT	INF	INFIRMARY
BUS	BUSINESS	EMBY	EMBASSY	INFO	INFORMATION
BVD	BOULEVARD	ESP	ESPLANADE	INT	INTERCHANGE
BY	BYPASS	EST	ESTATE	IS	ISLAND
CATH	CATHEDRAL	EX	EXCHANGE	JCT	JUNCTION
CEM	CEMETERY	EXPY	EXPRESSWAY	JTY	JETTY
CEN	CENTRE	EXT	EXTENSION	KG	KING
CFT	CROFT	F/O	FLYOVER	KNL	KNOLL
CH	CHURCH	FC	FOOTBALL CLUB	L	LAKE
CHA	CHASE	FK	FORK	LA	LANE
CHYD	CHURCHYARD	FLD	FIELD	LDG	LODGE
CIR	CIRCLE	FLDS	FIELDS	LGT	LIGHT
CIRC	CIRCUS	FLS	FALLS	LK	LOCK
CL	CLOSE	FM	FARM	LKS	LAKES
CLFS	CLIFFS	FT	FORT	LNDG	LANDING
CMP	CAMP	FTS	FLATS	LTL	LITTLE
CNR	CORNER	FWY	FREEWAY	LWR	LOWER
CO	COUNTY	FY	FERRY	MAG	MAGISTRATE
COLL	COLLEGE	GA	GATE	MAN	MANSIONS
COM	COMMON	GAL	GALLERY	MD	MEAD
COMM	COMMISSION	GDN	GARDEN	MDW	MEADOWS
CON	CONVENT	GDNS	GARDENS	MEM	MEMORIAL
COT	COTTAGE	GLD	GLADE	MI	MILL
COTS	COTTAGES	GLN	GLEN	MKT	MARKET
CP	CAPE	GN	GREEN	MKTS	MARKETS
CPS	COPSE	GND	GROUND	ML	MALL
CR	CREEK	GRA	GRANGE	MNR	MANOR
CREM	CREMATORIUM	GRG	GARAGE	MS	MEWS
CRS	CRESCENT	GT	GREAT	MSN	MISSION
CSWY	CAUSEWAY	GTWY	GATEWAY	MT	MOUNT
CT	COURT	GV	GROVE	MTN	MOUNTAIN
CTRL	CENTRAL	HGR	HIGHER	MTS	MOUNTAINS
CTS	COURTS	HL	HILL	MUS	MUSEUM

MWY	MOTORWAY	SE	SOUTH EAST		
N	NORTH	SER	SERVICE AREA		
NE	NORTH EAST	SH	SHORE		
NW	NORTH WEST	SHOP	SHOPPING		
O/P	OVERPASS	SKWY	SKYWAY		
OFF	OFFICE	SMT	SUMMIT		
ORCH	ORCHARD	SOC	SOCIETY		
OV	OVAL	SP	SPUR		
PAL	PALACE	SPR	SPRING		
PAS	PASSAGE	SQ	SQUARE		
PAV	PAVILION	ST	STREET		
PDE	PARADE	STN	STATION		
PH	PUBLIC HOUSE	STR	STREAM		
PK	PARK	STRD	STRAND		
PKWY	PARKWAY	SW	SOUTH WEST		
PL	PLACE	TDG	TRADING		
PLN	PLAIN	TER	TERRACE		
PLNS	PLAINS	THWY	THROUGHWAY		
PLZ	PLAZA	TNL	TUNNEL		
PR	PRINCE	TOLL	TOLLWAY		
PREC	PRECINCT	TPK	TURNPIKE		
PREP	PREPARATORY	TR	TRACK		
PRIM	PRIMARY	TRL	TRAIL		
PROM	PROMENADE	TWR	TOWER		
PRS	PRINCESS	U/P	UNDERPASS		
PRT	PORT	UNI	UNIVERSITY		
PT	POINT	UPR	UPPER		
PTH	PATH	V	VALE		
PZ	PIAZZA	VA	VALLEY		
QD	QUADRANT	VIAD	VIADUCT		
QU	QUEEN	VIL	VILLA		
QY	QUAY	VIS	VISTA		
R	RIVER	VLG	VILLAGE		
RBT	ROUNDABOUT	VLS	VILLAS		
RD	ROAD	VW	VIEW		
RDG	RIDGE	W	WEST		
REP	REPUBLIC	WD	WOOD		
RES	RESERVOIR	WHF	WHARF		
RFC	RUGBY FOOTBALL CLUB	WK	WALK		
RI	RISE	WKS	WALKS		
RP	RAMP	WLS	WELLS		
RW	ROW	WY	WAY		
S	SOUTH	YD	YARD		
SCH	SCHOOL	YHA	YOUTH HOSTEL		

POSTCODE TOWNS AND AREA ABBREVIATIONS

ABRD	Abbeydale Road	CHSW	Chesterfield south & west
ARMTH	Armthorpe	CLCR	Clay Cross
ATT	Attercliffe	CONI	Conisbrough
AU/AST/KP	Aughton/Aston/ Kiveton Park	CUD/GR	Cudworth/ Grimethorpe
AWLS/ASK	Adwick le Street/ Askern	DARN/MH	Darnall/ Meadowhall
BSLY	Barnsley	DEARNE	Wath upon Dearne/ Bolton upon Dearne
BSLYN/ROY	Barnsley north/ Royston	DIN	Dinnington
BSVR	Bolsover	DOD/DAR	Dodworth/ Darton
BTLY	Bentley	DON	Doncaster Town Centre
CHNE	Chesterfield north & east	DONS/BSCR	Doncaster south/ Bessacarr
CHPT/GREN	Chapeltown/ Grenoside		

DRON	Dronfield	MEX/SWTN	Mexborough/ Swinton
ECC	Ecclesall	MOS	Mosborough
ECK/KIL	Eckington/Killamarsh	NROS/TKH	New Rossington/ Tickhill
EPW	Epworth	OWL	Owlerton
FUL	Fulwood	RAW	Rawmarsh
GLV	Gleadless Valley	RCH	Rural Chesterfield
HACK/IN	Hackenthorpe/ Intake	RHAM	Rotherham
HAN/WDH	Handsworth/ Woodhouse	RHAM/THRY	Rotherham/ Thrybergh
HOR/CROF	Horbury/Crofton	SHEF	Sheffield
HOY	Hoyland	SHEFN	Sheffield north
HTFD	Hatfield	SHEFP/MNR	Sheffield Park/ Manor
KIMB	Kimberworth		
MALT	Maltby		

SHEFS	Sheffield south
ST/HB/BR	Stannington/ Hillsborough/ Bradfield
STKB/PEN	Stocksbridge/ Penistone
STV/CWN	Staveley/Clowne
TOT/DORE	Totley/Dore
WHHL	Wheatley Hills
WKFDW/WTN	Wakefield west/ Walton
WMB/DAR	Wombwell/ Darfield
WRKN	Worksop north
WRKS	Worksop south

Index - streets

Abb - Alb

A

Abbey Brook Cl *SHEFS* S8......152 C4
Abbey Brook Ct *SHEFS* S8.....152 C4
Abbey Brook Dr *SHEFS* S8.....152 C4
Abbey Crs *ABRD* S7.............151 H4
Abbey Cft *ABRD* S7.............151 H4
  CHNE S41.....................186 A2
  ECK/KIL S21...................176 A3
Abbeydale Pk
  TOT/DORE S17 *...............161 G1
Abbeydale Park Crs
  TOT/DORE S17.................161 F2
Abbeydale Park Ri
  TOT/DORE S17.................161 F1
Abbeydale Rd *ABRD* S7.........152 B2
Abbeydale Rd South
  TOT/DORE S17.................161 G2
Abbey Farm Vw
  CUD/GR S72....................21 H2
Abbeyfield Rd *ATT* S4...........115 F5
Abbey Gra *ABRD* S7.............151 H4
Abbey Gn *DOD/DAR* S75........30 C4
Abbey La *ABRD* S7..............151 H4
  BSLYN/ROY S71................21 E5
  ECC S11.......................151 H4
Abbey Lane Dell *SHEFS* S8....151 H4
Abbey Pl *ECK/KIL* S21..........176 A3
Abbey Sq *BSLYN/ROY* S71.......21 E3

Abbey View Rd *SHEFS* S8.....153 E2
Abbey Wk *BTLY* DN5............39 E5
Abbey Wy *DIN* S25.............147 H1
Abbots Cl *CUD/GR* S72.........22 A2
Abbotsford Dr *MALT* S66.......133 E1
Abbots Meadow *MOS* S20......157 G4
Abbots Rd *BSLYN/ROY* S71....21 F4
Abbott St *DONS/BSCR* DN4......6 A5
Abdy Rd *KIMB* S61..............96 B4
  RAW S62.......................84 D1
Aberconway Crs
  NROS/TKH DN11................91 F3
Abercorn Rd *WHHL* DN2.........57 C1
Abercrombie St *CHNE* S41.......5 F2
Aberford Gv *HOY* S74...........52 D2
Abingdon Gdns *KIMB* S61.......97 F3
Abingdon Rd *WHHL* DN2.........41 F5
Abney Cl *CHSW* S40...........186 C3
  GLV S14.......................140 C4
Abney Dr *GLV* S14..............140 C4
Abney Rd *GLV* S14..............140 C4
Acacia Av *CHSW* S40............93 H2
  MALT S66.....................108 C4
  MALT S66.....................110 B3
  STV/CWN S43.................189 E1
Acacia Ct *BTLY* DN5.............26 C5
Acacia Crs *ECK/KIL* S21........167 H3
Acacia Gv *CONI* DN12...........88 C3
  CUD/GR S72....................17 E2
Acacia Rd
  DONS/BSCR DN4...............58 B5
  SHEFN S5.....................103 E5

Acer Cl *DIN* S25................148 B5
  ECK/KIL S21...................168 A3
Acer Cft *ARMTH* DN3............42 D5
  DONS/BSCR DN4................74 D1
Ackworth Dr
  DARN/MH S9..................117 H3
Acorn Cft *KIMB* S61.............97 F4
Acorn Dr *ST/HB/BR* S6.........112 C5
Acorn Hl *ST/HB/BR* S6.........112 C5
Acorn Rdg *RCH* S42............191 F5
Acorn St *OWL* S3...............125 H2
Acorn Wy *CUD/GR* S72..........22 D1
  ST/HB/BR S6..................123 F1
Acre Cl *ARMTH* DN3.............29 F5
Acre Ga *CHPT/GREN* S35........80 B5
Acre Rd *CUD/GR* S72............22 A3
Acres Hill La *DARN/MH* S9....127 H4
Acres Hill Rd *DARN/MH* S9....127 H3
Acres Vw *RHAM* S60............119 H1
Acres View Cl *CHNE* S41.......187 F2
Acrewood Dr *MALT* S66.........108 B2
Acton Cl *AU/AST/KP* S26.......145 F1
Adastral Av *HACK/IN* S12......154 C3
Addison Rd *MALT* S66..........110 B3
  MEX/SWTN S64.................67 F3
  SHEFN S5.....................115 H2
Addison Sq *DIN* S25............134 D4
Addy Cl *ST/HB/BR* S6..........125 G2
Addy Dr *ST/HB/BR* S6..........125 F2
Adelaide La *OWL* S3...........125 H2
Adelaide Rd *ABRD* S7..........139 F4

Adelaide St *MALT* S66.........111 F5
Adelphi St *ST/HB/BR* S6.......125 G2
Adkins Dr *SHEFN* S5...........114 C1
Adkins Rd *SHEFN* S5...........114 C1
Adlard Rd *WHHL* DN2............41 F4
Adlington Crs *SHEFN* S5.......101 H5
Adlington Rd *SHEFN* S5........101 H5
Admiral Biggs Dr
  RHAM S60.....................130 A3
Admirals Crest *KIMB* S61.......95 H4
Adrian Crs *SHEFN* S5...........102 A5
Adsetts St *ATT* S4.............116 A3
Adwick Av *BTLY* DN5............26 B2
Adwick Ct *BSLYN/ROY* S71......20 D2
Adwick La *AWLS/ASK* DN6......26 A1
Adwick Pk *DEARNE* S63.........66 B5
Adwick Rd *MEX/SWTN* S64......66 D1
Agden Rd *ABRD* S7.............139 G2
Agnes Rd *BSLY* S70..............2 E6
Agnes Ter *BSLY* S70..............3 H3
Ainsdale Av *DEARNE* S63........53 F1
Ainsdale Ct *BSLYN/ROY* S71.....20 D2
Ainsdale Rd *BSLYN/ROY* S71....12 B4
Ainsley Cl *EPW* DN9.............75 H1
Ainsley Rd *FUL* S10............125 E3
Ainsty Rd *ABRD* S7.............139 H3
Aintree Av *DONS/BSCR* DN4....57 H3
  ECK/KIL S21..................166 B5
Aintree Cl *BTLY* DN5............38 C5
Aintree Dr *MEX/SWTN* S64......67 F2
Aire Cl *CHPT/GREN* S35.........80 C5
Airedale Rd *ST/HB/BR* S6.....113 G2

Aireton Cl *MALT* S66..........108 A4
Aireton Rd *BSLY* S70.............2 E3
Air Mount Cl *MALT* S66........108 A5
Aisby Dr *NROS/TKH* DN11.......91 G1
Aisthorpe Rd *SHEFS* S8........152 D2
Aitken Rd *MEX/SWTN* S64.......86 B3
Aizlewood Rd *ABRD* S7........139 H4
Akley Bank Cl
  TOT/DORE S17.................161 F3
Alba Cl *WMB/DAR* S73...........34 C1
Albanus Rdg *ST/HB/BR* S6.....123 F1
Albany Av *CHPT/GREN* S35......94 B2
Albany Cl *WMB/DAR* S73.........33 G4
Albany La *NROS/TKH* DN11......91 E2
Albany Rd *ABRD* S7............139 H3
  DONS/BSCR DN4................55 C5
  MEX/SWTN S64.................86 B2
  STKB/PEN S36..................76 D2
Albany St *RHAM/THRY* S65.......9 H5
Albert Av *STV/CWN* S43........180 B3
Albert Rd *DEARNE* S63..........37 C5
  DEARNE S63....................64 D1
  HACK/IN S12..................156 B2
  MEX/SWTN S64.................67 E3
  RAW S62.......................98 B2
  SHEFS S8.....................140 A4
  STV/CWN S43..................180 B3
Albert St *BSLY* S70..............3 C4
  CUD/GR S72....................17 E3
  DEARNE S63....................37 E2
  ECK/KIL S21..................174 D1
  MALT S66.....................111 F4

MEX/SWTN S64 ....66 B4
RHAM S60 ....8 C4
Albert Terrace Rd
 ST/HB/BR S6.................125 G2
Albion Dr DEARNE S63...........37 H2
Albion Pl DON DN1 ....7 F4
Albion Rd BSLYN/ROY S71 ...15 G4
 CHSW S40.........................4 E5
 RHAM S60 ....3 D4
Albion St ST/HB/BR S6.........10 B1
Albion Ter BSLY S70..............3 J7
 DONS/BSCR DN4................55 H4
Alcester Rd ABRD S7.............139 H3
Aldam Cl RHAM/THRY S65...107 F2
 TOT/DORE S17...................161 E4
Aldam Cft DONS/BSCR DN4...71 F2
 TOT/DORE S17...................161 E4
Aldam Wy TOT/DORE S17....161 E4
Aldbury Cl BSLYN/ROY S71...20 B1
Aldcliffe Crs
 DONS/BSCR DN4................71 F4
Aldene Av RAW S62...............85 F5
Aldene Gld ST/HB/BR S6......113 F5
Aldene Rd ST/HB/BR S6.......113 F2
Alderford Dr
 DONS/BSCR DN4................71 H4
Alder Gv DONS/BSCR DN4.....71 F1
 WMB/DAR S73.....................50 D1
Alder Holt Cl ARMTH DN3....43 E5
Alder La DARN/MH S9 ....128 C4
Alder Ms HOY S74.................62 A3
Alderney Rd
 SHEFP/MNR S2................140 A3
Aldersgate Cl
 NROS/TKH DN11.................91 G3
Alderson Av RAW S62...........85 F5
Alderson Dr BSLYN/ROY S71..20 A1
 WHHL DN2 ....7 J4
Alderson Rd SHEFP/MNR S2..140 A2
Alderson Rd
 SHEFP/MNR S2................139 H2
Alderson Rd North
 SHEFP/MNR S2................140 A1
Aldervale Cl MEX/SWTN S64..86 B3
Aldesworth Rd
 DONS/BSCR DN4................58 A4
Aldfield Wy SHEFN S5........115 F3
Aldham Cottages
 WMB/DAR S73 * 50 A1
Aldham Crs WMB/DAR S73...33 G4
Aldham House La
 WMB/DAR S73.....................49 H1
Aldred Cl ECK/KIL S21.........158 C5
Aldred Ct RHAM/THRY S65.....9 H6
Aldred Rd FUL S10.............125 E2
Aldred St RHAM/THRY S65.....9 H6
Aldrin Wy MALT S66...........110 C2
Aldwarke La
 RHAM/THRY S65.................98 C4
Aldwarke Rd RAW S62...........98 C4
Alexander St BTLY DN5.........39 H1
Alexandra Cl RHAM S61.......104 C1
Alexandra Gdns ECC S11.....139 F4
Alexandra Rd
 AU/AST/KP S26.................145 E2
 AWLS/ASK DN6 ....25 H1
 BTLY DN5...........................39 H1
 DONS/BSCR DN4................55 C5
 DRON S18.........................171 F1
 MEX/SWTN S64...................67 F3
 SHEFP/MNR S2................140 A3
Alexandra Rd East CHNE S35..5 K7
Alexandra Rd West
 CHSW S40.........................4 D3
Alexandra St MALT S66........111 E4
Alexandra Ter
 BSLYN/ROY S71 ....33 F2
 DOD/DAR S75......................18 D3
Alford Cl CHSW S40............191 G1
Alfred Rd DARN/MH S9 ....116 B5
Alfred St BSLYN/ROY S71 .....13 G5
Algar Cl SHEFP/MNR S2.......141 E3
Algar Dr SHEFP/MNR S2......141 F3
Algar Pl SHEFP/MNR S2.......141 E3
Algar Rd SHEFP/MNR S2.......141 E3
Alice Rd KIMB S61.................8 B3
Alice Wy DRON S18..............179 E1
Alison Cl AU/AST/KP S26.....145 F3
Alison Crs SHEFP/MNR S2....141 H1
Alison Dr AU/AST/KP S26.....145 F3
Allan St RHAM/THRY S65.......9 H5
Allatt Cl BSLY S70.................3 G7
Alldred Crs MEX/SWTN S64....86 A2
Allenby Cl SHEFS S8.............162 C1
Allenby Crs NROS/TKH DN11..91 E3
Allenby Dr SHEFS S8...........162 C1
Allendale BSLY S70................32 C5
Allendale Gdns BTLY DN5......55 F2
Allendale Rd BTLY DN5..........55 F2
 DOD/DAR S75......................19 G3
 HOY S74...........................61 H3
 RCH S42...........................195 F4
 RHAM/THRY S65.................107 E5
Allende Wy SHEFN S5..........127 H1
Allen Rd MOS S20................157 F3
Allen St OWL S3...................10 E1
Allerton St DON DN1..............6 D2
Allestree Dr DRON S18........170 A2
All Hallowes Dr MALT S66....110 C4

Alliance St ATT S4..............126 D1
Alliss Rd ARMTH DN3.............59 G5
Allott Cl RHAM/THRY S65....108 D1
Allott Crs HOY S74................62 C1
Allott St HOY S74..................61 F3
Allpits Rd BSVR S44.............193 H1
All Saints Wy
 AU/AST/KP S26.................145 G3
All Saints' Sq RHAM S60.........9 F4
Allsop Pl CHNE S41.............187 F1
Allt St RAW S62....................98 B2
Alma Crs DRON S18.............163 E5
Alma Rd CHPT/GREN S35.......80 B4
 RHAM S60 ....9 F6
Alma Rw RHAM S60.............120 A3
Alma St BSLY S70..................2 D4
 OWL S3............................126 A2
 WMB/DAR S73.....................50 B3
Alma St West CHSW S40........4 C5
Almholme La BTLY DN5.........27 H2
Almond Av ARMTH DN3.........42 D5
Almond Cl CUD/GR S72.........16 D5
Almond Cl MALT S66............110 B5
Almond Crs STV/CWN S43....183 E2
Almond Dr ECK/KIL S21.........168 A3
Almond Gld MALT S66..........121 G1
Almond Pl STV/CWN S43 * ..188 C2
Almond Rd
 DONS/BSCR DN4................58 B5
Almond Tree Rd
 AU/AST/KP S26.................158 D3
Alms Hill Crs ECC S11.........151 E2
Alms Hill Dr ECC S11..........151 F2
Almshill Gld ECC S11..........151 F2
Alms Hill Rd ECC S11..........151 F2
Alney Pl ST/HB/BR S6..........101 F5
Alnwick Dr HACK/IN S12.......141 H5
Alnwick Rd HACK/IN S12......141 H5
Alperton Cl BSLYN/ROY S71....21 F2
Alpha Rd RHAM/THRY S65....106 D2
Alpine Cl STKB/PEN S36..........76 C2
Alpine Gld STKB/PEN S36.......76 C2
Alpine Gv STV/CWN S43........181 E5
Alpine Rd ST/HB/BR S6.........125 F2
 STKB/PEN S36.....................76 C2
Alport Av HACK/IN S12.........155 G1
Alport Dr HACK/IN S12.........142 C5
Alport Gv HACK/IN S12........142 C5
Alport Pl HACK/IN S12.........155 G1
Alport Ri DRON S18.............170 B1
Alport Rd HACK/IN S12.........142 C5
Alric Dr BSLYN/ROY S71.........33 E1
 RHAM S60 ....10 C5
Alrich Ms STKB/PEN S36........76 B1
Alsing Rd DARN/MH S9.........117 E1
Alston Cl DONS/BSCR DN4.....73 H1
Alston Rd DONS/BSCR DN4....73 H2
Alton Cl DRON S18...............170 B3
 ECC S11............................151 G3
 RCH S42...........................191 F4
Alum Chine Cl CHNE S41......193 E4
Alverley La DONS/BSCR DN4..71 G4
Alverley Wy BSLY S70.............60 D2
Alwyn Av BTLY DN5...............39 E3
Amalfi Cl WMB/DAR S73.........34 D5
Ambassador Gdns
 ARMTH DN3......................43 E5
Amber Crs CHSW S40...........191 G3
Amber Cft STV/CWN S43......189 G2
Amberley St DARN/MH S9.....116 C4
Ambler Ri AU/AST/KP S26....145 E1
Ambleside Cl CHNE S41.......186 C2
 MOS S20..........................167 E2
 RHAM S60 * 118 A4
Ambleside Crs BTLY DN5........54 A4
Ambleside Dr BSVR S44.......196 C3
Ambleside Gv
 BSLYN/ROY S71 ....33 G2
Ambleside Wk DIN S25.........148 C2
Amen Cnr RHAM S60 * 8 E3
America La DEARNE S63.........64 C5
Amersall Ct BTLY DN5............39 E3
Amersall Crs BTLY DN5..........39 E2
Amersall Rd BTLY DN5...........39 E2
Amesbury Cl CHNE S41 * 187 E2
Amory's Holt Cl MALT S66...110 C1
Amory's Holt Dr MALT S66...110 C1
Amory's Holt Rd MALT S66...110 C1
Amory's Holt Wy MALT S66..110 B2
Amos Rd DARN/MH S9..........116 D2
Amy Rd BTLY DN5..................25 F2
Anchorage Crs BTLY DN5.......55 G1
Anchorage La BTLY DN5.........55 F1
Ancona Ri WMB/DAR S73.......34 D5
Ancote Cl DOD/DAR S75.........30 C1
Anderson Cl STV/CWN S43...180 C5
Andover Dr OWL S3.............126 A1
Andover St OWL S3..............126 A1
Andrew La FUL S10..............136 C5
Andrews Pl KIMB S61...........105 E1
Andwell La FUL S10.............136 C5
Anelay Rd DONS/BSCR DN4...71 F1
Anfield Rd
 DONS/BSCR DN4................74 A1
Angel La RAW S62..................83 H2
Angel St DEARNE S63............53 F4
 SHEF S1............................11 H4
Angel Yd CHSW S40 * 5 F4
Angerford Av SHEFS S8........153 E1
Anglesey Rd DRON S18........171 E3
Angleton Av
 SHEFP/MNR S2................142 A2

Angleton Cl
 SHEFP/MNR S2................142 A2
Angleton Gdns
 SHEFP/MNR S2................142 A2
Angleton Gn
 SHEFP/MNR S2................142 A2
Angleton Ms
 SHEFP/MNR S2................142 A2
Angram Rd CHPT/GREN S35...80 B5
Annan Rd DOD/DAR S75.........18 B2
Annat Pl CHPT/GREN S35.......80 A4
Annesley Cl CHNE S41.........193 E4
 SHEFS S8..........................152 D5
Annesley Rd SHEFS S8.........152 D5
Anne St DIN S25..................134 D2
Anns Rd SHEFP/MNR S2.......140 A3
Anns Rd North
 SHEFP/MNR S2................140 B3
Ann St RAW S62....................98 B3
Ansdell Rd BTLY DN5.............26 D5
Ansell Rd ECC S11................138 D2
Anson Gv RHAM S60............118 D4
Anson St SHEFP/MNR S2........11 K3
Ansten Crs DONS/BSCR DN4..58 A4
Anston Cl DIN S25................148 B2
Antrim Av FUL S10................10 A6
Anvil Cl ST/HB/BR S6..............86 C4
Anvil Crs CHPT/GREN S35....102 B1
Apley Rd DON DN1..................6 E6
Apollo St RAW S62................85 H4
Apostle Cl DONS/BSCR DN4...71 E2
Appleby Rd WHHL DN2...........57 C1
Appleby Wk DIN S25............148 D1
Applegarth Cl HACK/IN S12..141 G4
Applegarth Dr
 HACK/IN S12....................141 G4
Applehaigh Dr ARMTH DN3....29 E2
Applehaigh Gv
 BSLYN/ROY S71 ....12 A5
Applehaigh La
 HOR/CROF WF4.................12 A3
Applehaigh Vw
 BSLYN/ROY S71 ....12 A5
Applehurst Bank BSLY S70 * ..32 B2
Appleton Gdns BTLY DN5.......39 G2
Appleton Wy BSLY S70...........32 A5
 BTLY DN5...........................39 G2
Appletree Dr DRON S18.......171 E2
Appletree Rd BSVR S44........184 B5
Appletree Wy
 DONS/BSCR DN4................74 C3
Appleton Cl
 RHAM/THRY S65.................99 F5
April Cl BSLYN/ROY S71..........20 C3
April Dr BSLYN/ROY S71..........20 D3
Aqueduct St
 SHEFP/MNR S2................19 H4
Arbour Crs MALT S66............133 F1
Arbour Dr MALT S66.............133 F1
Arbourthorne Rd
 SHEFP/MNR S2................141 E4
The Arcade BSLY S70................3 F4
Archaeological Wy
 STV/CWN S43...................185 G3
Archdale Cl CHSW S40.........192 C5
 SHEFP/MNR S2................141 H2
Archdale Rd
 SHEFP/MNR S2 * 141 G2
Archer Ga ST/HB/BR S6........112 D3
Archer La ABRD S7...............139 F5
Archer Rd ABRD S7..............152 B2
 SHEFS S8..........................152 C2
Archery Cl MALT S66............121 F1
Archibald Rd ABRD S7..........139 G4
Arcon Pl RAW S62.................85 C5
Arcubus Av AU/AST/KP S26..145 F2
Ardeen Rd WHHL DN2.............7 K1
Arden Cl CHSW S40..............191 G1
Arden Ga DONS/BSCR DN4....71 F4
Ardmore St DARN/MH S9......116 C2
Ardron Wk RAW S62..............85 H5
Ardsley Av AU/AST/KP S26...145 G4
Ardsley Cl MOS S20.............155 H3
Ardsley Dr MOS S20............155 H3
Ardsley Gv MOS S20............155 H3
Ardsley Rd BSLY S70..............32 C5
 CHSW S40.........................191 F1
Arena Ct DARN/MH S9.........116 D4
Argyle Cl SHEFS S8...............58 B5
Argyle La SHEFS S8..............140 A5
Argyle Rd SHEFS S8.............140 A5
Argyll Av WHHL DN2..............7 F1
Arklow Cl CHNE S41.............192 D4
Arklow Rd HACK/IN S12.........57 E1
Arksey Common La
 BTLY DN5...........................27 G5
Arksey La BTLY DN5...............39 H1
Arkwright Rd BTLY DN5..........39 F5
Arley St SHEFP/MNR S2..........11 F7
Arlington Av
 AU/AST/KP S26.................145 H2
Arlott Wy CONI DN12.............70 C5
Armer St RHAM S60................8 C5
Armitage Rd
 DONS/BSCR DN4................71 F1
 STKB/PEN S36...................77 F3
Armley Rd DARN/MH S9........116 D4
Armroyd La HOY S74..............62 B4
Arms Park Dr MOS S20.........167 F2

Armstead Rd MOS S20.........157 F2
Armstrong Wk MALT S66......110 C2
Armthorpe La ARMTH DN3.....29 G2
 WHHL DN2 ....41 E5
Armyne Gv BSLYN/ROY S71...33 E1
Arncliffe Dr BSLY S70.............30 D1
 CHPT/GREN S35.................93 H1
Arnold Av BSLYN/ROY S71.....14 D4
 HACK/IN S12.....................154 D3
Arnold Crs MEX/SWTN S64....67 E2
Arnold Rd RHAM/THRY S65...106 D3
Arnold St ST/HB/BR S6..........114 A5
Arnside Cl CHNE S41............178 D5
Arnside Rd ABRD S7.............139 C5
 MALT S66..........................98 C1
Arran Hl RHAM/THRY S65.......99 H3
Arran Rd FUL S10.................124 D4
Arras St DARN/MH S9...........127 F2
Arthington St SHEFS S8........140 A4
Arthur Av BTLY DN5...............26 D5
Arthur Rd STKB/PEN S36.......77 H4
Arthur St BSLY S70.................32 A5
 BTLY DN5...........................26 D5
 RAW S62............................85 G4
Artisan Vw SHEFS S8...........140 A4
Arundel Av RHAM S60...........130 A3
 RHAM/THRY S65.................99 F5
Arundel Cl CHNE S41...........187 F1
 DRON S18.........................170 B2
Arundel Cottages
 RHAM S60 ....130 A3
Arundel Crs RHAM S60.........129 H3
Arundel Gdns
 BSLYN/ROY S71 ....12 C5
 BTLY DN5...........................39 F2
Arundel Ga SHEF S1..............11 C4
Arundel La SHEF S1..............11 H5
Arundell Dr BSLYN/ROY S71...21 F2
Arundel Rd CHPT/GREN S35...81 E5
 RHAM S60 * 130 A3
 RHAM/THRY S65...................9 K7
Arundel St RHAM S60............130 A3
 SHEF S1............................11 G6
Arundel Vw HOY S74.............62 C1
Ascension Cl MALT S66.........111 E4
Ascot Av DONS/BSCR DN4......57 H4
Ascot Cl MEX/SWTN S64.........67 F2
Ascot Dr BTLY DN5.................38 D4
 DIN S25............................134 D1
Ascot St SHEFP/MNR S2.......140 A1
Ashberry Cl DEARNE S63........37 F2
Ashberry Gdns
 ST/HB/BR S6.....................125 F2
Ashberry Rd ST/HB/BR S6.....125 F2
Ashbourne Cl CHSW S40.......186 A4
Ashbourne Gv
 HAN/WDH S13...................142 D1
Ashbourne Rd
 BSLYN/ROY S71 ....20 A1
 HAN/WDH S13...................142 D1
Ashburnham Gdns
 BTLY DN5...........................55 E2
Ashburton Cl
 AWLS/ASK DN6 ....25 E1
Ashbury Dr SHEFS S8..........153 G3
Ashbury La SHEFS S8...........153 G3
Ashby Ct BSLY S70.................2 D6
Ash Cl ECK/KIL S21...............168 A3
 RHAM/THRY S65.................107 F5
 STV/CWN S43....................177 F5
Ash Ct BTLY DN5...................54 D4
 MALT S66..........................110 B2
Ashcourt Dr
 DONS/BSCR DN4................71 H4
Ash Crs ECK/KIL S21.............174 B2
 MEX/SWTN S64...................66 C2
Ashcroft Dr CHNE S41..........179 H4
Ashdale Cl ARMTH DN3..........42 B1
Ash Dale Rd
 DONS/BSCR DN4................70 B4
Ashdell FUL S10...................125 E5
Ashdell La FUL S10...............125 E5
Ashdell Rd FUL S10..............125 E5
Ashdene Ct MEX/SWTN S64....86 B3
Ashdown Dr CHSW S40...........4 A7
Ashdown Gdns MOS S20......157 G2
Ashdown Pl BTLY DN5............39 H2
Asher Rd ABRD S7................139 H2
Ashes La RAW S62.................82 B3
Ashfield Cl ARMTH DN3..........43 E5
 DOD/DAR S75......................2 A1
 HACK/IN S12.....................154 B1
Ashfield Ct BSLY S70 * 32 D2
Ashfield Dr HACK/IN S12.......154 B1
Ashfield Rd CHNE S41..........193 E4
 DONS/BSCR DN4................42 B3
 STKB/PEN S36...................77 F2
Ashfield Wy MALT S66..........108 B2
Ashford Cl BSLYN/ROY S71 *..12 B4
Ashford Rd DRON S18..........170 B3
 ECC S11 * 139 F2
Ashgate Av CHSW S40.........191 G1

Ashgate Cl FUL S10.............125 E5
Ashgate La FUL S10.............125 E5
Ashgate Rd CHSW S40..........4 B2
 FUL S10............................125 E5
 RCH S42...........................186 A5
Ashgate Valley Rd
 CHSW S40...........................4 A2
Ash Gv ARMTH DN3...............43 E3
 AU/AST/KP S26.................159 G2
 BSLY S70............................32 D3
 CONI DN12.........................88 C2
 FUL S10............................125 F5
 MALT S66..........................108 C4
 MALT S66..........................111 F2
 RAW S62............................98 C1
 STV/CWN S43....................182 D2
Ash House La
 TOT/DORE S17...................150 D4
Ashland Rd ABRD S7............139 C5
Ashleigh Ct ECK/KIL S21.......167 E5
Ash La DRON S18.................164 B5
 ECK/KIL S21.......................173 E3
 STKB/PEN S36.....................77 G2
Ashleigh Av HACK/IN S12.....141 F5
Ashleigh Cl ECK/KIL S21.......174 C2
Ashleigh Crs ECK/KIL S21......174 C2
Ashleigh Dr HACK/IN S12......141 F5
Ashleigh Gdns KIMB S61........97 F4
Ashleigh Pl HACK/IN S12......141 F5
Ashleigh Rd STV/CWN S43.....177 F4
Ashleigh V BSLY S70..............32 C2
Ashley Cl ECK/KIL S21...........168 B2
Ashley Cft BSLYN/ROY S71....12 B5
Ashley Gv AU/AST/KP S26.....145 F5
Ashley La ECK/KIL S21..........168 B2
Ashmore Rd ECK/KIL S21......174 B1
Ash Mt RAW S62 * 98 B1
 RHAM/THRY S65...................9 G4
Ashopton Rd CHNE S41........186 C3
Ashover Cl SHEFS S8..............48 A1
Ashover Rd STV/CWN S43....189 G3
Ashpool Cl HAN/WDH S13.....143 E4
Ashpool Fold
 HAN/WDH S13...................143 E4
Ash Rdg MEX/SWTN S64........86 B1
Ash Rd CUD/GR S72...............17 F2
 DEARNE S63.......................65 F3
Ash St MOS S20...................166 C1
 ST/HB/BR S6.....................125 G1
 WMB/DAR S73.....................33 G5
Ashton Av BTLY DN5..............38 D1
Ashton Cl CHSW S40............191 G4
 ECK/KIL S21.......................168 A3
Ashton Dr ARMTH DN3...........29 E3
Ash Tree Cl CHSW S40.........191 G1
Ash Tree Rd STV/CWN S43....185 E4
Ashurst Cl ST/HB/BR S6........113 E5
Ashurst Dr ST/HB/BR S6.......113 E5
Ashurst Pl ST/HB/BR S6........113 E5
Ashurst Rd ST/HB/BR S6.......113 E5
Ash V CHSW S40..................191 F1
Ash Vw CHPT/GREN S35.........93 H2
 KIMB S61............................97 F5
Ashville NROS/TKH DN11........91 G3
Ashwell Cl CUD/GR S72..........17 E3
Ashwell Gv
 RHAM/THRY S65.................106 C1
Ashwell Rd HAN/WDH S13.....143 E4
Ashwood Cl ARMTH DN3.........75 E1
 CHPT/GREN S35.................80 A3
Ashwood Gv CUD/GR S72.......23 H4
Ashwood Rd
 CHPT/GREN S35.................80 A4
 RAW S62............................98 B2
Ashworth Dr KIMB S61...........96 B4
Askam Ct MALT S66..............108 D3
Askam Rd MALT S66.............108 D3
Askern Rd BTLY DN5...............26 C5
Askew Ct STKB/PEN S36...........77 G3
Askew Wy CHSW S40..............5 F7
Askrigg Cl DONS/BSCR DN4...74 B2
Asline Rd SHEFP/MNR S2.....140 A2
Aspen Cl ARMTH DN3............42 B1
 ECK/KIL S21.......................168 A2
Aspen Gv WMB/DAR S73.........51 E1
Aspen Rd ECK/KIL S21...........174 B2
Aspen Wy MEX/SWTN S64......86 A3
Aspley Cl CHSW S40.............191 F1
Asquith Rd BTLY DN5.............39 H1
 DARN/MH S9 * 103 H5
Astcote Ct ARMTH DN3..........29 E3
Aster Cl DIN S25..................148 D4
 MOS S20..........................157 F2
Aston Cl DRON S18...............163 C5
Aston La BSLYN/ROY S71........20 A1
Aston La AU/AST/KP S26.......131 F5
Aston St SHEFP/MNR S2.......126 D3
Astwell Gdns
 CHPT/GREN S35.................80 C5
Atebanks Ct
 DONS/BSCR DN4................71 H4
Athelstan Cl ARMTH DN3 *....142 C1
Athelstane Crs ARMTH DN3....29 F4
Athelstane Dr MALT S66........183 E2
Athelstane Rd CONI DN12......88 D1
Athelstan Rd
 HAN/WDH S13...................142 C1
Athersley Crs
 BSLYN/ROY S71 ....20 A1
Athersley Gdns MOS S20......156 A3
Athersley Rd
 BSLYN/ROY S71 ....20 A1

Farwater La *DRON* S18 ....170 D2
Fathers Gdns
 AU/AST/KP S26.........159 H3
Favell Rd *CUD* S3 ....10 C3
 RHAM/THRY S65 ....107 F2
Fawcett St *OWL* S3 ....10 C1
Fawn Cl *KIM* S42 ....195 F4
Fearnehough St
 DARN/MH S9 ....127 F2
Fearnley Rd *HOY* S74 ....61 G3
Fearnley Ri *HOY* S74 ....61 G3
Fearnville Gv
 BSLY/ROY S71 ....15 C1
Feeman Gdns
 CHPT/GREN S35 ....80 B5
Felkirk Vw *CUD* S72 ....58 B5
Fellbrigg Rd
 SHEFP/MNR S2 ....140 D3
Fellowsfield Wy *KIMB* S61 .....104 C2
Fell Rd *DARN/MH* S9 ....116 C5
Fell St *DARN/MH* S9 ....116 C5
Fenland Wy *CHSW* S40 ....192 A4
Fenney La *ECC* S11 ....151 E3
Fenn Rd *DOD/DAR* S75 ....60 D3
Fensome Wy *WMB/DAR* S73.....34 D4
Fenton Cl *ARMTH* DN3 ....42 D5
Fenton Cft *KIMB* S61 ....105 E4
Fenton Flds *KIMB* S61 ....105 E4
Fenton Rd *KIMB* S61 ....97 E4
Fenton St *BSLY* S70 * 2 E4
 ECK/KIL S21 ....174 B1
 KIMB S61 ....104 D2
Fentonville St *ECC* S11 ....139 G2
Fenton Wy *KIMB* S61 ....97 F4
Feoffees Rd
 SHEFP/MNR S2 ....140 D3
Ferguson St *DARN/MH* S9.....127 F1
Ferham Cl *KIMB* S61 ....105 E3
Ferham Park Av *KIMB* S61.....105 E3
Ferham Rd *KIMB* S61 ....105 E3
Fern Av *BTLY* DN5 ....39 G3
 MOS S20 ....157 F1
 STV/CWN S43 ....189 G1
Fern Bank *AWLS/ASK* DN6 ....25 F1
 KIMB S61 * 104 C2
Fernbank Cl *BSLY* S70 * 31 G3
Fernbank Dr *ARMTH* DN3........42 D2
 ECK/KIL S21 ....166 B5
Fern Cl *ECK/KIL* S21............166 B5
 WHHL DN2 ....41 F4
 RHAM/THRY S65 ....51 E1
Ferncroft Av *MOS* S20 ....166 C1
Ferndale Cl *DRON* S18 ....163 H5
Ferndale Dr *MALT* S66 ....108 C3
Ferndale Ri *DRON* S18 ....163 H5
 DRON S18................163 H5
Ferndale Rd *CONI* DN12 ....88 D1
Ferndale Vw *BTLY* DN5 ....39 E5
Fernhall Cl *ARMTH* DN3.........29 G4
Fernhall Cft *WMB/DAR* S73.....50 C2
Fern Hollow *MALT* S66 ....121 C1
Fernhurst Rd *WHHL* DN2........41 G4
Fernlea Cl *BTLY* DN5 ....39 F5
Fernlea Gv *CHPT/GREN* S35..102 B1
Fern Lea Gv *DEARNE* S63 ....52 D4
Ferneleigh Dr *RHAM* S60......118 B2
Fern Rd *ST/HB/BR* S6 ....124 D1
Fernvale Wk
 MEX/SWTN S64 ....86 B3
Fern Wy *ECK/KIL* S21 ....166 B5
Ferrand St *BSLY* S70 ....60 C1
Ferrara Cl *WMB/DAR* S73........34 C4
Ferrars Cl *DARN/MH* S9 ....117 H2
Ferrars Dr *DARN/MH* S9 ......117 G1
Ferrars Rd *DARN/MH* S9 ......117 G1
Ferrars Wy *DARN/MH* S9 ......117 H3
Ferrers Rd *WHHL* DN2 ....40 D5
Ferriby Rd *ST/HB/BR* S6 ......113 H2
Ferry Boat La *CONI* DN12 ....67 G5
Ferry La *CONI* DN12 ....69 E5
Ferry Moor La *CUD/GR* S72.....22 B1
Ferrymoor Wy *CUD/GR* S72......22 C1
Ferry Ter *CONI* DN12 * 69 E5
Ferry Vls *CONI* DN12 * 69 E5
Festival La *AU/AST/KP* S26...159 G3
Festival Rd *DEARNE* S63 ....65 F3
Fewton Wy
 DONS/BSCR DN4 ....57 F5
Fiddlers Dr *ARMTH* DN3.........59 F1
Field Av *ECK/KIL* S21 ....175 H3
Field Cl *DRON* S18 ....170 A1
 WMB/DAR S73 ....35 E4
Field Dr *CUD/GR* S72 ....21 G3
Fielder Ms *SHEFN* S5..........103 E5
Fielders Wy *CONI* DN12..........70 C5
Field Ga *NROS/TKH* DN11........91 F4
Field Head Rd *HOY* S74..........62 A2
Field Head Rd *HOY* S74 ....62 A3
Fieldhead Ms *SHEFS* S8 * 140 A3
Field House Rd *HOY* S74.........54 B5
Fieldhouse Wy *ATT* S4..........115 H5
Fielding Dr *MALT* S66 ....108 D5
Fielding Gv *RAW* S62............85 F4
Fielding Rd *ST/HB/BR* S6......114 A2
Field La *BSLY* S70 ....33 G3
 ECK/KIL S21 ....167 H3
 MALT S66 ....121 E5
Fieldside *ARMTH* DN3...........42 B1
Field Vw *RHAM* S60 ....118 C3
 STV/CWN S43............185 F3
Fieldview Pl *CHNE* S41 ....186 C3

Field Wy *RHAM* S60 ....8 E1
Fife Cl *DARN/MH* S9 ....103 C5
Fife St *BSLY* S70 ....2 D6
 DARN/MH S9 ....103 C5
Fife Wy *DARN/MH* S9 ....103 C5
Figtree La *SHEF* S1 ....11 G2
Filby Rd *BTLY* DN5 ....39 E5
Filey Av *BSLY/ROY* S71.........12 C5
Filey La *OWL* S3 ....10 C5
Filey St *FUL* S10 ....10 C5
Finch Cl *RHAM/THRY* S65.......99 H4
Finch Gn *DARN/MH* S9 ....103 C5
Finch Ri *AU/AST/KP* S26.......145 G4
Finch Rd *DONS/BSCR* DN4.......77 F2
Finchwell Cl *HAN/WDH* S13...128 D5
Finchwell Crs
 HAN/WDH S13 ....128 D5
Finchwell Rd
 HAN/WDH S13 ....128 D5
Findon Cft *ST/HB/BR* S6......113 C4
Findon Pl *ST/HB/BR* S6........113 C4
Findon Rd *ST/HB/BR* S6 ......113 C4
Findon St *ST/HB/BR* S6........113 H4
Finkle St *BTLY* DN5 ....39 H2
Finlay Rd *RHAM/THRY* S65 ...106 C1
Finlay St *OWL* S3 ....10 C1
Finsbury St *DIN* S25 ....134 A2
Firbeck Av *DIN* S25 ....134 C1
Firbeck Rd
 DONS/BSCR DN4 ....7 H6
 SHEFS S8 ....152 C2
Firbeck Wy
 NROS/TKH DN11..........91 H1
Fir Cl *DEARNE* S63 ....65 F3
Fircroft Av *SHEFN* S5 ....102 D4
Fircroft Rd *SHEFN* S5 ....103 E4
Firethorn Ri
 RHAM/THRY S65 ....119 F3
Firham Cl *BSLYN/ROY* S71......12 A5
Fir Pl *ECK/KIL* S21 ....168 A3
Fir Rd *ECK/KIL* S21 ....174 B1
Firsby La *CONI* DN12 ....88 A4
Firshill Av *ATT* S4 ....115 F4
Firshill Cl *ATT* S4 ....115 E4
Firshill Crs *ATT* S4 ....115 E4
Firshill Gld *SHEFN* S5 ....115 E4
Firshill Ri *ATT* S4 ....115 F4
Firshill Wk *ATT* S4.............115 F4
First Av *AWLS/ASK* DN6 ....25 F1
 RHAM/THRY S65 ....106 C1
First St *ST/HB/BR* S6 ....125 E2
 STV/CWN S43 ....181 F5
Firth Cft *STV/CWN* S43 * 180 B2
Firth Crs *MALT* S66 ....111 E4
 NROS/TKH DN11 ....91 E2
Firth Dr *ATT* S4 ....126 D1
Firth Park Av *SHEFN* S5 ......115 H1
Firth Park Crs *SHEFN* S5 .....115 H1
Firth Park Rd *SHEFN* S5 ......115 H1
Firth Rd *DEARNE* S63 ....64 B2
Firth St *BSLYN/ROY* S71........3 H2
 DONS/BSCR DN4 ....6 A7
 KIMB S61 ....97 G3
Firthwood Av *DRON* S18 ......163 H5
Firthwood Cl *DRON* S18 ......163 H5
Firthwood Rd *DRON* S18 ......163 H5
Fir Tree Dr *AU/AST/KP* S26...159 G3
Firtree Ri *CHPT/GREN* S35......94 A3
Fir Vale Pl *SHEFN* S5 * 115 C3
Firvale Rd *RCH* S42.............191 F4
Fir Vale Rd *SHEFN* S5 ....115 C3
Fish Dam La *BSLYN/ROY* S71...20 D1
Fisher Cl *CHSW* S40 ....192 B5
 RHAM S60 ....60 C1
Fisher La *DARN/MH* S9 ....128 A2
Fisher Rd *MALT* S66 ....111 F3
Fisher St *BTLY* DN5 ....26 D5
Fisher Ter *BTLY* DN5 ....39 G5
Fishponds Cl *RCH* S42 ....195 F5
Fishponds Rd
 HAN/WDH S13 ....142 A2
Fishponds Rd West
 HAN/WDH S13 ....142 A3
Fitzalan Rd *HAN/WDH* S13 ...142 D1
Fitzalan Sq *SHEF* S1............11 H3
Fitzgerald Rd *FUL* S10 ....124 D3
Fitzhubert Rd
 SHEFP/MNR S2 ....141 G2
Fitzmaurice Rd
 DARN/MH S9 ....127 H1
Fitzroy Rd *SHEFP/MNR* S2 ...140 B4
Fitzwalter Rd
 SHEFP/MNR S2 ....12 D6
Fitzwilliam Av *CONI* DN12......88 B1
Fitzwilliam Cit *RAW* S62........98 B2
Fitzwilliam Ga *SHEF* S1 ....11 F6
Fitzwilliam Rd
 RHAM/THRY S65 ....9 H2
 WMB/DAR S73 ....35 E4
Fitzwilliam Sq *KIMB* S61........97 F2
Fitzwilliam St *BSLY* S70 ....2 C5
 DEARNE S63 ....65 E5
 HOY S74 ....61 F3
 MEX/SWTN S64 ....86 A1
 OWL S3 ....10 D5
 RAW S62 ....98 A3
 WMB/DAR S73 ....62 D1

Five Oaks *BTLY* DN5 ....27 G4
Five Trees Cl
 TOT/DORE S17............161 G2
Five Trees Dr
 TOT/DORE S17............161 G2
Five Weirs Wk
 DARN/MH S9 ....127 F1
Flamsteed Crs *CHNE* S41 .....187 G3
Flanders Cl *KIMB* S61 ....95 F1
Flanderwell Av *MALT* S66 ....108 C3
Flanderwell Ct *MALT* S66 ....108 C3
Flanderwell Gdns
 MALT S66 ....108 C3
Flanderwell La *MALT* S66 ....108 C3
Flash La *MALT* S66 ....109 E5
 ST/HB/BR S6 ....122 C3
Flask Vw *ST/HB/BR* S6 ....112 C5
Flat La *CUD/GR* S72 ....36 A5
 RHAM S60 ....119 H3
Flat St *SHEF* S1 ....11 H3
Flatts Cl *RHAM* S60 ....130 A2
Flatts La *DEARNE* S63 ....66 C3
 RHAM S60 ....130 A2
Flaxby Rd *DARN/MH* S9 ......127 H2
Flax Lea *BSLY* S70 ....32 A5
Fleet Cl *DEARNE* S63 ....64 A1
Fleet Hill Crs
 BSLYN/ROY S71 ....20 A2
Fleetwood Av
 BSLYN/ROY S71 ....20 C2
Fleming Gdns *MALT* S66 .....108 B3
Fleming Pl *BSLY* S70 * 3 F6
Fleming Sq *DEARNE* S63 ......65 E2
Fleming Wy *MALT* S66 ....108 A4
Fletcher Av *DRON* S18 ....171 E2
Fleury Cl *GLV* S14 ....154 A1
Fleury Crs *GLV* S14 ....154 A1
Fleury Pl *GLV* S14 ....154 A1
Fleury Ri *GLV* S14 ....154 A1
Fleury Rd *GLV* S14 ....154 A1
Flint Rd *WHHL* DN2 ....41 C5
Flintson Av *STV/CWN* S43 ....180 B2
Flintway *DEARNE* S63 ....65 F5
Flockton Av *HAN/WDH* S13...143 F2
Flockton Crs
 HAN/WDH S13 ....143 F2
Flockton Dr *HAN/WDH* S13...143 G2
Flockton Rd *HAN/WDH* S13...143 G2
Flodden St *FUL* S10 ....124 D3
Floodgate Dr
 CHPT/GREN S35 ....102 B1
Flora St *ST/HB/BR* S6 ....125 G1
Florence Av
 AU/AST/KP S26...........145 F3
 DONS/BSCR DN4 ....55 C5
Florence Cl *CHSW* S40 ....195 F1
Florence Ri *WMB/DAR* S73.....34 D5
Florence Rd *RCH* S42..........195 E3
 SHEFS S8 ....152 C3
Flower St *DEARNE* S63 ....37 H5
Flowitt St *DONS/BSCR* DN4....55 H5
 MEX/SWTN S64 ....66 D3
Folderings La *STKB/PEN* S36...77 E5
Folder La *BTLY* DN5 ....54 A4
Folds Crs *SHEFS* S8............152 A4
Folds Dr *SHEFS* S8 ....152 A4
Folds La *SHEFS* S8 ....152 A4
The Fold *RHAM/THRY* S65 ...107 F1
Foley Av *WMB/DAR* S73........50 A3
Foley St *ATT* S4 ....126 C2
Foljambe Av *CHSW* S40 ......191 H4
Foljambe Crs
 NROS/TKH DN11..........90 D2
Foljambe Dr
 RHAM/THRY S65 ....99 G5
Foljambe Rd *CHSW* S40 ....4 D2
 RHAM/THRY S65 ....106 D1
 STV/CWN S43 ....188 C1
Foljambe St *RAW* S62 ....98 B2
Folkwood Gv *ECC* S11 ....138 A5
Follett Rd *SHEFN* S5...........102 C4
Fontwell Dr *MEX/SWTN* S64...67 E2
Foolow Av *CHSW* S40 ....192 B3
Forbes Rd *ST/HB/BR* S6 ......114 A5
Ford La *HACK/IN* S12 ....165 H3
 STKB/PEN S36 ....77 E1
Ford Rd *ECC* S11 ....138 C4
 ECK/KIL S21 ....165 G4
Fore Hill Av
 DONS/BSCR DN4 ....73 H2
Foremark Rd *SHEFN* S5 ......102 D5
Forest Ct *STV/CWN* S43 ......177 F5
Forest Edge *ECC* S11 ....151 F4
Forest Gra *DONS/BSCR* DN4...58 A4
Forest Rd *DONS/BSCR* DN4....71 E5
Forest Rd *BSLYN/ROY* S71.....14 D4
Forge Dr *CHSW* S40 ....4 C2
Forge La *ECK/KIL* S21 ....167 H1
 HOY S74 ....62 C4
 RHAM S60 ....8 E4
 SHEFP/MNR S2 ....11 F7
Forge Rd *AU/AST/KP* S26.....159 F2
Formby Ct *BSLYN/ROY* S71....20 D1
Forncett St *ATT* S4............126 D1
Fornham St *SHEF* S1 ....11 H6
Forres Av *FUL* S10 ....124 C4
Forres Rd *FUL* S10 ....124 D4
Forrester Av *MALT* S66 ....108 B3
Forrester's La *DRON* S18 .....163 G4
Forster Rd *DONS/BSCR* DN4...57 F5
Forth Av *DRON* S18 ....170 B1
Fort Hill Rd *DARN/MH* S9 ....116 B2
Fortway Rd *RHAM* S60 ....118 C2

Fossard Cl *WHHL* DN2 ....41 E4
Fossard Wy *BTLY* DN5 ....55 G4
Fossdale Rd *ABRD* S7 ....139 F5
Foster Rd *MALT* S66 ....108 B4
Foster St *BSLY* S70 ....32 D2
Foster Wy *CHPT/GREN* S35 ....80 B5
Foster's Cl *MEX/SWTN* S64.....66 A5
Foston Dr *CHSW* S40 ....186 B4
Fothergill Dr *ARMTH* DN3.......29 G4
Foulstone Rw
 WMB/DAR S73 ....49 H4
Foundry Ga *WMB/DAR* S73....49 H4
Foundry St *BSLY* S70 ....3 F6
 CHNE S41 ....187 G1
 HOY S74 ....61 G5
 RAW S62 ....98 B3
Fountain Ct *BSLYN/ROY* S71...14 C3
 NROS/TKH DN11..........91 H3
Fountain Prec *SHEF* S1 * 11 F3
Fountains Wy
 BSLYN/ROY S71 ....20 C2
Four Lands Cl *DOD/DAR* S75...18 A2
Fourth Av *AWLS/ASK* DN6 ......25 F4
Four Wells Dr *HACK/IN* S12..156 A2
Fowler Bridge Rd *BTLY* DN5...40 A2
Fowler Crs *NROS/TKH* DN11...91 E2
Fowler St *CHNE* S41 ....179 F4
Foxbrook Cl *CHSW* S40 ......191 H4
Foxbrook Dr *CHSW* S40 ......191 H4
Fox Cl *KIMB* S61 ....96 B4
Foxcote Wy *MALT* S66 ....108 D5
Fox Ct *MEX/SWTN* S64 ....86 B2
Fox Covert Cl *DEARNE* S63 *...53 E1
Fox Cft *HOY* S74 ....61 H3
Foxcroft Cha *ECK/KIL* S21 ...168 A2
Foxcroft Dr *ECK/KIL* S21 .....168 A2
Foxcroft Gv *ECK/KIL* S21 .....168 A2
Foxdale Av *HACK/IN* S12 .....141 H5
Foxencroft *BSLYN/ROY* S71....21 E3
Foxfield Av *BSLY* S70 ....65 H1
Foxfield Wk *BSLY* S70 ....32 D4
Fox Glen Rd *STKB/PEN* S36....77 E3
Foxglove Rd *SHEFN* S5 ....105 E5
Fox Gv *DONS/BSCR* DN4 ....70 C2
Foxhall La *FUL* S10 ....136 C4
Fox Hill Av *ST/HB/BR* S6 .....101 E4
Fox Hill Cl *ST/HB/BR* S6 .....101 E4
Fox Hill Crs *ST/HB/BR* S6 ....101 E4
Fox Hill Dr *ST/HB/BR* S6 .....101 E4
Fox Hill Pl *ST/HB/BR* S6 .....101 E3
Fox Hill Rd *ST/HB/BR* S6 .....101 E3
Fox Hill Wy *ST/HB/BR* S6 ....101 E3
Foxland Av *MEX/SWTN* S64....85 C1
Fox La *HACK/IN* S12 ....155 H4
 TOT/DORE S17............162 B2
Fox Lane Ct *HACK/IN* S12....155 E1
Fox Lane Vw *HACK/IN* S12...155 E1
Fox Rd *ST/HB/BR* S6 ....125 C1
Foxroyd Cl *STV/CWN* S43 .....73 F2
Foxstone Cl *STV/CWN* S43 ...189 H1
Fox St *KIMB* S61 ....104 C3
 OWL S3 ....10 C1
Foxwood Av *HACK/IN* S12....141 H4
Foxwood Cl *CHNE* S41 ....179 E5
Foxwood Dr *HACK/IN* S12....141 H4
Foxwood Gv *HACK/IN* S12....141 H4
Foxwood Rd *CHNE* S41 ....179 E4
 HACK/IN S12 ....141 H4
Foxwood Wy *CHNE* S41 ......179 E4
Foyers Wy *CHNE* S41 ....5 J4
Framlingham Pl
 SHEFP/MNR S2 ....140 D3
France Rd *ST/HB/BR* S6 ......112 D3
Frances Dr *RCH* S42 ....195 E3
Frances St *DON* DN1 ....6 D3
 RHAM S60 ....8 D2
France St *RAW* S62.............98 B3
Francis Cl *STV/CWN* S43 .....188 B2
Francis Crs North
 RHAM S60 ....120 B1
Francis Crs South
 RHAM S60 ....120 B1
Francis Dr *RHAM* S60 ....120 B1
Francis Gv *CHPT/GREN* S35....80 B4
Francus Royd
 BSLYN/ROY S71 ....15 G3
Franklin Crs *WHHL* DN2 * 7 J4
Franklyn Dr *STV/CWN* S43 ...182 B5
Franklyn Rd *CHSW* S40 ....4 B2
Frank Pl *DARN/MH* S9 ....116 C5
Frank Rd *BTLY* DN5 ....39 H4
Fraser Cl *SHEFS* S8 ....152 C2
Fraser Crs *SHEFS* S8 ....152 C2
Fraser Dr *SHEFS* S8 ....152 C2
Fraser Rd *RHAM* S60 ....9 J7
 SHEFS S8 ....152 C2
Frecheville St
 STV/CWN S43 ....181 H5
Frederick Av *BSLY* S70 ....2 D7
Frederick Dr
 CHPT/GREN S35 ....92 D5
Frederick St *DARN/MH* S9 ...127 H3
 DEARNE S63 ....37 H5
 DEARNE S63 * 64 D1
 MEX/SWTN S64 ....66 C3
 RHAM S60 ....9 G1
 SHEFS S8 ....152 C2
 WMB/DAR S73 ....35 A2
Frederic Pl *BSLY* S70 ....31 H3
Fred Mulley Rd *ATT* S4 ......126 D2

Freebirch Vw *CHNE* S41.......186 B2
Freedom Ct *ST/HB/BR* S6 * ...125 E1
Freedom Rd *ST/HB/BR* S6.....125 E1
Freeman Rd *MALT* S66 ....108 B4
Freeman St *BSLY* S70 ....3 H7
Freemans Yd *BSLY* S70 ....3 H5
Freesia Cl *CONI* DN12 ....88 D5
Freeston Pl *DARN/MH* S9 ....116 C5
French Ga *DON* DN1..............6 D3
French St *BTLY* DN5 ....26 D5
Fretson Cl *SHEFP/MNR* S2 ...141 G2
Fretson Gn
 SHEFP/MNR S2 ....141 G2
Fretson Rd *SHEFP/MNR* S2 ..141 G2
Fretson Road S
 SHEFP/MNR S2 ....141 G3
Fretwell Cl *MALT* S66 ....110 C2
Fretwell Rd *MALT* S66 ....109 H4
Friar Cl *ST/HB/BR* S6 ....123 H1
Friars Ga *DON* DN1 ....6 C1
Friars Rd *BSLYN/ROY* S71......21 E4
Frickley Rd *ECC* S11 ....138 B2
Frinton Cl *CHSW* S40 ....192 B5
Frithbeck Cl *ARMTH* DN3 ....42 D4
Frith Cl *HACK/IN* S12 ....141 H5
Frithhall La *RCH* S42 ....190 A2
Frith Rd *HACK/IN* S12 ....141 H5
Frithwood Dr *DRON* S18 .....171 G1
Frobisher Gv *MALT* S66 ......110 C2
Froggatt Cl *STV/CWN* S43 ...189 G3
Froggatt La *SHEF* S1 ....11 G5
Frogmore Cl *MALT* S66 ......108 D3
Front Rw *NROS/TKH* DN11 * ...91 H2
Front St *RHAM* S60 ....130 A3
Frostings Cl *CHPT/GREN* S35..93 E5
The Frostings
 CHPT/GREN S35 ....93 E5
Fulford Cl *CHSW* S40 ....191 G4
 DARN/MH S9 ....128 A2
Fulford Pl *DARN/MH* S9 ......128 A2
Fuller Dr *CHNE* S41 * 188 A3
Fullerton Av *CONI* DN12........88 D1
Fullerton Crs
 RHAM/THRY S65 ....99 G4
Fullerton Dr *RHAM* S60 ......118 C4
Fullerton Rd *RHAM* S60 ......118 C1
Fulmar Wy *KIMB* S61 ....82 C5
Fulmer Cl *BSLYN/ROY* S71......20 C2
Fulmere Crs *SHEFN* S5 ....101 G3
Fulmere Rd *SHEFN* S5 ....101 G3
Fulney Rd *ECC* S11 ....138 E2
Fulton Rd *ST/HB/BR* S6 ......125 E2
Fulwood Cha *FUL* S10 ....138 A2
Fulwood Dr
 DONS/BSCR DN4 ....71 H4
Fulwood Head Rd *FUL* S10 ..136 C4
Fulwood La *FUL* S10 ....136 B4
Fulwood Rd *FUL* S10 ....137 H3
Furlong Ct *DEARNE* S63 ....53 F2
Furlong Mdw *DEARNE* S63 ....63 F2
Furlong Rd *DEARNE* S63 ....53 G2
Furnace Hl *CHSW* S40 ....4 C3
 OWL S3 ....11 F1
Furnace La *HAN/WDH* S13 ...143 H4
 STV/CWN S43 ....188 D3
Furness Cl *DIN* S25 ....148 D1
 ST/HB/BR S6 ....112 D5
Furness Dene
 BSLYN/ROY S71 ....20 D2
Furness Rd *CHPT/GREN* S41..186 B4
Furniss Av *TOT/DORE* S17....160 D2
Furniss Ms *TOT/DORE* S17 ...161 E2
Furnival Cl *AU/AST/KP* S26...147 E5
Furnival Ga *SHEF* S1 ....11 G5
Furnival Rd
 DONS/BSCR DN4 ....55 C5
 AU/AST/KP S26...........147 E5
 SHEFP/MNR S2 ....11 J2
Furnival Sq *SHEF* S1 ....11 G5
Furnival St *SHEF* S1 ....11 G5
Furnival Wy *RHAM* S60 ....120 B5
Future Wk *CHSW* S40 * 4 E4
Fylde Cl *BSLYN/ROY* S71........20 D1

G

Gainsborough Cl *MALT* S66 ..108 B4
Gainsborough Rd
 DRON S18................170 C3
 ECC S11 ....139 F5
Gainsborough Wy
 BSLYN/ROY S71 ....20 B3
Gainsford Rd *DARN/MH* S9..128 A3
Gaitskell Cl *DEARNE* S63 ....53 F4
 MALT S66 ....111 F4
Gala Crs *MALT* S66 ....110 B2
Gallery La *RCH* S42 ....190 A5
Galley Dr *MOS* S20 ....156 D4
Gallow Tree Rd
 RHAM/THRY S65 ....107 F5
Galpharm Wy
 DOD/DAR S75 ....30 A2
Galsworthy Av *SHEFN* S5 ....114 C4
Galsworthy Cl
 DONS/BSCR DN4 ....71 F3
Galsworthy Rd *SHEFN* S5 ....114 D1
Galway Cl *BSLYN/ROY* S71.....12 C1
 RAW S62 ....98 B2
Gamston Rd *SHEFS* S8 ....139 H5
Gander La *STV/CWN* S43 .....184 B1

Gannow Cl ECK/KIL S21 ....168 D1
Ganton Pl BSLYN/ROY S71 .....14 C5
Ganton Rd ST/HB/BR S6 ......113 H2
Garbroads Crs
  RHAM/THRY S65 ....99 G4
Garbutt St DEARNE S63 ....53 F4
Garden Av ECK/KIL S21 ....175 H4
Garden Cl RHAM S60 ....119 G1
  STV/CWN S43 ....180 B3
Garden Ct BSLY S70 ....30 D1
Garden Crs RHAM S60 ....119 G2
Garden Dr WMB/DAR S73 ....51 E5
Gardeners Cl BSVR S44 ....196 D2
Garden Gv WMB/DAR S73 ....50 A5
Garden House Cl
  BSLYN/ROY S71 ....20 C2
Gardenia Rd ARMTH DN3 ....29 E4
Garden La BTLY DN5 ....69 F1
  RHAM S60 ....8 D3
Gardens La CONI DN12 ....88 D1
The Gardens
  DONS/BSCR DN4 ....73 H1
Garden St BSLY S70 ....3 F7
  DEARNE S63 ....64 C1
  DEARNE S63 ....64 C1
  KIMB S61 ....8 A3
  MEX/SWTN S64 ....66 D3
  SHEF S1 ....10 E2
  WMB/DAR S73 ....35 E5
Garden Wk RHAM S60 ....119 G2
Gardom Cl DRON S18 ....170 B2
Garfield Mt
  RHAM/THRY S65 ....9 H6
Garland Cl MOS S20 ....167 E1
Garland Cft MOS S20 ....167 E1
Garland Dr ST/HB/BR S6 ....112 D3
Garland Mt MOS S20 ....157 E5
Garland Wy MOS S20 ....167 E1
Garry Rd ST/HB/BR S6 ....113 H3
Garter St ATT S4 ....115 H5
Garth Cl DARN/MH S9 ....127 G2
Garth Wy DRON S18 ....170 D2
Gartrice Gdns MOS S20 ....167 G3
Gartrice Gv MOS S20 ....167 G3
Gashouse La ARMTH DN3 ....59 H3
Gate Crs DOD/DAR S75 ....30 B2
Gatefield Cl CHNE S41 ....186 C2
Gatefield Rd ABRD S7 ....139 G4
Gateway Cl RAW S62 ....98 A4
Gateway Ct RAW S62 ....98 A4
The Gateway RAW S62 ....98 A4
Gate Wood La ARMTH DN3 .....59 H3
Gattison La
  NROS/TKH DN11 ....91 F3
Gatty Rd SHEFN S5 ....102 D2
Gaunt Cl ECK/KIL S21 ....168 A2
  GLV S14 ....153 H2
  MALT S66 ....108 D3
Gaunt Dr GLV S14 ....153 H2
  MALT S66 ....108 D3
Gaunt Pl GLV S14 ....153 H1
Gaunt Rd GLV S14 ....153 H1
  MALT S66 ....108 D3
Gawber Rd DOD/DAR S75 ....2 A1
Gawtress Rw DEARNE S63 ....65 G2
Gayle Ct BSLY S70 ....2 D3
Gayton Cl DONS/BSCR DN4 .....71 G3
Geer La HACK/IN S12 ....165 E3
Gelders Pl DRON S18 ....171 E5
Geit St OWL S3 ....10 D5
Genn La BSLY S70 ....31 F4
Genoa Cl RHAM S60 ....34 C3
Genoa St MEX/SWTN S64 ....67 F3
The Gentre MALT S66 ....108 D4
George Pl RAW S62 ....98 B1
George Sq BSLY S70 * 3 F5
George St ARMTH DN3 ....42 B3
  BSLY S70 ....3 F5
  BSLY S70 ....48 A1
  BTLY DN5 ....26 C5
  CHNE S41 ....11 F1
  CUD/GR S72 ....35 H3
  DEARNE S63 ....37 E4
  HOY S74 ....62 A3
  RHAM S60 ....8 E3
  SHEF S1 ....11 G5
  STV/CWN S43 ....188 C1
  WMB/DAR S73 ....50 B3
George Yd BSLY S70 ....3 F4
Georgian Ms RHAM S60 ....129 G1
Gerald Cl BSLY S70 ....32 C3
Gerald Crs BSLY S70 ....32 D2
Gerald Pl BSLY S70 ....32 D2
Gerald Rd BSLY S70 ....32 D2
Gerald Wk DARN/MH S9 ....116 C5
Gerard Cl CHSW S40 ....191 G3
  SHEFS S8 ....140 B4
Gerard Rd RHAM S60 ....9 G7
Gerard St SHEFS S8 ....140 B4
Gervase Av SHEFS S8 ....162 C2
Gervase Dr SHEFS S8 ....162 C2
Gervase Pl SHEFS S8 ....162 C2
Gervase Rd SHEFS S8 ....162 C2
Gibbing Greaves Rd
  RHAM/THRY S65 ....107 G5
Gibbons Dr GLV S14 ....154 A3
Gibbons Wy GLV S14 ....154 A3
Gibraltar St SHEF S1 ....11 F1
Gibson La STKB/PEN S36 ....77 E1
Gifford Dr DONS/BSCR DN4 .....70 D2

Gifford Rd SHEFS S8 * 140 A3
Gilbert Av CHSW S40 ....191 H4
Gilbert Gv BSLY S70 ....32 D2
Gilberthorpe Dr
  RHAM/THRY S65 ....106 C3
Gilberthorpe Rd
  DONS/BSCR DN4 ....71 F1
Gilberthorpe St
  RHAM/THRY S65 ....9 K5
Gilbert Rw SHEFF/MNR S2 ....11 K4
Gilbert St SHEF S1 ....11 J3
Gildhurst Rd BSLY S70 ....60 D2
Giles Av DEARNE S63 ....64 C2
Gileswood Crs DEARNE S63 .....64 A2
Gill Cl MALT S66 ....121 G1
Gill Cft ST/HB/BR S6 ....123 C1
Gilleyfield Av
  TOT/DORE S17 ....161 E1
Gill Mdw ST/HB/BR S6 ....123 C1
Gillott La MALT S66 ....121 F1
Gillott Rd ST/HB/BR S6 ....121 G1
Gill St DON DN1 ....6 E6
  HOY S74 ....62 B5
Gilpin La ST/HB/BR S6 ....125 G2
Gilpin St ST/HB/BR S6 ....125 G2
Gilroyd La DOD/DAR S75 ....30 C5
Ginhouse La KIMB S61 ....105 G1
Gladstone La CHSW S41 ....179 H4
Gipsy La CHNE S41 ....179 H4
  DRON S18 ....172 C2
Gisborne Rd ECC S11 ....138 C4
Gisbourne Cl STV/CWN S43 ...182 B5
Glade Cl CHSW S40 ....187 E4
Glade Cft HACK/IN S12 ....141 C5
Glade Lea HACK/IN S12 ....141 C5
The Glade CHSW S40 ....4 A3
Glade Vw ARMTH DN3 ....4 B5
Gladstone Ms FUL S10 ....138 A1
Gladstone Rd CHSW S40 ....4 D2
  DONS/BSCR DN4 ....55 G4
  FUL S10 ....138 A1
  MALT S66 ....110 C2
Gladwin Gdns CHSW S40 ....191 H4
Gladys St RHAM/THRY S65 .....106 C5
Glaisdale Cl DIN S25 ....134 A2
Glamis Rd WHHL DN2 ....57 E2
Glasshouse La
  STV/CWN S43 ....180 B1
Glasshouse Rd
  MEX/SWTN S64 ....86 C4
Glasshouse St RHAM S60 ....38 D5
Glastonbury Gv BTLY DN5 ....27 G4
Gleadless Av HACK/IN S12 .....154 B1
Gleadless Bank
  HACK/IN S12 ....154 B1
Gleadless Common
  HACK/IN S12 ....141 F5
Gleadless Ct
  SHEFF/MNR S2 ....140 B4
Gleadless Mt HACK/IN S12 .....154 B1
Gleadless Ri HACK/IN S12 ......154 C2
Gleadless Rd GLV S14 ....141 E5
  HACK/IN S12 ....154 C2
  SHEFF/MNR S2 ....140 A3
Gleadless Vw HACK/IN S12 .....141 F1
Glebe Cl MEX/SWTN S64 ....86 A2
Glebe Ct CHNE S41 ....179 G4
Glebe Crs RHAM/THRY S65 ......99 G5
Glebe Farm Cl ARMTH DN3 .....42 C4
Glebeland Cl RAW S62 ....97 G4
Glebelands Rd
  STKB/PEN S36 ....77 E3
Glebe Rd FUL S10 ....125 E3
  MEX/SWTN S64 ....86 A2
Glebe St DONS/BSCR DN4 ....70 D2
  STV/CWN S43 ....177 F5
The Glebe Wy CHNE S41 ....11 G3
Gledhill Av STKB/PEN S36 ....44 C5
Gledhill Cl DRON S18 ....171 E2
Glenalmond Rd ECC S11 ....138 D3
Glenavon Cl STV/CWN S43 ....180 B1
Glencoe Dr SHEFF/MNR S2 ....126 C5
Glencoe Pl
  SHEFF/MNR S2 * 126 C5
Glencoe Rd SHEFF/MNR S2 ....126 C5
Glencoe Wy CHSW S40 ....186 B5
Glendale Cl DOD/DAR S75 ....30 D1
Glendale Rd BTLY DN5 ....54 B4
Gleneagles Cl CHSW S40 ....191 G4
Gleneagles Dr
  DONS/BSCR DN4 ....74 D2
Gleneagles Ri
  MEX/SWTN S64 ....86 B1
Gleneagles Rd DIN S25 ....134 D5
Glen Field Av
  DONS/BSCR DN4 ....55 G4
Glenfield Crs CHNE S41 ....187 F2
Glenholme Dr
  HAN/WDH S13 ....142 C3
Glenholme Pl
  HAN/WDH S13 ....142 C3
Glenholme Rd
  HAN/WDH S13 ....142 C3
Glenholme Wy
  HAN/WDH S13 ....142 C2
Glenmoor Av BSLY S70 ....30 D2
Glenmore Cl STV/CWN S43 ....189 E4
Glenmore Cft HACK/IN S12 ....141 H4
Glenmore Ri
  WMB/DAR S73 ....50 C4
Glenorchy Rd ABRD S7 ....139 F5

Glen Rd ABRD S7 ....139 G4
  ARMTH DN3 ....59 G5
The Glen FUL S10 ....138 D1
Glenthorne Cl CHSW S40 ....191 G2
Glentilt Rd ABRD S7 ....139 F5
Glen V DRON S18 ....170 D2
Glen View Rd SHEFS S8 ....152 C5
Glenville Cl HOY S74 ....61 H3
Glenwood Ct ST/HB/BR S6 .....113 F1
Glenwood Crs
  CHPT/GREN S35 ....94 B1
Glenwood Dr ST/HB/BR S6 .....113 F1
Gliwice Wy DONS/BSCR DN4 ...57 F4
Glossop Cl FUL S10 ....10 B4
Glossop Rd FUL S10 ....10 A6
Glossop's Cft CHNE S41 ....179 H4
Gloucester Crs FUL S10 ....10 A6
Gloucester Rd CHNE S41 ....187 F3
  KIMB S61 ....96 D5
Gloucester St FUL S10 ....10 B5
Glover Rd SHEFS S8 * 140 A3
  TOT/DORE S17 ....161 F5
Glumangate CHSW S40 ....5 F3
Glyn Av DON DN1 ....6 E1
Goathland Dr
  HAN/WDH S13 ....143 G3
Goathland Pl
  HAN/WDH S13 ....143 G3
Goathland Rd
  HAN/WDH S13 ....143 H3
Goddard Av STKB/PEN S36 ......76 B1
Goddard Hall Rd SHEFN S5 ....115 G3
Godley St BSLYN/ROY S71 ....12 B3
Godric Dr RHAM S60 ....118 B3
Godric Gn RHAM S60 ....118 B3
Godric Rd SHEFN S5 ....102 C2
Godstone Rd RHAM S60 ....9 G6
Goldcrest Wk KIMB S61 ....95 G1
Gold Cft BSLY S70 ....3 J7
Golden Smithies La
  MEX/SWTN S64 ....65 H5
Goldsborough Rd WHHL DN2 .....2 K3
Goldsmith Dr
  RHAM/THRY S65 ....106 D3
Goldsmith Rd
  DONS/BSCR DN4 ....72 A2
  RHAM/THRY S65 ....106 D3
Gold St BSLY S70 ....3 J6
Goldthorpe Rd DEARNE S63 .....53 F1
Gomersal La DRON S18 ....171 E2
Gomersall Av CONI DN12 ....88 B1
Gooder Av BSLYN/ROY S71 ....15 C1
Goodison Bvd
  DONS/BSCR DN4 ....74 A1
Goodison Crs ST/HB/BR S6 .....124 B1
Goodison Ri ST/HB/BR S6 ......124 B1
Goodwin Av RAW S62 ....85 F5
Goodwin Crs
  MEX/SWTN S64 ....66 B4
Goodwin Rd KIMB S61 ....97 E2
  SHEFS S8 ....140 A4
Goodwood Gdns
  DONS/BSCR DN4 ....57 H3
Goodyear Crs
  WMB/DAR S73 ....50 B3
Goore Av DARN/MH S9 ....127 H4
Goore Dr DARN/MH S9 ....127 H4
Goore Rd DARN/MH S9 ....127 H5
Gooseacre Av DEARNE S63 ......37 E1
Goosebutt St RAW S62 ....98 B2
Goose Carr La
  AU/AST/KP S26 ....146 D3
Goosecroft Av
  RHAM/THRY S65 ....99 G4
Goosehill Ct
  DONS/BSCR DN4 ....71 H4
Goose La MALT S66 ....108 C5
Gordon Av SHEFS S8 ....153 E5
Gordon Rd ECC S11 ....139 F2
Gordon St BSLY S70 ....33 E2
  DON DN1 ....6 B4
Gordon Ter
  RHAM/THRY S65 * 9 K5
Gorehill Cl DEARNE S63 ....53 H5
Gorman Cl CHNE S41 ....187 E1
Gorse Cl DEARNE S63 ....63 H2
Gorse St RHAM/THRY S65 ....109 F1
Gorse Dr ECK/KIL S21 ....168 B3
Gorseland Ct MALT S66 ....108 A5
Gorse La FUL S10 ....136 D3
The Gorse MALT S66 ....121 F1
Gorse Valley Rd CHNE S41 .....193 C5
Gorse Valley Vw CHNE S41 ....193 C5
Gorsey Brigg DRON S18 ....170 B2
Gosber St ECK/KIL S21 ....166 D5
Gosber Rd ECK/KIL S21 ....166 D5
Gosforth Cl DRON S18 * 170 D2
Gosforth Crs DRON S18 * 170 B3
Gosforth Dr DRON S18 ....170 B3
Gosforth Gn DRON S18 ....170 D2
Gosforth La DRON S18 ....170 B3
Gosling Gate Rd
  DEARNE S63 ....37 G5
Gotham Rd RHAM S60 ....118 C3
Gough Cl RHAM/THRY S65 ......107 E5
Goulding St MEX/SWTN S64 .....66 D4
Gowdall Gn BTLY DN5 ....26 D5
Gower Crs CHSW S40 ....186 C4
Gower St ATT S4 ....115 H5

Goyt Side Rd CHSW S40 ....4 A6
Goyt Ter CHSW S40 * 4 A5
Grace Rd CONI DN12 ....70 C5
Grace St BSLYN/ROY S71 ....13 J1
Grady Dr DONS/BSCR DN4 ....72 A3
Graftcivke Cl
  NROS/TKH DN11 ....91 H2
Grafton St BSLY S70 ....3 F6
  SHEFF/MNR S2 ....126 C5
Grafton Wy
  RHAM/THRY S65 ....9 G2
Graham Av RHAM S60 ....118 D5
Graham Rd ARMTH DN3 ....29 F4
  FUL S10 ....138 A2
Graham's Orch BSLY S70 ....3 F4
Grammar St ST/HB/BR S6 ....125 F1
Grampian Cl BTLY DN5 ....39 E5
  DOD/DAR S75 ....18 D5
Grampian Crs CHSW S40 ....186 A5
Granary Cl RCH S42 ....186 B5
Granary Ct DIN S25 ....148 B2
Granby Ct ARMTH DN3 ....45 E5
Granby Crs WHHL DN2 ....2 J5
Granby La NROS/TKH DN11 .....90 D2
Granby Rd SHEFN S5 ....115 H2
Grange Av AU/AST/KP S26 .....145 E1
  DONS/BSCR DN4 ....71 G1
  DRON S18 ....170 D2
Grange Cliffe Cl ECC S11 ....151 H1
Grange Cl CUD/GR S72 ....17 H1
  DONS/BSCR DN4 ....74 B2
  MALT S66 ....132 C2
Grange Ct BTLY DN5 ....39 G4
  DONS/BSCR DN4 ....74 B2
  MALT S66 ....108 B5
Grange Crs BSLYN/ROY S71 .....21 E5
  DEARNE S63 ....38 B3
  ECC S11 ....139 G2
Grange Crescent Rd
  ECC S11 ....139 G2
Grange Dr KIMB S61 ....96 B5
  MALT S66 ....109 H5
Grange Farm
  DONS/BSCR DN4 ....71 G4
Grange Farm Cl RHAM S60 ....118 D5
Grange Farm Dr
  AU/AST/KP S26 ....145 G4
Grangefield Av
  NROS/TKH DN11 ....91 F2
Grangefield Ter
  NROS/TKH DN11 ....91 F2
Grange La BSLYN/ROY S71 ....21 E5
  DONS/BSCR DN4 ....71 E4
  KIMB S61 ....96 B5
  MALT S66 ....111 F2
  NROS/TKH DN11 ....91 E2
  RHAM S60 ....118 A1
Grange Mill La
  DARN/MH S9 ....103 F1
Grangemill Pl
  STV/CWN S43 ....189 G1
Grange Pk ARMTH DN3 ....29 G2
Grange Park Av
  STV/CWN S43 ....188 D5
Grange Rd AWLS/ASK DN6 ....25 G4
  BSLYN/ROY S71 ....15 E1
  BTLY DN5 ....39 G4
  CUD/GR S72 ....17 H2
  DEARNE S63 ....63 H2
  DONS/BSCR DN4 ....74 B2
  ECC S11 ....139 G2
  MEX/SWTN S64 ....85 H1
  MOS S20 ....157 G2
  RAW S62 ....85 G4
  RHAM S60 ....119 H2
Grange St DEARNE S63 ....37 G2
The Grange KIMB S61 ....96 A4
Grange Vw DEARNE S63 * 37 E2
  DONS/BSCR DN4 ....74 B2
  HOY S74 ....48 D4
Grange View Crs KIMB S61 .....104 B1
Grange View Rd KIMB S61 ......104 B1
Grangewood Rd CHSW S40 ....192 B6
Granham Acre CUD/GR S72 .....17 G2
Grantham St
  NROS/TKH DN11 ....91 E2
Grantley Cl RHAM S60 ....74 B3
Granville Cl CHNE S41 ....193 F4
Granville Rd
  SHEFF/MNR S2 ....11 J6
  SHEFF/MNR S2 ....140 D1
Granville Sq Jct
  SHEFF/MNR S2 ....11 H6
Granville St DOD/DAR S75 ....19 F4
Granville Ter
  RHAM/THRY S65 ....9 K5
Grasby Ct MALT S66 ....108 D3
Grasmere Av WHHL DN2 ....57 G1
Grasmere Cl CHNE S41 ....186 D1
  DIN S25 ....134 C1
  STKB/PEN S36 ....44 D2
Grasmere Rd ABRD S7 ....53 H4
  BSLYN/ROY S71 ....3 J4
  CONI DN12 ....88 D1
  DRON S18 ....170 C2
Grassdale Vw HACK/IN S12 ....153 H2
Grassington Cl
  HACK/IN S12 ....156 B2
Grassington Dr
  HACK/IN S12 ....156 A2
Grassington Wy
  CHPT/GREN S35 ....80 D5

Grassmoor Cl HACK/IN S12 ....141 F4
Grassthorpe Rd
  HACK/IN S12 ....154 C1
Grattan St KIMB S61 ....104 C3
Graven Cl CHPT/GREN S35 .....100 D1
Gray Av AU/AST/KP S26 ....145 F1
Gray Cl RHAM/THRY S65 ....9 H1
Gray Gdns
  DONS/BSCR DN4 ....71 H2
Grays Ct CONI DN12 ....68 C4
Grayson Cl
  RHAM/THRY S65 ....108 D1
  STKB/PEN S36 ....77 E3
Grayson Rd KIMB S61 ....97 E2
Gray St HOY S74 ....62 C3
  MOS S20 ....166 C1
  OWL S3 ....126 B1
  STV/CWN S43 ....185 F2
Gray's Rd BSLYN/ROY S71 ....15 C5
Greasbro Rd DARN/MH S9 ......117 F2
Greasbrough La RAW S62 ....97 H1
Greasbrough Rd KIMB S61 ......97 H5
  RAW S62 ....98 A3
  RHAM S60 ....8 E1
Greasbrough St RHAM S60 ....8 D2
Great Bank Rd
  RHAM/THRY S65 ....107 G5
Great Broading
  DOD/DAR S75 ....18 D2
Great Central Av
  RHAM S60 ....55 H5
Great Cliffe Rd
  DOD/DAR S75 ....30 A2
Great Common Cl
  STV/CWN S43 ....177 H4
Great Cft DRON S18 ....170 B1
Great Eastern Wy RAW S62 ......98 B4
Great North Rd
  AWLS/ASK DN6 ....24 D1
Great Park Rd KIMB S61 ....104 C5
Greaves Cl ST/HB/BR S6 ....123 C1
Greaves Fold DOD/DAR S75 .....18 D5
  ST/HB/BR S6 ....123 C1
Greaves Rd KIMB S61 ....105 E2
  SHEFN S5 ....102 A1
Greaves St ST/HB/BR S6 ....114 D5
Greave Wy STV/CWN S43 ....188 A1
Green Acres HOY S74 ....62 A3
  RAW S62 ....85 E3
  STKB/PEN S36 ....45 E3
Greenacres Cl DRON S18 ....171 G4
Green Arbour Rd MALT S66 ....133 E1
Greenaway Dr BSVR S44 ....196 C4
Greenbank BSLYN/ROY S71 .....14 D3
Greenbank Dr CHSW S40 ....186 C5
Greenbank Wk CUD/GR S72 .....17 H5
Green Boulevarde
  DONS/BSCR DN4 ....58 A5
Green Brook Pl
  STKB/PEN S36 ....44 C4
Green Cha ECK/KIL S21 ....166 C5
Green Cl DRON S18 ....172 A5
  ECK/KIL S21 ....175 H3
  STV/CWN S43 ....189 G3
Green Ct MALT S66 ....108 C2
Green Croft RHAM S60 ....119 F1
Green Cross DRON S18 ....171 F1
Greendale Av RCH S42 ....190 C4
Green Farm Cl CHSW S40 ....186 C5
Greenfield Cl ARMTH DN3 ....29 C1
  ARMTH DN3 ....43 E5
  RHAM/THRY S65 ....107 F1
  SHEFS S8 ....162 D1
Greenfield Ct MALT S66 ....108 B3
  MEX/SWTN S64 ....53 H5
Greenfield Dr SHEFS S8 ....162 D1
Greenfield Gdns
  DONS/BSCR DN4 ....74 C1
  MALT S66 ....108 B3
Greenfield La
  DONS/BSCR DN4 ....55 G4
Greenfield Rd HOY S74 ....62 A1
  RHAM/THRY S65 ....107 F1
  SHEFS S8 ....162 D1
Greenfields ECK/KIL S21 ....166 C5
Greenfields Cl RHAM S60 ....118 C4
Greenfoot Cl DOD/DAR S75 ......19 F4
Greenfoot La DOD/DAR S75 ....2 C1
Greengate Cl CHSW S40 ....191 G2
Green Gate Cl DEARNE S63 .....53 F2
Greengate La
  CHPT/GREN S35 ....80 B5
Greengate Rd
  HAN/WDH S13 ....143 G4
Green Gn CHSW S40 ....191 G2
Greenhall Rd ECK/KIL S21 ......166 C5
Greenhead Gdns
  CHPT/GREN S35 ....94 A1
Greenhead La
  CHPT/GREN S35 ....81 E5
Greenhill Av BSLYN/ROY S71 ...19 G4
  MALT S66 ....109 H5
  SHEFS S8 ....152 C5
Greenhill Main Rd
  SHEFS S8 ....162 C1
Greenhill Pkwy SHEFS S8 ....162 B2
Greenhill Rd SHEFS S8 ....152 C5

Greenhouse La *FUL* S10 ......136 D5
Greenhouse Rd *WHHL* DN2 ....41 F4
Greenhow St *ST/HB/BR* S6...125 E2
Green Ings La *DEARNE* S63.....65 E1
Greenland Av *MALT* S66.........111 E1
Greenland Av South
   MALT S66.........................111 E2
Greenland Cl *DARN/MH* S9 ..128 A2
   DIN S25.........................148 B2
Greenland Ct *DARN/MH* S9 ..128 A1
Greenland Dr *DARN/MH* S9 ..128 A1
Greenland Rd
   DARN/MH S9..................116 D5
Greenlands Av
   NROS/TKH DN11................91 C1
Greenland Vw *BSLY* S70.........47 H1
   DARN/MH S9..................128 A2
Greenland Wy
   MALT S66.........................111 E2
Green La *ARMTH* DN3.............58 D4
   AU/AST/KP S26..............131 F5
   AWLS/ASK DN6.................25 E3
   BSLY S70..........................31 G5
   BTLY DN5...........................38 B1
   CHNE S41.......................188 B5
   CHPT/GREN S35.............102 C1
   DOD/DAR S75...................30 C4
   DRON S18.......................171 F1
   ECK/KIL S21...................168 A4
   HOR/CROF WF4................12 A3
   HOY S74............................61 E4
   KIMB S61.........................104 A2
   MALT S66.........................121 H5
   RAW S62............................84 B5
   RAW S62............................98 D1
   RHAM S60.......................118 B5
   ST/HB/BR S6..................125 H2
   STKB/PEN S36.................76 A1
Green Lea *DRON* S18.............170 A1
Greenleafe Av *WHHL* DN2 .....41 G3
Green Oak Av
   TOT/DORE S17................161 E4
Green Oak Crs
   TOT/DORE S17................161 E4
Green Oak Dr
   AU/AST/KP S26..............159 G3
   TOT/DORE S17................161 E4
Green Oak Gv
   TOT/DORE S17................161 E4
Green Oak Rd
   TOT/DORE S17................161 E4
Greenock St *ST/HB/BR* S6 ...113 H4
Green Pastures
   TOT/DORE S17................161 G1
Green Ri *RAW* S62..................84 D4
Green Rd *STKB/PEN* S36........44 D4
Greenset Vw
   BSLY/ROY S71..................14 C3
Greenside *CUD/GR* S72..........13 H5
   DOD/DAR S75...................30 C4
   HOR/CROF WF4................13 H1
   KIMB S61............................97 F3
Greenside Av
   AU/AST/KP S26..............159 G3
   CHNE S41.......................187 F2
   DOD/DAR S75...................14 A3
Greenside Cl *STV/CWN* S43...184 C2
Greenside La *HOY* S74............62 A2
Greenside Ms *HACK/IN* S12...156 B4
Green Spring Av *BSLY* S70 .....47 H5
Greens Rd *RHAM/THRY* S65..106 D3
Green St *BSLY* S70.................48 C1
   CHNE S41.......................179 G5
   DONS/BSCR DN4...............71 F2
   HOY S74............................62 B2
   RAW S62............................97 F2
   STKB/PEN S36.................77 G5
The Green *CHNE* S41............193 F5
   CONI DN12.......................67 G5
   DEARNE S63.....................53 E2
   DIN S25.........................148 B2
   MALT S66.......................108 C2
   MEX/SWTN S64................85 H1
   RHAM S60.......................119 F2
   STKB/PEN S36.................44 A2
   STV/CWN S43................185 E2
   TOT/DORE S17................160 D4
The Green Vw *CUD/GR* S72 ...13 H5
Greenway *AU/AST/KP* S26 ....159 H3
The Greenway *CHSW* S40......191 G4
The Greenway *SHEFS* S8.......152 D3
Greenwood Av *BSLY* S70........35 B5
   DARN/MH S9..................127 C4
   DONS/BSCR DN4...............55 F5
Greenwood Cl
   DARN/MH S9..................127 G4
Greenwood Crs
   DARN/MH S9..................127 G4
   MALT S66.......................108 C4
Greenwood Dr
   DARN/MH S9..................127 G4
Greenwood La
   HAN/WDH S13.................143 H3
Greenwood Rd
   CHPT/GREN S35...............80 D4
   DARN/MH S9..................127 H4
   MEX/SWTN S64................86 C4
Greenwood Ter *BSLY* S70 ....2 E3
Greenwood Wy
   DARN/MH S9..................127 G4
Greeton Dr
   CHPT/GREN S35.............100 A3

Gregg House Crs
   SHEFN S5........................102 D4
Gregg House Rd *SHEFN* S5...102 C3
Greggs Ct *BSLY* S70...............32 D2
Gregory Cl *STV/CWN* S43.....188 B1
Gregory La *STV/CWN* S43.....188 B1
Gregory Rd *SHEFS* S8...........140 A4
Grendon Vis
   RHAM/THRY S65 * 92 C1
Grenfell Rd *MEX/SWTN* S64...67 F3
Grenfolds Rd
   CHPT/GREN S35.............101 F1
Grenobank Rd
   CHPT/GREN S35.............101 F1
Greno Crs *CHPT/GREN* S35...101 F1
Greno Ga *CHPT/GREN* S35 ....93 E5
Grenomoor Cl
   CHPT/GREN S35.............101 E2
Greno Rd *MEX/SWTN* S64......86 B2
Grenoside Mt
   CHPT/GREN S35.............101 F2
Greno Vw *DOD/DAR* S75.........46 A3
   HOY S74............................61 G3
Greno View Rd
   CHPT/GREN S35...............80 B4
Greno Wood Ct
   CHPT/GREN S35...............93 E5
Grenville Pl *DOD/DAR* S75 .....19 F4
Grenville Rd
   DONS/BSCR DN4...............71 E2
Gresham Av *RHAM* S60.........118 C3
Gresham Rd *ST/HB/BR* S6 ....125 E1
Gresley Rd *DONS/BSCR* DN4..55 H4
   SHEFS S8........................162 B3
Grey Friars' Rd *DON* DN1.........6 C2
Greystock St *ATT* S4.............126 D1
Greystones Av *BSLY* S70 ....47 H1
   ECC S11.........................138 C3
Greystones Cl *ECC* S11.........138 C3
Greystones
   AU/AST/KP S26..............169 H2
Greystones Crs *ECC* S11.......138 C3
Greystones Dr *ECC* S11.........138 C3
Greystones Grange Crs
   ECC S11.........................138 C3
Greystones Grange Rd
   ECC S11.........................138 C3
Greystones Hall Rd
   ECC S11.........................138 C3
Greystones Ri *ECC* S11.........138 B3
Greystones Rd *ECC* S11.........138 B3
   RHAM S60.......................120 B3
Grice Cl *DONS/BSCR* DN4.......58 B3
Griffin Rd *MEX/SWTN* S64......65 H5
Griffiths Cl *RAW* S62..............98 B2
Griffiths Rd *CHPT/GREN* S35..80 C5
Grimesthorpe Rd *ATT* S4.....126 C1
Grimesthorpe Rd South
   ATT S4...........................126 C1
Grimpit Hl *HOR/CROF* WF4 ....12 A3
Grimsell Cl *ST/HB/BR* S6 ......101 F2
Grimsell Crs *ST/HB/BR* S6....101 F2
Grimsell Dr *ST/HB/BR* S6......101 F2
Grindlow Av *CHSW* S40.........192 B3
Grindlow Cl *GLV* S14.............140 C4
Grindlow Dr *GLV* S14.............140 C4
Grindon Cl *CHSW* S40...........186 C4
Grizedale Av *MOS* S20...........157 G3
Grizedale Cl *MOS* S20............157 G3
Grosvenor Crs *BTLY* DN5.........27 F5
   DONS/BSCR DN4...............70 D2
Grosvenor Dr *BSLY* S70............2 A4
Grosvenor Rd
   AWLS/ASK DN6.................25 F2
   RHAM/THRY S65.................9 H1
Grosvenor Sq
   SHEFP/MNR S2................139 H2
Grosvenor Ter
   DONS/BSCR DN4...............70 D2
Grouse Cft *ST/HB/BR* S6......125 E1
Grove Av *BTLY* DN5.................39 G5
   ST/HB/BR S6..................113 G2
Grove Bank *RHAM* S60..........106 A5
Grove Cl *DEARNE* S63............51 G5
   STKB/PEN S36.................44 D5
Grove Cottages
   CHSW S40 * 191 H2
Grove Farm Cl
   STV/CWN S43................188 C2
Grove Gdns *DEARNE* S63.........37 E3
   STV/CWN S43................188 D5
Grove Hill Rd *WHHL* DN2........41 G3
Grove House Ct
   TOT/DORE S17 * 161 E4
Grove Pl *DON* DN1..................3 G4
Grove Rd *ABRD* S7...............152 A2
   CHNE S41.......................187 G2
   DEARNE S63.....................51 F5
   RHAM S60..........................9 F6
   STKB/PEN S36.................77 H3
   STV/CWN S43................188 C4
   TOT/DORE S17................161 G3
Grove Sq *ST/HB/BR* S6..........114 C5
Grove Sq *BSLY* S70.................32 C5
   BSLY/ROY S71....................3 J5
   CHNE S41.......................193 E4
The Grove *CUD/GR* S72..........16 D3
   MALT S66.......................108 B4
   RAW S62............................98 C1
   RHAM/THRY S65.................2 E3
   ST/HB/BR S6..................113 E4
   TOT/DORE S17................160 D3
   WHHL DN2.........................41 E5

Grove V *WHHL* DN2................41 E5
Grove Wy *STV/CWN* S43.......188 D4
Guernsey Rd
   SHEFP/MNR S2................140 A3
Guest La *DONS/BSCR* DN4......70 D1
Guest Pl *RHAM* S60................106 B5
Guest Rd *DOD/DAR* S75...........2 D1
   ECC S11.........................139 E2
   RHAM S60.......................106 B5
Guest St *HOY* S74...................62 A1
Guilbert Av *MALT* S66............132 D2
Guildford Av *CHSW* S40.........191 H4
   SHEFP/MNR S2................140 D2
Guildford Ri
   SHEFP/MNR S2................140 D2
Guildford Rd
   BSLY/ROY S71..................12 B4
   WHHL DN2.........................41 F3
Guild Rd *RHAM/THRY* S65....106 D5
Guildway *AU/AST/KP* S26 ....147 E5
Guilford Wy
   SHEFP/MNR S2................141 E3
Guilthwaite Common La
   AU/AST/KP S26..............131 E2
Guilthwaite Crs *RHAM* S60...119 G3
Guilane Dr *DONS/BSCR* DN4...70 D2
Gunhills La *ARMTH* DN3..........43 E3
Gun La *OWL* S3......................11 H1
Gurney Rd *DONS/BSCR* DN4...71 H2
Gurth Av *ARMTH* DN3.............29 G5
Gurth Dr *MALT* S66...............133 E2
Gwendoline Ms
   DEARNE S63.....................65 F3
Gypsy La *WMB/DAR* S73.........50 C4

H

Habershon Dr
   CHPT/GREN S35 * 80 D5
Habershon Rd *KIMB* S61.........96 D5
Hackings Av *STKB/PEN* S36....44 C5
Hackness La *RHAM* S60.........118 B3
Hackthorn Rd *SHEFS* S8.......152 D2
Haddon Cl *CHSW* S40............191 G2
   DOD/DAR S75...................30 A3
   DRON S18.......................171 F1
Haddon Pl *STV/CWN* S43.......189 H1
Haddon Ri *MEX/SWTN* S64.....64 H7
Haddon Rd *BSLY/ROY* S71......20 B1
Haddon St *OWL* S3................125 H1
Haddon Wy
   AU/AST/KP S26..............145 H3
Haden St *ST/HB/BR* S6.........114 A4
Hadfield St *ST/HB/BR* S6......125 E2
   WMB/DAR S73...................50 C4
Hadleigh Cl *RAW* S62.............98 B2
Hadrian Rd *RHAM* S60...........118 C2
Hadrians Cl
   NROS/TKH DN11................91 G4
Hady Crs *CHNE* S41...............193 E1
Hady Hl *CHNE* S41....................5 K5
Hady La *CHNE* S41.................193 F2
Haggard Rd *ST/HB/BR* S6.....114 B4
Hagg Hl *ST/HB/BR* S6..........100 D4
   ST/HB/BR S6..................113 B4
Hagg La *FUL* S10...................123 H4
Hague Av *ECK/KIL* S21..........175 H3
   RAW S62............................85 E3
Hague Rw *SHEFP/MNR* S2....11 K4
Haids Cl *MALT* S66................110 D1
Haids La *MALT* S66................110 D1
Haids Rd *MALT* S66...............110 C1
Haig Crs *NROS/TKH* DN11......91 E3
Haigh Ct *DEARNE* S63............63 H2
Haigh Cft *STV/CWN* S43.......189 H1
Haigh Moor Cl
   HAN/WDH S13.................142 C2
Haigh Moor Dr *DIN* S25........134 A4
Haigh Moor Rd
   HAN/WDH S13.................142 D2
Haigh Moor Wy
   AU/AST/KP S26..............144 C3
   BSLY/ROY S71..................12 B5
Haigh Rd *DONS/BSCR* DN4.....71 G1
Hail Mary Dr
   HAN/WDH S13.................143 H2
Hakehill Cl *DONS/BSCR* DN4..73 H2
Halcyon Cl *HACK/IN* S12.......155 H2
Haldane Cl *CUD/GR* S72.........17 H1
Haldane Crs *BSVR* S44..........196 C2
Haldane Rd
   RHAM/THRY S65..............106 C1
Haldene *BSLY* S70...................48 B1
Haldyn Gdns *ARMTH* DN3 ......43 E4
Hale St *SHEFS* S8.................139 H4
Halesworth Cl *CHSW* S40......191 H4
Halesworth Rd
   HAN/WDH S13.................128 C5
Half Acre La *DRON* S18.........171 H3
Half Cft *STV/CWN* S43..........188 D2
Halfway Dr *MOS* S20.............167 E1
Halfway Gdns *MOS* S20.........167 E1
Halifax Av *CONI* DN12.............88 C1
Halifax Crs *BTLY* DN5.............39 F4
Halifax Rd *ST/HB/BR* S6.......101 F4
Halifax St *BSLY/ROY* S71........19 G3
Hallam Cha *FUL* S10.............123 H5

Hallam Cl *AU/AST/KP* S26....145 E1
   DONS/BSCR DN4.................7 J6
Hallam Ct *DEARNE* S63 * 52 D4
Hallamgate Rd *FUL* S10.......124 D5
Hallam Grange Cl *FUL* S10...137 E1
Hallam Grange Crs *FUL* S10..137 E1
Hallam Grange Cft *FUL* S10..137 E1
Hallam Grange Ri *FUL* S10 ...137 E1
Hallam Grange Rd *FUL* S10...137 E1
Hallam La *SHEF* S1.................11 G6
Hallam Rd *RHAM* S60............119 F2
Hallamshire Cl *FUL* S10........137 E2
Hallamshire Rd *FUL* S10.......137 E2
Hallam Wy *CHPT/GREN* S35..102 B1
Hall Av *HOY* S74.....................74 A5
   MEX/SWTN S64................67 F3
Hall Balk La *DOD/DAR* S75 ....19 F4
   NROS/TKH DN11................72 A5
Hall Bank *DOD/DAR* S75........19 F4
Hall Broome Gdns
   DEARNE S63.....................53 E2
Hallcar St *ATT* S4..................126 C2
Hall Cl *BSLY* S70.....................48 A3
   DEARNE S63.....................64 B1
   DIN S25.........................148 B2
   DRON S18.......................180 A1
Hall Close Av *RHAM* S60......120 A3
Hall Crs *RHAM* S60...............119 H2
Hall Cft *MALT* S66.................108 C5
Hallcroft Dr *ARMTH* DN3........59 E1
Hallcroft Ri *BSLY/ROY* S71.....15 F1
Hall Cross Av *WMB/DAR* S73..50 D4
Hall Dr *DEARNE* S63...............64 D3
Haller Cl *ARMTH* DN3.............42 E4
Hall Farm Cl
   AU/AST/KP S26..............131 E5
   CHNE S41.......................181 H5
Hall Farm Cft *DIN* S25..........134 D5
Hall Farm Ms *DEARNE* S63....37 F3
Hall Farm Ri *DEARNE* S63.....37 F3
Hallfield Cl *RCH* S42.............195 G3
Hall Field La *HOR/CROF* WF4..13 G2
Hall Flat La *DONS/BSCR* DN4..71 H2
Hallgate *DEARNE* S63.............37 F3
Hall Ga *DON* DN1....................6 D4
   MEX/SWTN S64................67 G3
   STKB/PEN S36.................44 D3
Hallgate Rd *FUL* S10............124 C5
Hall Gv *DOD/DAR* S75............14 A5
   RHAM S60..........................9 G7
   STV/CWN S43................188 C2
Halls Ct *SHEFS* S8................152 D2
Hallside Ct *ARMTH* DN3..........58 D4
   MOS S20.........................166 D2
Halls Rw *CHSW* S40 * 4 A5
Hall St *DEARNE* S63...............53 C1
   HOY S74............................62 A2
   RHAM S60..........................9 F2
   WMB/DAR S73...................50 C3
Hallsworth Av
   WMB/DAR S73...................62 C1
Hall Vw *CHNE* S41................187 E3
Hall View Rd
   NROS/TKH DN11................91 G4
Hall Villa La *BTLY* DN5............26 C2
Hallwood Ri
   CHPT/GREN S35...............93 F1
Hallwood Rd
   CHPT/GREN S35...............93 E1
Hallyburton Cl
   SHEFP/MNR S2................140 C4
Hallyburton Dr
   SHEFP/MNR S2................140 C4
Hallyburton Rd
   SHEFP/MNR S2................140 C4
Halmshaw *BTLY* DN5..............39 G2
Halsall Av *DARN/MH* S9........128 A4
Halsall Dr *DARN/MH* S9........127 H4
Halsall Rd *DARN/MH* S9........128 A4
Halsbury Rd
   RHAM/THRY S65..............106 C1
Halton Cl *CHNE* S41..............179 E5
Halton Ct *HACK/IN* S12.........155 H2
Hamble *DOD/DAR* S75 * 14 A4
Hambledon Cl *CHNE* S41.......179 E5
Hambleton Cl *DOD/DAR* S75..18 D5
   HOY S74............................62 A4
Hameline Cl *CONI* DN12.........88 D1
Hamilton Cl
   DONS/BSCR DN4.................7 H7
   MEX/SWTN S64................67 G2

Hamilton Ms
   DONS/BSCR DN4.................7 J6
Hamilton Park Rd *BTLY* DN5..38 D4
Hamilton Rd *DEARNE* S63......37 H4
   DONS/BSCR DN4.................7 H7
   MALT S66.......................111 F4
   SHEFN S5.......................115 H2
Hammerton Rd
   ST/HB/BR S6..................114 A5
Hammerton St
   WMB/DAR S73...................50 A1
Hammond St *OWL* S3.............10 C1
Hampden Rd
   MEX/SWTN S64................67 E4
Hamper La *STKB/PEN* S36......45 F1
Hampole Dr *DEARNE* S63........37 E3
Hampson Gdns *ARMTH* DN3...29 G4
Hampton Rd *SHEFN* S5.........115 G3
   WHHL DN2..........................7 J3
Hampton St *CHNE* S41.........193 F5
Hanbury Cl *BSLY/ROY* S71.....20 D3
   CHSW S40.......................186 A4
   DONS/BSCR DN4...............71 G4
   DRON S18.......................170 D2
Handby St *CHNE* S41............193 F4
Handley Cl *STV/CWN* S43.....180 B2
Handley Rd *STV/CWN* S43....180 B2
Handley St *ATT* S4................126 B2
Hands Rd *FUL* S10................125 E3
Handsworth Av
   DARN/MH S9..................128 A3
Handsworth Crs
   DARN/MH S9..................128 B4
Handsworth Gdns
   ARMTH DN3.....................43 E4
Handsworth Grange Cl
   HAN/WDH S13.................143 E2
Handsworth Grange Crs
   HAN/WDH S13.................143 E1
Handsworth Grange Rd
   HAN/WDH S13.................143 E1
Handsworth Rd
   DARN/MH S9..................128 A4
Hanging Water Cl *FUL* S10...138 D3
Hangingwater Rd *ECC* S11...138 B3
Hangram La *ECC* S11............150 B3
Hangsman La *DIN* S25..........134 A2
Hangthwaite La
   AWLS/ASK DN6.................25 H4
Hanley Cl *HACK/IN* S12.........156 B2
Hanmoor Rd *ST/HB/BR* S6...100 D3
Hannah Rd *HAN/WDH* S13....143 H3
Hannas Royd *DOD/DAR* S75...30 C3
Hanover Cl *OWL* S3.................10 C6
Hanover Sq *DEARNE* S63........37 G2
   OWL S3............................10 D6
Hanover St *DEARNE* S63.........37 G2
   OWL S3............................10 C5
Hanover Wy *OWL* S3...............10 C5
Hanslope Vw *ARMTH* DN3......29 E2
Hanson Rd *STKB/PEN* S36....112 D4
Hanwell Cl *CHPT/GREN* S35..102 A1
Harbord Rd *SHEFS* S8...........152 C3
Harborough Av
   SHEFP/MNR S2................141 G1
Harborough Cl
   SHEFP/MNR S2................127 G5
Harborough Dr
   SHEFP/MNR S2................127 G5
Harborough Hill Rd
   BSLY/ROY S71....................3 H4
Harborough Ri
   SHEFP/MNR S2................127 G5
Harborough Rd
   SHEFP/MNR S2................127 G5
Harborough Wy
   SHEFP/MNR S2................141 G1
Harbury St *HAN/WDH* S13....144 A2
Harcourt Cl *CHNE* S41..........193 E5
   DONS/BSCR DN4...............73 C1
Harcourt Crs *FUL* S10...........125 F4
Harcourt Ri
   CHPT/GREN S35...............94 B2
Harcourt Rd *FUL* S10............125 F4
Harcourt Ter
   RHAM/THRY S65.................9 K5
Hardcastle Av
   HAN/WDH S13.................143 E3
Hardcastle Gdns
   HAN/WDH S13.................143 E3
Hardcastle Rd
   HAN/WDH S13.................143 E4
   STKB/PEN S36.................44 D4
Harden Cl *DOD/DAR* S75.........18 C5
   STKB/PEN S36.................44 D4
Hardhurst Rd *DRON* S18.......179 E1
Hardie Cl *MALT* S66...............111 F5
Hardie Pl *RAW* S62..................85 F5
   STV/CWN S43................185 F5
Hardie St *ECK/KIL* S21..........174 D1
Harding Av *RAW* S62...............84 D3
Harding Cl *RAW* S62................84 D4
Harding St *DARN/MH* S9.......127 H1
Hardwick Av *STV/CWN* S43 ...180 B3
Hardwick Cl
   AU/AST/KP S26 * 145 H3
   BSLY S70..........................48 A1
   DRON S18.......................171 F1
   HOR/CROF WF4................13 G1
   STV/CWN S43................185 G2
Hardwick Crs
   BSLY/ROY S71..................15 E5
   ECC S11.........................139 E2

Hardwicke Rd
RHAM/THRY S65 ....9 H1
Hardwick Gv DOD/DAR S75...30 B4
Hardwick La
AU/AST/KP S26 ....146 C2
Hardwick St CHNE S41.........5 G1
Hardwicks Yd CHSW S40 *.....4 B5
Hardy Pl ST/HB/BR S6.........125 F2
Hardy Rd WHHL DN2.........40 C4
Hardy St RHAM S60.........8 C2
Harefield Rd ECC S11.........139 F1
Harehill Crs RCH S42.........194 D3
Harehill Rd CHSW S40.........192 B5
Harehills Rd RHAM S60.........9 H6
Harewood Av ARMTH DN3...29 F3
AWLS/ASK DN6 ....24 D2
BSLY S70.........30 D1
Harewood Ct
NROS/TKH DN11.........91 H3
Harewood Gv MALT S66.........108 D3
Harewood Rd WHHL DN2.........7 H3
Harewood Wy ECC S11.........151 G3
Hargrave Pl
RHAM/THRY S65.........99 H4
Harland St ECC S11.........139 G1
Harlech Cl CHPT/GREN S35...80 D5
Harlech Gn FUL S10.........136 D1
Harlech Gv FUL S10.........136 D1
Harlech Md FUL S10.........136 D1
Harlesthorpe Av
STV/CWN S43.........185 F2
Harlesthorpe La
STV/CWN S43.........185 E1
Harleston St ATT S4.........126 C1
Harley Rd ECC S11.........138 B5
RAW S62.........81 H2
Harlington Ct CONI DN12...68 C4
Harlington Rd
MEX/SWTN S64.........53 H5
Harmer La SHEF S1.........11 H4
Harmony Wy RHAM S60.........129 G1
Harney Cl DARN/MH S9.........128 A2
Harold Av AWLS/ASK DN6...25 E2
BSLY/ROY S71.........22 B5
Harold Cft KIMB S61 *.........97 G2
Harold St ST/HB/BR S6.........125 F1
Harperhill Cl CHSW S40.........192 B5
Harriet Cl BSLY S70 *.........32 A3
Harrington Ct
BSLY/ROY S71.........21 E3
Harrington Rd
SHEF/MNR S2.........140 A2
Harrington St DON DN1.........6 D2
Harrison La FUL S10.........136 D3
Harrison Rd ST/HB/BR S6...113 H5
Harris Rd ARMTH DN3.........42 B4
ST/HB/BR S6.........113 H2
Harrogate Dr CONI DN12...68 A5
Harrogate Rd
AU/AST/KP S26.........145 E4
Harrop Dr MEX/SWTN S64...86 A2
Harrop La FUL S10.........136 D4
Harrowden Rd
DARN/MH S9.........117 G2
WHHL DN2.........40 D4
Harrow Rd ARMTH DN3.........43 E5
Harrow St ECC S11.........10 D5
Harry Firth Cl DARN/MH S9.127 G2
Harry Rd DOD/DAR S75.........18 D4
Hartcliff Rd STKB/PEN S36...44 C3
Hartfield Cl CHNE S41.........192 D5
Hartfield Rd KIMB S61.........105 H3
Hartford Rd SHEFS S8.........153 E2
Hart Hl RAW S62.........84 D3
Harthill Rd CONI DN12.........88 C2
Hartington Av ABRD S7.........152 A2
Hartington Ct
STV/CWN S43.........185 G2
Hartington Dr
BSLY/ROY S71.........19 H3
Hartington Rd ABRD S7...152 A2
CHNE S41.........5 K6
DRON S18.........171 F1
KIMB S61.........105 E3
Hartington Vw
STV/CWN S43.........182 B3
Hartland Av MOS S20.........157 G3
Hartland Ct MOS S20 *.........157 G2
Hartland Crs ARMTH DN3...29 F5
Hartland Dr MOS S20.........157 G3
Hartland Wy CHNE S41.........179 G5
Hartley Brook Av
SHEFN S5.........102 C3
Hartley Brook Rd
SHEFN S5.........102 C3
Hartley Cl MEX/SWTN S64...86 B2
Hartley La KIMB S61.........8 C2
Hartley St MEX/SWTN S64...66 D4
SHEF/MNR S2.........140 A3
Hartop Av
SHEF/MNR S2.........140 C4
Hartopp Cl SHEF/MNR S2...140 C4
Hartopp Dr
SHEF/MNR S2.........140 C4
Hartopp Rd
SHEF/MNR S2.........140 C4
Hartshead SHEF S1.........11 G2

Hartshead Sq SHEF S1 *.....11 H2
Hartside Cl CHSW S40.........186 D3
Harvest Cl ARMTH DN3.........29 G4
BSLY S70.........48 A1
DONS/BSCR DN4.........55 F5
MALT S66.........110 A4
Harvest La OWL S3.........126 A1
Harvest Rd MALT S66.........108 B4
Harvest Wy RCH S42.........186 A4
Harvey Clough Ms
SHEFS S8.........153 E2
Harvey Clough Rd
SHEFS S8.........153 E2
Harvey Ct BSVR S44.........196 C2
Harvey Cl 193 C2
CHPT/GREN S35.........94 A1
Harvey St BSLY S70 *.........2 D6
STKB/PEN S36.........77 F2
Harwell Rd SHEF/MNR S2...139 H5
Harwich Rd
SHEFP/MNR S2.........141 E1
Harwood Cl
SHEFP/MNR S2.........139 H2
Harwood Dr MOS S20.........156 D4
Harwood Gdns MOS S20...157 E4
Harwood St
SHEFP/MNR S2.........140 A2
Harwood Ter
BSLY/ROY S71.........21 E5
Haslam Ct BSVR S44.........196 C2
CHNE S41.........5 G1
Haslam Crs SHEFS S8.........162 B2
Haslam Pl MALT S66.........111 F2
Haslam Rd NROS/TKH DN11...91 F2
Hasland Rd CHNE S41.........193 E3
CHNE S41.........193 H4
CHSW S40.........5 H7
Haslehurst Rd
SHEF/MNR S2.........127 E5
Haslemere Cl BTLY DN5.....39 C4
Haslemere Gv BTLY DN5.....39 G4
Hassop Cl DRON S18.........186 C3
DRON S18.........171 G1
Hassop Rd STV/CWN S43...182 B4
Hastilar Cl SHEFP/MNR S2...141 H2
Hastilar Rd SHEFP/MNR S2...141 G2
Hastilar Rd South
HAN/WDH S13.........142 A3
Hastings Cl CHNE S41.........186 D3
Hastings Mt ABRD S7.........152 A1
Hastings Rd ABRD S7.........152 A1
CHNE S41.........193 H4
CHSW S40.........5 H7
Hatchell Dr DONS/BSCR DN4..74 C3
Hatchellwood Vw
DONS/BSCR DN4.........74 D3
Hatfield Cl BSLYN/ROY S71...14 C5
Hatfield Crs DIN S25.........134 A3
Hatfield Gdns
BSLYN/ROY S71.........12 B5
Hatfield House Ct
SHEFN S5 *.........102 D4
Hatfield House Cft
SHEFN S5.........102 D4
Hatfield House La
SHEFN S5.........102 C5
Hatfield La ARMTH DN3.........29 H5
MEX/SWTN S64.........66 B3
RHAM/THRY S65.........9 H1
Hathern Cl STV/CWN S43...188 D5
Hathersage Rd
TOT/DORE S17.........150 B4
Hatton Cl DRON S18.........170 B3
Hatton Dr CHSW S40.........186 B4
Hatton Rd ST/HB/BR S6.........114 A5
Haugh La ECC S11.........138 B5
Haugh Rd RAW S62.........84 D3
Haughton Rd SHEFS S8.........152 D3
Havelock St BSLY S70 *.........2 D6
FUL S10.........10 B5
WMB/DAR S73.........35 E5
Havercroft Rd RHAM S60...120 A1
Havercroft Ter ECK/KIL S21...167 H1
Haverdale Rd DOD/DAR S75...2 C7
Haverhill Gv WMB/DAR S73...50 C2
Haverlands La BSLY S70.......47 F1
Haverlands Rdg BSLY S70...47 H1
Hawes Cl MEX/SWTN S64...67 G2
Hawfield Ct
DONS/BSCR DN4.........55 G4
Hawke Cl RAW S62.........84 C4
Hawke Rd WHHL DN2.........40 D5
Hawke St DARN/MH S9.........116 C4
Hawk Hill La MALT S66.........133 E4
Hawkins Av CHPT/GREN S35...93 G1
Hawkshead Av DRON S18...170 B2
Hawkshead Crs DIN S25.....148 D2
Hawkshead Rd ATT S4.........116 B3
Hawksley Av CHSW S40.........4 D1
ST/HB/BR S6.........114 A4
Hawksley Cl ARMTH DN3.....42 D4
Hawksley Ct ARMTH DN3...42 D3
Hawksley Ms ST/HB/BR S6..114 A4
Hawksley Rd ST/HB/BR S6..114 A4
Hawksway ECK/KIL S21.........166 B5
Hawksworth Cl
RHAM/THRY S65.........107 E2
Hawksworth Rd
RHAM/THRY S65.........107 E2
ST/HB/BR S6.........125 F1
Hawkwell Bank
BSLYN/ROY S71.........33 G2

Hawley St DRON S18.........172 C2
RAW S62.........98 B1
SHEF S1.........11 F2
Haworth Bank RHAM S60...119 F3
Haworth Cl BSLYN/ROY S71...20 B4
Haworth Crs RHAM S60.........119 F3
Hawshaw La HOY S74.........61 G2
Hawthorn Av ARMTH DN3...42 D2
MALT S66.........110 B3
MOS S20.........156 D4
STV/CWN S43.........188 B5
Hawthorn Cl STV/CWN S43...184 D2
Hawthorn Av DIN S25.........148 B5
DRON S18.........165 E5
RAW S62.........98 C1
STKB/PEN S36.........76 B1
Hawthorne Cha
MEX/SWTN S64.........66 A5
Hawthorne Cl ECK/KIL S21...168 B3
STV/CWN S43.........177 E5
Hawthorne Crs
DOD/DAR S75.........30 A2
MEX/SWTN S64.........66 A3
Hawthorne Cft
DEARNE S63.........37 E5
Hawthorne Dr DEARNE S63...53 F3
Hawthorne Gv BTLY DN5.....26 D5
Hawthorne Pl
AU/AST/KP S26.........145 G3
Hawthorne Rd DEARNE S63...53 E3
The Hawthornes MOS S20...157 F1
Hawthorne St BSLY S70.........2 E7
CHSW S40.........192 C5
CUD/GR S72.........17 E1
ST/HB/BR S6.........124 C1
Hawthorn Wy CUD/GR S72..17 E1
Hawthorn Hl STV/CWN S43...175 F5
Hawthorn Rd
CHPT/GREN S35.........80 C4
ECK/KIL S21.........174 B1
RHAM S60.........113 H4
Haxby Cl HAN/WDH S13.........142 C4
Haxby Pl HAN/WDH S13.........142 C4
Haxby St HAN/WDH S13.........142 C5
Haybrook Ct
TOT/DORE S17.........161 E3
Haydn Rd MALT S66.........111 H4
Haydock Cl MEX/SWTN S64...42 F2
Haydon Gv MALT S66.........108 B3
Hayes Ct MOS S20.........167 E2
Hayes Dr MOS S20.........166 D2
Hayfield Cl DOD/DAR S75...30 A3
DRON S18.........170 B2
RCH S42.........195 F4
STV/CWN S43.........182 B5
Hayfield Crs HACK/IN S12...155 E2
Hayfield Dr HACK/IN S12...155 F2
Hayfield La EPW DN9.........75 G4
Hayfield Pl HACK/IN S12...155 F2
Hayfield Vw HACK/IN S12...155 E2
Hayford Wy STV/CWN S43...182 A5
Hay Green La BSLY S70.........60 D1
Hayhurst Crs MALT S66.........111 E4
Hayland St DARN/MH S9...116 D2
Haylock Cl DOD/DAR S75...18 A4
Haymarket SHEF S1.........11 H4
Haythorne Wy MEX/SWTN S64...86 B2
Haywood Av
STKB/PEN S36.........77 F2
Haywood Cl
RHAM/THRY S65.........107 E2
Haywood La STKB/PEN S36...77 F2
Hazel Av ECK/KIL S21.........168 A3
Hazelbadge Crs
HACK/IN S12.........155 G2
Hazel Cl DRON S18.........171 G3
Hazel Ct DRON S18.........171 F3
RHAM/THRY S65.........109 E1
Hazel Dr CHSW S40.........191 H4
RCH S42.........195 H4
Hazel Gv ARMTH DN3.........43 E3
CHPT/GREN S35.........94 A2
CONI DN12.........88 D2
MALT S66.........108 C4
NROS/TKH DN11.........91 F3
STV/CWN S43.........183 E2
Hazel Rd ECK/KIL S21.........174 C1
MALT S66.........110 B3
Hazelshaw DOD/DAR S75...30 C4
Hazelwood BSLYN/ROY S71...20 A2
Hazelwood Cl DRON S18...170 A2
Hazelwood Dr
MEX/SWTN S64.........86 B3
Hazelbarrow Cl SHEFS S8...163 F1
Hazelbarrow Crs SHEFS S8..163 F1
Hazelbarrow Dr SHEFS S8...163 F1
Hazelbarrow Gv SHEFS S8...163 G1
Hazelbarrow Rd SHEFS S8...163 F1
Hazledene Crs CUD/GR S72...17 F3
Hazledene Rd CUD/GR S72...17 E3
Hazlehurst Av CHNE S41...187 G4
Hazlehurst Cl
RHAM/THRY S65.........99 F5
Hazlehurst La CHNE S41...187 G4
SHEFS S8.........164 B1
Hazlewood Dr
STV/CWN S43.........177 F5
Headford Gdns OWL S3.........10 D5
Headford Gv OWL S3.........10 D5

Headford Ms OWL S3.........10 D6
Headford St OWL S3.........10 D5
Headingley Cl ARMTH DN3...29 F2
Headingley Wy CONI DN12...70 C5
Headland Cl STV/CWN S43...188 C2
Headland Dr FUL S10.........124 C4
Headland Rd FUL S10.........124 C4
Headlands Rd HOY S74.........61 H2
Heads La STKB/PEN S36.........76 C5
Heath Av ECK/KIL S21.........168 B3
Heath Bank Rd WHHL DN2...41 G3
Heathcote Dr CHNE S41.........193 G4
Heathcote St ATT S4.........115 H3
Heath Ct DONS/BSCR DN4...70 D1
Heatherbank
DONS/BSCR DN4.........74 A1
Heather Cl RHAM S60.........106 A5
Heather Ct WHHL DN2 *.........41 G3
Heatherdale Rd MALT S66...111 F3
Heather Gdns CHNE S41 *...193 G5
Heather Knowle
DOD/DAR S75.........30 C3
Heather Lea Av
TOT/DORE S17.........160 C1
Heather Lea Pl
TOT/DORE S17.........160 C1
Heather Rd SHEFN S5.........116 A1
Heather Vale Cl
CHNE S41.........193 G5
Heather Vale Rd CHNE S41...193 G5
Heather Wy RCH S42.........190 B5
Heatherwood Cl WHHL DN2..41 G4
Heathfield Cl CHSW S40.........4 A3
Heathfield Ct ARMTH DN3...29 G1
DRON S18.........170 D2
RCH S42.........190 D5
Heathfield Rd HACK/IN S12..155 F1
Heathfields BSLY S70.........32 B2
Heath Gv DEARNE S63.........52 D4
Heath Rd ST/HB/BR S6.........101 F5
STKB/PEN S36.........77 F2
Heaton Cl DRON S18.........170 B2
Heatons Bank RAW S62.........85 G5
Heaton St CHSW S40.........191 G2
Heavens Wlk
DONS/BSCR DN4.........56 B4
Heavygate Av FUL S10.........125 E1
Heavygate Rd FUL S10.........125 E1
Hedgehill Rd STKB/PEN S36...44 A3
Hedge Hill Rd
STKB/PEN S36.........44 A3
Hedley Dr STV/CWN S43...188 B1
Heeley Bank Rd
SHEF/MNR S2.........140 B3
Heeley Gn SHEF/MNR S2...140 B4
Heelis St BSLY S70.........3 G6
Heighton Vw
AU/AST/KP S26.........145 F1
Helena Cl BSLY S70.........2 B1
Helena St MEX/SWTN S64...67 E3
Helensburgh Cl
DONS/BSCR DN4.........2 B2
Hellaby Hall Rd MALT S66...109 H4
Hellaby La MALT S66.........109 H4
Hellaby Vw MALT S66.........108 D2
Helliwell La STKB/PEN S36...77 H4
Helmsley Av MOS S20.........166 D1
Helmsley Cl
AU/AST/KP S26.........145 E4
CHNE S41.........186 C2
Helmton Dr SHEFS S8.........153 E2
Helmton Rd SHEFS S8.........152 D3
Helston Cl CHNE S41.........192 D4
Helston Crs BSLYN/ROY S71...15 F3
Helston Ri ABRD S7.........152 A1
Hemingfield Rd
WMB/DAR S73.........49 H4
Hemmingway Cl
RHAM S60.........130 A4
Hemper Gv SHEFS S8.........162 B1
Hemper La SHEFS S8.........162 B2
Hemp Pits Rd BTLY DN5.....40 B1
Henderson Gln
BSLYN/ROY S71.........15 E1
Hendon St HAN/WDH S13...142 D1
Hengist Rd BTLY DN5.........55 E3
Henley Av SHEFS S8.........153 F5
Henley Grove Rd KIMB S61...8 A2
Henley Ri KIMB S61.........105 E1
KIMB S61.........105 E1
Henley Wd WHHL DN2.........41 G5
Henley Wy KIMB S61.........105 E2
Hennings Cl
DONS/BSCR DN4.........73 F1
Henry Cl CUD/GR S72.........16 D1
Henry Ct RAW S62.........98 B3
Henry La NROS/TKH DN11...90 D2
Henry Pl MEX/SWTN S64...67 G4
Henry Rd DEARNE S63.........53 F5
Henry St BSLY S70.........32 C5
CHNE S41.........187 H1
CHPT/GREN S35.........80 A4
ECK/KIL S21.........166 D5
OWL S3.........125 H2
RHAM/THRY S65.........9 F5
WMB/DAR S73.........50 D1
Henshall St BSLY S70.........3 J7
Heppenstall La
DARN/MH S9.........127 F1
Heptinstall St BSLY S70.........32 B5
Hepworth Dr
AU/AST/KP S26.........145 F3

Hepworth Rd
DONS/BSCR DN4.........71 F1
Herald Rd WHHL DN2.........42 A1
Herbert Rd ABRD S7.........139 G4
BTLY DN5.........39 G5
Herbert St KIMB S61.........104 C2
MEX/SWTN S64.........67 F3
Herdings Ct HACK/IN S12...154 C2
Herdings Rd HACK/IN S12...154 C2
Herdings Vw HACK/IN S12...154 C2
Hereford Dr STV/CWN S43...188 D1
Hereford Rd WHHL DN2.........41 F3
Hereford St SHEF S1.........11 F7
Hereward Ct CONI DN12.........89 C1
Hereward Rd SHEFN S5.........102 B5
Hereward's Rd SHEFS S8...153 H4
Heritage Dr STV/CWN S43...184 D1
Hermitage St
SHEFP/MNR S2.........10 E7
Hermit Hl DOD/DAR S75.........60 A2
Hermit La DOD/DAR S75.....18 B5
Heron Ct CONI DN12.........89 C1
WHHL DN2.........63 H1
Heron Dr DEARNE S63.........63 H1
Heron Hi AU/AST/KP S26...145 G4
Heron Mt SHEFP/MNR S2...127 E5
Herons Wy BSLY S70.........47 H5
DONS/BSCR DN4.........72 B1
Herrick Gdns
DONS/BSCR DN4.........72 A2
Herries Av SHEFN S5.........115 E2
Herries Dr SHEFN S5.........115 E2
Herries Pl SHEFN S5.........115 E2
Herries Rd ST/HB/BR S6...114 A2
Herringthorpe Av
RHAM S60.........106 D5
Herringthorpe Cl
RHAM/THRY S65.........106 D4
Herringthorpe Gv
RHAM/THRY S65.........107 E5
Herringthorpe La
RHAM/THRY S65.........107 E4
Herringthorpe Valley Rd
RHAM S60.........120 A1
RHAM/THRY S65.........107 E4
Herriot Dr CHSW S40.........192 D3
Herschell Rd ABRD S7.........139 H3
Hesketh Dr ARMTH DN3.....29 G3
Hesley Bar KIMB S61.........94 D2
Hesley Ct MEX/SWTN S64...86 A2
Hesley Gra KIMB S61.........95 H4
Hesley La KIMB S61.........96 A4
Hesley Ms KIMB S61.........96 A4
Hesley Rd NROS/TKH DN11...91 F3
SHEFN S5.........102 C2
Hesley Ter SHEFN S5.........102 C3
Heslow Gv KIMB S61.........95 H1
Hessey St HAN/WDH S13...142 D4
Hessle Rd ST/HB/BR S6.........113 H2
Hewers Holt STV/CWN S43...177 F5
Hewitt St MEX/SWTN S64...67 G3
Hexthorpe Rd
DONS/BSCR DN4.........6 A5
Heyhouse Dr
CHPT/GREN S35.........81 E4
Heyhouse Wy
CHPT/GREN S35.........80 D4
Heysham Gn
BSLYN/ROY S71.........20 D2
Heywood St STV/CWN S43...188 C1
Heywood Vw
STV/CWN S43.........177 G5
Hibberd Pl ST/HB/BR S6...113 G4
Hibberd Rd ST/HB/BR S6...113 G4
Hibbert Ter BSLY S70 *.........31 H3
Hickingwood La
STV/CWN S43.........185 F1
Hickinwood Crs
STV/CWN S43.........185 F1
Hickleton Ct DEARNE S63...37 E3
Hickleton Gn CONI DN12...68 B5
Hickmott Rd ECC S11 *.........139 F2
Hickson Dr RHAM/THRY S65...21 E3
Hicks St OWL S3.........126 A1
Hides Gn BSVR S44.........196 D2
Hides St DARN/MH S9.........116 D4
High Alder Rd
DONS/BSCR DN4.........57 G5
Higham Common Rd
DOD/DAR S75.........18 A5
Higham La DOD/DAR S75...30 A1
High Ash Dr DIN S25.........148 B5
High Balk DOD/DAR S75...19 F3
High Bank
RHAM/THRY S65 *.........99 G4
Highbury Av
DONS/BSCR DN4.........58 A5
Highbury Crs
DONS/BSCR DN4.........58 A5
Highbury Rd CHNE S41.........187 F4
Highcliffe Ct
MEX/SWTN S64.........66 C5
Highcliffe Dr ECC S11.........138 B3
MEX/SWTN S64.........66 B5
Highcliffe Pl ECC S11.........138 B4
Highcliffe Rd ECC S11.........138 B3
High Cft HOY S74.........62 A3
High Croft Dr
BSLYN/ROY S71.........14 D5
Higher Albert St CHNE S41...5 F1
Highfield Av BSLY S70.........31 H4
BSLYN/ROY S71.........20 A1

CHNE S41 .....187 E3
DEARNE S63 .....37 F5
Highfield Cottages
MEX/SWTN S64 * 66 D2
Highfield Ct WMB/DAR S73 .....50 A2
Highfield Gv DEARNE S63 .....64 A1
Highfield La CHNE S41 .....187 E3
HAN/WDH S13 .....129 F5
Highfield Pk MALT S66 .....111 F4
Highfield Pl
SHEFP/MNR S2 .....140 A2
Highfield Range
WMB/DAR S73 .....35 E3
Highfield Ri ST/HB/BR S6 .....123 F2
Highfield Rd BSVR S44 .....196 D3
CHNE S41 .....187 F4
CONI DN12 .....89 F2
DON DN1 .....6 E2
KIMB S61 .....97 G4
MEX/SWTN S64 .....65 H5
WMB/DAR S73 .....35 E4
Highfields Crs DRON S18 .....171 E3
High Field Spring
HAN/WDH S13 .....129 E4
Highfields Rd DRON S18 .....171 G3
Highfield Ter CHNE S41 * 187 G1
Highfield Vw RHAM S60 .....129 G1
Highfield View Rd
CHNE S41 .....187 F4
Highfield Vls
RHAM/THRY S65 * 99 G3
High Fisher Ga DON DN1 .....6 D2
Highgate DARN/MH S9 .....117 G2
WMB/DAR S73 .....51 F3
Highgate Cl
NROS/TKH DN11 .....91 G4
Highgate Ct DEARNE S63 .....37 E5
Highgate Dr DRON S18 .....171 G4
Highgate La DEARNE S63 .....53 F1
DRON S18 .....171 G4
High Gate Wy CUD/GR S72 .....17 E2
Highgreave SHEFN S5 .....102 C3
High Greave Av SHEFN S5 .....102 B2
High Greave Ct SHEFN S5 .....102 C3
High Greave Pl
RHAM/THRY S65 .....107 E2
High Greave Rd
RHAM/THRY S65 .....107 E2
Highgrove Cl CHNE S41 .....187 G1
Highgrove Ct
DONS/BSCR DN4 .....74 C2
High Hazel Ga RHAM S60 .....130 A3
High Hazel Crs RHAM S60 .....129 G1
High Hazel Rd RHAM S60 .....130 A3
High Hazels Cl
DARN/MH S9 * 128 B3
High Hazels Md
DARN/MH S9 .....128 B3
High Hazels Rd
STV/CWN S43 .....184 A1
High House Farm Ct
AU/AST/KP S26 .....159 F3
High House Ter
ST/HB/BR S6 .....114 B5
Highland Rd STV/CWN S43 .....180 A1
High La HACK/IN S12 .....155 G4
MALT S66 .....132 C4
High Lee La STKB/PEN S36 .....45 F1
High Leys Rd STV/CWN S43 .....185 E4
Highlow Cl CHSW S40 .....186 C4
Highlow Vw RHAM S60 .....118 C3
High Matlock Av
ST/HB/BR S6 .....123 H1
High Matlock Rd
ST/HB/BR S6 .....112 D5
Highmill Av MEX/SWTN S64 .....65 G5
Highmoor Av
AU/AST/KP S26 .....159 G3
Highnam Crescent Rd
FUL S10 .....125 E4
High Nook Rd DIN S25 .....135 E5
High Pavement Rw
SHEFP/MNR S2 .....126 C3
High Rdg BSLY S70 .....31 H5
Highridge Cl CONI DN12 .....89 F2
High Rd DONS/BSCR DN4 .....70 C2
High Royd Av CUD/GR S72 .....21 H1
High Royd La HOY S74 .....48 B5
STKB/PEN S36 .....45 C1
Highroyds BSLY S70 .....31 H5
Highstone Av BSLY S70 .....31 G3
Highstone Crs BSLY S70 .....31 H4
Highstone La BSLY S70 .....31 H4
Highstone Rd BSLY S70 .....31 H4
Highstone V BSLY S70 .....31 G3
High Storrs Cl ECC S11 .....138 D4
High Storrs Crs ECC S11 .....138 C3
High Storrs Dr ECC S11 .....138 C4
High Storrs Ri ECC S11 .....138 C3
High Storrs Rd ECC S11 .....138 C4
High St AU/AST/KP S26 .....145 G2
BSLY S70 .....2 E4
BSLY S70 .....32 B5
BSLYN/ROY S71 .....15 F1
BSLYN/ROY S71 .....20 C3
BSVR S44 .....196 D3
BTLY DN5 .....39 H2
CHNE S41 .....179 G4
CHPT/GREN S35 .....102 B1
CHSW S40 .....5 F4
CONI DN12 .....89 E1
CUD/GR S72 .....17 E2
DEARNE S63 .....65 F2

DIN S25 .....148 B4
DOD/DAR S75 .....30 B3
DON DN1 .....6 C3
DRON S18 .....170 D1
DRON S18 .....172 C2
ECK/KIL S21 .....166 C5
HOY S74 .....62 A2
KIMB S61 .....104 C2
MALT S66 .....111 E3
MEX/SWTN S64 .....67 E4
MOS S20 .....166 C1
RAW S62 .....98 B2
RHAM S60 .....9 F4
RHAM S60 .....119 H3
SHEF S1 .....11 H3
STKB/PEN S36 .....44 D4
STV/CWN S43 .....177 E4
STV/CWN S43 .....180 B3
STV/CWN S43 .....182 A4
STV/CWN S43 .....184 D3
STV/CWN S43 .....188 D1
TOT/DORE S17 .....160 D1
WMB/DAR S73 .....50 B2
High Street La
SHEFP/MNR S2 .....11 K3
High Street Ms MOS S20 .....166 C1
Highthorn Rd
MEX/SWTN S64 .....86 B2
Highthorn Vls
MEX/SWTN S64 * 86 C2
Highton St ST/HB/BR S6 .....125 E1
High Trees RHAM S60 * 119 H1
TOT/DORE S17 .....160 D1
High Vw BSLYN/ROY S71 .....15 F1
SHEF S1 .....115 E4
High View Cl CHNE S41 .....193 F2
WMB/DAR S73 .....35 E3
Highwood Pl ECK/KIL S21 .....166 C5
Highwoods Crs
MEX/SWTN S64 .....66 C3
Highwoods Rd
MEX/SWTN S64 .....66 C3
High Wood Wy
STV/CWN S43 .....184 C1
High Wray Cl ECC S11 .....151 H1
Hilary Wy AU/AST/KP S26 .....145 F3
Hillberry Ri CHSW S40 .....195 F1
Hill Cl RHAM/THRY S65 .....107 F5
ST/HB/BR S6 .....123 C1
Hillcote Cl FUL S10 .....137 H1
Hillcote Ms FUL S10 .....137 H1
Hillcote Ms FUL S10 .....137 H1
Hillcote Ri FUL S10 .....137 H1
Hillcrest DEARNE S63 .....37 E5
Hill Crest HOY S74 .....61 G3
RHAM/THRY S65 * 99 G3
Hillcrest Dr DIN S25 .....148 B4
RHAM/THRY S65 .....99 G3
Hillcrest Gv STV/CWN S43 .....182 B3
Hillcrest Ri STKB/PEN S36 .....77 H3
Hill Crest Rd
CHPT/GREN S35 .....93 H1
RHAM/THRY S65 .....106 D2
Hillcrest Rd CHNE S41 .....193 F5
STKB/PEN S36 .....77 H3
WHHL DN2 .....41 E4
Hillcrest Wy MALT S66 .....108 B1
Hill End Rd DOD/DAR S75 .....14 A5
Hill Farm Cl DEARNE S63 .....36 D3
Hillfoot Ct TOT/DORE S17 .....160 D4
Hillfoot Rd TOT/DORE S17 .....160 D4
Hillhouses La RCH S42 .....195 E4
Hillman Dr STV/CWN S43 .....189 C3
Hill Park Gv DOD/DAR S75 .....30 B2
Hillsborough Barracks
ST/HB/BR S6 * 114 B5
Hillsborough Pl
ST/HB/BR S6 * 114 A4
Hillsborough Rd
DONS/BSCR DN4 .....58 A5
ST/HB/BR S6 .....114 A4
Hills Cl BTLY DN5 .....55 E3
RAW S62 .....66 D3
Hillside BSLYN/ROY S71 .....33 G2
DIN S25 .....148 B2
MOS S20 .....166 C1
Hill Side RHAM S60 .....119 H3
Hillside Av DRON S18 .....171 E3
Hillside Ct BTLY DN5 .....54 B5
KIMB S61 .....97 H5
Hillside Dr CHSW S40 .....191 H5
HOY S74 .....62 B3
STV/CWN S43 .....183 E3
Hillside Gv CUD/GR S72 .....17 H2
Hillside Rd WHHL DN2 .....41 C3
Hills Rd STKB/PEN S36 .....77 H3
Hill St BSLYN/ROY S71 .....33 E2
HOY S74 .....62 C3
SHEFP/MNR S2 .....139 H1
WMB/DAR S73 .....35 E3
Hill Top BSVR S44 .....196 D2
Hilltop CUD/GR S72 .....17 H1
Hill Top Cl BSLYN/ROY S71 .....7 F4
Hill Top Cl HOR/CROF WF4 .....12 B3
KIMB S61 .....104 B3
Hilltop Cl MALT S66 .....110 B2
Hill Top Cl RHAM S60 .....118 A3
Hill Top Crs MOS S20 .....156 D4
WHHL DN2 .....41 G3
Hilltop Gdns CONI DN12 .....88 B2
Hilltop Gn SHEFN S5 .....114 D1

Hill Top La CHPT/GREN S35 .....100 D1
DOD/DAR S75 .....18 D4
KIMB S61 .....104 B3
RHAM/THRY S65 .....107 H2
Hill Top Ri CHPT/GREN S35 .....101 F2
Hill Top Rd CHPT/GREN S35 .....101 F2
CONI DN12 .....88 B2
ST/HB/BR S6 .....122 A1
BSLY S70 .....47 H5
Hilltop Rd CHNE S41 .....179 G4
DRON S18 .....171 E5
RCH S42 .....194 D3
Hilltop Wy DRON S18 .....171 E4
Hill Turrets Cl ECC S11 .....151 F1
Hill Vw East KIMB S61 .....104 B1
Hill View Rd KIMB S61 .....104 B1
STV/CWN S43 .....188 C1
Hilton Dr CHPT/GREN S35 .....102 B1
Hilton St DOD/DAR S75 .....2 C1
Hindburn Cl
DONS/BSCR DN4 .....73 C1
Hinde House Crs ATT S4 .....116 A2
Hinde House Cft ATT S4 .....116 A2
Hinde House La ATT S4 .....115 H3
Hinde St ATT S4 .....116 A3
Hindewood La ATT S4 .....116 A3
Hindle St BSLY S70 .....2 D5
Hind Rd RHAM S60 .....120 A2
Hipley Cl CHSW S40 .....186 B4
Hipper St CHSW S40 .....5 C5
Hipper St South CHSW S40 .....5 C5
Hipper St West CHSW S40 .....4 C5
Hirst Common La
ST/HB/BR S6 .....100 C3
Hirst Dr RHAM/THRY S65 .....107 F2
Hirst Ga MEX/SWTN S64 .....67 G3
Hobart St ECC S11 .....139 H2
Hobson Av ST/HB/BR S6 .....114 C5
Hobson Dr ST/HB/BR S6 .....114 C5
Hockley La RCH S42 .....195 G5
Hodder St DOD/DAR S75 .....80 D5
Hodgkinson Av
STKB/PEN S36 .....44 D3
Hodgson St SOWL S3 .....10 E6
Hodroyd Cl CUD/GR S72 .....17 F3
Hodroyd Cottages
CUD/GR S72 .....17 H2
Hodroyd La CUD/GR S72 .....17 F3
Hodster La CUD/GR S72 .....23 H3
Hogarth Ri DRON S18 .....170 D2
Holbeach Dr CHSW S40 .....192 A4
Holbeck Av BSVR S44 .....197 F2
Holbeck Cl CHNE S41 .....5 F6
Holbein Cl DRON S18 .....170 D3
Holberry Cl FUL S10 .....10 C5
Holberry Gdns FUL S10 .....10 B5
Holbourne Gv
CHPT/GREN S35 .....80 B2
Holbrook Av MOS S20 .....157 F5
Holbrook Cl CHSW S40 .....191 C4
MOS S20 .....157 F5
Holbrook Dr
HAN/WDH S13 .....141 H4
Holbrook Gn MOS S20 .....157 F5
Holbrook Pl STV/CWN S43 .....189 C2
Holbrook Ri MOS S20 .....157 F4
Holbrook Rd
HAN/WDH S13 .....141 H3
Holburn Av DRON S18 .....171 E1
Holden Ct BSLY S70 .....2 E5
Holderness Dr
AU/AST/KP S26 .....145 F2
Holdings Rd
SHEFP/MNR S2 .....140 D1
Hole House La
STKB/PEN S36 .....76 D2
Holgate WMB/DAR S73 .....35 H5
Holgate Av SHEFN S5 .....101 H3
Holgate Crs SHEFN S5 .....102 A3
Holgate Dr SHEFN S5 .....102 A3
Holgate Mt BSLY S70 .....31 H4
Holgate Rd SHEFN S5 .....102 A3
Holgate Wy MALT S66 .....111 F2
Holkham Ri ECC S11 .....151 F3
Holland Cl RAW S62 .....85 F4
Holland Pl
SHEFP/MNR S2 * 140 A1
Holland Rd CHNE S41 .....179 F4
CHPT/GREN S35 .....80 B4
SHEFP/MNR S2 .....140 A1
Holland St SHEF S1 .....10 E3
Hollies Cl DRON S18 .....171 G3
Hollinberry La
CHPT/GREN S35 .....79 H2
Hollin Busk La
STKB/PEN S36 .....77 E4
Hollin Busk Rd
STKB/PEN S36 .....77 E3
Hollin Cl CHNE S41 .....186 C1
NROS/TKH DN11 .....91 H1
Hollin Cft DOD/DAR S75 .....30 C2
Hollindale Dr HACK/IN S12 .....142 A5
Holling Cft STKB/PEN S36 * 77 C2
Holling Hill La MALT S66 .....107 H5
Hollingswood Wy
MALT S66 .....108 C2
Hollingwood Crs
STV/CWN S43 .....181 E5
Holling's La MALT S66 .....108 C1
RHAM/THRY S65 .....99 H4
Hollin Hill Rd STV/CWN S43 .....185 G3
Hollin Moor La MALT S66 .....108 A5
Hollins Cl ST/HB/BR S6 .....124 B2

Hollins Dr ST/HB/BR S6 .....124 B2
Hollinsend Av HACK/IN S12 .....142 A5
Hollinsend Pl HACK/IN S12 .....142 A5
Hollinsend Rd HACK/IN S12 .....154 C2
Hollins La ST/HB/BR S6 .....124 C1
Hollins Spring Av DRON S18 .....171 E3
Hollins Spring Rd
DRON S18 .....171 E3
The Hollins DOD/DAR S75 .....30 C4
Hollins Wood Gv
CUD/GR S72 .....22 A3
Hollis Cl RAW S62 .....84 C3
Hollis Cft HAN/WDH S13 .....143 E4
SHEF S1 .....10 E2
Hollis La CHNE S41 .....5 H5
Hollowdene DOD/DAR S75 .....18 D4
Hollowgate RHAM S60 .....9 G6
Hollow Ga BTLY DN5 .....69 E3
CHPT/GREN S35 .....93 F1
RHAM S60 .....119 H3
Hollowgate Av DONS/BSCR DN4 .....51 G5
Hollow La MOS S20 .....166 D2
The Hollows
DONS/BSCR DN4 .....74 A2
Holly Av BTLY DN5 .....39 G3
Hollybank Av HACK/IN S12 .....142 A4
Hollybank Crs HACK/IN S12 .....142 A4
Hollybank Dr HACK/IN S12 .....142 A4
Hollybank Rd HACK/IN S12 .....142 A4
Hollybank Wy HACK/IN S12 .....142 B4
Holly Bush Dr DEARNE S63 .....37 F3
Holly Cl CHPT/GREN S35 .....93 H2
ECK/KIL S21 .....167 H3
Holly Crs MALT S66 .....108 C5
Holly Dene ARMTH DN3 .....42 C2
Holly Dr BTLY DN5 .....26 D5
Holly Farm CUD/GR S72 .....17 E1
Holly Gdns HACK/IN S12 .....142 A4
Holly Grove Rd STV/CWN S43 .....152 B5
Holly Gv DEARNE S63 .....37 E5
DEARNE S63 .....65 F4
HACK/IN S12 .....142 A4
NROS/TKH DN11 .....91 G3
Holly La SHEF S1 * 11 F3
Holly Mt MALT S66 .....108 C5
Holly St DON DN1 .....56 A4
SHEF S1 .....11 F3
Holly Ter AU/AST/KP S26 .....144 D2
DONS/BSCR DN4 .....71 F1
Hollythorpe Cl CHNE S41 .....193 F6
Hollythorpe Crs SHEFS S8 .....153 E1
Hollythorpe Ri SHEFS S8 .....153 F1
Hollythorpe Rd SHEFS S8 .....153 F1
Hollytree Av MALT S66 .....85 H5
Hollywell Cl RAW S62 .....84 B1
Holmebank Cl CHSW S40 .....4 B2
Holmebank East CHSW S40 .....4 B2
Holmebank Vw CHNE S41 .....186 C5
Holmebank West CHSW S40 .....4 B2
Holme Cl ST/HB/BR S6 .....114 A4
Holme Ct DEARNE S63 .....53 E1
Holmefield Cl ARMTH DN3 .....43 E5
Holme Hall Crs CHSW S40 .....186 B4
Holme La CHPT/GREN S35 .....101 F2
ST/HB/BR S6 .....113 H5
Holme Oak Wy
ST/HB/BR S6 .....112 C5
Holme Park Av CHNE S41 .....186 B2
Holme Rd CHNE S41 .....187 C3
Holmes Carr Crs
NROS/TKH DN11 .....90 C2
Holmes Carr Rd
DONS/BSCR DN4 .....73 H2
NROS/TKH DN11 .....90 D1
Holmes Ct KIMB S61 * 8 A5
Holmes Crs RHAM S60 .....130 B3
Holmesdale Cl DRON S18 .....163 F5
Holmesdale Rd DRON S18 .....163 F5
Holmesfield KIMB S61 * 104 C2
Holmes La CONI DN12 .....87 F3
Holmes Market DON DN1 .....6 E1
Holmes Rd MALT S66 .....108 D5
The Holmes DON DN1 .....6 B1
Holme Wood Ct
ARMTH DN3 * 29 G5
Holme Wood Gdns
DONS/BSCR DN4 .....74 A1
Holme Wood La
ARMTH DN3 .....43 F4
Holm Flatt St RAW S62 .....98 A3
Holmhirst Cl SHEFS S8 .....152 C3
Holmhirst Dr SHEFS S8 .....152 C2
Holmhirst Rd SHEFS S8 .....152 C2
Holmhirst Wy SHEFS S8 .....152 C2
Holmley Bank DRON S18 .....163 E5
Holmley La DRON S18 .....163 E5
Holmoak Cl MEX/SWTN S64 .....86 B2
Holmshaw Cl ARMTH DN3 .....29 C4
Holmshaw Dr
HAN/WDH S13 .....142 C2
Holmshaw Gv
HAN/WDH S13 .....142 C2
Holt La House Gv ABRD S7 .....152 B2
Holtwood Rd ATT S4 .....115 F5
Holwick Ct BSLY S70 .....2 E4
Holy Cl CHNE S41 .....179 G3
Holymoor Rd RCH S42 .....190 B5
Holyoake Av
HAN/WDH S13 .....142 C1

Holyrood Av FUL S10 .....136 D1
Holyrood Rd MALT S66 .....108 D3
Holyrood Rd WHHL DN2 .....7 K3
Holyrood Vw FUL S10 .....136 D1
Holywell Hts ATT S4 .....116 C2
Holywell La CONI DN12 .....89 C2
Holywell Pl
RHAM/THRY S65 * 9 C5
Holywell Rd ATT S4 .....116 B3
MEX/SWTN S64 .....86 B2
Holywell St CHNE S41 .....5 G3
Homecroft Rd DEARNE S63 .....37 F5
Homefield Crs BTLY DN5 .....39 E2
Homeport Ms CHNE S41 .....5 G1
Homestead Cl SHEFN S5 .....102 D4
Homestead Dr RAW S62 .....85 F4
RHAM S60 .....118 B3
Homestead Rd SHEFN S5 .....102 C5
The Homestead BTLY DN5 .....39 H1
Honeysuckle Cl
DONS/BSCR DN4 .....57 G5
WMB/DAR S73 .....51 E1
Honeysuckle Rd
SHEFN S5 * 116 B1
Honeywell Cl
BSLYN/ROY S71 .....3 C1
Honeywell Gv
BSLYN/ROY S71 .....19 H3
Honeywell La DOD/DAR S75 .....19 G4
Honeywell Pl
BSLYN/ROY S71 .....19 H4
Honeywell St
BSLYN/ROY S71 .....19 H4
Honister Cl DEARNE S63 .....64 A1
Hoober Av ECC S11 .....138 C5
Hoober Ct RAW S62 .....84 D3
Hoober Fld DEARNE S63 .....84 B1
Hoober Hall La RAW S62 .....63 H5
Hoober La RAW S62 .....84 A2
Hoober Rd ECC S11 .....138 C5
Hoober St DEARNE S63 .....64 B2
Hoober Vw RAW S62 .....84 D3
WMB/DAR S73 .....50 C4
Hood Green Rd
DOD/DAR S75 .....46 A3
Hoodhill Rd RAW S62 .....81 H2
Hoole La FUL S10 .....125 E5
Hoole Rd FUL S10 .....125 E4
Hoole St CHNE S41 .....193 F4
ST/HB/BR S6 .....125 E1
Hooton La MALT S66 .....110 C4
Hooton Rd MEX/SWTN S64 .....86 D4
Hope Av DEARNE S63 .....64 A3
Hopedale Rd HACK/IN S12 .....155 F1
Hopefield Av HACK/IN S12 .....155 F1
Hope Rd CHPT/GREN S35 .....100 A3
Hope St BSLYN/ROY S71 .....21 F1
CHSW S40 .....4 B4
DOD/DAR S75 .....2 C2
DOD/DAR S75 .....14 A4
MEX/SWTN S64 .....67 E4
RHAM S60 .....8 C2
STKB/PEN S36 .....77 E2
WMB/DAR S73 .....50 C3
Hope Street Extension
RHAM S60 .....8 D2
Hopewell St BSLY S70 .....32 D2
Hopwood La ST/HB/BR S6 .....123 E3
Hopwood St BSLY S70 .....2 E2
Horace St RHAM S60 .....9 H6
Horbiry End
AU/AST/KP S26 .....147 E5
Horbury La CHPT/GREN S35 .....93 G2
Horbury Rd CUD/GR S72 .....16 D4
Hornbeam Cl
CHPT/GREN S35 .....93 H2
SHEFN S5 .....181 E4
Hornbeam Rd MALT S66 .....108 B3
Hornby St BSLY S70 .....31 H3
Horndean Rd SHEFN S5 .....115 H3
Horner Cl STKB/PEN S36 .....76 D2
Horner Rd ABRD S7 .....139 H3
Hornes La DOD/DAR S75 .....14 A3
Horninglow Cl
DONS/BSCR DN4 .....74 C2
SHEFN S5 .....115 C1
Hornsby Rd SHEFN S5 .....115 H3
Hornscroft Rd BSVR S44 .....196 D3
Hornthorpe Rd
ECK/KIL S21 .....174 B1
Hornthwaite Hill Rd
STKB/PEN S36 .....44 A3
Horse Carr Vw
BSLYN/ROY S71 .....33 G2
Horse Chestnut Cl CHSW S40 .....5 F7
Horsefair Cl MEX/SWTN S64 .....66 A5
Horsehead La BSVR S44 .....197 E2
Horsehills La ARMTH DN3 .....42 C5
Horsemoor Rd DEARNE S63 .....36 D2
Horseshoe Cl
AU/AST/KP S26 .....159 G2
Horse Shoe Ct
DONS/BSCR DN4 .....71 F1
Horseshoe Gdns
AU/AST/KP S26 .....159 F2
Horsewood Cl BSLY S70 .....30 D2
Horsewood Rd
HAN/WDH S13 .....143 H2
RCH S42 .....191 F4
Horsley Cl CHSW S40 .....186 A4
Horton Cl MOS S20 .....167 E1
Horton Dr MOS S20 .....167 E1

Horton Vw ARMTH DN3.........29 E2
Houfton Crs BSVR S44..........196 C1
Houfton Rd BSVR S44............196 C1
Hough Cl CHSW S40.....................5 G7
Hough La WMB/DAR S73........49 H4
Houghton Rd DEARNE S63.....36 C2
DIN S25...................................147 H2
Houldsworth Crs BSVR S44..196 C1
Houldsworth Dr CHNE S41...193 G2
Hound Hill La BSLY S70 ....31 F5
DEARNE S63..............................66 B1
Hounsfield Crs
RHAM/THRY S65 ....107 F2
Hounsfield La FUL S10............10 C4
Hounsfield Rd OWL S3.............10 C3
RHAM/THRY S65 ....107 F2
House Park Ga
CHPT/GREN S35 ....92 B5
Housley La CHPT/GREN S35...80 D5
Housley Pk CHPT/GREN S35...81 E5
Houstead Rd DARN/MH S9...128 B4
Howard Dr CHNE S41............179 G3
Howard La SHEF S1.................11 H5
Howard Rd MALT S66.............108 D4
MALT S66..............................111 F3
ST/HB/BR S6.........................125 E2
Howards Cl MALT S66...........133 G1
Howard St BSLY S70................31 H3
DIN S25...................................135 E4
RHAM/THRY S65 ....9 F3
SHEF S1....................................11 H4
WMB/DAR S73..........................35 G5
Howarth Dr RHAM S60..........118 D5
Howarth Rd RHAM S60..........118 D4
Howbrook Cl
CHPT/GREN S35 ....80 A3
Howbrook La
CHPT/GREN S35 ....79 F1
Howden Cl DONS/BSCR DN4..73 G2
STV/CWN S43......................182 B4
Howden Rd DARN/MH S9.....116 C5
Howdike La
RHAM/THRY S65 ....87 F4
Howell Gdns DEARNE S63......37 E3
Howells Pl STV/CWN S43......182 D3
Howlett Cl RHAM S60...........120 B3
Howlett Dr RHAM S60...........118 C5
Howse St HOY S74...................62 C2
Howson Cl
RHAM/THRY S65 ....109 E1
Howson Rd STKB/PEN S36.....77 F2
Hoylake Av CHSW S40...........191 G5
Hoylake Dr MEX/SWTN S64...86 B2
Hoyland Rd HOY S74...............61 F3
OWL S3...................................114 C5
Hoyland St MALT S66..............111 F3
WMB/DAR S73..........................50 B3
Hoyle Mill Rd BSLY S70............32 D2
Hoyle St OWL S3.......................10 E1
Hucklow Av CHSW S40..........192 B3
STV/CWN S43.......................189 G2
Hucklow Rd SHEFN S5...........115 H2
Hucknall Av CHSW S40..........186 C5
Huddersfield Rd
DOD/DAR S75........................19 E3
STKB/PEN S36 ....44 C2
Hudson Av HOR/CROF WF4....12 B3
Hudson Hvn
WMB/DAR S73 *....................49 H1
Hudson Mt BSVR S44.............197 E4
Hudson Rd HAN/WDH S13....144 A2
KIMB S61...............................96 C4
Humberside Wy
BSLYN/ROY S71 ....20 D1
Humphrey Rd SHEFS S8........152 C5
Humphries Av RAW S62...........84 D4
Hundall La CHNE S41............179 G2
DRON S18..............................172 B4
Hungerhill Cl KIMB S61 ....104 B1
Hungerhill La ARMTH DN3......29 E5
Hunger Hill La RHAM S60.......120 A3
Hungerhill Rd KIMB S61..........96 B5
Hunger Hill Rd RHAM S60.......119 H2
Hunloke Av CHSW S40...............4 C7
CHSW S40.............................191 H3
Hunloke Crs CHSW S40..............4 B7
Hunloke Vw RCH S42..............195 H3
Hunningley Cl BSLY S70...........32 D3
Hunningley La BSLY S70 ....32 D3
Hunsdon Rd ECK/KIL S21........166 C5
Hunshelf La
CHPT/GREN S35 ....94 B4
Hunshelf Pk STKB/PEN S36....77 E1
Hunshelf Rd
CHPT/GREN S35 ....93 H1
STKB/PEN S36 ....76 D1
Hunsley St ATT S4.................116 A4
Hunster Gv
NROS/TKH DN11....................91 F3
Hunstone Av SHEFS S8 ....163 E1
Hunt Cl BSLYN/ROY S71 *........20 C3
Hunter Hill Rd ECC S11...........139 E3
Hunter House Rd ECC S11.....138 D3
Hunter Rd ST/HB/BR S6.........113 H4
Hunters Cha DIN S25.............134 D3
Hunters Cl DIN S25.................134 D2
Hunters Cottages
DOD/DAR S75 *......................30 C1
Hunters Ct DIN S25................134 D2
Hunters Dr DIN S25................134 D3
Hunters Gdns DIN S25...........134 D2
ST/HB/BR S6.........................112 D3
Hunters Gn DIN S25...............134 D2
Hunters Pk DIN S25...............134 D2
Hunters Ri DOD/DAR S75........30 C1
Hunters Wy DIN S25..............134 D2
Hunter's Av BSLY S70 ....30 C2
Hunter's La
HAN/WDH S13 ....142 A4
Huntingdon Av BSVR S44......197 E3
Huntingdon Crs ECC S11 ....139 G2
Huntingdon Rd WHHL DN2.....57 G1
Huntington St BTLY DN5.........26 D5
Huntington Wy MALT S66 ....110 C1
Huntingtower Rd ECC S11 ...138 D3
Hunt La BTLY DN5.....................39 H5
Huntley Cl STV/CWN S43.......189 F1
Huntley Gv ECC S11...............138 B4
Huntley Rd ECC S11...............138 C4
Huntsman Rd
DARN/MH S9 ....128 B3
STV/CWN S43......................182 A4
Huntsmans Gdns
DARN/MH S9 ....117 E5
Hunt St HOY S74......................61 F3
Hurl Dr HACK/IN S12.............141 F5
Hurley Cft DEARNE S63...........64 A1
Hurlfield Av HACK/IN S12......141 G5
Hurlfield Ct HACK/IN S12 ......141 F4
Hurlfield Dr HACK/IN S12......141 F4
MALT S66..............................108 D2
Hurlfield Rd HACK/IN S12 .....141 F5
Hurlingham Cl ECC S11 ....152 A1
Hurlstone Cl ARMTH DN3........29 G4
Hursley Cl MOS S20...............157 G4
Hursley Dr MOS S20..............157 G4
Hurst Gn CHPT/GREN S35......80 B4
Hurst La EPW DN9...................75 H5
Hutchings Crs
STV/CWN S43......................184 D1
Hutchinson La ABRD S7........152 B2
Hutchinson Rd ABRD S7 ....152 B2
RAW S62...............................85 G5
Hutcliffe Dr SHEFS S8...........152 B3
Hutcliffe Wood Rd
SHEFS S8 ....152 B3
Hutcliffe Wood Vw
SHEFS S8 ....152 B4
Hut La ECK/KIL S21...............168 C4
Hutton Rd KIMB S61................96 C5
Huxterwell Dr
DONS/BSCR DN4 ....71 H4
Hyacinth Cl SHEFN S5...........116 B1
Hyacinth Rd SHEFN S5..........116 B1
Hyde Park Ter
SHEFP/MNR S2...................126 C4
Hyde Park Wk
SHEFP/MNR S2...................126 C4
Hyland Crs DONS/BSCR DN4 ..70 D2
Hyman Cl DONS/BSCR DN4....70 D1
Hyndley Rd BSVR S44............196 C1

I

Ians Wy CHSW S40................186 C5
Ibbotson Rd ST/HB/BR S6.....125 E1
Ickles Wy RHAM S60..............105 F5
Icknield Wy RHAM S60..........118 C4
Ida Gv MALT S66...................110 B2
Ida's Rd ECK/KIL S21.............166 D4
Idsworth Rd SHEFN S5...........115 H2
Ilam Cl STV/CWN S43............189 G3
Ilkley Crs AU/AST/KP S26.....145 E4
Ilkley Rd SHEFN S5................102 D5
Illsley Rd WMB/DAR S73 ....35 E4
Imperial Buildings
RHAM S60 *............................9 F4
Imperial Crs WHHL DN2 ....7 J2
Imrie Pl AU/AST/KP S26.........159 H3
Indstry Rd BSLYN/ROY S71.....15 G5
Industry Rd
BSLYN/ROY S71 ....15 G5
DARN/MH S9 ....128 A2
Industry St ST/HB/BR S6 ......125 E1
Infield La DARN/MH S9 ....128 A3
Infirmary Rd CHNE S41.............5 H1
RAW S62...............................98 C3
ST/HB/BR S6........................125 G1
Ingbirchworth Rd
STKB/PEN S36 ....44 A2
Ingelow Av SHEFN S5............102 B4
Ingfield Av DARN/MH S9 ....117 G2
Ingleborough Cft
CHPT/GREN S35 ....80 D5
Ingleborough Dr BTLY DN5.....55 E3
Ingleby Cl DRON S18.............170 A2
Ingle Gv BTLY DN5 ....55 E3
Ingleton Rd CHNE S41...........192 D5
Ingleton Wk BSLY S70 ....2 D3
Inglewood Av MOS S20 ....157 G4
Inglewood Ct MOS S20 * 157 G4
Inglewood Dell MOS S20 ....157 G4
Ingram Ct
SHEFP/MNR S2....................126 D5
Ingram Rd
SHEFP/MNR S2....................126 D5
Ingsfield La DEARNE S63.........52 C3
Ingshead Av RAW S62 ....98 C1
Ings La BTLY DN5......................27 G5
BTLY DN5...............................55 E3
CUD/GR S72...........................35 F3
Ings Rd BTLY DN5....................39 H5
BTLY DN5...............................69 F2
WMB/DAR S73........................51 E1
Ings Wy BTLY DN5...................27 F5
Inkerman Cottages
CHSW S40 * 191 G1
Inkerman Rd
WMB/DAR S73.......................35 E5
Inkersall Dr MOS S20............157 E5
Inkersall Green Rd
STV/CWN S43 ....189 F1
Inkersall Rd STV/CWN S43....182 A5
Innovation Wy
DOD/DAR S75 ....19 E3
Insley Gdns
DONS/BSCR DN4 ....74 A1
Intake Crs DOD/DAR S75.........30 B4
Intake Gdns DOD/DAR S75.....18 D5
Intake La CUD/GR S72.............17 E4
DOD/DAR S75 ....18 D5
Intake Rd BSVR S44..............196 B1
Interchange Wy
BSLYN/ROY S71 ....3 H3
Ireland Cl STV/CWN S43 ....182 B5
Ireland St STV/CWN S43........182 B4
Iron Cliff Rd BSVR S44...........196 C1
Irongate CHSW S40....................5 G4
Ironside Cl GLV S14 ....153 H3
Ironside Pl GLV S14 ....154 A2
Ironside Rd GLV S14..............153 H3
Ironstone Crs
CHPT/GREN S35 ....80 D4
Ironstone Dr
CHPT/GREN S35 ....80 D4
Irving St DARN/MH S9..........128 A3
Irwell Gdns
DONS/BSCR DN4 ....57 H3
Island Cl RHAM S60...............119 H1
Islay St FUL S10 ....124 D4
Issott St BSLYN/ROY S71.........19 H4
Ivan Brook Cl DRON S18 *.....170 A2
Ivanhoe Cl BTLY DN5................55 F1
Ivanhoe Ms
AU/AST/KP S26...................145 E2
Ivanhoe Rd ARMTH DN3 ....42 B1
CONI DN12.............................88 D1
DONS/BSCR DN4 ....71 E1
MALT S66..............................133 E1
ST/HB/BR S6.........................124 C1
Ivanhoe Wy BTLY DN5.............55 F1
Ivor Gv DONS/BSCR DN4.........55 G5
Ivy Cl CHNE S41 ....179 G4
NROS/TKH DN11....................91 G2
Ivy Cottage La FUL S10..........137 G4
Ivy Ct CUD/GR S72 ....21 H1
SHEFS S8 ....153 G3
Ivy Dr FUL S10 ....125 F3
Ivy Farm Cl BSLYN/ROY S71 ...15 H3
STV/CWN S43......................185 E3
Ivy Farm Cft
RHAM/THRY S65 ....99 F5
Ivy Gv FUL S10 * 125 F3
Ivy Hall Rd SHEFN S5.............103 E2
Ivy House Ct EPW DN9.............75 H1
Ivy La MOS S20 ....157 G1
Ivy Park Rd FUL S10 ....124 A5
Ivy Side Cl ECK/KIL S21.........168 B2
Ivyside Gdns ECK/KIL S21 .....168 B2
Ivy Spring Cl RCH S42............195 H3
Ivy Ter BSLY S70 ....3 K6

J

Jack Close Orch
BSLYN/ROY S71 ....12 C5
Jackson Crs RAW S62..............84 D4
Jackson St CUD/GR S72...........21 G1
DEARNE S63..........................37 G5
Jacksons Yd BSLY S70 * 2 D4
Jacobs Cl SHEFN S5...............103 E5
Jacobs Dr SHEFN S5..............103 E5
Jacques Pl BSLYN/ROY S71.....20 D5
Jago Av STV/CWN S43 ....185 G2
Jamaica St ATT S4 ....115 G5
James Andrew Cl
SHEFS S8 ....162 D1
James Andrew Crs
SHEFS S8 ....162 C1
James Andrew Cft
SHEFS S8 ....162 D1
James St BSLY S70 ....32 C5
BSLYN/ROY S71 ....3 H2
CHNE S41 ....187 G3
DARN/MH S9 ....128 A4
MEX/SWTN S64 ....67 H3
RHAM S60 ....8 B4
James Walton Dr MOS S20...167 F1
James Walton Pl MOS S20....167 F1
James Walton Vw
MOS S20..............................167 F1
Janson St DARN/MH S9.........116 C4
Jardine Cl DARN/MH S9 ....103 G5
Jardine St DARN/MH S9.........103 H5
WMB/DAR S73........................50 B3
Jarratt St DON DN1....................6 E6
Jarrow Rd ECC S11 ....139 F2
Jasmine Av MOS S20 ....157 F2
Jasmine Cl CONI DN12.............89 F2
Jaunty Av HACK/IN S12 ....154 D2
Jaunty Cl HACK/IN S12 ....154 D2
Jaunty Crs HACK/IN S12 ....154 D2
Jaunty Dr HACK/IN S12 ....154 D1
Jaunty La HACK/IN S12..........154 D1
Jaunty Mt HACK/IN S12.........155 E2
Jaunty Pl HACK/IN S12 ....154 D2
Jaunty Rd HACK/IN S12.........155 E2
Jaunty Vw HACK/IN S12.........155 E2
Jaunty Wy HACK/IN S12........154 D1
Jay La AU/AST/KP S26...........145 G4
Jebb Gdns CHSW S40............191 G2
Jedburgh Dr DARN/MH S9 ...103 G5
Jedburgh St DARN/MH S9....103 G5
Jeffcock Rd
CHPT/GREN S35 ....80 C4
DARN/MH S9 ....128 A3
Jefferson Av WHHL DN2 ....41 H1
Jeffery Crs STKB/PEN S36 ......77 F3
Jeffery St
SHEFP/MNR S2 *.................140 B4
Jenkin Av DARN/MH S9.........116 C2
Jenkin Cl DARN/MH S9..........116 C1
Jenkin Dr DARN/MH S9.........116 C2
Jenkin Rd DARN/MH S9 ....116 C1
Jenkinson Gv ARMTH DN3......42 B4
Jenkin Wood Cl MALT S66.....108 C2
Jennings Cl
RHAM/THRY S65 ....9 H1
Jepson Rd CHNE S41 ....193 E5
SHEFN S5..............................103 F5
Jericho St OWL S3....................10 C1
Jermyn Av HACK/IN S12........155 G1
Jermyn Cl HACK/IN S12 ....155 H2
Jermyn Crs HACK/IN S12.......155 H2
Jermyn Cft DOD/DAR S75.......30 B3
Jermyn Dr HACK/IN S12 ....155 H2
Jermyn Wy HACK/IN S12.......155 G2
Jersey Rd SHEFP/MNR S2.....140 A3
Jervis Pl STV/CWN S43..........189 F3
Jesmond Av
BSLYN/ROY S71 ....15 F1
Jesop Ct DIN S25...................134 D3
Jessamine Rd SHEFN S5........103 E5
Jessell St DARN/MH S9.........127 F2
Jessop St SHEF S1....................11 F6
Jewitt Rd KIMB S61 ....96 C4
Joan La MALT S66...................110 C4
Joan Royd La
STKB/PEN S36 ....44 B5
Jockell Dr RAW S62..................98 B1
Jockey Rd STKB/PEN S36........45 H4
John Calvert Rd
HAN/WDH S13 ....143 H4
John Hibbard Av
HAN/WDH S13 ....144 A3
John Hibbard Cl
HAN/WDH S13 ....144 A3
John Hibbard Crs
HAN/WDH S13 ....144 A3
John Hibbard Ri
HAN/WDH S13 ....144 A3
Johnson Ct CONI DN12............70 C5
RHAM/THRY S65 ....9 J6
Johnson La CHPT/GREN S35...94 B5
Johnson St DOD/DAR S75.........2 C3
OWL S3 ....126 B2
STKB/PEN S36 ....76 D2
Johnstone Cl CHSW S40.........192 B3
John St AWLS/ASK DN6 ....25 G1
BSLY S70..................................3 G5
BSLY S70................................48 A1
CHSW S40 ....4 B4
CUD/GR S72...........................35 H3
DEARNE S63..........................37 F2
ECK/KIL S21..........................166 D5
MEX/SWTN S64 ....67 E4
RHAM S60 ....8 C5
SHEFP/MNR S2....................140 A1
STV/CWN S43......................184 D3
STV/CWN S43......................188 C1
WMB/DAR S73........................50 A2
John Ward St
HAN/WDH S13 ....143 H3
John West St STKB/PEN S36 ..76 D3
Joiner St OWL S3......................11 H1
Jones Av WMB/DAR S73 ....49 H2
Jordan Crs KIMB S61 ....104 C4
Jordanthorpe Gn SHEFS S8..163 G2
Jordanthorpe Pkwy
SHEFS S8 ....163 E3
Jordanthorpe Vw
SHEFS S8 ....163 G1
Joseph Fletcher Dr
RCH S42...............................195 F5
Josephine Rd KIMB S61 ....105 E3
Joseph Rd FUL S10 ....125 E2
Joseph St BSLY S70....................3 G6
CUD/GR S72...........................23 E1
ECK/KIL S21..........................166 D5
RHAM S60 ....8 C2
Joshua Rd ABRD S7 ....139 G3
Josselin Ct CHPT/GREN S35....93 H1
Jossey La BTLY DN5..................38 D2
Jowitt Cl MALT S66.................111 F5
Jowitt Rd ECC S11...................138 D4
Jubb Cl RHAM/THRY S65.......107 F5
Jubilee Cottages
RHAM S60 *.........................118 B3
Jubilee Crs ECK/KIL S21........168 C1
STV/CWN S43......................185 G2
Jubilee Gdns
BSLYN/ROY S71 ....12 D5
Jubilee Rd DARN/MH S9 ....127 H1
DON DN1 ....40 C5
Jubilee St RHAM S60..............105 H5
Judith Rd AU/AST/KP S26 .....145 F4
Judy Rw BSLYN/ROY S71 ....20 C3
Julian Rd DARN/MH S9..........116 D1
Julian Wy DARN/MH S9.........116 D1
Jumble La KIMB S61 ....95 E4
Junction Cl WMB/DAR S73 .....50 D4
Junction Rd ECC S11 ....139 E2
HAN/WDH S13 ....143 H3
NROS/TKH DN11....................91 E3
Junction St BSLY S70................32 B2
WMB/DAR S73........................50 D4
June Rd HAN/WDH S13 ....143 H4
Juniper Cl STV/CWN S43.......181 E4
Juniper Ri ECK/KIL S21 ....168 A3

K

Kariba Cl CHNE S41 ....5 J4
Kashmir Gdns
DARN/MH S9 ....127 H2
Katherine St MALT S66..........133 E1
Kathleen Gv DEARNE S63 ....37 H4
Kay Crs RAW S62 ....84 C3
Kaye Pl FUL S10....................125 F3
Kaye St BSLYN/ROY S71 ....3 G2
Kay St HOY S74........................61 F3
Kay's Ter BSLY S70 ....33 E3
Kea Park Cl MALT S66...........109 G4
Kearsley La CONI DN12...........88 D3
Kearsley Rd
SHEFP/MNR S2....................140 A2
Keats Dr DIN S25...................135 F5
Keats Gv STKB/PEN S36 ....44 D2
Keats Rd CHNE S41................187 F1
DONS/BSCR DN4 ....71 H2
ST/HB/BR S6........................101 F3
Keble Martin Wy
DEARNE S63..........................64 D2
Keble Sq DEARNE S63.............64 D2
Kedleston Cl CHNE S41 ....186 C2
Keepers Cl NROS/TKH DN11...91 H2
SHEFN S5..............................102 D5
Keetons Hl SHEFP/MNR S2...139 H2
ECC S11 *.............................139 H2
Keilder Ct CHSW S40..............191 H3
Keir Pl RAW S62 ....85 H5
Keir St BSLY S70........................2 D3
Keir Ter BSLY S70......................2 D3
Kelburn Av CHSW S40 ....191 G3
Kelby Cft DOD/DAR S75 ....18 B2
Kelgate MOS S20....................166 D2
Kelham Bank DON DN1............56 A4
Kelham Island OWL S3 ....126 A2
Kelham St DON DN1.................56 A4
Kelly St DEARNE S63................37 G5
Kelsey Gdns
DONS/BSCR DN4 ....74 A3
Kelsey Ter BSLY S70 * 31 H3
Kelso Dr DONS/BSCR DN4.......70 D1
Kelvin Ct KIMB S61...................96 A4
Kelvin Gv WMB/DAR S73.........50 C3
Kelvin St MEX/SWTN S64.........67 E3
RHAM/THRY S65 ....99 F5
Kemp Cl ECK/KIL S21 ....168 A2
Kempton Gdns
MEX/SWTN S64 ....67 G2
Kempton Park Rd BTLY DN5..38 D5
Kempton St
DONS/BSCR DN4 ....57 H3
Kempwell Dr RAW S62 ....85 F3
Kenbourne Gv ABRD S7.........139 G3
Kenbourne Rd ABRD S7.........139 G3
Kendal Av DIN S25 ....148 C3
Kendal Cl BTLY DN5 *..............54 A4
Kendal Crs BSLY S70................48 A1
CONI DN12.............................89 F1
Kendal Dr DEARNE S63............53 E4
DRON S18.............................170 C2
Kendal Green Rd BSLY S70......47 G1
Kendal Gv BSLYN/ROY S71......33 G2
Kendal Rd BTLY DN5 ....39 G3
CHNE S41 ....187 E1
ST/HB/BR S6.........................113 H4
Kendal V BSLY S70 ....48 A1
Kendray St BSLY S70..................3 G4
Kenilworth Cl BTLY DN5...........38 D4
Kenilworth Pl ECC S11 ....139 E2
Kenilworth Rd
DONS/BSCR DN4 ....71 E1
Kenmare Crs WHHL DN2.........57 E1
Kennedy Dr DEARNE S63.........53 F2
Kennedy Rd SHEFS S8...........152 C3
Kenneth St
RHAM/THRY S65 ....9 G2
Kennet V CHSW S40...............186 D5
Kenning Hall Cl
SHEFP/MNR S2....................140 D3
Kenninghall Dr
SHEFP/MNR S2....................140 D3
Kenninghall Mt
SHEFP/MNR S2....................140 D3
Kenninghall Rd
SHEFP/MNR S2....................140 D3
Kennington Av
AWLS/ASK DN6 ....24 D2
Kennington Gv CONI DN12.....70 C5
Kenrock Cl BTLY DN5...............40 C1
Kensington Av
STKB/PEN S36 ....44 A2
Kensington Cha FUL S10 ......136 D2
Kensington Cl DIN S25 ....134 A3
Kensington Ct FUL S10 ....136 D2
Kensington Dr FUL S10.........136 D1
Kensington Pk FUL S10.........136 C2

Kensington Rd
  DOD/DAR S75 ....2 C1
Kent Av RAW S62 ....85 E4
Kent Cl BSLYN/ROY S71........12 C5
  CHNE S41 ....187 F4
Kent House Cl
  HACK/IN S12 ....155 G5
Kentmere Cl DRON S18........170 C2
Kentmere Dr
  DONS/BSCR DN4 ....73 F1
Kentmere Wy
  STV/CWN S43 ....189 C1
Kent Rd DONS/BSCR DN4 ......71 H2
  KIMB S61 ....96 C5
  SHEFS S8 ....140 B4
Kent St CHNE S41 ....193 E4
Kenwell Dr TOT/DORE S17...161 H3
Kenwood Av ABRD S7 ....139 C3
Kenwood Bank ECC S11 .....139 F2
Kenwood Cl BSLY S70 ....32 D2
Kenwood Park Rd
  ABRD S7 ....139 G2
Kenwood Ri MALT S66 ....108 C3
Kenwood Rd ABRD S7 ....139 F3
Kenworthy Rd BSLY S70 ....31 G5
  STKB/PEN S36 ....76 D3
Kenyon Rd CHNE S41 ....193 C5
Kenyon St SHEF S1 ....10 C2
Keppel Dr KIMB S61 ....95 H4
Keppel Pl SHEFS S5 ....103 E3
Keppel Rd KIMB S61 ....95 H4
  SHEFN S5 ....103 E3
Keppel View Rd KIMB S61 ...104 B1
Kepple Cl NROS/TKH DN11...91 F4
Keresforth Cl BSLY S70 ....2 B7
Keresforth Hall Rd
  BSLY S70 ....31 F3
Keresforth Hill Rd BSLY S70...30 A6
Kerwin Cl
  DOD/DAR S75 ....30 B4
Kerwin Cl TOT/DORE S17....150 C5
Kerwin Dr TOT/DORE S17....150 C5
Kerwin Rd TOT/DORE S17....150 C5
Kestrel Av KIMB S61 ....95 G1
Kestrel Cl BSVR S44 ....196 C1
  ECK/KIL S21 ....167 H1
Kestrel Dr AWLS/ASK DN6.....25 F1
  ECK/KIL S21 ....166 E5
Kestrel Gn SHEFP/MNR S2...127 E5
Kestrel Ri AU/AST/KP S26 ....144 C3
  BSLY S70 ....47 H5
Keswick BTLY DN5 ....39 G2
Keswick Cl BSVR S44 ....196 C3
  ST/HB/BR S6 ....113 E4
Keswick Crs RHAM S60 ....118 B5
Keswick Dr CHNE S41 ....186 C2
Keswick Pl DRON S18 ....170 B2
Keswick Wk
  BSLYN/ROY S71 ....33 H1
Keswick Wy DIN S25 ....148 D2
Kettlebridge Rd
  DARN/MH S9 ....127 G4
Ketton Av SHEFS S8 ....153 E2
Ketton Wk DOD/DAR S75 ....2 A1
Kevin Gv MALT S66 ....109 H4
Kew Ct MEX/SWTN S64 ....86 A2
Kew Crs HACK/IN S12 ....154 B3
Key Av HOY S74 ....62 A2
Key Hill La CUD/GR S72 ....17 H1
Keyworth Pl
  HAN/WDH S13 ....143 E4
Keyworth Rd ST/HB/BR S6...114 A3
Khartoum Rd ECC S11 ....139 F2
Kibworth Cl CHNE S41 ....193 E5
Kidsley Cl CHSW S40 ....186 A4
Kieran Cl DIN S25 ....134 A3
Kier Hardie Wy
  NROS/TKH DN11 ....91 G3
Kilburn Rd DRON S18 ....170 A2
Kildale Gdns MOS S20 ....166 D1
Kildonan Gv HACK/IN S12....155 G2
Kilham La ARMTH DN3 ....59 H4
Killamarsh La ECK/KIL S21...169 E2
Kilner Wy ST/HB/BR S6 ....114 B1
Kilnhurst Rd RAW S62 ....83 G5
  RHAM/THRY S65 ....87 E4
Kiln Rd KIMB S61 ....104 D1
Kilton Hl OWL S3 ....126 B1
Kilton Pl OWL S3 ....126 B1
Kilvington Av
  HAN/WDH S13 * 141 H3
Kilvington Crs
  HAN/WDH S13 ....141 H3
Kilvington Rd
  HAN/WDH S13 ....141 H3
Kimberley Av DARN/MH S9...127 F1
Kimberworth Park Rd
  KIMB S61 ....96 C5
Kimberworth Rd KIMB S61...104 D2
Kinder Gdns SHEFN S5 ....102 B4
Kinder Rd STV/CWN S43 .....189 F3
King Av MALT S66 ....111 F4
  NROS/TKH DN11 ....91 E2
King Ecgbert Rd
  TOT/DORE S17 ....161 E2
King Edward Rd
  DONS/BSCR DN4 ....55 H5
King Edwards
  Gdns BSLYN/ROY S71 ....20 D1
King Edward St
  BSLYN/ROY S71 ....20 D1
Kingfield Rd ECC S11 ....139 F3
Kingfisher Cl WHHL DN2 ....41 F3

Kingfisher Ct BSVR S44 ....196 C1
  NROS/TKH DN11 ....91 G2
Kingfisher Dr WMB/DAR S73...51 E4
Kingfisher Gv
  AU/AST/KP S26 ....144 C3
Kingfisher Ri KIMB S61 ....82 C5
Kingfisher Rd
  AWLS/ASK DN6 ....25 F1
King Georges Cl
  NROS/TKH DN11 ....90 D3
King George Sq ARMTH DN3...29 F3
King George Ter BSLY S70 *....32 B2
King George's Rd
  NROS/TKH DN11 ....90 D2
King James St
  ST/HB/BR S6 ....125 F1
Kings Ar DON DN1 * 6 C4
Kings Cl STV/CWN S43 ....185 F3
Kings Coppice
  TOT/DORE S17 ....160 D2
Kings Cft BSLY S70 ....48 C1
Kingscroft Cl
  TOT/DORE S17 ....151 E5
Kingsgate DON DN1 ....6 D4
Kingsgate Flats DON DN1 ....6 D4
Kingsley Av BTLY DN5 ....55 F5
  CHSW S40 ....192 B4
Kingsley Cl BSLYN/ROY S71...20 A1
Kingsley Crs ARMTH DN3 ....42 D4
Kingsley Dr
  RHAM/THRY S65 ....109 F1
Kingsley Park Av ABRD S7....151 H1
Kingsley Park Gv ABRD S7 ...151 H1
Kingsley Rd AWLS/ASK DN6....25 E2
Kingsmead Dr ARMTH DN3 ....59 F5
Kingsmede Av CHSW S40 .....191 H3
Kings Ms ECK/KIL S21 ....167 E5
Kings Rd WMB/DAR S73 ....54 D4
Kingstone Pl BSLY S70 ....31 F5
Kingstone Rd WHHL DN2 ....57 F1
Kingston St ATT S4 ....115 C5
King St AU/AST/KP S26 ....145 E2
  BSLY S70 ....3 H6
  CHPT/GREN S35 ....81 E5
  DEARNE S63 ....37 G5
  DON DN1 ....6 E2
  HOY S74 ....6 C5
  MEX/SWTN S64 ....66 B5
  SHEF S1 ....11 H2
  STV/CWN S43 ....180 D5
  STV/CWN S43 ....185 E3
King St North CHNE S41 ....187 G2
King St South CHSW S40 ......192 C5
Kingsway DEARNE S63 ....37 E2
Kings Wy RHAM S60 ....118 C3
Kingsway WMB/DAR S73 ....50 B5
Kingsway Gv NROS/TKH DN11...91 G4
Kingsway Gv DEARNE S63 .....37 E2
Kingswood Av DIN S25 ....134 C1
  MOS S20 ....156 A3
Kingswood Cl CHNE S41 ......186 D1
  MOS S20 ....155 H3
Kingswood Crs HOY S74 ....62 A1
Kingswood Cft MOS S20 * 156 A3
Kingswood Gv MOS S20 ....156 A3
Kingwell Crs BSLY S70 ....31 H4
Kingwell Cft BSLY S70 ....32 A5
Kingwell Rd BSLY S70 ....32 A5
King's Crs CONI DN12 ....70 B5
King's Rd CUD/GR S72 ....17 E5
  DON DN1 ....7 F2
  MEX/SWTN S64 ....67 F3
King's St CUD/GR S72 ....23 E1
Kinharvie Rd SHEFN S5 ....114 D1
Kinnaird Av SHEFN S5 ....102 C4
Kinnaird Pl SHEFN S5 ....102 C4
Kinnaird Rd SHEFN S5 ....102 C4
Kinsey Rd CHPT/GREN S35 .....80 A4
Kipling Av DONS/BSCR DN4....71 F2
Kipling Cl DRON S18 ....171 G4
Kipling Rd CHNE S41 ....187 F1
Kirby Cl CHNE S41 ....193 E5
Kirby Rw KIMB S61 * 95 E1
Kirby St MEX/SWTN S64 ....67 E5
Kirk Balk HOY S74 ....61 H2
Kirkby Av BSLYN/ROY S71 ......15 E4
  BTLY DN5 ....39 G4
  HACK/IN S12 ....154 C1
Kirkby Dr HACK/IN S12 ....154 C1
Kirkby Rd HACK/IN S12 ....154 C1
Kirkby Vw HACK/IN S12 ....154 C2
Kirkcroft Av ECK/KIL S21 .....168 B1
  KIMB S61 ....95 C1
Kirkcroft Cl KIMB S61 ....95 F1
Kirkcroft Dr ECK/KIL S21 ......168 A2
Kirkcroft La ECK/KIL S21 ......168 B2
Kirk Cross Crs
  BSLYN/ROY S71 ....15 C2
Kirkdale Cl CHSW S40 ....192 D4
Kirkdale Crs HAN/WDH S13...143 F1
Kirkdale Dr HAN/WDH S13 ...143 F1
Kirkfield Wy BSLYN/ROY S71...15 G2
Kirkhall Cl ARMTH DN3 ....43 E5
Kirklands Cl BSLYN/ROY S71...20 C4
Kirklands Dr BSLYN/ROY S71...15 H5
Kirkland Gdns
  BSLYN/ROY S71 ....20 A2
Kirklands Dr RAW S62 ....85 E5
Kirkstall Cl BTLY DN5 ....38 D5
  DIN S25 ....148 B5
  RHAM S60 ....118 A3

Kirkstall Rd BSLYN/ROY S71...14 C5
  ECC S11 ....139 E2
Kirkstead Abbey Ms
  KIMB S61 ....95 G4
Kirkstead Gdns
  HAN/WDH S13 ....144 A3
Kirkstead Rd KIMB S61 ....103 G2
Kirkstone Cl BTLY DN5 ....39 G2
Kirkstone Rd CHNE S41 ....186 C1
  ST/HB/BR S6 ....114 A5
Kirk St ATT S4 ....126 C1
  DONS/BSCR DN4 ....55 H3
Kirk Wy BSLYN/ROY S71 ....20 D4
Kirkwood Cl STKB/PEN S36.....45 F4
Kirton Rd ATT S4 ....115 C5
Kitchen Wood La
  DRON S18 ....170 A3
Kitchin Rd WMB/DAR S73 ....49 H2
Kitson Dr BSLYN/ROY S71 ......15 G3
Kiveton La AU/AST/KP S26 ...147 F4
Knab Cl ABRD S7 ....139 E5
Knab Cft ABRD S7 ....139 E5
Knab Ri ABRD S7 ....139 E5
Knab Rd ABRD S7 ....139 E5
Knapton Av RAW S62 ....85 E5
Knaresboro Rd ABRD S7 ......152 A2
Knaresborough Cl
  AU/AST/KP S26 ....145 E3
Knaresborough Rd
  CONI DN12 ....88 B2
Knaves Mire Av DIN S25 ......134 A3
Knavesmire Gdns
  DONS/BSCR DN4 ....57 H3
Knifesmithgate CHSW S40 ......5 F4
Knighton Cl CHNE S41 ....192 D5
Knollbeck Av WMB/DAR S73...51 E5
Knoll Beck Cl DEARNE S63 .....53 E1
Knoll Beck Crs
  WMB/DAR S73 ....51 E5
Knollbeck La WMB/DAR S73....51 E5
Knoll Cl STKB/PEN S36 ....77 E2
Knoll Cottages
  STKB/PEN S36 * 60 C3
Knoll Drift DOD/DAR S75 * 60 B3
The Knoll CHSW S40 ....190 D2
Knoll St DRON S18 ....163 H5
Knowle Cl ST/HB/BR S6 ....123 C1
Knowle Cft TOT/DORE S17 ...160 C1
Knowle Gn TOT/DORE S17 ....160 C1
Knowle La ECC S11 ....138 B5
Knowle Rd BSLY S70 ....32 B4
  SHEFN S5 ....102 B3
Knowles Av STKB/PEN S36 .....77 F3
Knowles St STKB/PEN S36 ......45 F4
Knowle Top MOS S20 ....167 E1
Knowsley St BSLY S70 ....2 C5
Knutton Crs SHEFN S5 ....101 G3
Knutton Ri SHEFN S5 ....101 G2
Knutton Rd SHEFN S5 ....101 G3
Kyle Cl ECK/KIL S21 ....175 H2
  SHEFN S5 ....101 G3
Kyle Crs SHEFN S5 ....101 G3
Kynance Crs RHAM S60 ....118 B5

L

Laburnam Gv BSLY S70 ....48 B1
Laburnum Av MALT S66 ....108 B3
Laburnum Cl BSVR S44 ....197 E3
  CHPT/GREN S35 ....94 A2
  DIN S25 ....148 A5
Laburnum Dr ARMTH DN3 ......43 E3
Laburnum Gv CONI DN12 ....88 C2
  ECK/KIL S21 ....168 A3
  STKB/PEN S36 ....76 D3
Laburnum Pde MALT S66 .....110 B3
Laburnum Rd BTLY DN5 ....26 C5
Laburnum Rd
  DONS/BSCR DN4 ....71 F2
  MALT S66 ....110 B3
  MEX/SWTN S64 ....66 B4
Laburnum St STV/CWN S43...181 F5
Laceby Cl MALT S66 ....108 D2
Laceby Ct BSLY S70 ....31 E3
Ladies Spring Gv
  TOT/DORE S17 * 161 G1
Ladock Cl BSLYN/ROY S71 ......20 B4
Lady Bank Dr
  DONS/BSCR DN4 ....56 C4
Ladybank Rd MOS S20 ....166 D2
Ladybank Vw ECK/KIL S21 ....166 D4
Ladybower La
  STV/CWN S43 ....189 H1
Ladycroft DEARNE S63 ....53 E3
Lady Cft DEARNE S63 ....65 E2
Lady Croft La
  WMB/DAR S73 ....63 E1
Ladycroft Rd ARMTH DN3 ....58 D1
Lady Ida's Dr ECK/KIL S21 ....166 A4
Ladymead BSLYN/ROY S71 .....20 B3
Lady Oak Rd
  RHAM/THRY S65 ....107 E1
Ladyroyd Cft CUD/GR S72 ......21 H1
Ladysmith Av ABRD S7 ....139 F4
Ladywood Dr CHNE S41 ....186 C2
Ladywood Rd CUD/GR S72 .....23 F1
Lady's Br OWL S3 ....11 H1
Laird Av ST/HB/BR S6 ....113 C3
Laird Dr ST/HB/BR S6 ....113 C3
Laird Rd ST/HB/BR S6 ....113 C3
Lairds Wy STKB/PEN S36 ....45 E3

Laithe Cft DOD/DAR S75 ....30 B3
Laithes Cl BSLYN/ROY S71 ......15 F5
Laithes Crs BSLYN/ROY S71 ....14 D5
Laithes La BSLYN/ROY S71 .....14 D5
Lakeen Rd WHHL DN2 ....7 K1
Lakeland Cl CUD/GR S72 ....21 H2
Lakeland Dr DIN S25 ....148 C2
Lake Lands RCH S42 ....195 F5
Lake Rd AWLS/ASK DN6 ....25 G4
Lakeside RCH S42 ....195 F5
Lakeside Bvd
  DONS/BSCR DN4 ....73 E1
Lakeside Cl CHNE S41 ....180 A2
  MALT S66 ....108 C1
Lakeside Ct DEARNE S63 ....63 H1
Lake View Av CHSW S40 ....191 G3
Lambcote Wy MALT S66 ....111 F2
Lambcroft Vw
  HAN/WDH S13 ....143 G4
Lamb Dr SHEFN S5 ....114 B1
Lambecroft BSLYN/ROY S71 ...15 G3
Lambert Fold DOD/DAR S75 ....30 C3
Lambert Rd BSLY S70 ....32 C3
Lamberts La
  RHAM/THRY S65 ....99 G3
Lambert St OWL S3 ....11 F2
Lambert Wk BSLY S70 ....32 C3
  DEARNE S63 ....51 G5
Lambeth Rd
  DONS/BSCR DN4 ....71 H1
Lamb Hill Cl HAN/WDH S13...142 B3
Lamb La BSLYN/ROY S71 ....20 C2
  WRKN S81 ....135 G2
Lambra Rd BSLYN/ROY S71 ......3 H5
Lambrell Av
  AU/AST/KP S26 ....159 G3
Lambrell Gn
  AU/AST/KP S26 ....159 G3
Lamb Rd SHEFN S5 ....114 B1
Lanark Dr MEX/SWTN S64 ......67 G1
Lanark Gdns WHHL DN2 ....41 G5
Lancar Ct BSLYN/ROY S71 ......20 A3
Lancaster Av ARMTH DN3 ....29 F3
  WHHL DN2 ....42 A5
Lancaster Ga BSLY S70 ....3 F4
Lancaster Rd CHNE S41 ....187 E1
  STKB/PEN S36 ....76 D2
Lancaster St BSLY S70 ....2 C5
  DEARNE S63 ....37 G1
  OWL S3 ....125 H2
Lancelot Cl CHSW S40 ....191 H4
Lancing Cl SHEFP/MNR S2 ....140 A2
Landsdowne Av CHNE S41 ....187 E2
Landseer Cl DRON S18 ....170 C3
  GLV S14 ....153 H3
Landseer Ct MALT S66 ....108 B3
Landseer Dr GLV S14 ....153 H3
Landseer Pl GLV S14 ....154 A3
Lane Cl CHPT/GREN S35 ....80 D4
Lane End RHAM S60 ....119 G3
Lane End Vw RHAM S60 ....119 G3
Laneham Cl
  DONS/BSCR DN4 ....73 H2
Lane Head Av RAW S62 * 85 G5
Lane Head Rd
  TOT/DORE S17 ....160 C4
Laneside Cl DONS/BSCR DN4...55 G4
The Lanes RHAM/THRY S65...106 D2
The Lane ECK/KIL S21 ....176 B2
Lang Av BSLYN/ROY S71 ....21 E5
Lang Crs BSLYN/ROY S71 ....21 E5
Langdale Dr BTLY DN5 ....39 F2
  DIN S25 ....165 G5
Langdale Rd
  BSLYN/ROY S71 ....3 H5
  DOD/DAR S75 ....18 A2
Langdale Sq STV/CWN S43 ...188 B1
Langdale Wy DIN S25 ....148 B5
Langdon Rd KIMB S61 ....104 C1
Langdon St ECC S11 ....139 H2
Langdon Wk BSLY S70 * 2 D3
Langer Field Av CHSW S40 ...192 C5
Langer La RCH S42 ....195 E3
Langer St DONS/BSCR DN4 .....55 E3
Langford Cl DOD/DAR S75 ......30 C3
Langford Cft CHSW S40 ....5 G7
Langhurst Rd CHSW S40 ....186 A4
Langley Cl CHSW S40 ....186 A4
Langley St
  RHAM/THRY S65 ....107 F2
Langsett Av ST/HB/BR S6 .....113 G2
Langsett Ct ST/HB/BR S6 .....114 B5
Langsett Ct
  DONS/BSCR DN4 ....57 F5
Langsett Crs ST/HB/BR S6 ....114 B5
Langsett Gv ST/HB/BR S6 .....125 F1
Langsett Ri ST/HB/BR S6 ......125 F1
Langsett Rd
  BSLYN/ROY S71 ....20 B5
  ST/HB/BR S6 ....114 B5
Langsett Rd South
  CHPT/GREN S35 ....100 A3
Langthwaite La BTLY DN5 ....35 H5
Langthwaite Rd BTLY DN5 ......39 H1
Langton Gdns ARMTH DN3 .....58 C5
Langtree Av CHNE S41 ....179 G5
Langwith Rd BSVR S44 ....196 B5
Lansbury Av
  CHPT/GREN S35 ....93 H1
  MALT S66 ....111 F3
  NROS/TKH DN11 ....91 G2
  STV/CWN S43 ....182 D2
Lansbury Ct ECK/KIL S21 ......166 D5

Lansbury Pl RAW S62 ....86 A5
Lansbury Rd ECK/KIL S21 .....166 D5
Lansdowne Ct DEARNE S63 ....37 E3
Lansdowne Crs
  MEX/SWTN S64 ....86 B1
Lansdowne Rd
  STV/CWN S43 ....188 B2
  WHHL DN2 ....41 G5
Lanyon Wy BSLYN/ROY S71 ....20 B4
Lapwater Rd KIMB S61 ....96 D3
Lapwing V KIMB S61 ....82 C5
Larch Av ECK/KIL S21 ....168 A3
  EPW DN9 ....75 H5
  MALT S66 ....108 C4
Larch Cl WMB/DAR S73 ....35 E5
Larch Dr ARMTH DN3 ....42 D4
The Larches
  MEX/SWTN S64 ....86 A1
Larchfield Pl
  BSLYN/ROY S71 ....20 D2
Larchfield Rd
  DONS/BSCR DN4 ....71 F1
Larch Gv AU/AST/KP S26 ......145 H2
  CHPT/GREN S35 ....94 A3
  CONI DN12 ....88 C3
Larch Hl DARN/MH S9 ....128 C4
Larch Ms RHAM/THRY S65....106 D1
Larch Pl BSLY S70 ....32 C4
Larch Rd ECK/KIL S21 ....174 B1
  MALT S66 ....110 B2
Larch Wy CHSW S40 ....186 D4
Larkhill Cl RAW S62 ....98 C5
Larkspur Cl ARMTH DN3 ....82 B1
Larwood Gv CONI DN12 ....70 C5
Latchmoor Cl DOD/DAR S75...19 F3
Latham Sq ARMTH DN3 ....29 F2
  ECC S11 ....138 C3
Lathe Rd RHAM S60 ....120 A2
Lathkill Av STV/CWN S43 ......189 F3
Lathkill Cl HAN/WDH S13 ......142 A3
Lathkill Rd HAN/WDH S13 .....142 A3
Latin Gdns BTLY DN5 ....38 C3
Lauder Rd BTLY DN5 ....39 G4
Lauder St ATT S4 ....115 H3
Laudsdale Cl
  RHAM/THRY S65 ....107 F2
Laudsdale Rd
  RHAM/THRY S65 ....107 F1
Laughton Common Rd
  MALT S66 ....133 G3
Laughton Mdw DIN S25 ....134 A2
Laughton Rd DARN/MH S9 ....116 D2
  DIN S25 ....134 D5
  DONS/BSCR DN4 ....55 H3
  MALT S66 ....133 F1
Launce Rd SHEFN S5 ....101 H5
Laurel Av BSLY S70 ....32 D3
  BTLY DN5 ....39 F5
  MALT S66 ....108 C4
Laurel Cl STV/CWN S43 ....181 E5
Laurel Dr ECK/KIL S21 ....168 A4
Laurel Garth Cl CHNE S41 .....179 H3
Laurel Rd ARMTH DN3 ....42 D3
Laurel St DONS/BSCR DN4 .....71 C1
Laurence Cl CHNE S41 ....179 G4
Lavender Cl CONI DN12 ....89 F2
Lavender Ct BSLY S70 ....32 C3
Laverack St HAN/WDH S13...142 D1
Laverdene Av
  TOT/DORE S17 ....161 E3
Laverdene Cl
  TOT/DORE S17 ....161 E4
Laverdene Dr
  TOT/DORE S17 ....161 E4
Laverdene Rd
  TOT/DORE S17 ....161 E4
Laverdene Wy
  TOT/DORE S17 ....161 E4
Laverock Wy SHEFN S5 ....102 D4
Lavinia Rd CHPT/GREN S35 ...101 F2
Lawn Av AWLS/ASK DN6 ....24 D1
  DON DN1 ....7 F5
Lawn Garth BTLY DN5 ....39 F3
Lawn Rd DON DN1 ....7 F5
The Lawns ECC S11 ....138 D4
The Lawn DRON S18 ....171 F1
Lawnswood Dr DEARNE S63 ...53 E3
Lawrence Cl DOD/DAR S75 .....18 A4
  MALT S66 ....108 B4
Lawrence Dr
  MEX/SWTN S64 ....86 A1
Lawson Rd FUL S10 ....124 D5
Lawton La RHAM S60 ....119 E1
Laxey Rd ST/HB/BR S6 ....124 A2
Laxfield Cl CHSW S40 ....191 G4
Laxton Cl MALT S66 ....110 B2
Laxton Rd BSLYN/ROY S71 ......14 C1
Laycock Av AU/AST/KP S26...145 G3
Layden Dr BTLY DN5 ....38 C2
Layden Wy DON DN1 ....7 F5
Laytham Dr DON S18 ....170 A2
Leabrook Rd DRON S18 ....170 A2
Leach La MEX/SWTN S64 ....67 F4
Leadbeater Dr
  HACK/IN S12 ....141 G5
Leadbeater Rd
  HACK/IN S12 ....141 F5
Leader Rd ST/HB/BR S6 ....113 H3
Leadhill Rd CHSW S40 ....186 A5
Leadley St DEARNE S63 ....37 G5

Leadmill Rd *SHEFP/MNR* S2 ....11 H6
Leadmill St *SHEF* S1............11 H6
Leaf Cl *MALT* S66................111 F2
Leaholme *BSVR* S44 * 196 A2
Leake Rd *ST/HB/BR* S6........114 A2
Leamington Gdns
.........*WHHL* DN2................41 G5
Leamington St *FUL* S10........125 E5
Leander Ct *STV/CWN* S43 *..182 B4
Lea Rd *BSLYN/ROY* S71........15 F5
.........*DRON* S18................171 E2
Lease Gate Rd *RHAM* S60 ....119 H2
The Leas *BTLY* DN5 ....39 F5
The Lea *MEX/SWTN* S64........85 H2
.........*MOS* S20................156 D3
Leaton Cl *ST/HB/BR* S6........112 D3
Leavy Greave *FUL* S10..........10 C4
Leavygreave Rd *OWL* S3........10 C3
Leawood Pl *ST/HB/BR* S6......123 H1
Ledbury Rd *BSLYN/ROY* S71...19 H1
Ledsham Ct *HOY* S74..............62 D1
Ledsham Rd *RHAM* S60........106 C5
Ledstone Rd *SHEFS* S36........152 C1
Lee Av *STKB/PEN* S36 ....77 F2
Leebrook Av *MOS* S20..........156 B4
Leebrook Cl *MOS* S20..........156 B4
Leebrook Dr *MOS* S20..........156 B4
Lee Brook La *RAW* S62..........83 G1
Lee Cft *MALT* S66................111 G4
.........*SHEF* S1....................9 F2
Leedham Cl *SHEFS* S5..........103 F5
Leedham Rd
.........*RHAM/THRY* S65........107 E5
.........*SHEFS* S5................103 F5
Leeds Av *DIN* S25................148 C1
Leeds Rd *DARN/MH* S9........127 G1
Lee House La *STKB/PEN* S36..76 B3
Lee La *BSLYN/ROY* S71..........14 C2
Lee Rd *CHNE* S41................193 G2
.........*ST/HB/BR* S6............112 D3
Lees Av *DIN* S25................148 C1
Lees Hall Av *SHEFS* S8........153 E1
Lees Hall Pl *SHEFS* S8........140 B5
Lees Hall Rd *SHEFS* S8........140 B5
Lees House Ct *SHEFS* S8 *....153 E1
Leeswood Cl *CHNE* S41........186 D1
Leewood Cl *DEARNE* S63......63 H2
Leger Ct *WHHL* DN2 * 7 G5
Leger Wy *WHHL* DN2 ....57 E2
Legion Dr *AU/AST/KP* S26....145 G3
Leicester Av *WHHL* DN2........57 E2
Leicester Rd *DIN* S25..........135 E4
Leicester Wk *OWL* S3............10 C2
Leigh St *DARN/MH* S9..........116 C5
Leighton Dr *BSLYN/ROY* S71...3 G1
Leighton Dr *GLV* S14............154 B2
Leighton Pl *GLV* S14............154 B2
Leighton Rd *GLV* S14............154 B2
Leighton Vw *GLV* S14............141 E5
Leinster Av *WHHL* DN2..........41 E5
Lemont Rd *TOT/DORE* S17....161 E4
Lennox Rd *ST/HB/BR* S6........113 H5
.........*WHHL* DN2..................41 E5
Lenton St *SHEFP/MNR* S2 ....11 H7
Leonard Ct *SHEFP/MNR* S2 ..141 H3
Leopold Av *DIN* S25............134 D5
Leopold St *BSLY* S70 ....2 D6
.........*DIN* S25................134 D4
.........*SHEF* S1....................11 F3
Leppings La *ST/HB/BR* S6....114 A2
Lepton Gdns *BSLY* S70..........32 D4
Lescar La *ECC* S11................139 E2
Lesley Rd *DEARNE* S63........37 G5
Leslie Av *CONI* DN12 ....88 C1
.........*MALT* S66................110 B4
Leslie Rd *BSLY* S70................32 D5
.........*ST/HB/BR* S6............115 G3
Lesmond Crs *CUD/GR* S72......36 A4
Lestermoor Av
.........*AU/AST/KP* S26........159 G3
Letard Dr *RHAM* S60............118 C3
Letsby Av *DARN/MH* S9........128 C1
Levens Wy *CHNE* S41............187 E1
Leverick Dr *RAW* S62............86 A4
Leverton Dr *ECC* S11............139 H1
Leverton Gdns *ECC* S11 *......139 H1
Leverton Wy
.........*RHAM/THRY* S65........99 G5
Leveson St *ATT* S4................126 D2
Levet Rd *DONS/BSCR* DN4....58 B4
Lewdendale *BSLY* S70............48 A1
Lewden Garth *BSLY* S70 *......48 D1
Lewes Rd *CONI* DN12............88 D2
Lewis Rd *BSLYN/ROY* S71......14 D1
.........*HAN/WDH* S13..........142 A3
Lewyns Dr *DONS/BSCR* DN4..58 B4
Leybourne Rd *KIMB* S61........96 C5
Leyburn Cl *CHSW* S40..........186 D4
.........*DONS/BSCR* DN4........74 B1
Leyburn Dr *AU/AST/KP* S26..145 E2
Leyburn Gv
.........*CHPT/GREN* S35..........81 E5
Leyburn Rd *ABRD* S7............139 H4
Ley End *BSLY* S70..................47 H1
Leyfield Ct *ARMTH* DN3..........43 E5
Leyfield Pl *WMB/DAR* S73......50 D1
Leyfield Rd *TOT/DORE* S17..160 D5
The Leylands *DOD/DAR* S75...18 C3
Leys Cl *DONS/BSCR* DN4........74 B2
Leys La *DIN* S25................135 F4
Liberty Cl *ST/HB/BR* S6........124 A2
Liberty Dr *ST/HB/BR* S6........124 A2

Liberty Hl *ST/HB/BR* S6........124 A2
Liberty Pl *ST/HB/BR* S6........124 A2
Liberty Rd *ST/HB/BR* S6........124 A2
Library Cl *KIMB* S61..............78 C2
Lichen Cl *ARMTH* DN3............42 B1
Lichfield Rd *CHSW* S40........191 G4
.........*WHHL* DN2..................40 D4
Lichfield St *WHHL* DN2........118 D3
Lichford Rd
.........*SHEFP/MNR* S2........140 C4
Lidgate La *CUD/GR* S72........16 D1
Lidget Cl *AU/AST/KP* S26....144 D4
.........*DONS/BSCR* DN4........74 A1
Lidget La *DEARNE* S63............37 H3
.........*DOD/DAR* S75..............60 B3
.........*RHAM/THRY* S65........109 E3
Lidget Gra *HOY* S74..............81 C1
Lidgett La *DIN* S25..............134 D5
Lidgett Wy *BSLYN/ROY* S71...12 C5
Lidsters La *DIN* S25............148 C4
Liffey Av *WHHL* DN2..............41 E5
Lifford Pl *HOY* S74................62 D3
Lifford Rd *WHHL* DN2............40 D5
Lifford St *DARN/MH* S9........117 G1
Lilac Av *STKB/PEN* S36............76 D3
Lilac Cl *DIN* S25................148 B4
Lilac Crs *HOY* S74................62 A1
Lilac Farm Cl *MALT* S66......108 B5
Lilac Gv *BSVR* S44................197 F3
.........*CONI* DN12................88 C2
.........*DONS/BSCR* DN4........58 B5
.........*MALT* S66................108 C4
.........*SHEFS* S5................110 B3
Lilac Rd *ARMTH* DN3..............43 E5
.........*MOS* S20................157 F2
.........*SHEFN* S5................116 A1
Lilac St *STV/CWN* S43..........181 E5
Lilian St *RHAM* S60................9 H6
Lilian St South *RHAM* S60......9 H6
Lilford Rd *BTLY* DN5..............59 G5
Lilly Hall Cl *MALT* S66..........110 B2
Lilly Hall Rd *MALT* S66........110 C3
Lillymede Cl *CHSW* S40........195 F1
Limb La *TOT/DORE* S17........150 D5
Limbreck Ct *BTLY* DN5..........39 G1
Limbrick Cl *ST/HB/BR* S6......113 H5
Limbrick Rd *ST/HB/BR* S6....114 A5
Lime Ct *BTLY* DN5..................54 D4
Limecroft Vw *ECK* S42..........199 F2
Limedale Vw *ARMTH* DN3......29 C1
Limegrove *RHAM* S60..........106 C5
Lime Gv *BSLYN/ROY* S71........15 G3
.........*CHPT/GREN* S35..........94 A2
.........*MALT* S66................111 F3
.........*MEX/SWTN* S64............86 B2
.........*STKB/PEN* S36............76 C3
Limekiln Fields Rd
.........*BSVR* S44................196 D2
Limekilns *DIN* S25..............148 B2
Limekiln Wy *STV/CWN* S43..177 F5
Limelands Rd *DIN* S25..........134 C5
Lime Rd *ECK/KIL* S21..........174 B2
Limes Av *DOD/DAR* S75........14 A2
.........*DOD/DAR* S75............14 A2
Limes Cl *DOD/DAR* S75..........14 A2
Limestone Cottage La
.........*ST/HB/BR* S6............100 D5
Lime St *MOS* S20................157 F1
.........*ST/HB/BR* S6............125 G1
Limesway *DOD/DAR* S75........18 D4
.........*MALT* S66................110 D3
Lime Tree Av *ECK/KIL* S21....168 A3
.........*ARMTH* DN3................42 D3
Limetree Av
.........*AU/AST/KP* S26........159 G2
Lime Tree Rd
.........*DONS/BSCR* DN4..........7 C6
Limetree Av *MALT* S66........133 F1
Limetree Cl *STV/CWN* S43..188 D4
Lime Tree Ct
.........*DONS/BSCR* DN4..........7 H7
Lime Tree Crs
.........*NROS/TKH* DN11..........91 G3
.........*RAW* S62....................85 H5
Limpool Cl *DONS/BSCR* DN4..74 B2
Limpsfield Rd
.........*DARN/MH* S9............116 C3
Linacre Rd *CHSW* S40..........186 B5
.........*RCH* S42................186 A5
Linaker Rd *ST/HB/BR* S6......124 D2
Linburn Cl *BSLYN/ROY* S71...12 A5
Linburn Rd *SHEFS* S8..........153 H1
Linby Rd *BSLYN/ROY* S71......14 D4
Lincoln Gdns *DEARNE* S63....37 F5
Lincoln Rd *WHHL* DN2............40 D4
Lincolnshire Wy
.........*ARMTH* DN3................43 F4
Lincoln St *CHSW* S40..........192 C4
.........*DARN/MH* S9............116 D2
.........*MALT* S66................111 E4
.........*NROS/TKH* DN11..........91 G3
.........*RHAM* S60..................9 H7
Lincroft Dr *RAW* S62..............98 B3
Lindale Cl *DIN* S25..............134 D5
Lindale Gdns *DEARNE* S63....53 H1
Lindale Rd *CHNE* S41..........186 D1
The Lindales *DOD/DAR* S75....2 A3
Linden Av *CHSW* S40............191 F3
.........*DRON* S18................163 F5
.........*MALT* S66................108 C4
.........*SHEFS* S8................152 C1

Linden Ct *CHPT/GREN* S35....94 B5
Linden Crs *STKB/PEN* S36......76 D2
Linden Gv *MALT* S66............110 B3
Linden Park Gv *CHSW* S40......4 B3
Linden Rd *CHPT/GREN* S35....94 B5
.........*DEARNE* S63................64 B2
Linden Wk *BTLY* DN5..............26 C3
Lindholme Dr
.........*NROS/TKH* DN11..........91 H1
Lindholme Gdns *MOS* S20....156 C3
Lindhurst Rd
.........*BSLYN/ROY* S71..........14 C4
Lindisfarne Ct *CHSW* S40....191 G3
Lindisfarne Rd *DRON* S18....171 F5
Lindley Crs *DEARNE* S63........37 F5
Lindley Rd *SHEFN* S5..........115 H2
Lindley St *RHAM/THRY* S65......9 G2
Lindley's Cft
.........*AU/AST/KP* S26........147 F5
Lindrick Av *MEX/SWTN* S64..86 C1
Lindrick Cl *CUD/GR* S72........17 E3
.........*DONS/BSCR* DN4........73 G3
Lindrick Dr *ARMTH* DN3........42 D5
Lindrick Gdns *CHSW* S40....191 G4
Lindrick Wy *STV/CWN* S43..184 B1
Lindsay Av *SHEFN* S5..........102 A4
Lindsay Cl *SHEFN* S5..........102 A4
Lindsay Crs *SHEFN* S5........102 A4
Lindsay Dr *SHEFN* S5..........102 A4
Lindsay Pl *AU/AST/KP* S26..145 F5
Lindsay Rd *SHEFN* S5..........102 B4
Lindsey Cl *DONS/BSCR* DN4..73 H3
Lindum Dr *MALT* S66............108 C5
Lindum Ter
.........*RHAM/THRY* S65 *........9 H4
Lingamore Leys
.........*DEARNE* S63................37 F1
Lingard Ct *DOD/DAR* S75........2 D2
Lingard St *DOD/DAR* S75........2 D1
Lingfield Cl *MALT* S66..........109 E5
Lingfield Dr *BTLY* DN5............38 D5
Ling Field Rd *BTLY* DN5..........24 A2
Lingfoot Av *SHEFS* S8..........163 F2
Lingfoot Cl *SHEFS* S8..........163 F2
Lingfoot Crs *SHEFS* S8........163 F2
Lingfoot Dr *SHEFS* S8..........163 F2
Lingfoot Pl *SHEFS* S8..........163 F2
Lingmoor Cl
.........*DONS/BSCR* DN4........71 E2
Lingodell Cl *DIN* S25............134 C1
Ling Rd *CHSW* S40..............191 H4
Lings La *MALT* S66..............108 C5
The Lings *ARMTH* DN3............43 F5
.........*MALT* S66................108 D5
Lingthwaite *DOD/DAR* S75....30 C3
Link Rw *SHEFP/MNR* S2......126 C3
Links Rd *DRON* S18............171 F3
Linkswood Av *WHHL* DN2......41 G3
Linkswood Rd
.........*RHAM/THRY* S65..........99 F5
The Link *DOD/DAR* S75..........30 C4
Linkway *WHHL* DN2................41 H4
Linley La *HACK/IN* S12..........142 B5
Linnet Mt *KIMB* S61................95 F1
Linscott Cl *CHNE* S41..........186 D2
Linscott Rd *SHEFS* S8..........152 C3
Linthwaite La *RAW* S62..........63 E5
Linton Cl *BSLY* S70................30 D2
Linton Rd *CHSW* S40............191 G4
Lipp Av *ECK/KIL* S21............168 A1
Liskeard Pl *AWLS/ASK* DN6...25 E2
Lisle Rd *RHAM* S60..............106 C5
Lismore Rd *MALT* S66..........140 B5
Lister Av *DONS/BSCR* DN4......55 H5
.........*HACK/IN* S12............154 D1
.........*RHAM* S60................120 C3
Lister Cl *CHNE* S41..............154 D1
.........*HACK/IN* S12............154 D1
Lister Ct *WHHL* DN2..............41 E5
Lister Crs *HACK/IN* S12........154 D1
Lister Dr *HACK/IN* S12..........154 D2
Lister La *OWL* S3................125 H2
Lister Pl *HACK/IN* S12..........154 D2
Lister Rd *ST/HB/BR* S6........125 E1
Lister St *RHAM/THRY* S65........9 G5
Lister Wy *HACK/IN* S12........154 D1
Little Brind Rd *CHNE* S41....186 B2
Little Common La *ECC* S11....151 F2
.........*KIMB* S61..................80 A3
Little Leeds *HOY* S74............62 A2
Little London Pl *SHEFS* S8....139 H4
Little London Rd *SHEFS* S8..139 G5
Little Matlock Gdns
.........*ST/HB/BR* S6............123 H1
Little Matlock Wy
.........*ST/HB/BR* S6............123 H1
Littlemoor *CHNE* S41..........186 D2
.........*ECK/KIL* S21............167 E5
Littlemoor Av
.........*AU/AST/KP* S26........159 G3
Littlemoor Crs *CHNE* S41....186 D2

Littlemoor La
.........*DONS/BSCR* DN4..........55 H4
Littlemoor St
.........*DONS/BSCR* DN4..........55 H3
Little New Cl *DOD/DAR* S75...18 D4
Little Norton Av *SHEFS* S8..163 E1
Little Norton Dr *SHEFS* S8..153 E5
Little Norton La *SHEFS* S8..153 E5
Little Norton Wy *SHEFS* S8..163 E1
Little Westfields
.........*BSLYN/ROY* S71..........12 A5
Little Wood Dr
.........*HACK/IN* S12............154 B2
Little Wood Rd
.........*HACK/IN* S12............154 C2
Littleworth St
.........*DONS/BSCR* DN4..........55 H3
Littleworth Wy *MALT* S66....111 F2
Littleworth Cl
.........*NROS/TKH* DN11..........91 H2
Littleworth La
.........*BSLYN/ROY* S71..........20 D4
.........*NROS/TKH* DN11..........91 H2
Litton Cl *STV/CWN* S43........189 G1
Litton Wk *BSLY* S70................2 C3
Liverpool Av *WHHL* DN2........40 D4
Liverpool St *DARN/MH* S9....116 B4
Livesey St *ST/HB/BR* S6......114 B4
Livingstone Av *WHHL* DN2....40 C5
Livingstone Crs
.........*BSLYN/ROY* S71..........20 B2
Livingstone Rd
.........*CHPT/GREN* S35..........80 C5
Livingstone Ter *BSLY* S70 * 3 F6
Livington Rd
.........*DARN/MH* S9............127 G1
.........*RAW* S62....................98 B3
Lloyd St *ATT* S4................115 H3
Loakfield Dr *SHEFN* S5........101 H2
Lobelia Cl *DIN* S25............148 B3
Lobelia Crs *ARMTH* DN3........29 F4
Lobwood *BSLY* S70................32 A5
Lobwood La *BSLY* S70............32 B5
Lockeaflash Crs *BSLY* S70......32 D4
Locke Av *BSLY* S70................31 G3
Locke Rd *DOD/DAR* S75........30 C4
Lockesley Av *CONI* DN12......88 C1
Locke St *BSLY* S70................31 F3
Lock House Rd
.........*DARN/MH* S9............117 E3
Locking Dr *ARMTH* DN3........43 F5
Lock La *DARN/MH* S9..........117 G1
Lockoford La *CHNE* S41........187 G3
Locksley Av *ARMTH* DN3......29 F5
Locksley Dr *MALT* S66........132 D1
Locksley Gdns *BSLY* S70........60 D2
Lock St *ST/HB/BR* S6............125 G1
Lockton Cl *CHPT/GREN* S35...80 A3
Lockwood Av *DIN* S25..........148 B5
Lockwood Cl
.........*RHAM/THRY* S65........107 E3
Lockwood La *BSLY* S70..........31 H5
Lockwood Rd *DEARNE* S63....37 G4
.........*DON* DN1....................4 A5
.........*RHAM/THRY* S65........107 E2
Lodge Cl *STV/CWN* S43......189 F3
Lodge Dr *RAW* S62................81 H2
.........*RCH* S42................195 G3
Lodge Farm Cl *DIN* S25........148 B2
.........*RCH* S42................191 G5
Lodge Hill Dr
.........*AU/AST/KP* S26........159 F3
.........*CHPT/GREN* S35..........79 E5
Lodge La *AU/AST/KP* S26....145 F4
.........*DIN* S25..................135 F4
.........*FUL* S10..................123 E5
.........*KIMB* S61..................95 E1
Lodge Moor Rd *FUL* S10......136 C2
Lodge Pl *STV/CWN* S43......189 G3
Lodge Wy *RHAM* S60............118 C3
Loganberry Cl *MALT* S66......90 C3
Logan Rd *DARN/MH* S9........128 B3
Loicher La *CHPT/GREN* S35...94 D5
Lomas Cl *ST/HB/BR* S6........112 C5
Lombard Cl *DOD/DAR* S75....19 C4
Lombard Crs *WMB/DAR* S73...34 C5
Londale Cft *BSLYN/ROY* S71...99 G5
London Rd *SHEFP/MNR* S2..139 H1
London Rd South
.........*SHEFS* S8................140 A3
London St *STV/CWN* S43......180 B3
London Wy *KIMB* S61............95 E2
Long Acre *BSLYN/ROY* S71...15 F3
Longacre Cl *MOS* S20..........157 G5
Longacre Rd *MOS* S20..........157 G5
Longacre Vw *MOS* S20..........157 G5
Longcar La *BSLY* S70..............2 D7
Long Cswy *BSLYN/ROY* S71...20 C4
Longcliffe Cl *DOD/DAR* S72...17 E2
Longcliff Wk *CHSW* S40......186 C5
Long Cl *DONS/BSCR* DN4......170 D4
Longcroft Crs *DRON* S18......170 A1
Longedge Gv *RCH* S42........195 H4
Longedge La *RCH* S42..........195 H4
Longedge Ri *RCH* S42..........195 G3
Longfellow Dr
.........*RHAM/THRY* S65........106 D4
Longfellow Rd
.........*DONS/BSCR* DN4........72 A2
Longfield Cl *WMB/DAR* S73...49 H1

Long Field Dr *ARMTH* DN3....29 C5
Longfield Dr
.........*DONS/BSCR* DN4........73 H2
.........*RHAM/THRY* S65........108 C1
Longfield Gra *CHNE* S41......186 C5
Long Field Rd *ARMTH* DN3...29 G4
Longfield Rd *FUL* S10..........124 D2
Longfields Crs *HOY* S74........61 H2
Longfields Rd
.........*BSLYN/ROY* S71..........15 F4
Longford Cl
.........*TOT/DORE* S17 *........161 G3
Longford Crs
.........*TOT/DORE* S17..........161 G3
Longford Dr
.........*TOT/DORE* S17..........161 F4
Longford Rd
.........*TOT/DORE* S17..........161 F4
Longford Spinney
.........*TOT/DORE* S17..........161 F4
Long Henry Rw
.........*SHEFP/MNR* S2..........11 K4
Longlands *BSVR* S44............197 E2
Longlands Av
.........*AU/AST/KP* S26........159 G3
Long Lands La *BTLY* DN5......24 B3
Long La *BTLY* DN5................54 B1
.........*ECK/KIL* S21............168 C2
.........*ECK/KIL* S21............173 E2
.........*FUL* S10..................124 B3
.........*RHAM* S60................130 B1
.........*ST/HB/BR* S6............122 A2
.........*ST/HB/BR* S6............123 H2
.........*STKB/PEN* S36............45 F5
.........*STV/CWN* S43............173 E4
Longley Av West *SHEFN* S5..114 D2
Longley Cl *DOD/DAR* S75......18 A3
.........*SHEFN* S5................115 F2
Longley Crs *SHEFN* S5........115 F1
Longley Dr *SHEFN* S5..........115 F1
Longley Farm Vw
.........*SHEFN* S5................115 F2
Longley Hall Gv *SHEFN* S5..115 F2
Longley Hall Ri *SHEFN* S5..115 F2
Longley Hall Rd *SHEFN* S5..115 F2
Longley Hall Wy *SHEFN* S5..115 G1
Longley Ings *STKB/PEN* S36..45 F5
Longley La *SHEFN* S5..........115 F2
Longley Spring *HOY* S74........81 C1
Longley St *DOD/DAR* S75......18 A3
Long Line *ECC* S11..............150 B3
Longman Rd *BSLY* S70............3 F1
Longridge Rd
.........*BSLYN/ROY* S71..........20 D1
Long Rd *MALT* S66..............133 E5
Longshaw Cl *STV/CWN* S43..189 H2
Longside Wy *DOD/DAR* S75...18 C5
Longstone Crs
.........*HACK/IN* S12............155 F1
Longthwaite Cl *DIN* S25......134 C1
Longton Rd *ARMTH* DN3......29 G2
Longwood Cl *MALT* S66......108 B1
Lonsdale Av *BSLYN/ROY* S71..33 H2
.........*WHHL* DN2..................57 F2
Lonsdale Cl *DIN* S25............148 B2
Lonsdale Rd *ST/HB/BR* S6..114 A5
Loosemore Dr
.........*HACK/IN* S12............141 F5
Lopham Cl *OWL* S3..............126 B2
Lopham St *OWL* S3..............126 B2
Lordens Hl *DIN* S25............135 G4
Lord Roberts Rd *CHSW* S40..195 G1
Lords Cl *BSVR* S44..............196 D3
.........*CONI* DN12................70 C4
Lordsmill St *CHNE* S41..........5 H6
Lord St *BSLYN/ROY* S71........20 C5
.........*RHAM/THRY* S65........106 C2
Lorna Rd *MEX/SWTN* S64......67 E3
Lorne Cl *DRON* S18..............170 B1
Lorne Rd *DEARNE* S63..........36 D2
Loscoe Gv *DEARNE* S63........37 F5
Lothian Rd *WHHL* DN2..........41 G5
Louden Cl *KIMB* S61..............95 H4
Louden Rd *KIMB* S61............95 H4
Lounde Cl *BTLY* DN5..............54 C4
Loundes Rd *DRON* S18........172 A5
Loundes Wood Av
.........*CHNE* S41................186 C1
Lound Rd *DARN/MH* S9......128 B4
Lound Side *CHPT/GREN* S35..94 B1
Loundsley Green Rd
.........*CHSW* S40................186 B5
Louth Rd *ECC* S11..............138 D3
Love La *OWL* S3......................11 G1
Lovell St *ATT* S4................126 D2
Loversall Ct
.........*DONS/BSCR* DN4........71 H3
Love St *OWL* S3....................11 G1
Lovetot Av *AU/AST/KP* S26..145 F2
Lovetot Rd *AU/AST/KP* S26..127 E2
.........*KIMB* S61..................95 F4
Lowburn Rd *HAN/WDH* S13..142 A3
Low Common *ECK/KIL* S21..176 B4
Low Common Rd *DIN* S25....134 B4
Low Cft *BSLYN/ROY* S71........15 F3
Lowcroft *WMB/DAR* S73........50 D2
Low Cudworth *CUD/GR* S72...21 H2
Lowedges Cl *SHEFS* S8........162 C2
Lowedges Crs *SHEFS* S8......162 C2
Lowedges Dr *SHEFS* S8........162 D2
Lowedges Pl *SHEFS* S8........162 C2

Lowedges Rd *SHEFS* S8 ....162 B3
Lowe La *DOD/DAR* S75 ....46 B2
Lowell Av *DONS/BSCR* DN4 ....71 H2
Lower Castlereagh St
   BSLY S70 ....3 F5
Lower Dolcliffe Rd
   MEX/SWTN S64 ....66 D3
Lower Farm La *BSLY* S70 ......48 D1
Lower Grove Rd *CHSW* S40 ....4 E4
The Lower Limes *BSLY* S70 ...48 B1
Lower Malton Rd *BTLY* DN5 ...39 E3
Lower Mill Cl *DEARNE* S63 .....54 F1
Lower Thomas St *BSLY* S70 .....3 F6
Lower Unwin St
   STKB/PEN S36 ....44 D4
Lower York St
   WMB/DAR S73 * 50 B2
Lowfield Av *HACK/IN* S12 ....155 G4
   KIMB S61 ....97 F1
Lowfield Cl *ARMTH* DN3 ....29 G1
Lowfield Farm
   DEARNE S63 * 53 G3
Lowfield Gv *DEARNE* S63 ....53 G4
Lowfield Mdw *DEARNE* S63 ....53 F4
Lowfield Rd *DEARNE* S63 ....53 F4
   WHHL DN2 ....41 G3
Lowfields *STV/CWN* S43 ......182 C4
Lowgate *BTLY* DN5 ....39 E3
Lowgates *STV/CWN* S43 .....182 B4
Low Golden Smithies
   MEX/SWTN S64 ....66 A4
Low Grange Rd *DEARNE* S63..37 E2
Low Grange Sq *DEARNE* S63..37 E2
Lowhouse Rd *SHEFN* S5 ....108 C3
Low Laithes Vw
   WMB/DAR S73 ....49 H1
Lowlands Cl *BSLYN/ROY* S71 ..20 D2
   BTLY DN5 ....26 D4
Low La *KIMB* S61 ....105 E1
Low Matlock La
   ST/HB/BR S6 ....113 E5
Low Pasture Cl
   DOD/DAR S75 ....30 C3
Low Pavement *CHSW* S40 ....5 G4
Low Riddings *MALT* S66 ......108 C3
Low Rd *BSVR* S44 ....184 B4
   CONI DN12 ....89 E1
   DONS/BSCR DN4 ....71 G1
Low Rd East
   DONS/BSCR DN4 ....70 D2
Low Rd West
   DONS/BSCR DN4 ....70 D2
Lowry Dr *DRON* S18 ....170 D2
Low St *DOD/DAR* S75 ....30 D4
Lowther Rd *DON* DN1 ....40 C5
   ST/HB/BR S6 ....114 B3
Lowton Wy *MALT* S66 ....109 A4
Low Vw *DOD/DAR* S75 ....30 A3
Low Wood Cl
   MEX/SWTN S64 * 86 A2
Loxley Av *WMB/DAR* S73 ....50 A3
Loxley Cl *CHSW* S40 ....191 F1
Loxley New Rd
   ST/HB/BR S6 ....113 H5
Loxley Pk *ST/HB/BR* S6 ......113 C5
Loxley Rd *BSLYN/ROY* S71 ....21 F4
   ST/HB/BR S6 ....112 A2
Loxley View Rd *FUL* S10 .....124 D2
Loy Cl *KIMB* S61 ....97 E3
Lucas Rd *CHNE* S41 ....187 E4
Lucas St *ATT* S4 ....115 C5
Ludgate Cl *NROS/TKH* DN11 ...91 G4
Ludham Cl *CHNE* S41 ....187 F2
Lugano Gv *WMB/DAR* S73 .....34 C4
Luke La *ST/HB/BR* S6 ....113 F3
Lulworth Cl *BSLY* S70 ....32 B2
Lumley Crs *MALT* S66 ....111 G3
Lumley St *ATT* S4 ....115 C4
Lump La *CHPT/GREN* S35.......93 E5
Lumsdale Rd *STV/CWN* S43 .189 G1
Luna Cft *HACK/IN* S12 ....154 B5
Lunbreck Rd
   DONS/BSCR DN4 ....70 C3
Lund Av *BSLYN/ROY* S71 ....21 H4
Lund Cl *BSLYN/ROY* S71 ....21 F4
Lund Crs *BSLYN/ROY* S71 .....21 F4
Lundhill Cl *WMB/DAR* S73 .....50 C4
Lundhill Farm Ms
   WMB/DAR S73 ....50 B5
Lundhill Gv *WMB/DAR* S73 ....50 C4
Lund Hill La *BSLYN/ROY* S71 ..13 F5
Lundhill Rd *WMB/DAR* S73 .....50 C5
Lund La *BSLYN/ROY* S71 ....21 F4
Lundwood Cl *MOS* S20 ....156 C3
Lundwood Dr *MOS* S20 ....156 C3
Lundwood Gv *MOS* S20 ....156 C3
Lundy Rd *DRON* S18 ....171 E3
Lunn Rd *CUD/GR* S72 ....21 H1
Lupton Crs *SHEFS* S8 ....162 D3
Lupton Dr *SHEFS* S8 ....162 D2
Lupton Rd *SHEFS* S8 ....162 D3
Luterel Dr *AU/AST/KP* S26 ...145 F2
Lutterworth Dr
   AWLS/ASK DN6 ....25 E1
Lych Gate Cl
   DONS/BSCR DN4 ....74 C1
Lydden Cl *STV/CWN* S43 .....188 C1
Lydford Av *CHNE* S41 ....179 H5
Lydgate Cft *FUL* S10 ....124 D4
Lydgate Dr *RCH* S42 ....195 E4
Lydgate Hall Crs *FUL* S10 ...124 C4
Lydgate La *FUL* S10 ....124 C4

Lymegate *DEARNE* S63 ....63 H2
Lyme St *RHAM* S60 ....8 C5
Lyminster Rd *ST/HB/BR* S6 ...101 E4
Lyminton La *ARMTH* DN3 ......130 A3
Lymister Av *RHAM* S60 ....119 F2
Lyncroft Cl *RHAM* S60 * 118 D4
Lyndale Av *ARMTH* DN3 ....42 A1
Lynden Av *AWLS/ASK* DN6 .....25 E2
Lyndhurst Bank
   STKB/PEN S36 ....44 D4
Lyndhurst Cl *ECC* S11 ....139 F2
Lyndhurst Crs *ARMTH* DN3 .....29 E4
Lyndhurst Rd *ECC* S11 ....139 F2
Lynham Av *BSLY* S70 ....60 D2
Lynmouth Rd *ABRD* S7 ....139 G5
Lynn Pl *DARN/MH* S9 ....116 D4
Lynthwaite Cl
   WMB/DAR S73 ....63 H1
Lynton Av *RHAM* S60 ....119 G1
Lynton Dr *ARMTH* DN3 ....29 E5
Lynton Rd *ECC* S11 ....139 F2
Lynwood Dr *BSLYN/ROY* S71...15 G3
   MEX/SWTN S64 ....66 D3
Lyons Cl *ATT* S4 ....115 C5
Lyons Rd *ATT* S4 ....115 C5
Lyons St *ATT* S4 ....115 C5
Lytham Av *BSLYN/ROY* S71 ....20 D2
   DIN S25 ....148 D1
Lytham Cl *DONS/BSCR* DN4....74 D2
Lyttleton Crs *STKB/PEN* S36...44 C5
Lytton Av *SHEFN* S5 ....101 G4
Lytton Cl *DONS/BSCR* DN4 ....71 H2
Lytton Crs *SHEFN* S5 ....101 G4
Lytton Dr *SHEFN* S5 ....101 G4
Lytton Rd *SHEFN* S5 ....101 G4

M

Mabel St *RHAM* S60 ....9 J6
Macaulay Crs *ARMTH* DN3 .....43 E4
Machin St *RAW* S62 ....84 C3
Machins Ct *DRON* S18 ....171 E1
Machon Bank *ABRD* S7 ....139 G4
Machon Bank Rd *ABRD* S7 ...139 F4
Mackenzie Crs
   CHPT/GREN S35 ....93 F2
   FUL S10 ....10 B6
Mackenzie St *ECC* S11 ....139 G2
Mackinnon Av
   AU/AST/KP S26 ....159 H3
Macmanus Av *RAW* S62 ....85 F3
Macnaghten Rd
   DOD/DAR S75 ....60 D3
Macro Rd *WMB/DAR* S73 ....50 C4
Madehurst Gdns
   SHEF/MNR S2 ....140 B3
Madehurst Ri
   SHEF/MNR S2 ....140 B3
Madehurst Rd
   SHEF/MNR S2 ....140 B3
Madehurst Vw
   SHEF/MNR S2 ....140 B3
Madin St *STV/CWN* S43 ....189 F3
Madingley Cl
   DONS/BSCR DN4 ....71 G3
Madin St *CHNE* S41 ....5 F1
Mafeking Pl
   CHPT/GREN S35 ....81 E5
Magellan Rd *MALT* S66 ....110 C2
Magna Cl *MALT* S66 ....108 A3
Magna Crs *MALT* S66 ....108 A3
Magna La *RHAM/THRY* S65 ....99 F5
Magnolia Cl *ARMTH* DN3 ....29 F4
   CUD/GR S72 ....17 F2
   DIN S25 ....148 B5
Magpie Gv *SHEF/MNR* S2 ....127 E5
Mahon Av *RAW* S62 ....85 F5
Maidstone Rd
   ST/HB/BR S6 ....101 F5
Maidwell Wy *ARMTH* DN3 ......29 E3
Main Av *CUD/GR* DN12 ....70 D3
   TOT/DORE S17 ....161 H4
Main St *ARMTH* DN3 ....58 D4
   AU/AST/KP S26 ....145 E3
   BSVR S44 ....196 C4
   BTLY DN5 ....54 B5
   CHPT/GREN S35 ....101 E1
   DEARNE S63 ....37 G5
   DIN S25 ....148 B3
   EPW DN9 ....75 H1
   HACK/IN S12 ....112 B6
   KIMB S61 ....97 G3
   MALT S66 ....108 D4
   MEX/SWTN S64 ....66 D4
   RAW S62 ....82 C2
   RAW S62 ....85 G5
   RHAM S60 ....129 H2
   STV/CWN S43 ....50 A2
Mair Ct *RHAM* S60 ....119 G3
Makin St *MEX/SWTN* S64 ......67 G3
Malcolm Cl *BSLY* S70 ....32 D2
Malham Ct *CHSW* S40 ....186 D4
   CUD/GR S72 ....17 E1
Malham Gdns *BSLY* S70 ....2 D3

Malham Gdns *MOS* S20 ....166 D1
Malham Gv *MOS* S20 ....167 E1
Malham Pl *CHPT/GREN* S35.....80 D5
Malham Tarn Ct
   DONS/BSCR DN4 ....57 F5
Malia Rd *CHNE* S41 ....188 A3
Malinda St *OWL* S3 ....125 H2
Malinder Cl *ECK/KIL* S21 .....168 B2
Malin Rd *RHAM/THRY* S65 ....107 F1
   ST/HB/BR S6 ....113 C5
Malkin St *CHNE* S41 ....5 H3
Mallard Av *ARMTH* DN3 ....29 F4
Mallard Ct *DONS/BSCR* DN4...71 F2
   KIMB S61 ....95 G1
Mallard Ct *STV/CWN* S43 * ..182 B4
Mallard Dr *ECK/KIL* S21 ......167 H1
Mallory Av *RAW* S62 ....85 E5
Mallory Cl *CHNE* S41 ....179 E3
Mallory Dr *MEX/SWTN* S64 ....67 F2
Mallory Rd
   RHAM/THRY S65 ....107 E1
Mallory Wy *CUD/GR* S72 ....17 E5
Malon Wy *HAN/WDH* S13 .....143 F1
Malson Wy *CHNE* S41 ....187 F3
Maltby St *DARN/MH* S9 ....116 C5
Malthouse La *RCH* S42 ....194 B4
Malthouse Rd
   BSLYN/ROY S71 * 3 H5
Malting La *ATT* S4 ....11 K1
Maltings Ct *ARMTH* DN3 ....29 E4
The Maltings *RHAM* S60 ....9 F7
Maltkiln St *RHAM* S60 ....9 F6
Malton Av *AU/AST/KP* S26 ...145 G3
Malton Pl *BSLYN/ROY* S71 ....15 C5
Malton Rd *BTLY* DN5 ....38 D3
   WHHL DN2 ....41 F5
Malton St *ATT* S4 ....115 C5
Maltravers Cl
   SHEF/MNR S2 ....127 E5
Maltravers Crs
   SHEF/MNR S2 ....126 D4
Maltravers Pl
   SHEF/MNR S2 ....127 E4
Maltravers Rd
   SHEF/MNR S2 ....127 E4
Maltravers Ter
   SHEF/MNR S2 ....127 E5
Maltravers Wy
   SHEF/MNR S2 ....127 E4
Malvern Cl *CHNE* S41 ....39 E5
Malvern Cl *DOD/DAR* S75 .....18 C5
Malvern Dr *MALT* S66 ....108 B2
Malvern Rd *CHSW* S40 ....4 C2
   DARN/MH S9 ....127 H2
   WHHL DN2 ....41 F5
Malvern Wy *MALT* S66 ....108 B2
Malwood Wy *MALT* S66 ....111 F2
Manchester Rd *FUL* S10 ....124 A4
   STKB/PEN S36 ....76 B1
Mandeville St *DARN/MH* S9...128 A2
Mangham Rd *KIMB* S61 ....97 H5
Mangham Wy *KIMB* S61 ....97 H5
Manifold Av *STV/CWN* S43 ...189 H1
Manknell Rd *CHNE* S41 ....187 G1
Mannering Rd
   DONS/BSCR DN4 ....71 E2
Manners St *OWL* S3 ....125 H1
Manor Ap *KIMB* S61 ....104 D2
Manor Av *DEARNE* S63 ....37 C5
   STV/CWN S43 ....188 D2
Manor Cl *AU/AST/KP* S26 * ..147 F5
   DEARNE S63 ....64 B1
   MALT S66 ....110 D3
   RAW S62 ....84 C3
Manor Court Rd *BSVR* S44 ...196 C4
Manor Crs *CHSW* S40 ....191 H1
   CUD/GR S72 ....17 H4
   DRON S18 ....170 D2
   RHAM S60 ....118 B4
Manor Ct *AU/AST/KP* S26 ....147 F5
   BTLY DN5 ....69 F3
   CHSW S40 ....191 H1
   DIN S25 ....148 C5
   RHAM S60 ....120 A3
   STV/CWN S43 ....188 D2
Manor Dr *BSLY* S70 ....31 H5
Manor Est *BTLY* DN5 ....26 B3
Manor Farm
   AU/AST/KP S26 ....131 F5
   AWLS/ASK DN6 ....25 F1
   BSLYN/ROY S71 ....15 H4
Manor Farm Ct
   ECK/KIL S21 ....168 B3
   MOS S20 * 157 G2
   RHAM S60 ....99 H2
Manor Farm Dr
   MEX/SWTN S64 ....86 A1
Manor Farm Gdns *DIN* S25 ..148 B4
Manor Farm Ms
   MOS S20 * 157 G2
Manor Flds *KIMB* S61 ....104 C2
Manor Gdns *BSLYN/ROY* S71...33 G2
   BTLY DN5 ....54 B4
Manor Gv *BSLYN/ROY* S71 ....15 F3
   CUD/GR S72 ....17 H4
   STV/CWN S43 ....177 E4
Manor House Cl *HOY* S74 ....62 A2
Manor House Dr *BTLY* DN5 ....39 F1
Manor House Rd *KIMB* S61 ...104 C1

Manor Laith Rd
   SHEF/MNR S2 ....126 D5
Manor La *DIN* S25 ....135 E3
   MEX/SWTN S64 ....67 E1
   SHEF/MNR S2 ....141 E1
Manor Oaks Cl
   SHEF/MNR S2 ....127 E4
Manor Oaks Ct
   SHEF/MNR S2 ....126 D4
Manor Oaks Dr
   SHEF/MNR S2 ....126 C4
Manor Oaks Gdns
   SHEF/MNR S2 ....126 D4
Manor Oaks Pl
   SHEF/MNR S2 ....127 E5
Manor Oaks Rd
   SHEF/MNR S2 ....126 C4
Manor Occupation Rd
   BSLYN/ROY S71 ....12 B5
Manor Park Av
   SHEF/MNR S2 ....141 F1
Manor Park Centre
   SHEF/MNR S2 ....127 F5
Manor Park Cl
   SHEF/MNR S2 ....141 F1
Manor Park Ct
   SHEF/MNR S2 ....141 F1
Manor Park Crs
   SHEF/MNR S2 ....141 F1
Manor Park Dr
   SHEF/MNR S2 ....141 F1
Manor Park Pl
   SHEF/MNR S2 ....127 F5
Manor Park Ri
   SHEF/MNR S2 ....127 F5
Manor Park Rd
   SHEF/MNR S2 ....127 F5
Manor Park Wy
   SHEF/MNR S2 ....141 F1
Manor Pl *RAW* S62 ....98 C1
Manor Ri *AU/AST/KP* S26 .....159 F2
   BTLY DN5 ....26 C3
   CHSW S40 ....191 G1
   CUD/GR S72 ....21 G1
   DEARNE S63 ....37 G2
   DEARNE S63 ....64 A1
   DIN S25 ....134 D3
   ECK/KIL S21 ....168 B3
   MALT S66 ....111 E3
   MEX/SWTN S64 ....86 B1
   RHAM S60 ....118 B4
   STV/CWN S43 ....177 E4
   STV/CWN S43 ....188 D4
Manor Sq *DEARNE* S63 ....36 D2
Manor St *BSLYN/ROY* S71 .....15 H4
Manor Vw *CUD/GR* S72 ....17 E2
   MOS S20 * 167 E1
Manor Wy *AU/AST/KP* S26 ...147 F5
   DEARNE S63 ....53 F5
   HOY S74 ....62 A1
   SHEF/MNR S2 ....127 E4
Manse Ct *DONS/BSCR* DN4...58 C5
Manse Farm Ms
   CUD/GR S72 ....16 D5
Mansel Av *SHEFN* S5 ....101 F3
Mansel Crs *SHEFN* S5 ....101 F3
Mansel Rd *SHEFN* S5 ....101 E3
Mansfeldt Crs *CHNE* S41 .....187 E5
Mansfeld Crs *ARMTH* DN3 ....42 B3
Mansfield Dr *HACK/IN* S12 ...141 H4
Mansfield Rd
   AU/AST/KP S26 ....158 D2
   BSLYN/ROY S71 ....14 C4
   BSVR S44 ....197 E5
   CHNE S41 ....193 F5
   ECK/KIL S21 ....168 D2
   HACK/IN S12 ....141 H4
   RHAM S60 ....99 E5
Manton Dr *SHEF/MNR* S2 .....11 H7
Manvers Ct
   AU/AST/KP S26 ....145 F3
   DIN S25 ....148 B1
Manvers Pk *DEARNE* S63 ......66 A2
Manvers Rd
   AU/AST/KP S26 ....145 F3
   BSVR S44 ....189 E5
   MEX/SWTN S64 ....66 D5
   MOS S20 ....157 F1
   ST/HB/BR S6 ....96 B5
Manvers Wy *DEARNE* S63 .....65 G1
Maori Av *DEARNE* S63 ....53 F5
Maple Av *DONS/BSCR* DN4 ....58 B5
   MALT S66 ....110 B3
Maplebeck Dr
   DARN/MH S9 ....117 G2
Maplebeck Rd
   DARN/MH S9 ....117 H2
Maple Cl *BSLY* S70 ....32 B3
Maple Croft Crs
   DARN/MH S9 ....116 B1
Maple Croft Rd
   DARN/MH S9 ....116 B1
Maple Dr *ECK/KIL* S21 ....168 A3
   MALT S66 ....108 B3
Maple Gv *AU/AST/KP* S26 ....145 H2
   CONI DN12 ....88 B3
   DARN/MH S9 ....128 C4
   STKB/PEN S36 ....76 B2
Maple Pl *CHPT/GREN* S35 .....94 A2
Maple Rd *AU/AST/KP* S26 ....159 G2
   DOD/DAR S75 ....60 B5
   MEX/SWTN S64 ....66 D3

Maple St *STV/CWN* S43 ....189 F1
Maplewood Av *MALT* S66 .....108 B1
Mapperley Rd *DRON* S18 .....170 A2
Mappin St *SHEF* S1 ....10 D3
Mappin's Rd *RHAM* S60 ......129 G2
Mapplebeck Rd
   CHPT/GREN S35 ....80 C4
Mapplewell Dr
   DOD/DAR S75 ....14 A4
Maran Av *WMB/DAR* S73 ......35 G5
Marbeck Cl *DIN* S25 ....134 B4
Marcham Dr *MOS* S20 ....157 G1
March St *CONI* DN12 ....89 E2
March St *CONI* DN12 ....89 E1
   DARN/MH S9 ....116 D5
March Vale Ri *CONI* DN12 .....89 E2
Marchwood Av
   ST/HB/BR S6 ....124 A1
Marchwood Dr
   ST/HB/BR S6 ....113 E5
Marchwood Rd
   ST/HB/BR S6 ....113 E5
Marcliff Cl *MALT* S66 ....107 H5
Marcliff Crs *MALT* S66 ....107 H5
Marcliff La *MALT* S66 ....107 H5
Mardale Ct *CHNE* S41 ....179 E5
Marden Rd *ABRD* S7 ....139 G4
Margaret Cl
   AU/AST/KP S26 ....145 F4
   WMB/DAR S73 ....34 D5
Margaret Rd *WMB/DAR* S73...50 C3
Margaret St *MALT* S66 ....111 F5
   SHEF S1 ....11 G7
Margate Dr *ATT* S4 ....115 H4
Margetson Crs *SHEFN* S5 ....101 H3
Margetson Dr *SHEFN* S5 .....101 G3
Margetson Rd *SHEFN* S5 .....101 H3
Marian Rd *ARMTH* DN3 ....29 E3
Marigold Cl *SHEFN* S5 ....116 A1
Marina Rd *WMB/DAR* S73 .....34 C5
Marine Dr *CHNE* S41 ....5 K4
Marion Rd *ST/HB/BR* S6 ......113 H2
Markbrook Dr
   CHPT/GREN S35 ....80 A3
Market Cl *BSLYN/ROY* S71 ......3 J5
Market H *BSLY* S70 ....3 F4
Market Pde *BSLY* S70 ....3 G4
Market Pl *BSVR* S44 ....196 D2
   CHSW S40 ....5 F4
   CUD/GR S72 ....16 D5
   DON DN1 ....6 D2
   SHEF S1 ....11 H2
The Market Pl *MOS* S20 * 157 E3
Market Rd *DON* DN1 ....6 D2
Market Sq *RHAM/THRY* S65 * ...9 F3
Market St *AWLS/ASK* DN6 .....25 F5
   BSLY S70 ....3 F4
   CHPT/GREN S35 ....94 B1
   CUD/GR S72 ....16 D5
   DEARNE S63 ....36 D3
   ECK/KIL S21 ....166 D5
   HAN/WDH S13 ....143 G4
   HOY S74 ....62 A1
   MEX/SWTN S64 ....66 C5
   RHAM S60 ....8 E4
   STKB/PEN S36 ....44 B4
   STV/CWN S43 ....182 A4
Markfield Dr *MALT* S66 ....108 A3
Markham Av *ARMTH* DN3 ......42 C3
   CONI DN12 ....88 C1
Markham Cottages
   CONI DN12 * 88 C1
Markham Crs
   STV/CWN S43 ....182 B4
Markham Rd *CHSW* S40 ....4 E5
Markland Av *STV/CWN* S43...185 G2
Markland Crs *STV/CWN* S43..185 G3
Markland La *STV/CWN* S43 ..185 G5
Mark La *FUL* S10 ....137 E4
Mark St *BSLY* S70 ....2 E5
Marlborough Av *BTLY* DN5 ....55 F2
Marlborough Cl
   DEARNE S63 ....37 E2
   DIN S25 ....148 B1
Marlborough Ri
   AU/AST/KP S26 ....145 G4
Marlborough Rd *FUL* S10 .....125 E4
   WHHL DN2 ....7 J2
Marlborough Ter *BSLY* S70 .....2 E6
Marcliffe Rd *ST/HB/BR* S6 ...113 C2
Marlfield Cft
   CHPT/GREN S35 ....102 B3
Marlow Cl *MALT* S66 ....108 D5
   WHHL DN2 ....41 G5
Marlowe Dr
   RHAM/THRY S65 ....106 D4
Marlowe Rd
   RHAM/THRY S65 ....106 D4
Marlow Rd *WHHL* DN2 ....41 G5
Marmion Rd *ECC* S11 ....138 C3
Marples Cl *SHEFS* S8 ....139 H3
Marples Dr *SHEFS* S8 ....139 H3
Marrick Ct *CHPT/GREN* S35 ...93 H1
Marrion Rd *RAW* S62 ....85 E5
Marriott La *ABRD* S7 ....152 B2
Marriott Pl *RAW* S62 ....84 D4
Marriott Rd *ABRD* S7 ....152 B2
   MEX/SWTN S64 ....66 C4
Marrison Dr *ECK/KIL* S21 ....168 A2
Marr Ter *FUL* S10 ....138 B1

Marsala Wk *WMB/DAR* S73 ....**34** D4
Marsden La *OWL* S3 ....**10** E2
Marsden Pl *CHSW* S40 * **4** F5
CHSW S40 * **5** F2
Marsden Rd
STKB/PEN S36 * **77** E2
Marsden St *CHSW* S40 ....**5** F3
Marshall Av
DONS/BSCR DN4 ....**71** G1
Marshall Cl *RAW* S62 ....**98** B2
Marshall Gv *DEARNE* S63 ....**65** F3
Marshall Rd *SHEFS* S8 ....**152** D3
Marsh Av *DRON* S18 ....**163** F5
Marsh Cl *MOS* S20 ....**166** C2
Marshfield *BSLY* S70 ....**47** H4
Marshfield Cl
STV/CWN S43 ....**182** C4
Marsh Ga *BTLY* DN5 ....**6** A1
Marsh House Rd *ECC* S11 ....**138** B5
Marsh La *ARMTH* DN3 ....**28** C1
BTLY DN5 ....**27** F4
FUL S10 ....**124** B4
Marsh Rd *BTLY* DN5 ....**39** H5
Marsh St *RHAM* S60 ....**8** D7
STKB/PEN S36 ....**77** F2
WMB/DAR S73 ....**50** C2
Marsh Vw *ECK/KIL* S21 ....**174** B1
Marson Av *AWLS/ASK* DN6 ......**24** D2
Marston Cl *DRON* S18 ....**179** G2
Marston Crs *BSLYN/ROY* S71 ..**19** H1
Marstone Crs
TOT/DORE S17 ....**161** E3
Marston Rd *FUL* S10 ....**124** D3
Martin Cl *AU/AST/KP* S26 .....**145** E1
BSLY S70 ....**87** H5
ST/HB/BR S6 ....**125** G2
Martin La *ECK/KIL* S21 ....**166** C5
Martin Crs *SHEFN* S5 ....**102** B3
Martindale Cl
STV/CWN S43 ....**181** G5
Martin La *HOY* S74 ....**48** D4
Martin Ri *ECK/KIL* S21 ....**166** C5
KIMB S61 ....**82** C5
Martins Rd *BSLYN/ROY* S71 ....**21** E4
Martin St *ST/HB/BR* S6 ....**10** E1
Marton Rd *BTLY* DN5 ....**26** B2
Marvell Rd *BTLY* DN5 ....**38** D4
Mary Ann Cl *BSLYN/ROY* S71 ...**20** D5
Mary Ann St *CHNE* S41 ....**179** F2
Maryhill Cl *RHAM* S60 ....**130** B3
Mary La *WMB/DAR* S73 ....**35** F5
Mary St *CUD/GR* S72 ....**36** A4
ECK/KIL S21 ....**166** D5
RHAM S60 ....**8** D3
SHEFP/MNR S2 ....**11** G7
Mary's Pl *DOD/DAR* S75 ....**18** D7
Masbrough St *RHAM* S60 ....**8** B5
Masefield Cl *DIN* S25 ....**135** E5
Masefield Rd *DEARNE* S63 ......**64** C1
HAN/WDH S13 ....**142** A3
WHHL DN2 ....**41** G3
Masham Ct *DONS/BSCR* DN4 ...**58** A5
Masham Rd
DONS/BSCR DN4 ....**74** A1
Mason Av *AU/AST/KP* S26 ......**145** F1
Mason Crs *HAN/WDH* S13 ....**142** B3
Mason Dr *AU/AST/KP* S26 ......**145** E1
Mason Gv *HAN/WDH* S13 ....**142** B3
Mason Lathe Rd *SHEFN* S5 ....**103** E4
Mason St *DEARNE* S63 ....**37** G5
Masons Wy *BSLY* S70 ....**32** C4
Mason Wy *HOY* S74 ....**61** H1
Massey Rd *HAN/WDH* S13 ....**143** H5
Masson Cl *RHAM* S60 ....**186** D4
Mastall La *BTLY* DN5 ....**27** G5
Masters Crs *SHEFS* S5 ....**102** B4
Masters Rd *SHEFN* S5 ....**102** B4
Mastin Av *STV/CWN* S43 ....**180** C1
Mather Av *DARN/MH* S9 ....**127** H5
Mather Cl *DARN/MH* S9 ....**127** H4
Mather Crs *DARN/MH* S9 ....**127** H4
Mather Dr *DARN/MH* S9 ....**127** H4
Mather Rd *DARN/MH* S9 ....**127** H4
Matilda La *SHEF* S1 ....**11** H6
Matilda St *SHEF* S1 ....**11** F5
Matilda Wy *SHEF* S1 ....**11** F5
Matlock Dr *STV/CWN* S43 ......**189** G4
Matlock Rd *BSLYN/ROY* S71 ....**20** B1
RCH S42 ....**191** G5
ST/HB/BR S6 ....**125** E2
Mattersey Cl
DONS/BSCR DN4 ....**74** A3
Matthew Gap
STKB/PEN S36 ....**44** A2
Matthews Av *DEARNE* S63 ....**64** D2
Matthews Cl *DEARNE* S63 ....**64** D3
Matthews Dr *MALT* S66 ....**121** F1
Matthews Fold *SHEFS* S8 .....**153** D4
Matthews La *SHEFS* S8 ....**153** C4
Matthew St *OWL* S3 ....**10** E1
Maugerhay *SHEFS* S8 ....**153** C4
Maulays Ct *NROS/TKH* DN11 ....**91** H3
Mauncer Crs
HAN/WDH S13 ....**143** F3
Mauncer Dr *HAN/WDH* S13 ......**143** F3
Mauncer La *HAN/WDH* S13 ......**143** H4
Maun Wy *SHEFN* S5 ....**115** G1
Maurice St *RAW* S62 ....**98** B3
Mawfa Av *GLV* S14 ....**153** H3
Mawfa Crs *GLV* S14 ....**153** H3
Mawfa Dr *GLV* S14 ....**153** H3
Mawfa La *GLV* S14 ....**153** H3
Mawfield Rd *DOD/DAR* S75 .....**18** B3

Maxey Pl *SHEFS* S8 ....**140** A4
Maxfield Av *FUL* S10 ....**125** E4
Maxwell St *ATT* S4 ....**126** C1
Maxwell Rd *ATT* S4 ....**126** C1
Maxwell Wy *ATT* S4 ....**180** A3
DONS/BSCR DN4 ....**71** G2
Maycock Av *KIMB* S61 ....**96** B4
May Day Gn *BSLY* S70 ....**3** G4
May Day Green Ar *BSLY* S70 * ..**3** G4
Mayfield *BSLYN/ROY* S71 ....**20** B3
STKB/PEN S36 ....**45** H5
Mayfield Crs *BSLY* S70 ....**31** G4
NROS/TKH DN11 ....**91** F3
CHSW S40 ....**191** G2
FUL S10 ....**137** E5
Mayfields *BTLY* DN5 ....**38** D1
Mayflower Cr *HACK/IN* S12 ....**141** H4
Mayflower Rd
DONS/BSCR DN4 ....**70** C3
Mayflower Wy
WMB/DAR S73 ....**50** C3
Maynard Rd *CHSW* S40 ....**4** F7
RHAM S60 ....**120** A1
May Rd *ST/HB/BR* S6 ....**113** H4
May Ter *ST/HB/BR* S6 ....**2** A4
Maythorne Cl *DOD/DAR* S75 ..**14** A4
May Tree Cl *MOS* S20 ....**157** E4
Maytree Cl *MOS* S20 ....**157** E1
May Tree Cft *MOS* S20 ....**157** E4
May Tree La *MOS* S20 ....**157** E4
McConnel Crs
NROS/TKH DN11 ....**90** D2
McGregor's Wy *CHSW* S40 .....**195** H1
McIntyre Rd *STKB/PEN* S36 ....**76** D3
McKenzie Wy
AU/AST/KP S26 ....**159** H3
McLaren Crs *MALT* S66 ....**111** E4
McLintock Wy *BSLY* S70 ....**2** D4
McLoughlin Wy
AU/AST/KP S26 ....**159** H3
McMahon Av *STV/CWN* S43 ....**189** F3
Meaburn Cl
DONS/BSCR DN4 ....**74** B1
Meadow Av *CUD/GR* S72 ....**22** B3
RAW S62 ....**84** D4
Meadow Bank Av *ABRD* S7 .....**139** F3
Meadowbank Cl *KIMB* S61 ....**105** E3
Meadow Bank Rd *ECC* S11 ....**139** F3
KIMB S61 ....**104** A5
Meadow Cl *BSVR* S44 ....**196** D4
DRON S18 ....**163** G4
RHAM/THRY S65 ....**99** G5
STV/CWN S43 ....**177** G5
STV/CWN S43 ....**180** B4
Meadow Ct *BSLYN/ROY* S71 ....**15** H1
Meadowcourt
DARN/MH S9 ....**116** D2
Meadow Crs *BSLYN/ROY* S71 ...**12** D5
CUD/GR S72 ....**35** G3
MOS S20 ....**166** B1
Meadow Cft *ARMTH* DN3 ....**29** G5
BTLY DN5 ....**54** C5
CUD/GR S72 ....**17** E1
MEX/SWTN S64 ....**86** A3
Meadowcroft Gdns
MOS S20 ....**157** E5
Meadowcroft Gld *MOS* S20 ..**157** E5
Meadowcroft Ri *MOS* S20 ...**157** E5
Meadow Dr *BSLYN/ROY* S71 ....**20** D5
CHPT/GREN S35 ....**93** G1
MEX/SWTN S64 ....**86** A1
Meadowfield Dr *HOY* S74 .....**62** A4
Meadow Field Rd
ARMTH DN3 ....**29** G1
Meadowgate *DEARNE* S63 .....**63** H2
WMB/DAR S73 ....**51** E4
Meadow Gate Av *MOS* S20 ...**157** H2
Meadow Gate Cl *MOS* S20 ...**157** H4
Meadow Gate La *MOS* S20 ...**157** H4
Meadowgate Pk
ECK/KIL S21 ....**168** A1
Meadowgates *DEARNE* S63 ....**53** E2
Meadow Gv *TOT/DORE* S17 ..**161** E4
Meadow Grove Rd
TOT/DORE S17 ....**160** D2
Meadowhall Rd
DARN/MH S9 ....**116** D2
KIMB S61 ....**104** B4
Meadowhall Wy
DARN/MH S9 ....**116** D2
Meadowhead *SHEFS* S8 ....**152** D5
Meadow Head Av
SHEFS S8 ....**162** C1
Meadow Head Dr
SHEFS S8 ....**152** D5
Meadow House Dr *FUL* S10 ..**137** H1
Meadowland Ri
CUD/GR S72 ....**22** A2
Meadowlands *BSVR* S44 ....**197** F2
Meadow La *MALT* S66 ....**111** E4
MEX/SWTN S64 ....**67** E5
WMB/DAR S73 ....**35** F5
Meadowpark Cft *DIN* S25 ....**134** C5
Meadow La S *BSLYN/ROY* S71 ..**15** H1
Meadows Ct
NROS/TKH DN11 ....**91** H3
Meadowside Cl *RCH* S42 ......**191** H4
Meadows Rd *DEARNE* S63 * ...**65** H2
The Meadows
AU/AST/KP S26 ....**147** E5
DOD/DAR S75 ....**18** A3

Meadow St *BSLYN/ROY* S71 .....**3** H2
DIN S25 ....**134** A3
KIMB S61 ....**105** E3
OWL S3 ....**10** D1
Meadow Ter *ECC* S11 ....**139** E2
The Meadow *BTLY* DN5 ....**54** C4
Meadow Vw *BSLY* S70 ....**32** A3
CHSW S40 ....**191** E4
STV/CWN S43 ....**185** F3
Meadow View Cl *HOY* S74 ....**61** H5
Meadow View Dr
RHAM/THRY S65 ....**109** E1
Meadow View Rd
MEX/SWTN S64 ....**86** B3
SHEFS S8 ....**152** D5
Meadow Wk *ARMTH* DN3 ....**29** G4
Meadow Wy
MEX/SWTN S64 ....**66** D4
Meadstead Dr
BSLYN/ROY S71 ....**15** F1
Meadstead Fold
BSLYN/ROY S71 ....**15** F1
The Meads *SHEFS* S8 ....**153** F5
The Meadway
TOT/DORE S17 ....**160** D1
Meakin St *CHNE* S41 ....**193** F4
Mears Cl *STKB/PEN* S36 ....**45** F3
The Mede *AWLS/ASK* DN6 .....**24** D2
Medina Wy *DOD/DAR* S75 ....**18** A2
Medley Vw *CONI* DN12 ....**89** F2
Medlock Cl *HAN/WDH* S13 ...**129** E5
Medlock Crs *HAN/WDH* S13 ..**129** E5
Medlock Dr *HAN/WDH* S13 ...**145** E1
Medlock Rd *CHSW* S40 ....**191** G4
HAN/WDH S13 ....**145** E1
Medlock Wy *HAN/WDH* S13 ...**129** E5
Medway Cl *DOD/DAR* S75 ....**18** B2
Medway Pl *WMB/DAR* S73 ......**50** D4
Meersbrook Av *SHEFS* S8 ...**139** H5
Meersbrook Park Rd
SHEFS S8 ....**140** A4
Meersbrook Rd *SHEFS* S8 ...**140** B5
Meetinghouse Cft
HAN/WDH S13 ....**143** G4
Meetinghouse La
HAN/WDH S13 ....**143** G4
SHEF S1 ....**11** G2
Mekyll Cl *MALT* S66 ....**108** B3
Melbeck Ct *CHPT/GREN* S35 ...**93** C1
Melbourne Av
AU/AST/KP S26 ....**145** G2
DEARNE S63 ....**52** D3
FUL S10 ....**125** E3
Melbourne Rd
DONS/BSCR DN4 ....**71** E2
STKB/PEN S36 ....**76** C2
Melbourn Rd *FUL* S10 ....**125** E2
Melciss Rd *MALT* S66 ....**108** A5
Melford Dr
DONS/BSCR DN4 ....**71** G4
Melfort Gln *FUL* S10 ....**124** A4
Mell Av *HOY* S74 ....**61** H2
Melling Av *BTLY* DN5 ....**55** E2
Melling Cl *CHSW* S40 ....**192** B4
Melling Ct *CHSW* S40 ....**192** B4
Mellington Cl *SHEFS* S8 ....**153** C3
Mellor Lea Farm Cha
CHPT/GREN S35 ....**94** B4
Mellor Lea Farm Dr
CHPT/GREN S35 ....**94** B4
Mellor Lea Farm Garth
CHPT/GREN S35 ....**94** B4
Mellor Rd *WMB/DAR* S73 ....**50** B3
Mellor Wy *CHSW* S40 ....**192** C5
Mellow Fields Rd *DIN* S25 ..**134** B5
Mellwood Gv
WMB/DAR S73 ....**50** A5
Melrose Cl *CHSW* S40 ....**191** C1
DONS/BSCR DN4 ....**71** E4
MALT S66 ....**132** D1
Melrose Gv *RHAM* S60 ....**119** G2
Melrose Rd *OWL* S3 ....**126** B5
Melrose Wy *BSLYN/ROY* S71 ...**15** G5
Meltham La *CHNE* S41 ....**187** H3
Melton Av *DEARNE* S63 ....**37** G5
WMB/DAR S73 ....**51** F5
Melton Ct *AU/AST/KP* S26 ...**146** A3
Meltonfield *DEARNE* S63 .....**37** H5
Meltonfield Cl *ARMTH* DN3 ...**43** E5
Melton Gdns *BTLY* DN5 ....**54** B5
Melton Gn *DEARNE* S63 ....**64** C2
Melton Gv *MOS* S20 ....**156** A3
Melton High St *DEARNE* S63 ..**64** C1
Melton Rd *BTLY* DN5 ....**54** B4
Melton St *MEX/SWTN* S64 .....**67** G4
WMB/DAR S73 ....**51** F5
Melton Ter *BSLY* S70 ....**32** C5
Melton Wood Gv *BTLY* DN5 ...**54** B4
Melville Av *DONS/BSCR* DN4 ..**71** G1
Melville Crs *STV/CWN* S43 ..**185** C4
Melville Dr *SHEFP/MNR* S2 ..**141** G2
Melville St *WMB/DAR* S73 .....**50** B2
Melvinia Crs *DOD/DAR* S75 ..**19** F3
Melwood Gv *ARMTH* DN3 ....**59** E1
Mendip Cl *BTLY* DN5 * **39** E5
DOD/DAR S75 ....**18** D5
Mendip Crs *CHSW* S40 ....**186** B5
Mendip Ri *RHAM* S60 ....**118** D3
Merbeck Dr *CHPT/GREN* S35 ..**80** B4
Merbeck Gv *CHPT/GREN* S35 ..**80** C3
Mercaston Cl *CHSW* S40 .....**186** A4

Mercel Av *ARMTH* DN3 ....**43** E2
Merchants Wy *WHHL* DN2 ......**41** G1
Mercia Dr *TOT/DORE* S17 ....**161** E2
Meredith Crs
DONS/BSCR DN4 ....**71** H2
Meredith Rd *ST/HB/BR* S6 ..**113** H4
Mere Gv *ARMTH* DN3 ....**42** C3
Mere La *ARMTH* DN3 ....**42** C3
Merlin Av *BSVR* S44 ....**196** C1
Merlin Cl *AWLS/ASK* DN6 .....**25** F1
BSLY S70 ....**115** G1
Merlin La *RHAM* S60 ....**115** G1
SHEFN S5 ....**115** G1
Merrian Cft *STV/CWN* S43 * .**180** C3
Merrick Cl *CHSW* S40 ....**186** D4
Merrill Rd *DEARNE* S63 ....**37** E1
Merton La *DARN/MH* S9 ......**103** H5
Merton Rd *DARN/MH* S9 ......**103** H5
Metcalfe Av *ECK/KIL* S21 ...**168** A2
Methley Cl *HACK/IN* S12 ....**141** F4
Methley St *CUD/GR* S72 ......**21** H1
Mexborough Rd
DEARNE S63 ....**53** F4
Meynell Cl *CHSW* S40 ....**191** C2
Meynell Crs *SHEFN* S5 ......**101** F5
Meynell Rd *SHEFN* S5 ....**101** F5
Michael Cl *RCH* S42 ....**195** C2
Michael Cft *DEARNE* S63 .....**64** D2
Michael Rd *BSLYN/ROY* S71 ..**21** E5
Mickelden Wy
DOD/DAR S75 ....**18** A2
Micklebring Gv *CONI* DN12 ..**88** C3
Micklebring Wy *MALT* S66 ...**199** H4
Mickley La *TOT/DORE* S17 ...**161** F4
Middle Av *RAW* S62 ....**85** F5
Middle Bank
DONS/BSCR DN4 ....**56** C5
Middleburn Cl *BSLY* S70 ......**32** A3
Middlecliff Cl *MOS* S20 ....**157** E4
Middlecliff La *CUD/GR* S72 ..**35** G2
CUD/GR S72 ....**36** A1
Middlecliff Ri *MOS* S20 ....**157** E4
Middlecroft Rd
STV/CWN S43 ....**189** G2
Middle Dr *RHAM* S60 ....**119** F3
Middlefield Cl
TOT/DORE S17 ....**160** C2
Middlefield Cft
TOT/DORE S17 ....**160** C2
Middlefield Rd
DONS/BSCR DN4 ....**73** H1
RHAM S60 ....**118** D3
Middlefields Dr *RHAM* S60 ..**120** A3
Middlegate *BTLY* DN5 ....**38** D7
Middleham Rd
DONS/BSCR DN4 ....**74** A1
Middle Hay Cl *GLV* S14 .....**141** E4
Middle Hay Pl *GLV* S14 .....**141** E5
Middle Hay Ri *GLV* S14 .....**141** E5
Middle Hay Vw *GLV* S14 .....**141** E5
Middle La *CHPT/GREN* S35 ....**92** D5
RHAM/THRY S65 ....**9** K3
ST/HB/BR S6 ....**124** C1
Middle La South
RHAM/THRY S65 ....**106** C3
Middle Ox Cl *MOS* S20 ......**167** F2
Middle Ox Gdns *MOS* S20 ...**167** F2
Middle Pavement
CHSW S40 * **5** F4
Middle Pl *RHAM/THRY* S65 ..**106** C3
Middlesex St *BSLY* S70 ....**31** H3
Middle St *BSVR* S44 ....**197** F4
Middleton Av *DIN* S25 ......**134** C5
Middleton Dr *STV/CWN* S43 .**189** F4
Middleton La
CHPT/GREN S35 ....**101** F1
Middleton Rd
RHAM/THRY S65 ....**9** K4
Middletown Mdw
STV/CWN S43 ....**177** E5
Middlewood Cha
ST/HB/BR S6 ....**113** G1
Middlewood Dr *KIMB* S61 ....**96** A4
ST/HB/BR S6 ....**113** G1
Middlewood Dr East
ST/HB/BR S6 ....**100** B5
Middlewood Rd
ST/HB/BR S6 ....**113** G1
Middlewood Rd North
CHPT/GREN S35 ....**100** B4
Middlewoods
DOD/DAR S75 ....**30** C3
Middlewoods Wy
BSLYN/ROY S71 ....**15** F4
Midfield Rd *FUL* S10 ....**124** C3
Midhill Rd *SHEFP/MNR* S2 ...**140** B5
Midhope Wy *DOD/DAR* S75 .....**18** A2
Midhurst Rd *ST/HB/BR* S6 ...**112** D5
Midland Cl *CHNE* S41 * **192** D5
Midland Rd *BSLYN/ROY* S71 ..**12** D5
KIMB S61 ....**8** A4
MEX/SWTN S64 ....**66** C5
Midland St *BSLY* S70 ....**3** G4
RAW S62 ....**82** D1
SHEF S1 ....**11** G7
Midland Ter *CHNE* S41 * **192** D5
Midland Wy *STV/CWN* S43 ...**184** A1
Midvale Av *ST/HB/BR* S6 ....**125** G1
Midvale Rd *ST/HB/BR* S6 ....**125** G1
Milano Ri *WMB/DAR* S73 ......**34** D5

Milbanke St *DON* DN1 ....**6** E1
Milburn Crt *MOS* S20 ....**157** G4
Milburn Gv *MOS* S20 ....**157** G4
Milden Pl *BSLY* S70 ....**23** F3
Milden Rd *ST/HB/BR* S6 .....**113** G2
Milefield La *CUD/GR* S72 .....**17** G5
Milefield Vw *CUD/GR* S72 ....**17** H5
Miles Cl *SHEFN* S5 ....**115** E3
Miles Rd *CHP/GREN* S35 ......**80** C4
SHEFN S5 ....**114** D3
Mileswood Cl *CUD/GR* S72 ...**23** H4
Milethorn La *DON* DN1 ....**40** B5
Milford Av *HOY* S74 ....**62** D2
Milford Rd *STV/CWN* S43 ....**189** C4
Milford St *DARN/MH* S9 .....**116** D4
Milgate St *BSLYN/ROY* S71 ...**12** D5
Milgrove Crs
CHPT/GREN S35 ....**80** B3
Milking La *STV/CWN* S43 ....**184** B5
Millais Ri *MALT* S66 ....**108** B2
Millard La *MALT* S66 ....**111** E4
Millbank Cl *CHPT/GREN* S35 ..**80** B5
Mill Cl *RHAM* S60 ....**105** C5
CHPT/GREN S35 ....**94** A5
Milldale Cl *CHSW* S40 ......**186** C4
Milldale Rd *TOT/DORE* S17 ..**161** F3
Milldyke Ct *RHAM* S60 ......**120** B3
Millennium Wy *CHNE* S41 ...**179** E5
Miller Av *STV/CWN* S43 .....**183** E2
Miller Cft *HAN/WDH* S13 ....**143** E4
Miller Dale Dr *RHAM* S60 * .**118** D5
Miller Rd *ABRD* S7 ....**139** H3
Millers Dl *BSLY* S70 ....**48** A1
Miller St *STKB/PEN* S36 ......**77** H2
Mill Field Ct *ARMTH* DN3 ....**29** C1
Millfield Rd *BTLY* DN5 ......**40** A2
Mill Ga *BTLY* DN5 ....**39** H2
Mill Gn *STV/CWN* S43 ....**181** H4
Mill Green Wy
STV/CWN S43 ....**185** E2
Mill Hvn *DIN* S25 ....**148** B3
Millhill *ARMTH* DN3 ....**59** E1
Mill HI *RHAM* S60 ....**120** A3
WMB/DAR S73 ....**49** H1
Mill Hill Cl *BTLY* DN5 ....**55** F2
Mill Hills *AU/AST/KP* S26 ...**147** F5
Millhouses La *ECC* S11 .....**151** H1
Millhouses Cl *ECC* S11 .....**151** H1
Millhouses La *ABRD* S7 .....**152** A2
ECC S11 ....**138** C5
Millhouses St *HOY* S74 ......**62** A3
Millicent Sq *MALT* S66 .....**111** E4
Millindale *MALT* S66 ....**111** E4
BSVR S44 ....**196** D1
BTLY DN5 ....**70** B1
CHSW S40 ....**64** C3
DEARNE S63 ....**64** C3
DIN S25 ....**148** B3
DONS/BSCR DN4 ....**70** C2
DRON S18 ....**171** F2
ECK/KIL S21 ....**175** C1
RAW S60 ....**82** B1
RHAM S60 ....**129** H3
STKB/PEN S36 ....**77** H2
TOT/DORE S17 ....**161** F3
Mill Meadow Gdns
MOS S20 ....**157** H4
Millmoor La *RHAM* S60 ....**8** B5
Millmoor Rd
DONS/BSCR DN4 ....**58** A5
WMB/DAR S73 ....**50** D1
Millmount Rd *HOY* S74 ....**62** B2
SHEFS S8 ....**139** H5
Millrace Dr *DEARNE* S63 .....**53** E1
Mill Rd *CHPT/GREN* S35 ......**94** B5
ECK/KIL S21 ....**167** E4
RHAM S60 ....**129** H3
Mill Road Cl *CHPT/GREN* S35 .**94** B5
Millsands *OWL* S3 ....**11** H1
Millside *CUD/GR* S72 ....**39** H2
Millside Ct *BTLY* DN5 ....**39** H2
Millside Wk *CUD/GR* S72 .....**17** E1
Millstone Cl *DRON* S18 .....**170** B1
Millstone Dr
AU/AST/KP S26 ....**145** E2
Millstream Cl *BTLY* DN5 .....**54** D4
Mill Stream Cl *CHSW* S40 ..**191** G3
Mill St *ARMTH* DN3 ....**42** D4
CHNE S41 ....**5** H4
KIMB S61 ....**97** F2
RHAM S60 ....**8** E7
STV/CWN S43 ....**185** E2
Millthorpe Rd *SHEFN* S5 ...**102** D5
Milltown Cl *DEARNE* S63 .....**52** D4
Mill Wk *BSVR* S44 ....**196** D1
Millwood Rd
DONS/BSCR DN4 ....**71** F3
Mill Wood Vw
ST/HB/BR S6 ....**112** C5
Milner Av *STKB/PEN* S36 ......**44** B3
Milner Cl *MALT* S66 ....**109** E3
Milner Ga *CONI* DN12 ....**69** G5
Milner Gate Ct *CONI* DN12 ..**89** F1
Milner Rd
DONS/BSCR DN4 ....**71** F1
Milnes St *BSLY* S70 * **3** J7
Milne St *DOD/DAR* S75 ....**18** A3
Milnrow Crs *SHEFN* S5 .....**101** H3
Milnrow Dr *SHEFN* S5 ......**101** H3
Milnrow Rd *SHEFN* S5 ......**101** H3
Milnrow Vw *SHEFN* S5 ......**101** H3
Milton Av *BTLY* DN5 ....**55** F1

Milton Cl *HOY S74* 62 B1
   KIMB S61 ....97 F2
   WMB/DAR S73 ....51 F5
Milton Ct *MEX/SWTN S64*....66 A5
Milton Crs *CHSW S40*.........192 C4
   HOY S74............................62 A3
Milton Gv *ARMTH DN3*...........42 D4
   WMB/DAR S73 ....50 C3
Milton La *DIN S25* 23 H5
Milton Pl *STV/CWN S43*.......182 B5
Milton Rd *ABRD S7* 139 G3
   ARMTH DN3 ....59 G4
   CHPT/GREN S35 ....93 F1
   DIN S25..........................135 E5
   HOY S74............................62 A4
   MEX/SWTN S64.................67 E5
   RHAM/THRY S65................9 J1
Milton St *CUD/GR S72* 23 H5
   MALT S66........................110 D4
   MEX/SWTN S64.................66 A5
   OWL S3............................10 D6
   RHAM S60..........................9 C5
Milton Wk *DON DN1*.................6 C5
Minden Cl *MALT S66*............108 B5
Minden Ct *BTLY DN5*..............39 H2
Minimum Ter *CHSW S40*..........4 C6
Minna Rd *OWL S3*.................115 F5
Minneymoor Hl *CONI DN12*....69 F5
Minneymoor La *CONI DN12*....89 F1
Minster Cl *CHPT/GREN S35*..102 C1
   DONS/BSCR DN4 ....74 C1
Minster Rd
   CHPT/GREN S35 ....102 B1
Minster Wy *BSLYN/ROY S71*...20 D4
Minto Rd *ST/HB/BR S6*.........113 H5
Miriam Av *CHSW S40*...........191 E4
Mission Fld *WMB/DAR S73*....51 F5
Mitchell Cl *BSLY S70*..............32 D5
Mitchell Rd *SHEFS S8* 152 D2
   WMB/DAR S73 ....34 A5
Mitchell St *OWL S3*................10 C2
   STV/CWN S43 ....185 F2
Mitchells Wy
   WMB/DAR S73 ....50 A1
Mitchell Wy *STV/CWN S43*...180 C3
Mitchell's St *BSLY S70*............33 E5
Mitchelson Av
   DOD/DAR S75...................30 A3
Moat Cl *MALT S66*................108 C2
Moat Cft *BTLY DN5*................39 F1
Moat Hills Ct *BTLY DN5*..........39 C1
Moat House Wy *CONI DN12*...69 E5
Moatlands *MALT S66*............121 G2
Moat La *MALT S66*................121 G2
Modena Ct *WMB/DAR S73*.....34 C4
Moffat Gdns *WHHL DN2*........41 H1
Moffatt Rd *SHEFF/MNR S2*...140 B3
Molineaux Cl *SHEFN S5*........102 C3
Molineaux Rd *SHEFN S5*.......102 C3
Molineux Av *STV/CWN S43*..181 H5
Molloy Pl *SHEFS S8*..............140 A4
Molloy St *SHEFS S8*..............140 A5
Mona Av *FUL S10*..................12 C5
Mona Cl *DONS/BSCR DN4*....55 H5
   FUL S10..........................125 E2
Mona St *DOD/DAR S75*............2 C3
Monckton Rd *SHEFN S5*.......116 B1
Moncrieffe Rd *ABRD S7*.......139 G4
Monksbridge Rd *DIN S25*.....134 A4
Monks Cl *KIMB S61*................96 A4
Monkspring *BSLY S70*............32 C5
Monks Wy *BSLYN/ROY S71*....20 D4
Monk Ter *BSLYN/ROY S71*......21 E2
Monkton Wy
   BSLYN/ROY S71................12 C4
Monkwood Rd *CHNE S41*.....186 E1
   RAW S62...........................85 E4
Monmouth Rd *WHHL DN2*.....41 H1
Monmouth St *FUL S10*...........10 C5
Monnies End *STV/CWN S43*.184 C1
   STV/CWN S43 ....189 F3
Monsal Crs *BSLYN/ROY S71*....8 C5
   STV/CWN S43 ....189 F3
Monsal St *DEARNE S63*..........37 E2
Montague Av *CONI DN12*.......69 F5
Montague Ct *WMB/DAR S73*...17 E4
   DON DN1...........................6 E1
   ECC S11.........................139 G1
Montague St *BTLY DN5*.........55 E3
Montagu St *MEX/SWTN S64*..67 F4
Monteney Crs *SHEFN S5*.....102 A1
Monteney Gdns *SHEFN S5*...102 A2
Monteney Rd *SHEFN S5*.......102 A2
Montfort Dr *OWL S3*.............126 B1
Montgomery Av *ABRD S7*....139 G3
Montgomery Dr *ABRD S7*....139 G3
Montgomery Gdns
   WHHL DN2.........................41 G5
Montgomery Rd *ABRD S7*....139 G3
   DEARNE S63.....................37 E2
Montgomery Terrace Rd
   OWL S3 *.........................125 H2
Montrose Av *WHHL DN2*........41 F5
Montrose Pl *DRON S18*........170 B1
Montrose Rd *ABRD S7*.........139 E5
Monument Dr *CUD/GR S72*....17 H2
Monyash Cl *STV/CWN S43*...189 G2
Moonpenny Wy *DRON S18*...171 E2
Moonshine La *SHEFN S5*......114 D1
Moonshine Wy *SHEFN S5*....114 C1
Moorbank Cl *DOD/DAR S75*...19 E3
   FUL S10..........................123 H4
   WMB/DAR S73 ....49 H1
Moorbank Dr *FUL S10*..........124 A4

Moorbank Rd *FUL S10*..........123 H4
   WMB/DAR S73 ....33 H5
Moorbank Vw
   WMB/DAR S73 ....33 H5
Moorbridge Crs
   WMB/DAR S73 ....51 F4
Moor Crs *MOS S20*...............166 C1
Moorcroft Cl *FUL S10*...........137 F3
Moorcroft Dr *FUL S10*...........137 F3
Moorcroft Rd *FUL S10*...........137 F3
Moordale Vw *RAW S62*..........86 A4
Moor End Rd *FUL S10*..........125 E3
Moore St *SHEF S1*....................9 C3
Moore Street Jct *OWL S3*......10 D7
Moor Farm Av *MOS S20*........156 B5
Moor Farm Carth *MOS S20*..156 B5
Moor Farm Ri *MOS S20*........156 B5
Moorfield Av *BSVR S44*........197 E3
   RHAM/THRY S65............108 D2
Moorfield Cl
   RHAM/THRY S65............108 D2
Moorfield Dr *ARMTH DN3*.......42 D5
Moorfield Gv
   RHAM/THRY S65............108 D2
Moorfield Sq *BSVR S44*........197 E3
Moor Gap *ARMTH DN3*...........59 F5
Moorgate Av *FUL S10*..........125 F3
   RHAM S60.......................106 A5
Moorgate Crs *DRON S18*......171 F5
Moorgate Gv *RHAM S60*......106 A5
Moorgate La *RHAM S60*.......106 A5
Moorgate Rd *RHAM S60*........9 G7
   RHAM S60.......................106 A5
Moorgate St *RHAM S60*..........9 F4
Moor Green Cl
   DOD/DAR S75...................18 C5
Moorhay Cl *CHNE S41*..........186 B2
Moor Head *SHEF S1*...............11 F5
Moorhead Wy *MALT S66*.......109 F4
Moorhouse Cl *RHAM S60*......120 B3
Moorhouse La *RHAM S60*......120 A3
Moorland Av *BSLY S70*...........30 D2
Moorland Ct *DEARNE S63*......51 G5
Moorland Dr *STKB/PEN S36*...76 C2
Moorland Gv
   DONS/BSCR DN4 ....57 G4
Moorland Pl *ST/HB/BR S6*....123 C1
Moorlands *MALT S66*............107 H5
Moorlands Crs *RHAM S60*......108 A1
Moorland Ter *CUD/GR S72*......22 A2
Moorland Vw
   AU/AST/KP S26...............145 G3
   DEARNE S63.....................51 C5
   DRON S18.......................172 C2
   HACK/IN S12...................154 C3
Moorland View Rd
   CHSW S40......................191 C3
Moor La *ARMTH DN3*.............29 E2
   BSLY S70..........................60 D3
   BSVR S44.......................197 E3
Moor La North
   RHAM/THRY S65............108 D1
Moor La South
   RHAM/THRY S65............108 D2
Moorlawn Av *RCH S42*..........190 C5
Moor Oaks Rd *FUL S10*........125 E4
Moorpark Av *CHSW S40*.......191 G4
Moor Rd *DEARNE S63*.............65 F1
Moorside *STV/CWN S43*.......188 B2
Moorside Av *STKB/PEN S36*...44 C4
Moorside Cl *MOS S20*...........156 C5
Moorside Av *FUL S10*...........124 D2
Moorsyde Crs *FUL S10*..........124 D2
The Moor *SHEF S1*.................11 F6
Moorthorpe Dell *MOS S20*....156 B4
Moorthorpe Gdns
   MOS S20........................156 A3
Moorthorpe Gn *MOS S20*.....155 H3
Moorthorpe Ri *MOS S20*.......156 B4
Moorthorpe Vw *MOS S20*.....156 B4
   MOS S20........................156 A3
Moortop Rd *DRON S18*.........172 D2
Moor Va *MOS S20*................155 H3
Moor Valley Cl *MOS S20*......156 A4
Moor Vw *ARMTH DN3*............59 F5
Moorview *KIMB S61*..............96 A5
Moorview Cl *RCH S42*..........195 G4
   STV/CWN S43 ....188 B2
Moorview Ct *KIMB S61*..........96 A5
Moor View Dr *SHEFS S8* *....152 C3
Moor View Rd *SHEFS S8*.....152 C3
   STV/CWN S43 ....182 C4
Moor View Ter *ECC S11*........138 A5
Moorwinstow Cft
   TOT/DORE S17................161 E1
Moorwood La
   ST/HB/BR S6...................122 B3
Moorwoods Av
   CHPT/GREN S35 ....81 E5
Moorwoods La
   CHPT/GREN S35 ....93 H1
Moray Pl *DRON S18*..............170 B1
Mordaunt Rd
   SHEFF/MNR S2...............141 F4
Morgan Av *SHEFN S5*..........114 C1
Morgan Cl *SHEFN S5*...........114 D1
Morgan Rd *SHEFN S5*..........114 C2
   WHHL DN2.........................57 G1
Morland Cl *GLV S14*.............154 B2

Morland Dr *GLV S14*.............154 B2
Morland Pl *GLV S14*..............154 B2
Morland Rd *GLV S14*............154 A2
Morley Av *CHSW S40*...........186 C5
Morley Cl *DRON S18*............170 A2
Morley Pl *CONI DN12*.............88 D2
Morley Rd *DON DN1*...............40 C5
   KIMB S61..........................96 C5
Morley St *RAW S62*................98 B2
   ST/HB/BR S6...................113 H5
Morpeth Gdns *OWL S3*..........10 D1
Morpeth St *OWL S3*...............10 D1
   RHAM S60..........................9 C3
Morrall Rd *SHEFN S5*...........101 H2
Morrell St *MALT S66*.............111 E4
Morris Av *CHNE S41*.............187 E4 •
   RAW S62...........................85 F5
Morrison Av *MALT S66*.........111 E2
Morrison Dr
   NROS/TKH DN11...............91 F3
Morrison Pl *WMB/DAR S73*....35 E4
Morrison Rd *WMB/DAR S73*...34 D4
Mortain Rd *RHAM S60*..........119 F3
Mortains *AU/AST/KP S26*.....147 F4
Morthcroft *CUD/GR S72* 17 E2
Morthen Hall La *MALT S66*...121 F5
Morthen La *MALT S66*...........131 F1
Morthen Rd *MALT S66*..........121 F5
Mortimer Dr *STKB/PEN S36*...44 C5
Mortimer Hts *STKB/PEN S36*..44 C5
Mortimer Rd *MALT S66*.........111 G4
   STKB/PEN S36..................44 C5
Mortimer St *SHEF S1*.............11 H6
Mortlake Rd *SHEFN S5*........115 G2
Mortomley Cl
   CHPT/GREN S35 ....80 C4
Mortomley La
   CHPT/GREN S35 ....80 C4
Morton Cl *BSLYN/ROY S71*....20 D2
Morton Gdns *MOS S20*.........167 F2
Morton La *ECC/KIL S21*........173 E2
Morton Pl *CHPT/GREN S35*..101 E1
Morton Rd *MEX/SWTN S64*...67 F3
Morven Av *BSVR S44* *.........197 E4
Mosborough Hall Dr
   MOS S20........................167 E3
Mosborough Moor
   MOS S20........................156 B5
Mosbrough Rd
   HAN/WDH S13................141 H3
Moss Cl *MALT S66*...............108 B5
Mossdale Av *MOS S20*.........166 D1
Mossdale Cl *BTLY DN5*..........39 E3
Moss Dr *ECC/KIL S21*..........168 B3
Mossebrook Ct
   ECK/KIL S21...................167 E4
Moss Gv *HACK/IN S12*.........156 D1
Moss Rd *TOT/DORE S17*......160 B4
Moss Vw *MOS S20*...............166 B2
Moss Wy *MOS S20*...............156 C3
Motehall Dr
   SHEFF/MNR S2...............141 E1
Motehall Pl *SHEFF/MNR S2*..141 H1
Motehall Rd *SHEFF/MNR S2*..141 G1
Motehall Wy
   SHEFF/MNR S2...............141 G1
The Motte *KIMB S61*..............104 D1
Mottram St *BSLYN/ROY S71*.....3 C3
Mound Rd *CHSW S40*..........192 C3
Mount Av *CUD/GR S72* 36 A1
Mountbatten Dr
   CHPT/GREN S35 ....93 F1
Mountcastle St *CHNE S41* *..187 F1
Mount Cl *BSLY S70*................31 H3
Mount Crs *HOY S74*................61 H2
Mountenoy Rd *RHAM S60*.......9 F7
Mountfield Wy *DIN S25*.........134 A3
Mountford Cft
   TOT/DORE S17................161 E3
Mount Pleasant *BSLY S70*.......48 B1
   CHNE S41 *....................179 G3
   DONS/BSCR DN4 ....71 G1
Mount Pleasant Cl
   STV/CWN S43 ....181 E5
Mount Pleasant Rd
   DEARNE S63.....................65 F4
   ECC S11.........................139 H2
   KIMB S61............................8 A2
Mount Rd *CHPT/GREN S35*...80 B5
   OWL S3..........................114 D5
Mount St *BSLY S70*..................2 E7
   BSLYN/ROY S71................33 F2
   ECC S11.........................139 H1
   KIMB S61............................8 A2
Mount Ter *DEARNE S63*.........64 A2
   WMB/DAR S73 ....50 A2
The Mount *ARMTH DN3*.........42 C1
   MALT S66........................108 B2
Mount Vernon Av *BSLY S70*...31 H3
Mount Vernon Crs *BSLY S70*..32 A4
Mount Vernon Rd *BSLY S70*...31 H4
Mount View Av *SHEFS S8*....153 E2
Mount View Gdns
   SHEFS S8......................153 E2
Mount View Rd *SHEFS S8*....153 E2
Mousehole Cl
   RHAM/THRY S65..............99 G5
Mousehole La
   RHAM/THRY S65..............99 G5
Mowbray Gdns
   RHAM/THRY S65............107 E1
Mowbray Pl
   RHAM/THRY S65............107 E1

Mowbray St *OWL S3*............126 A2
   RHAM/THRY S65............107 E1
Moxon Cl *STKB/PEN S36*........77 F3
Mucky La *BSLYN/ROY S71*.....33 G1
   STKB/PEN S36..................76 B4
Muglet La *MALT S66*.............111 H4
Muirdale Av
   DONS/BSCR DN4..............74 D2
   MEX/SWTN S64.................66 D2
Muirfield Cl *CHNE S41*..........187 H3
Mulberry Cl *BTLY DN5*...........38 D5
   DEARNE S63.....................37 E5
   RAW S62...........................98 B3
   RCH S42.........................195 G3
Mulberry Ct *DONS/BSCR DN4..70 D1
Mulberry Crs *STV/CWN S43*..181 F5
Mulberry Rd *DIN S25*............148 C2
   ECK/KIL S21...................174 B1
Mulberry St *SHEF S1*.............11 H5
Mulberry Wy *ARMTH DN3*.....58 D1
   ECK/KIL S21...................167 H3
Mulehouse Rd *FUL S10*........124 C3
Mundella Pl *SHEFS S8*.........153 E2
Munsbrough La *KIMB S61*......97 E4
Munsbrough Ri *KIMB S61*.......97 E5
Murdoch Pl *BSLYN/ROY S71*..14 C5
Murdock Rd *SHEFN S5*..........101 H5
Murrayfield Dr *MOS S20*.......167 G2
Murray Rd *ECC S11*..............138 D4
   ECK/KIL S21...................168 C1
   RAW S62...........................98 B3
Musard Pl *STV/CWN S43*.....181 H5
Musgrave Crs *SHEFN S5*.....115 E3
Musgrave Dr *SHEFN S5*.......115 E3
Musgrave Pl *SHEFN S5*........115 E3
Musgrave Rd *SHEFN S5*.......114 D3
Mushroom La *FUL S10*..........10 A3
Muskoka Av *ECC S11*...........138 A4
Muskoka Dr *ECC S11*...........138 A4
Mutual St *DONS/BSCR DN4...55 H3
Myers Grove La
   ST/HB/BR S6..................113 E5
Myers La *ST/HB/BR S6*.........112 A1
Myers St *WMB/DAR S73*........50 A1
Mylnhurst Rd *ECC S11*..........151 H1
Mylor Ct *BSLYN/ROY S71*......20 C4
Mylor Rd *ECC S11*.................138 A4
Myrtle Crs *MALT S66*.............108 C4
Myrtle Gv *AU/AST/KP S26*.....159 E5
   STV/CWN S43 ....181 E5
Myrtle Rd *SHEFP/MNR S2*.....52 A2
   WMB/DAR S73 ....50 A2
Myrtle Springs Dr
   HACK/IN S12...................141 F5
Myrtle St *DOD/DAR S75*...........2 B3
Mysten Cft *DOD/DAR S75*......19 F3
Myton Rd *DARN/MH S9*........127 G3

N

Nabeel Ct *RHAM S60*...............9 H7
Nairn Dr *DRON S18*...............170 B2
Nairn St *FUL S10*..................124 D4
Nancy Crs *CUD/GR S72*.........23 F1
Nancy Rd *CUD/GR S72*..........23 F1
Nanny Hl *STKB/PEN S36*.......77 E2
Nanny Marr Rd
   WMB/DAR S73 ....35 F4
Napier Mt *BSLY S70*...............31 H4
Napier St *ECC S11*................139 G1
Narrow La *DIN S25*................148 C3
Naseby Av *BTLY DN5*.............38 D4
Naseby St *ATT S4*.................116 C2
Nathan Ct *MOS S20*..............157 F4
Nathan Dr *MOS S20*..............157 F3
Nathan Gv *MOS S20*.............157 F4
Navan Rd *SHEFP/MNR S2*....141 G3
Navigation Wy
   WMB/DAR S73 ....34 B5
Navvy La *BSLYN/ROY S71*.....12 D2
Naylor Gv *DOD/DAR S75*........30 B3
Naylor St *RAW S62*.................98 B3
Neale Bank *STV/CWN S43*...188 B2
Neale Rd *WHHL DN2*.............41 F2
Neale St *STV/CWN S43*........188 C2
Nearcroft Rd *KIMB S61*.........104 D1
Nearfield Rd
   DONS/BSCR DN4 ....73 H2
Needham Wy *ABRD S7*........139 E5
Needlewood *DOD/DAR S75*...30 B4
Neepsend La *OWL S3*...........125 G1
Neild Rd *HOY S74*..................62 C2
Neill Rd *ECC S11*..................139 E2
Nelson Av *BSLYN/ROY S71*....20 A3
Nelson Cl *RHAM S60*............118 D4
Nelson Pl *CHPT/GREN S35*....93 F1
Nelson Rd *MALT S66*.............111 F3
   ST/HB/BR S6...................113 F3
Nelson St *BSLY S70* *...............3 F5
   CHNE S41 *....................187 G3
   DONS/BSCR DN4 ....6 C4
Nemesia Cl *DIN S25*.............148 A4
Nesbit St *BSVR S44*..............197 F4
Nesfield Cl *CHNE S41*...........186 D1
Nesfield Wy *SHEFN S5*.........102 D5
Nether Av *CHPT/GREN S35*....93 F5
   ECK/KIL S21...................168 A2
Nether Cantley La
   ARMTH DN3.....................58 D3

Nether Cl *RCH S42*...............195 G5
Nether Crs *CHPT/GREN S35*...93 F5
Nethercroft *DOD/DAR S75*......18 A2
Nether Croft Rd
   STV/CWN S43 ....188 C2
Netherdene Rd *DRON S18*....171 E2
Nether Edge Rd *ECC S11*.....139 G5
Nether Farm Cl
   STV/CWN S43 ....188 C4
Netherfield *HOY S74*..............62 B2
Netherfield Cl
   STKB/PEN S36..................77 H2
   STV/CWN S43 ....188 C4
Netherfield Cft *CUD/GR S72*...16 D2
Netherfield La *RAW S62*..........98 B2
Netherfield Rd *CHSW S40*....191 E4
   FUL S10..........................124 C4
Netherfields Crs *DRON S18*...171 E3
Netherfield Vw
   RHAM/THRY S65............107 F1
Nethergate *ST/HB/BR S6*.....123 F2
Nethergreen Av
   ECK/KIL S21...................168 B1
Nethergreen Ct
   ECK/KIL S21...................168 B1
Nethergreen Gdns
   ECK/KIL S21...................168 B1
Nethergreen Rd *ECC S11*.....138 A2
   ECK/KIL S21...................168 B1
Nether Hall Rd *DON DN1*.........6 D3
Nether La *CHPT/GREN S35*....93 F5
Netherleigh Rd *CHSW S40*....191 F1
Nether Ley Av
   CHPT/GREN S35 ....94 A1
Nether Ley Ct
   CHPT/GREN S35 ....94 A1
Nether Ley Cft
   CHPT/GREN S35 ....94 A1
Nether Ley Gdns
   CHPT/GREN S35 ....94 A1
Nethermoor Av
   ECK/KIL S21...................168 B1
Nethermoor Cl
   ECK/KIL S21...................168 B1
Nethermoor Dr
   ECK/KIL S21...................168 B1
   MALT S66........................121 G2
Nethermoor La
   ECK/KIL S21...................168 B1
Nethermoor Rd *RCH S42*......195 G5
Nether Oak Cl *MOS S20*.......157 H5
Nether Oak Dr *MOS S20*.......157 H5
Nether Oak Vw *MOS S20*......157 H5
Nether Shire La *SHEFN S5*...102 C2
Nether Springs Rd
   BSVR S44.......................196 C1
Netherthorpe
   STV/CWN S43 ....182 C4
Netherthorpe Cl
   ECK/KIL S21...................168 A1
   STV/CWN S43 ....182 B5
Netherthorpe La
   ECK/KIL S21...................168 A1
Netherthorpe Pl *OWL S3*.......10 D1
Netherthorpe Rd *OWL S3*......10 C3
   STV/CWN S43 ....182 B4
Netherthorpe St *OWL S3*.......10 D1
Netherthorpe Wk *OWL S3*.....10 D1
Netherthorpe Wy *DIN S25*....148 C1
Netherwood Rd
   WMB/DAR S73 ....34 B5
Nettleham Rd *SHEFS S8*......152 D2
Neville Av *BSLY S70*...............32 C3
Neville Cl *BSLY S70*................32 D3
   OWL S3..........................126 B2
   STV/CWN S43 ....189 H1
Neville Crs *BSLY S70*..............32 D3
Neville Dr *OWL S3*................126 B1
Neville Rd *KIMB S61*...............96 D5
Neville St *RHAM S60*..............8 D5
Nevis Cl *CHSW S40*..............186 C5
Newark *MOS S20*..................157 E5
Newark Rd *MEX/SWTN S64*...66 C3
Newark St *DARN/MH S9*.......116 C5
   NROS/TKH DN11...............91 E2
New Barlborough Cl
   STV/CWN S43 ....184 D1
New Beetwell St *CHSW S40*....5 F4
Newbiggin Cl *RAW S62*..........98 A2
Newbiggin Dr *RAW S62*.........98 A2
Newbold Av *CHNE S41*.........187 E3
Newbold Back La
   CHSW S40......................186 D4
Newbold Dr *CHNE S41*.........187 E3
Newbold Rd *CHNE S41*.............4 E1
Newbold Ter *BTLY DN5*..........39 F4
Newbolt Rd
   DONS/BSCR DN4 ....71 H2
Newbould Crs *MOS S20*.......157 G2
Newbould La *FUL S10*..........125 E5
Newbridge Dr *CHNE S41*......179 G5
Newbridge Dr
   STV/CWN S43 ....188 B1
Newbridge Gv
   BSLYN/ROY S71................20 B4
Newbridge La *CHNE S41*......179 H5
   STV/CWN S43 ....188 B1
Newburn Dr *DARN/MH S9*....117 C2
Newbury Rd *FUL S10*............124 D3
Newbury Wy *BTLY DN5*..........38 D4
Newby Crs
   DONS/BSCR DN4 ....71 G3
Newby Rd *CHNE S41*............186 C5

Newcastle Cl DIN S25 .... 148 C1
Newcastle St SHEF S1 .... 10 E3
New Chapel Av
  STKB/PEN S36 .... 44 C5
Newcomen Rd BTLY DN5 .... 39 C5
Newcroft Cl MOS S20 .... 157 H2
New Cross Dr
  HAN/WDH S13 .... 143 E4
New Cross Wy
  HAN/WDH S13 .... 143 E4
Newdale Av CUD/GR S72 .... 21 G2
New Droppingwell Rd
  KIMB S61 .... 103 H3
Newent La FUL S10 .... 124 D3
Newfield Av BSLYN/ROY S71 .... 20 D3
Newfield Crs DEARNE S63 .... 64 D3
  TOT/DORE S17 .... 160 C1
Newfield Cft
  TOT/DORE S17 .... 150 C5
Newfield Farm Cl GLV S14 .... 141 E5
Newfield Green Rd
  SHEFP/MNR S2 .... 140 D4
Newfield La TOT/DORE S17 .... 160 C1
Newfield Pl TOT/DORE S17 .... 160 C1
Newgate Cl
  CHPT/GREN S35 .... 80 B4
Newhall Av MALT S66 .... 121 G2
New Hall Crs STKB/PEN S36 .... 76 B1
New Hall La STKB/PEN S36 .... 76 A2
New Hall Rd CHSW S40 .... 191 H2
Newhall Rd ARMTH DN3 .... 29 G4
  ATT S4 .... 116 A4
  DARN/MH S9 .... 116 B5
Newhaven Cl CHSW S40 .... 191 F3
New Hl CONI DN12 .... 89 E1
Newhill Rd BSLYN/ROY S71 .... 20 A2
  DEARNE S63 .... 64 D3
New Ings ARMTH DN3 .... 42 C4
Newington Av CUD/GR S72 .... 16 D4
Newington Dr
  AU/AST/KP S26 .... 145 G3
Newington Rd ECC S11 .... 139 E2
Newland Av CUD/GR S72 .... 21 G1
  MALT S66 .... 110 D2
Newland Cl DHNE S41 .... 5 G1
Newland Gdns CHNE S41 .... 187 G4
Newland Rd
  BSLYN/ROY S71 .... 14 C5
Newlands Av CHSW S40 .... 191 G1
  HACK/IN S12 .... 141 G4
Newlands Cl
  DONS/BSCR DN4 .... 74 B1
Newlands Dr BTLY DN5 .... 39 F5
  HACK/IN S12 .... 141 G4
Newlands Gv HACK/IN S12 .... 141 H4
Newlands Rd HACK/IN S12 .... 141 G4
Newlands Wy
  WMB/DAR S73 .... 51 E4
  NROS/TKH DN11 .... 91 G2
New La BTLY DN5 .... 54 A4
Newlyn Dr BSLYN/ROY S71 .... 20 B4
Newlyn Pl SHEFS S8 .... 152 D2
Newlyn Rd SHEFS S8 .... 152 D2
Newman Av
  BSLYN/ROY S71 .... 15 G3
Newman Cl DARN/MH S9 .... 103 H5
Newman Ct RHAM S60 .... 119 G5
Newman Dr DARN/MH S9 .... 103 G5
Newman Rd DARN/MH S9 .... 116 C1
  RHAM S60 .... 119 G2
Newmarch St
  DARN/MH S9 .... 117 G1
Newmarket Cl
  DONS/BSCR DN4 .... 57 H3
New Mdw RAW S62 .... 84 D3
New Queen St CHNE S41 .... 4 E1
New Rd DEARNE S63 .... 65 F2
  DIN S25 .... 148 A2
  DOD/DAR S75 .... 14 A3
  DOD/DAR S75 .... 60 B5
  DRON S18 .... 172 C2
  KIMB S61 .... 103 H4
  RCH S42 .... 195 E4
  STKB/PEN S36 .... 77 F2
  STV/CWN S43 .... 177 F4
  WMB/DAR S73 .... 63 F1
Newsam Rd MEX/SWTN S64 .... 86 B2
New School Cl MOS S20 .... 166 C1
New School Ct MOS S20 .... 166 C1
New School Rd MOS S20 .... 166 C1
Newsham Rd SHEFS S8 .... 139 H5
New Smithy Av
  STKB/PEN S36 .... 44 A2
New Smithy Dr
  STKB/PEN S36 .... 44 A2
Newsome Av
  WMB/DAR S73 .... 49 H2
New Station Rd BSVR S44 .... 196 D3
  MEX/SWTN S64 .... 66 C5
Newstead Av HACK/IN S12 .... 155 G3
Newstead Cl DRON S18 .... 170 A2
  HACK/IN S12 .... 155 G2
Newstead Dr HACK/IN S12 .... 155 G3
Newstead Gv HACK/IN S12 .... 155 G2
Newstead Pl HACK/IN S12 .... 155 G3
Newstead Ri HACK/IN S12 .... 155 G3
Newstead Rd
  BSLYN/ROY S71 .... 14 C4
  BTLY DN5 .... 39 F1
  HACK/IN S12 .... 155 G2
Newstead Wy HACK/IN S12 .... 155 G3

New St BSLY S70 .... 3 F6
  BSLY S70 .... 48 C1
  BSLYN/ROY S71 .... 15 G1
  BSLYN/ROY S71 .... 33 E2
  BSVR S44 .... 196 D1
  BTLY DN5 .... 39 G2
  CHPT/GREN S35 .... 80 B3
  CHSW S40 .... 5 F6
  CUD/GR S72 .... 23 E1
  DEARNE S63 .... 53 F4
  DIN S25 .... 134 C1
  DOD/DAR S75 .... 30 B4
  DON DN1 .... 6 C7
  KIMB S61 .... 95 F2
  KIMB S61 .... 97 F2
  MEX/SWTN S64 .... 67 H5
  MOS S20 .... 157 G5
  RAW S62 .... 98 B1
  RHAM S60 .... 129 H1
  SHEF S1 .... 11 G2
  WMB/DAR S73 .... 62 D1
New Street Bus Link
  MOS S20 .... 157 G5
New Street La
  SHEFP/MNR S2 .... 11 K2
Newton Av STKB/PEN S36 .... 76 B1
Newton Chamber Rd
  CHPT/GREN S35 .... 80 D3
Newton Chambers Rd
  CHPT/GREN S35 .... 80 D4
Newton Cl CHPT/GREN S35 .... 81 E4
Newton Dr BTLY DN5 .... 55 F2
  RHAM/THRY S65 .... 106 C3
Newton Gdns
  CHPT/GREN S35 .... 81 E4
Newton La BTLY DN5 .... 55 F2
  SHEF S1 .... 11 G6
  STKB/PEN S36 .... 76 B1
Newton Pl KIMB S61 .... 95 F3
Newton Gn CUD/GR S72 .... 21 H2
New Wortley Rd KIMB S61 .... 8 B3
Niagara Rd ST/HB/BR S6 .... 114 A1
Nicholas La DEARNE S63 .... 37 E5
Nicholas St BSLY S70 .... 2 D5
  CHNE S41 .... 193 F5
Nicholson Av DEARNE S63 .... 64 D3
  DOD/DAR S75 .... 18 A3
Nicholson Pl SHEFS S8 .... 140 B4
Nicholson Rd
  DONS/BSCR DN4 .... 55 G4
  SHEFS S8 .... 140 A4
Nichols Rd ST/HB/BR S6 .... 124 C2
Nickerwood Dr
  AU/AST/KP S26 .... 145 F4
Nicklety Ct RHAM S60 .... 129 F1
Nidderdale Pl MALT S66 .... 108 C3
Nidderdale Rd KIMB S61 .... 96 D3
Nidd Rd DARN/MH S9 .... 127 G2
Nidd Rd East DARN/MH S9 .... 127 G2
Nightingale Cl CHNE S41 .... 5 F2
  RHAM S60 .... 9 F7
Nightingale Ct RHAM S60 .... 9 F6
Nightingale Cft KIMB S61 .... 82 C5
Nightingale Rd
  CHPT/GREN S35 .... 101 F1
Nikolas Rd ECK/KIL S21 .... 175 H2
Nile St FUL S10 .... 125 E5
Nine Trees MALT S66 .... 121 H4
Ninian Gv DONS/BSCR DN4 .... 58 A5
Nobel Wy DIN S25 .... 134 B3
Noble St HOY S74 .... 62 B3
Noblethorpe Rd
  MEX/SWTN S64 .... 86 D4
Nodder Rd HAN/WDH S13 .... 142 A3
Noehill Pl SHEFP/MNR S2 .... 141 H1
Noehill Rd SHEFP/MNR S2 .... 141 H1
Nookery Cl MALT S66 .... 111 F2
Nooking Cl ARMTH DN3 .... 43 E4
Nook La ST/HB/BR S6 .... 123 G1
  STKB/PEN S36 .... 45 E5
The Nook FUL S10 .... 125 F3
Nora St DEARNE S63 .... 37 H4
Norborough Rd
  DARN/MH S9 .... 117 G2
  WHHL DN2 .... 40 D5
Norbreck Rd
  DONS/BSCR DN4 .... 70 C3
Norbriggs Rd STV/CWN S43 .... 183 E4
Norbrook Wy RHAM S60 .... 120 B3
Norburn Dr ECK/KIL S21 .... 168 B2
Norbury Cl CHSW S40 .... 186 B4
  DRON S18 .... 170 B2
Norcroft BSLY S70 .... 31 H4
Norcross Gdns
  WMB/DAR S73 .... 35 F5
Norfolk Cl BSLYN/ROY S71 .... 20 B3
  RCH S42 .... 191 F4
Norfolk Ct
  RHAM/THRY S65 * 9 G3
Norfolk Dr DIN S25 .... 148 C2
Norfolk Hl CHPT/GREN S35 .... 93 E5
Norfolk Hill Cft
  CHPT/GREN S35 .... 93 E5
Norfolk La SHEF S1 * 11 G4

Norfolk Park Av
  SHEFP/MNR S2 .... 140 D1
Norfolk Park Dr
  SHEFP/MNR S2 .... 140 C1
Norfolk Park Rd
  SHEFP/MNR S2 .... 11 K7
Norfolk Pl MALT S66 .... 111 E3
Norfolk Rd CUD/GR S72 .... 36 A1
  DONS/BSCR DN4 .... 71 H2
  SHEFP/MNR S2 .... 11 K5
Norfolk Rw SHEF S1 .... 11 G3
Norfolk St RHAM/THRY S65 .... 9 G3
  SHEF S1 .... 11 G4
Norfolk Wy RHAM S60 .... 119 G2
Norgreave Wy MOS S20 .... 167 E1
Norman Cl BSLY S70 .... 32 A5
  BSLYN/ROY S71 .... 20 C3
Norman Crs BTLY DN5 .... 38 D3
  NROS/TKH DN11 .... 91 E2
Normancroft Crs
  SHEFP/MNR S2 .... 142 A1
Normancroft Dr
  SHEFP/MNR S2 .... 141 H1
Normancroft Wy
  SHEFP/MNR S2 .... 141 H1
Normandale Av
  ST/HB/BR S6 .... 112 D4
Normandale Rd
  ST/HB/BR S6 .... 114 B5
Norman St DARN/MH S9 .... 116 C5
  DEARNE S63 .... 37 G2
Normanton Gdns ATT S4 .... 115 G5
Normanton Gv
  HAN/WDH S13 .... 142 D4
Normanton
  HI HACK/IN S12 .... 142 A4
Normanton Spring Ct
  HAN/WDH S13 .... 142 C4
Normanton Spring Rd
  HAN/WDH S13 .... 142 C5
Normanville Av RHAM S60 .... 118 B3
Norrels Dr RHAM S60 .... 106 B5
Norrel's Cft RHAM S60 .... 106 B5
Norris Rd ST/HB/BR S6 .... 113 H4
Norroy St ATT S4 .... 126 D1
Norstead Crs MALT S66 .... 109 E3
Northampton Rd
  WHHL DN2 .... 41 G5
North Bridge Rd BTLY DN5 .... 6 B2
North Church St SHEF S1 .... 11 G2
North Cliff Rd CONI DN12 .... 68 D5
North Cl BSLYN/ROY S71 .... 15 G1
  DRON S18 .... 172 A5
Northcote Av
  SHEFP/MNR S2 .... 140 B4
Northcote Rd
  DOD/DAR S75 .... 2 A3
Northcote Ter
  SHEFP/MNR S2 .... 140 B4
North Crs ECK/KIL S21 .... 158 C5
  RHAM/THRY S65 .... 106 C2
North Dr RHAM S60 .... 105 E2
Northern Av
  SHEFP/MNR S2 .... 141 E3
Northern Common
  DRON S18 .... 161 H5
North Farm Ct
  AU/AST/KP S26 .... 145 H2
Northfield Av FUL S10 .... 124 D2
  RAW S62 .... 85 F4
Northfield Cl FUL S10 .... 125 E2
Northfield Ct MALT S66 .... 108 B4
Northfield La MALT S66 .... 108 A4
Northfield Rd BTLY DN5 .... 55 H1
  FUL S10 .... 124 D3
  RHAM S60 .... 9 F2
Northfields STV/CWN S43 .... 185 F3
Northgate DOD/DAR S75 .... 19 E4
North Ga MEX/SWTN S64 .... 67 G3
North Hill Rd SHEFN S5 .... 101 H5
Northlands BSLYN/ROY S71 .... 12 C5
Northlands Rd SHEFN S5 .... 101 H5
Northmoor Cl
  STV/CWN S43 * 188 D2
North Moor Vw
  STV/CWN S43 .... 188 D2
North Pitt St KIMB S61 .... 104 D3
North Pl DOD/DAR S75 .... 18 D4
  RHAM/THRY S65 .... 106 C2
North Qd SHEFN S5 .... 102 D5
North Rd BSLYN/ROY S71 .... 12 D5
  RHAM/THRY S65 .... 106 D2
  STV/CWN S43 .... 185 E2
North Royds Wd
  BSLYN/ROY S71 .... 14 D3
Northside Rd DEARNE S63 .... 65 F2
North St DONS/BSCR DN4 .... 6 E7
  MEX/SWTN S64 .... 66 C5
  RAW S62 .... 85 H4
  RHAM S60 .... 8 C2
  WMB/DAR S73 .... 35 E4
North Swaithe Cl BTLY DN5 .... 26 C5
North Ter CHNE S41 * 192 D5
Northumberland Av
  HOY S74 .... 62 A1
  WHHL DN2 .... 41 F5
Northumberland Rd
  FUL S10 .... 125 E4
Northumberland Wy
  BSLYN/ROY S71 .... 33 F2
North View St BSVR S44 .... 196 B3
Northwood ST/HB/BR S6 .... 100 C5

Northwood Dr
  ST/HB/BR S6 .... 100 B5
Northwood Pl
  ST/HB/BR S6 .... 113 F1
Norton Av CHSW S40 .... 191 E4
  GLV S14 .... 153 H4
  HACK/IN S12 .... 154 D3
Norton Church Glebe
  SHEFS S8 .... 153 F4
Norton Church Rd
  SHEFS S8 .... 153 F4
Norton Green Cl SHEFS S8 .... 153 G4
Norton Hammer La
  SHEFS S8 .... 152 C1
Norton La SHEFS S8 * 163 E1
Norton Lees Cl SHEFS S8 * 153 E1
Norton Lees Crs SHEFS S8 .... 153 E1
Norton Lees La SHEFS S8 .... 153 E1
Norton Lees Rd SHEFS S8 .... 139 H5
Norton Lees Sq SHEFS S8 .... 153 E1
Norton Ms SHEFS S8 .... 153 G4
Norton Park Av SHEFS S8 .... 153 F5
Norton Park Crs SHEFS S8 .... 153 F5
Norton Park Dr SHEFS S8 .... 153 F5
Norton Park Rd SHEFS S8 .... 163 E1
Norton Vw SHEFS S8 .... 153 E1
Norton Rd DEARNE S63 .... 64 D1
  GLV S14 .... 154 A3
  WHHL DN2 .... 41 F5
Norville Crs WMB/DAR S73 .... 35 F4
  DEARNE S63 .... 37 G2
Norwich Gdns ATT S4 * 115 G5
Norwich Rd
  DONS/BSCR DN4 .... 73 H2
Norwood Av CHNE S41 .... 193 F5
  MALT S66 .... 110 D2
  SHEFN S5 .... 113 F3
Norwood Cl MALT S66 .... 110 D2
  SHEFN S5 .... 113 F3
Norwood Crs
  AU/AST/KP S26 .... 159 G4
  ECK/KIL S21 .... 168 D1
Norwood Dr BTLY DN5 .... 26 C4
  DOD/DAR S75 .... 18 A2
  SHEFN S5 .... 113 F3
Norwood Grange Dr
  SHEFN S5 .... 115 F2
Norwood Pl ECK/KIL S21 .... 168 D1
Norwood Rd CONI DN12 .... 85 E2
  SHEFN S5 .... 115 F3
Norwood St
  RHAM/THRY S65 .... 99 F5
Nostell Fold DOD/DAR S75 .... 30 B4
Nostell Pl DONS/BSCR DN4 .... 73 H2
Nottingham Cliff OWL S3 .... 126 A1
Nottingham Cl
  BSLYN/ROY S71 .... 33 G3
  BTLY DN5 .... 38 D4
  DIN S25 .... 148 B5
  RCH S42 .... 195 E4
Nottingham Dr RCH S42 .... 195 H4
Nottingham St SHEFS S8 .... 115 F5
  RHAM/THRY S65 .... 9 G5
Norton La HOR/CROF WF4 .... 12 C2
Novara Cl BSLY S70 .... 32 B2
Novello St MALT S66 .... 111 G4
Nowill Cl SHEFS S8 .... 140 A4
Nowill Pl SHEFS S8 .... 140 A4
Nunnery Crs RHAM S60 .... 129 G1
Nunnery Dr
  SHEFP/MNR S2 .... 127 F3
Nunnery Sq
  SHEFP/MNR S2 * 127 E4
Nunnery Ter
  SHEFP/MNR S2 .... 127 E4
Nunnington Wy
  ARMTH DN3 .... 29 E3
Nursery Crs DIN S25 .... 148 B2
Nursery Dr BSVR S44 .... 196 C3
  CHPT/GREN S35 .... 102 B1
  RHAM S60 .... 129 G1
Nursery Gdns BSLY S70 .... 33 E3
Nursery Gv
  CHPT/GREN S35 .... 102 B1
Nursery La BTLY DN5 .... 70 A1
  OWL S3 .... 9 F2
Nursery Rd AU/AST/KP S26 .... 145 E2
  DIN S25 .... 148 C1
Nursery St BSLY S70 .... 3 F7
  OWL S3 .... 9 F2
Nuttall Pl SHEFP/MNR S2 .... 126 D4
Nutwell Cl DONS/BSCR DN4 .... 74 D4
Nutwell La ARMTH DN3 .... 42 D4

○

Oadby Dr CHNE S41 .... 193 E5
Oak Av DEARNE S63 .... 65 G3
Oak Bank Av CHNE S41 .... 179 H3
Oakbank Cl MEX/SWTN S64 .... 86 B3
Oakbank Ct
  TOT/DORE S17 * 161 E3
Oakbrook Rd ECC S11 .... 138 B2
Oak Cl ECK/KIL S21 .... 168 A3
  HOY S74 .... 61 G3
  MALT S66 .... 108 C3
  MEX/SWTN S64 .... 66 C3
  STV/CWN S43 .... 188 B2
Oak Ct BTLY DN5 .... 54 D4
Oakcrest DONS/BSCR DN4 .... 74 D4
Oakcroft CHNE S41 .... 195 F4
Oak Crs HOR/CROF WF4 .... 13 H1
  RCH S42 .... 195 F4
Oakdale BSLY S70 .... 32 B5
Oakdale Cl ARMTH DN3 .... 42 B1
Oakdale Pl KIMB S61 .... 104 D3
Oak Dr
  DONS/BSCR DN4 .... 70 C4
Oakdale Rd DIN S25 .... 148 C3
  ECC S11 .... 139 F4
  KIMB S61 .... 104 D4
Oakdell DRON S18 .... 163 H5
Oakdene NROS/TKH DN11 .... 91 F3
Oak Dr ARMTH DN3 .... 42 C2
Oaken Wood Cl KIMB S61 .... 95 G1
Oaken Wood Rd KIMB S61 .... 95 F1
Oakes Gn DARN/MH S9 .... 127 F1
Oakes Park Vw GLV S14 .... 153 H3
Oakes St DARN/MH S9 .... 103 H5
Oakfern Gv CHPT/GREN S35 .... 80 B3
Oakfield Av CHSW S40 .... 191 F3
Oakfield Wk DOD/DAR S75 .... 18 D5
Oak Gv CONI DN12 .... 88 D2
Oakham Dr OWL S3 .... 125 H1
Oakham Pl DOD/DAR S75 .... 2 A1
Oak Haven Av CUD/GR S72 .... 36 A1
Oakhill Rd ABRD S7 .... 139 F4
  DRON S18 .... 171 G1
  WHHL DN2 .... 41 F4
Oakholme Ms FUL S10 .... 139 E1
Oakholme Rd FUL S10 .... 139 E1
Oakland Rd ST/HB/BR S6 .... 113 H4
Oaklands DONS/BSCR DN4 .... 75 E3
  MALT S66 .... 121 G2
Oaklands Av
  BSLYN/ROY S71 .... 20 D3
Oaklands Dr
  DONS/BSCR DN4 .... 57 H3
Oaklands Gdns
  DONS/BSCR DN4 .... 73 H1
Oaklands Pl DEARNE S63 .... 65 E3
Oaklea BSLY S70 .... 48 C1
  DEARNE S63 .... 37 G3
Oak Lea KIMB S61 .... 97 F3
Oak Lea Av DEARNE S63 .... 64 C1
Oakley Av CHSW S40 .... 4 C3
Oakley Rd HAN/WDH S13 .... 128 C5
Oak Lodge Rd
  CHPT/GREN S35 .... 80 C5
Oak Mdw RHAM/THRY S65 .... 106 D1
Oak Pk FUL S10 .... 124 D5
Oak Park Ri BSLY S70 * 32 A3
Oak Rd ARMTH DN3 .... 42 C2
  CUD/GR S72 .... 17 F2
  DEARNE S63 .... 37 F2
  DEARNE S63 .... 65 G3
  HACK/IN S12 .... 154 C3
  MALT S66 .... 110 B3
  MEX/SWTN S64 .... 66 C3
  MOS S20 .... 157 F1
Oakroyd Crs CUD/GR S72 .... 23 E1
Oaks Av STKB/PEN S36 .... 56 C5
Oaks Crs BSLY S70 .... 65 G4
Oaks Dr STKB/PEN S36 .... 32 C2
Oaks Fold Av SHEFN S5 .... 103 E3
Oaks Fold Rd SHEFN S5 .... 103 E3
Oaks Fold Rd SHEFN S5 .... 103 E4
Oaks La BSLY S70 .... 32 C2
  KIMB S61 .... 96 A5
  SHEFN S5 .... 103 E4
Oak St BSLY S70 .... 2 D5
  CUD/GR S72 .... 23 E2
  MOS S20 .... 156 C5
  SHEFS S8 .... 140 A3
  STV/CWN S43 .... 181 E5
Oak Ter AU/AST/KP S26 .... 144 D2
  DON DN1 .... 56 A4
Oaktree Av MALT S66 .... 108 C4
Oaktree Cl MALT S66 .... 59 G4
Oak Tree Rd ARMTH DN3 .... 59 G4
  STV/CWN S43 .... 185 E4
Oakwell MALT S66 .... 111 E2
Oakwell La BSLYN/ROY S71 .... 3 J5
Oakwell Ter BSLYN/ROY S71 .... 3 K6
Oakwell Vw BSLYN/ROY S71 .... 3 K5
  BSLYN/ROY S71 .... 32 B1
Oakwood Av
  BSLYN/ROY S71 .... 12 B5
  SHEFN S5 .... 101 H2
Oakwood Cl BSLY S70 .... 48 C1
Oakwood Crs
  BSLYN/ROY S71 .... 15 F1
  RAW S62 .... 85 G5
Oakwood Dr ARMTH DN3 .... 42 C5
  RHAM S60 .... 119 G1
Oakwood Gv RHAM S60 .... 106 C3
Oakwood Hall Dr
  RHAM S60 .... 119 F2
Oakwood Rd
  BSLYN/ROY S71 .... 12 B5
  DONS/BSCR DN4 .... 71 F1
Oakwood Rd East
  RHAM S60 .... 119 G1
Oakwood Rd West
  RHAM S60 .... 119 F1
Oakwood Wy
  STV/CWN S43 .... 182 D2
  MOS S20 .... 167 E2
Oakworth Cl DOD/DAR S75 .... 18 D4
Oakworth Dr MOS S20 .... 166 D2
Oakworth Gv MOS S20 .... 166 D2
Oakworth Vw MOS S20 .... 166 D2
Oates Av RAW S62 .... 98 C1

Oates Cl KIMB S61..................105 E2
Oates St KIMB S61..................105 E2
Oats Orch MOS S20.................166 D2
Oberon Crs WMB/DAR S73.......34 D4
Oborne Cl RHAM/THRY S65....109 E1
Occupation Cl
　STV/CWN S43.....................177 E5
Occupation La
　HACK/IN S12......................155 H2
　ST/HB/BR S6.....................112 D3
Occupation Rd CHNE S41......187 F1
　RAW S62.................................81 H2
　RAW S62.................................98 A2
Ochre Dike Cl MOS S20 *.......157 E3
Ochre Dike La MOS S20...........156 D3
Octavia Cl RHAM S60...............118 C2
Odeon Ar DON DN1 *..................6 D4
Odom Ct SHEFP/MNR S2.........140 B4
Offridge Cl STV/CWN S43........185 F4
Ogden Rd WHHL DN2..................41 H2
Oil Mill Fold RHAM S60................9 F5
Oldale Cl HAN/WDH S13...........143 G3
Oldale Ct HAN/WDH S13..........143 G4
Oldale Gv HAN/WDH S13.........143 G4
Old Anna Lane or
　Long La STKB/PEN S36...........44 A2
Old Bakery Cl CHNE S41..........179 G4
Old Brick Works La
　CHNE S41.............................187 G3
Old Clifton La
　RHAM/THRY S65.......................9 J5
Oldcoates Cl DIN S25...............134 D3
Oldcotes Rd DIN S25................135 E2
Old Cottage Cl
　HAN/WDH S13......................143 H3
Old Cross La RHAM/THRY S63...65 F2
Old Doncaster Rd
　DEARNE S63..........................65 H2
Old Farm Ct MEX/SWTN S64.....54 D4
Oldfield Av CONI DN12...............88 B1
　ST/HB/BR S6.......................123 H1
Oldfield Cl HOY S74....................62 A2
Oldfield Gv ST/HB/BR S6.........123 H2
Oldfield Rd
　RHAM/THRY S65..................107 F2
　ST/HB/BR S6.......................123 H1
Oldfield Ter ST/HB/BR S6........123 H2
Old Fulwood Rd FUL S10.........137 H3
Old Garden Dr
　RHAM/THRY S65.......................9 K2
Oldgate La RHAM/THRY S65........9 G3
Old Guildhall Yd DON DN1 *.........6 C3
Old Hall Cl BTLY DN5...................54 C5
　DIN S25................................134 B1
　MALT S66 *..........................108 D4
Old Hall Dr MALT S66................108 D4
Old Hall Ms MALT S66...............108 D4
Old Hall Pl BTLY DN5...................39 H2
Old Hall Rd BSLY S70..................47 F5
　BTLY DN5................................39 G1
　CHSW S40.............................191 H2
　DARN/MH S9........................116 C2
Old Hall Wk CUD/GR S72 *.........36 A1
Oldhay Ct TOT/DORE S17.........160 D2
Old Hay Gdns
　TOT/DORE S17.....................160 C2
Old Hay La TOT/DORE S17.......160 C2
Old Hexthorpe
　DONS/BSCR DN4....................55 F4
Old House La CHSW S40..........186 D3
Old La MOS S20.........................167 F1
Old Manor Dr
　STKB/PEN S36........................45 H5
Old Mill Dr CHNE S41...............186 A2
Old Mill La BSLY S70.....................3 F2
Old Mill Rd CONI DN12...............89 F1
Old Oak Vw BSLY S70.................32 C2
Old Park Av SHEFS S8..............162 B1
Old Park Rd SHEFS S8..............162 B1
Old Pheasant Ct CHSW S40.....191 H4
Old Quarry Av
　AU/AST/KP S26....................159 F2
Old Quarry Cl
　STV/CWN S43.......................177 F5
Old Retford Rd
　HAN/WDH S13......................143 G1
Oldridge Cl CHSW S40..............186 A3
　CHSW S40.............................191 E1
　CONI DN12...............................88 B3
Oldroyd Av CUD/GR S72............23 E1
Old School Av ARMTH DN3........42 D4
　HOY S74...................................62 A1
　KIMB S61..................................97 G2
　RCH S42.................................190 B5
Old School Ct DOD/DAR S75.....18 A2
Old School Dr SHEFS S10.........102 B4
Old School La BSVR S44...........193 H2
　RHAM S60..............................129 H1
Old School Wy WHHL DN2........40 C5
Old Sheffield Rd RHAM S60.........8 E7
Old Ship La CHSW S40..................5 G5
Old Station Dr ABRD S7............152 B2
Old St SHEFP/MNR S2..............126 C3
Old Town Hall RHAM S60.............9 F3
Old Warren V RAW S62..............95 E4
Oldwell Cl TOT/DORE S17........160 D4
Old Whittington La
　DRON S18..............................172 A5
Old Wortley Rd KIMB S61........106 C1
Olive Cl AU/AST/KP S26...........145 F3
Olive Crs HACK/IN S12.............154 C3

Olive Grove Rd
　SHEFP/MNR S2.....................140 B2
Olive Rd MOS S20.....................166 D1
　STKB/PEN S36........................76 D2
Oliver Rd ABRD S7....................152 A1
　DONS/BSCR DN4.....................71 G1
Olivers Dr DARN/MH S9............128 B3
Olivers Mt DARN/MH S9............128 C3
Oliver St MEX/SWTN S64............66 D3
Olivers Wy RHAM S60...............118 B5
Olivet Rd SHEFS S8...................148 D5
Ollerton Rd BSLYN/ROY S71......14 D4
Onchan Rd ST/HB/BR S6...........124 A2
Onslow Rd ECC S11...................138 D3
Orange St SHEF S1......................10 E5
Orchard Av DIN S25...................148 C1
Orchard Cl ARMTH DN3.............29 E3
　BSLYN/ROY S71......................20 C2
　BSVR S44...............................197 E3
　MEX/SWTN S64........................67 E3
　RHAM S60..............................129 H1
　SHEFN S5...............................102 B2
　STV/CWN S43.........................185 E3
Orchard Crs SHEFN S5.............102 B2
Orchard Cft
　AU/AST/KP S26....................159 F2
　DOD/DAR S75..........................30 C3
Orchard Flatts Crs KIMB S61.....97 E4
Orchard Gdns DIN S25..............148 B4
Orchard Gv MALT S66...............108 C1
Orchard La AU/AST/KP S26.....159 F3
　MOS S20................................157 F3
　SHEF S1....................................11 F3
Orchard Lea Dr
　AU/AST/KP S26 *.................145 F3
Orchard Ms DARN/MH S9...........39 F5
　DEARNE S63............................64 D2
　ECK/KIL S21............................168 B2
　RHAM S60..............................129 H1
Orchard Rd ST/HB/BR S6.........125 E1
Orchard Sq DRON S18...............170 D1
　SHEF S1....................................11 G3
Orchard St DEARNE S63.............53 C1
　DONS/BSCR DN4.....................55 H4
　SHEF S1....................................11 G3
　STKB/PEN S36.........................77 H3
　WMB/DAR S73..........................50 B2
Orchards Wy CHSW S40............191 G3
The Orchard DEARNE S63..........37 E3
　DIN S25.................................148 C2
Orchard Vw BSVR S44...............196 D4
Orchard View Rd
　CHSW S40..............................186 C5
Orchard Vls
　RHAM/THRY S65 *...................99 H3
Orchard Wk BSLYN/ROY S71.......3 G1
Orchard Wy DEARNE S63...........37 F2
　RHAM S60..............................118 C5
Orchard Wls MALT S66.............108 C5
Orchid Vw DIN S25....................148 A4
Ordnance Ter KIMB S61 *.........104 D3
Orgreave Cl HAN/WDH S13......143 G1
Orgreave Crs
　HAN/WDH S13......................143 G1
Orgreave Dr HAN/WDH S13.....143 G1
Orgreave La HAN/WDH S13.....143 G1
Orgreave Pl HAN/WDH S13......129 F5
Orgreave Ri HAN/WDH S13......143 H1
Orgreave Rd RHAM S60............129 G2
Orgreave Wy
　HAN/WDH S13......................143 G2
Oriel Rd FUL S10........................137 G3
Oriel Wy BSLYN/ROY S71...........20 D4
Ormesby Cl DIN S18...................170 A2
Ormesby Crs BTLY DN5...............39 E5
Ormesby Wy MALT S66.............109 E4
Ormes Meadow MOS S20.........156 C3
Ormond Cl RCH S42...................191 F5
　SHEFS S8...............................163 F2
Ormond Dr SHEFS S8................163 F2
Ormond Rd SHEFS S8................163 F2
Ormond Wy SHEFS S8...............163 F1
Ormsby Cl DONS/BSCR DN4......71 G4
Ormsby Rd CHNE S41................187 F2
Orpen Dr GLV S14......................154 A3
Orpen Wy GLV S14.....................154 A3
Orwell Cl WMB/DAR S73.............50 D4
Osberton Pl ECC S11.................139 E2
Osberton St RAW S62..................85 H5
　RHAM/THRY S65......................99 E5
Osbert Rd RHAM S60.................119 H1
Osborne Av
　AU/AST/KP S26....................145 G2
　AWLS/ASK DN6........................24 D2
Osborne Ct ECC S11..................139 E3
Osborne Dr AU/AST/KP S26.....147 F5
Osborne Ms BSLY S70...................3 K6
Osborne Rd
　AU/AST/KP S26....................147 F5
　ECC S11..................................139 E3
　WHHL DN2...................................7 H1
Osborne St BSLY S70....................3 K6
Osgathorpe Crs ATT S4.............115 G4
Osgathorpe Dr ATT S4...............115 H4
Osgathorpe Rd ATT S4..............115 G4
Osmaston Rd SHEFS S8............152 D3
Osmond Dr SHEFS S8..................32 A5
Osmond Pl BSLY S70 *.................32 A5
Osmund Rd ECK/KIL S21...........166 B5
Osprey Av BSLY S70.....................47 H5
Osprey Cl AWLS/ASK DN6...........25 F1

Osprey Gdns
　SHEFP/MNR S2.....................127 E5
Osprey Rd AU/AST/KP S26.......145 G4
Oswestry Rd SHEFN S5.............102 C5
Oswin Av DONS/BSCR DN4........55 F5
Otley Cl CONI DN12......................89 F1
Otter St DARN/MH S9.................127 F1
Oughtibridge La
　CHPT/GREN S35...................100 A2
Oughton Wy ATT S4..................115 H5
Oulton Cl MALT S66...................109 E3
Oulton Dr CUD/GR S72...............17 E5
Oulton Ri MEX/SWTN S64...........67 H2
Ouseburn Cft DARN/MH S9......127 G2
Ouseburn Rd DARN/MH S9.......127 G2
Ouseburn St DARN/MH S9........127 G2
Ouse Rd RHAM S60....................127 G2
Ouslethwaite Ct BSLY S70..........31 G4
Ouson Gdns BSLYN/ROY S71.....15 G3
Outgang La DIN S25...................134 A2
　MALT S66................................111 F5
Outram Rd CHNE S41................187 F3
　SHEFP/MNR S2.....................127 E5
Oval Rd RHAM/THRY S65..........106 D2
The Oval AWLS/ASK DN6.............24 D1
　CONI DN12...............................69 E5
　DIN S25.................................148 C2
　DONS/BSCR DN4.....................57 C4
　HOR/CROF WF4........................12 B3
　SHEFN S5...............................115 G1
Overcroft Ri
　TOT/DORE S17.....................160 C4
Overdale Av BSLY S70.................32 B4
Overdale Gdns
　TOT/DORE S17.....................160 C2
Overdale Ri TOT/DORE S17.......160 C2
Overdale Rd WMB/DAR S73........50 C4
Overend Cl GLV S14...................153 H1
Overend Rd GLV S14.................153 H1
Overend Wy GLV S14.................153 H1
Oversley Rd WHHL DN2..............40 D4
Oversley St DARN/MH S9..........117 C1
Overton Cl STV/CWN S43..........182 B3
Overton Rd ST/HB/BR S6..........113 H2
Owen Cl RHAM/THRY S65............9 H1
　ST/HB/BR S6.........................101 F3
Owen Falls Av CHNE S41..............5 K3
Owen Pl ST/HB/BR S6................101 F3
Owlcotes Vw BSVR S44..............196 D4
Owler Car La DRON S18.............164 A3
Owler La ATT S4.........................115 H3
Owlings Pl ST/HB/BR S6............113 G4
Owlings Rd ST/HB/BR S6...........113 G4
Owlthorpe Av MOS S20.............156 B5
Owlthorpe Cl MOS S20..............156 B5
Owlthorpe Dr MOS S20..............156 B5
Owlthorpe Greenway
　MOS S20................................157 E4
Owlthorpe Gv MOS S20.............156 B5
Owlthorpe La MOS S20..............156 B5
Owlthorpe Ri MOS S20...............156 B5
Owram St WMB/DAR S73 *..........35 E5
Ox Carr ARMTH DN3...................42 C4
Ox Close La KIMB S61..................96 C5
Oxclose Dr DRON S18................170 A2
Oxclose La DRON S18................170 A2
Oxclose Park Gdns
　MOS S20................................167 F2
Oxclose Park Rd MOS S20........167 F1
Oxclose Park Rd North
　MOS S20................................167 F2
Oxclose Park Vw MOS S20........167 F2
Oxcroft La BSVR S44..................197 E1
Oxcroft Wy STV/CWN S43.........184 B1
Oxford Cl KIMB S61 *..................97 G3
　STV/CWN S43.......................188 D1
Oxford Pl BSLYN/ROY S71..........33 E2
　DON DN1...................................6 C6
Oxford Rd STV/CWN S43...........188 D1
Oxford St BSLY S70......................32 A3
　BSLYN/ROY S71......................33 E2
　CHSW S40.............................192 C5
　DOD/DAR S75..........................14 A4
　MEX/SWTN S64........................66 C3
　NROS/TKH DN11......................91 E2
　RHAM/THRY S65........................8 B5
　ST/HB/BR S6.............................10 B1
Oxford Vls
　RHAM/THRY S65 *.................106 C2
Ox HI MOS S20...........................167 G3
Oxley Cl STKB/PEN S36................76 C6
Oxley Ct RHAM S60....................106 B5
Oxley Gv RHAM S60...................106 B5
Oxspring Bank SHEFN S5..........114 B2
Oxspring La STKB/PEN S36.........45 H3
Oxted Rd DARN/MH S9..............116 C2
Oxton Dr DONS/BSCR DN4.........70 D2
Oxton Rd BSLYN/ROY S71...........15 E4

Packer's Rw CHSW S40.................5 G4
Pack Horse La
　CHPT/GREN S35.....................80 C3
Packington Rd
　DONS/BSCR DN4.....................74 C1
Packman Rd DEARNE S63...........64 B5
Packman Wy DEARNE S63..........64 B5
Packwood Cl MALT S66.............111 E2
Paddington Rd DIN S25.............134 A3

Paddock Cl BTLY DN5...................39 E5
　DOD/DAR S75..........................14 A4
　RCH S42.................................195 F4
Paddock Crs
　SHEFP/MNR S2.....................141 E5
Paddock Cft
　MEX/SWTN S64........................65 H5
Paddock Dr MALT S66...............108 C2
Paddock Gv CUD/GR S72...........17 C5
Paddock Rd DOD/DAR S75.........14 A3
The Paddocks
　AU/AST/KP S26....................145 G3
　BTLY DN5................................38 D5
　BTLY DN5................................69 F2
　RHAM/THRY S65..................109 E3
　STV/CWN S43.......................183 E3
The Paddock
　AWLS/ASK DN6........................25 G1
　KIMB S61..................................95 H2
　WMB/DAR S73..........................35 E3
　WMB/DAR S73..........................50 A5
Paddock Vw
　AU/AST/KP S26....................147 E5
Padley Cl DOD/DAR S75.............30 A3
Padley Wy SHEFN S5.................102 C5
Padua Ri WMB/DAR S73..............34 D5
Page Hall Rd SHEFN S5.............102 B5
Pagenall Dr
　AU/AST/KP S26....................145 F2
Paget St DARN/MH S9................116 B5
Pagnell Av DEARNE S63..............36 D3
Paisley Cl STV/CWN S43............189 G1
Palermo Fold
　WMB/DAR S73..........................34 D4
Palgrave Crs SHEFN S5.............101 G5
Palgrave Rd SHEFN S5..............101 F5
Palington Gv
　DONS/BSCR DN4.....................58 A4
Pall MI BSLY S70............................3 F5
Palm Av ARMTH DN3...................43 E1
Palmer Cl STKB/PEN S36.............44 C5
Palmer Crs DRON S18................171 F2
Palmer Rd DARN/MH S9............128 A1
Palmerston Av MALT S66...........110 C2
Palmerston Rd FUL S10..............10 A4
Palmer St DARN/MH S9.............127 F2
　DONS/BSCR DN4.......................7 F7
Palmers Wy MALT S66...............132 D1
Palm Gv CONI DN12.....................88 C3
Palm Hollow Cl MALT S66.........107 H5
Palm La ST/HB/BR S6................125 E1
Palm St DOD/DAR S75...................2 C1
　ST/HB/BR S6.........................125 E1
Palterton La BSVR S44...............196 A5
Pamela Dr DONS/BSCR DN4......70 C2
Pangbourne Rd
　DEARNE S63............................37 E1
Pantry Gn BSLY S70 *.................48 C1
Pantry HI BSLY S70.....................48 C1
Pantry Well BSLY S70..................48 C1
Paper Mill Rd SHEFN S5............102 D2
The Parade HOY S74 *.................61 H3
　RAW S62...................................85 E4
Paradise La SHEF S1....................11 G2
Paradise Sq SHEF S1...................11 G2
Paradise St SHEF S1....................11 G2
Parish Wy BSLYN/ROY S71.........20 D4
Park Av ARMTH DN3...................42 B3
　BSLY S70....................................2 B5
　BSLYN/ROY S71......................14 D5
　BTLY DN5................................55 C4
　CHPT/GREN S35......................94 A2
　CONI DN12...............................89 E2
　CUD/GR S72.............................16 D5
　DIN S25.................................148 C1
　DRON S18..............................171 F1
　FUL S10..................................138 D2
　MEX/SWTN S64........................67 E3
　RHAM S60..............................130 B3
　STKB/PEN S36.........................44 B3
Park Cl DEARNE S63...................37 F2
Park Crs BSLYN/ROY S71...........15 H1
　CHPT/GREN S35....................102 B1
　DEARNE S63............................53 C5
　DONS/BSCR DN4.....................70 C3
　FUL S10....................................10 A6
Park Dr STKB/PEN S36.................76 D2
　AU/AST/KP S26....................144 D3
　BTLY DN5................................54 C4
　CHNE S41..................................5 J7
Parkdrive DOD/DAR S75.............46 D1
Park Drive Wy
　STKB/PEN S36.........................76 D1
Park End Rd DEARNE S63...........53 F5
Parker Av BSVR S44...................193 H1
Parkers La TOT/DORE S17.........160 C5
Parker St BSLY S70.......................2 D1
Parker's La FUL S10...................125 E4
Parker's Rd FUL S10..................125 E4
Park Farm DRON S18.................170 A1
Park Farm Ms ECK/KIL S21.......176 D2
Parkfield Ct RAW S62...................98 B3
Parkfield Rd RHAM/THRY S65....98 B1
Parkgate DEARNE S63.................37 H5
　DRON S18..............................171 G1

Parkgate Av CONI DN12.............88 C1
Parkgate Cl MOS S20................156 A5
Parkgate Cft MOS S20...............156 A5
Parkgate Dr MOS S20................156 A4
Parkgate La ECK/KIL S21...........180 C1
Park Grange Cft
　SHEFP/MNR S2.....................140 C2
Park Grange Dr
　SHEFP/MNR S2.....................140 C2
Park Grange Mt
　SHEFP/MNR S2.....................140 C2
Park Grange Ri
　SHEFP/MNR S2.....................140 C2
Park Grange Rd
　SHEFP/MNR S2.....................140 B1
Park Grange Vw
　SHEFP/MNR S2.....................140 D2
Park Gv BSLY S70...........................2 E7
　MALT S66...............................108 D4
　RAW S62...................................85 F4
　STKB/PEN S36.........................76 D1
Park Hall Av RCH S42.................191 E4
Park Hall Cl RCH S42..................191 F5
Park Hall Gdns RCH S42............191 F4
Parkhall La ECK/KIL S21.............176 B1
Parkhead Cl
　BSLYN/ROY S71......................12 A5
Parkhead Ct ECC S11.................151 F1
Parkhead Crs ECC S11...............151 F1
Parkhead Rd ECC S11................151 F1
Park HI ARMTH DN3 *..................29 G2
　AU/AST/KP S26....................144 D3
　ECK/KIL S21............................167 E5
Park Hill Gdns
　AU/AST/KP S26....................144 D3
Parkhill Rd WMB/DAR S73...........50 C2
Park Hollow WMB/DAR S73.........50 C3
Park House La
　DARN/MH S9.........................117 H4
Parkinson St DON DN1................40 B5
Parkland Dr
　NROS/TKH DN11.....................91 H2
　RCH S42.................................195 G5
Parklands ARMTH DN3................42 B1
Parklands Av DIN S25.................134 C5
Parklands Cl
　NROS/TKH DN11.....................91 G2
Parklands Vw
　AU/AST/KP S26....................145 G5
Parkland Vw
　BSLYN/ROY S71......................21 F2
Park La CHNE S41.......................187 F2
　CHPT/GREN S35......................77 F1
　CUD/GR S72.............................23 F4
　DIN S25.................................134 A3
　DONS/BSCR DN4.....................57 G3
　FUL S10....................................10 A6
　RHAM/THRY S65......................99 H4
Park Lane Ct
　RHAM/THRY S65......................99 H3
Park Mt RHAM/THRY S65.............99 H4
Park Nook RHAM/THRY S65........99 G4
Park Pl RHAM/THRY S65............106 D2
Park Rd BSLY S70........................31 G3
　BTLY DN5................................39 G1
　CHSW S40.................................5 F5
　CONI DN12...............................88 D2
　DEARNE S63............................37 E2
　DEARNE S63............................65 E3
　DON DN1...................................6 E3
　MEX/SWTN S64........................86 A1
　RHAM/THRY S65....................106 C2
　ST/HB/BR S6...........................124 B1
Park Side CHNE S41 *................177 F2
Parkside BSLYN/ROY S71...........15 H3
　DOD/DAR S75..........................19 F3
Parkside La ST/HB/BR S6..........123 H2
Parkside Ms BSLY S70.................32 A5
Parkside Rd HOY S74...................61 F4
　ST/HB/BR S6...........................114 A3
Parkside Vw CHNE S41..............186 B3
Parkson Rd RHAM S60...............119 H2
Park Spring Dr
　SHEFP/MNR S2.....................140 C2
Park Spring Pl
　SHEFP/MNR S2.....................140 C2
Park Spring Rd CUD/GR S72......22 D3
Park Spring Wy
　SHEFP/MNR S2.....................140 C2
Park Sq CHPT/GREN S35............80 D4
Park Square Jct
　SHEFP/MNR S2.......................11 J3
Parkstone Crs MALT S66...........109 H5
Parkstone Delph
　HACK/IN S12.........................154 C3
Parkstone Wy WHHL DN2...........41 G3
Park St AU/AST/KP S26..............145 E3
　BSLY S70....................................2 E7
　CHSW S40.............................192 C5
　KIMB S61....................................8 A3
　RAW S62...................................85 F5
　STV/CWN S43.......................177 F4
　WMB/DAR S73..........................50 B3
Park Ter CHPT/GREN S35...........94 B2
　DON DN1...................................6 E5
　RHAM/THRY S65......................99 G4
Park Vale Dr
　RHAM/THRY S65......................99 H4
Park Vw AWLS/ASK DN6..............25 G2
　BSLYN/ROY S71......................12 D5
　CHNE S41..............................193 H5

P

CUD/GR S72 .... 17 E1
DOD/DAR S75 .... 30 B3
KIMB S61 .... 97 F3
MALT S66 .... 111 F3
STV/CWN S43 .... 177 H4
Park View Av *MOS* S20 ...... 167 E1
Park View Rd
CHPT/GREN S35 .... 94 A2
DEARNE S5 .... 14 A3
KIMB S61 .... 104 A4
ST/HB/BR S6 .... 114 A3
Park Wy *AWLS/ASK* DN6 ...... 25 F1
Parkway *ARMTH* DN3 .... 42 D5
Parkway Av *DARN/MH* S9 ... 127 F3
Parkway Cl *DARN/MH* S9 .. 127 F3
Parkway Dr *DARN/MH* S9 .. 127 G4
Parkway North *WHHL* DN2 ... 40 D4
Parkway South *WHHL* DN2 .. 41 E4
Parkwood Ri *ARMTH* DN3 ... 29 G2
Parkwood Rd *OWL* S3 .... 114 C5
Parliament St *ECC* S11 ... 139 C1
Parma Ri *WMB/DAR* S73 ...... 34 C5
Parsley Hay Cl
HAN S13 .... 142 D1
Parsley Hay Dr
HAN S13 .... 142 D1
Parsley Hay Gdns
HAN S13 .... 142 D1
Parsley Hay Rd
HAN S13 .... 142 D1
Parsonage Cl *MOS* S20 ...... 166 D2
Parsonage Cs
ST/HB/BR S6 .... 125 E1
Parsonage St *ST/HB/BR* S6 .. 125 E1
Parson Cross Rd
ST/HB/BR S6 .... 96 B5
Partridge Cl *ECK/KIL* S21 .. 166 B5
Partridge Flatt Rd
DONS/BSCR DN4 .... 74 B2
Partridge Pl
AU/AST/KP S26 .... 145 G4
Partridge Ri
DONS/BSCR DN4 .... 74 B2
Partridge Vw
SHEFP/MNR S2 .... 127 E5
Parwich Cl *CHSW* S40 ...... 186 A4
Pashley Cft *WMB/DAR* S73 ... 49 H3
Passfield Rd
NROS/TKH DN11 .... 91 G3
Passhouses Rd *ATT* S4 ...... 115 F4
Pasture Cl *ARMTH* DN3 ...... 42 D5
Pasture Gv *ECK/KIL* S21 ... 166 C5
Pasture Rd *WMB/DAR* S73 .. 51 H1
Pastures Br
MEX/SWTN S64 * 67 C3
Pastures Ct *MEX/SWTN* S64 .. 67 H3
NROS/TKH DN11 .... 91 H3
Pastures La *BTLY* DN5 ...... 68 C1
Pastures Rd
MEX/SWTN S64 .... 68 A3
The Pastures
AU/AST/KP S26 .... 147 E5
MEX/SWTN S64 .... 67 H3
Paternoster Rw *SHEF* S1 .... 11 H5
Paterson Cl *STKB/PEN* S36 .. 76 C1
Paterson Ct *STKB/PEN* S36 .. 76 C1
Paterson Cft *STKB/PEN* S36 .. 76 C1
Paterson Gdns
STKB/PEN S36 .... 76 C1
Paterson Rd *DIN* S25 ...... 135 E4
Patmore Rd *DONS/BSCR* DN4 .. 102 D5
Paton Gv *STV/CWN* S43 ...... 188 B1
Patrick Stirling Ct
DONS/BSCR DN4 .... 55 G4
Patterdale Cl *DRON* S18 .... 170 C2
Patterdale Wy *DIN* S25 ...... 148 D2
The Pavement
SHEFP/MNR S2 .... 11 K3
Pavilion Cl *STV/CWN* S43 .. 185 E4
Pavilion La *RHAM* S60 ...... 118 B2
Pavilion Wy *SHEFS* S8 ...... 102 D5
Pavillion Ct *CONI* DN12 .... 70 C5
Paxton Crs *ARMTH* DN3 ...... 42 B5
Paxton La *FUL* S10 .... 10 A5
Paxton Rd *CHNE* S41 .... 188 A4
Payler Cl *SHEFP/MNR* S2 .... 141 G2
Payne Crs *RAW* S62 .... 85 E4
Peacock Cl *ECK/KIL* S21 ... 166 B5
KIMB S61 .... 82 B5
Pea Fields La
CHPT/GREN S35 .... 79 F1
Peakdale Crs *HACK/IN* S12 .. 142 C5
Peake Av *CONI* DN12 .... 88 C1
Peak La *MALT* S66 .... 110 C5
Peak Pl *STV/CWN* S43 ...... 189 H2
Peak Rd *BSLYN/ROY* S71 * .. 15 F5
Peaks Mt *MOS* S20 .... 157 E2
Pearce Cl
DONS/BSCR DN4 .... 71 F1
Pearce Ms *RAW* S62 .... 98 B1
Peak Vw *STV/CWN* S43 ...... 184 D1
Peak View Rd *CHSW* S40 .... 186 D5
Pearce La *RCH* S42 .... 194 C4
Pearce Rd *DARN/MH* S9 ...... 128 A4
Pearce Wk *DARN/MH* S9 ...... 128 A4
Pearl St *ECC* S11 .... 139 G2
Pearmain Dr *MALT* S66 ...... 119 H1
Pea Royd La *STKB/PEN* S36 .. 77 E1
Pearson Crs *WMB/DAR* S73 .. 49 H1
Pearson Gdns *BSVR* S44 .... 196 A4
Pearson Pl *SHEFS* S8 ...... 152 C1
Pearsons Cft *CHNE* S41 .... 186 C3
Pearson St *STKB/PEN* S36 .. 76 D1

Pearson's Cl
RHAM/THRY S65 .... 107 E5
Pearson's Fld
WMB/DAR S73 .... 50 B2
Pear St *ECC* S11 .... 139 G1
Peartree Av *RCH* S42 ...... 195 E4
DEARNE S63 .... 37 E2
Pear Tree Av *MALT* S66 .... 108 C4
Pear Tree Cl *CUD/GR* S72 .. 23 H5
ECK/KIL S21 .... 168 A3
RHAM S60 .... 118 D4
STV/CWN S43 .... 189 E1
Peartree Orch
BSLYN/ROY S71 .... 12 D4
Pear Tree Rd *SHEFN* S5 .... 102 D3
Pearwood Crs
DONS/BSCR DN4 .... 71 F3
Peasehill Cl *BSLY* S70 .... 3 F6
Peashill St *RAW* S62 ...... 98 B1
Peatfield Rd *ECK/KIL* S21 .. 168 D1
Peckham Rd
CHPT/GREN S35 .... 80 D5
Pedley Av *MOS* S20 .... 157 E4
Pedley Cl *MOS* S20 .... 157 E4
Pedley Dr *MOS* S20 * 157 E5
Pedley Gv *MOS* S20 .... 157 E4
Peel Cl *MALT* S66 .... 110 C2
Peel Pde *BSLY* S70 .... 2 E4
Peel Pl *BSLYN/ROY* S71 .... 20 A4
Peel Sq *BSLY* S70 .... 3 F4
Peel St *BSLY* S70 .... 2 E4
FUL S10 .... 125 E5
Peel Ter *FUL* S10 .... 10 B4
Peggars Cl *STV/CWN* S43 ... 177 F5
Pell's Cl *DON* DN1 * 6 C4
Pembrey Ct *MOS* S20 ...... 157 C3
Pembroke Av
DONS/BSCR DN4 .... 71 G2
Pembroke Cl *CHSW* S40 * ... 191 G3
Pembroke Crs
CHPT/GREN S35 .... 80 B5
DIN S25 .... 148 B4
Pembroke Ri *BTLY* DN5 .... 38 D4
KIMB S61 .... 104 D3
Pembroke Rd *DRON* S18 ..... 171 E3
Pembroke St *ECC* S11 ...... 139 G1
KIMB S61 .... 104 D3
Pendeen Rd *ECC* S11 .... 138 B2
Pendlebury Gv *HOY* S74 .... 61 G3
Pendle Cft *MOS* S20 ...... 157 H4
Pengeston Rd
STKB/PEN S36 .... 64 B4
Peniston Boundary Wk
STKB/PEN S36 .... 45 G1
Penistone Ct
STKB/PEN S36 * 45 E3
Penistone Rd
CHPT/GREN S35 .... 93 E5
OWL S3 .... 125 C1
ST/HB/BR S6 .... 114 A3
Penistone Rd North
ST/HB/BR S6 .... 114 A1
Peniston St *DON* DN1 ...... 6 E2
Penley St *ECC* S11 .... 139 G2
Penmore Gdns *CHNE* S41 .... 193 E4
Penmore La *CHNE* S41 ...... 193 E4
Penmore Vw *STKB/PEN* S36 .. 76 D4
Pennine Wy *CHSW* S40 ...... 186 C4
DOD/DAR S75 .... 18 D5
Pen Nook Cl *STKB/PEN* S36 .. 77 G4
Pen Nook Ct *STKB/PEN* S36 .. 77 G4
Pen Nook Gdns
STKB/PEN S36 .... 77 G4
Pen Nook Gld
STKB/PEN S36 .... 77 G4
Penns Rd *SHEFP/MNR* S2 .... 140 C4
Penny Engine La
ECK/KIL S21 .... 167 E4
Pennyfields *DEARNE* S63 ... 52 D3
Penny Hill La
AU/AST/KP S26 .... 131 H3
MALT S66 .... 132 C3
Penny La *TOT/DORE* S17 .... 160 C3
Penny Piece La *DIN* S25 ... 148 B2
Penny Piece Pl *DIN* S25 ... 148 B2
Pennywell Dr *RAW* S62 ..... 190 B5
Penrhyn Rd *ECC* S11 .... 139 E3
Penrhyn Wk
BSLYN/ROY S71 .... 33 G2
Penrith Cl *SHEFN* S5 ...... 114 C2
Penrith Crs *SHEFN* S5 ..... 114 C2
Penrith Gv *BSLYN/ROY* S71 .. 33 F2
Penrith Rd *SHEFN* S5 ...... 114 C2
Penrose Pl *HAN/WDH* S13 ... 143 E4
Penthorpe Cl *HACK/IN* S12 .. 141 G4
Pentland Cl *CHSW* S40 ..... 186 C4
Pentland Gdns *MOS* S20 .... 156 D3
Pentland Rd *DRON* S18 ..... 170 B2
Penton St *SHEF* S1 * 11 F3
Penwood Wk *MALT* S66 ...... 108 B1
Penyghent Cl
CHPT/GREN S35 .... 80 D5
Pepper Cl *KIMB* S61 .... 96 B3
Pepper St *HOY* S74 .... 49 E5
Percy St *OWL* S3 .... 125 H2
RHAM/THRY S65 .... 9 G4
Peregrine Dr *BSLY* S70 .... 47 H5
Perigree Rd *SHEFS* S8 ..... 152 C2
Periwood Av *SHEFS* S8 ..... 152 B2
Periwood Cl *SHEFS* S8 ..... 152 C2
Periwood Dr *SHEFS* S8 ..... 152 C2

Periwood Gv *SHEFS* S8 ..... 152 C2
Periwood La *SHEFS* S8 ..... 152 C2
Perkyn Rd *SHEFN* S5 ...... 102 C2
Perkyn Ter *SHEFN* S5 ...... 102 C2
Perran Gv *BTLY* DN5 .... 39 F5
Perseverance St *BSLY* S70 .. 2 C4
Persimmon Cl
NROS/TKH DN11 .... 91 F4
Perth Cl *MEX/SWTN* S64 .... 67 G2
Petal Cl *MALT* S66 .... 111 F2
Peterborough Cl *FUL* S10 .. 137 E1
Peterborough Dr *FUL* S10 .. 137 E1
Peterborough Rd *FUL* S10 .. 137 E1
Peterdale Cl *STV/CWN* S43 .. 188 C1
Peterdale Rd *STV/CWN* S43 .. 188 C1
Peterfoot Wy
BSLYN/ROY S71 .... 15 F3
Petersgate *BTLY* DN5 ...... 39 F2
Peter St *KIMB* S61 .... 104 C2
MALT S66 .... 133 E1
Peters Yd *ATT* S4 * 116 A4
Petre St *ATT* S4 .... 115 H5
Pettyclose La *CHNE* S41 ... 188 B4
Petworth Cft
BSLYN/ROY S71 .... 12 B5
Petworth Dr *ECC* S11 ...... 151 F3
Pevensey Av *CHNE* S41 ..... 187 E3
Peveril Crs *BSLYN/ROY* S71 .. 15 E5
Peveril Rd *BSVR* S44 ...... 196 C1
CHNE S41 .... 187 F2
ECC S11 .... 138 D3
ECK/KIL S21 .... 167 E4
Pexton Rd *ATT* S4 .... 115 G4
Pheasant Bank
NROS/TKH DN11 .... 91 G2
Philadelphia Dr
ST/HB/BR S6 .... 125 C2
Philadelphia Gdns
ST/HB/BR S6 .... 125 C2
Philadelphia Gv
ST/HB/BR S6 .... 125 C2
Philip Rd *BSLY* S70 ...... 22 B2
Phillimore Rd *DARN/MH* S9 .. 127 H1
Phillips Rd *ST/HB/BR* S6 .. 112 D3
Phoenix Ct *HACK/IN* S12 ... 155 C4
Phoenix Gv *RHAM* S60 ...... 118 B3
Phoenix La *DEARNE* S63 .... 37 G3
Phoenix Rd *DARN/MH* S9 .... 117 G1
HACK/IN S12 .... 155 C4
Piccadilly Rd *RHAM* S60 ... 119 H4
CHNE S41 .... 5 J5
Piccadilly Rd *CHNE* S41 .... 5 J5
MEX/SWTN S64 .... 86 A2
Pickard Crs *HAN/WDH* S13 .. 142 B2
Pickard Dr *HAN/WDH* S13 ... 142 B2
Pickburn La *BTLY* DN5 ..... 24 A4
Pickering Crs
AU/AST/KP S26 .... 145 E4
Pickering Rd *BTLY* DN5 .... 26 A4
OWL S3 .... 114 D5
Pickering St
DARN/MH S9 * 116 D4
Pickhill's Av *DEARNE* S63 .. 37 H4
Pickmere Rd *FUL* S10 ...... 124 D3
Pickton Cl *CHSW* S40 ...... 191 H2
Pickup Crs *WMB/DAR* S73 ... 50 B4
Pickwick Dr *RHAM* S60 ..... 129 F1
Piece End *CHPT/GREN* S35 .. 80 B3
Piece End Cl
CHPT/GREN S35 .... 80 B3
The Pieces North
RHAM S60 .... 119 H4
The Pieces South
RHAM S60 .... 119 H4
Pigeon Bridge Wy
AU/AST/KP S26 .... 145 H4
Pighills La *DRON* S18 ..... 163 F4
Pike Cl *CHSW* S40 .... 186 B4
Pike Lowe Gv
DOD/DAR S75 .... 14 B4
Pike Rd *RHAM* S60 .... 118 C3
Pikes La *BSLY* S70 .... 3 J7
Pilley Gn *DOD/DAR* S75 .... 60 B3
Pilley Hl *DOD/DAR* S75 .... 30 B4
Pilley La *DOD/DAR* S75 .... 60 B3
Pinchfield Ct *MALT* S66 ... 121 F1
Pinchfield Holt *MALT* S66 .. 121 F1
Pinchfield La *MALT* S66 ... 121 F1
Pinchmill Hollow *MALT* S66 121 F2
Pinch Mill La *RHAM* S60 ... 120 C3
Pinchwell Vw *MALT* S66 .... 121 F1
Pindale Av *STV/CWN* S43 ... 189 G2
Pindar Oaks Cottages
BSLY S70 .... 32 B2
Pindar Oaks St *BSLY* S70 .. 32 B2
Pindar St *BSLY* S70 .... 32 B2
Pine Av *DIN* S25 .... 148 B5
Pine Cl *BSLY* S70 .... 22 B1
ECK/KIL S21 .... 168 A3
HOY S74 .... 62 A3
MALT S66 .... 108 C3
Pine Cft *CHPT/GREN* S35 ... 94 A2
Pinecroft Wy
CHPT/GREN S35 .... 94 A2
Pinefield Av *ARMTH* DN3 ... 29 G1
Pinefield Rd *ARMTH* DN3 ... 29 G1
Pine Gv *CONI* DN12 .... 88 C3
Pinehall Dr *BSLYN/ROY* S71 .. 20 D3
Pine Hall Rd *ARMTH* DN3 ... 29 G1
Pinehurst Ri *MEX/SWTN* S64 .. 86 B1
Pine Rd *DONS/BSCR* DN4 .... 58 B5
The Pines *FUL* S10 .... 137 E2

Pine St *STV/CWN* S43 ...... 189 E1
Pine Vw *CHSW* S40 .... 191 F1
Pine Wk *MEX/SWTN* S64 ..... 86 B3
Pinewood Av *ARMTH* DN3 .... 42 D2
DONS/BSCR DN4 .... 71 E3
Pinewood Cl *CUD/GR* S72 ... 23 H4
MEX/SWTN S64 .... 86 A1
RCH S42 .... 190 C4
Pinfold Cl *BSLYN/ROY* S71 .. 15 E2
MEX/SWTN S64 .... 86 A1
RCH S42 .... 190 C4
Pinfold Ct *ARMTH* DN3 ..... 29 F1
Pinfold Gdns *CUD/GR* S72 .. 22 A2
Pinfold Hl *BSLY* S70 ...... 32 A4
Pinfold Lands
MEX/SWTN S64 .... 67 C4
Pinfold la *BSLYN/ROY* S71 .. 15 C2
OWL S3 .... 115 E5
RHAM S60 .... 9 H6
WMB/DAR S73 .... 35 F5
Pinfold St *ECK/KIL* S21 ... 166 D5
SHEF S1 .... 11 F3
Pingle Av *ABRD* S7 .... 152 A2
Pingle Gra *STV/CWN* S43 ... 188 C2
Pingle Rd *ABRD* S7 .... 152 A2
ECK/KIL S21 .... 168 C1
Pingles Crs
RHAM/THRY S65 .... 99 G4
Pinner Rd *ECC* S11 .... 139 E3
Pinstone St *SHEF* S1 ...... 11 G4
Pioneer Cl *DEARNE* S63 .... 66 A2
Pipe House La *RAW* S62 .... 85 F4
Piper Cl *SHEFN* S5 .... 115 E1
Piper Crs *SHEFN* S5 .... 115 E1
Pipering Lane (East)
BTLY DN5 .... 39 F3
Pipering Lane (West)
BTLY DN5 .... 39 E3
Piper La *AU/AST/KP* S26 ... 145 H2
RCH S42 .... 190 C4
Piper Rd *SHEFN* S5 .... 115 F1
Pipeyard La *ECK/KIL* S21 .. 166 C5
Pippin Ct *MALT* S66 .... 110 B2
Pipworth Gv
SHEFP/MNR S2 .... 142 A1
Pipworth La *ECK/KIL* S21 .. 167 E4
Pisgah House Rd *FUL* S10 .. 137 H1
Pitch Cl *STV/CWN* S43 ..... 185 E4
Pitchford La *FUL* S10 ..... 137 H1
Pithouse La
AU/AST/KP S26 .... 158 B3
MOS S20 .... 158 A2
Pit La *HACK/IN* S12 .... 141 C4
KIMB S61 .... 95 F3
RHAM S60 .... 130 B3
Pitman Rd *CONI* DN12 ...... 68 A5
Pitsmoor Rd *OWL* S3 .... 126 A1
Pittam Cl *ARMTH* DN3 ...... 42 D4
Pitt Cl *SHEF* S1 .... 10 D4
Pitt Cl *SHEF* S1 * 10 D4
Pitt St *BSLY* S70 .... 2 E5
ECK/KIL S21 .... 174 C1
KIMB S61 .... 104 D3
MEX/SWTN S64 .... 67 C3
SHEF S1 .... 10 D4
WMB/DAR S73 .... 34 C5
Pitt St West *BSLY* S70 .... 2 D5
Plane Cl *DONS/BSCR* DN4 ... 58 B5
Plane Dr *MALT* S66 .... 108 C4
Plane Tree Wy *DIN* DN9 .... 75 H5
Plank Ga *CHPT/GREN* S35 ... 100 A1
STKB/PEN S36 .... 78 A4
Plantation Av
BSLYN/ROY S71 .... 15 H1
DIN S25 .... 134 D4
DONS/BSCR DN4 .... 74 D4
Plantation Cl *CHSW* S40 ... 186 A4
MALT S66 .... 110 D2
Plantation Ct *DIN* S25 .... 134 D4
Plantation Rd
DONS/BSCR DN4 .... 72 A4
SHEFS S8 .... 140 A4
Plantin Ri *MOS* S20 * 167 E1
The Plantin *MOS* S20 ...... 167 E1
Platts Dr *MOS* S20 .... 157 G1
Platts La *CHPT/GREN* S35 .. 100 A2
Platt St *OWL* S3 .... 8 B4
Pleasant Av *BSVR* S44 ..... 197 E5
Pleasant Cl *HACK/IN* S12 .. 141 H4
Pleasant Pl *CHSW* S40 * ... 4 A4
Pleasant Rd *HACK/IN* S12 .. 141 H4
Pleasant Vw *CUD/GR* S72 ... 22 A3
Pleasley Rd *AU/AST/KP* S26 131 E3
RHAM S60 .... 119 H4
Plover Ct *NROS/TKH* DN11 .. 91 G2
SHEFP/MNR S2 .... 127 E5
Plover Cft *KIMB* S61 ...... 82 C5
Plover Dr *BSLY* S70 .... 47 H5
Plover Wy *BSVR* S44 .... 193 H1
Plowright Cl *GLV* S14 ..... 140 D5
Plowright Dr *GLV* S14 ..... 140 D5
Plowright Wy *GLV* S14 ..... 140 D5
Plumber St *BSLY* S70 ...... 2 C4
Plumbley Hall Ms *MOS* S20 166 C2
Plumbley Hall Rd *MOS* S20 .166 C1
Plumbley La *MOS* S20 ...... 166 B2
Plumb Leys *RHAM* S60 ...... 130 A3
Plum La *OWL* S3 .... 11 G5
Plumper's Rd *DARN/MH* S9 117 F2
Plumpton Av
MEX/SWTN S64 .... 67 G2
Plumpton Gdns
DONS/BSCR DN4 .... 74 C2

Plumpton Pk *CUD/GR* S72 ... 17 E2
Plumpton Park Rd
DONS/BSCR DN4 .... 74 C3
Plum St *OWL* S3 .... 11 G1
Plunket Rd *WHHL* DN2 ...... 7 J1
Plymouth Rd *ABRD* S7 ...... 139 G5
Pocket Handkerchief La
STV/CWN S43 .... 147 F2
Pocknedge La *RCH* S42 ..... 190 B5
Pogmoor La *DOD/DAR* S75 ... 18 C5
Pogmoor Rd *DOD/DAR* S75 ... 2 A2
Polka Ct *OWL* S3 .... 126 A1
Pollard Av *SHEFN* S5 ...... 114 C1
Pollard Crs *SHEFN* S5 ..... 114 C1
Pollard La *SHEFN* S5 ...... 114 C1
Pollard St *KIMB* S61 ...... 104 C3
Pollitt St *DOD/DAR* S75 ... 2 D1
Pollyfox Wy *DOD/DAR* S75 .. 30 A3
Polyfields La *BSVR* S44 ... 197 E4
Pomona St *ECC* S11 .... 139 G1
Pond Cl *ST/HB/BR* S6 ...... 123 H1
Pond Hl *SHEF* S1 * 11 J3
Pond La *RCH* S42 .... 195 E5
Pond Rd *ST/HB/BR* S6 ...... 123 H1
Pond Sq *SHEF* S1 .... 11 J4
Pond St *BSLY* S70 .... 3 F6
CHSW S40 .... 5 F4
SHEF S1 .... 11 J4
Pondwell Dr *STV/CWN* S43 .. 188 C2
Pontefract Rd
BSLYN/ROY S71 .... 3 J5
CUD/GR S72 .... 17 E3
DEARNE S63 .... 64 B1
Pool Dr *DONS/BSCR* DN4 .... 74 D2
Poole Pl *DARN/MH* S9 ...... 128 A3
Poole Rd *DARN/MH* S9 ...... 127 H5
Pools La *BSLYN/ROY* S71 ... 16 A1
Pool Sq *SHEF* S1 .... 11 G3
Pool's La *ECK/KIL* S21 .... 173 E4
Pope Av *CHSW* S40 .... 191 F3
Poplar Av *ARMTH* DN3 ...... 59 F4
DRON S18 .... 171 G4
ECK/KIL S21 .... 168 A3
MEX/SWTN S64 .... 66 D2
Poplar Dr *DEARNE* S63 ..... 65 F4
Poplar Gld *MALT* S66 ...... 108 B5
Poplar Gv *BSLYN/ROY* S71 .. 21 E5
CONI DN12 .... 88 D2
DONS/BSCR DN4 .... 70 C4
MEX/SWTN S64 .... 66 B5
RHAM/THRY S65 .... 109 E1
Poplar Pl *ARMTH* DN3 ...... 42 D4
CHNE S41 .... 187 F1
Poplar Ri *MALT* S66 .... 110 B2
Poplar Rd *ECK/KIL* S21 .... 174 C1
WMB/DAR S73 .... 50 C3
Poplars Rd *BSLY* S70 ...... 32 B3
The Poplars *CONI* DN12 .... 88 D2
Poplar St *CUD/GR* S72 ..... 23 F2
Poplar Ter *BSLYN/ROY* S71 .. 13 G2
BTLY DN5 .... 39 H2
Poplar Wy *RHAM* S60 .... 129 E2
Popple St *ATT* S4 .... 116 A3
Poppyfields Wy
ARMTH DN3 .... 75 E1
Porter Av *DOD/DAR* S75 .... 2 A2
Porter Brook Vw *ECC* S11 .. 139 F2
Porter St *STV/CWN* S43 .... 182 A4
Porter Ter *DOD/DAR* S75 ... 18 D5
Portland Av
AU/AST/KP S26 .... 145 G3
BSVR S44 .... 197 E3
Portland Buildings
SHEFP/MNR S2 * 125 C2
Portland Cl *CHNE* S41 ..... 5 G3
DIN S25 .... 134 C5
Portland Crs *BSVR* S44 .... 197 E3
Portland La *SHEF* S1 ...... 10 D4
Portland Pl *DON* DN1 ...... 6 C5
MALT S66 .... 111 E3
Portland Rd *MOS* S20 ...... 157 G3
NROS/TKH DN11 .... 91 H4
Portland St *BSLY* S70 ..... 32 B2
MEX/SWTN S64 .... 66 B5
ST/HB/BR S6 .... 125 G2
STV/CWN S43 .... 185 G2
Portobello St *SHEF* S1 .... 10 D3
Portsea Rd *ST/HB/BR* S6 ... 113 H4
Port House La
STKB/PEN S36 .... 76 D3
Potterdyke Av *RAW* S62 .... 85 F3
Potter Hl *KIMB* S61 .... 97 G3
Potter Hill La
CHPT/GREN S35 .... 80 A4
Potteric Carr Rd
DONS/BSCR DN4 .... 56 C4
Potters Cl *CHNE* S41 ...... 179 H4
Potters Ga *CHPT/GREN* S35 .. 80 A4
Pottery Cl *RAW* S62 .... 98 B1
Pottery La *RAW* S62 .... 98 C1
Pottery La East *CHNE* S41 .. 187 H1
Pottery La West *CHNE* S41 .. 187 G2
Pottery Rd *KIMB* S61 ...... 105 E4
Poucher St *RHAM/THRY* S65 .. 104 A3
Poulton St *BSLYN/ROY* S71 .. 20 D1

Powder Mill La BSLY S70....48 C2
Powell Dr ECK/KIL S21....168 A2
Powell St BSLY S70....48 B1
  OWL S3....10 B2
Power Station Rd BTLY DN5...55 H1
Powley Rd ST/HB/BR S6....101 E4
Poynton Av
  AU/AST/KP S26....131 G4
Poynton Dr DIN S25....134 D3
Poynton Wy AU/AST/KP S26..131 G4
Poynton Wood Crs
  TOT/DORE S17....161 G2
Poynton Wood Gld
  TOT/DORE S17....161 G2
Prescott Rd ST/HB/BR S6...113 G2
President Wy ATT S4....126 C2
Preston Av HOY S74....62 C1
Preston St SHEFS S8....140 A3
Preston Wy BSLYN/ROY S71...20 D1
Prestwich St DARN/MH S9..103 H5
Prestwold Wy CHNE S41 ...193 E5
Priest Croft La
  BSLYN/ROY S71....34 D2
Priestfield Gdns CHNE S41..186 B2
Priestley Av RAW S62....85 H4
Priestley Cl DONS/BSCR DN4..71 F3
Priestley St SHEFP/MNR S2..140 B1
Primrose Av RHAM S60....118 D5
  SHEFN S5....103 E5
  WMB/DAR S73....34 D5
Primrose Cir
  NROS/TKH DN11....91 G3
Primrose Cl ECK/KIL S21 ...168 C1
Primrose Crs MOS S20....157 F2
Primrose Dr
  CHPT/GREN S35....102 B1
  ST/HB/BR S6....125 G1
Primrose La ECK/KIL S21...158 C5
Primrose Pk RHAM S60 *....8 D1
Primrose Pl
  DONS/BSCR DN4....57 F5
Primrose Wy HOY S74....62 A3
Primulas Cl DIN S25....148 A4
Prince Arthur St
  DOD/DAR S75....2 C2
Princegate DON DN1....6 D4
Prince of Wales Rd
  DARN/MH S9....128 A4
  SHEFP/MNR S2....141 G3
Princess Cl SHEFP/MNR S2..141 H2
Princess Dr DEARNE S63....37 G3
  STKB/PEN S36....77 E4
Princess Gdns
  WMB/DAR S73....50 B3
Princess Gv DOD/DAR S75....60 A3
Princess Rd DEARNE S63....53 C1
  DRON S18....171 E1
  MEX/SWTN S64....67 F3
Princess St ATT S4....126 C2
  AWLS/ASK DN6....25 F3
  BSLY S70....2 E5
  CHNE S41....2 E1
  CUD/GR S72....23 E1
  DEARNE S63....64 D1
  DIN S25....134 A3
  HOY S74....61 F3
  STV/CWN S43....180 D5
  WMB/DAR S73....50 A2
Princes St RHAM S60....8 B4
Prince St MEX/SWTN S64....66 B4
Prince's Crs CUD/GR DN12....70 B5
Prince's Rd DONS/BSCR DN4..57 F4
Prince's Sq ARMTH DN3....29 F3
Prince St DON DN1....6 E4
Pringle Rd RHAM S60....118 B3
Printing Office St DON DN1..6 C4
Prior Rd CONI DN12....88 D2
Priory Av ECC S11....139 H2
Priory Cl BSLY S70....47 H3
  CHPT/GREN S35....94 A5
  CONI DN12....69 E5
  MEX/SWTN S64 *....67 G4
Priory Crs BSLYN/ROY S71...21 F4
Priory Pl ARMTH DN3....139 H2
  BSLYN/ROY S71....21 E3
  DON DN1....6 C4
Priory Rd ABRD S7....139 G3
  BSLYN/ROY S71....21 E3
  CHPT/GREN S35....94 A5
  DEARNE S63....53 E3
Priory Wk DON DN1....6 D4
Priory Wy AU/AST/KP S26..145 G3
Pritchard Cl HACK/IN S12...116 B2
Private Dr STV/CWN S43...189 E1
Probert Av DEARNE S63....37 F5
Proctor Pl ST/HB/BR S6....96 B2
Progress Dr MALT S66....108 D5
Prominence Wy MALT S66..108 B1
Prospect STKB/PEN S36....44 A3
Prospect Cl MALT S66....108 D5
Prospect Dr TOT/DORE S17..161 F3
Prospect Pl DON DN1....6 C6
  TOT/DORE S17....161 G2
Prospect Rd BTLY DN5....26 C3
  CHNE S41....179 F4
  DEARNE S63....53 E2
  DRON S18....163 G5
  SHEFP/MNR S2....140 A3
  TOT/DORE S17....161 G3
Prospect St BSLY S70....2 D4
  CUD/GR S72....16 D5

Prospect Ter CHSW S40....4 C1
Providence Ct BSLY S70....3 F7
Providence Rd
  ST/HB/BR S6....124 D1
Providence St KIMB S61....97 G3
  RHAM S60....8 C5
  WMB/DAR S73....50 D1
Psalter La ECC S11....138 D3
Psalters Dr STKB/PEN S36...45 G5
Psalters La KIMB S61....104 D2
Pullman Cl STV/CWN S43..182 B3
Pump Houses
  STV/CWN S43 *....183 E4
Purbeck Av CHSW S40....186 D5
Purbeck Cl MOS S20....156 D3
Purbeck Gv MOS S20....156 D3
Purbeck Rd MOS S20....156 D3
Purcell Cl MALT S66....111 G4
Purslove Cl MALT S66....109 E5
Pye Bank Cl OWL S3....126 A1
Pye Bank Dr OWL S3....126 A1
Pye Bank Rd OWL S3....126 A1
Pym Rd MEX/SWTN S64....67 G3
Pynot Rd CHNE S41....179 H4

Q

The Quadrant
  TOT/DORE S17....161 E3
Quail Ri BSLYN/ROY S71....127 E5
Quaker Cl DEARNE S63....64 D3
Quaker La BSLYN/ROY S71...33 F2
  DONS/BSCR DN4....70 D2
Quantock Wy CHSW S40....186 B4
Quarry Bank La
  CUD/GR S72....21 H1
Quarry Bank Rd CHNE S41....5 K6
Quarry Cl RHAM S60....118 A4
Quarryfield La MALT S66....110 D1
Quarry Field La MALT S66...121 F1
Quarry Flds MALT S66....121 F1
Quarry Hl ECK/KIL S21....173 F1
  HACK/IN S12....156 A5
  RHAM S60....9 F5
Quarry Hill Ct DEARNE S63...65 E4
Quarry Hill Rd DEARNE S63..65 E4
Quarry La ARMTH DN3....59 F5
  AWLS/ASK DN6....25 E3
  CHSW S40....191 G2
  DIN S25....148 B2
  ECC S11....139 E4
  KIMB S61....8 C1
Quarry Rd BSVR S44....196 D1
  DRON S18....172 C2
  ECK/KIL S21....168 A1
  HAN/WDH S13....128 C4
  HOY S74....48 D4
  TOT/DORE S17....161 E3
Quarry St BSLY S70....3 H6
  BSLYN/ROY S71....20 A2
  CUD/GR S72....16 D5
  MEX/SWTN S64....67 F4
  RAW S62....85 F5
Quarry Vale Gv
  HACK/IN S12....155 E1
Quarry Vale Rd
  HACK/IN S12....155 E1
Queen Av MALT S66....111 E4
  NROS/TKH DN11....91 E2
Queen Gdns WMB/DAR S73..50 B3
Queen Mary Cl
  SHEFP/MNR S2....141 F3
Queen Mary Crs
  ARMTH DN3....29 F3
  SHEFP/MNR S2....141 G2
Queen Mary Gv
  SHEFP/MNR S2....141 F3
Queen Mary Ms
  SHEFP/MNR S2....141 G3
Queen Mary Ri
  SHEFP/MNR S2....141 F3
Queen Mary Rd CHSW S40 ..191 F3
  SHEFP/MNR S2....141 G3
Queen Mary's Rd
  NROS/TKH DN11....91 E2
Queens Acre
  MEX/SWTN S64 *....66 B5
Queens Av AU/AST/KP S26..159 G3
Queensberry Rd WHHL DN2...58 B4
Queens Crs HOY S74....61 E3
Queens Dr DOD/DAR S75....2 B1
  DOD/DAR S75....19 E4
Queens Gdns DOD/DAR S75..2 B1
  HOY S74....61 E3
Queensgate
  CHPT/GREN S35 *....101 F1
  DON DN1....6 D5
Queens Pk CONI DN12....70 B5
Queens Rd AU/AST/KP S26..145 E3
  BSLYN/ROY S71....3 H1
  CUD/GR S72....23 F1
  SHEFP/MNR S2....140 B2
Queen St BSLY S70....3 H6
  CHPT/GREN S35....81 G5
  CHSW S40....4 E2
  DEARNE S63....37 G3
  DIN S25....134 D3
  DONS/BSCR DN4....55 H5
  ECK/KIL S21....167 E5

  HOY S74....61 E3
  MEX/SWTN S64....66 B5
  MOS S20....166 C2
  RAW S62....85 G4
  RHAM/THRY S65....106 C2
  SHEF S11....11 G2
  STKB/PEN S36....45 E3
  STV/CWN S43....180 D5
Queen St North CHNE S41..187 G1
Queensway BSLY S70....48 B1
  BSLYN/ROY S71....12 C5
  CUD/GR S72....23 E1
  DOD/DAR S75....19 E4
  HOY S74....62 B2
  RHAM S60....119 F2
Queenswood Cl
  ST/HB/BR S6....113 F1
Queenswood Dr
  ST/HB/BR S6....113 F1
Queenswood Ga
  ST/HB/BR S6....113 F1
Queenswood Rd
  ST/HB/BR S6....113 F1
Queen Victoria Rd
  TOT/DORE S17....161 F3
Queen's Av CUD/GR S72....35 H3
  DOD/DAR S75....2 D4
  MEX/SWTN S64....66 B4
Queen's Ct BTLY DN5....39 G4
Queen's Crs CONI DN12....70 B5
Queen's Dr BTLY DN5....39 G4
  CUD/GR S72....16 D1
  DOD/DAR S75....30 B3
Queen's Rd CUD/GR S72....17 E3
  DON DN1....7 F1
  MOS S20....157 F1
Queen's Rw OWL S3....10 E1
Queen's Ter MEX/SWTN S64...67 E3
Queen Wy WMB/DAR S73....49 H5
Quest Av WMB/DAR S73....49 H5
Quiet La FUL S10....137 F4
Quilter Rd MALT S66....111 G4
Quintec Cl KIMB S61....98 A5
Quoit Gn DRON S18....171 F2
Quorn Dr CHSW S40....186 A4

R

Raby Rd WHHL DN2....40 D5
Raby St DARN/MH S9....117 G1
Racecommon La BSLY S70...31 F3
Racecommon Rd BSLY S70...2 D7
Racecourse Mt CHNE S41..187 F1
Racecourse Rd CHNE S41..187 F1
  MEX/SWTN S64....65 G5
Race St BSLY S70....2 E5
Racker Wy ST/HB/BR S6..113 H5
Rackford Rd DIN S25....148 C3
Radburn Rd
  NROS/TKH DN11....91 E4
Radcliffe Cl BTLY DN5....39 E1
Radcliffe La BTLY DN5....39 E1
Radcliffe Rd BSLYN/ROY S71..14 D4
  BTLY DN5....26 C5
Radford Cl
  RHAM/THRY S65....109 E1
Radley Av MALT S66....108 A4
Radnor Cl MOS S20....157 G3
Radnor Wy WHHL DN2....41 G5
Raeburn Cl GLV S14....154 A3
Raeburn Pl GLV S14....154 A2
Raeburn Rd GLV S14....154 A3
Raeburn Wy GLV S14....154 A3
Ragusa Dr NROS/TKH DN11...91 F4
Rail Mill Wy RAW S62....98 B4
Rails Rd ST/HB/BR S6....123 E3
Railway Av RHAM S60....129 G2
Railway Ct DONS/BSCR DN4..56 B4
Railway Ter CHNE S41 *..192 D5
  RHAM S60 *....8 D4
Railway Vw DEARNE S63....37 G5
Rainborough Ct
  DEARNE S63....63 H2
Rainborough Ms
  DEARNE S63....64 B1
Rainborough Rd
  DEARNE S63....64 B2
Rainbow Av HACK/IN S12..156 B1
Rainbow Crs HACK/IN S12..156 C1
Rainbow Dr HACK/IN S12..156 C1
Rainbow Gv HACK/IN S12..156 C1
Rainbow Pl HACK/IN S12..156 C1
Rainbow Rd HACK/IN S12..156 C1
Rainford Dr BSLYN/ROY S71..20 D1
Rainford Sq ARMTH DN3....29 F2
Rainton Gv DOD/DAR S75...18 D4
Rainton Rd DON DN1....7 F6
Raintree Ct BTLY DN5....39 F5
Raisen Hall Pl SHEFN S5....115 E2
Raisen Hall Rd SHEFN S5..114 D1
Rake's La NROS/TKH DN11...73 E5
Raleigh Ct WHHL DN2....57 H4
Raleigh Dr CHPT/GREN S35...93 F1
Raleigh Rd SHEFP/MNR S2..140 B1
Raleigh Ter DONS/BSCR DN4..71 E2
Raley St BSLY S70....2 C7
Ralph Ellis Dr STKB/PEN S6..76 D3
Ralph Rd STV/CWN S43....182 C4

Ralston Ct MOS S20....166 D2
Ralston Crs MOS S20....167 E2
Ralston Gv MOS S20....166 D2
Ramper Av STV/CWN S43..185 E4
Rampton Rd ABRD S7....139 H3
Ramsay Crs BTLY DN5....39 F4
Ramsden Rd
  DONS/BSCR DN4....55 C3
  RHAM S60....9 H7
Ramsey Av CHSW S40....191 H5
Ramsey Rd FUL S10....125 E3
Ramshaw Cl CHNE S41....186 C2
Ramshaw Rd DRON S18....172 A5
Ramsker Dr ARMTH DN3....42 D5
Ramsworth Cl BTLY DN5....39 E5
Ranby Rd ECC S11....138 D3
Randall Pl SHEFP/MNR S2..138 D5
Randall St ECK/KIL S21....174 B1
  SHEFP/MNR S2....140 A1
Randerson Dr
  MEX/SWTN S64....86 C2
Rands La ARMTH DN3....43 E3
Ranelagh Dr ECC S11....138 D5
Ranfield Ct MALT S66....191 G4
Ranfield Ct
  RHAM/THRY S65....109 E1
Rangeley Rd ST/HB/BR S6..124 C2
Ranmoor Cliffe Rd FUL S10..138 A1
Ranmoor Cl CHNE S41 *....193 E4
Ranmoor Crs FUL S10....138 B1
Ranmoor Park Rd FUL S10..138 B1
Ranmoor Ri FUL S10....138 B1
Ranmoor Rd FUL S10....138 A1
Ranskill Ct DARN/MH S9...117 E5
Ranworth Rd MALT S66....109 E4
Ranyard Rd
  DONS/BSCR DN4....71 F1
Raseby Av MOS S20....157 E3
Raseby Cl MOS S20....157 E3
Raseby Pl MOS S20....157 E3
Rasen Ct MEX/SWTN S64....67 F2
Ratcliffe Cl CHNE S41....193 E5
Ratcliffe Rd ECC S11....139 F2
Ratten Rw DOD/DAR S75....30 A4
Ravencar Rd ECK/KIL S21..166 B5
Ravencarr Pl
  SHEFP/MNR S2....141 G1
Ravencarr Rd
  SHEFP/MNR S2....141 G1
Raven Dr KIMB S61....82 C5
Raven Edge
  RHAM/THRY S65....108 D3
Ravenfield Cl MOS S20....156 A3
Ravenfield Dr
  BSLYN/ROY S71....20 A1
Ravenfield Rd ARMTH DN3...43 E5
Ravenfield St CONI DN12....68 B5
Ravenholt BSLY S70....48 A1
Raven La CUD/GR S72....13 G3
Raven Mdw MEX/SWTN S64..86 A3
Ravenna Cl BSLY S70....32 B2
Raven Rd ABRD S7....139 F4
Ravenscar Cl CONI DN12....68 B5
Ravenscourt Wy MOS S20...48 B1
Ravenscroft Av
  HAN/WDH S13....142 C2
Ravenscroft Cl
  HAN/WDH S13....142 C2
Ravenscroft Ct
  HAN/WDH S13....142 C2
Ravenscroft Crs
  HAN/WDH S13....142 C2
Ravenscroft Dr
  HAN/WDH S13....142 C2
Ravenscroft Ov
  HAN/WDH S13....142 C2
Ravenscroft Pl
  HAN/WDH S13....142 C2
Ravenscroft Rd
  HAN/WDH S13....142 C2
Ravenscroft Wy
  HAN/WDH S13....142 C2
Ravensdale Cl
  STV/CWN S43....189 G3
Ravensdale Rd DRON S18...170 A2
Ravenshaw Cl
  DOD/DAR S75....18 D4
Ravensmead Ct
  DEARNE S63....53 E3
Ravens Wk CONI DN12....89 G1
Ravenswood Dr MALT S66..108 B1
Ravenswood Rd CHSW S40..186 A4
Ravensworth Rd DON DN1....7 F6
The Ravine SHEFN S5....103 E2
Rawmarsh Hl RAW S62....98 B2
Rawmarsh Rd RHAM S60....9 F1
Rawson Cl DONS/BSCR DN4..58 B4
Rawsons Bank
  CHPT/GREN S35....102 B3
Rawson Spring Rd
  ST/HB/BR S6....114 B2
Rawson Spring Wy
  ST/HB/BR S6....114 B2
Raybould Rd KIMB S61....96 D5
Rayleigh Av STV/CWN S43..188 D3
Rayls Rd AU/AST/KP S26....147 F5
Rayls Rd AU/AST/KP S26....147 F5
Raymond Av CUD/GR S72....23 F1
Raymond Rd BSLY S70....32 D3
  BTLY DN5....39 G3
Raynald Rd SHEFP/MNR S2..141 G1
Reader Crs MEX/SWTN S64...66 B4

Reaper Crs CHPT/GREN S35...80 C5
Reasbeck Ter
  BSLYN/ROY S71....19 H2
Reasby Av
  RHAM/THRY S65....108 D1
Reavill Cl DIN S25....134 D3
Rebecca Ms BSLY S70....3 G7
Rebecca Rw BSLY S70....3 G7
Recreation Cl MALT S66....133 F1
Recreation Cl
  STV/CWN S43....185 G1
Recreation La
  NROS/TKH DN11....91 E2
Recreation Rd
  AWLS/ASK DN6....25 F3
  DEARNE S63....65 F1
  STV/CWN S43....188 D4
Rectory Cl BSLYN/ROY S71...15 H3
  DEARNE S63....36 D2
  ECK/KIL S21....167 E4
  STKB/PEN S36....77 E2
  WMB/DAR S73....50 B3
Rectory Dr RCH S42....194 D3
Rectory Gdns DON DN1....7 G1
  RAW S62....85 G4
Rectory La DEARNE S63....168 B2
  RCH S42....194 D3
Rectory Ms BTLY DN5....54 D5
Rectory Rd ECK/KIL S21....168 B2
  STV/CWN S43....182 A4
  STV/CWN S43....185 C2
Rectory St RAW S62....98 B2
Rectory Wy BSLYN/ROY S71..20 D4
Redacre Cl BSVR S44....197 F2
Redbourne Rd BTLY DN5....39 H1
Redbrook Av CHNE S41....192 D4
Redbrook Ct DOD/DAR S75...19 E3
Redbrook Gv MOS S20....156 A2
Redbrook Rd DOD/DAR S75..18 C3
Redbrook Vw
  DOD/DAR S75....19 E3
Redbrook Wk
  DOD/DAR S75....19 E3
Redcar Cl CONI DN12....88 A1
Redcar Rd FUL S10....125 E4
Redcliffe Cl DOD/DAR S75..18 D5
Redfearn St BSLYN/ROY S71..3 H2
Redfern Av MOS S20....156 D4
Redfern Ct MOS S20....156 D4
Redfern Dr MOS S20....156 D4
Redfern Gv MOS S20....156 D4
Red Fern Gv STKB/PEN S36...76 D3
Redgrave Pl MALT S66....108 B3
Redgrove Wy CHSW S40....191 G4
Redhall Cl ARMTH DN3....29 G5
Red Hill OWL S3....32 C5
Redhill Av BSLY S70....32 C5
Redhouse Cl STV/CWN S43..180 B2
Red House La
  AWLS/ASK DN6....24 B1
Redland La ABRD S7....152 B2
Redland Wy MALT S66....110 C2
Red La CHNE S41....180 A5
  FUL S10....139 E1
Red Lion Yd RHAM S60....9 F1
Redmarsh Av RAW S62....85 E4
Redmires La FUL S10....136 B1
Redmires Rd FUL S10....136 D1
Rednall Cl DONS/BSCR DN4..55 H5
Red Oak La ST/HB/BR S6....112 C5
Redrock Rd RHAM S60....119 G2
Redscope Crs KIMB S61....96 B4
Redscope Rd KIMB S61....96 B4
Redthorne Wy CUD/GR S72..16 D1
Redthorn Rd
  HAN/WDH S13....142 D2
Redthorpe Crest
  DOD/DAR S75....18 C3
Redvers Buller Rd
  CHSW S40....192 C3
Redwood Av
  BSLYN/ROY S71....15 G1
  ECK/KIL S21....168 A3
Redwood Cl HOY S74....61 H3
  STV/CWN S43....189 E1
Redwood Dr MALT S66....110 A3
Redwood Gln
  CHPT/GREN S35....93 H2
Reedham Dr MALT S66....109 E4
Reeves Wy ARMTH DN3....42 B4
Regent Av ARMTH DN3....43 E5
Regent Cl HOY S74....62 A3
Regent Crs BSLYN/ROY S71..14 D5
Regent Gdns BSLY S70....2 C2
Regent Sq DON DN1....6 E4
Regent St BSLY S70
  DONS/BSCR DN4....71 G1
  HOY S74....61 E3
  KIMB S61....104 D3
  SHEF S11....104 D3
  STV/CWN S43....184 D2
Regent St South BSLY S70 *..3 G2
Regents Wy
  AU/AST/KP S26....145 G3
Regent Ter DON DN1....7 F4
  OWL S3....10 D3
Regina Crs CUD/GR S72....17 G1
Reginald Rd BTLY DN5....32 D3
  WMB/DAR S73 *....50 D3
Rembrandt Dr DRON S18...170 C2
Remington Av SHEFN S5....101 H4
Remington Dr SHEFN S5....101 H4

Remington Rd SHEFN S5 .... 101 H3
Remount Rd KIMB S61 .... 96 B4
Remount Wy KIMB S61 .... 96 H4
Rempstone Dr CHNE S41 .... 192 D5
Renathorpe Rd SHEFN S5 ...... 102 D3
Rencliffe Av RHAM S60 .... 119 F1
Reneville CI SHEFN S5 .... 102 A1
Reneville Crs SHEFN S5 .... 102 A1
Reneville Dr SHEFN S5 .... 102 A1
Reneville Rd RHAM S60 .... 105 H5
Reney Av SHEFS S8 .... 162 B2
Reney Crs SHEFS S8 .... 162 B2
Reney Dr SHEFS S8 .... 162 B2
Reney Rd SHEFS S8 .... 162 B2
Renishaw Av RHAM S60 .... 119 H2
Renishaw Rd STV/CWN S43 .... 183 C1
Renshaw CI
    CHPT/GREN S35 .... 80 A3
Renshaw Rd ECC S11 .... 138 C4
Renville CI RAW S62 .... 85 E4
Renway Rd RHAM S60 .... 106 C5
Repton CI CHSW S40 .... 186 A4
Repton PI DRON S18 .... 170 A2
Reresby Crs RHAM S60 .... 120 A2
Reresby Dr RHAM S60 .... 120 A2
Reresby Rd RHAM S60 .... 119 H2
Reservoir Rd
    AU/AST/KP S26 .... 131 E3
    FUL S10 .... 125 E4
Reservoir Ter CHSW S40 .... 4 C1
Retford Rd HAN/WDH S13 ...... 143 E1
Retford Wk
    NROS/TKH DN11 .... 91 H2
Revell CI RHAM/THRY S65 ...... 107 F2
Revill CI MALT S66 .... 110 D2
Revill Ct DIN S25 .... 134 D3
Revill La HAN/WDH S13 .... 143 C4
Rex Av ABRD S7 .... 151 H1
Rex Cnr DON DN1 * 6 E2
Reynard Crs ECK/KIL S21 ...... 175 H3
Reynard La ST/HB/BR S6 ...... 123 F2
Reynolds CI DRON S18 .... 170 C3
    MALT S66 .... 108 B4
Rhodes Av CHNE S41 .... 187 E4
    KIMB S61 .... 96 C4
Rhodes Cottages
    STV/CWN S43 .... 185 F2
Rhodes Rd RHAM S60 .... 120 A2
Rhodesia Rd CHSW S40 .... 191 F2
Rhodes St SHEFP/MNR S2 ...... 11 K4
Rhodes Ter BSLY S70 .... 3 J6
Ribble CI CHPT/GREN S35 ...... 80 D5
Ribblesdale Dr
    HACK/IN S12 .... 155 H4
Ribble Wy SHEFN S5 .... 115 G1
Riber Av BSLYN/ROY S71 .... 15 E5
Riber CI ST/HB/BR S6 .... 112 D5
    STV/CWN S43 .... 189 C4
Riber Ter CHSW S40 .... 189 C4
Ribston Ct DARN/MH S9 .... 127 H3
Ribston Ms DARN/MH S9 ...... 127 H3
Ribston PI DARN/MH S9 .... 127 H3
Ribston Rd DARN/MH S9 ...... 127 H3
Richard Av BSLYN/ROY S71 .... 20 A1
Richard La NROS/TKH DN11 .... 91 E2
Richard Rd BSLYN/ROY S71 .... 20 A1
    RHAM S60 .... 9 H7
Richards Ct
    SHEFP/MNR S2 * 140 B4
Richards Rd SHEFP/MNR S2 .. 140 A3
Richard St BSLY S70 .... 2 D5
Richards Wy RAW S62 .... 85 G5
Rich Farm CI BTLY DN5 .... 27 F4
Richmond Av
    HAN/WDH S13 .... 142 C1
Richmond CI CHSW S40 .... 192 A4
Richmond Ct
    HAN/WDH S13 .... 142 B3
Richmond Farm Ms
    HAN/WDH S13 .... 142 B3
Richmond Gv
    HAN/WDH S13 .... 142 B3
Richmond Hall Av
    HAN/WDH S13 .... 142 B2
Richmond Hall Crs
    HAN/WDH S13 .... 142 B3
Richmond Hall Dr
    HAN/WDH S13 .... 142 B2
Richmond Hall Rd
    HAN/WDH S13 .... 142 B2
Richmond Hall Wy
    HAN/WDH S13 .... 142 B3
Richmond Hill Rd
    BTLY DN5 .... 55 E3
    HAN/WDH S13 * 142 B4
Richmond Park Av
    HAN/WDH S13 .... 128 C5
    KIMB S61 .... 104 B5
Richmond Park CI
    HAN/WDH S13 .... 142 C1
Richmond Park Crs
    HAN/WDH S13 .... 128 C5
Richmond Park Cft
    HAN/WDH S13 .... 128 B5
Richmond Park Dr
    HAN/WDH S13 .... 142 C1
Richmond Park Gv
    HAN/WDH S13 .... 142 B1
Richmond Park Ri
    HAN/WDH S13 .... 128 B5
Richmond Park Rd
    HAN/WDH S13 .... 142 C1

Richmond Park Vw
    HAN/WDH S13 .... 142 C1
Richmond Park Wy
    HAN/WDH S13 .... 142 C1
Richmond PI
    HAN/WDH S13 .... 142 B3
Richmond Rd BTLY DN5 .... 38 D3
    DEARNE S63 .... 37 E2
    HAN/WDH S13 .... 142 A4
    KIMB S61 .... 104 C3
Richmond St BSLY S70 * 2 C5
    OWL S3 .... 126 B1
Richworth Rd
    HAN/WDH S13 .... 142 D2
Rickley Pitt Cottages
    DOD/DAR S75 * 47 F3
Ricknald CI AU/AST/KP S26 ... 131 F5
Ridal Av STKB/PEN S36 .... 76 C1
Ridal CI STKB/PEN S36 .... 76 C1
Ridal Cft STKB/PEN S36 .... 76 C1
Riddings CI MALT S66 .... 133 F1
    SHEFP/MNR S2 .... 141 G3
Riddings Cft CHNE S41 .... 186 C3
Ridd Wy RCH S42 .... 195 G4
Rider Rd ST/HB/BR S6 .... 114 A4
Ridge Balk La
    AWLS/ASK DN6 .... 24 D2
Ridgedale Rd BSVR S44 .... 196 D3
Ridgehill Av HACK/IN S12 ..... 141 G5
Ridgehill Gv HACK/IN S12 ..... 141 H5
Ridge Rd AWLS/ASK DN6 .... 25 F5
    ECK/KIL S21 .... 173 G1
    RHAM/THRY S65 .... 9 H3
The Ridge FUL S10 .... 137 G1
Ridge View CI
    DARN/MH S9 .... 116 C1
Ridge View Dr
    DARN/MH S9 .... 116 C1
Ridgewalk Wy BSLY S70 .... 31 H4
Ridgeway DRON S18 .... 163 H5
    RHAM/THRY S65 .... 107 E2
    STV/CWN S43 .... 185 F3
Ridgeway Av BSVR S44 .... 197 E2
Ridgeway CI MALT S66 .... 109 C5
    RHAM/THRY S65 .... 107 F2
Ridgeway Crs
    BSLYN/ROY S71 .... 15 G3
    HACK/IN S12 .... 141 G4
    HACK/IN S12 .... 141 G4
Ridgeway Dr HACK/IN S12 .... 141 G4
Ridgeway Moor
    HACK/IN S12 .... 165 G3
Ridgeway Rd HACK/IN S12 .... 141 G5
    RHAM S60 .... 118 B4
    SHEFP/MNR S2 .... 141 G3
Ridgeway West
    STV/CWN S43 .... 185 E4
Ridgewood Av ARMTH DN3 ... 42 B1
Ridgway Av WMB/DAR S73 ..... 35 E4
Riding CI DONS/BSCR DN4 ..... 74 D2
    MALT S66 .... 108 A4
Ridings Av BSLYN/ROY S71 .... 20 C5
The Ridings BSLYN/ROY S71 ... 20 C2
Rig CI KIMB S61 .... 96 D5
Rig Dr MEX/SWTN S64 .... 65 G5
Riggs High Rd
    ST/HB/BR S6 .... 122 D2
Riggs Low Rd
    ST/HB/BR S6 .... 122 D2
Riley Av DONS/BSCR DN4 ...... 71 F2
Riley Rd DEARNE S63 .... 65 F3
Rimington Rd
    DARN/MH S9 * 50 B2
Rimini Ri WMB/DAR S73 .... 34 C5
Ringer La STV/CWN S43 .... 185 E3
Ringer Wy STV/CWN S43 ...... 185 E3
Ringinglow Rd BSLY S11 ...... 150 B1
Ringstead Av FUL S10 .... 124 B5
Ringstead Crs FUL S10 .... 124 B5
Ringway DEARNE S63 .... 52 D3
Ringwood Av CHNE S41 .... 187 E2
Ringwood CI STV/CWN S43 ... 189 G1
Ringwood Crs MOS S20 .... 157 G3
Ringwood Dr MOS S20 .... 157 G3
Ringwood Gv MOS S20 .... 157 G3
Ringwood Rd MOS S20 .... 157 G3
Ringwood Vw
    STV/CWN S43 .... 188 D1
Ripley Gv DOD/DAR S75 .... 18 D3
Ripley St ST/HB/BR S6 .... 114 A5
Ripon Av WHHL DN2 .... 40 D4
Ripon St DARN/MH S9 .... 127 F2
Ripon Wy AU/AST/KP S26 ..... 145 E3
Rippon Crs RAW S62 .... 85 F4
Rippon Crs ST/HB/BR S6 ..... 113 H4
Rippon Rd ST/HB/BR S6 .... 113 H4
Risedale Rd DEARNE S63 .... 53 G1
The Rise CUD/GR S72 .... 17 H2
    DIN S25 .... 148 C3
    MEX/SWTN S64 .... 85 H1
Rising St OWL S3 .... 126 E1
Rivelin Bank ST/HB/BR S6 .... 113 H5
Rivelin Mill Br ST/HB/BR S6 . 123 E4
Rivelin Park Crs
    ST/HB/BR S6 .... 124 B1
Rivelin Park Dr
    ST/HB/BR S6 .... 124 B1
Rivelin Park Rd
    ST/HB/BR S6 .... 124 C1
Rivelin Rd ST/HB/BR S6 .... 124 C1
Rivelin Ter ST/HB/BR S6 .... 124 C1

Rivelin Valley Rd
    ST/HB/BR S6 .... 123 E4
River Bank
    CHPT/GREN S35 .... 100 A2
Riverdale Av FUL S10 .... 138 B2
Riverdale Dr FUL S10 .... 138 C1
Riverdale Pk
    STV/CWN S43 .... 182 C3
Riverdale Rd BTLY DN5 .... 39 E2
    FUL S10 .... 138 C2
Riverhead BTLY DN5 .... 58 B4
Riverside CI CONI DN12 .... 69 E5
    DONS/BSCR DN4 .... 55 F4
    ST/HB/BR S6 .... 113 F4
    WMB/DAR S73 .... 35 G4
Riverside Ct DIN S25 .... 134 A2
Riverside Crs RCH S42 .... 190 B5
Riverside Dr BTLY DN5 .... 54 C4
Riverside Gdns DEARNE S63 .. 53 F4
    EPW DN9 .... 75 H1
Riverside Prec RHAM S60 ...... 8 C7
Riverside Rd BSVR S44 .... 196 B2
    RHAM S60 .... 8 B7
River Ter ST/HB/BR S6 .... 114 A4
River Vw CHSW S40 * 5 H1
River Wy EPW DN9 .... 75 H1
Riviera Mt BTLY DN5 .... 39 H5
Riviera Pde BTLY DN5 .... 39 H5
Rix Rd MEX/SWTN S64 .... 86 B3
Roache Dr DEARNE S63 .... 53 E1
Roach Rd ECC S11 .... 139 E2
Robert Av BSLYN/ROY S71 ..... 20 D5
Robert CI DRON S18 .... 178 E1
Robert Dr SHEFS S8 .... 162 D1
Roberts Av BSLYN/ROY S71 ... 89 F2
Roberts Cv AU/AST/KP S26 .. 145 G3
Robertshaw Crs
    STKB/PEN S36 .... 77 F3
Robertson Dr ST/HB/BR S6 .. 124 C1
Robertson Rd
    ST/HB/BR S6 .... 124 C1
Roberts Rd DONS/BSCR DN4 ... 6 A7
Roberts St CUD/GR S72 * 16 C5
    WMB/DAR S73 * 50 A3
Robert St BSLY S70 * 48 A1
    RHAM S60 .... 8 B4
Robey St ATT S4 .... 115 H3
Robincroft CHSW S40 .... 192 D5
Robincroft Rd RCH S42 .... 194 D3
Robinets Rd KIMB S61 .... 97 E3
Robin Hood Av
    BSLYN/ROY S71 .... 12 D5
Robin Hood Cha
    ST/HB/BR S6 .... 112 C5
Robin Hood Crs ARMTH DN3 .. 42 C1
Robin Hood Rd ARMTH DN3 ... 42 C1
    DARN/MH S9 * 103 G5
Robin La BSLYN/ROY S71 ...... 12 D5
    MOS S20 .... 157 F1
Robin PI AU/AST/KP S26 ...... 145 G4
Robins Ri AU/AST/KP S26 ..... 145 G3
Robinson Rd
    SHEFP/MNR S2 .... 126 C5
Robinson St RHAM S60 .... 105 H5
Rob Royd DOD/DAR S75 .... 30 B4
Rob Royd La BSLY S70 .... 31 F4
Roche MOS S20 * 157 E5
Roche CI BSLYN/ROY S71 .... 20 B4
Roche End AU/AST/KP S26 ... 147 E5
Rocher Av CHPT/GREN S35 ... 101 G2
Rocher Cv CHPT/GREN S35 ... 101 G2
Rochester CI FUL S10 .... 137 E1
Rochester Dr FUL S10 .... 137 E1
Rochester Rd
    BSLYN/ROY S71 .... 20 B3
    DIN S25 .... 148 B5
    FUL S10 .... 137 E1
Rochester Rw BTLY DN5 .... 38 D5
Rockcliffe Houses
    RAW S62 * 98 B2
Rockcliffe Rd RAW S62 .... 98 B2
Rockingham CI BSLY S70 .... 60 C2
    CHSW S40 .... 191 G1
    DRON S18 .... 170 A2
    SHEF S1 .... 11 F6
Rockingham Ct
    BSLYN/ROY S71 .... 3 J4
Rockingham Ga LSHEF S11 ..... 11 F5
Rockingham La LSHEF S11 ..... 11 F4
Rockingham Rd
    DOD/DAR S75 .... 30 C5
    MEX/SWTN S64 .... 65 H5
    RAW S62 .... 85 G5
Rockingham Rw BSLY S70 .... 60 D2
Rockingham St BSLY S70 .... 60 C2
    BSLYN/ROY S71 .... 19 G3
    HOY S74 .... 61 E2
    SHEF S1 .... 10 E3
Rockingham Wy SHEF S1 .... 11 F5
Rockland Vis
    BSLYN/ROY S71 * 99 G4
Rocklea CI MEX/SWTN S64 ..... 86 A1
Rockley Av WMB/DAR S73 ..... 49 H4
Rockley CI CHSW S40 .... 192 B5
Rockley Crs BSLY S70 .... 60 C1
Rockley La DOD/DAR S75 .... 47 E2
Rockley Mdw BSLY S70 .... 31 E3
Rockley Nook WHHL DN2 ...... 41 F3
Rockley Rd ST/HB/BR S6 ..... 113 H2
Rockley Vw DOD/DAR S75 ...... 60 B2

Rockliffe Av
    DONS/BSCR DN4 .... 71 E2
    ECC S11 .... 139 F2
Rock Mt HOY S74 .... 62 B2
Rock Mount Rd
    DARN/MH S9 .... 103 H5
Rockside STV/CWN S43 * 185 E2
Rock Side Rd STKB/PEN S36 .. 44 A3
Rock St BSLY S70 .... 2 D5
    OWL S3 .... 126 B2
Rockwood CI
    CHPT/GREN S35 .... 93 G1
Rocliffe CI DIN S25 .... 134 B4
Roden Wy RAW S62 .... 84 C3
Rodge Cft CHNE S41 .... 179 G5
Rodger Rd HAN/WDH S13 .... 143 H1
Rodger St HAN/WDH S13 .... 8 B2
Rodman Dr HAN/WDH S13 .. 143 H2
Rodman St HAN/WDH S13 .. 143 H2
Rod Moor Rd
    TOT/DORE S17 .... 161 H4
Rodney Hl ST/HB/BR S6 .... 112 D4
Rodsley CI CHSW S40 .... 186 A6
Rodwell CI RHAM S60 .... 130 A3
Rodwood Av
    STV/CWN S43 .... 177 E4
Roebuck Hl HOY S74 .... 49 H5
Roebuck Rd ST/HB/BR S6 .... 125 F3
Roebuck St WMB/DAR S73 ..... 50 C4
Roecar CI CHNE S41 .... 179 H4
Roe Croft CI BTLY DN5 .... 54 B3
Roehampton Ri
    BSLYN/ROY S71 .... 33 F2
    BTLY DN5 .... 38 D5
    DARN/MH S9 .... 118 A3
Roe La OWL S3 .... 115 H4
Roger Rd BSLYN/ROY S71 ...... 15 G1
Rojean Rd CHPT/GREN S35 ... 101 F1
Rokeby Dr SHEFN S5 .... 102 A3
Rokeby Rd SHEFN S5 .... 102 A3
Rolleston Av MALT S66 .... 110 C3
Rolleston Rd SHEFN S5 .... 102 C5
Rollin Dr ST/HB/BR S6 .... 113 H3
Rolling Dales CI MALT S66 .... 110 C1
Rolls Crs RAW S62 .... 84 C3
Roman Ct KIMB S61 .... 96 D5
Roman Crs RAW S62 .... 85 E5
    RHAM S60 .... 8 B4
Romandale Gdns
    SHEFP/MNR S2 .... 142 A1
Roman Rdg AWLS/ASK DN6 ... 24 D3
Roman Ridge Rd
    DARN/MH S9 .... 116 D1
Roman Rd WHHL DN2 .... 7 G5
Roman St DEARNE S63 .... 37 G1
Romeley Crs STV/CWN S43 .. 184 D3
Romeley La BSVR S44 .... 184 D3
Romney CI MALT S66 .... 108 B3
Romney Dr DRON S18 .... 170 C2
Romney Gdns
    SHEFP/MNR S2 .... 140 B4
Romsdal Rd FUL S10 * 125 E3
Romwood Av
    MEX/SWTN S64 .... 65 G5
Ronald Rd DARN/MH S9 ...... 128 A3
    DONS/BSCR DN4 .... 55 G5
Ronksley Crs SHEFN S5 .... 102 D3
Ronksley La ST/HB/BR S6 ..... 122 A4
Ronksley Rd SHEFN S5 .... 102 D3
Rood La STV/CWN S43 .... 185 E3
Rookdale CI DOD/DAR S75 ... 18 D3
Rookery Bank
    STKB/PEN S36 .... 77 H3
Rookery Cha STKB/PEN S36 .. 77 H3
Rookery CI AU/AST/KP S26 ... 159 G2
    STKB/PEN S36 .... 77 H3
Rookery Dell STKB/PEN S36 .. 77 H3
Rookery Ri STKB/PEN S36 ..... 77 H3
Rookery Rd MEX/SWTN S64 ... 85 H1
The Rookery MEX/SWTN S64 ... 85 H1
Rookery V STKB/PEN S36 ..... 77 H3
Rook Hl BSLY S70 .... 32 C5
Roper Hl FUL S10 .... 136 B3
Rosamond Av
    TOT/DORE S17 .... 161 G2
Rosamond CI
    TOT/DORE S17 .... 161 G2
Rosamond Dr
    TOT/DORE S17 .... 161 G3
Rosamond Gld
    TOT/DORE S17 .... 161 G2
Rosamond PI
    TOT/DORE S17 .... 161 G2
Rosa Rd FUL S10 .... 125 E3
Roscoe Bank ST/HB/BR S6 ... 124 B3
Roscoe Dr ST/HB/BR S6 ...... 124 B3
Roscoe Mt ST/HB/BR S6 ...... 124 B3
Roscoe Rd OWL S3 .... 125 H2
Rose Av DONS/BSCR DN4 ..... 55 H5
    MOS S20 .... 157 F2
    STV/CWN S43 .... 185 G1
    WMB/DAR S73 .... 35 H5
Roseberry CI HOY S74 .... 62 A4
Roseberry St BSLY S70 .... 32 D2
Rosebery St KIMB S61 .... 105 G3
Rosebery Ter BSLY S70 * 3 J6
Rose CI RHAM S60 .... 118 D3
Rose Ct DONS/BSCR DN4 ..... 85 A5
    MALT S66 .... 108 A5
Rose Crs BTLY DN5 .... 39 E3
    RAW S62 .... 85 H5
    STV/CWN S43 .... 183 G2
Rosedale Av CHSW S40 .... 192 D4

Rosedale Gdns BSLY S70 .... 2 B4
    ECC S11 .... 139 F2
Rosedale Rd AU/AST/KP S26 . 145 G2
    BTLY DN5 .... 38 D3
    ECC S11 .... 139 F2
Rosedale Vw RCH S42 .... 191 F5
Rosedale Wy MALT S66 .... 108 C3
Rose Dr MALT S66 .... 108 B4
Rose Garth Av
    AU/AST/KP S26 .... 145 G2
Rosegarth CI BTLY DN5 .... 39 E3
Rose Garth CI CHNE S41 ..... 193 G5
Rosegreave DEARNE S63 .... 37 F5
Rose Gv ARMTH DN3 .... 42 C4
    WMB/DAR S73 .... 49 H1
Rose Hl CHSW S40 .... 4 C4
    DONS/BSCR DN4 .... 57 G4
    MOS S20 .... 156 B5
Rosehill Av RAW S62 .... 85 G4
Rose Hill CI MOS S20 .... 156 B5
    STKB/PEN S36 .... 44 D4
Rosehill Cottages
    DOD/DAR S75 * 30 C4
Rosehill Ct BSLY S70 .... 3 F1
    BSVR S44 .... 196 D3
Rose Hill Ct
    DONS/BSCR DN4 .... 57 G3
Rose Hill Dr DOD/DAR S75 .... 30 B3
    MOS S20 .... 156 B5
Rose Hill East CHSW S40 .... 5 F4
Rose Hill Ms MOS S20 .... 156 B5
Rose Hill Ri DONS/BSCR DN4 . 57 G3
Rosehill Rd RAW S62 .... 85 F5
Rose Hill Vw MOS S20 .... 156 B5
Rose Hill West CHSW S40 .... 4 E4
Rose La OWL S3 .... 133 H1
Roselle St ST/HB/BR S6 .... 114 A4
Rosemary CI BTLY DN5 .... 63 F3
Rosemary Rd MALT S66 .... 108 A4
    MOS S20 .... 157 F1
Rose PI WMB/DAR S73 .... 50 A1
Rose Tree Av CUD/GR S72 ..... 16 C5
Rose Tree CI CUD/GR S72 ..... 16 C5
Rose Wy ECK/KIL S21 .... 168 B3
Rosewell Ct
    RHAM/THRY S65 .... 106 C3
Rose Wood CI CHNE S41 ..... 186 D5
Roslin Rd FUL S10 .... 125 E4
Rossendale CI CHSW S40 ..... 192 A4
Rosser Av HACK/IN S12 .... 154 B3
Rossetti Mt MALT S66 .... 108 A3
Rossington Br
    DONS/BSCR DN4 .... 74 D4
Rossington Rd ECC S11 .... 139 E2
Rossington St CONI DN12 ...... 68 B4
Rossiter Rd KIMB S61 .... 97 G3
Rosslyn Av AU/AST/KP S26 .. 145 G2
Rosslyn Crs BTLY DN5 .... 26 D5
Ross St DARN/MH S9 .... 128 B3
Rosston Rd MALT S66 .... 111 F3
Roston CI DRON S18 .... 170 B2
Rothay CI DRON S18 .... 170 C3
Rothay Rd ATT S4 .... 116 B3
Rothbury CI MOS S20 .... 157 G3
Rothbury Ct MOS S20 .... 157 G3
Rothbury Wy RHAM S60 ..... 118 C3
Rother Av STV/CWN S43 ..... 188 B3
Rother Crs RHAM S60 .... 130 A3
Rother Cft HOY S74 .... 62 A2
Rotherham CI ECK/KIL S21 .. 158 D5
Rotherham Rd
    AU/AST/KP S26 .... 145 G3
    BSLYN/ROY S71 .... 20 A1
    BSVR S44 .... 197 G5
    DEARNE S63 .... 64 B2
    DIN S25 .... 134 A3
    ECK/KIL S21 .... 167 F3
    ECK/KIL S21 .... 169 E4
    HAN/WDH S13 .... 129 F5
    MALT S66 .... 110 A3
    MOS S20 .... 167 F1
    RHAM S60 .... 119 H3
    RHAM S60 .... 129 H1
    STV/CWN S43 .... 177 H1
    WMB/DAR S73 .... 35 H5
Rotherham Rd North
    MOS S20 .... 167 F1
Rotherham Roundwalk
    KIMB S61 .... 96 A3
    RAW S62 .... 83 F3
    RHAM S60 .... 119 E1
    RHAM/THRY S65 .... 107 F4
Rotherham St
    DARN/MH S9 * 116 C5
Rotherhill CI
    RHAM/THRY S65 .... 106 C2
Rothermoor Av
    AU/AST/KP S26 .... 159 G3
Rother Rd RHAM S60 .... 118 D1
Rotherside Rd ECK/KIL S21 .. 167 F4
Rotherstoke CI RHAM S60 .... 106 A3
Rother St WMB/DAR S73 .... 51 E5
Rother Ter RHAM S60 .... 118 D1
Rothervale CI MOS S20 .... 157 G1
Rothervale Rd CHSW S40 .... 192 C4
Rother Valley Wy MOS S20 .. 157 H5
Rother View Gdns
    AU/AST/KP S26 .... 144 G3
Rother View Rd RHAM S60 .. 118 D1
Rother Wy CHNE S41 .... 187 H3
    MALT S66 .... 109 G3

Rotherway *RHAM* S60..........119 E4
Rotherwood Av
 HAN/WDH S13..........143 H2
Rotherwood Cl *BTLY* DN5....38 D4
Rotherwood Crs *MALT* S66...133 E1
Rotherwood Rd
 ECK/KIL S21..........168 C1
Rothesay Cl *BTLY* DN5..........39 F5
Roughbirchworth La
 STKB/PEN S36..........45 H5
Rough La *CHPT/GREN* S35.....78 C3
 CHPT/GREN S35..........92 D5
Roughwood Rd *KIMB* S61.....96 C4
Roundel St *DARN/MH* S9 ...127 F2
Round Green La
 DOD/DAR S75..........46 D1
Roundhill Cottages
 ECK/KIL S21 *..........166 B4
Roundhill Ct
 DONS/BSCR DN4..........57 F5
Roundwood Ct *BSLY* S70.....48 A1
Roundwood Gv *RAW* S62.....98 C1
Roundwood Wy
 WMB/DAR S73..........34 D5
Rowan Cl *BSLY* S70..........31 H3
 CHPT/GREN S35..........94 A2
 DEARNE S63..........37 E5
Rowan Ct *WHHL* DN2..........41 G4
Rowan Dr *DEARNE* S63..........37 E5
 DOD/DAR S75..........39 C4
 MALT S66..........108 C4
Rowan Garth *BTLY* DN5.........9 G4
Rowan Mt *WHHL* DN2..........41 F4
Rowan Ri *MALT* S66..........110 B3
Rowan Rd *ECK/KIL* S21....174 B2
 STV/CWN S43..........183 E3
Rowan Tree Dell
 TOT/DORE S17..........161 E5
Rowan Tree Rd
 ECK/KIL S21..........167 H2
Rowborn Dr
 CHPT/GREN S35..........100 B5
Rowdale Crs *HACK/IN* S12 ..142 B5
Rowell La *ST/HB/BR* S6.....112 B5
Rowena Av *ARMTH* DN3..........42 B1
Rowena Dr *BTLY* DN5...........8 C4
Rowena Rd *CONI* DN12 *......88 D1
Rowenfields *DIN* S25..........149 F1
Rowland Pl *DON* DN1...........6 C5
Rowland Rd
 SHEFP/MNR S2..........140 A2
Rowland St *BSLYN/ROY* S71..12 D5
 OWL S3..........126 A2
Rowley Wy *MALT* S66..........108 B1
Rowms La *MEX/SWTN* S64.....26 D5
Rowsley Crs *STV/CWN* S43 ..189 C1
Rowsley St *SHEFP/MNR* S2...140 B1
Roxby Cl *DONS/BSCR* DN4.....73 H3
Roxton Av *SHEFS* S8..........152 D5
Roxton Ct *SHEFS* S8..........152 C4
Royal Av *DON* DN1.............7 F2
Royal Ct *DOD/DAR* S75..........18 A1
 HOY S74..........62 B2
Royale Cl *ECK/KIL* S21....167 E5
Royal Oak Ct *STV/CWN* S43 ..183 E2
Royal St *BSLY* S70.............3 F4
Royd Av *CUD/GR* S72..........21 H1
Royd Cl *BSLY* S70..........47 H1
Royd Ct *STKB/PEN* S36..........77 F4
Roydfield Cl *MOS* S20..........156 D3
Roydfield Dr *MOS* S20..........156 D3
Roydfield Gv *MOS* S20..........156 D3
Royd La *STKB/PEN* S36..........77 F4
Roydmoor Ct *STKB/PEN* S36..44 A2
Royds Av *RHAM* S60..........120 A2
Royds Close Crs
 RHAM/THRY S65..........99 G4
Royds La *HOY* S74..........62 D3
Royds Moor HI *RHAM* S60 ...120 C3
The Royd *STKB/PEN* S36..........77 F4
Roy Kilner Rd
 WMB/DAR S73..........49 H1
 MOS S20..........156 A3
Royston Av *BTLY* DN5..........39 C3
 MOS S20..........156 A3
Royston Cl *MOS* S20..........156 A3
Royston Gv *MOS* S20 *......156 A3
Royston HI *HOY* S74..........61 H1
Royston La *BSLYN/ROY* S71..15 G2
Royston Rd *CUD/GR* S72....156 D3
Rubens Cl *DRON* S18..........170 D2
Rubens Rw *SHEFP/MNR* S2..126 C4
Rud Broom Cl
 STKB/PEN S36..........44 B4
Rud Broom La
 STKB/PEN S36..........44 B3
Rudyard Rd *ST/HB/BR* S6......114 A4
Rufford Av *BSLYN/ROY* S71..15 E4
Rufford Cl *CHSW* S40...........4 C7
 HOR/CROF WF4..........13 C1
Rufford Rd *MOS* S20..........158 C3
 HOR/CROF WF4..........13 C1
Rufford Ri *DEARNE* S63..........53 E1
 MOS S20..........156 C3
Rufford Rd *DONS/BSCR* DN4 ..7 J7
Rufus La *NROS/TKH* DN11....90 D2
Rugby St *OWL* S3..........126 A1
Rundle Dr *ABRD* S7..........139 C3
Rundle Rd *ABRD* S7..........139 C3
 STKB/PEN S36..........76 D2
Runnymede Rd *WHHL* DN2....57 F2
Rupert Rd *ABRD* S7..........139 C3
Rural Crs *ARMTH* DN3..........59 F5
Rural La *ST/HB/BR* S6..........113 F2

Ruscombe Pl
 BSLYN/ROY S71..........15 G3
Rushby St *ATT* S4..........116 A3
Rushdale Av *SHEFS* S8......140 A5
Rushdale Mt *SHEFS* S8......140 A5
Rushdale Rd *SHEFS* S8......140 A5
Rushdale Ter *SHEFS* S8......140 A4
Rushen Mt *CHSW* S40......195 F1
Rushey Cl *RAW* S62..........85 E3
Rushley Av *TOT/DORE* S17...150 D5
Rushley Cl *TOT/DORE* S17...150 D5
Rushley Dr *TOT/DORE* S17...150 D5
Rushley Rd *TOT/DORE* S17...160 D1
Rushton Dr *BSLYN/ROY* S71...12 C5
Ruskin Av *MEX/SWTN* S64......67 F2
Ruskin Cl *DEARNE* S63..........64 C1
Ruskin Dr *ARMTH* DN3..........43 E4
Ruskin Rd *DONS/BSCR* DN4....71 C2
Ruskin Sq *SHEFS* S8..........140 A4
The Rusk *BTLY* DN5 *........177 F5
Russell Cl *AU/AST/KP* S26...144 D3
 BSLYN/ROY S71..........20 B2
Russell Ct *ECC* S11..........151 C3
Russell Pl *MALT* S66..........111 F2
Russell Rd *MEX/SWTN* S64...86 C4
Russell St *OWL* S3..........126 A2
 RHAM/THRY S65...........9 H1
Russett Cl *MALT* S66..........110 B2
Rustlings Rd *ECC* S11......138 C2
Ruston Cl *CHSW* S40......186 B3
Ruston Dr *BSLYN/ROY* S71...12 C5
Ruthin St *ATT* S4..........116 A4
Ruth Sq *FUL* S10..........10 B5
Ruthven Dr
 DONS/BSCR DN4..........70 D1
Ruthyn Av *STV/CWN* S43 ....177 E4
Rutland Av *BSVR* S44......196 C3
 DIN S25..........148 B1
Rutland La *NROS/TKH* DN11...90 D2
Rutland Pk *FUL* S10......125 E5
Rutland Rd *WMB/DAR* S73...49 H3
Rutland St *CHSW* S40...........4 D4
 OWL S3..........126 A1
 DON DN1.............7 F2
 OWL S3..........126 A1
Rutland Wy *DOD/DAR* S75.......2 A1
 OWL S3..........125 H2
Ryan Dr *HAN/WDH* S13......144 A3
Ryan Pl *RAW* S62..........98 B2
Rydal Cl *DEARNE* S63..........53 E4
 DRON S18..........170 B2
 STKB/PEN S36..........44 D2
Rydal Ct *DONS/BSCR* DN4......71 G4
Rydal Crs *CHNE* S41......187 E1
Rydalhurst Av
 ST/HB/BR S6..........113 F2
Rydall Pl *BTLY* DN5..........39 F2
Rydal Rd *DIN* S25..........148 D1
Rydal Ter *BSLYN/ROY* S71.....3 J5
Rydal Wy *MEX/SWTN* S64......67 C2
Rye Bank *RHAM* S60......120 B3
Rye Cft *BSLYN/ROY* S71.....20 A1
 CONI DN12..........89 C1
Ryecroft Bank *HOY* S74.....61 H1
Ryecroft Glen Rd
 TOT/DORE S17..........151 G5
Ryecroft Rd *RAW* S62..........86 A5
Ryecroft Vw
 TOT/DORE S17..........150 D5
Ryefield Gdns *ECC* S11......138 C5
Rye Flatt La *CHSW* S40......191 F3
Ryegate Crs *FUL* S10......124 C4
Ryegate Rd *FUL* S10......124 D4
Ryehill Av *CHSW* S40......191 E2
Ryeview Gdns *KIMB* S61......97 H4
Ryhill Dr *MOS* S20..........156 A3
Rykneld Ri *RCH* S42..........195 C4
Ryle Rd *ABRD* S7..........139 C4
Rylstone Ct *HACK/IN* S12 ..156 B3
Rylstone Gv *HACK/IN* S12 ..156 B3
Rylstone Wk *BSLY* S70..........32 D4
Ryton Av *WMB/DAR* S73.....50 D4
Ryton Cl *MALT* S66..........111 E3
Ryton Rd *DIN* S25..........148 B3
Ryton Wy *DONS/BSCR* DN4..74 C2

S

Sackerville Ter *ECK/KIL* S21..167 H1
Sackville Rd *RCH* S42......191 F4
Sackville Rd *FUL* S10......124 D3
Sackville St *BSLY* S70...........2 D3
Saddler Av *MOS* S20......156 D4
Saddler Cl *MOS* S20......156 D4
Saddler Gn *MOS* S20......156 D4
Saddler Gv *MOS* S20......156 D4
Saddletree Vw
 STV/CWN S43..........182 D2
Sadler Ga *BSLY* S70 *..........3 F3
Sadler's Ga *WMB/DAR* S73...50 A1
Saffron Ct *WMB/DAR* S73....50 C4
St Agnes' Rd
 DONS/BSCR DN4...........7 K6
St Aidan's Av
 SHEFP/MNR S2..........140 D2
St Aidan's Cl
 SHEFP/MNR S2..........141 E1
St Aidan's Dr
 SHEFP/MNR S2..........141 E1

St Aidan's Mt
 SHEFP/MNR S2..........141 E2
St Aidan's Pl
 SHEFP/MNR S2..........141 E2
St Aidan's Rd
 SHEFP/MNR S2..........140 D1
St Aidan's Wy
 SHEFP/MNR S2..........141 E2
St Albans Cl *FUL* S10......137 G1
St Albans Ct *MALT* S66......108 B5
St Albans Dr *FUL* S10......137 F1
St Albans Rd *FUL* S10......137 F1
St Alban's Wy *MALT* S66....108 B5
St Andrew Rd
 STKB/PEN S36..........77 G3
St Andrews Cl
 DONS/BSCR DN4..........74 D2
 MALT S66..........108 C2
St Andrews Crs *HOY* S74......62 A2
St Andrews Ri *HOY* S74 *...191 G4
St Andrews Rd *HOY* S74......62 A2
St Andrews Wk *RHAM* S60 ..118 A3
St Andrews Wy
 BSLYN/ROY S71..........33 G3
St Andrew's La *ECC* S11....139 F3
 MEX/SWTN S64..........88 D2
St Andrew's Rd *CONI* DN12 ..88 D2
 ECC S11..........139 F3
St Andrew's Sq
 DEARNE S63..........53 E3
St Andrew's Ter
 DONS/BSCR DN4...........7 F7
St Andrew's Wy
 ARMTH DN3..........29 F1
St Annes Dr *BSLYN/ROY* S71...15 H5
St Anne's Rd
 DONS/BSCR DN4..........57 E3
St Ann's Rd *RHAM/THRY* S65...9 G1
 STKB/PEN S36..........77 F2
St Ann's Rbt
 RHAM/THRY S65...........9 H2
St Anthony Rd *FUL* S10....124 C3
St Augustines Av
 CHSW S40..........192 C3
St Augustines Dr
 CHSW S40..........192 C3
St Augustines Mt
 CHSW S40..........192 C3
St Augustines Ri
 CHSW S40..........192 C4
St Augustines Rd
 CHSW S40..........192 B4
 DONS/BSCR DN4..........57 G4
St Austell Dr *DOD/DAR* S75 ..18 A3
St Barbara's Cl *MALT* S66 ..110 C4
St Barbara's Rd
 WMB/DAR S73..........34 D5
St Barnabas La
 SHEFP/MNR S2..........140 A2
St Barnabas Rd
 SHEFP/MNR S2..........140 A2
St Bartholomews Ri
 DONS/BSCR DN4..........57 H4
St Bartholomew's Cl
 MALT S66..........110 C4
St Barts Ter *BSLY* S70...........3 H7
St Bede's Rd *RHAM* S60.......8 C4
St Benedicts Ct
 SHEFP/MNR S2..........140 D2
St Catherines Wy
 DOD/DAR S75..........18 D5
St Catherine's Av
 DONS/BSCR DN4..........55 H5
St Cecilia's Rd
 DONS/BSCR DN4...........7 K7
St Chad's Wy *BTLY* DN5......54 C5
 CHNE S41..........187 G1
St Charles St *DARN/MH* S9 ..127 E1
St Christophers
 BSLYN/ROY S71..........33 G3
St Christopher's Crs
 BTLY DN5..........39 E4
St Clements
 BSLYN/ROY S71..........33 G3
 BTLY DN5 *..........38 D4
St David Rd *STKB/PEN* S36...77 G3
St Davids Dr *BSLYN/ROY* S71..33 F2
 RHAM S60..........118 A3
 BTLY DN5..........38 D4
 DIN S25..........148 B5
St David's Ri *CHSW* S40....191 H4
St David's Rd *CONI* DN12 ....88 D1
St Dominic's Cl *BTLY* DN5....54 B5
St Edmund's Av *MALT* S66...133 E2
St Edwards Av *BSLY* S70......2 C7
St Elizabeth Cl
 SHEFP/MNR S2..........140 B2
St Eric's Rd *DONS/BSCR* DN4..57 H5
St Francis Bvd
 BSLYN/ROY S71..........15 H5
St Francis Cl *FUL* S10......124 A5
 MALT S66..........108 C2
St George Ga *DON* DN1...........6 D3
St George Pl *STKB/PEN* S36...77 G3
St Georges Cl *OWL* S3......10 C2
St Georges Dr *RHAM* S60 ..118 A3
St George's Av
 MEX/SWTN S64..........65 H5
St George's Cl *OWL* S3......10 C2
St George's Rd *BSLY* S70......2 E5
St George's Ter *OWL* S3......10 D3
St Giles Cl *CHSW* S40......192 D4
St Giles Ga *BTLY* DN5..........38 D5

St Giles Sq *CHPT/GREN* S35 ...93 H1
St Helen Rd *STKB/PEN* S36...77 G4
St Helens Av
 BSLYN/ROY S71..........20 B1
St Helens Bvd
 BSLYN/ROY S71..........20 B1
St Helens Cl *DEARNE* S63 ....36 D2
 RHAM S60..........130 B4
St Helens Ct *HOY* S74 *......62 C2
St Helen's Av
 BSLYN/ROY S71..........20 B2
St Helen's Cl *CHNE* S41.......5 F2
St Helen's Rd
 DONS/BSCR DN4...........7 K6
St Helen's Sq *ARMTH* DN3...29 F3
St Helen's St *CHNE* S41.......5 F2
 HOY S74..........62 C2
St Helier Dr *DOD/DAR* S75 ..18 D5
St Hilda Av *BSLY* S70...........2 A4
St Hilda Cl *STKB/PEN* S36...77 G4
St Hildas Cl *DEARNE* S63 ....37 G1
St Hilda's Rd
 DONS/BSCR DN4...........7 K6
St James Av *DIN* S25..........29 F3
St James Cl *ARMTH* DN3......29 F3
 CHNE S41 *..........193 E3
 DEARNE S63..........65 G2
St James Rw *SHEF* S1..........11 G3
St James St *DON* DN1...........6 B6
St James Wk
 HAN/WDH S13..........143 H2
St James' Gdns
 DONS/BSCR DN4..........55 H4
St James' Br
 DONS/BSCR DN4...........6 B6
St James' St *SHEF* S1..........11 G3
St Joan Av *STKB/PEN* S36...77 G4
St Johns Av *MALT* S66......108 C3
St Johns Cl *RCH* S42......191 F5
St Johns Pl *STV/CWN* S43 ..181 H5
St Johns Vls *CUD/GR* S72 *..21 H1
St Johns Wk
 BSLYN/ROY S71..........15 H1
St John's Av *DOD/DAR* S75 ..30 A4
 RHAM/THRY S65..........106 C1
 STKB/PEN S36..........44 C4
St John's Ct *DIN* S25......134 C1
 MALT S66..........108 C3
St John's Crs *STV/CWN* S43..185 F3
St John's Dr *DIN* S25......134 C1
St John's Mt *CHNE* S41....187 F1
St John's Rd *BSLY* S70...........3 F7
 CHNE S41..........187 F1
 CUD/GR S72..........21 H1
 DIN S25..........134 C1
 DONS/BSCR DN4..........55 G5
 DRON S18..........172 A3
 MEX/SWTN S64..........66 A5
 RHAM/THRY S65..........106 C1
 SHEFP/MNR S2..........126 D3
 STKB/PEN S36..........77 H3
St Joseph's Ct *DIN* S25....134 C4
St Joseph's Gdns *BSLY* S70 ..32 B2
St Joseph's Rd
 HAN/WDH S13..........143 H2
St Lawrence Av *BSVR* S44 ..197 F4
St Lawrence Ct
 AWLS/ASK DN6..........25 E1
St Lawrence Glebe
 DARN/MH S9..........117 G2
St Lawrence Rd
 DARN/MH S9..........117 G1
St Leger Cl *DIN* S25......134 A3
St Leger Wy *DIN* S25......134 D3
St Leonards Cl *SHEFN* S5...115 F1
St Leonards Dr *CHNE* S41...193 E3
St Leonards Wy
 BSLYN/ROY S71..........33 G3
St Leonard's Av
 RHAM/THRY S65..........99 H4
St Leonard's Cl *DIN* S25...134 C5
St Leonard's Cft
 RHAM/THRY S65..........99 H3
St Leonard's La
 RHAM/THRY S65...........9 K2
St Leonard's Lea *BTLY* DN5..39 E4
St Leonard's Pl
 RHAM/THRY S65...........9 H3
St Leonard's Rd
 RHAM/THRY S65...........9 H3
St Lukes Wy
 BSLYN/ROY S71 *..........20 C4
St Margaret Av
 STKB/PEN S36..........77 G3
St Margaret's Dr *CHSW* S40....4 E3
 MEX/SWTN S64..........65 H5
St Margaret's Rd
 CHPT/GREN S35..........102 B1
 DONS/BSCR DN4...........7 K6
St Mark Rd *STKB/PEN* S36...77 G3
St Mark's Crs *FUL* S10......125 F5
St Mark's Rd *CHSW* S40.......4 B8
St Martin Cl *STKB/PEN* S36..77 G3
St Martins Cl *CHSW* S40....187 E4
 DOD/DAR S75..........18 D5
St Martin's Av *BTLY* DN5....54 B5
St Martin's Cl *CHNE* S41...186 D3
St Mary Crs *STKB/PEN* S36...77 G4
St Marys Rd *WMB/DAR* S73...50 A3

St Mary's Cl *CHPT/GREN* S35 ...94 A5
St Mary's Crs *DON* DN1 *........7 J1
 MEX/SWTN S64..........66 A5
 RHAM S60..........129 C1
St Mary's Gdn *SHEF* S1.....48 A3
St Mary's Ga *BSLY* S70...........3 F3
 CHNE S41...........5 H5
 SHEFP/MNR S2..........10 E7
St Mary's La
 CHPT/GREN S35..........94 A5
St Mary's Pl *BSLY* S70...........3 F3
St Mary's Rd *DEARNE* S63...37 H4
 DON DN1..........40 C5
 RAW S62..........98 C1
 SHEF S1..........11 G7
 WMB/DAR S73..........35 F5
St Mary's Sq *STKB/PEN* S36..44 D3
St Mary's Vw *KIMB* S61......97 F5
St Mary's Wk *BTLY* DN5.....54 B5
St Matthews Cl
 ECK/KIL S21..........175 H2
St Matthews Wy
 BSLYN/ROY S71..........20 C4
St Matthias Rd
 STKB/PEN S36..........77 G4
St Michaels Av
 BSLYN/ROY S71..........20 D1
 NROS/TKH DN11..........91 C1
St Michaels Cl *DEARNE* S63...37 F5
St Michael's Av
 MEX/SWTN S64..........66 B4
St Michael's Cl
 CHPT/GREN S35 *..........102 B5
St Michael's Crs
 CHPT/GREN S35..........102 B1
St Michael's Rd
 CHPT/GREN S35..........102 B1
 DONS/BSCR DN4..........57 H4
St Nicholas Cl *ARMTH* DN3 ...29 E5
St Nicolas Rd *RAW* S62......85 G5
St Oswald's Dr *ARMTH* DN3...29 E5
St Owens Dr *DOD/DAR* S75 ..18 D5
St Pancras Cl *DON* DN1....134 A3
St Patrick Rd *STKB/PEN* S36..77 G3
St Patrick's Rd *WHHL* DN2...57 F3
St Patrick's Wy *BTLY* DN5...38 D4
St Paul Cl *AU/AST/KP* S26 ..147 E5
 STKB/PEN S36..........77 G3
St Pauls Cl *DON* DN1......134 A2
St Pauls Pde
 BSLYN/ROY S71..........33 F2
 SHEF S1..........11 G4
St Pauls Rd *DOD/DAR* S75 ....2 B1
 DOD/DAR S75..........19 E4
St Paul's Pde *BTLY* DN5.....38 D5
St Peter Av *STKB/PEN* S36...77 H3
St Peter's Ga *RHAM* S60....118 A4
 SHEF S1..........11 K4
St Peter's Ga *DEARNE* S63 ....37 E1
St Peter's Rd *CONI* DN12......88 D2
 DON DN1..........71 E1
St Peter's Ter *BSLY* S70...........3 J6
St Philip's Dr *CHNE* S41....192 D4
St Philip's Rd *OWL* S3......10 C1
St Phillip's Cl *MALT* S66 *...110 C4
St Quentin Cl
 TOT/DORE S17..........161 G3
St Quentin Dr
 TOT/DORE S17..........161 H3
St Quentin Mt
 TOT/DORE S17..........161 H3
St Quentin Ri
 TOT/DORE S17..........161 H3
St Quentin Vw
 TOT/DORE S17..........161 H3
St Ronan's Rd *ABRD* S7.....139 H3
St Sepulchre Ga *DON* DN1.....6 C4
St Sepulchre Ga West
 DONS/BSCR DN4...........6 B5
St Stephens Wk *BTLY* DN5...39 E5
St Stephen's Dr
 AU/AST/KP S26..........145 F2
St Stephen's Rd
 RHAM/THRY S65...........9 H2
St Stephen's Wk *OWL* S3 ....10 B2
St Thomas Rd *FUL* S10....124 D4
St Thomas St *SHEF* S1......10 E3
St Thomas's Cl
 DONS/BSCR DN4..........71 E2
St Thomas' St *CHSW* S40 ..191 G2
St Ursula's Rd
 DONS/BSCR DN4...........7 K4
St Veronica Rd
 STKB/PEN S36..........77 G4
St Vincent Av
 AWLS/ASK DN6..........24 D1
 DON DN1...........7 F2
St Vincent Rd *DON* DN1.......7 F2
St Vincent's Av *ARMTH* DN3..75 F5
St Wandrilles Cl
 CHPT/GREN S35..........94 B5
St Wilfrid's Rd
 DONS/BSCR DN4..........57 G4
 SHEFP/MNR S2..........140 A2
St Withold Av *MALT* S66....133 E1
Salcey Sq *CHSW* S40...........4 A7
Salcombe Cl *DOD/DAR* S75 ..14 A4
Sale HI *FUL* S10..........124 D5
Salerno Wy *WMB/DAR* S73...34 C4

Sale St *HOY* S74..........**61** E3
Salisbury Av *CHNE* S41....**187** E2
............*DRON* S18............**171** E3
Salisbury Crs *CHNE* S41....**187** F2
Salisbury Rd
............*DONS/BSCR* DN4........**55** G4
............*DRON* S18............**171** F4
............*FUL* S10.............**124** D4
............*MALT* S66.............**110** D2
Salisbury St *DOD/DAR* S75......**2** D1
............*DOD/DAR* S75..........**19** F4
Salt Box Gv
............*CHPT/GREN* S35........**101** E2
Salt Box La
............*CHPT/GREN* S35........**101** E2
Saltergate *CHSW* S40...........**4** D3
Salter Oak Cft
............*BSLYN/ROY* S71.........**15** C3
Saltersbrook Rd *DEARNE* S63....**37** F5
Saltersbrook Rd
............*WMB/DAR* S73............**34** D3
Salter's Wy *STKB/PEN* S36......**44** D4
Salvin Crs *STV/CWN* S43.......**185** E2
Samson St *SHEFP/MNR* S2......**126** C5
Samuel Cl *SHEFP/MNR* S2......**140** D3
Samuel Ct *SHEFP/MNR* S2......**140** D3
Samuel Pl *SHEFP/MNR* S2......**140** D3
Samuel La *DOD/DAR* S75.......**18** D4
............*SHEFP/MNR* S2.........**140** D3
Samuel Sq *DOD/DAR* S75.......**18** D4
Samuel St *DONS/BSCR* DN4.....**71** F2
Sanctuary Flds *DIN* S25........**148** A1
Sandal Ct *KIMB* S61............**61** F1
Sandal Beat La *WMB/DAR* S73....**34** E3
Sandal Beat Rd *WHHL* DN2......**57** C2
Sandal Carr Rd *ARMTH* DN3....**29** E4
Sandall La *ARMTH* DN3.........**28** D3
Sandall Pk *WHHL* DN2 *.........**41** G2
Sandall Park Dr *WHHL* DN2.....**41** F4
Sandall Ri *WHHL* DN2............**41** F4
Sandall Stones Rd
............*ARMTH* DN3...........**28** D4
Sandall Vw *DIN* S25...........**134** A2
Sandall Rd *CONI* DN12...........**88** C2
Sandalwood Cl *WHHL* DN2......**41** F3
Sandalwood Ri
............*MEX/SWTN* S64..........**86** B3
Sandbeck Cl *BSLYN/ROY* S71...**19** H4
Sandbeck Pl *ECC* S11..........**139** F3
Sandbeck Rd
............*DONS/BSCR* DN4...........**7** J6
............*NROS/TKH* DN11.........**91** G3
Sandbed Rd *OWL* S3............**114** C5
Sandbergh Rd *KIMB* S61........**96** C4
Sandby Cl *GLV* S14...........**154** A3
Sandby Cft *GLV* S14..........**154** A3
Sandby Dr *GLV* S14...........**154** A3
Sandcliffe Rd *WHHL* DN2.......**41** F4
Sandcroft Cl *HOY* S74..........**61** G3
Sanday Dr
............*RHAM/THRY* S65.........**108** D2
Sanderson St *DARN/MH* S9....**116** B5
Sandford Ct *BSLY* S70............**2** D6
Sandford Grove Rd
............*ABRD* S7.............**139** G4
Sandford Rd
............*DONS/BSCR* DN4.........**71** G2
Sandhill La *RAW* S62..........**85** H4
Sandhill Ri *EPW* DN9..........**75** H1
Sandhill Rd *RAW* S62..........**85** H5
Sandhills Rd *BSVR* S44........**197** E3
Sandhurst Rd
............*DONS/BSCR* DN4.........**74** C1
Sandiway *CHSW* S40...........**191** G4
Sandown Cl *ECK/KIL* S21......**166** B5
Sandown Gdns
............*DONS/BSCR* DN4.........**57** H3
Sandown Rd
............*MEX/SWTN* S64.........**67** F2
Sandpiper Rd *KIMB* S61........**82** F5
Sandpit Hl *ARMTH* DN3.........**59** F5
Sandringham Av
............*RHAM* S60............**119** H3
Sandringham Cl *CHNE* S41....**187** F1
............*STKB/PEN* S36.........**44** B4
............*STV/CWN* S43.........**188** D5
Sandringham Pl *FUL* S10.....**136** D2
............*RHAM/THRY* S65.......**108** D1
Sandringham Rd
............*DARN/MH* S9...........**103** C5
............*WHHL* DN2..............**7** K3
Sandrock Dr
............*DONS/BSCR* DN4.........**74** A1
Sands Cl *GLV* S14............**154** A1
Sandstone Av
............*DARN/MH* S9...........**116** B2
............*RCH* S42.............**116** B2
Sandstone Cl *DARN/MH* S9....**116** C1
Sandstone Dr
............*DARN/MH* S9...........**116** B2
Sandstone Rd
............*DARN/MH* S9...........**116** B2
Sandwith Rd
............*AU/AST/KP* S26........**147** E5
Sandy Acres Cl *MOS* S20....**157** F4
Sandy Acres Dr *MOS* S20....**157** F4
Sandybridge La
..................................**13** H5
Sandycroft Crs
............*DONS/BSCR* DN4.........**71** E2
Sandy Flat La *MALT* S66.....**121** F2

Sandygate *DEARNE* S63........**65** F4
Sandygate Grange Dr
............*FUL* S10.............**124** A5
Sandygate Gv *FUL* S10.......**123** H5
Sandygate Pk *FUL* S10.......**123** G5
Sandygate Park Crs
............*FUL* S10.............**123** H5
Sandygate Park Rd
............*FUL* S10.............**123** H5
Sandygate Rd *FUL* S10.......**123** H4
Sandy La *DONS/BSCR* DN4.......**7** K7
............*HOY* S74..............**49** E3
Sandymount Rd
............*DEARNE* S63..........**65** G3
Sanforth St *CHNE* S41.......**187** G3
Sankey Sq *DEARNE* S63........**37** F5
Sarah Ct *ARMTH* DN3..........**43** C3
Sarah St *KIMB* S61.............**8** A5
Sargeson Rd *ARMTH* DN3.......**42** B4
Sark Rd *SHEFP/MNR* S2.......**140** A3
Saundby Ct *DONS/BSCR* DN4..**73** G1
Saunderson Rd
............*STKB/PEN* S36.........**44** B2
Saunders Pl
............*SHEFP/MNR* S2........**127** E4
Saunders Rd
............*SHEFP/MNR* S2........**127** E4
Saunders Rw
............*WMB/DAR* S73..........**50** A3
Savage La *TOT/DORE* S17....**160** D1
Savile St *ATT* S4............**126** C2
Savile St East *ATT* S4......**126** D1
Savile St Jct *OWL* S3........**126** B2
Savile Hall La *DOD/DAR* S75..**30** B4
Savile Rd *DEARNE* S63........**65** E3
............*DOD/DAR* S75..........**30** C4
............*RHAM* S60............**119** H3
Saville St *CUD/GR* S72........**16** D5
............*RHAM/THRY* S65........**99** E5
Saville Ter *BSLY* S70..........**3** F7
Sawdon Rd *ECC* S11..........**139** G1
Sawn Moor Av *MALT* S66.....**133** F1
Sawn Moor Rd *MALT* S66.....**133** F2
Sawston Ct *DONS/BSCR* DN4..**71** G4
Saxon Ct *DONS/BSCR* DN4.....**74** B2
Saxon Crs *BSLY* S70...........**32** A5
Saxonlea Av
............*SHEFP/MNR* S2........**142** A1
Saxonlea Ct
............*SHEFP/MNR* S2........**142** A1
Saxonlea Crs
............*SHEFP/MNR* S2........**142** A1
Saxonlea Dr
............*SHEFP/MNR* S2........**141** H1
Saxon Rd *KIMB* S61..........**104** B3
............*SHEFS* S8.............**140** A4
Saxon Rw *CONI* DN12..........**89** C1
Saxon St *CUD/GR* S72.........**21** H1
Saxton Av *DONS/BSCR* DN4....**57** C5
Saxton Cl *CHNE* S41.........**193** E4
............*HOY* S74..............**62** D1
Saxton Dr *RHAM* S60.........**119** F3
Sca Fell Pl *DIN* S25.........**148** D2
Scaftworth Cl
............*DONS/BSCR* DN4.........**73** G1
Scammadine Cl *RHAM* S60....**118** C4
Scarborough Cl *DIN* S25....**148** C1
Scarborough La
............*NROS/TKH* DN11.........**90** D2
Scarborough Rd
............*DARN/MH* S9...........**128** A2
............*MALT* S66.............**108** B4
Scarbrough Crs *MALT* S66....**111** E4
Scarfield Cl *BSLYN/ROY* S71..**33** F2
Scargill Cft *OWL* S3...........**11** G2
Scar La *BSLYN/ROY* S71........**33** F2
Scarlet Oak Meadow
............*ST/HB/BR* S6..........**111** H4
Scarll Rd *DONS/BSCR* DN4.....**55** G4
Scarsdale Cl *DRON* S18......**171** F3
Scarsdale Crs
............*STV/CWN* S43.........**188** D2
Scarsdale Cross *DRON* S18..**171** F2
Scarsdale Rd *CHNE* S41.....**187** G1
............*DRON* S18.............**171** F2
............*SHEFS* S8............**152** D2
Scarsdale St *BSVR* S44......**196** B4
............*DIN* S25.............**179** G2
Scarth Av *DONS/BSCR* DN4....**55** H5
Scawsby La *BTLY* DN5..........**38** D7
Scawthorpe Av *BTLY* DN5.....**38** D7
Sceptone Gv *CUD/GR* S72......**17** E1
Schofield Dr *WMB/DAR* S73...**35** E4
Schofield Pl *WMB/DAR* S73...**35** E4
Schofield Rd *STKB/PEN* S36..**77** F2
............*WMB/DAR* S73..........**34** D4
Schofield St *MEX/SWTN* S64..**66** D3
Schole Av *STKB/PEN* S36.....**44** C3
Schole Hill La *DOD/DAR* S75..**44** B4
Scholes Gn *KIMB* S61.........**95** H3
Scholes La *KIMB* S61.........**95** G3
Scholes Ri *CHPT/GREN* S35..**102** B1
Scholes Vw *CHPT/GREN* S35..**94** B5
Scholey St *MALT* S66........**108** B4
Scholey Rd *WHHL* DN2.........**41** F3
Scholfield Rd *MOS* S20......**167** E1
School Board La *CHSW* S40....**4** B4
School Cl *AU/AST/KP* S26....**159** F2
............*MOS* S20............**167** F1
School Ct *DON* DN1 *..........**6** E1
Schoolfield Dr *RAW* S62.......**85** F4

Schoolfield Cl *BSVR* S44....**197** F3
School Green La *FUL* S10....**137** F3
School Gv *AU/AST/KP* S26....**145** G5
School Hl *CUD/GR* S72.......**16** C5
............*RHAM* S60............**98** A3
School La *ARMTH* DN3..........**58** D5
............*CHPT/GREN* S35.........**93** E5
............*DRON* S18............**171** E2
............*ECK/KIL* S21.........**165** G5
............*RAW* S62.............**98** A3
............*RHAM/THRY* S65........**99** H3
............*SHEFP/MNR* S2.......**126** C4
............*SHEFS* S8............**162** D1
............*ST/HB/BR* S6........**123** G2
School Lane Cl *SHEFS* S8...**153** G4
School Rd *AU/AST/KP* S26...**159** E3
............*CHNE* S41............**187** G2
............*CHPT/GREN* S35.........**80** C4
............*DIN* S25.............**134** B1
............*FUL* S10.............**124** A5
............*MALT* S66............**133** F1
............*MOS* S20............**157** G2
School St *AU/AST/KP* S26...**145** E3
............*BSLY* S70.............**2** C5
............*CUD/GR* S72..........**16** D4
............*CUD/GR* S72..........**23** H5
............*DEARNE* S63..........**37** F2
............*DEARNE* S63..........**53** E3
............*DIN* S25.............**134** D4
............*DOD/DAR* S75...........**2** C1
............*DOD/DAR* S75..........**14** A3
............*RHAM/THRY* S65........**99** H4
............*WMB/DAR* S73..........**63** E1
School Wk *CONI* DN12..........**88** B4
............*MALT* S66............**110** D3
Scotia Cl *SHEFP/MNR* S2....**141** F2
Scotia Dr *SHEFP/MNR* S2....**141** F2
Scotland St *OWL* S3...........**10** E1
Scot La *DON* DN1..............**6** D3
Scott Av *CONI* DN12...........**88** C2
Scott Cl *MALT* S66...........**133** E1
Scott Crs *ARMTH* DN3..........**29** E4
Scott Hl *BTLY* DN5............**54** B5
Scott St *ATT* S4.............**115** G4
Scott St *ATT* S4.............**116** A4
Scott Wk *MALT* S66...........**110** B2
Scott Wy *CHPT/GREN* S35......**93** H2
Scovell Av *RAW* S62...........**85** E4
Scowerdons Cl
............*HACK/IN* S12.........**142** D5
Scowerdons Dr
............*HACK/IN* S12.........**142** D5
Scraith Wood Dr *SHEFN* S5..**114** B2
Scrooby Dr *KIMB* S61..........**97** G3
Scrooby La *KIMB* S61.........**97** H3
Scrooby Pl *KIMB* S61.........**97** H3
Scrooby St *KIMB* S61.........**97** H3
Seabrook Rd
............*SHEFP/MNR* S2........**126** D5
Seagrave Crs *HACK/IN* S12..**154** D1
Seagrave Crs *HACK/IN* S12..**154** C2
Seagrave Dr *CHNE* S41......**193** E5
............*HACK/IN* S12.........**154** D1
Seagrave Rd *HACK/IN* S12...**154** C1
Searby Rd *MALT* S66.........**108** D2
Searson Av *BSVR* S44.......**196** D3
Seaton Cl *SHEFP/MNR* S2....**127** F5
Seaton Crs *SHEFP/MNR* S2...**127** F5
Seaton Gdns
............*NROS/TKH* DN11.........**91** F4
Seaton Pl *SHEFP/MNR* S2....**127** F5
Seaton Wy *SHEFP/MNR* S2...**127** F5
Sebastion Vw *RHAM* S60....**118** C2
Second Av *AWLS/ASK* DN6.....**25** C3
Second La *DIN* S25..........**148** C5
............*DIN* S25.............**121** G2
Sedan St *ATT* S4............**115** C5
Sedbergh Crs *CHNE* S41....**186** D2
Sedge Cl *MALT* S66.........**108** D1
Sedgefield Wy
............*MEX/SWTN* S64.........**67** F2
Sedgemoor Cl *CHSW* S40....**186** B5
Sedgley Rd *ST/HB/BR* S6...**114** F3
Sefton Rd *FUL* S10.........**138** A3
Selborne Rd *FUL* S10.......**124** C4
Selborne St
............*RHAM/THRY* S65.........**9** G1
Selbourne Cl *DOD/DAR* S75...**18** A2
Selby Cl *AU/AST/KP* S26....**145** G5
............*CHSW* S40............**191** G4
Selby Rd *BSLYN/ROY* S71 *..**14** D5
............*SHEFN* S5............**115** H3
............*WHHL* DN2..............**41** E5
Selhurst Crs
............*DONS/BSCR* DN4.........**74** A1
Selhurst Rd *CHNE* S41......**187** F4
Selkirk Rd *WHHL* DN2..........**41** G4
Sellars Rd *KIMB* S61..........**96** C5
Sellers St *SHEFS* S8.........**139** H3
Selly Oak Gv *SHEFS* S8.....**163** G2
Selly Oak Rd *SHEFS* S8.....**163** G2
Selmer Ct *STV/CWN* S43....**188** B1
Selwood Flats
............*RHAM/THRY* S65 *.......**9** K2
Selwyn St *BSVR* S44........**197** F4
............*RHAM/THRY* S65.........**9** H1
Senior Rd *DARN/MH* S9.....**128** A3
............*DONS/BSCR* DN4.........**55** C3
Seniors Pl *CHPT/GREN* S35..**80** D5
Sennen Cft *BSLYN/ROY* S71...**20** B4
Setcup La *ECK/KIL* S21......**174** C1
Seth Ter *BSLY* S70............**3** K6

Setts Wy *RCH* S42...........**195** H3
Sevenairs Fold *MOS* S20....**157** E2
Sevenairs Rd *MOS* S20......**157** E2
Sevenairs Vw *MOS* S20......**157** E2
Sevenfields Ct
............*ST/HB/BR* S6..........**113** G3
Sevenfields La
............*ST/HB/BR* S6..........**113** G3
Severn Ct *FUL* S10.........**125** F4
Severn Rd *FUL* S10.........**125** F4
Severnside Dr
............*HAN/WDH* S13.........**143** E3
Severnside Gdns
............*HAN/WDH* S13.........**143** E3
Severnside Pl
............*HAN/WDH* S13.........**143** E3
Sexton Dr *MALT* S66.........**108** D5
Seymore Rd
............*AU/AST/KP* S26.......**145** G5
Seymour La *STV/CWN* S43...**185** E4
Seymour Rd *MALT* S66.......**111** F4
Shackleton Rd *WHHL* DN2.....**41** H1
Shackleton Vw
............*STKB/PEN* S36.........**44** C4
Shady Side *DONS/BSCR* DN4..**55** G4
Shaftesbury Av *CHSW* S40....**4** A3
............*WHHL* DN2..............**42** B2
Shaftesbury Dr *HOY* S74.....**61** H3
Shaftesbury St *BTLY* DN5....**27** E1
Shaftholme Rd *BTLY* DN5.....**27** F2
Shafton Hall Dr *CUD/GR* S72..**16** D1
Shafton Rd *RHAM* S60.......**119** H3
Shaftsbury Av
............*AWLS/ASK* DN6.........**24** D2
Shaftsbury Sq
............*RHAM/THRY* S65.........**9** G2
Shakespeare Av *BTLY* DN5...**55** F1
Shakespeare Crs
............*DRON* S18............**171** G3
Shakespeare Dr *DIN* S25...**135** E5
Shakespeare Rd *BTLY* DN5...**55** F1
............*DEARNE* S63..........**64** D1
............*RHAM/THRY* S65.......**106** B1
Shalesmoor *OWL* S3............**11** F1
Shalesmoor Jct *OWL* S3....**125** H2
Shambles St *BSLY* S70..........**2** D5
The Shambles *CHNE* S41....**187** F2
Shamrock Pl *STV/CWN* S43..**183** G2
Shap Cl *CHSW* S40..........**186** B5
Shardlow Gdns
............*DONS/BSCR* DN4.........**74** B2
Sharlston Gdns
............*NROS/TKH* DN11.........**91** H2
Sharman Cl *DRON* S18......**172** C2
Sharpe Av *SHEFS* S8........**152** C5
Sharpfield Av *RAW* S62.......**85** E3
Sharrard Cl *HACK/IN* S12...**141** H5
Sharrard Dr *HACK/IN* S12...**141** H5
Sharrard Gv *HACK/IN* S12...**141** H5
Sharrard Rd *HACK/IN* S12...**141** H5
Sharrow La *ECC* S11.........**139** G2
Sharrow St *ECC* S11.........**139** G2
Sharrow Vale Rd *ECC* S11...**139** E2
Sharrow Vw *ABRD* S7........**139** G2
Shaw Ct *ARMTH* DN3..........**43** E5
Shawfield Cl *ARMTH* DN3....**29** G1
Shawfield Rd
............*BSLYN/ROY* S71..........**2** C5
Shaw La *BSLY* S70.............**2** C5
............*BSLYN/ROY* S71.........**15** H4
............*DOD/DAR* S75..........**30** A3
............*WHHL* DN2..............**41** H2
Shaw Rd *CONI* DN12...........**70** B5
............*RHAM/THRY* S65.......**106** C1
Shawsfield Rd *RHAM* S60....**106** B5
Shaw St *BSLY* S70..............**2** C5
............*CHNE* S41............**187** G2
Shaw Wood Wy *WHHL* DN2....**41** H3
Shaw's Rw *CHSW* S40........**191** H2
Shay House La
............*STKB/PEN* S36.........**76** D3
Shay Rd *STKB/PEN* S36.......**76** D2
The Shay *DONS/BSCR* DN4....**74** A1
Sheaf Bank *SHEFP/MNR* S2..**140** A3
Sheaf Cl *CONI* DN12..........**89** F2
Sheaf Ct *BSLY* S70............**32** D3
Sheaf Crs *DEARNE* S63........**53** F4
Sheaf St *SHEFS* S11..........**11** J4
Sheardown St
............*DONS/BSCR* DN4.........**6** A5
Sheards Cl *DRON* S18.......**170** D2
Sheards Dr *DRON* S18.......**170** C2
Sheards Wy *DRON* S18......**170** C2
Shearman Av *KIMB* S61.......**96** D4
Shearwood Rd *FUL* S10......**10** A4
Sheep Bridge La
............*NROS/TKH* DN11.........**91** H1
Sheepcote Rd *ECK/KIL* S21..**168** A2
Sheep Cote Rd *RHAM* S60...**120** B1
Sheep Dike La *MALT* S66....**121** G4
Sheepcote Rd *BSLYN/ROY* S71..**14** C4
Sheffield La *SHEFP/MNR* S2..**127** F5
Sheffield Pkwy
............*SHEFP/MNR* S2........**126** D3
Sheffield Rd *BSLY* S70.........**3** H6
............*BSLY* S70.............**60** D1
............*CHNE* S41............**187** G2
............*CONI* DN12............**69** H5
............*CONI* DN12............**88** B3
............*DARN/MH* S9.........**117** E3

............*DIN* S25.............**148** A3
............*DONS/BSCR* DN4.........**70** B3
............*DRON* S18............**162** D5
............*ECK/KIL* S21.........**168** A1
............*ECK/KIL* S21.........**176** B3
............*HACK/IN* S12.........**156** A2
............*HACK/IN* S13.........**143** E4
............*HOY* S74..............**61** G3
............*MOS* S20............**155** H3
............*RHAM* S60............**8** C7
............*RHAM* S60............**117** H1
............*STKB/PEN* S36.........**45** E3
............*STV/CWN* S43.........**184** D5
............*STV/CWN* S43.........**185** H3
Sheffield Round Wk
............*ECC* S11.............**150** C2
............*SHEFS* S8............**152** B5
Sheldon Av *CONI* DN12.......**89** F2
Sheldon La *ST/HB/BR* S6....**123** C1
Sheldon Rd *ABRD* S7.........**139** G4
............*CHSW* S40............**186** B4
............*SHEFS* S8.............**76** D2
Sheldon Rw *OWL* S3...........**11** J1
Sheldon St *SHEFP/MNR* S2..**140** A1
Sheldrake Cl *KIMB* S61.......**95** F1
Shelley Av *DONS/BSCR* DN4..**71** H4
Shelley Cl *STKB/PEN* S36....**44** D2
Shelley Dr *ARMTH* DN3........**43** E5
............*BSLYN/ROY* S71.........**20** B5
............*DIN* S25.............**135** F5
............*DRON* S18............**171** G4
............*RHAM/THRY* S65.......**106** D4
Shelley Gv *BTLY* DN5.........**55** F1
Shelley Ri *AWLS/ASK* DN6....**25** E2
Shelley Rd
............*RHAM/THRY* S65.......**106** D3
Shelley Wy *DEARNE* S63......**64** C1
Shenstone Dr
............*RHAM/THRY* S65.......**106** D5
Shenstone Rd
............*RHAM/THRY* S65.......**106** D5
............*ST/HB/BR* S6..........**113** H2
Shepcote La *STV/CWN* S9...**117** G5
Shepcote Ter *BSLY* S70 *......**32** C2
Shepcote Wy *DARN/MH* S9..**117** G5
Shephard's Ci *CONI* DN12....**68** B5
Shepherd Dr
............*CHPT/GREN* S35.........**80** C5
Shepherd La *DEARNE* S63....**37** F3
Shepherd St *OWL* S3..........**10** E1
Shepley Cft *CHPT/GREN* S35..**80** C5
Shepley St *CHSW* S40..........**4** A1
Sheppard Rd
............*DONS/BSCR* DN4.........**71** G1
Shepperson Rd
............*ST/HB/BR* S6..........**113** H3
Sherburn Ga
............*CHPT/GREN* S35.........**80** D5
Sherburn Rd
............*BSLYN/ROY* S71.........**14** C5
Sherde Rd *ST/HB/BR* S6....**125** F1
Sheridan Av
............*DONS/BSCR* DN4.........**72** A2
Sheridan Ct *BSLYN/ROY* S71..**20** B4
Sheridan Dr
............*RHAM/THRY* S65.......**107** G3
Sheringham Cl
............*DONS/BSCR* DN4.........**55** D4
Sherwood Av *ARMTH* DN3....**29** F5
............*BTLY* DN5..............**38** D4
............*CONI* DN12............**88** C2
Sherwood Crs *RHAM* S60......**9** G5
Sherwood Dr
............*DONS/BSCR* DN4.........**71** E3
Sherwood Gln *ABRD* S7......**151** H4
Sherwood Pl *DRON* S18.....**170** B2
Sherwood Rd *DRON* S18.....**170** B2
............*ECK/KIL* S21.........**168** C1
............*NROS/TKH* DN11.........**91** G3
Sherwood St
............*BSLYN/ROY* S71..........**3** H4
............*BSVR* S44............**196** B4
............*MOS* S20............**192** D3
Sherwood Wy *CUD/GR* S72....**16** C3
Shetland Rd *DRON* S18......**171** F3
Shield Av *BSLY* S70...........**31** H5
Shinwell Av *STV/CWN* S43...**189** F2
Shay Hl *RHAM* S60.............**9** F5
Shipman Ct *MOS* S20........**166** D1
Shipton St *ST/HB/BR* S6....**125** G2
Shirburn Gdns
............*DONS/BSCR* DN4.........**58** A4
Shirebrook Rd *SHEFS* S8...**140** A4
Shirecliffe Cl *OWL* S3......**115** F5
Shirecliffe La *OWL* S3......**115** G5
Shirecliffe Rd *SHEFN* S5...**115** G5
Shiregreen La *SHEFN* S5...**103** C5
Shiregreen Ter *SHEFN* S5..**102** D4
Shirehall Crs *SHEFN* S5....**102** D2
Shirehall Rd *SHEFN* S5.....**102** D5
Shire Oak Dr *HOY* S74.......**62** D3
Shireoaks Rd *DRON* S18....**170** C1
Shireoaks Wy *CUD/GR* S72...**17** H4
Shirec Cl *BTLY* DN5..........**54** B4
Shirewood Cl *DEARNE* S63...**63** H2
Shirland Av *BSLYN/ROY* S71..**20** A1
Shirland Ct *DARN/MH* S9...**127** F1
Shirland La *DARN/MH* S9...**127** F1
Shirland La *DARN/MH* S9...**127** G2
Shirland Ms *DARN/MH* S9...**127** G2
Shirland Pl *DARN/MH* S9...**127** H2
Shirland St *CHNE* S41........**5** G1

Shirley Cl CHSW S40..............186 B4
Shirley Rd DONS/BSCR DN4....55 C4
Shooters Hill Dr
  NROS/TKH DN11.................91 H3
Shoreham Dr RHAM S60......119 F3
Shoreham Rd RHAM S60.....120 B1
Shoreham St SHEF S1............11 H5
  SHEFP/MNR S2.................140 A2
Shore La FUL S10..................124 C5
Shorland Dr RHAM S60.......130 A3
Shortbrook Bank MOS S20..157 E5
Shortbrook Cl MOS S20......157 E5
Shortbrook Cft MOS S20 *..157 F5
Shortbrook Cl MOS S20......157 F5
Shortbrook Rd MOS S20.....157 E5
Shortbrook Wy MOS S20.....157 E5
Short Cl RCH S42.................190 B5
Shortfield Ct
  BSLYN/ROY S71................14 C4
Short La DONS/BSCR DN4......73 F1
  ST/HB/BR S6.....................122 C2
Shorts La TOT/DORE S17....160 B2
Short Wood Cl BSLY S70......47 H4
Shotton Wk DON DN1.............6 C6
Shrewsbury Cl
  MEX/SWTN S64.................66 D3
  STKB/PEN S36...................44 D3
Shrewsbury Rd
  SHEFP/MNR S2...................11 J6
  STKB/PEN S36...................44 D3
Shrewsbury Ter KIMB S61..104 D3
Shroggs Head Cl
  WMB/DAR S73...................35 F4
Shrogswood Rd RHAM S60..120 B1
Shubert Cl HAN/WDH S13..143 F2
Shude Hl SHEF S1..................11 J3
Shunters Drift
  STV/CWN S43...................177 F5
Shuttle Cl NROS/TKH DN11..91 G3
Shuttleworth Cl
  NROS/TKH DN11.................91 G3
Sicey Av SHEFN S5...............102 D3
Sicey La SHEFN S5...............102 D5
Sicklebrook La DRON S18..164 A4
Sidcop Rd CUD/GR S72..........16 D4
Siddall St SHEF S1.................11 G6
Sidings Ct DONS/BSCR DN4..56 C5
The Sidings Rbt
  DONS/BSCR DN4...................6 E7
The Sidings STV/CWN S43..185 F1
Sidlaw Cl CHSW S40.............186 C4
Sidney Rd WHHL DN2.............57 F1
Sidney St MEX/SWTN S64.....66 B5
  SHEF S1.............................11 G6
Sidons Cl KIMB S61................96 C4
Siemens Cl DARN/MH S9....117 G2
Siena Cl WMB/DAR S73........34 C4
Sike La STKB/PEN S36...........44 A5
Sikes Rd DIN S25..................148 B3
Silkstone Cl DOD/DAR S75....60 B3
  HACK/IN S12....................155 G1
Silkstone Crs HACK/IN S12..155 F1
Silkstone Dr HACK/IN S12..155 G1
Silkstone Rd HACK/IN S12..155 G1
Silkstone Vw HOY S74..........49 E5
Silver Birch Av FUL S10......137 G3
Silverdale Cl ARMTH DN3.....59 G5
  CHNE S41..........................179 E5
  ECC S11...........................138 C5
Silverdale Crs ECC S11........138 C5
Silverdale Cft ECC S11........151 C1
Silverdale Dr
  BSLYN/ROY S71................20 D2
Silverdale Gdns ECC S11....151 H1
Silverdale Gld ECC S11........151 H1
Silverdale Rd ECC S11........151 G1
Silverdales DIN S25.............135 G4
Silver Hill Rd ECC S11.........138 D5
Silver Jubilee Cl WHHL DN2..41 G4
Silver Mill Rd
  SHEFP/MNR S2.................140 A2
Silvermoor Dr
  RHAM/THRY S65.............108 D1
Silverstone Av CUD/GR S72..17 E5
Silver St BSLY S70...................3 F6
  DOD/DAR S75.....................30 B4
  DON DN1.............................6 D3
  RHAM/THRY S65................99 C4
  SHEF S1.............................11 F2
Silver Street Head SHEF S1..11 F2
Silver Well Dr
  STV/CWN S43...................189 H1
Silverwood Cl DEARNE S63..65 H1
Simcrest Av ECK/KIL S21..168 B3
Simmonite Rd KIMB S61........96 D5
Simons Wy WMB/DAR S73....33 H5
Simpson Pl MEX/SWTN S64..66 D3
Sims Cft CHNE S41...............180 A3
Sims St SHEF S1....................11 F2
Sincil Wy DONS/BSCR DN4..74 A1
Singleton Crs ST/HB/BR S6..114 A5
Singleton Gv ST/HB/BR S6..114 A5
Singleton Rd ST/HB/BR S6..114 A5
Sitka Cl BSLYN/ROY S71.......15 F2
Sitwell MOS S20 *...............157 E5
Sitwell Cl CHSW S40...........192 B3
  STKB/PEN S36...................76 C2
Sitwell Dr RHAM S60...........119 G3
Sitwell Gv MEX/SWTN S64...86 B1
  RHAM S60.........................119 G2

Sitwell La MALT S66.............121 F1
Sitwell Park Rd RHAM S60..120 B1
Sitwell Pl ABRD S7...............139 H2
Sitwell Rd ABRD S7..............139 H2
Sitwell St ECK/KIL S21........174 C1
Sitwell V RHAM S60.............119 F1
Sitwell Vw RHAM S60..........120 B3
Sivilla Rd MEX/SWTN S64.....86 B3
Skeldale Dr CHSW S40........192 D4
Skelton Cl HAN/WDH S13..143 G5
Skelton Gv HAN/WDH S13..143 F4
Skelton La HAN/WDH S13..143 F4
  MOS S20...........................143 F4
Skelton Rd SHEFS S8...........140 A5
Skelwith Cl ATT S4..............116 B3
  CHNE S41..........................186 D1
Skelwith Dr ATT S4..............116 B3
Skelwith Rd ATT S4..............116 B3
Skew Hill La
  CHPT/GREN S35...............100 D1
Skiddaw Cl CHSW S40........186 D3
Skiers Hall La HOY S74........62 B4
Skiers Vw Rd HOY S74.........61 G3
Skinnerthorpe Rd ATT S4..115 H5
Skipton Cl CONI DN12..........68 A5
Skipton Rd ATT S4...............115 C4
Skipwith Gdns
  NROS/TKH DN11.................91 E3
Skye Edge Av
  SHEFP/MNR S2.................126 D5
Skye Edge Rd
  SHEFP/MNR S2.................126 D5
Slack La CHSW S40.............191 F1
  CUD/GR S72.......................13 H4
Slade Rd MEX/SWTN S64......86 A1
Slag La STV/CWN S43..........173 F5
Slaidburn Av
  CHPT/GREN S35.................80 D5
Slate St SHEFP/MNR S2......140 B3
Slayleigh Av FUL S10..........137 G2
Slayleigh Delph FUL S10....137 G2
Slayleigh Dr FUL S10...........137 H2
Slayleigh La FUL S10...........137 G2
Slayley Hl STV/CWN S43....184 C2
Slayley Vw STV/CWN S43..184 C2
Slayley View Rd
  STV/CWN S43...................177 F5
Sleaford St DARN/MH S9 *..127 F1
Sledgate Dr MALT S66........120 D1
Sledgate La MALT S66........120 D1
Slinn St FUL S10..................125 E5
Slitting Mill La DARN/MH S9..127 F1
Sloade La HACK/IN S12.......165 F1
Smallage La HAN/WDH S13..144 C1
Smalldale Rd HACK/IN S12..155 G1
Smawell La HOR/CROF WF4..12 B2
Smeaton Cl
  RHAM/THRY S65.............108 D1
Smeaton St RHAM/THRY S65..139 H2
Smeckley Wood Cl
  CHNE S41..........................178 C3
Smelter Wood Av
  HAN/WDH S13.................142 C3
Smelter Wood Cl
  HAN/WDH S13 *...............142 C3
Smelter Wood Crs
  HAN/WDH S13.................142 D3
Smelter Wood Dr
  HAN/WDH S13.................142 C3
Smelter Wood La
  HAN/WDH S13.................142 C3
Smelter Wood Pl
  HAN/WDH S13.................142 C3
Smelter Wood Ri
  HAN/WDH S13.................142 D3
Smelter Wood Rd
  HAN/WDH S13.................142 C3
Smelter Wood Wy
  HAN/WDH S13.................142 C3
Smillie Rd NROS/TKH DN11..91 G3
Smith Av STV/CWN S43.......189 F2
Smith Crs CHNE S41............193 F3
Smithey Cl CHPT/GREN S35..80 B5
Smithfield OWL S3.................11 F1
Smithfield Av CHNE S41......193 E5
Smithfield Rd HACK/IN S12..154 C3
Smithies La DOD/DAR S75..19 G3
Smithies Rd MEX/SWTN S64..66 A4
Smithies St BSLYN/ROY S71..14 C4
Smithley La WMB/DAR S73..49 G1
Smith Rd STKB/PEN S36......76 C2
Smithson Av BSVR S44........197 E3
Smith Sq DONS/BSCR DN4..71 F1
Smith St CHPT/GREN S35.....94 A1
  DONS/BSCR DN4................71 F1
  WMB/DAR S73...................50 C2
Smithy Bridge La
  WMB/DAR S73...................63 F1
Smithy Brook Rd
  ECK/KIL S21.....................176 A3
Smithy Carr Av
  CHPT/GREN S35.................93 H1
Smithy Carr Cl
  CHPT/GREN S35.................93 H1
Smithy Cl KIMB S61...............96 D5
Smithy Cft DRON S18...........170 A1
Smithy Fold La
  CHNE S41............................79 E4
Smithy Moor La
  STKB/PEN S36...................76 A1

Smithy Wood Crs SHEFS S8..152 C1
Smithy Wood La
  DOD/DAR S75.....................30 B4
Smithy Wood Rd
  CHPT/GREN S35.................94 C2
  SHEFS S8..........................152 C1
Snail Hl RHAM S60...................9 F4
Snailsden Wy DOD/DAR S75..14 B4
Snaithing La FUL S10..........138 A1
Snaithing Park Cl
  FUL S10............................138 A1
Snaithing Park Rd
  FUL S10............................138 A1
Snake La CONI DN12............89 F2
Snape Hl DRON S18..............171 E1
Snape Hill Crs DRON S18..163 E5
Snapehill Crs DRON S18....171 E1
Snape Hill Dr DRON S18 *..163 F5
Snape Hill La DRON S18....171 E1
Snape Hill Rd
  WMB/DAR S73...................35 E5
Snelston Cl DRON S18.........170 A2
Snetterton Cl CUD/GR S72..17 E5
Snig Hl OWL S3.....................11 H2
Snipe Rd ECK/KIL S42..........190 B5
Snowberry Cl
  MEX/SWTN S64.................86 A3
Snowden Ter
  WMB/DAR S73...................50 B2
Snowdon La ECK/KIL S21..164 D5
Snowdon Wy RHAM S60.....118 D5
Snow La OWL S3...................11 F1
Snydale Rd CUD/GR S72......16 D5
Soaper La DRON S18...........171 E1
Soap House La
  HAN/WDH S13.................144 A3
Society St DON DN1.................6 D4
Sokell Av WMB/DAR S73.....50 A3
Solly St OWL S3....................10 D2
Solway Ri DRON S18............170 B1
Somercotes Rd
  HACK/IN S12....................142 B5
Somersall Cl CHSW S40.....191 E3
Somersall La CHSW S40.....191 E4
  CHSW S40.........................191 E3
Somersall Park Rd
  CHSW S40.........................191 E3
Somersall Willows
  CHSW S40.........................191 E3
Somersby Av BTLY DN5.......55 F1
  RCH S42............................191 F5
Somerset Dr STV/CWN S43..188 D1
Somerset Rd DON DN1..........6 E6
  OWL S3.............................126 B1
Somerset St BSLY S70 *........2 D3
  CUD/GR S72.......................21 H1
  MALT S66..........................111 F4
  OWL S3.............................126 B1
Somerton Dr
  DONS/BSCR DN4................74 A1
Somerville Ter
  ST/HB/BR S6.....................125 F1
Somin Ct DONS/BSCR DN4..72 A3
Sopewell Rd KIMB S61........104 B3
Sorby Rd AU/AST/KP S26..144 D3
Sorby St ATT S4...................126 C2
Sorby Wy MALT S66............121 F1
Soresby St CHSW S40............5 F4
Sorrel Rd MALT S66............108 C3
Sorrelsykes Cl RHAM S60..119 H4
Sorrento Wy
  WMB/DAR S73...................34 D4
Sothall Cl MOS S20.............157 F2
Sothall Ct MOS S20.............157 F2
Sothall Gn MOS S20...........157 F2
Sothall Ms MOS S20...........157 F2
Sough Hall Av KIMB S61......95 H1
Sough Hall Cl KIMB S61......95 H1
Sough Hall Crs KIMB S61....95 F1
Sough Hall Rd KIMB S61.....95 F2
Soughley La
  CHPT/GREN S35.................78 A1
  FUL S10............................136 C2
Sousa St MALT S66..............111 G4
Southall St SHEFS S8..........140 A4
South Av MEX/SWTN S64.....85 H1
Southbourne Rd FUL S10..125 E5
South Cl BSLYN/ROY S71.....15 C2
  DRON S18.........................172 A5
Southcote Dr DRON S18....170 B2
South Cft CUD/GR S72..........17 E1
Southcroft Gdns ABRD S7..139 H4
Southdown Av CHSW S40..186 C5
South Dr BSLYN/ROY S71....15 G2
  DEARNE S63.....................52 D4
Southend Pl
  SHEFP/MNR S2.................127 E5
Southend Ter
  SHEFP/MNR S2.................127 E5
Southey Av SHEFN S5.........115 E1
Southey Cl SHEFN S5..........114 D1
Southey Crs MALT S66........111 D1
  SHEFN S5.........................114 D1
Southey Dr SHEFN S5.........115 E1
Southey Green Cl
  SHEFN S5.........................114 D1
Southey Green Rd
  SHEFN S5.........................101 F5
Southey Hall Dr SHEFN S5..114 D1

Southey Hall Rd SHEFN S5..114 D1
Southey Hl SHEFN S5..........101 G5
Southey Pl SHEFN S5..........114 D1
Southey Ri SHEFN S5..........114 D1
Southey Rd MALT S66........111 E3
Southfield Dr DRON S18....171 G3
Southfield La DEARNE S63..36 D3
Southfield Mt DRON S18....171 G3
Southfield Rd ARMTH DN3..22 A3
  CUD/GR S72.......................22 A3
Southfields STV/CWN S43..185 F3
Southgate CUD/GR S72.......17 F2
Southgate Dr
  DOD/DAR S75.....................17 F2
  ECK/KIL S21.....................167 E5
  HOY S74.............................62 A3
  STKB/PEN S36...................45 E4
Southgate Ct ECK/KIL S21..167 E5
Southgate Crs
  STV/CWN S43...................185 F1
Southgate Wy
  STV/CWN S43...................181 F2
South Grimesthorpe Rd
  ATT S4..............................126 C1
Southgrove Rd FUL S10......139 F1
Southlands Wy
  AU/AST/KP S26................145 G3
South La SHEF S1..................11 F7
Southlea Av HOY S74...........62 B3
Southlea Cl HOY S74............62 B3
Southlea Dr HOY S74...........62 A3
Southlea Rd HOY S74..........62 B3
South Lodge Ct CHSW S40..191 F1
Southmoor Av ARMTH DN3..42 C5
Southmoor Cl
  STV/CWN S43...................188 D5
Southmoor La ARMTH DN3..42 C5
South Pde DON DN1...............7 F4
  OWL S3.............................126 A2
South Pl CHSW S40.................5 G5
  WMB/DAR S73...................18 D4
South Rd CHPT/GREN S35...80 B4
  DOD/DAR S75.....................30 B2
  KIMB S61..........................104 C3
  ST/HB/BR S6.....................125 E1
Southsea Rd
  HAN/WDH S13.................143 E4
South St AWLS/ASK DN6...25 F5
  BSLY S70............................2 B4
  CHSW S40.........................134 D4
  DIN S25............................134 D4
  DOD/DAR S75.....................30 B4
  DONS/BSCR DN4.................6 E7
  KIMB S61..........................104 B3
  MALT S66..........................133 F1
  MOS S20...........................166 D2
  RAW S62.............................85 G5
  WMB/DAR S73...................18 D4
South St North
  STV/CWN S43...................180 B2
South Street Pk
  SHEFP/MNR S2...................11 K3
South Ter MALT S66 *.............9 F5
South Vw MOS S20.............167 G1
  WMB/DAR S73...................35 E5
South View Cl
  ST/HB/BR S6.....................113 E4
South View Crs ABRD S7..139 H3
South View Ri
  ST/HB/BR S6.....................113 E3
South View Rd ABRD S7....139 H2
  HOY S74.............................61 H2
South View Ter MALT S60..129 G2
Southwell Gdns
  AU/AST/KP S26................144 C3
Southwell Ri
  MEX/SWTN S64.................67 F2
Southwell Rd ATT S4..........116 B3
  RAW S62.............................85 H5
Southwell St DOD/DAR S75..2 C3
Southwood ST/HB/BR S6...113 G1
Southwood La DRON S18..171 E4
Southwood Dr
  STV/CWN S43...................185 F3
Southwood Gv
  ST/HB/BR S6.....................113 G1
Spa Brook Cl HACK/IN S12..155 H1
Spa Brooke Dr
  HACK/IN S12....................142 D5
Spa La CHNE S41.................143 C5
  HAN/WDH S13.................143 C5
Spa Lane Cft
  HAN/WDH S13.................143 G4
Spalton Rd RAW S62............92 B2
Spansyke St
  DONS/BSCR DN4.................6 A5
Spark La DOD/DAR S75........14 A4
Sparrowbusk Cl
  MEX/SWTN S64...............177 F5
Spartan Av MALT S66.........110 B1
Spa View Av HACK/IN S12..155 H2
Spa View Dr HACK/IN S12..155 H2
Spa View Pl HACK/IN S12..155 H2
Spa View Rd HACK/IN S12..155 H2
Spa View Ter HACK/IN S12..155 H2
Spa View Wy HACK/IN S12..155 H2
Spa Well Crs RHAM S60 *..89 G2
Speetley Vw STV/CWN S43..177 F4
Speeton Rd ST/HB/BR S6...114 A5
Speighthill Crs RCH S42..195 E3
Spencer Av STV/CWN S43..182 D4

Spencer Ct RHAM S60.........120 B3
Spencer Dr
  RHAM/THRY S65.............108 D1
Spencer Gn RHAM S60.......120 B3
Spencer Rd SHEFP/MNR S2..140 A3
Spencer St BSLY S70.............2 E7
  BSVR S44..........................196 C4
  CHSW S40............................5 F2
  MEX/SWTN S64.................66 C3
Spenser Rd
  RHAM/THRY S65.............106 C4
Spey Cl RHAM/THRY S65....14 A5
Spilsby Cl DONS/BSCR DN4..74 C2
Spink Hall Cl STKB/PEN S36..77 E3
Spink Hall La STKB/PEN S36..76 D5
Spinkhill Av HAN/WDH S13..142 A2
Spinkhill Dr HAN/WDH S13..142 B2
Spinkhill La ECK/KIL S21..176 A1
Spinkhill Rd ECK/KIL S21..168 C4
  HAN/WDH S13.................142 B3
Spinkhill Vw ECK/KIL S21..175 H2
Spinner Cft CHSW S40............5 G7
Spinners Rd WHHL DN2......40 C3
Spinney Cl RHAM S60..........119 C1
Spinneyfield RHAM S60......119 C2
Spinney Hl BTLY DN5............54 B5
The Spinney ARMTH DN3...29 C1
  DONS/BSCR DN4................71 F3
Spital Brook Cl CHSW S40..135 J3
Spitalfields OWL S3............126 B2
Spital Gdns CHNE S41...........5 K7
Spital Gv NROS/TKH DN11..91 G2
Spital Hl ATT S4...................126 C2
Spital La CHNE S41.................5 J5
  OWL S3.............................126 B2
Spital St OWL S3.................126 B2
Spittal Gn BSVR S44...........196 C4
Spofforth Rd DARN/MH S9..127 G2
Spooner Dr ECK/KIL S21..168 A2
Spooner Rd FUL S10............125 E4
Spoon Gld ST/HB/BR S6.....123 C1
Spoonhill Rd ST/HB/BR S6..124 B1
Spoon La ST/HB/BR S6........123 E1
Spoon Ms ST/HB/BR S6......123 C1
Spoon Wy ST/HB/BR S6......123 C1
Spotswood Cl GLV S14........154 A1
Spotswood Dr GLV S14......141 E5
Spotswood Mt GLV S14......153 H1
Spotswood Pl GLV S14........153 H1
Spout La ST/HB/BR S6.........112 B5
Spout Spinney
  ST/HB/BR S6.....................123 F1
Springbank WMB/DAR S73..35 C5
Springbank Cl
  BSLYN/ROY S71................15 G4
Spring Bank Rd CHSW S40...4 D3
  CONI DN12..........................88 D3
Spring Cl ECK/KIL S21........194 B3
Spring Close Dell GLV S14..154 B1
Spring Close Mt GLV S14..154 B1
Spring Close Vw GLV S14..154 A1
Spring Crs BTLY DN5............54 B4
Spring Cft KIMB S61.............96 D5
Springcroft Dr BTLY DN5..39 E2
Spring Dr WMB/DAR S73....51 E5
Spring Farm
  HOR/CROF WF4.................12 A3
Springfield DEARNE S63 *..52 C3
Springfield Av CHSW S40......4 A3
  ECC S11...........................139 E5
Springfield Cl ABRD S7......152 A1
  ARMTH DN3........................43 E5
  ECK/KIL S21.....................166 C5
  STV/CWN S43...................185 E3
  WMB/DAR S73...................35 F5
Springfield Ct BTLY DN5....39 E5
Springfield Crs BSVR S44..196 C1
  HOY S74.............................61 G3
  WMB/DAR S73...................35 F5
Springfield Gln ABRD S7..151 H1
Springfield Pl BSLY S70 *....2 A2
Springfield Rd ABRD S7....152 A1
  CUD/GR S72.......................17 H5
  HOY S74.............................61 F3
  MALT S66..........................108 A4
  MEX/SWTN S64.................86 C4
Springfields DOD/DAR S75..18 C3
Springfield St BSLY S70........2 B4
Spring Gdns
  BSLYN/ROY S71................20 C3
  DON DN1.............................6 C4
  HOY S74.............................62 A2
Spring Gv BSLYN/ROY S71..15 H4
Spring Hl FUL S10...............125 E3
Springhill Av WMB/DAR S73..51 E5
Spring Hill Cl BTLY DN5.....54 B4
Spring Hill Rd FUL S10......125 E3
Spring House Rd FUL S10..125 E3
Spring La BSLYN/ROY S71..15 G4
  BTLY DN5............................54 B1
Springmount Dr MALT S66..141 E2
Spring Pl CHSW S40 *............5 F3
Spring St BSLY S70.................3 F6
  RHAM/THRY S65.................9 H5
Spring Vale Av BSLY S70....47 H1
Springvale Cl MALT S66.....110 D2
Springvale Gv
  STKB/PEN S36...................45 E3
Springvale Rd CUD/GR S72..22 D2
  FUL S10............................125 F3

Spring Vale Rd STV/CWN S43 ......188 C1
Springvale Wk ST/HB/BR S6 ......125 F2
Spring View Rd FUL S10 ..125 E3
Spring Wk RHAM/THRY S65 ...9 G3
Spring Water Av HACK/IN S12 ......155 H1
Spring Water Cl HACK/IN S12 ......155 H1
Spring Water Dr HACK/IN S12 ......155 H1
Spring Wy DON DN1 ......40 C5
Springwell Av MOS S20......157 E1
Springwell Cl MALT S66......111 E2
Springwell Crs MOS S20......157 E1
Springwell Dr MOS S20......157 E1
Springwell Gdns DONS/BSCR DN4 ......71 F2
Springwell Gv MOS S20......157 E1
Springwell La DONS/BSCR DN4 ......71 F2
Springwell Park Dr STV/CWN S43 ......189 G2
Springwood Av AU/AST/KP S26 ......145 H1
Springwood Cl ARMTH DN3...59 E5
Spring Wood Cl CHNE S41 ...186 C1
Springwood Ct AU/AST/KP S26 ......145 F1
STV/CWN S43 * 180 B2
Springwood Gv DEARNE S63 ......37 E3
Springwood La CHPT/GREN S35 ......80 A5
Springwood Rd BTLY DN5 ......39 E2
HOY S74......61 G3
SHEFS S8 ......140 A4
Springwood Vw STKB/PEN S36 ......45 F4
Sprotbrough Rd BTLY DN5...55 F2
Spruce Av BSLYN/ROY S71...15 F1
MALT S66......108 B4
Spruce Ri ECK/KIL S21 ......168 A3
Spurley Hey Gv STKB/PEN S36 ......77 E3
Spurr St SHEFP/MNR S2......140 B2
The Square East MALT S66...108 C2
The Square BSLY S70......2 C7
CUD/GR S72......23 F1
RAW S62 ......62 H1
The Square West MALT S66..108 B2
Stables Ct BSVR S44......197 F3
The Stables MEX/SWTN S64...65 H4
Stacey Cl RAW S62 ......17 H5
Stacey Dr RHAM/THRY S65...99 G3
Stacye Av HAN/WDH S13 ....143 H4
Stacye Ri HAN/WDH S13 ....143 H4
Stadium Ct RAW S62......98 A4
Stadium Wy DARN/MH S9...127 F2
RHAM S60......98 A5
Stafford Cl DRON S18......170 A1
Stafford Crs RHAM S60......119 F3
Stafford Dr RHAM S60......119 F3
Stafford Gv BSLY S70......60 D3
Stafford La SHEFP/MNR S2...126 D5
Stafford Rd AWLS/ASK DN6...25 F2
SHEFP/MNR S2......126 D5
Staffordshire Cl MALT S66...111 F3
Stafford St SHEFP/MNR S2..126 C5
Stafford Wy CHPT/GREN S35 ......93 H1
Stag Cl RHAM S60......120 A1
Stag Crs RHAM S60......120 A1
Stag La RHAM S60......119 H1
Stag Willow Cl RHAM S60...106 D5
Stainborough Cl DOD/DAR S75......30 B4
Stainborough La DOD/DAR S75......46 A5
Stainborough Rd DOD/DAR S75......30 B4
STV/CWN S43...31 H5
DOD/DAR S75......60 B2
Staindrop Cl CHPT/GREN S35 ......80 C4
Staindrop Vw CHPT/GREN S35 ......81 E5
Stainley Cl DOD/DAR S75...18 D3
Stainmore Av MOS S20......157 G3
Stainton Cl BSLYN/ROY S71...19 G1
Stainton La MALT S66......111 F1
Stainton Rd ECC S11......138 C3
Stainton St CONI DN12......68 B5
Stairfoot Wy BSLY S70......33 E3
Stair Rd ATT S4 ......115 G4
Stalker Lees Rd ECC S11 ....139 F2
Stamford Rd MALT S66......109 B1
Stamford St DARN/MH S9...116 B5
Stampers Hl BSLY S70......47 F3
Stanage Ri HACK/IN S12......142 B5
Stanbury Ri DOD/DAR S75....18 D4
Stancil La NROS/TKH DN11...90 A4
Standhill Crs BSLYN/ROY S71...14 C5
Standish Av SHEFN S5......115 E4
Standish Bank SHEFN S5 ....115 E3
Standish Cl SHEFN S5......115 E3
Standish Dr SHEFN S5......115 E3
Standish Gdns SHEFN S5 ....115 E3
Standish Rd SHEFN S5......115 E3
Standish Wy SHEFN S5......115 E4
Standon Crs DARN/MH S9...103 F4

Standon Dr DARN/MH S9 ...103 F4
Standon Rd DARN/MH S9 ...103 G4
Stand Pk CHNE S41 * 187 G2
Stand Rd CHNE S41......187 F2
Staneford Ct MOS S20......156 D4
Stanford Cl MALT S66......111 G4
Stanford Rd DRON S18......170 A2
Stanford Wy RCH S42......191 F4
Stanhope Gdns DOD/DAR S75......2 B1
Stanhope Rd DON DN1......40 C5
HACK/IN S12......142 A5
Stanhope St BSLY S70......2 C4
Stanier Wy ECK/KIL S21 ....175 H3
Staniforth Av ECK/KIL S21 ...166 B5
Staniforth Rd DARN/MH S9 ......127 G2
Stanley Av STV/CWN S43 ...189 F2
Stanley Gdns DONS/BSCR DN4......6 A7
Stanley Gv AU/AST/KP S26 ...145 G2
Stanley La OWL S3......126 B2
Stanley Rd BSLY S70......33 E2
BTLY DN5......38 D3
CHPT/GREN S35 ......80 C5
SHEFS S8 ......140 B5
STKB/PEN S36 ......77 E3
Stanley Sq ARMTH DN3......29 F3
Stanley St BSLY S70......2 C4
CHNE S41......5 K6
CUD/GR S72......22 A2
ECK/KIL S21 ......168 B1
OWL S3......126 B2
Stanley Ter MALT S66......110 B4
Stannington Gln ST/HB/BR S6 ......124 A1
Stannington Rd ST/HB/BR S6 ......113 G5
Stannington View Rd FUL S10......124 C3
Stanton Crs HACK/IN S12.....155 F1
Stanwell Av DARN/MH S9 ...103 G5
Stanwell St DARN/MH S9 ...103 G5
Stanwood Av ST/HB/BR S6..124 B1
Stanwood Crs ST/HB/BR S6 ......124 B1
Stanwood Dr RCH S42......191 F4
ST/HB/BR S6 ......124 B1
Stanwood Ms ST/HB/BR S6 ......124 B1
Stanwood Rd ST/HB/BR S6..124 B1
Stapleton Rd DONS/BSCR DN4......70 D3
Star La BSLY S70......2 E4
Starling Md SHEFP/MNR S2 ......127 E5
Starnhill Cl CHPT/GREN S35...94 C5
Station La ATT S4 ......116 C2
CHNE S41......179 G4
CHPT/GREN S35 ......100 A1
STV/CWN S43......180 B4
Station Rd ARMTH DN3......29 F1
AU/AST/KP S26......159 H3
BSLY S70......2 C3
BSLY S70......48 C1
BSLYN/ROY S71......12 B5
BSLYN/ROY S71......21 F2
BSVR S44......196 B2
BTLY DN5......27 F5
CHNE S41......5 H4
CHNE S41......187 H1
CHPT/GREN S35 ......94 C5
CONI DN12......69 E5
DARN/MH S9 * 128 A3
DEARNE S63......37 F2
DEARNE S63......65 F2
DIN S25......134 A2
DOD/DAR S75......30 A5
ECK/KIL S21 ......175 F1
HAN/WDH S13 ....143 H3
MEX/SWTN S64......67 E4
MOS S20......166 D1
NROS/TKH DN11......91 G2
RHAM S60......8 B4
RHAM S60......129 G1
STKB/PEN S36 ......78 A2
STV/CWN S43......185 E2
STV/CWN S43......188 A1
WMB/DAR S73......50 C2
Station St MEX/SWTN S64...66 B5
Station Vw DIN S25......134 A2
Staton Av MOS S20......157 G1
Staton La DRON S18......172 C2
The Statutes RHAM S60......8 D4
Staunton Cl CHSW S40......195 G1
Staunton Rd DONS/BSCR DN4......74 C1
Staveley La ECK/KIL S21 ....174 A4
STV/CWN S43......181 F1
Staveley Rd SHEFS S8......140 A3
STV/CWN S43......180 C3
Staveley St CONI DN12......70 B5
Steade Rd ABRD S7......139 H3
Steadfield Rd HOY S74......61 F4
Steadfold Gdns MALT S66...133 G1
Steadfolds Cl MALT S66......133 G1
Steadfolds La MALT S66......133 F1
Steadfolds Ri MALT S66......133 G1
The Steadlands RAW S62......84 D4

Stead La HOY S74......61 F3
Stead St ECK/KIL S21......166 D5
Steele Av STV/CWN S43 ....189 F3
Steele St HOY S74......61 F4
Steel La BSVR S44......197 G2
Steelhouse La OWL S3......11 G1
Steel La BSVR S44......197 G2
Steel St KIMB S61......105 E4
Steeping Ct STV/CWN S43...188 C1
Steep La RCH S42......194 A3
STKB/PEN S36 ......45 F2
Steeplegate CHSW S40......5 G4
Steeton Ct HOY S74......62 C2
Stemp St ECC S11......139 H2
Stenton Rd SHEFS S8......162 D1
Stephen Dr CHPT/GREN S35 ......100 D1
FUL S10......124 B4
Stephen Hl FUL S10......124 B4
Stephen Hill Rd FUL S10 ....124 B4
Stephen La CHPT/GREN S35 ......100 D1
Stephenson Pl CHSW S40 ......5 G4
Stephenson Rd STV/CWN S43......182 A5
Stepney St SHEFP/MNR S2...11 K2
Stepping La CHPT/GREN S35...92 D5
Sterland St CHSW S40......4 C4
Sterndale Rd ABRD S7......152 A2
Sterry Cl STV/CWN S43 ....185 E4
Steven Cl CHPT/GREN S35...93 H2
Steven Crs CHPT/GREN S35...93 H1
Steven Pl CHPT/GREN S35...93 H1
Stevenson Dr DOD/DAR S75...18 A3
RHAM/THRY S65 ......106 D4
Stevenson Rd DARN/MH S9 ......127 E1
DONS/BSCR DN4 ......71 H2
Stevenson Wy DARN/MH S9 ......127 E1
Stevens Rd DONS/BSCR DN4..55 H4
Stewart Rd ECC S11......139 F2
Stewarts Rd RAW S62......85 G5
Stewart St DON DN1 ......6 B5
Sticking La DEARNE S63......66 C1
Stillman Cl CHNE S41......193 E4
Stirling Cl HOY S74......62 C2
Stirling St DON DN1......6 C6
Stockarth Cl CHPT/GREN S35 ......100 B5
Stockarth La CHPT/GREN S35 ......100 A5
Stockarth Pl ST/HB/BR S6...100 B5
Stockbridge La DONS/BSCR DN4 ......73 F1
Stockbridge La BTLY DN5 ....27 E5
Stockbridge Works STKB/PEN S36 ......77 F1
Stockil Rd DONS/BSCR DN4...7 G6
Stockley Vw BSVR S44......197 E4
Stock Rd SHEFP/MNR S2......141 E1
Stocks Green Ct TOT/DORE S17......160 C4
Stocks Green Dr TOT/DORE S17......160 D4
Stocks Hl HACK/IN S12......154 A5
Stockton Cl OWL S3 * 126 B1
Stockwell Av AU/AST/KP S26......159 G4
Stockwell Gn BSLYN/ROY S71......20 A3
Stockwell La AU/AST/KP S26......159 F4
Stock's La DOD/DAR S75......2 B4
RAW S62......98 B1
Stoke St DARN/MH S9......127 E2
Stoket La AU/AST/KP S26 ...131 H2
Stokewell Rd DEARNE S63...64 C1
Stoneacre Av HACK/IN S12..156 B2
Stoneacre Cl HACK/IN S12..156 B3
Stoneacre Dr HACK/IN S12..156 B3
Stoneacre Ri HACK/IN S12..156 B2
Stonebridge La CUD/GR S72...36 A1
Stonecliffe Dr STKB/PEN S36 ......76 C4
Stonecliffe Pl SHEFP/MNR S2 ......141 G1
Stonecliffe Rd SHEFP/MNR S2 ......141 G1
Stone Cl DRON S18......163 G5
RHAM/THRY S65 ......108 D2
Stone Close Av DONS/BSCR DN4 ......55 H3
Stone Crs MALT S66......108 B4
Stonecroft Rd TOT/DORE S17......161 E3
Stone Cross Dr BTLY DN5 ....54 B3
Stonecross Gdns DONS/BSCR DN4 ......58 C5
Stonedale Cl MOS S20......166 D1
Stone Delf FUL S10......137 G1
Stone Font Gv AU/AST/KP S26......145 E3
Stonehill Ri BTLY DN5......38 D2
CUD/GR S72......21 H1
Stone Hill Dr AU/AST/KP S26......145 E3

Stone La HAN/WDH S13 ....143 E5
STV/CWN S43......180 B2
Stone Leigh DOD/DAR S75 ...60 B4
Stoneleigh Cl DEARNE S63...65 F5
Stoneleigh Cft BSLY S70 * ...31 H3
Stoneley Cl HACK/IN S12....154 C4
Stoneley Crs HACK/IN S12...154 C4
Stoneley Dr HACK/IN S12....154 C4
Stoneley Dell HACK/IN S12..154 C4
Stonelow Crs DRON S18......171 H1
Stonelow Rd DRON S18......171 F1
Stonely Brook MALT S66....108 D3
Stone Moor Rd STKB/PEN S36 ......76 C4
Stone Park Cl MALT S66 * ...111 F3
Stone Rd DRON S18......163 G4
Stone Rw CHSW S40......4 C5
Stone Row Ct DOD/DAR S75...60 B4
Stonerow Wy RHAM S60......98 A5
Stone St BSLYN/ROY S71......19 G3
MOS S20......166 D1
Stonewood Ct FUL S10......123 H5
Stonewood Gv FUL S10......123 H5
HOY S74......61 H4
Stoney Cft HOY S74......61 F3
Stoneycroft La RCH S42......194 A3
Stoney Ga CHPT/GREN S35...80 B3
Stoney Royd BSLYN/ROY S71......14 D3
Stonyford Rd WMB/DAR S73......50 D1
Stoops Cl MALT S66......186 D3
Stoops La DONS/BSCR DN4...73 F1
Stoops Rd DONS/BSCR DN4...73 F1
Stopes Rd ST/HB/BR S6......122 A5
Storey St SHEFP/MNR S2......140 B1
Storey St MEX/SWTN S64......66 A5
Storey's Ga WMB/DAR S73...49 H2
Storforth La CHNE S41......193 E5
CHSW S40......192 C5
Storforth Lane Ter CHNE S41......193 E4
Storrs Br ST/HB/BR S6......112 A3
Storrs Bridge La ST/HB/BR S6 ......112 A3
Storrs Hall Rd ST/HB/BR S6 ......112 B5
Storrs La CHPT/GREN S35...79 H1
ST/HB/BR S6 ......112 B5
Storrs Mill La BSLYN/ROY S71......22 C5
Storrs Rd CHSW S40......191 F2
Storrs Wood Vw CUD/GR S72......22 B3
Storth Av FUL S10......138 A2
Storth La AU/AST/KP S26 ...159 G2
FUL S10......138 A1
Stortholme Ms FUL S10......138 A1
Storth Pk FUL S10......137 H3
Stotfold Dr DEARNE S63......37 E2
Stothard Rd FUL S10......124 D3
Stottercliffe Rd STKB/PEN S36 ......44 B3
Stour Cl STV/CWN S43......188 C1
Stour La ST/HB/BR S6......113 F2
Stovin Cl DARN/MH S9......127 H1
Stovin Dr DARN/MH S9......127 H1
Stovin Gdns DARN/MH S9...116 D5
Stow Bridge La RHAM S60...131 G1
Stowe Av ABRD S7......152 A1
Stradbroke Av HAN/WDH S13 ....142 B5
Stradbroke Cl HAN/WDH S13 ....142 C3
Stradbroke Crs HAN/WDH S13 ....142 C3
Stradbroke Dr HAN/WDH S13 ....142 C3
Stradbroke Pl HAN/WDH S13 ....142 C3
Stradbroke Ri CHSW S40 ....191 G4
Stradbroke Rd HAN/WDH S13 ....142 B5
Stradbroke Wy HAN/WDH S13 ....142 C3
Strafford Av BSLY S70......31 H4
HOY S74......62 C2
Strafford Pl KIMB S61......95 E1
Strafford Rd KIMB S61......96 C5
Strafford Wk DOD/DAR S75...31 H4
Straight La DEARNE S63......37 G5
Stratford Rd FUL S10......137 H1
Stratford Wy MALT S66......109 E5
Strathmore Gv DEARNE S63......65 F2
Strathmore Rd WHHL DN2......7 K3
Strathtay Rd ECC S11......138 D3
Stratton Rd BSVR S44......196 D2
Strauss Crs MALT S66......111 F4
Strawberry Av SHEFN S5....102 B3
Strawberry Gdns BSLYN/ROY S71......12 C5
Strawberry Lee La TOT/DORE S17......160 B3
Straw La ST/HB/BR S6 * 125 G2
Streatfield Crs NROS/TKH DN11......91 E3
Streetfields MOS S20......166 D2
Street La MOS S20......167 E2
Street La RAW S62......83 G1
Strelley Av SHEFS S8......152 C4
Strelley Rd BSLYN/ROY S71...14 C4
SHEFS S8 ......152 B4

Stretton Cl DONS/BSCR DN4...58 C5
Stretton Rd BSLYN/ROY S71...20 A2
ECC S11......139 E3
The Stride CHSW S40 * 192 B5
Stringers Cft RHAM S60......120 B3
Strutt Rd OWL S3......125 E5
Stuart Cl CHNE S41......188 A3
Stuart Gv CHPT/GREN S35...94 A2
Stuart Rd CHPT/GREN S35...94 B2
Stuart St DEARNE S63......37 G2
Stubbin Cl RAW S62......84 D4
Stubbing House La CHPT/GREN S35 ......100 C2
Stubbing La CHPT/GREN S35 ......112 C1
Stubbing Rd CHSW S40......192 B5
Stubbin La RAW S62......84 D3
SHEFN S5......102 C5
Stubbin Rd RAW S62......84 B4
Stubbs Crs KIMB S61......96 D5
Stubbs Rd WMB/DAR S73......52 A1
Stubley Cl DRON S18......170 C1
Stubley Cft DRON S18......170 B1
Stubley Dr DRON S18......170 C1
Stubley Hollow DRON S18...170 C1
Stubley La DRON S18......170 B1
Stubley Pl DRON S18......170 C1
Studfield Crs ST/HB/BR S6...113 F3
Studfield Dr ST/HB/BR S6...113 F3
Studfield Gv ST/HB/BR S6...113 F4
Studfield Hl ST/HB/BR S6...113 F3
Studfield Ri ST/HB/BR S6...113 F3
Studfield Rd ST/HB/BR S6...113 F4
Studley Ct DARN/MH S9 * ..128 A3
Studley Gdns ARMTH DN3...29 E3
Studmoor Rd KIMB S61......96 A5
Stump Cross Gdns DEARNE S63......52 D3
Stump Cross Rd DEARNE S63......65 E3
Stumperlowe Av FUL S10 ...138 A2
Stumperlowe Cl FUL S10 ...138 A2
Stumperlowe Crescent Cft FUL S10......137 H2
Stumperlowe Cft FUL S10...137 H1
Stumperlowe Hall Cha FUL S10......137 H1
Stumperlowe Hall Rd FUL S10......137 H3
Stumperlowe La FUL S10 ...137 H2
Stumperlowe Park Rd FUL S10......137 H2
Stumperlowe Vw FUL S10...137 H1
Stupton Rd DARN/MH S9 ...116 C2
Sturge Cft SHEFP/MNR S2...140 B4
Sturton Cft RHAM/THRY S65...99 G5
Sturton Rd ATT S4......115 G4
Sudbury Cl DRON S18......170 A1
Sudbury Dr AU/AST/KP S26..145 G3
Sudbury St OWL S3......125 H2
Sudhall Cl CHNE S41......186 D1
Suffolk Cl DIN S25......148 C2
Suffolk Rd DONS/BSCR DN4...71 H2
SHEFP/MNR S2 ......11 H5
Sulby Gv BSLY S70......32 D4
Summerdale Rd CUD/GR S72......21 G2
Summerfield RHAM/THRY S65......9 H4
Summerfield Crs STV/CWN S43......188 C1
Summerfield Rd CHSW S40......4 E7
DRON S18......163 F5
Summerfield St ECC S11......10 C7
Summer La BSLYN/ROY S71...12 B5
DOD/DAR S75......2 C2
TOT/DORE S17......160 C4
WMB/DAR S73......49 G3
Summerley Lower Rd DRON S18......172 A1
Summerley Rd DRON S18....172 A1
Summer Rd BSLYN/ROY S71...12 B5
Summerskill Gn STV/CWN S43......189 G2
Summer St BSLY S70......2 D5
OWL S3......10 B2
Summer Vw BSLYN/ROY S71...15 F1
Summerwood Cft DRON S18......170 D1
Summerwood La DRON S18......162 D5
Summerwood Pl DRON S18......170 D1
Sumner Rd RHAM/THRY S65......9 J1
Sunderland St ECC S11......139 G1
Sunderland Ter BSLY S70......3 K6
Sundew Cft CHPT/GREN S35...80 B5
Sundew Gdns CHPT/GREN S35......80 B5
Sundown Pl HAN/WDH S13..142 D2
Sundown Rd HAN/WDH S13......142 D2
Sun Lea Flats RHAM/THRY S65 * 9 J3
Sunningdale Cl CHSW S40 ..192 A4
DONS/BSCR DN4 ......74 D2
MEX/SWTN S64......86 B2
Sunningdale Dr CUD/GR S72...17 E3
Sunningdale Mt ECC S11 ....138 D5

Sunningdale Ri CHSW S40.....191 G4
Sunningdale Rd DIN S25.....148 D1
　WHHL DN2.....41 E5
Sunny Bank FUL S10.....10 C7
　HOY S74.....62 B2
Sunnybank Crs RHAM S60.....118 C4
Sunny Bank Dr
　CUD/GR S72.....21 H3
Sunny Bank Ri HOY S74.....62 C2
Sunny Bank Rd
　STKB/PEN S36.....77 E5
Sunny Bar DON S1.....6 D3
Sunnybrook Cl HOY S74.....62 A4
Sunny Brook Cl
　STV/CWN S43.....185 E3
Sunnyside ARMTH DN3.....29 E5
　ARMTH DN3.....59 C5
Sunnyside Cl DIN S25.....148 C2
Sunny Springs CHNE S41.....5 G1
Sunnyvale Av
　TOT/DORE S17.....160 D4
Sunnyvale Rd
　TOT/DORE S17.....160 D4
Surbiton St DARN/MH S9.....116 D4
Surrey Cl BSLY S70.....31 H3
Surrey La SHEF S1.....11 H5
Surrey Pl SHEF S1.....11 H4
Surrey St DONS/BSCR DN4.....11 H4
　SHEF S1.....11 G4
Surtees Cl MALT S66.....110 C1
Sussex Rd ATT S4.....126 C2
　CHPT/GREN S35.....94 A1
Sussex St ATT S4.....126 C3
　OWL S3.....126 C2
Suthard Cross Rd
　FUL S10 *.....124 D3
Sutherland Rd ATT S4.....126 D1
Sutherland St ATT S4.....126 D1
Sutton Av BSLYN/ROY S71.....14 D4
Sutton Crs STV/CWN S43.....189 G2
Sutton Hall Rd BSVR S44.....196 B4
Sutton Rd ARMTH DN3.....29 F2
Sutton St OWL S3.....126 C2
Sutton Vw BSVR S44.....197 E4
Swaddale Av CHNE S41.....187 H3
Swaddale Cl CHNE S41.....187 H3
Swaith Av BTLY DN5.....39 F3
Swaithe Av BTLY DN5.....39 F3
Swaithedale BSLY S70.....32 C5
Swaithe Vw BSLY S70.....32 D5
Swale Cl DEARNE S63.....53 E4
Swaledale Dr WMB/DAR S73.....50 C2
Swaledale Rd ABRD S7.....139 F5
Swale Rd KIMB S61.....97 E3
Swallow Cl BSLY S70.....40 B4
Swallow Ct NROS/TKH DN11.....92 C2
Swallow Crs RAW S62.....85 H5
Swallow La AU/AST/KP S26.....145 G4
Swallow Wood Cl
　RHAM S60.....130 A3
Swallowwood Ct
　DEARNE S63.....63 H2
Swallow Wood Ct
　HAN/WDH S13.....143 E4
Swallow Wood Rd
　AU/AST/KP S26.....144 C3
Swamp Wk ST/HB/BR S6.....114 B5
Swanbourne Pl SHEFN S5.....102 C5
Swanbourne Rd SHEFN S5.....102 C4
Swanee Rd BSLY S70.....32 B4
Swannington Cl
　DONS/BSCR DN4.....74 C1
Swan Rd AU/AST/KP S26.....145 G4
Swan St BTLY DN5.....39 H1
　RHAM S60.....9 F6
Swanwick St CHNE S41.....179 G4
Swarcliffe Rd DARN/MH S9.....127 G2
Swathwick Cl RCH S42.....195 E3
Swathwick La RCH S42.....194 C3
Sweyn Cft BSLY S70 *.....32 A5
Swifte Rd RHAM S60.....119 E3
Swift Ri AU/AST/KP S26.....159 H3
Swift St CHPT/GREN S35.....101 F1
Swift St DOD/DAR S75.....2 D2
Swift Wy SHEFP/MNR S2.....127 E5
Swinburne Av
　AWLS/ASK DN6.....25 E2
　DONS/BSCR DN4.....71 H2
Swinburne Pl
　RHAM/THRY S65.....106 D4
Swinston Hill Gdns
　DIN S25.....135 E5
Swinston Hill Rd DIN S25.....149 G2
Swinton Rd MEX/SWTN S64.....66 D4
Swinton St OWL S3.....126 C4
Swithland Cl CHNE S41.....192 D5
Sycamore Av ARMTH DN3.....43 E3
　AU/AST/KP S26.....159 F3
　CHSW S40.....4 B7
　CUD/GR S72.....16 C5
　DRON S18.....163 E5
　MALT S66.....108 C4
Sycamore Cl BSVR S44.....197 E4
Sycamore Cl ECC S11.....109 E3
　MEX/SWTN S64.....66 C3
Sycamore Crs DEARNE S63.....65 F3
Sycamore Dr
　BSLYN/ROY S71.....15 E1
　BSVR S44.....193 F1
　ECK/KIL S21.....168 A3

Sycamore Farm Cl
　MALT S66.....121 F1
Sycamore Gv CONI DN12.....88 C2
　DONS/BSCR DN4.....58 B5
Sycamore House Rd
　SHEFN S5.....155 F2
Sycamore La STV/CWN S43.....177 F5
　STV/CWN S43.....181 E5
Sycamore Rd
　CHPT/GREN S35.....102 B1
　MEX/SWTN S64.....66 C3
　RHAM/THRY S65.....98 D5
　STKB/PEN S36.....76 C3
　STV/CWN S43.....180 D5
The Sycamores BTLY DN5.....39 C2
Sycamore St DOD/DAR S75.....2 B3
　MOS S20.....156 C5
Sycamore Vw BTLY DN5.....54 D4
Sycamore Wk STKB/PEN S36.....44 D3
Syday La ECK/KIL S21.....176 B2
Sydney Rd ST/HB/BR S6.....125 F3
Sydney St CHSW S40.....4 B4
Syke Cft BSLYN/ROY S71.....12 C4
Sykes Av DOD/DAR S75.....2 D2
Sykes St MEX/SWTN S64.....86 B2
Sykes St BSLY S70.....31 F3
Sylvan Cl CHNE S41.....192 D3
Sylvester Av
　DONS/BSCR DN4.....56 A4
Sylvester Gdns SHEF S1.....11 G6
Sylvester St SHEF S1.....11 F7
Sylvestria Ct
　NROS/TKH DN11.....91 G2
Sylvia Cl HAN/WDH S13 *.....143 H3
Sylvia Rd DRON S18.....178 D1
Symes Gdns
　DONS/BSCR DN4.....58 B4
Symonds Av RAW S62.....84 C3
Symons Crs SHEFN S5.....101 H4

T

Tadcaster Cl CONI DN12.....88 A1
Tadcaster Crs SHEFS S8.....152 D1
Tadcaster Rd SHEFS S8.....152 D1
Tadcaster Wy SHEFS S8.....152 D1
Taddington Rd CHSW S40 *.....186 B4
Talbot Crs CHNE S41.....193 F5
　SHEFP/MNR S2.....11 K5
Talbot Gdns SHEFP/MNR S2.....126 C5
Talbot Pl MEX/SWTN S64.....66 C5
　SHEFP/MNR S2.....126 C4
　STKB/PEN S36.....44 C3
Talbot St CHNE S41.....193 F5
　SHEFP/MNR S2.....11 K5
Tallys End STV/CWN S43.....177 E5
Talmont Rd ECC S11.....138 D4
Tamar Cl DOD/DAR S75.....18 A4
Tanfield Cl BSLYN/ROY S71.....12 A5
Tanfield Rd ST/HB/BR S6.....114 B3
Tanfield Wy MALT S66.....108 B5
Tankersley La HOY S74.....60 D4
Tank Row BSLYN/ROY S71.....32 D1
Tannery Cl HAN/WDH S13.....143 F4
Tannery St HAN/WDH S13.....143 F4
Tansley Dr CHSW S40.....186 A4
　DARN/MH S9.....103 H5
Tansley St DARN/MH S9.....103 H5
Tansley Wy STV/CWN S43.....189 G3
Tap La CHSW S40.....4 C4
Taplin Rd ST/HB/BR S6.....113 H4
Tapton Bank FUL S10.....124 C5
Tapton Crescent Rd
　FUL S10.....124 D5
Tapton Hl Rd FUL S10.....124 C5
Tapton House Rd FUL S10.....124 D5
Tapton La CHNE S41.....5 H3
Tapton Lock Hl CHNE S41.....187 H5
Tapton Ms FUL S10.....124 D4
Tapton Park Mt FUL S10.....138 B1
Tapton Park Rd FUL S10.....138 B1
Tapton Ter CHNE S41.....5 H2
Tapton V CHNE S41.....188 A4
Tapton View Rd CHNE S41.....187 F4
Taptonville Crs FUL S10.....124 D5
Taptonville Rd FUL S10.....125 E4
Tapton Wy STV/CWN S43.....188 D5
Tarleton Cl ARMTH DN3.....29 G3
Tasker Rd FUL S10.....124 D4
Tasman Gv MALT S66.....110 C2
Tatenhill Gdns
　DONS/BSCR DN4.....74 C2
Taunton Av DARN/MH S9.....116 D1
Taunton Gdns
　MEX/SWTN S64.....67 G4
Taunton Gv DARN/MH S9.....103 H5
Taverner Cl CHPT/GREN S35.....80 B2
Taverner Cft
　CHPT/GREN S35.....80 C3
Taverner Wy
　CHPT/GREN S35.....80 C3
Tavistock Rd ABRD S7.....139 H4
Tavy Cl DOD/DAR S75.....18 A2
Tayworth Cl DOD/DAR S75.....14 A5
　DRON S18.....170 B1
Taylor Crs CHNE S41.....193 F5
　CUD/GR S72.....23 E2
Taylor Rw BSLY S70.....3 H6
　DEARNE S63 *.....64 D2

Taylors Cl RAW S62.....98 A4
Taylors Ct RAW S62.....98 A4
Taylors La RAW S62.....98 A3
Tay St CONI DN12.....89 F1
Tay St ST/HB/BR S6.....10 A1
T Benedict Ct
　SHEFP/MNR S2.....140 D2
Teesdale Rd HACK/IN S12.....155 H4
　KIMB S61.....96 D3
Telford Crs STV/CWN S43.....182 B4
Telford Rd BTLY DN5.....39 F5
Telson Cl MEX/SWTN S64.....65 G5
Temperance St
　MEX/SWTN S64.....86 B1
Tempest Av WMB/DAR S73.....35 E3
Templar Cl MALT S66.....132 D1
Temple Cres MALT S66.....108 D5
Temple Gdns
　DONS/BSCR DN4.....74 B1
Temple Rd RHAM S60.....117 H1
Templestowe Ga CONI DN12.....89 C1
Temple Wy BSLYN/ROY S71.....20 D4
Ten Acre Rd KIMB S61.....104 D1
Tenby Gdns
　DONS/BSCR DN4.....71 G1
Ten Lands La
　HOR/CROF WF4.....13 F2
Tennyson Av ARMTH DN3.....42 D4
　BTLY DN5.....55 F1
　CHSW S40.....4 A6
　MEX/SWTN S64.....67 F2
Tennyson Cl DIN S25.....135 E5
　STKB/PEN S36.....44 A2
Tennyson Ri DEARNE S63.....64 C1
Tennyson Rd
　BSLYN/ROY S71.....20 B3
　BTLY DN5.....39 H1
　MALT S66.....111 E4
　RHAM/THRY S65.....106 D3
　ST/HB/BR S6.....125 F1
Ten Pound Wk
　DONS/BSCR DN4.....56 B5
Tenter Balk La
　AWLS/ASK DN6.....25 E2
Tenterden Rd SHEFN S5.....105 F5
Tenter Hl STKB/PEN S36.....44 A2
Tenter La DONS/BSCR DN4.....70 C2
Tenter Rd DONS/BSCR DN4.....70 C2
Tenters Gn BSLY S70.....47 H1
Tenter St RHAM S60.....8 C2
　SHEF S1.....11 F2
Terminus Rd ABRD S7.....152 A2
Terrace Rd RAW S62.....98 B3
Terrey Rd TOT/DORE S17.....161 E3
Terry Rd DARN/MH S9.....116 D5
Tetney Rd FUL S10.....138 B1
Tewitt Rd BTLY DN5.....26 C3
Teynham Dr SHEFN S5.....114 D2
Teynham Rd SHEFN S5.....114 C2
Thackeray Av RAW S62.....85 H4
Thames St RHAM S60.....8 D3
Thealby Gdns
　DONS/BSCR DN4.....73 C1
Theatre La CHNE S41.....5 H3
Thellusson Av BTLY DN5.....38 C3
Theobald Av
　DONS/BSCR DN4.....7 H6
Theobald Cl
　DONS/BSCR DN4.....7 G7
Thicket Dr MALT S66.....111 F2
Thicket La BSLY S70.....48 C1
Third Av AWLS/ASK DN6.....25 G3
Thirlmere Dr DIN S25.....148 D2
　DRON S18.....171 E1
Thirlmere Gdns
　ARMTH DN3.....29 F4
Thirlmere Rd ABRD S7.....139 C5
　BSLYN/ROY S71.....3 J4
　CHNE S41.....186 C2
Thirlwall Av CONI DN12.....88 C1
Thirlwell Rd SHEFS S8.....140 A4
Thirsk Cl CONI DN12.....88 A1
Thistley Ct CUD/GR S72.....17 H4
Thomas St AU/AST/KP S26.....159 H3
　BSLY S70.....3 G6
　BSLY S70.....32 A5
　MEX/SWTN S64.....86 C4
　SHEF S1.....10 E5
　WMB/DAR S73.....35 E3
Thompson Cl CHNE S41.....187 G1
　MALT S66.....110 C1
　RAW S62.....84 C3
Thompson Dr
　MEX/SWTN S64.....86 A2
Thompson Gdns
　CHPT/GREN S35.....80 A3
Thompson Rd ECC S11.....139 F1
　WMB/DAR S73.....50 B3
Thompson St CHNE S41.....187 G1
Thomson Av
　DONS/BSCR DN4.....71 F1
Thomson Cl DEARNE S63.....65 F2
Thoresby Av
　BSLYN/ROY S71.....20 B3
　DONS/BSCR DN4.....7 J7
　STV/CWN S43.....185 G2
Thoresby Cl
　AU/AST/KP S26.....145 H3
Thoresby Pl
　STV/CWN S43 *.....189 G3
Thoresby Rd
　ST/HB/BR S6.....114 A5

Thornborough Cl
　SHEFP/MNR S2.....140 C3
Thornborough Pl
　SHEFP/MNR S2.....140 C3
Thornborough Rd
　SHEFP/MNR S2.....140 B3
Thornbridge Av
　HACK/IN S12.....155 F2
Thornbridge Crs CHSW S40.....195 F1
Thornbridge Dr
　HACK/IN S12.....155 F2
Thornbridge Gv
　HACK/IN S12.....155 F2
Thornbridge La
　HACK/IN S12.....155 F2
Thornbridge Pl
　HACK/IN S12.....155 G2
Thornbridge Ri
　HACK/IN S12.....155 G2
Thornbridge Rd
　HACK/IN S12.....155 F2
Thornbridge Wy
　HACK/IN S12.....155 G2
Thornbrook Cl
　CHPT/GREN S35.....81 F5
Thornbrook Gdns
　CHPT/GREN S35.....81 E5
Thornbrook Ms
　CHPT/GREN S35.....81 E5
Thorncliffe Cl
　AU/AST/KP S26.....144 D4
Thorncliffe La
　CHPT/GREN S35.....80 D4
Thorncliffe Rd
　CHPT/GREN S35.....81 E3
Thorncliffe Vw
　CHPT/GREN S35.....81 E3
Thorncliff Wy DOD/DAR S75.....60 C3
Thorndale Rd RHAM S60.....118 C4
Thorndene Cl CHNE S41.....187 H3
Thorndon Wy CHSW S40.....191 G4
Thorne Cl BSLYN/ROY S71.....14 C5
Thornely Av DOD/DAR S75.....30 B2
Thorne Rd ABRD S7.....139 C5
　ARMTH DN3.....6 E5
　DON S1.....6 E5
　WHHL DN2.....41 E4
Thornfield Av CHSW S40.....191 F3
Thorn Garth BTLY DN5.....39 G4
Thornham Cl ARMTH DN3.....42 D5
Thornham La ARMTH DN3.....43 H4
Thornhill Av RHAM S60.....118 B5
　WHHL DN2.....41 F4
Thornhill Edge RHAM S60.....8 C3
Thornhill Pl DEARNE S63.....65 E2
Thorn La WHHL DN2.....28 D5
Thornley Brook
　DEARNE S63.....36 D2
Thornley Sq DEARNE S63.....36 D2
Thorn Rd MEX/SWTN S64.....86 B2
Thornsett Gdns
　TOT/DORE S17.....161 F1
Thornsett Rd ABRD S7.....139 G2
Thorntondale Rd BTLY DN5.....38 D4
Thornton Pl DRON S18.....170 A2
Thornton Rd BSLY S70.....32 C3
Thornton St KIMB S61.....104 C4
Thornton Ter BSLY S70.....32 C3
Thorntree Cl KIMB S61.....95 F3
Thorntree La DOD/DAR S75.....2 C1
Thorntree Rd KIMB S61.....95 F3
Thornwell Gv CUD/GR S72.....21 G1
Thornwell La KIMB S61.....88 B5
Thornwood Ct DEARNE S63.....37 E1
Thorogate RAW S62.....95 H4
Thorold Pl ARMTH DN3.....29 F2
Thorp Cl SHEFP/MNR S2.....140 D2
Thorpe Av DRON S18.....168 D3
Thorpe Cl CHNE S41.....187 F1
Thorpe Dr MOS S20.....157 G4
Thorpefield Cl KIMB S61.....95 F1
Thorpefield Dr KIMB S61.....95 F1
Thorpe Gn MOS S20.....156 D3
Thorpehall Rd ARMTH DN3.....29 G4
Thorpe House Av SHEFS S8.....153 F1
Thorpe House Ri SHEFS S8.....153 E1
Thorpe House Rd
　SHEFS S8.....153 F1
Thorpe La BTLY DN5.....54 B4
Thorpe St KIMB S61.....95 F3
Thorpleigh Rd
　STV/CWN S43.....182 D4
Three Hills Cl
　RHAM/THRY S65.....99 H3
Three Nooks La CUD/GR S72.....16 D3
Threshfield Wy
　HACK/IN S12.....155 F3
Thrumpton Rd
　BSLYN/ROY S71.....14 D3
Thrush Av RHAM S60.....118 D4
Thrush St ST/HB/BR S6.....125 G1
Thruxton Cl CUD/GR S72.....17 E4
Thrybergh Ct CONI DN12.....68 D5
Thrybergh Hall Rd RHAM S60.....85 H5
Thundercliffe Rd KIMB S61.....103 H2
Thurbrook Gdns MALT S66.....133 E1
Thurlstone Rd
　STKB/PEN S36.....44 D2
Thurnscoe Bridge La
　DEARNE S63.....37 F4

Thurnscoe La CUD/GR S72.....36 B1
Thurnscoe Rd DEARNE S63.....53 E3
Thurstan Av BSLY S70.....32 C5
Tiber Vw RHAM S60.....118 C2
Tickhill Rd DONS/BSCR DN4.....71 G3
Tickhill Sq CONI DN12.....68 B5
Tickhill St CONI DN12.....68 B4
Tickhill Wy NROS/TKH DN11.....91 G3
Tideswell Cl STV/CWN S43.....189 C1
Tideswell Rd SHEFS S8.....102 D5
Tiercel Ms DIN S25.....134 C4
Tilford Rd HAN/WDH S13.....143 G4
Tillotson Cl SHEFS S8.....140 A4
Tillotson Ri SHEFS S8.....140 A4
Tilts La BTLY DN5.....27 F1
Timothy Wood Av BSLY S70.....47 H5
Tingle Bridge Av
　WMB/DAR S73.....63 E1
Tingle Bridge Crs
　WMB/DAR S73.....63 E1
Tingle Bridge La
　WMB/DAR S73.....63 E1
Tingle Cl WMB/DAR S73.....63 E1
Tinker La FUL S10.....124 D2
　HOY S74.....61 E2
Tinker Rd RAW S62.....85 G3
Tinsley Park Cl
　DARN/MH S9.....117 E5
Tinsley Park Rd
　DARN/MH S9.....116 D5
Tinsley Rd HOY S74.....61 H1
Tippit La CUD/GR S72.....22 A2
Tipton St DARN/MH S9.....116 C2
Tiverton Cl MEX/SWTN S64.....86 D3
Tissington Cl CHSW S40.....186 B4
Tithe Barn Av
　HAN/WDH S13.....143 F3
Tithe Barn Cl
　HAN/WDH S13.....143 G3
Tithe Barn Ct
　MEX/SWTN S64.....53 H5
Tithe Barn La
　HAN/WDH S13.....143 G4
Tithe Barn Wy
　HAN/WDH S13.....143 F3
Tithe Laithe HOY S74.....62 A2
Titterton Cl DARN/MH S9.....127 G1
Titterton St DARN/MH S9.....127 G1
Toad La MALT S66.....132 D2
Tockwith Rd DARN/MH S9.....127 H2
Todmorden Cl CONI DN12.....68 A5
Todwick Rd
　AU/AST/KP S26.....147 G2
　SHEFS S8.....152 C1
Tofts La ST/HB/BR S6.....123 C3
Toftstead ARMTH DN3.....42 D5
Toftwood Av FUL S10.....124 C3
Toftwood Rd FUL S10.....124 D3
Togo St DEARNE S63.....37 E3
Toll Bar Av HACK/IN S12.....141 H5
Toll Bar Cl HACK/IN S12.....141 E5
Toll Bar Dr HACK/IN S12.....141 E5
Toll Bar Rd HACK/IN S12.....141 E5
　MEX/SWTN S64.....65 H5
　RHAM/THRY S65.....107 G5
Tollbridge Rd
　STV/CWN S43.....182 D4
Tollgate Cl CUD/GR S72.....17 F2
Toll House Md MOS S20.....166 C1
Tom La FUL S10.....137 H1
Tomlinson Rd HOY S74.....62 B2
Tompson Hl
　CHPT/GREN S35.....79 H4
Tooker Rd RHAM S60.....9 G6
Topcliffe Rd BSLYN/ROY S71.....20 A2
Top Field La
　RHAM/THRY S65.....107 F1
Top Fold BSLYN/ROY S71 *.....3 G2
Top Hall Rd DONS/BSCR DN4.....74 B5
Toppham Dr SHEFS S8.....162 D2
Toppham Rd SHEFS S8.....162 D2
Toppham Wy SHEFS S8.....162 D2
Top Pingle Cl STV/CWN S43.....188 C2
Top Rd BSVR S44.....193 H2
Top Rw BSLYN/ROY S71 *.....3 G2
Top Side CHPT/GREN S35.....92 D5
Top Tree Wy
　RHAM/THRY S65.....99 H3
Torbay Rd ATT S4.....115 H5
Tor Cl BSLYN/ROY S71.....20 B2
Torksey Cl DONS/BSCR DN4.....74 A2
Torksey Rd SHEFN S5.....102 C5
Torne Cl DONS/BSCR DN4.....74 C2
Torry Ct HAN/WDH S13.....143 H3
Tortmayns AU/AST/KP S26.....147 E5
Torver Dr DEARNE S63.....53 E4
Tor Wy RHAM S60.....118 D5
Torwood Dr SHEFS S8.....162 C1
Totley Brook Cl
　TOT/DORE S17.....160 D3
Totley Brook Cft
　TOT/DORE S17 *.....160 D3
Totley Brook Gln
　TOT/DORE S17.....160 D3
Totley Brook Gv
　TOT/DORE S17.....160 D3
Totley Brook Rd
　TOT/DORE S17.....160 D3
Totley Brook Wy
　TOT/DORE S17.....160 D3
Totley Cl BSLYN/ROY S71.....15 F5
Totley Grange Cl
　TOT/DORE S17 *.....160 D4

Totley Grange Rd
TOT/DORE S17 ....160 D4
Totley Hall Cft
TOT/DORE S17 ....160 D5
Totley Hall Dr
TOT/DORE S17 ....160 D4
Totley Hall La
TOT/DORE S17 ....160 D4
Totley Hall Md
TOT/DORE S17 ....160 D5
Totley La *TOT/DORE* S17 ....161 G4
Totley Mt *STV/CWN* S43 ....188 B1
Towcester Wy
MEX/SWTN S64 ....67 G2
Tower Cl *BTLY* DN5 ....38 D1
SHEFP/MNR S2 ....140 C2
Tower Crs *SHEFP/MNR* S2 ...197 E4
Tower Dr *SHEFP/MNR* S2 ...140 C2
Tower St *BSLY* S70 ....31 G3
Town End *BSVR* S44 ....196 D2
DRON S18 ....172 B2
Town End Av
AU/AST/KP S26 ....145 F2
Townend Av
RHAM/THRY S65 ....99 G4
Townend Cl *RHAM* S60 ....130 A3
Townend La *STKB/PEN* S36 ...77 G4
Town End Rd
CHPT/GREN S35 ....101 H1
Townend St *FUL* S10 ....125 E3
Town Flds *DON* DN1 * 7 F4
Town Fields Av
CHPT/GREN S35 ....102 B1
Townfield Vls *DON* DN1 * 7 F3
Towngate *STKB/PEN* S36 ....44 A2
Townhead Rd
TOT/DORE S17 ....160 C1
Townhead St *SHEF* S1 ....11 F3
Townlands Cl
WMB/DAR S73 ....50 D1
Town La *KIMB* S61 ....96 B4
Town Moor Av *WHHL* DN2 ....7 H2
Town St *DARN/MH* S9 ....117 F1
RHAM S60 ....105 H5
Town View Av *BTLY* DN5 ....38 A2
Town Wells Ct *DIN* S25 ....148 B3
Toyne St *FUL* S10 ....124 D3
Trafalgar Rd *ST/HB/BR* S6...101 E5
Trafalgar St *SHEF* S1 ....10 E4
Traffic Ter *CHNE* S41 * 192 D5
STV/CWN S43 ....181 F2
Trap La *ECC* S11 ....138 A4
Travey Rd *SHEFP/MNR* S2 ...141 G3
Travis Gdns
DONS/BSCR DN4 ....55 F4
Travis Pl *FUL* S10 ....10 C6
Tredis Cl *BSLYN/ROY* S71....20 B4
Treecrest Ri *DOD/DAR* S75 ...19 G3
Treefield Cl *KIMB* S61 ....97 E3
Treelands *DOD/DAR* S75 ....18 D4
Treeneuk Cl *CHSW* S40 ....191 F1
Tree Root Wk *FUL* S10 ....125 F4
Treeton La *RHAM* S60......129 H2
Treetown Crs *RHAM* S60....130 A2
Treherne Rd *RHAM* S60......9 J7
Trelawney Wy *BSLY* S70....31 H5
Trent Cl *CONI* DN12 ....70 C5
Trent Gdns *ARMTH* DN3 ....29 F2
Trent Gv *DRON* S18 ....163 F5
Trentham Cl *RHAM* S60......118 D4
Trenton Cl *HAN/WDH* S13 ...143 H4
Trenton Ri *HAN/WDH* S13 ...143 H4
Trent St *DARN/MH* S9 ....127 E1
Trent Ter *CONI* DN12 * 69 E5
Treswell Crs *ST/HB/BR* S6 *..114 A4
Trevorrow Crs *CHSW* S40.....5 G7
Trewan Ct *BSLYN/ROY* S71 ...20 B4
Trickett Rd *CHPT/GREN* S35...80 A3
ST/HB/BR S6 ....114 A5
Trinity Cl *CHNE* S41 ....4 E1
Trinity St *OWL* S3 ....11 F1
Trippet La *SHEF* S1 ....11 F3
Tristford Cl *RHAM* S60......129 H1
Troon Cl *CHSW* S40 ....191 G4
Troon Wk *DIN* S25 ....134 D5
Troughbrook Rd
STV/CWN S43 ....181 F5
Troutbeck Cl *DEARNE* S63....37 E3
Troutbeck Rd *ABRD* S7......152 C1
Trowell Wy *BSLYN/ROY* S71...14 D4
Trueman Gn *MALT* S66......110 C2
Trueman Ter
BSLYN/ROY S71 ....21 E5
Truman Gv *STKB/PEN* S36 ...77 H2

Truman St *BTLY* DN5 ....39 G1
Truro Av *WHHL* DN2 ....41 G2
Truro Ct *BSLYN/ROY* S71 .....20 B4
Truswell Av *FUL* S10 ....124 C4
Truswell Rd *FUL* S10 ....124 C4
Tudor Cl *CUD/GR* S72 ....23 E1
Tudor Rd *AWLS/ASK* DN6 .....25 G4
WHHL DN2 ....4 D1
Tudor St *DEARNE* S63 ....37 G2
NROS/TKH DN11............91 F1
STV/CWN S43 ....182 B4
Tudor Wy *BSLY* S70 ....32 A5
Tuffolds Cl *RHAM ECC* S11...138 D4
Tulip Tree Cl *MOS* S20 ....144 C5
Tullibardine Rd *ECC* S11...138 D4
Tumbling La *BSLYN/ROY* S71...21 F1
Tummon Rd
SHEFP/MNR S2 ....127 E5
Tummon St *KIMB* S61......8 A5
Tune St *BSLY* S70 ....3 J7
WMB/DAR S73 ....50 A3
Tunstall Gn *CHSW* S40 ....4 A7
Tunstall Wy *CHSW* S40 ....4 A7
Tunwell Av *SHEFN* S5......102 B2
Tunwell Dr *SHEFN* S5......102 B2
Tunwell Greave *SHEFN* S5...102 A2
Turie Av *SHEFN* S5......102 A3
Turie Crs *SHEFN* S5......102 A3
Turnberry Cl *CHSW* S40 ....191 G4
Turnberry Ct *BTLY* DN5 ....39 G2
Turnberry Gv *CUD/GR* S72 *...17 E3
Turnberry Wy *DIN* S25......148 D1
Turnbull Cl *CHSW* S40 ....192 B3
Turner Av *WMB/DAR* S73....49 H2
Turner Cl *DRON* S18 ....170 D2
RAW S62 ....98 C2
Turner Dr *STV/CWN* S43 ...189 F2
Turner La *RHAM* S60......119 H3
Turners La *FUL* S10 ....125 E5
Turner St *CUD/GR* S72......36 A1
SHEFP/MNR S2 ....137 H2
Turner's Cl *HOY* S74 ....62 B1
Turnesc Gv *DEARNE* S63......37 F3
Turnoaks La *CHSW* S40.....192 C5
Turnpike Cft
CHPT/GREN S35 ....93 E5
Turnshaw Av
AU/AST/KP S26 ....145 E1
Turnshaw Farm
AU/AST/KP S26 ....131 H4
Turton Rd *RHAM/THRY* S65 ...109 F1
Tuscany Gdns *BSLY* S70......32 B2
Tutbury Gdns
DONS/BSCR DN4 ....74 C1
Tuxford Crs *BSLYN/ROY* S71...20 D5
Twelve Lands Cl
DOD/DAR S75 ....60 C3
The Twenty Lands
RHAM S60............130 A4
Twentywell Ct
TOT/DORE S17 ....161 H2
Twentywell La
TOT/DORE S17 ....161 G1
Twentywell Ri
TOT/DORE S17 ....161 H1
Twentywell Rd
TOT/DORE S17 ....161 H3
Twentywell Vw
TOT/DORE S17 ....161 H3
Twibell St *BSLYN/ROY* S71 ....3 J1
Twickenham Cl *MOS* S20...167 E3
Twickenham Cr *MOS* S20...167 E2
Twickenham Crs *MOS* S20...167 E3
Twickenham Gld *MOS* S20...167 E3
Twickenham Gln *MOS* S20...167 F3
Twickenham Gv *MOS* S20...167 E2
Twigg Ct *MEX/SWTN* S64 ...168 A6
Twitchill Dr *HAN/WDH* S13 ...143 F4
Twyford Cl *MEX/SWTN* S64 ...65 G5
Tyas Pl *MEX/SWTN* S64 * 67 F3
Tyas Rd *SHEFN* S5......102 A2
Tye Rd *MOS* S20 ....157 G2
Tyers Hill Cottages
BSLYN/ROY S71 * 34 B2
Tyler St *DARN/MH* S9......116 D1
Tyler Wy *DARN/MH* S9......116 D1
Tylney Rd *CHSW* S40 ....191 F5
Tynedale Ct *ARMTH* DN3 ....29 G3
Tynker Av *MOS* S20 ....157 G2
Tyzack Rd *SHEFS* S8......152 C3

U

Ulley Crs *HAN/WDH* S13 ....141 H3
Ulley La *AU/AST/KP* S26 ....145 G2
Ulley Rd *HAN/WDH* S13 ....141 H3
Ulley Vw *AU/AST/KP* S26 ....131 F5
Ullswater Av *MOS* S20 ....167 G2
Ullswater Cl *DEARNE* S63......148 C1
DIN S25 ....148 C1
DRON S18 ....170 C1
MOS S20 ....167 G2
Ullswater Dr *DRON* S18 ....170 C1
Ullswater Pl *DRON* S18 ....170 C1
Ullswater Rd
BSLYN/ROY S71 ....33 H2
MEX/SWTN S64 ....67 H2
Ulrica Dr *MALT* S66......133 E1
Ulverston Rd *CHNE* S41 ....186 D2
SHEFS S8 ....152 C1

Undercliffe Rd
ST/HB/BR S6............124 B2
Undergate Rd *DIN* S25......134 C3
Underhill *DON* DN1 ....88 B1
Underhill La *ST/HB/BR* S6...100 D4
Underhill Rd *STV/CWN* S43...177 F5
Underwood Av *BSLY* S70......32 B4
Underwood Rd *SHEFS* S8 ...152 D1
Union Ct *BSLY* S70............3 H6
Union Dr *ECC* S11......139 F4
Union Rd *ABRD* S7......139 F4
ECC S11 ....139 F4
Union St *BSLY* S70............6 C5
DON DN1 ....6 C5
KIMB S61 ....8 B4
SHEF S1............11 G5
Union Wk *CHSW* S40 * 5 F3
Unity Pl *RHAM* S60......9 F5
University Sq Jct *OWL* S3 ...10 C3
Unstone-Dronfield By-Pass
CHNE S41 ....178 C2
DRON S18 ....162 D5
Unstone Hl *DRON* S18......171 H3
Unstone Rd *CHNE* S41......179 F1
Unstone St *SHEFP/MNR* S2...140 A1
Unwin Crs *STKB/PEN* S36...44 D4
Unwin St *STKB/PEN* S36...44 D4
Upland Ri *ARMTH* DN3......43 E4
Uplands Rd *ARMTH* DN3......43 E4
Uplands Wy *RAW* S62......85 E5
Upper Albert Rd *SHEFS* S8...140 B5
Upper Allen St *OWL* S3......10 D2
Upper Clara St *KIMB* S61...104 D3
Upper Cliffe Rd
DOD/DAR S75 ....30 A2
Upper Croft Cl
STV/CWN S43 ....188 C2
Upperfield Cl *MALT* S66...110 D2
Upperfield Rd *MALT* S66...110 C3
Upper Folderings
DOD/DAR S75 ....30 B3
Upper Forest Rd
BSLYN/ROY S71 ....14 D4
Upper Gate Rd
ST/HB/BR S6............123 F2
Upper Hanover St *FUL* S10...10 C4
OWL S3 ....10 C4
Upper Hoyland Rd *HOY* S74...61 G1
Upper Ley Ct
CHPT/GREN S35 ....94 A1
Upper Ley Dell
CHPT/GREN S35 ....94 A1
Upper Lum Cl *CHNE* S41...193 F2
Upper Lunns Cl
BSLYN/ROY S71 ....16 A1
Upper May Day Green Ar
BSLY S70 * 3 G4
Upper Millgate *RHAM* S60 *...9 F4
Upper Moor St
CHSW S40 * 191 F2
Upper Newbold Cl
CHNE S41 ....186 B2
Upper New St *BSLY* S70......3 G6
Upper Rye Cl *RHAM* S60...103 E5
Upper School La *DRON* S18...171 E2
Upper Sheffield Rd
BSLY S70 ....32 A4
Upperthorpe *ST/HB/BR* S6...125 F2
Upperthorpe Gln
ST/HB/BR S6............125 F2
Upperthorpe Rd
ECK/KIL S21 ....168 B3
ST/HB/BR S6............125 G2
Upper Valley Rd *SHEFS* S8...140 A5
Upper Whiston La
RHAM S60............120 A5
Upperwood Hall
WMB/DAR S73 * 34 D4
Upperwood Rd
WMB/DAR S73 ....34 C4
Upper Wortley Rd
KIMB S61 ....95 E2
Upton Cl *MALT* S66......110 C1
WMB/DAR S73 ....49 H1
Upwell Hl *ATT* S4......116 A3
Upwell La *ATT* S4......116 A3
Upwell St *ATT* S4......116 A3
Upwood Cl *CHNE* S41......186 A4
Upwood Rd *ST/HB/BR* S6...113 H5
Urban Rd *DONS/BSCR* DN4...55 H4
Urch Cl *CONI* DN12......89 E2
Uttley Cl *DARN/MH* S9......127 H1
Uttley Cft *DARN/MH* S9......127 H1
Uttley Dr *DARN/MH* S9......127 H1
Uttoxeter Av *MEX/SWTN* S64...67 G2

V

Vaal St *BSLY* S70......32 B2
Vainor Rd *ST/HB/BR* S6......113 G2
Vale Av *RHAM/THRY* S65......99 H4
Vale Cl *BSVR* S44......196 D3
DRON S18 ....171 F2
Vale Ct *RHAM/THRY* S65......99 H4
Vale Crs *RHAM/THRY* S65......99 H4
Vale Gv *ST/HB/BR* S6......113 E4
Valentine Cl *SHEFN* S5......102 C4
Valentine Crs *SHEFN* S5......102 C4
Valentine Rd *SHEFN* S5......102 C4
Vale Rd *OWL* S3......114 D5
RHAM/THRY S65 ....99 H4

Valiant Gdns *BTLY* DN5 ......55 E2
Valley Crs *CHNE* S41......5 K6
Valley Dr *ARMTH* DN3......59 F5
DEARNE S63 ....64 D2
ECK/KIL S21 ....168 B1
Valley Gv *BSLYN/ROY* S71...21 F2
Valley Rd *BSVR* S44......196 D4
CHNE S41 ....5 K6
CHPT/GREN S35 ....80 C5
ECK/KIL S21 ....168 B1
HACK/IN S12 ....156 C3
MEX/SWTN S64 ....85 H1
SHEFS S8 ....140 A4
STV/CWN S43 ....183 E2
Valley Vw *BSVR* S44 * 197 E5
Valley View Cl *CHNE* S41...193 G5
ECK/KIL S21 ....174 C1
Valley Wy *HOY* S74......62 A3
STV/CWN S43 ....50 C3
Vancouver Dr *DEARNE* S63...52 D3
Varley Gdns *MALT* S66......108 B3
Varney Rd *DEARNE* S63......65 E3
Vaughan Av *DON* DN1......6 E2
Vaughan Rd *DOD/DAR* S75...18 D4
Vauxhall Cl *DARN/MH* S9...103 H5
Vauxhall Rd *DARN/MH* S9...103 H5
Velvet Wood Cl
DOD/DAR S75 ....18 C4
Venetian Crs
WMB/DAR S73 ....34 D5
Ventnor Cl *DONS/BSCR* DN4...71 F1
Ventnor Pl *ABRD* S7......139 H2
Venture Wy *CHNE* S41......179 F5
Venus Ct *RHAM* S60......118 C2
Verdant Wy *SHEFN* S5......102 D4
Verdon St *OWL* S3......126 B2
Verelst Av *AU/AST/KP* S26...145 F4
Vere Rd *ST/HB/BR* S6......114 A2
Verger Cl *NROS/TKH* DN11...91 G2
Vernon Cl *BSLY* S70......31 H5
Vernon Crs *BSLY* S70......31 H5
Vernon Delph *FUL* S10......124 B4
Vernon Dr *CHPT/GREN* S35...80 D5
Vernon Rd *BSLY* S70......31 H5
CHSW S40 ....4 A4
RHAM S60 ....119 H1
TOT/DORE S17 ....161 G4
Vernon St *BSLY* S70......60 D2
BSLYN/ROY S71 ....3 F2
HOY S74 ....61 G3
Vernon St North
BSLYN/ROY S71 ....3 F2
Vernon Ter *FUL* S10......124 C5
Vernon Wy *DOD/DAR* S75 *...18 D4
Verona Ri *WMB/DAR* S73...35 E5
Vesey St *RAW* S62......98 B2
Vicarage Cl
CHPT/GREN S35 ....101 E1
DONS/BSCR DN4 ....74 C1
HOY S74 ....62 A2
MEX/SWTN S64 ....67 G4
RHAM/THRY S65 ....107 F1
Vicarage Crs
CHPT/GREN S35 ....101 E1
Vicarage La *BSLYN/ROY* S71...15 G1
RHAM/THRY S65 ....9 F4
TOT/DORE S17 ....160 D1
Vicarage Rd
CHPT/GREN S35 ....101 E1
DARN/MH S9 ....116 B5
Vicarage Wy *CHNE* S41......4 D3
Vicar Crs *WMB/DAR* S73...35 F5
Vicar La *CHSW* S40......5 G4
HAN/WDH S13 ....143 F3
SHEF S1 ....11 G2
Vicar Rd *DEARNE* S63......64 D1
WMB/DAR S73 ....35 F5
Vickers Dr *SHEFN* S5......115 H1
Vickers Rd *CHPT/GREN* S35...80 B4
SHEFN S5 ....115 H2
Victoria Av *RHAM/THRY* S65...9 K5
STV/CWN S43 ....182 B5
Victoria Cl *STKB/PEN* S36...76 D2
Victoria Cottages
MEX/SWTN S64 ....66 C3
Victoria Ct *ECC* S11......139 F4
Victoria Crs *BSLY* S70......60 C1
DOD/DAR S75 ....2 D2
Victoria Crs West
DOD/DAR S75 ....2 D2
Victoria Gv *STV/CWN* S43...188 D4
Victoria La *NROS/TKH* DN11...91 G2
Victorian Crs *WHHL* DN2...7 K5
Victoria Park Rd
STV/CWN S43 ....188 D4
Victoria Quays
SHEFP/MNR S2 * 11 J2
Victoria Rd *AWLS/ASK* DN6...25 H1
BSLY S70 ....23 E2
BSLYN/ROY S71 ....26 D5
BTLY DN5 ....26 D5
CONI DN12 ....70 B5
DEARNE S63 ....64 D1
DONS/BSCR DN4 ....55 H5
FUL S10 ....10 B7
MEX/SWTN S64 ....67 E3
MOS S20 ....157 F1
RAW S62 ....98 B2
STKB/PEN S36 ....77 E2
WMB/DAR S73 ....50 D3

Victoria Station Rd
SHEFP/MNR S2............11 J1
Victoria St *BSLY* S70............2 E3
BSVR S44 ....197 E4
CHNE S41 ....5 F2
CUD/GR S72 ....16 D5
DIN S25 ....135 E4
DRON S18 ....170 D1
HOY S74 ....62 B2
MALT S66 ....111 E5
MEX/SWTN S64 ....86 C4
OWL S3 ....10 D4
RHAM S60 ....8 B5
RHAM S60 ....129 H1
STKB/PEN S36 ....44 D3
STKB/PEN S36 ....76 D2
STV/CWN S43 ....180 D5
WMB/DAR S73 ....35 F4
Victoria St North
SHEFN S5 ....179 F4
Victoria St West *CHSW* S40...191 G2
Victoria Ter *BSLY* S70............3 J7
Victoria Vw *CHNE* S41 * 187 F1
Victoria Wy *MALT* S66......110 B2
Victor Rd *TOT/DORE* S17...161 F1
Victor St *ST/HB/BR* S6......114 B5
Victor Ter *BSLY* S70............3 K6
Viewland Cl *CUD/GR* S72...22 A2
Viewlands Cl *MALT* S66...109 E5
STKB/PEN S36 ....44 D1
View Rd *RHAM/THRY* S65...106 C1
SHEFP/MNR S2 ....140 A3
View Tree Cl *RAW* S62......81 H2
Vikinglea Cl
SHEFP/MNR S2 * 141 H1
Vikinglea Dr
SHEFP/MNR S2 ....141 H2
Vikinglea Gld
SHEFP/MNR S2 ....141 H1
Vikinglea Rd
SHEFP/MNR S2 ....141 H1
Villa Gdns *BTLY* DN5......26 C2
Village Ct *CUD/GR* S72......17 E5
Village St *AWLS/ASK* DN6...25 F1
Villa Park Rd
DONS/BSCR DN4 ....58 A5
Villa Rd *AWLS/ASK* DN6......25 F2
Villas Rd *BSVR* S44......196 B3
Villiers Cl *SHEFP/MNR* S2...141 E5
Villiers Dr *SHEFP/MNR* S2...141 E4
Vincent Crs *CHSW* S40......191 F2
Vincent La *CHSW* S40......191 F2
Vincent Rd *ABRD* S7......139 H2
BSLYN/ROY S71 ....21 E4
MALT S66 ....108 D2
Vine Cl *BSLYN/ROY* S71......20 C3
RHAM S60 ....8 C4
Viola Bank *STKB/PEN* S36...76 D2
Violet Av *MOS* S20......157 E2
Violet Bank Rd *ABRD* S7...139 G4
Vivian Rd *SHEFN* S5......115 H2
Vizard Rd *HOY* S74......62 B2
Vulcan Rd *DARN/MH* S9...116 D3

W

Wadbrough Rd *ECC* S11......139 F1
Waddington Rd
DOD/DAR S75 ....18 D5
Waddington Wy
RHAM/THRY S65 ....98 C4
Wade Cl *RHAM* S60......106 B5
Wade Meadow
ST/HB/BR S6............113 G3
Wade St *ATT* S4......116 A3
DOD/DAR S75 ....18 D5
Wadsley La *ST/HB/BR* S6...113 G2
Wadsley Park Crs
ST/HB/BR S6............113 G3
Wadsworth Av
HACK/IN S12 ....142 A5
Wadsworth Cl
HACK/IN S12 ....142 B5
Wadsworth Dr
HACK/IN S12 ....142 B4
RAW S62 ....84 C3
Wadsworth Rd
HACK/IN S12 ....142 A5
MALT S66 ....108 D5
Wadworth Av
NROS/TKH DN11............91 H2
Wadworth Ri
RHAM/THRY S65 ....99 G5
Wadworth St *CONI* DN12...68 C4
Wagon Rd *KIMB* S61......97 F3
Wain Av *CHNE* S41......5 J4
Waingate *OWL* S3......11 H2
Wainwright Av
HAN/WDH S13 ....142 B2
WMB/DAR S73 ....49 H2
Wainwright Crs
HAN/WDH S13 ....142 A2
Wainwright Pl
WMB/DAR S73 ....49 H2
Wainwright Rd
DONS/BSCR DN4 ....7 G6
KIMB S61 ....96 D5
Wakefield Rd
BSLYN/ROY S71 ....19 H1
Wakelam Dr *ARMTH* DN3...42 B4

Wake Rd *ABRD* S7 ....**139** G3
Walbank Rd *ARMTH* DN3 ......**43** E4
Walbert Av *DEARNE* S63 ....**37** E3
Walbrook *BSLY* S70................**48** B1
Walden Av *BTLY* DN5..............**39** E1
Walden Rd *SHEFP/MNR* S2 ...**140** B3
Walders Av *ST/HB/BR* S6 ......**113** G2
Walders La *STKB/PEN* S36 ....**77** E5
Walesmoor Av
  AU/AST/KP S26 ....**159** G3
Wales Pl *AU/AST/KP* S26 .....**125** F1
Wales Rd *AU/AST/KP* S26 .....**159** F3
Waleswood Rd *MOS* S20 ......**158** A1
Waleswood Vw
  AU/AST/KP S26 ....**145** F4
Waleswood Wy
  AU/AST/KP S26 ....**158** D2
Walford Rd *ECK/KIL* S21.......**168** A1
Walgrove Av *CHSW* S40 ....**4** A7
Walgrove Rd *CHSW* S40 ....**4** B7
Walker Cl *CHPT/GREN* S35 ....**101** E1
Walker La *RHAM/THRY* S65 ......**9** G3
Walker Pl *RHAM/THRY* S65.......**9** G3
Walker Rd *DOD/DAR* S75 ....**60** D3
  KIMB S61 ....**96** D5
Walkers La *ECK/KIL* S21........**168** B2
Walker St *MEX/SWTN* S64 .....**66** C5
  OWL S3 ....**126** B2
  RAW S62 ....**85** H5
Walker Vw *RAW* S62 ....**85** H5
Walkley Bank Cl
  ST/HB/BR S6.........................**114** A5
Walkley Bank Rd
  ST/HB/BR S6.........................**124** D1
Walkley Crescent Rd
  ST/HB/BR S6.........................**124** D1
Walkley La *ST/HB/BR* S6 ......**114** A5
Walkley Rd *ST/HB/BR* S6 .....**125** E1
Walkley St *ST/HB/BR* S6 ......**125** F2
Walkley Ter *ST/HB/BR* S6 .....**124** C1
The Walk *BSLY* S70................**70** C6
Wallace Rd *DONS/BSCR* DN4...**71** E2
  OWL S3 ....**114** D5
Waller Rd *ST/HB/BR* S6 ....**124** C1
Walling Cl *DARN/MH* S9 ....**116** D2
Walling Rd *DARN/MH* S9 ......**116** D2
Wallsend Cottages
  CHNE S41...............................**187** E4
Walney Fold
  BSLYN/ROY S71 ....**20** D1
Walnut Cl *BSLY* S70 * **31** H3
Walnut Dr *DIN* S25................**134** D5
  ECK/KIL S21 ....**168** A3
Walnut Gv *MEX/SWTN* S64 ...**66** D2
Walnut Pl *CHPT/GREN* S35 ...**102** C3
Walpole Cl *DONS/BSCR* DN4...**71** F3
Walpole Gv *AU/AST/KP* S26 ..**145** F1
Walseker La
  AU/AST/KP S26 ....**169** G1
Walsham Dr *BTLY* DN5 ....**39** E3
Walstow Crs *ARMTH* DN3 ....**42** A4
Walters Rd *MALT* S66 ....**111** F3
Walter St *RHAM* S60 ....**8** B5
  ST/HB/BR S6 ....**114** B5
Waltham Cft *CHNE* S41 ....**193** E5
Waltham Gdns *MOS* S20 ......**157** G3
Waltham St *BSLY* S70 ....**3** H6
Waltheof Rd
  SHEFP/MNR S2 ....**141** G2
Walton Back La *RCH* S42 ......**190** D4
Walton Cl *CHPT/GREN* S35 ....**80** A3
  CHSW S40 ....**191** F4
  DRON S18 ....**170** A1
Walton Crs *CHSW* S40 ....**4** A7
Walton Dr *CHSW* S40 ....**4** B7
Walton Drive Ct *CHSW* S40 ......**4** B7
Walton Fields Rd
  CHSW S40 ....**191** H2
Walton Rd *CHSW* S40 ....**191** H3
  ECC S11 ....**139** F1
Walton St *DOD/DAR* S75 ....**19** E4
Walton St North
  DOD/DAR S75 ....**18** D4
Walton Wk *CHSW* S40 ....**4** A7
Walton Wy *RCH* S42 ....**195** E3
Wannop St *RAW* S62 ....**98** B3
Wansfell Rd *ATT* S4 ....**116** B3
Wansfell Ter *BSLYN/ROY* S71....**3** J5
The Wapping
  RHAM/THRY S65.....................**87** G4
Warburton Cl
  SHEFP/MNR S2 ....**140** C3
Warburton Gdns
  SHEFP/MNR S2 ....**140** C3
Warburton Rd
  SHEFP/MNR S2 ....**140** C3
Ward Cl *STKB/PEN* S36 ....**44** D4
Warde-Aldam Crs
  MALT S66..............................**108** A4
Warde Av *DONS/BSCR* DN4 ....**71** F2
Warden Cl
  DONS/BSCR DN4 ....**58** C5
Warden St *RHAM* S60 ....**118** D1
Wardgate Wy *CHSW* S40 ......**186** A4
Ward La *STV/CWN* S43 ....**177** F3
Wardlow Cl *CHSW* S40 ....**192** B4
Wardrew Rd *HACK/IN* S12 ....**142** B5
Ward Pl *ABRD* S7 ....**139** H2
Wardsend Rd *ST/HB/BR* S6...**114** B2
Wardsend Rd North
  ST/HB/BR S6 ....**114** A1
Ward St *STKB/PEN* S36 ....**44** D4

Wareham Ct *MOS* S20 ....**157** G3
Wareham Gv *DOD/DAR* S75 ....**30** C2
Warehouse La *DEARNE* S63 .....**65** E2
Warley Rd *SHEFP/MNR* S2 ....**141** E1
Warminster Cl *SHEFS* S8 ....**153** E1
Warminster Crs *SHEFS* S8 .....**153** F1
Warminster Dr *SHEFS* S8 ....**153** F2
Warminster Pl *SHEFS* S8 ....**153** F2
Warminster Rd *SHEFS* S8 ......**153** E1
Warmsworth Halt
  DONS/BSCR DN4 ....**70** B4
Warmsworth Rd
  DONS/BSCR DN4 ....**70** B4
Warner Av *DOD/DAR* S75 ....**18** D5
Warner Pl *DOD/DAR* S75 ....**2** A2
Warner Rd *DOD/DAR* S75 ....**18** D5
  ST/HB/BR S6 ....**113** H5
Warner St *CHNE* S41 ....**5** J7
Warning Dr
  DONS/BSCR DN4 ....**74** C3
Warning Tongue La
  DONS/BSCR DN4 ....**74** D4
Warren Av *RAW* S62 ....**85** G4
Warren Cl *BSLYN/ROY* S71 .....**12** D4
  DONS/BSCR DN4 ....**70** C2
  WHHL DN2 ....**41** F3
Warren Crs *BSLY* S70 ....**31** H3
  ECK/KIL S21 ....**173** G1
Warren Dr *KIMB* S61 ....**104** D1
Warreners Dr
  RHAM/THRY S65.....................**99** H4
Warren Gdns
  CHPT/GREN S35 ....**81** E3
Warren Mt *KIMB* S61 ....**104** D1
Warren House La *MALT* S66 ..**108** D3
Warren La *CHPT/GREN* S35 ....**80** D2
  DONS/BSCR DN4 ....**74** B3
Warren Mt *KIMB* S61 ....**104** D1
Warren Pl *BSLY* S70 ....**31** H3
Warren Quarry La *BSLY* S70 ......**3** G7
Warren Ri *DRON* S18 ....**163** G5
Warren Rd *MALT* S66 ....**108** B4
Warren St *ATT* S4 ....**126** D2
Watson St *HOY* S74 ....**61** F3
Watt La *FUL* S10 ....**124** B5
Waveney Dr *DOD/DAR* S75 .....**18** A4
Waverley Av *CONI* DN12 ....**89** F1
  DONS/BSCR DN4 ....**71** E1
  MALT S66 ....**133** F1
The Warren
  NROS/TKH DN11 ....**91** G1
Warren V *MEX/SWTN* S64 ......**85** G2
  RAW S62 ....**85** G2
Warren Vale Rd
  MEX/SWTN S64 ....**65** G5
Warren Vw *BSLY* S70 ....**3** G7
  HOY S74 ....**61** G4
Warrington Rd *FUL* S10 ....**125** F3
Warris Cl *KIMB* S61 ....**96** C5
Warris Pl *SHEFP/MNR* S2 ......**126** D4
Warsop Rd *BSLYN/ROY* S71 ...**14** C3
Warwick Rd *BSLYN/ROY* S71 ..**20** B4
  MALT S66 ....**110** A3
Warwick St *CHSW* S40 ....**192** D5
  FUL S10 ....**125** E3
  RHAM S60 ....**9** G6
Warwick St South
  RHAM S60 * **9** H6
Warwick Ter *FUL* S10 ....**125** E3
Warwick Wy *DIN* S25 ....**148** C2
Wasdale Av *MOS* S20 ....**167** E2
Washfield Crs *RHAM* S60 ......**130** A3
Washfield La *RHAM* S60 ....**130** A3
Washford Rd *DARN/MH* S9 ...**127** E1
Wash House La *CHSW* S40 ....**191** G2
Washington Av *CONI* DN12 ....**88** B1
  WMB/DAR S73 ....**49** H3
Washington Cl *DIN* S25 ....**134** B5
Washington Gv *BTLY* DN5 ......**39** G3
Washington Rd
  AWLS/ASK DN6 ....**25** F2
  CHPT/GREN S35 ....**94** B5
  DEARNE S63 ....**53** F1
  ECC S11 ....**139** H2
Washington St
  MEX/SWTN S64 ....**67** F3
Wasteneys Rd
  *WATCH House La *BTLY* DN5 ....**39** F4
Watchley Gdns *DEARNE* S63 ...**37** E5
Watch St *HAN/WDH* S13 ....**143** H2
Waterdale *DON* S1...................**64** D5
Waterdale Cl *BTLY* DN5 ....**54** D5
Waterdale Rd *BSLY* S70 ....**47** H1
Waterfield Ms *MOS* S20 ....**157** E4
Waterfield Pl *BSLY* S70 ....**33** E2
Waterford Rd *OWL* S3 ....**114** C5
Water Hall La *STKB/PEN* S36 ..**44** D2
Waterhall Vw
  STKB/PEN S36 ....**44** D2
Waterhouse Cl
  RHAM/THRY S65.....................**99** G5
Wateringbury Gv
  STV/CWN S43 ....**182** B4
Watering Place Rd
  STKB/PEN S36 ....**44** A3
Water La *BSVR* S44 ....**196** B4
  RAW S62 ....**62** C5
  RHAM S60 ....**8** E6
  TOT/DORE S17 ....**161** F1
Waterloo Ct *DIN* S25 ....**5** D2
Waterloo Rd *BSLY* S70 ....**3** C5
Waterloo Wk *OWL* S3 ....**125** H1
Watermead *DEARNE* S63 ....**53** F4
Watermeade *ECK/KIL* S21 ....**174** B1
Water Meadow La
  CHNE S41..............................**186** B3

Water Royd Dr
  DOD/DAR S75 ....**30** B3
Waterside Dr *MALT* S66 ....**108** C1
Waterside Pk
  WMB/DAR S73 * **57** E5
Waterside Vw *CONI* DN12 ....**69** E5
Water Slacks Cl
  HAN/WDH S13 ....**143** F4
Water Slacks Dr
  HAN/WDH S13 ....**143** F4
Water Slacks Rd
  HAN/WDH S13 ....**143** F4
Watersmeet Rd
  ST/HB/BR S6.........................**113** H5
Water St *OWL* S3 ....**11** G1
  RHAM/THRY S65 ....**9** F3
Waterthorpe Cl *MOS* S20 * ...**157** F5
Waterthorpe Crs *MOS* S20 ...**157** F5
Waterthorpe Gdns
  MOS S20 ....**157** E5
Waterthorpe Gld *MOS* S20 ...**157** F5
Waterthorpe Glen *MOS* S20 .**157** F5
Waterthorpe Greenway
  MOS S20 ....**156** D2
Waterthorpe Ri *MOS* S20 .....**157** E5
Watery St *OWL* S3 ....**125** H2
Wath Rd *ABRD* S7 ....**139** G4
  DEARNE S63 ....**52** D4
  HOY S74 ....**62** C4
  MEX/SWTN S64 ....**64** C5
  WMB/DAR S73 ....**50** D4
Wath Wood Bottom
  DEARNE S63 ....**65** E5
Wath Wood Dr
  MEX/SWTN S64 ....**64** C5
Wath Wood Rd *DEARNE* S63 ...**65** F4
Watkinson Gdns *MOS* S20 ....**157** F3
Watnall Rd
  BSLYN/ROY S71 ....**14** D4
Watson Cl *KIMB* S61 ....**104** D1
Watson Gln *KIMB* S61 ....**104** D1
Watson La *RCH* S42 ....**194** C4
Watson Rd *FUL* S10 * **125** E5
  KIMB S61 ....**104** D1
Watson St *HOY* S74 ....**61** F3
Watt La *FUL* S10 ....**124** B5
Waveney Dr *DOD/DAR* S75 .....**18** A4
Waverley Av *CONI* DN12 ....**89** F1
Waverley Ct *BTLY* DN5 ....**26** C3
Waverley Rd *DARN/MH* S9 ...**128** A3
Waverley Vw *RHAM* S60 ....**129** G2
Waycliffe *BSLYN/ROY* S71 ......**20** C4
Wayford Av *CHNE* S41 ....**192** D3
Wayland Av *BSLY* S70 ....**31** H5
Wayland Rd *ECC* S11 ....**139** F2
Wayside *STV/CWN* S43 ....**188** B1
The Way *CHSW* S40 * **4** E7
Weakland Cl *HACK/IN* S12 ...**155** H1
Weakland Crs *HACK/IN* S12 .**155** H2
Weakland Dr *HACK/IN* S12 ..**155** H2
Weakland Wy *HACK/IN* S12 .**155** H2
Weaver Dr *DOD/DAR* S75 ....**18** A4
Weavers Cl *CHPT/GREN* S35 ...**93** E5
Webb Av *STKB/PEN* S36 ....**77** C3
Webbs Av *ST/HB/BR* S6 ....**97** G4
Webster Cl *KIMB* S61 ....**104** A1
Webster Ct *SHEFS* S8 ....**187** E4
Webster Crs *KIMB* S61 ....**104** B1
Webster Cft *CHNE* S41 ....**179** F4
Webster St *DARN/MH* S9 .....**116** D3
Wedgewood Cl *CHNE* S41 .....**194** B2
Weedon St *DARN/MH* S9 .....**116** D2
Weet Shaw Cl *CUD/GR* S72 ....**17** E2
Weet Shaw La *CUD/GR* S72 ...**16** C3
Weetwood Dr *ECC* S11 ....**138** C5
Weetwood Rd *RHAM* S60 ....**94** C5
Weigh La *SHEFP/MNR* S2 * ...**126** C4
Weir Cl *HOY* S74 ....**62** A3
Weir Head *DARN/MH* S9 ......**116** D3
Welbeck Cl *DRON* S18 ....**170** A1
  STV/CWN S43 ....**189** H3
Welbeck Ct *STV/CWN* S43 ....**189** H3
Welbeck Dr *AU/AST/KP* S26 .**145** H3
  RCH S42 ....**195** E3
Welbeck Ms *MALT* S66 ....**121** F1
Welbeck Rd *BSVR* S44 ....**197** E3
  DONS/BSCR DN4 ....**7** H5
  ST/HB/BR S6 ....**124** D1
Welbeck St *DOD/DAR* S75 ....**2** C2
Welbeck Vls *BSVR* S44 * **197** E2
Welbury Gdns *MOS* S20 ....**157** H1
Welby Pl *SHEFS* S8 ....**152** D1
Welfare Av *CHSW* S40 ....**4** A4
  CONI DN12 ....**88** C2
Welfare Rd *DEARNE* S63 ....**53** H5
  DEARNE S63 ....**37** E2
Welham Dr *RHAM* S60 ....**106** A5
Welland Cl *DOD/DAR* S75 ....**18** A4
  OWL S3 ....**125** H1
Welland Ct *DOD/DAR* S75 ....**18** A4
Welland Gdns *HOY* S74 ....**62** C2
Wellbourne Cl
  CHPT/GREN S35 ....**94** C2
Wellcarr Rd *SHEFS* S8 ....**153** E5
Wellcliffe Cl *MALT* S66 ....**108** C3
Well Court La *CUD/GR* S72 .....**36** B4

Wellcroft Cl *WHHL* DN2 ....**41** G4
Wellcroft Gdns *MALT* S66 ....**109** E5
Welleseley Rd *FUL* S10 ....**10** A1
Wellfield Cl *HACK/IN* S12 ....**155** C4
  ST/HB/BR S6 ....**10** A1
Wellfield Gdns
  BSLYN/ROY S71 ....**20** C4
Wellfield Gv *STKB/PEN* S36 ....**44** D1
Wellfield Rd *DOD/DAR* S75 ......**2** C2
  KIMB S61 ....**96** C4
  ST/HB/BR S6 ....**125** F2
Wellgate *CONI* DN12 ....**89** E1
  RHAM S60 ....**9** F4
Wellgate Mt *RHAM* S60 ....**9** G5
Wellgate Ter *RHAM* S60 ....**9** G5
Well Green Rd
  ST/HB/BR S6.........................**123** F2
Wellhead Rd *SHEFS* S8 ....**140** A4
Well Hill Gv *BSLYN/ROY* S71 ..**12** C5
Well House La
  STKB/PEN S36 ....**44** D2
Wellhouse Wy
  STKB/PEN S36 ....**44** D1
Wellingley Rd
  DONS/BSCR DN4 ....**72** A3
Wellington Av *DIN* S25 ....**148** B1
Wellington Cl
  BSLYN/ROY S71 ....**20** B3
Wellington Crs *BSLY* S70 ....**32** C5
Wellington Gv *BTLY* DN5 ....**39** G3
Wellington Pl *BSLY* S70 * **2** C5
Wellington Rd
  ST/HB/BR S6 ....**124** A2
Wellington St *BSLY* S70 ....**3** F1
  DEARNE S63 ....**53** C1
  MEX/SWTN S64 ....**67** E3
  SHEF S1 ....**10** E5
  STV/CWN S43 ....**180** B2
Welling Wy *KIMB* S61 ....**104** C2
Well La *AU/AST/KP* S26 ....**131** E5
  BSLYN/ROY S71 ....**20** C2
  RHAM S60 ....**130** A3
  ST/HB/BR S6 ....**113** F2
Well Meadow Dr *OWL* S3 ......**10** D1
Well Meadow St *OWL* S3 ....**10** D1
Well Pl *SHEFS* S8 ....**140** A4
Well Rd *SHEFS* S8 ....**140** A4
Wells Cl *DOD/DAR* S75 ....**14** A4
Wellspring Cl *RCH* S42 ....**195** H3
  STV/CWN S43 ....**177** F5
Well Spring Cl
  STV/CWN S43 * **188** C2
Wells Rd *DIN* S25 ....**148** B3
Wells St *BSVR* S44 ....**197** F4
Well View Rd *KIMB* S61 ....**104** B1
The Wellway *MALT* S66 ....**98** B2
Welney Pl *ST/HB/BR* S6 ....**96** E5
Welshpool Pl *CHSW* S40 * **4** A7
Welton Cl *DONS/BSCR* DN4 ...**73** G2
Welwyn Cl *CHSW* S40 ....**191** H1
  HACK/IN S12 ....**154** D1
Welwyn Rd *HACK/IN* S12 ....**154** D1
Wembley Av *CONI* DN12 ....**88** C1
Wembley Cl *WHHL* DN2 ....**41** G5
Wendel Gv *HOY* S74 ....**62** D2
Wenlock Cl *CHSW* S40 ....**186** D5
Wenlock Crs *CHSW* S40 ....**186** C5
Wenlock St
  HAN/WDH S13 * **142** D1
Wensley Ct *ATT* S4 ....**116** A3
Wensley Crs
  DONS/BSCR DN4 ....**74** B1
Wensley St *ATT* S4 ....**116** A2
Wensley Dale Dr
  RHAM S60 ....**118** D5
Wensleydale Rd *BTLY* DN5 .....**38** B7
  KIMB S61 ....**96** B3
Wensley Gdns *ATT* S4 ....**116** A2
Wensley Gn *ATT* S4 ....**116** A2
Wensley Rd *BSLYN/ROY* S71 ..**116** A3
Wensley St *ATT* S4 ....**116** A2
  DEARNE S63 ....**53** D1
Wensley Wy *STV/CWN* S43 ..**189** G1
Wentworth Av
  AU/AST/KP S26 ....**145** H4
  CHSW S40 ....**192** A4
  ECC S11 ....**151** F3
Wentworth Cl *KIMB* S61 ....**95** E1
Wentworth Ct *KIMB* S61 ....**97** F2
Wentworth Crs
  DOD/DAR S75 ....**14** A4
  STKB/PEN S36 ....**44** D3
Wentworth Dr
  DOD/DAR S75 ....**14** A4
  RAW S62 ....**98** B2
Wentworth Gdns
  MEX/SWTN S64 ....**86** A3
Wentworth Mdw
  DEARNE S63 ....**37** E2
Wentworth Ms
  DOD/DAR S75 ....**14** A4
  HOY S74 ....**48** D4
Wentworth Pl *KIMB* S61 ....**96** A4
Wentworth Rd *BSLY* S70 ....**48** D4
  DOD/DAR S75 ....**14** A4
  DRON S18 ....**170** A2
  HOY S74 ....**48** D4
  KIMB S61 ....**95** F1
  RAW S62 ....**84** D5

  STKB/PEN S36 ....**44** C2
  WHHL DN2 ....**40** C5
Wentworth St *BSLY* S70 ....**60** C1
  BSLYN/ROY S71 ....**19** G4
Wentworth Vw *HOY* S74 ....**62** A3
  WMB/DAR S73 ....**50** B4
Wentworth Wy *DIN* S25 ....**149** E1
  DOD/DAR S75 ....**30** B4
  DOD/DAR S75 ....**30** B4
Wescoe Av *CUD/GR* S72 ....**36** A1
Wesley Av *AU/AST/KP* S26 ...**145** F1
Wesley Ct *KIMB* S61 ....**95** F1
Wesley La *FUL* S10 ....**124** D4
Wesley Pl *DIN* S25 ....**148** B4
Wesley Rd *AU/AST/KP* S26 ...**145** F1
  CHPT/GREN S35 ....**80** A4
Wesley St *BSLY* S70 ....**3** G5
Wessenden Cl *DOD/DAR* S75 ..**30** C1
Wessex Cl *STV/CWN* S43 ......**188** D1
Wessex Gdns
  TOT/DORE S17 ....**160** D3
Wessington Dr
  STV/CWN S43 ....**189** G1
West Acre *STKB/PEN* S36 ....**44** C3
  DEARNE S63 ....**52** D4
  DONS/BSCR DN4 ....**71** G1
  RAW S62 ....**163** F5
  WMB/DAR S73 ....**49** F5
Westbank Cl *DRON* S18 ....**168** A4
Westbank Dr *DIN* S25 ....**148** B4
West Bank Ri *DIN* S25 ....**148** B4
West Bank St *OWL* S3 ....**11** G2
West Bars *CHSW* S40 ....**4** E4
West Bawtry Rd *RHAM* S60 ..**118** D3
Westbourne Gdns
  DONS/BSCR DN4 ....**71** F1
Westbourne Gv *CHSW* S40 ...**191** F1
  DOD/DAR S75 ....**19** E4
Westbourne Rd *FUL* S10 ......**139** G1
Westbourne Ter *BSLY* S70 ....**2** B4
Westbridge Rd
  STV/CWN S43 ....**177** G4
Westbrook Bank *ECC* S11 .....**139** F2
Westbrook Cl *DRON* S18 ....**168** A4
Westbrook Dr *CHSW* S40 .....**190** D2
Westbrook Rd
  CHPT/GREN S35 ....**94** A1
Westbury Av
  CHPT/GREN S35 ....**94** B2
Westbury Cl *DOD/DAR* S75 .....**18** D3
Westbury St *DARN/MH* S9 ...**127** F2
Westby Cl *RHAM/THRY* S65 ..**109** E1
Westby Crs *RHAM* S60 ....**118** D4
West Carr Rd *RHAM* S60 ......**134** B4
West Cl *KIMB* S61 ....**104** C1
West Crs *STKB/PEN* S36 ....**45** C4
  STKB/PEN S36 ....**76** C2
West Croft Ct
  STV/CWN S43 ....**189** F4
Westcroft Crs *MOS* S20 ....**157** E5
Westcroft Dr *MOS* S20 ....**157** E5
Westcroft Gdns *MOS* S20 ....**157** E5
Westcroft Gln *MOS* S20 ....**167** E1
Westcroft Gv *MOS* S20 ....**157** E5
West Don St *ST/HB/BR* S6 ...**125** C1
West End *STV/CWN* S43 ....**177** E4
West End Av
  BSLYN/ROY S71 ....**15** E1
  BTLY DN5................................**39** G3
West End Bungalows
  STV/CWN S43 * **177** E4
West End Ct
  NROS/TKH DN11 ....**91** H3
West End Crs
  BSLYN/ROY S71 ....**15** E1
West End La
  NROS/TKH DN11 ....**90** D1
West End Rd *DEARNE* S63 ......**64** B1
West End Vw *ECK/KIL* S21 ...**174** C1
Westerdale Rd *BTLY* DN5 ....**38** D4
Western Av *DIN* S25 ....**134** C5
Western Cl *DIN* S25 ....**134** C5
Western Rd *FUL* S10 ....**124** D5
  RHAM/THRY S65.....................**106** C2
Western Ter *BSLY* S70 ....**2** E2
Western Ter *WMB/DAR* S73 .....**50** A2
Westerton Dr *MALT* S66 ......**109** E5
West Farm La
  RHAM/THRY S65.....................**107** F1
Westfield Av
  AU/AST/KP S26 ....**145** E1
  CHSW S40 ....**191** F3
  HACK/IN S12 ....**154** A3
  STKB/PEN S36 ....**44** A2
West Field Bank
  STV/CWN S43 ....**177** E4
Westfield Centre *MOS* S20 ...**157** E5
Westfield Cl *CHSW* S40 ....**191** F2
Westfield Crs *DEARNE* S63 ....**36** D2
  MOS S20 ....**156** D5
Westfield Cft *DEARNE* S63 ....**36** D2
Westfield Gdns *CHSW* S40 ...**191** F2
Westfield La *ECK/KIL* S21 ....**156** B2
  ECK/KIL S21 ....**173** G3
  STKB/PEN S36 ....**44** A2
Westfield Northway
  MOS S20 ....**157** E5
Westfield Rd *ARMTH* DN3 ....**42** C4
  DEARNE S63 ....**64** A2
  DONS/BSCR DN4 ....**55** H4

DRON S18........**171** G3
ECK/KIL S21........**168** A3
MALT S66........**108** D4
RAW S62........**98** A2
WMB/DAR S73........**64** A1
Westfields *BSLYN/ROY* S71........**12** K5
Westfield Southway
MOS S20........**157** E5
West HI *BSLY* S70........**2** C4
West Garth *DIN* S25........**134** D4
Westgate *BSLY* S70........**2** E4
BSLYN/ROY S71........**20** B3
Westgate *RHAM* S60........**9** F5
STKB/PEN S36........**44** D4
West Green Av
BSLYN/ROY S71........**21** F1
West Green Dr *ARMTH* DN3........**29** E3
West Gv *BSLYN/ROY* S71........**12** A5
WHHL DN2........**41** E5
Westhaven *CUD/GR* S72 *........**22** A2
West HI *KIMB* S61........**104** A3
Westhill La *OWL* S3........**10** D4
Westholme Rd
DONS/BSCR DN4........**6** A7
West Kirk La *CUD/GR* S72........**36** A3
West Laith Ga *DON* DN1........**6** C4
Westland CI *MOS* S20........**157** E4
Westland Gdns *MOS* S20........**156** D4
Westland Gv *MOS* S20........**157** E5
Westland Rd *MOS* S20........**157** E4
West La *AU/AST/KP* S26........**144** D1
West Lea *CHSW* S40........**191** F2
STV/CWN S43........**184** D2
Westlea Vw *STV/CWN* S43........**184** D2
Westleigh *CHSW* S40........**4** C2
West MI *MOS* S20 *........**157** E2
Westminster Av *FUL* S10........**137** F1
Westminster Buildings
DON DN1 *........**6** D3
Westminster CI *FUL* S10........**137** F1
MALT S66........**119** J4
Westminster Crs *FUL* S10........**137** F1
WHHL DN2........**41** G5
West Moor Crs
DOD/DAR S75........**30** C1
West Moor La *ARMTH* DN3........**43** F1
Westmoor Rd
STV/CWN S43........**188** D5
Westmore CI *DEARNE* S63........**37** E5
Westmoreland St
ST/HB/BR S6........**125** G2
Westmount St
DONS/BSCR DN4........**71** F2
Westmorland Wy *BTLY* DN5........**54** A4
Westmount Av *DEARNE* S63........**51** G5
Westnall Rd *SHEFN* S5........**102** D2
Westnall Ter *SHEFN* S5........**102** D2
Weston CI *CHSW* S40........**186** A3
Weston Rd *DONS/BSCR* DN4........**71** F2
Weston St *OWL* S3........**10** C2
Weston Vw *FUL* S10........**125** E4
Westover Rd *FUL* S10........**124** A5
West Park Dr
AU/AST/KP S26........**144** D3
West Pinfold
BSLYN/ROY S71........**15** G1
Westpit HI *DEARNE* S63........**64** A1
West PI *BTLY* DN5........**39** H1
West Qd *SHEFN* S5........**115** H1
West Rd *DOD/DAR* S75........**18** D5
MEX/SWTN S64........**66** D3
Westside Gra
DONS/BSCR DN4........**55** G5
West St *BSLY* S70........**48** B1
BSLYN/ROY S71........**12** D5
CHSW S40........**4** D2
CONI DN12........**89** E1
DEARNE S63........**37** C4
DEARNE S63........**65** F2
DIN S25........**148** B4
DON DN1........**5** C4
DRON S18........**170** D1
ECK/KIL S21........**174** C1
HOY S74........**61** G2
MEX/SWTN S64........**66** D4
MOS S20........**157** F2
SHEF S1........**10** E4
STV/CWN S43........**185** G1
WMB/DAR S73........**50** A2
West Street La *SHEF* S1........**11** F3
Westthorpe Fields Rd
ECK/KIL S21........**168** A4
Westthorpe Rd
ECK/KIL S21........**168** B3
West Vale Gv
RHAM/THRY S65........**99** H4
West Vw *BSLY* S70........**31** G3
BSVR S44........**197** E4
CUD/GR S72........**22** A2
STV/CWN S43........**177** E4
STV/CWN S43........**181** H5
West View CI
TOT/DORE S17........**161** F2
West View Crs *DEARNE* S63........**53** E1
West View La
TOT/DORE S17........**161** F2
West View Rd *CHNE* S41........**187** E3
KIMB S61........**104** A3
MEX/SWTN S64........**67** G4
Westville Rd *DOD/DAR* S75........**2** C1

West Wy *BSLY* S70........**2** E5
Westwell PI *MOS* S20........**166** D2
Westwick Crs *SHEFS* S8........**162** B1
Westwick Gv *SHEFS* S8........**162** B1
Westwick La *RCH* S42........**190** B2
Westwood Av
ST/HB/BR S6........**113** F1
STV/CWN S43........**189** G1
Westwood CI *ST/HB/BR* S6........**113** F1
STV/CWN S43........**189** G4
Westwood Ct *BSLY* S70........**2** E2
CHPT/GREN S35........**80** B3
Westwood Dr
STV/CWN S43........**189** G4
Westwood Drive Gdns
STV/CWN S43........**189** F4
Westwood La
STV/CWN S43........**188** D5
Westwood New Rd
CHPT/GREN S35........**80** A4
DOD/DAR S75........**60** B5
Westwood Rd *BSVR* S44........**189** E5
ECC S11........**138** B2
Wetherby CI *BTLY* DN5........**38** D5
Wetherby Dr
AU/AST/KP S26........**145** E3
MEX/SWTN S64........**67** F2
Wetlands La *CHNE* S41........**192** A4
Wet Moor La *DEARNE* S63........**64** D1
Whaley Rd *DOD/DAR* S75........**18** B2
Wharf CI *MEX/SWTN* S64........**66** C5
Wharfedale Dr
CHPT/GREN S35........**93** G1
Wharfedale Rd
DOD/DAR S75........**18** C4
Wharf La *CHNE* S41........**5** C1
STV/CWN S43........**182** B3
Wharf Rd *DARN/MH* S9........**117** F1
DON DN1........**40** B5
MEX/SWTN S64........**86** C3
Wharf St *BSLYN/ROY* S71........**3** J1
MEX/SWTN S64........**86** C3
SHEFP/MNR S2........**11** J2
Wharncliffe Av *DOD/DAR* S75........**30** C4
Wharncliffe Av
AU/AST/KP S26........**145** G2
DEARNE S63........**65** F2
Wharncliffe CI *HOY* S74........**61** H4
RAW S62........**84** D3
Wharncliffe HI
RHAM/THRY S65 *........**9** G3
Wharncliffe Rd
CHPT/GREN S35........**80** B4
FUL S10........**10** C6
Wharncliffe St *BSLY* S70........**2** D4
BSLYN/ROY S71........**15** H4
DONS/BSCR DN4........**55** G3
Wharton Av
AU/AST/KP S26........**145** F1
Wharton Dr *CHNE* S41........**5** J3
Wheatacre Rd
STKB/PEN S36........**77** E2
Wheata Dr *SHEFN* S5........**102** A2
Wheata PI *SHEFN* S5........**102** A3
Wheata Rd *SHEFN* S5........**102** A3
Wheatbridge Rd *CHSW* S40........**4** C4
Wheat CIt *CONI* DN12........**89** G1
Wheatcroft Rd *RAW* S62........**85** H5
Wheatcrofts *BSLY* S70........**2** C4
Wheatfield CI *ARMTH* DN3........**29** G1
Wheatfield Crs *SHEFN* S5........**102** D3
Wheatfield Dr *DEARNE* S63........**37** F3
Wheathill CI *STV/CWN* S43........**188** D5
Wheathill La *STV/CWN* S43........**188** C5
Wheatlands Rd *RCH* S42........**195** E3
Wheatley CI
BSLYN/ROY S71........**19** H3
Wheatley Gv
HAN/WDH S13........**142** C1
Wheatley Hall Rd
WHHL DN2........**40** D4
Wheatley La *DON* DN1........**6** E1
Wheatley PI *CONI* DN12 *........**68** B5
Wheatley Rd *BSLY* S70........**33** E3
BTLY DN5........**26** C5
KIMB S61........**96** C5
MEX/SWTN S64........**86** C4
Wheatley St *CONI* DN12........**89** E1
Wheeldon Crs
STV/CWN S43........**188** B2
Wheeldon St *OWL* S3........**10** D3
Wheel La *CHPT/GREN* S35........**101** F1
The Wheel *CHPT/GREN* S35........**101** C1
Wheldrake Rd *SHEFN* S5........**115** H2
Whernside Av
CHPT/GREN S35........**80** D5
Whinacre CI *SHEFS* S8........**163** F2
Whinacre PI *SHEFS* S8........**163** F2
Whinby Cft *DOD/DAR* S75........**30** B3
Whinby Rd *DOD/DAR* S75........**30** A2
The Whines *KIMB* S61........**97** G1
Whinfell CI *AWLS/ASK* DN6........**25** F1
Whinfell Ct *ECC* S11........**151** E3
Whin Gdns *DEARNE* S63........**37** F1
Whin Hill Rd
DONS/BSCR DN4........**57** H5
Whinmoor Rd
CHPT/GREN S35........**80** A4
Whinside Crs *DEARNE* S63........**37** E1
The Whins *RAW* S62........**84** C5

Whiphill CI *DONS/BSCR* DN4........**74** A1
Whiphill La *ARMTH* DN3........**43** E5
Whiphill Top La *ARMTH* DN3........**59** G5
Whirlow Court Rd *ECC* S11........**151** F3
Whirlowdale CI *ECC* S11........**151** E3
Whirlowdale Crs *ABRD* S7........**151** H2
Whirlowdale Ri *ECC* S11........**151** E3
Whirlowdale Rd *ECC* S11........**151** F3
Whirlow Grange Av
ECC S11........**151** E3
Whirlow Grange Dr
ECC S11........**151** E3
Whirlow Gn *ECC* S11........**151** F3
Whirlow Gv *ECC* S11........**151** F3
Whirlow La *ECC* S11........**151** E2
Whirlow Ms *ECC* S11 *........**151** F2
Whirlow Park Rd *ECC* S11........**151** F4
Whisperwood Dr
DONS/BSCR DN4........**71** H4
Whiston Brook Vw
RHAM S60........**120** A3
Whiston Gra *RHAM* S60........**119** G3
Whiston Gn *RHAM* S60........**119** H4
Whiston Gv *RHAM* S60........**106** B5
Whiston V *RHAM* S60........**119** H3
Whitaker CI
NROS/TKH DN11........**91** F4
Whitbourne CI
BSLYN/ROY S71........**19** H2
Whitburn Rd *DON* DN1........**2** E6
Whitby Rd *DARN/MH* S9........**127** H3
NROS/TKH DN11........**91** E2
Whitcomb Dr
NROS/TKH DN11........**91** F4
Whitebank CI *CHNE* S41........**192** D3
Whitecotes CI *CHSW* S40........**192** A4
Whitecotes La *CHSW* S40........**192** A4
Whitecotes Pk *CHSW* S40........**192** B4
White Cft *SHEF* S1........**10** E2
Whitecroft Crs *RHAM* S60........**118** C4
White Cross Av *CUD/GR* S72........**21** H2
White Cross Ct *CUD/GR* S72........**21** H2
White Cross La *BSLY* S70........**32** D5
White Cross Mt *CUD/GR* S72........**22** A2
White Cross Ri *BSLY* S70........**32** D5
White Cross Rd *CUD/GR* S72........**21** H2
White Edge CI *CHSW* S40........**186** A4
White Ga *DIN* S25........**148** D2
Whitehall Rd *KIMB* S61........**96** D2
White Hart Cnr
ECK/KIL S21........**167** E4
Whitehead Av
STKB/PEN S36........**77** F3
Whitehead CI *DIN* S25........**134** C5
Whitehead St
STV/CWN S43........**182** B4
White Hill Av *RHAM* S60........**118** C4
Whitehill Av *RHAM* S60........**118** C4
White Hill Dr *RHAM* S60........**118** C5
White Hill Gv *BSLY* S70 *........**30** C1
Whitehill La *RHAM* S60........**118** C3
Whitehill Rd *RHAM* S60........**118** C4
White Hill Ter *BSLY* S70........**30** C1
Whitehouse La
ST/HB/BR S6........**125** F1
Whitehouse Rd
ST/HB/BR S6........**125** F1
Whitehouses *CHSW* S40........**5** J7
White La *CHPT/GREN* S35........**81** F4
HACK/IN S12........**154** C2
Whitelea Gv
MEX/SWTN S64........**66** D4
White Leas *CHSW* S40........**186** B5
Whitelee Rd
MEX/SWTN S64........**66** C5
Whiteley La *FUL* S10........**137** G3
Whiteley Wood CI *ECC* S11........**138** A3
Whiteley Wood Rd
ECC S11........**138** A3
Whitelow La
TOT/DORE S17........**160** A1
White Rd *STV/CWN* S43........**182** C4
White Rose Ct *BTLY* DN5........**40** A1
White Rose Wy
DONS/BSCR DN4........**56** C5
Whites Croft Vw
STV/CWN S43........**177** E5
White Thorns CI *SHEFS* S8........**163** F3
White Thorns Dr *SHEFS* S8........**163** F3
White Thorns Vw
SHEFS S8........**163** F2
Whiteways CI *ATT* S4........**115** H4
Whiteways Dr *ATT* S4........**115** H4
Whiteways PI *ATT* S4........**115** H4
Whiteways Rd *ATT* S4........**115** H4
Whitewood CI
BSLYN/ROY S71........**15** F1
White's La *SHEFP/MNR* S2........**126** D4
Whitfield Gdns *WRKN* S81........**149** H4
Whitfield Rd *FUL* S10........**137** G3
RAW S62........**84** C3
Whiting St *SHEFS* S8........**140** A4
Whitley Carr
CHPT/GREN S35........**93** G4
Whitley Cft *CHPT/GREN* S35........**94** B4
Whitley La *CHPT/GREN* S35........**93** F5
Whitley Vw *CHPT/GREN* S35........**94** B4
Whitley View Rd *KIMB* S61........**103** H4
Whitney CI *DONS/BSCR* DN4........**71** E3
Whittier Rd
DONS/BSCR DN4........**71** G2
EPW DN9........**75** H4
Whittington HI *CHNE* S41........**179** G5
Whittington La *DRON* S18........**179** H1

Whittington Rd
STV/CWN S43........**180** C2
Whittingtons Ct *WHHL* DN2........**41** G2
Whittington St *DON* DN1........**40** B5
Whittington Wy *CHNE* S41........**179** G5
Whitting Valley Rd
CHNE S41........**179** G5
Whitton CI *DONS/BSCR* DN4........**73** G2
Whitwell Crs *STKB/PEN* S36........**76** C3
Whitwell La *STKB/PEN* S36........**76** C3
Whitwell Rd *DARN/MH* S9........**128** B3
Whitwell Vw
NROS/TKH DN11 *........**91** H2
Whitworth La
DARN/MH S9........**116** C5
Whitworth Rd *CHNE* S41........**187** F3
FUL S10........**137** G2
Whitworth St *DEARNE* S63........**37** G5
Whybourne Ter *RHAM* S60 *........**9** G5
Wicker CI *DEARNE* S63........**65** E1
Wicker *OWL* S3........**11** J1
Wicker La *OWL* S3........**11** J1
Wickersley Rd *RHAM* S60........**106** C5
Wickethern Rd *ARMTH* DN3........**43** E4
Wicket Wy *CONI* DN12........**70** C5
Wickfield CI *HACK/IN* S12........**142** D5
Wickfield Dr *HACK/IN* S12........**142** C5
Wickfield Gv *HACK/IN* S12........**142** C5
Wickfield PI *HACK/IN* S12........**142** C5
Wickfield Rd *HACK/IN* S12........**155** H1
Wicklow La *WHHL* DN2........**41** E5
Widdop CI *HAN/WDH* S13........**142** B2
Widdop Cft *HAN/WDH* S13........**142** B2
Wigfield Dr *BSLY* S70........**31** H5
Wigfull Rd *ECC* S11........**139** G1
Wigley Rd *STV/CWN* S43........**189** G3
Wignall Av *MALT* S66........**107** H5
Wikeley Wy *STV/CWN* S43........**188** B2
Wike Rd *BSLYN/ROY* S71........**21** E5
Wilberforce Rd *DIN* S25........**148** B3
WHHL DN2........**40** D5
Wilbrook Ri *DOD/DAR* S75........**18** C3
Wilby Carr Gdns
DONS/BSCR DN4........**58** B4
Wilby La *BSLY* S70........**3** J6
Wilcox CI *ST/HB/BR* S6........**101** F4
Wilcox Rd *ST/HB/BR* S6........**101** E4
Wild Av *RAW* S62........**84** C4
Wilden CIt *STV/CWN* S43........**188** A1
Wildene Dr *MEX/SWTN* S64........**67** G2
Wildflower CI
NROS/TKH DN11........**91** E4
Wilding CI *STV/CWN* S43........**182** D5
Wilding Wy *KIMB* S61........**104** C1
Wilford Rd *BSLYN/ROY* S71........**14** C3
Wilfred CI *DARN/MH* S9........**127** G2
Wilfred Dr *DARN/MH* S9........**127** G2
Wilfred St *RHAM* S60........**96** D2
Wilfrid Rd *DARN/MH* S9........**127** G2
Wilkinson Av
NROS/TKH DN11........**91** G3
Wilkinson CI *STV/CWN* S43........**195** G1
Wilkinson Dr *STV/CWN* S43........**189** F2
Wilkinson La *FUL* S10........**10** C4
Wilkinson Rd *HOY* S74........**62** C5
Wilkinson St *BSLY* S70........**1** D4
FUL S10........**10** B4
Willan Dr *RHAM* S60........**129** G2
Willbury Dr *HACK/IN* S12........**141** G4
Willey St *OWL* S3........**11** J1
William CI *MOS* S20 *........**166** D2
William Crs *MOS* S20........**166** D1
William La *NROS/TKH* DN11........**90** D2
Williamson Rd *ECC* S11........**139** F3
William St *BTLY* DN5........**39** F4
William St *BSLY* S70........**32** A5
CHNE S41........**187** G3
DEARNE S63........**37** E5
ECK/KIL S21........**166** D5
FUL S10........**10** C6
MEX/SWTN S64........**66** C5
RAW S62........**98** C4
RHAM S60........**9** H5
WMB/DAR S73........**50** A2
William St North *CHNE* S41........**179** F4
Willingham CI *MOS* S20........**157** G4
Willingham Gdns
MOS S20 *........**157** G3
Willington Rd *SHEFN* S5........**102** C5
Willis Rd *ST/HB/BR* S6........**113** H5
Wilman Rd
BSLYN/ROY S71........**21** F4
Willoughby St *ATT* S4........**115** H2
Willow Av *DONS/BSCR* DN4........**58** B5
RAW S62........**98** C1
Willow Bank
BSLYN/ROY S71........**19** F3
RHAM/THRY S65........**106** D1
Willow Beck
HOR/CROF WF4........**12** A2
Willow CI *CUD/GR* S72........**16** D5
DIN S25........**148** B5
HOY S74........**61** G3
MALT S66........**108** C3
RHAM S60........**118** D5
Willow Ct *MALT* S66........**108** B4
Willow Crs *CHPT/GREN* S35........**94** A2
EPW DN9........**75** H4
Willowcroft *DEARNE* S63 *........**52** D4
Willowdale CI *BTLY* DN5........**54** D5

Willow Dr *CONI* DN12........**70** C5
DARN/MH S9........**128** C4
MALT S66........**108** C3
MEX/SWTN S64........**66** D3
STV/CWN S43........**183** E2
Willow Dro *HOR/CROF* WF4........**15** F1
Willow Garth *RAW* S62........**85** G5
Willowgarth Av *RHAM* S60........**118** C5
Willowgarth CI
HOR/CROF WF4........**13** G1
Willow Garth Rd *CHNE* S41........**186** C1
Willow Gv *AU/AST/KP* S26........**145** H2
Willow La *DEARNE* S63........**53** F4
NROS/TKH DN11........**91** G2
Willowlees Ct
DONS/BSCR DN4........**74** A1
Willow Rd *ARMTH* DN3........**45** E5
DEARNE S63........**37** F2
ECK/KIL S21........**168** A3
MALT S66........**110** B5
STKB/PEN S36........**76** D2
The Willows *KIMB* S61........**96** B4
STKB/PEN S36........**45** H5
Willow St *BSLY* S70........**2** D6
CONI DN12........**89** F1
Willow Tree Dr
STV/CWN S43........**185** F4
Willow Wk *BTLY* DN5 *........**26** C4
Wilmington Dr
DONS/BSCR DN4........**72** D1
Wilsden Gv *DOD/DAR* S75........**18** D3
Wilson Av *DOD/DAR* S75........**85** E5
STKB/PEN S36........**34** D4
STV/CWN S43........**185** G1
Wilson Dro *HOR/CROF* WF4........**15** F1
Wilson Gv *BSLYN/ROY* S71........**21** F3
Wilson PI *SHEFS* S8........**140** A4
Wilson Rd *DRON* S18........**163** G4
ECC S11........**139** E2
STKB/PEN S36........**77** H3
Wilthorpe Av *DOD/DAR* S75........**19** E3
Wilthorpe Crs *DOD/DAR* S75........**19** E3
Wilthorpe Farm Rd
DOD/DAR S75........**19** E3
Wilthorpe Gdns *MOS* S20........**156** A3
Wilthorpe Gn *DOD/DAR* S75........**19** E3
Wilthorpe La *DOD/DAR* S75........**18** D3
Wilthorpe Rd *DOD/DAR* S75........**18** C3
Wilton CI *RAW* S62........**98** B1
Wilton Ct *KIMB* S61........**105** E2
Wilton Gdns *KIMB* S61........**105** E2
Wilton La *KIMB* S61........**105** E5
Wilton PI *FUL* S10........**10** B6
Wiltshire Rd *WHHL* DN2........**57** G1
Wimborne Crs *CHNE* S41........**187** E2
Winberry Av *DIN* S25........**148** C3
Wincanton CI
MEX/SWTN S64........**67** G2
Winchester Av *FUL* S10........**137** F2
WHHL DN2........**41** E4
Winchester Ct
RHAM/THRY S65 *........**9** G3
Winchester Crs *FUL* S10........**137** F2
Winchester Dr *FUL* S10........**137** F2
Winchester Rd *CHNE* S41........**187** E2
FUL S10........**137** F2
Winchester Wy
BSLYN/ROY S71........**33** G3
BTLY DN5........**38** D4
RHAM S60........**118** A3
Wincobank Av *SHEFN* S5........**116** A1
Wincobank CI *SHEFN* S5........**116** B1
Wincobank La *ATT* S4........**116** B3
Wincobank Rd *SHEFN* S5........**116** B1
Windermere Av *DRON* S18........**170** C2
WHHL DN2........**41** G5
Windermere Dr *DIN* S25........**148** C4
Windermere Crs
ARMTH DN3........**29** F3
Windermere Rd *ABRD* S7........**139** G5
BSLYN/ROY S71........**3** J4
CHNE S41........**186** C2
STKB/PEN S36........**34** D2
Winders Cnr *STV/CWN* S43........**184** B1
Winders PI *WMB/DAR* S73........**50** B3
Windgate HI *CONI* DN12........**69** F5
Windham CI *BSLYN/ROY* S71........**33** G3
Windhill Av *MEX/SWTN* S64........**67** G3
Windhill Crs *MEX/SWTN* S64........**67** G2
Windhill La *MEX/SWTN* S64........**67** G2
The Windings *DEARNE* S63........**37** G3
Windle Rd *DONS/BSCR* DN4........**58** C4
Windle Sq *ARMTH* DN3........**29** F5
Windmere Av *DEARNE* S63........**53** C1
Windmill Av *CONI* DN12........**89** F2
CUD/GR S72........**17** H4
Windmill Balk La
AWLS/ASK DN6........**25** F3
Windmill CI *BSVR* S44........**196** D1
Windmill Ct *AWLS/ASK* DN6........**25** F2
KIMB S61........**105** E2
WMB/DAR S73........**49** H3
Windmill Greenway
MOS S20........**167** E3
Windmill Hill La
CHPT/GREN S35........**93** G2
Windmill La *DRON* S18........**172** C5
SHEFN S5........**116** A1
STKB/PEN S36........**44** A3

Windmill Rd *DIN* S25...............148 C2
  WMB/DAR S73.............49 H3
Windmill Wy *STV/CWN* S43...188 A1
Windsor Av *STKB/PEN* S36 ....44 A2
Windsor Cl *CHSW* S40 ....191 C3
  MALT S66 ....35 H5
Windsor Crs *BSLYN/ROY* S71..20 B4
  CUD/GR S72.........................55 H5
Windsor Dr *DOD/DAR* S75 *...50 B3
  DRON S18............................170 A2
  MEX/SWTN S64 ....67 C2
  RCH S42 ....195 E3
Windsor Gdns *DEARNE* S63 ....37 C2
Windsor Ri *AU/AST/KP* S26...145 C4
Windsor Rd *CONI* DN12 * 68 D5
  KIMB S61............................95 F2
  SHEFS S8 ....139 H4
  WHHL DN2 ....7 H1
Windsor Sq *DEARNE* S63........37 C2
Windsor St *ATT* S4................126 D1
  DEARNE S63 ....37 C2
  HOY S74..............................61 H4
Windsor Wk *BTLY* DN5 ....39 E4
  CHNE S41...........................193 E3
  DIN S25 ....148 A5
Windy Fields Rd *RCH* S42 .....190 B5
Windy House La
  SHEFP/MNR S2...................141 F3
Windy Rdg *AU/AST/KP* S26...145 E1
Winfield Rd *DEARNE* S63 ....65 E3
Wingerworth Av *SHEFS* S8...162 B1
Wingerworth Wy
  CHSW S40 ....192 B5
Wingfield Cl *DRON* S18........170 A3
  KIMB S61............................97 E3
Wingfield Ct *KIMB* S61 * 96 D4
Wingfield Crs *HACK/IN* S12...142 A5
Wingfield Rd
  BSLYN/ROY S71.....................20 A1
  KIMB S61............................96 C3
Winholme *ARMTH* DN3 ....42 D4
Winifred Ter *RHAM* S60.............8 C3
Winkley Ter *SHEFN* S5...........103 E4
Winlea Av *RHAM/THRY* S65...107 G5
Winnat Pl *STV/CWN* S43.......189 G2
Winn Cl *ST/HB/BR* S6 ....113 H1
Winn Dr *ST/HB/BR* S6.............113 H1
Winn Gdns *ST/HB/BR* S6........113 H1
Winn Gv *ST/HB/BR* S6 ....100 C5
Winnipeg Rd *BTLY* DN5...........39 F4
Winsford Rd *ST/HB/BR* S6 ....101 E4
Winster Cl *BSLY* S70 ....47 H5
Winster Rd *ST/HB/BR* S6.......114 A3
  STV/CWN S43 ....189 G1
Winston Av *STKB/PEN* S36 .....76 B1
Winter Av *BSLYN/ROY* S71.....12 C4
  DOD/DAR S75 ....2 A2
Winter Hill La *KIMB* S61.........104 C2
Winterhill Rd *KIMB* S61 ....104 B3
Winter Rd *DOD/DAR* S75...........2 A3
Wintersett Rd
  DONS/BSCR DN4 ....57 F5
Winter St *OWL* S3......................10 D2
Winter Ter *DOD/DAR* S75 ....2 A2
Winterton Cl
  DONS/BSCR DN4 ....73 H2
Winterton Gdns
  HACK/IN S12 ....156 C2
Winterwell Rd *DEARNE* S63.....64 C1
Winton Cl *BSLY* S70 ....32 A3
Winton Rd *WHHL* DN2 ....57 F1
Wisbech Cl *CHSW* S40...........192 A4
Wisconsin Dr
  DONS/BSCR DN4 ....73 E1
Wiseton Rd *ECC* S11 ....139 E1
Wisewood Av
  ST/HB/BR S6......................113 G4
Wisewood La
  ST/HB/BR S6......................113 G4
Wisewood Pl
  ST/HB/BR S6......................113 G4
Wisewood Rd
  ST/HB/BR S6......................113 G4
Wishing Well Gn
  AU/AST/KP S26...................144 D3
Wiston Wy *CHNE* S41.............193 E5
Witham Cl *CHNE* S41..............188 A3
Witham Ct *CHSW* S40.............191 C1
  DOD/DAR S75 ....18 A4
Witham Rd *FUL* S10...............125 E5
Withens Av *ST/HB/BR* S6......113 H2
Witney St *SHEFS* S8..............140 A3
Wivelsfield Rd
  DONS/BSCR DN4 ....70 D1
Woburn Cl *DONS/BSCR* DN4...71 E3
Woburn Pl *DOD/DAR* S75.........30 B4
  ECC S11............................151 F5
Wolfe Cl *CHSW* S40...............191 H3
Wolfe Dr *ST/HB/BR* S6...........101 E4
Wolfe Rd *ST/HB/BR* S6...........101 F4
Wollaton Av
  TOT/DORE S17....................161 G3
Wollaton Cl
  BSLYN/ROY S71.....................14 C4
Wollaton Dr *TOT/DORE* S17...161 G4
Wollaton Rd
  TOT/DORE S17....................161 F4
Wolseley Rd *SHEFS* S8..........139 H3
Wolsey Av *WHHL* DN2 ....57 F1
Wolverley Rd
  HAN/WDH S13 ....143 E4
Wombell Av *DEARNE* S63........65 E3

Wombwell La *BSLY* S70...........33 F3
  HOY S74..............................48 D3
Wombwell Rd *HOY* S74............62 A1
Wood Acres *BSLY* S70 ....18 C3
Woodall La *AU/AST/KP* S26...169 G2
Woodall Rd *ECK/KIL* S21 ....168 D3
  RHAM/THRY S65................107 E4
Woodall Rd South
  RHAM/THRY S65................107 E5
Woodbank Crs *SHEFS* S8.......139 H5
Woodbank Rd
  ST/HB/BR S6......................122 D3
Woodbine Rd
  DARN/MH S9 ....116 B5
Woodbourne Gdns
  DOD/DAR S75 ....60 C3
Woodbourn Hl
  DARN/MH S9 ....127 F2
Woodbourn Rd
  DARN/MH S9 ....127 F3
Woodburn Dr
  CHPT/GREN S35 ....94 B1
Woodbury Cl *DARN/MH* S9 ....103 C4
Woodbury Rd
  DARN/MH S9 ....103 G4
Wood Cliffe *FUL* S10..............124 A1
Wood Cl *CHPT/GREN* S35........94 C2
  RAW S62.............................85 E4
  RCH S42 ....194 D3
  RHAM/THRY S65..................84 D1
Woodcock Cl *KIMB* S61............96 D4
Woodcock Pl
  SHEFP/MNR S2...................126 D4
Woodcock Rd *HOY* S74............62 A1
Wood Cft *KIMB* S61 ....96 D5
Woodcross Av
  DONS/BSCR DN4 ....74 C1
Wood End Av *STKB/PEN* S36...113 C5
Woodend Cl *ST/HB/BR* S6......113 G5
Woodend Ct *DOD/DAR* S75......30 C4
Woodend Dr *ST/HB/BR* S6 .....113 G5
Woodfarm Av
  ST/HB/BR S6......................124 B1
Woodfarm Cl *ST/HB/BR* S6....124 A1
Woodfarm Dr
  ST/HB/BR S6......................124 A1
Woodfarm Pl *ST/HB/BR* S6....124 A1
Woodfield Av
  MEX/SWTN S64 ....67 F3
Woodfield Cl
  WMB/DAR S73.......................35 E4
Woodfield Rd *ARMTH* DN3 ....43 E5
  DEARNE S63 ....64 E2
  DONS/BSCR DN4 ....71 G1
  FUL S10............................124 D3
Wood Flds *RHAM* S60 * 106 A5
Woodfield Vls *RHAM* S60 * 106 A5
Woodfield Wy
  DONS/BSCR DN4 ....71 H4
  DONS/BSCR DN4 ....72 C2
Wood Fold *OWL* S3.................115 E5
Woodfoot Rd *RHAM* S60 ....119 F3
Woodgrove Rd
  DARN/MH S9 ....103 H4
  RHAM/THRY S65................107 E2
Woodhall Cl *WMB/DAR* S73......35 E4
Woodhall Rd
  MEX/SWTN S64 ....86 B1
Woodhall Rd
  WMB/DAR S73.......................35 E5
Woodhead Dr *HOY* S74............48 D4
Woodhead La *HOY* S74............49 E4
Woodhead Rd
  CHPT/GREN S35 ....78 D2
  SHEFP/MNR S2...................140 A2
Woodholm Pl *ECC* S11...........138 D5
Woodholm Rd *ECC* S11..........138 D5
Woodhouse Av *MOS* S20........157 F1
Woodhouse Cl *RAW* S62..........85 H3
Woodhouse Ct *MOS* S20........144 A5
Woodhouse Crs *MOS* S20......157 F1
Woodhouse La *BSVR* S44........196 B1
  MOS S20............................144 A5
  STV/CWN S43 ....183 E1
Woodhouse Rd
  HACK/IN S12 ....141 H4
  HOY S74..............................61 H3
  WHHL DN2 ....40 C4
Woodkirk Rd *STKB/PEN* S36 ...45 F4
Woodknot Ms
  DONS/BSCR DN4 ....71 H4
Woodlaithes Rd *MALT* S66.....108 C1
Woodland Av *DIN* S25 * 148 C3
Woodland Cl *MALT* S66..........121 G1
  RHAM S60.........................129 F2
Woodland Dr *BSLY* S70............30 D2
  DIN S25 ....148 D3
  HACK/IN S12 ....154 D3
Woodland Gdns *MALT* S66.....111 F3
Woodland Gv *DEARNE* S63......65 F4
  STV/CWN S43 ....177 E5
  STV/CWN S43 ....185 G2
Woodland Pl
  TOT/DORE S17....................161 F3
Woodland Rd
  DEARNE S63 ....65 H4
  SHEFS S8 ....152 B3
Woodlands *STV/CWN* S43.....188 B2
Woodlands Av *MOS* S20.........144 B5
Woodlands Cl
  AU/AST/KP S26...................145 F1
Woodlands Crs
  MEX/SWTN S64 ....85 G1

Woodlands Farm
  RHAM S60.........................130 A3
Woodlands Rd
  AWLS/ASK DN6 ....25 F3
  HOY S74..............................49 E5
The Woodlands
  ARMTH DN3 ....43 E3
Woodlands Vw
  AWLS/ASK DN6 * 25 E3
  HOY S74..............................62 A1
  WMB/DAR S73.......................53 E3
Woodland Ter *CUD/GR* S72......23 F2
  CUD/GR S72.........................21 H2
  HACK/IN S12 ....154 D3
  MEX/SWTN S64 ....67 G4
Woodland View Rd
  ST/HB/BR S6 * 124 C1
Woodland Vls
  CUD/GR S72 *.......................23 F1
  DOD/DAR S75 * 60 C3
Wood Wd Wy
  SHEFS S8 ....107 E5
Wood La *BSLYN/ROY* S71........14 C2
  DARN/MH S9 ....118 A5
  MALT S66 ....121 C1
  MALT S66 ....132 C2
  RHAM S60.........................130 B4
  RHAM S60.........................124 B1
Wood Lane Cl
  ST/HB/BR S6......................124 A1
Woodlea Gdns
  DONS/BSCR DN4 ....74 B1
Woodlea Gv *ARMTH* DN3 ....42 D4
Woodlea Wy *WHHL* DN2 ....41 G3
Woodleys Av *RAW* S62............85 E3
Woodman Dr
  BSLYN/ROY S71.....................15 H4
Woodmere Dr *CHNE* S41........180 A2
Woodmoor St
  BSLYN/ROY S71.....................15 H4
Woodnook Gv *ECK/KIL* S21 ...173 G1
Wood Park Vw
  BSLYN/ROY S71.....................14 D3
Woodpecker Cl
  AU/AST/KP S26...................145 G4
Wood Rd *KIMB* S61 ....96 D5
  ST/HB/BR S6......................113 H4
Woodrove Av
  HAN/WDH S13 ....141 H3
Woodrove Cl
  HAN/WDH S13 ....141 H3
Woodroyd Av
  BSLYN/ROY S71.....................15 G3
Woodroyd Cl
  BSLYN/ROY S71.....................15 G3
Wood Royd Rd
  STKB/PEN S36 ....77 G2
Wood Seats
  CHPT/GREN S35 ....93 F3
Woodseats Cl *SHEFS* S8........152 C1
Woodseats House Rd
  SHEFS S8 ....152 D3
Woodseats Rd *SHEFS* S8.......152 C1
Woodsetts Rd *CONI* DN12 ......69 G5
Woodsett Wk *CONI* DN12 ....69 G5
Woodside Av *DEARNE* S63......65 F3
  ECK/KIL S21 ....168 D1
Woodside Cl *CHSW* S40.........186 B5
Woodside Ct
  AWLS/ASK DN6 ....25 E3
  MALT S66 ....121 C1
Woodside Gdns
  DOD/DAR S75 ....19 F3
Woodside Ri *CHNE* S41 ....193 E4
  DOD/DAR S75 ....19 F3
  DONS/BSCR DN4 ....71 E2
  ST/HB/BR S6 ....50 A3
Wood Syke *DOD/DAR* S75........30 C3
Wood View *RHAM* S60.............118 D1
Wood View Pl *RHAM* S60.......118 D1
Woodview Cl *RCH* S42...........195 F4
Woodview La
  DOD/DAR S75 ....18 D4
Wood Vw *CONI* DN12...............89 G2
  HOY S74..............................62 C3
Woodview Ter *ECC* S11..........138 A2

Wood Wk *BSLYN/ROY* S71......12 C4
  HOY S74..............................49 E5
  MEX/SWTN S64 ....66 D2
  WMB/DAR S73.......................49 G5
The Woodway *MALT* S66........108 B2
Wood's Riding *MALT* S66........108 B2
Woofindin Av *ECC* S11...........138 A3
Woofindin Rd *FUL* S10 ....137 H5
Wooldale Cl *MOS* S20............156 A3
Wooldale Cft *MOS* S20...........156 A3
Wooldale Dr *MOS* S20............156 A3
Wooldale Gdns *MOS* S20.......156 A3
Wooley Av *WMB/DAR* S73........50 A3
Woolley Rd *STKB/PEN* S36......76 C2
Woolley Wood Rd
  SHEFN S5..........................103 E2
Wootton Ct
  RHAM/THRY S65..................99 G4
Worcester Av *WHHL* DN2 ....40 D3
Worcester Cl *FUL* S10............137 F1
Worcester Dr *FUL* S10...........137 F1
Worcester Rd *FUL* S10...........137 E1
Wordsworth Av *DIN* S25.........135 E5
  DONS/BSCR DN4 ....71 H2
  SHEFN S5..........................114 C1
  STKB/PEN S36 ....44 C4
Wordsworth Cl *SHEFN* S5......101 G3
Wordsworth Crs
  SHEFN S5..........................101 G5
Wordsworth Dr *BTLY* DN5.......55 F1
  RHAM/THRY S65................106 C3
Wordsworth Pl *DRON* S18......171 G4
Wordsworth Rd
  BSLYN/ROY S71.....................20 B3
  CHNE S41...........................187 F1
  DEARNE S63 ....64 C1
Work Bank La
  STKB/PEN S36 ....44 B2
Workhouse La *OWL* S3............11 G1
Worksop Rd
  AU/AST/KP S26...................145 F3
  AU/AST/KP S26...................146 B3
  DARN/MH S9 ....127 G1
  DIN S25 ....182 D3
  STV/CWN S43 ....182 D3
Works Rd *STV/CWN* S43........181 F3
Worral Av *RHAM* S60..............130 A3
Worral Cl *BSLY* S70 ....31 H4
Worral Ct *ARMTH* DN3.............29 G5
Worrall Rd *CHPT/GREN* S35....80 C5
Worry Goose La *RHAM* S60....120 A2
Worsborough Vw
  DOD/DAR S75 ....60 B2
Worsbrough Rd *BSLY* S70........47 H5
  HOY S74..............................48 D4
Worsley Cl *BSLY* S70 ....32 B4
Worthing Crs *CONI* DN12 ....89 F1
Worthing Rd *DARN/MH* S9 ....127 E3
Wortley Av *MEX/SWTN* S64.....86 B1
  WMB/DAR S73.......................49 H1
Wortley Dr
  CHPT/GREN S35 ....94 C2
Wortley Ms *KIMB* S61...............95 E2
Wortley Rd
  CHPT/GREN S35 ....80 A3
  KIMB S61............................104 C1
  STKB/PEN S36 ....77 H2
Wortley St *BSLY* S70 ....3 F5
Wortley Vw *HOY* S74................74 D4
Wostenholm Rd *ABRD* S7 ......139 H3
Wragby Rd *ECC* S11...............138 C2
Wragg Rd *SHEFP/MNR* S2......127 E5
Wreakes La *DRON* S18...........162 D5
Wrelton Cl *BSLYN/ROY* S71.....15 F1
Wren Bank
  SHEFP/MNR S2...................127 E5
Wren Park Cl *CHSW* S40........192 B5
  HACK/IN S12 ....155 G5
Wrenpark Rd *RCH* S42...........194 D3
Wrens Wy *BSLY* S70 ....47 H5
Wright Crs *WMB/DAR* S73........50 B3
Wrightson Av
  DONS/BSCR DN4 ....70 D3
Wrightson Ter *BTLY* DN5..........39 H4
Wright St *DIN* S25..................148 C2
Wright's Hl *ECC* S11..............139 H1
Wroxham Cl *MALT* S66...........109 E4
Wroxham Dr *MALT* S66...........109 E4
Wroxham Wy *BTLY* DN5...........39 E5
  MALT S66 ....109 E4
Wulfric Cl *SHEFP/MNR* S2......141 E2
Wulfric Pl *SHEFP/MNR* S2.......141 E2
Wulfric Rd *ECK/KIL* S21..........166 C5
  SHEFP/MNR S2...................141 F3
Wyatt Av *ECC* S11..................139 E4
Wybourn House Rd
  SHEFP/MNR S2...................127 E4
Wybourn Ter
  SHEFP/MNR S2...................127 E4
Wychwood Cl
  DONS/BSCR DN4 ....71 F4
Wychwood Cft *MOS* S20........157 G3
Wychwood Gln *MOS* S20........157 G3
Wychwood Gv *MOS* S20........157 G3
Wycombe St
  BSLYN/ROY S71.....................21 E5
Wyedale Cft *MOS* S20............157 G3
The Wynd *ECK/KIL* S21..........175 H4
Wyndthorpe Av
  DONS/BSCR DN4 ....74 A1
Wyn Gv *WMB/DAR* S73............64 A1

Wynmoor Crs
  WMB/DAR S73.......................51 E5
Wynyard Rd *ST/HB/BR* S6.....113 H3
Wythburn Rd *CHNE* S41.........186 C2
Wyvern Gdns
  TOT/DORE S17....................161 F1

Y

Yarborough Ter *BTLY* DN5........39 H5
Yardley Sq *OWL* S3 * 10 D2
Yarmouth St *DARN/MH* S9.....116 D3
Yarncliff Cl *CHSW* S40............186 D4
Yarwell Dr *MALT* S66..............110 C2
Yates Cl *MALT* S66.................121 G1
Yealand Cl *AWLS/ASK* DN6......25 F1
Yearling Cha
  MEX/SWTN S64 ....65 H5
Yeldersley Cl *CHSW* S40........186 B4
Yeomans Rd *ST/HB/BR* S6.....125 G2
Yewdale *BSLY* S70....................32 B5
Yew Greave Crs *SHEFN* S5....101 H2
Yews La *SHEFN* S5.................101 C2
Yews Av *BSLY* S70....................32 B5
Yews La *BSLY* S70 ....32 B4
Yews Pl *BSLY* S70 ....32 B3
The Yews *RHAM/THRY* S65 * 9 G3
Yew Ter *CONI* DN12 *................69 E5
Yew Tree Av *DIN* S25..............148 D3
Yew Tree Crs
  NROS/TKH DN11.................91 G1
Yew Tree Dr *CHSW* S40...........191 E4
  DARN/MH S9 ....117 H3
  ECK/KIL S21 ....168 A3
Yew Tree Rd *MALT* S66...........110 A2
Yoredale Av
  CHPT/GREN S35 ....80 D5
York Gdns *DONS/BSCR* DN4....57 H4
York La *MALT* S66...................121 F5
York Ms *DEARNE* S63..............37 G2
York Ri *AU/AST/KP* S26..........145 E3
York Rd *AWLS/ASK* DN6...........25 H5
  BTLY DN5.............................38 D2
  DARN/MH S9 ....128 A2
  RHAM/THRY S65....................9 H2
  STKB/PEN S36 ....76 D2
Yorkshire Wy *ARMTH* DN3.......43 F4
York St *BSLY* S70.......................2 E5
  CHNE S41...........................193 E5
  CUD/GR S72.........................23 G1
  DEARNE S63 ....37 G1
  HOY S74..............................62 A1
  MEX/SWTN S64 ....66 D3
  NROS/TKH DN11.................91 E1
  SHEF S1..............................11 G2
  WMB/DAR S73.......................50 B2
Youlgreave Dr
  HACK/IN S12 ....142 B5
Young St *DON* DN1....................6 D4
Yvonne Gv *WMB/DAR* S73.......49 H2

Z

Zamor Crs *MALT* S66..............133 E2
Zetland Rd *HOY* S74.................62 D3
  WHHL DN2 ....7 J1
Zion La *DARN/MH* S9..............127 F1
Zion Pl *DARN/MH* S9..............127 F1
Zion Ter *BSLY* S70 ....33 E3

Abbeydale Golf Club
TOT/DORE S17 ....**161** H1
Abbeydale
Grange School
ABRD S7 ....**152** B1
Abbeydale Park
Sports Club
TOT/DORE S17 ....**161** G1
Abbeydale Primary
School
ABRD S7 ....**139** H4
Abbey Lane Primary
School
SHEFS S8 ....**152** C3
Abbey Special School
KIMB S61 ....**104** A2
Abercrombie Primary
School
CHNE S41 ....**5** H1
ACE Business Centre
OWL S3 ....**3** G4
Acorn Business Park
SHEFS S8 ....**152** C1
Acres Hill Primary School
DARN/MH S9 ....**127** H4
Adult & Community
Learning Unit
ST/HB/BR S6 ....**10** A1
Adwick Leisure Centre
AWLS/ASK DN6 ....**25** F3
Adwick Park Junior School
AWLS/ASK DN6 ....**25** F2
Adwick Washington Infant
School
AWLS/ASK DN6 ....**25** G3
Aldham Industrial
Estate
WMB/DAR S73 ....**34** A3
The Alhambra Shopping
Centre
BSLY S70 ....**3** G5
All Saints Catholic High
School
SHEFP/MNR S2 ....**11** K7
Alma Leisure Park
CHSW S40 ....**5** H7
Amber Business Centre
RHAM S60 ....**9** F2
Ambergate Clinics
KIMB S61 ....**105** F3
Anchorage Lower School
BTLY DN5 ....**39** E4
Anchorage Upper School
BTLY DN5 ....**38** C4
Anns Grove J & I School
SHEFS S8 ....**140** A3
Anston Brook Primary
School
DIN S25 ....**148** B3
Anston Greenlands J & I
School
DIN S25 ....**148** B1
Anston Hillcrest Primary
School
DIN S25 ....**148** B4
Anston Park J & I School
DIN S25 ....**148** D1
Apperknowle Community
Primary School
DRON S18 ....**172** B2
Arbourthorne Community
Primary School
SHEFP/MNR S2 ....**140** D4
Ardsley House Hotel
BSLYN/ROY S71 ....**33** G2
Arksey Primary School
BTLY DN5 ....**27** F5
Armthorpe Community
Centre
ARMTH DN3 ....**42** D4
The Armthorpe School
ARMTH DN3 ....**42** C3
Armthorpe Southfield
Primary School
ARMTH DN3 ....**42** D5
Armytage Industrial
Estate
CHNE S41 ....**179** G5
Ashdell Preparatory
School
FUL S10 ....**124** D5
Ashgate Croft Special
School
CHSW S40 ....**186** C5
Ashley Industrial Estate
RHAM S60 ....**9** F2
Ash Lodge Medical
Centre
CHSW S40 ....**191** H2
Ashville Medical Centre
BSLY S70 ....**32** D2
Aston CE Primary School
AU/AST/KP S26 ....**145** G3
Aston Comprehensive
School
AU/AST/KP S26 ....**144** D1
Aston Fence J & I School
HAN/WDH S13 ....**144** C2
Aston Hall CC
AU/AST/KP S26 ....**146** A3
Aston Lodge Primary
School
AU/AST/KP S26 ....**145** G4

Aston Springwood
Primary School
AU/AST/KP S26 ....**145** G2
Athersley North Primary
School
BSLYN/ROY S71 ....**14** C4
Athersley South Primary
School
BSLYN/ROY S71 ....**14** D5
Athron Industrial Unit
DON DN1 ....**6** E1
Atlas Business Park
CHPT/GREN S35 ....**94** C5
Attercliffe Cemetery
DARN/MH S9 ....**116** B5
Aughton Primary School
AU/AST/KP S26 ....**145** F1
Badsley Moor Infant
School
RHAM/THRY S65 ....**106** D3
Bailey House
(Council Building)
RHAM S60 ....**8** E2
Balby Carr Community
Sports College
DONS/BSCR DN4 ....**72** A2
Balby Street J & I School
CONI DN12 ....**68** D5
Balifield Primary School
HAN/WDH S13 ....**143** E2
Bankwood Lane
Industrial Estate
NROS/TKH DN11 ....**90** D1
Bankwood Primary School
GLV S14 ....**140** D5
Barbot Hall
Industrial Estate
KIMB S61 ....**97** H5
Barlborough Hall School
STV/CWN S43 ....**177** F2
Barlborough Primary
School
STV/CWN S43 ....**177** F4
Barnsley Business
Innovation Centre
CUD/GR S72 ....**16** D5
Barnsley Cemetery
BSLY S70 ....**3** K7
Barnsley College
BSLY S70 ....**3** F2
STKB/PEN S36 ....**44** D3
Barnsley College
(Belle Vue)
DOD/DAR S75 ....**3** F1
Barnsley District
General Hospital
DOD/DAR S75 ....**2** A2
Barnsley FC
(Oakwell Stadium)
BSLYN/ROY S71 ....**3** K4
Barnsley Municipal
Golf Club
DOD/DAR S75 ....**14** A2
Barnsley Private Clinic
DOD/DAR S75 ....**2** E1
Barrow Hill
STV/CWN S43 ....**181** E3
Barrow Hill Primary
School
STV/CWN S43 ....**181** F3
Barrow Hill Railway
Centre
STV/CWN S43 ....**181** E3
The Base
BSLY S70 ....**3** G5
Beauchief Golf Club
SHEFS S8 ....**151** H4
The Beauchief Hotel
ABRD S7 ....**151** H4
Beevor Industrial Estate
BSLYN/ROY S71 ....**20** B5
Beighton Cemetery
MOS S20 ....**157** H2
Beighton Health Centre
MOS S20 ....**157** F1
Beighton Infant School
MOS S20 ....**157** H2
Belgrave Medical Centre
SHEFP/MNR S2 ....**140** A2
Bentley Colliery CC
BTLY DN5 ....**26** D5
Bentley Health Centre
BTLY DN5 ....**39** G1
Bentley High Street
Primary School
BTLY DN5 ....**39** H2
Bentley New Village
Primary School
BTLY DN5 ....**26** D5
Bents Green Special School
ECC S11 ....**138** A5
Bessacarr Primary School
DONS/BSCR DN4 ....**57** G5
Best Western Elton Hotel
MALT S66 ....**108** D3
Best Western Mosborough
Hall Hotel
MOS S20 ....**166** D2
Best Western
The Consort Hotel
MALT S66 ....**121** H5
Birch Hall Golf Club
DRON S18 ....**179** E1

Birdholme Infant School
CHSW S40 ....**192** C5
Birdwell Health Centre
BSLY S70 ....**60** D2
Birdwell Primary School
BSLY S70 ....**60** D1
Birkdale Preparatory
School
FUL S10 ....**139** E1
Birkdale School
FUL S10 ....**139** E1
Birk Hill Infant School
ECK/KIL S21 ....**174** B1
Birkwood Primary School
CUD/GR S72 ....**22** A2
Birley Community College
HACK/IN S12 ....**155** F3
Birley Community
Primary School
HACK/IN S12 ....**155** F2
Birley Health Centre
HACK/IN S12 ....**155** F5
Birley Spa Community
Primary School
HACK/IN S12 ....**155** H1
Birleywood Golf Club
HACK/IN S12 ....**155** G3
Blackburn Primary School
KIMB S61 ....**103** H3
Bluebell Medical Centre
SHEFN S5 ....**116** B1
Bolsover Business Park
BSVR S44 ....**196** B2
Bolsover Castle
BSVR S44 ....**196** D2
Bolsover CE Junior School
BSVR S44 ....**196** D2
Bolsover Clinic
BSVR S44 ....**197** E3
Bolsover Infant School
BSVR S44 ....**197** E2
Bolsover Local Hospital
BSVR S44 ....**197** F2
Bolton Medical Centre
DEARNE S63 ....**53** E3
Bolton upon Dearne
Cemetery
DEARNE S63 ....**53** E2
Bolton upon Dearne
Infant School
DEARNE S63 ....**53** E3
Bonaroma Training
Academy
RHAM/THRY S65 ....**99** H3
Boythorpe Cemetery
CHSW S40 ....**4** C7
Bracken Moor
Sports Club
STKB/PEN S36 ....**77** E3
Bradmarsh Business Park
RHAM S60 ....**8** D7
Bramley Grange
Primary School
MALT S66 ....**109** E3
Bramley Sunnyside Infant
School
MALT S66 ....**108** C3
Brampton Cortonwood
Infant School
WMB/DAR S73 ....**51** E5
Brampton Ellis CE
Infant School
DEARNE S63 ....**64** C2
Brampton Ellis CE Junior
School
DEARNE S63 ....**64** B1
Brampton Primary School
CHSW S40 ....**4** B4
Brantwood School
for Girls
ECC S11 ....**139** F3
Brightside Infant School
DARN/MH S9 ....**116** D2
Brimington Cemetery
STV/CWN S43 ....**188** B2
Brimington Clinic
STV/CWN S43 ....**188** C1
Brinsworth Clinic
RHAM S60 ....**118** B3
Brinsworth
Comprehensive School
RHAM S60 ....**118** A4
Brinsworth Howarth
Primary School
RHAM S60 ....**118** C5
Brinsworth Manor Junior
School
RHAM S60 ....**118** B3
Brinsworth Medical
Centre
RHAM S60 ....**118** A3
Brinsworth Whitehill
Primary School
RHAM S60 ....**118** C5
Brockwell Primary
School
CHSW S40 ....**186** D5
Brookfield Community
School
CHSW S40 ....**191** E2
Brookhouse Junior
School
MOS S20 ....**157** H2

Broombank Road
Industrial Estate
CHNE S41 ....**178** C3
Broomhill Clinic
FUL S10 ....**125** E5
Broomhill Infant School
FUL S10 ....**125** E5
Broomhill Medical Centre
FUL S10 ....**125** F5
Broom Lane Medical
Centre
RHAM S60 ....**119** G1
Broom Valley J&I School
RHAM S60 ....**106** A4
Brunswick Primary School
HAN/WDH S13 ....**143** H3
Burncross Cemetery
CHPT/GREN S35 ....**93** H1
Burngreave Cemetery
ATT S4 ....**115** G5
Burns Medical Centre
DONS/BSCR DN4 ....**58** A5
Burton Road Business Park
BSLYN/ROY S71 ....**21** E5
Burton Road Primary
School
BSLYN/ROY S71 ....**20** A4
Business & Innovation
Barnsley Centre
DOD/DAR S75 ....**18** D3
Business Training Centre
DON DN1 ....**6** D7
Busk Meadow Infant
School
SHEFN S5 ....**115** E2
Byron Wood Primary
School
SHEFN S5 ....**115** F5
Calow CE Primary School
CHNE S41 ....**193** H1
Calow Lane Industrial
Estate
CHNE S41 ....**193** G4
The Campanile Hotel
DONS/BSCR DN4 ....**57** F4
Canklow Meadows
Industrial Estate
RHAM S60 ....**118** D3
Canklow Woods J & I
School
RHAM S60 ....**118** D2
Cantley Health Centre
DONS/BSCR DN4 ....**58** B5
Cantley Sycamore Primary
School
DONS/BSCR DN4 ....**74** A1
Carbrook Hall Industrial
Estate
DARN/MH S9 ....**116** D3
Carfield Primary School
SHEFS S8 ....**140** B5
Caribbean Sports Club
CHPT/GREN S35 ....**102** C1
Carlton Industrial Estate
BSLYN/ROY S71 ....**15** G4
Carlton Park Hotel
RHAM S60 ....**106** A5
Carlton Primary School
BSLYN/ROY S71 ....**15** H4
Carrfield Medical Centre
SHEFP/MNR S2 ....**140** B4
Carr House Centre
DONS/BSCR DN4 ....**7** J6
Carter Knowle Junior
School
ABRD S7 ....**139** F5
Castle Hills Primary School
BTLY DN5 ....**39** E2
Castle Industrial Estate
BSVR S44 ....**196** B2
Castle Market
SHEFP/MNR S2 ....**11** J2
Castle Street Medical
Centre
BSVR S44 ....**196** D2
Catcliffe Primary School
RHAM S60 ....**129** H1
Cathedral Church of
St Peter & St Paul
SHEF S1 ....**11** G2
Cavendish Junior School
CHNE S41 ....**187** F1
Cedar School
DONS/BSCR DN4 ....**71** F2
Centenary Industrial
Park
SHEFS S8 ....**139** G5
Central Business Park
RHAM S60 ....**8** D4
Centre in the Park
SHEFP/MNR S2 ....**140** D2
Centurion Business Park
KIMB S61 ....**105** E4
Centurion Retail Park
BTLY DN5 ....**39** H5
Century Business Centre
DEARNE S63 ....**51** G4
Chapel Green Community
College
CHPT/GREN S35 ....**80** D5
Charles Clifford
Dental Hospital
FUL S10 ....**10** A4

Charnock Hall Primary
School
HACK/IN S12 ....**154** D3
Charter Gallery Museum
CONI DN12 ....**88** D1
Chaucer School
SHEFN S5 ....**101** G4
Chesterfield &
North Derbyshire
Royal Hospital
STV/CWN S43 ....**193** G1
Chesterfield Bowl
CHSW S40 ....**192** D5
Chesterfield Caravan &
Leisure Centre
CHNE S41 ....**179** E3
Chesterfield College
CHNE S41 ....**5** H4
Chesterfield Crematorium
STV/CWN S43 ....**188** B3
Chesterfield FC
(Recreation Ground)
CHSW S40 ....**4** D2
Chesterfield Golf Club
RCH S42 ....**191** H5
Chesterfield Museum
CHNE S41 ....**5** H4
Chesterfield Newspaper
Office
CHNE S41 ....**5** H4
Chesterfield RFC
CHNE S41 ....**187** G4
Chesterfield Small
Business Centre
CHNE S41 ....**187** G1
Chesterfield Trading Estate
CHNE S41 ....**178** B3
Childrens Hospital
FUL S10 ....**10** A4
Child Welfare & School
Clinic
RHAM/THRY S65 ....**9** K1
Christ Church CE Primary
School
CHNE S41 ....**187** G4
Cineworld
CHSW S40 ....**5** H7
DARN/MH S9 ....**117** E4
City Road Cemetery
SHEFP/MNR S2 ....**141** E1
City Road Crematorium
SHEFP/MNR S2 ....**141** E2
Civic Theatre
BSLY S70 ....**3** G4
Claremont Hospital
FUL S10 ....**123** H5
Clarence Industrial
Trading Estate
CHNE S41 ....**187** G1
Clayliffe Business Park
DOD/DAR S75 ....**18** A2
Clayfield Industrial Estate
DONS/BSCR DN4 ....**71** G4
Clifford CE Infant School
ECC S11 ....**139** F2
Clifford Dental Hospital
FUL S10 ....**10** A4
Clifford Lister Business
Centre
MALT S66 ....**108** A5
Clifton-A Community
Arts School
RHAM/THRY S65 ....**106** B2
Clifton Park Museum
RHAM/THRY S65 ....**9** H4
Clocktower Business
Centre
STV/CWN S43 ....**181** E3
Clough House Medical
Centre
SHEF S1 ....**11** G7
Clowne Cemetery
STV/CWN S43 ....**184** C1
Clowne Infant School
STV/CWN S43 ....**185** E3
Clowne Junior School
STV/CWN S43 ....**185** E3
Clowne Welfare Sports
Club
STV/CWN S43 ....**184** D3
Coit Primary School
CHPT/GREN S35 ....**94** A2
Coleridge Primary School
RHAM/THRY S65 ....**106** C1
The Colonnades Shopping
Centre
DON DN1 ....**6** C4
Concord Junior School
SHEFN S5 ....**103** F5
Concord Park Golf Club &
Sports Centre
SHEFN S5 ....**103** E4
Conisbrough Castle
CONI DN12 ....**89** E1
Conisbrough Cemetery
CONI DN12 ....**88** D3
Contour Health Centre
RHAM S60 ....**9** F6
Copley Junior School
BTLY DN5 ....**54** B5
Courtyard by Marriott
Hotel
RHAM S60 ....**119** E3

Crooked Spire Church
CHSW S40 ....5 G4
Crookes Cemetery
FUL S10 ....124 C4
Crookhill Park Municipal
Golf Club
CONI DN12 ....89 H4
Crucible Theatre
SHEF S1 ....11 H3
Crystal Peaks Shopping &
Leisure Centre
MOS S20 ....157 E3
Cudworth Churchfield
Primary School
CUD/GR S72 ....16 D5
Cudworth Pontefract Road
Primary School
CUD/GR S72 ....16 D4
Curlew Junior School
WHHL DN2 ....41 G1
Cusworth Country Park
BTLY DN5 ....54 D1
Cutlers Hotel
SHEF S1 ....11 H3
Dalton Foljambe Primary
School
RHAM/THRY S65 ....99 G5
Dalton Health Centre
RHAM/THRY S65 ....99 F5
Dalton Listerdale Primary
School
RHAM/THRY S65 ....107 G5
Danum Hotel
DON DN1 ....6 D4
Danum School Technology
College
WHHL DN2 ....41 H5
Darfield All Saints CE
Primary School
WMB/DAR S73 ....35 F5
Darfield CC
WMB/DAR S73 ....35 F4
Darfield Health Centre
WMB/DAR S73 ....35 F5
Darfield Upperwood J & I
School
WMB/DAR S73 ....34 D4
Darfield Valley Primary
School
WMB/DAR S73 ....50 D1
Darnall Cemetery
DARN/MH S9 ....128 A2
Darnall Health Centre
DARN/MH S9 ....128 A2
Days Inn
AU/AST/KP S26 ....169 F3
Dead Earnest Theatre
ST/HB/BR S6 ....125 E1
Dearne Carrfield Primary
School
DEARNE S63 ....53 E1
Dearne Highgate Primary
School
DEARNE S63 ....37 E5
Dearne High School
DEARNE S63 ....53 G1
Dearne Valley College
DEARNE S63 ....66 A3
Dearne Valley College
(Rockingham Centre)
DEARNE S63 ....65 E2
Deepcar St Johns CE
Junior School
STKB/PEN S36 ....77 G3
Deer Park Primary School
RCH S42 ....195 F4
Denaby Ings Visitor
Centre
MEX/SWTN S64 ....68 B2
Denaby Lane Industrial
Estate
CONI DN12 ....68 A5
Denaby Main Primary
School
CONI DN12 ....68 B4
Department for Education
& Skills
SHEF S1 ....10 E7
Devonshire Green Medical
Centre
OWL S3 ....10 E4
Dinnington Business
Centre
DIN S25 ....134 C3
Dinnington Clinic
DIN S25 ....134 D5
Dinnington
Comprehensive School
DIN S25 ....134 D3
Dinnington Primary
School
DIN S25 ....134 D4
Dinnington RFC
DIN S25 ....135 F4
Dinnington St Joseph's RC
Primary School
DIN S25 ....134 D4
Dobcroft Infant School
ECC S11 ....151 H1
Dobcroft Junior School
ABRD S7 ....151 H2
Dodworth CE School
DOD/DAR S75 ....30 A4

Dodworth Health Centre
DOD/DAR S75 ....30 B3
Dodworth Keresforth
Road Primary School
DOD/DAR S75 ....30 C4
Dodworth Primary School
DOD/DAR S75 ....30 B3
The Dome Leisure Centre
DONS/BSCR DN4 ....57 F4
Doncaster Balby Central
First School
DONS/BSCR DN4 ....55 G4
Doncaster Civic Theatre
DON DN1 ....6 E4
The Doncaster Clinic
WHHL DN2 ....57 E2
Doncaster College
DON DN1 ....6 D1
Doncaster College & School
for the Deaf
WHHL DN2 ....7 K4
Doncaster Gate Hospital
RHAM/THRY S65 ....9 G4
Doncaster Golf Club
DONS/BSCR DN4 ....74 C3
Doncaster Leisure Park
DONS/BSCR DN4 ....57 F4
Doncaster Museum &
Art Gallery
DON DN1 ....6 E4
Doncaster Old (Hyde Park)
Cemetery
DON DN1 ....6 C7
Doncaster Racecourse
WHHL DN2 ....57 F3
Doncaster Racecourse
Exhibition Centre
WHHL DN2 ....57 E2
Doncaster Railport
DONS/BSCR DN4 ....56 B5
Doncaster Road Junior
School
MEX/SWTN S64 ....67 G4
Doncaster Road Primary
School
BSLY S70 ....3 J6
Doncaster Rovers FC
DONS/BSCR DN4 ....57 E3
Doncaster Royal Infirmary
WHHL DN2 ....41 E5
Doncaster Town CC
WHHL DN2 ....7 G4
Doncaster Town Moor
Golf Club
DONS/BSCR DN4 ....57 E3
Don Valley School &
Performing Arts College
DLVS DN5 ....38 D2
Don Valley Stadium
DARN/MH S9 ....127 C1
Dore House Farm
Industrial Estate
HAN/WDH S13 ....143 C1
Dore Primary School
TOT/DORE S17 ....160 D2
Dore & Totley Golf Club
TOT/DORE S17 ....162 A3
Dorothy Hyman Stadium
CUD/GR S72 ....22 A1
Drake House Retail Park
MOS S20 ....156 D2
Dronfield Cemetery
DRON S18 ....171 F3
The Dronfield Henry
Fanshawe School
DRON S18 ....171 E2
Dronfield Junior School
DRON S18 ....171 E2
The Dronfield School
DRON S18 ....170 D1
Dronfield Sports Centre
DRON S18 ....170 D2
Dunston Primary School
CHNE S41 ....186 D1
Dunston Trading Estate
CHNE S41 ....179 E4
Dykeshall Medical Centre
ST/HB/BR S6 ....113 H3
East Dene Primary School
RHAM/THRY S65 ....106 C1
East Herringthorpe
Cemetery
RHAM/THRY S65 ....107 F3
East Hill Secondary
School
SHEFN/MNR S2 ....140 C2
Eastwood Trading Estate
RHAM/THRY S65 ....98 C5
Ecclesall CE Junior School
ECC S11 ....138 C4
Ecclesall Infant School
ECC S11 ....138 B4
Ecclesall Medical Centre
ECC S11 ....138 D5
Ecclesfield Cemetery
CHPT/GREN S35 ....93 H5
Ecclesfield Comprehensive
School
CHPT/GREN S35 ....94 A3
Ecclesfield Health Centre
CHPT/GREN S35 ....94 B5
Ecclesfield Primary School
SHEFN S5 ....102 A1

Eckington Camms CE
Primary School
ECK/KIL S21 ....166 D4
Eckington Cemetery
MOS S20 ....167 E3
Eckington Health Centre
ECK/KIL S21 ....167 E5
Eckington Junior School
ECK/KIL S21 ....166 D5
Eckington School
ECK/KIL S21 ....166 A5
Eckington Swimming Pool
ECK/KIL S21 ....167 E5
Edenthorpe
Canon Popham CE
Primary School
ARMTH DN3 ....29 F4
Edenthorpe Hall Primary
School
ARMTH DN3 ....29 G5
Edlington Victoria Primary
School
CONI DN12 ....70 A5
The Edmunds Primary
School
BSLY S70 ....32 B5
Edward Sheerien
Secondary School
BSLYN/ROY S71 ....20 B1
Ellesmere Teaching School
ATT S4 ....126 C1
The Ellis CE Primary
School
WMB/DAR S73 ....50 A5
The Elmhirst School
BSLY S70 ....48 D1
Elsecar CE Primary School
HOY S74 ....62 D3
Elsecar Heritage Centre
HOY S74 ....62 C4
Elsworth House School
MALT S66 ....109 G3
Emmanuel Anglican-
Methodist Junior School
DRON S20 ....156 D4
EPPic Theatre
SHEFN S5 ....102 A1
Euro Link Business Park
DONS/BSCR DN4 ....56 C4
Fan Road Industrial Estate
STV/CWN S43 ....182 B4
Far Lane Medical Centre
ST/HB/BR S6 ....113 H3
Ferham House Clinic
KIMB S61 ....105 E3
Ferham Primary School
KIMB S61 ....8 A5
Fernbank School
AWLS/ASK DN6 ....25 G1
Fields End Business Park
DEARNE S63 ....37 G2
Fire Police Museum
OWL S3 ....11 F2
Firs Hill Community
Primary School
ATT S4 ....115 F4
Firth Park Medical Centre
SHEFN S5 ....115 H1
Firth Park School &
Community College
SHEFN S5 ....102 D4
Fir Vale School
ATT S4 ....115 H3
Flanderwell J & I School
MALT S66 ....108 B3
The Foulstone School
WMB/DAR S73 ....35 F5
Foundry Street Industrial
Estate
CHNE S41 ....187 G1
Foxhill Medical Centre
ST/HB/BR S6 ....101 F3
Fox Hill Primary School
ST/HB/BR S6 ....101 F3
Foxwood Industrial Park
CHNE S41 ....179 F5
Frenchgate Shopping
Centre
DON DN1 ....6 C3
Fullerton House School
CONI DN12 ....68 B5
The Garrison Hotel
ST/HB/BR S6 ....114 B4
Gateway Industrial
Estate
RAW S62 ....98 A4
Gawber Primary School
DOD/DAR S75 ....18 C4
Gilbert Heathcote Infant
School
CHNE S41 ....187 F1
Gillott Industrial Estate
BSLY S70 ....2 D3
Gladys Buxton School
DRON S18 ....171 G1
Gleadless Clinic
HACK/IN S12 ....154 D2
Gleadless Primary School
HACK/IN S12 ....141 H5
Globe Business Centre
ST/HB/BR S6 ....125 H2
Goldthorpe Health Centre
DEARNE S63 ....53 F1

Goldthorpe Industrial
Estate
DEARNE S63 ....52 D1
Goldthorpe Primary
School
DEARNE S63 ....37 G5
Gooseacre Primary School
DEARNE S63 ....37 E1
Gorseybrigg Infant School
DRON S18 ....170 B2
Gorseybrigg Primary
School
DRON S18 ....170 B2
Grand St Leger Hotel
DONS/BSCR DN4 ....7 J5
Grange Lane Industrial
Estate
BSLYN/ROY S71 ....33 E2
Grange Lane Infant School
NROS/TKH DN11 ....90 D3
Grange Park Golf Club
KIMB S61 ....95 G5
Grasmere School
BSLY S70 ....33 E2
Graves Art Gallery
SHEF S1 ....11 G4
Greasborough Lane
Cemetery
RAW S62 ....98 A1
Greasbrough Health Centre
KIMB S61 ....97 F3
Greasbrough J & I School
KIMB S61 ....97 F3
Great Houghton Cemetery
CUD/GR S72 ....23 H5
Great Houghton Clinic
CUD/GR S72 ....36 A1
Greenacre School
BSLY S70 ....31 E3
Green Arbour Special
School
MALT S66 ....133 E1
Greendale Shopping
Centre
DRON S18 ....171 F1
Greenfield Primary School
HOY S74 ....62 B2
Greengate Lane Primary
School
CHPT/GREN S35 ....80 C4
Greenhill Health Centre
SHEFS S8 ....162 C2
Greenhill Primary School
SHEFS S8 ....162 C1
Greenlands J & I School
DARN/MH S9 ....127 H3
Greensprings Touring Park
DOD/DAR S75 ....47 E4
Greenway Natural Health
Centre
TOT/DORE S17 ....161 E4
Grenoside Crematorium
CHPT/GREN S35 ....100 D2
Grenoside Primary School
CHPT/GREN S35 ....93 E5
Greystones First School
ECC S11 ....138 C3
Greystones Medical
Centre
ECC S11 ....138 D3
Greystones Primary
School
ECC S11 ....138 D3
Grimethorpe Cemetery
CUD/GR S72 ....23 F2
Grimethorpe Hall
CUD/GR S72 ....17 H4
Grimethorpe Ladywood
Primary School
CUD/GR S72 ....23 F1
Grove Street Primary
School
BSLYN/ROY S71 ....3 J4
Gunhills Lane Industrial
Estate
ARMTH DN3 ....43 E3
Hackenthorpe Medical
Centre
HACK/IN S12 ....156 A2
Hady Primary School
CHNE S41 ....193 F2
Halfway Infant School
MOS S20 ....167 E1
Halfway Junior School
MOS S20 ....167 E1
Hallam FM Arena
DARN/MH S9 ....116 D5
Hallam Primary School
FUL S10 ....137 G1
Hallamshire Business
Park
ECC S11 ....10 C7
Hallamshire Golf Club
FUL S10 ....123 G5
Hallamshire Natural
Health Centre
ECC S11 ....139 E2
Hall Cross Lower School
DONS/BSCR DN4 ....57 F5
Hall Cross School
DON DN1 ....7 F3
Hallowes Golf Club
DRON S18 ....171 F4

Handsworth Branch Clinic
HAN/WDH S13 ....142 D1
Handsworth Cemetery
HAN/WDH S13 ....129 E5
Handsworth Christian
School
HAN/WDH S13 ....128 D5
Handsworth Road
Medical Centre
HAN/WDH S13 ....142 D1
Hanover Medical Centre
FUL S10 ....10 C6
Hartington Industrial
Estate
STV/CWN S43 ....182 A2
Hasland Hall Community
School
CHNE S41 ....193 F5
Hasland Infant School
CHNE S41 ....193 E4
Hasland Junior School
CHNE S41 ....193 E4
Hatchell Wood Primary
School
DONS/BSCR DN4 ....74 C2
Hatfield Primary School
SHEFN S5 ....102 A3
Haugh Road Cemetery
RAW S62 ....85 E5
Havercroft Health Centre
HOR/CROF WF4 ....13 H1
Hawthorn Primary School
DONS/BSCR DN4 ....58 A4
Hayfield Lane Primary
School
EPW DN9 ....75 H4
The Hayfield School
EPW DN9 ....75 H4
Heather Garth Primary
School
DEARNE S63 ....52 D2
Heeley Business Centre
SHEFP/MNR S2 ....140 A2
Heeley City Farm
SHEFP/MNR S2 ....140 A3
Heeley Retail Park
SHEFS S8 ....152 D2
Hellaby Hall Hotel
MALT S66 ....109 H4
Hellaby Industrial Estate
MALT S66 ....109 G3
Henry Bradley Infant
School
STV/CWN S43 ....188 C1
Heritage Community
School
STV/CWN S43 ....184 D2
Heritage Park Community
School
SHEFP/MNR S2 ....140 C1
Herringthorpe J & I School
RHAM/THRY S65 ....106 D5
Herringthorpe Leisure
Centre
RHAM S60 ....106 C5
Herringthorpe Stadium
RHAM S60 ....106 C5
Hexthorpe Business Park
DONS/BSCR DN4 ....6 A5
Hexthorpe Primary
School
DONS/BSCR DN4 ....55 F4
Highfield Hall Primary
School
CHNE S41 ....187 F3
Highfields Primary School
AWLS/ASK DN6 ....25 F5
High Greave Infant
School
RHAM/THRY S65 ....107 E1
High Green Health Centre
CHPT/GREN S35 ....80 B3
High Green Primary School
CHPT/GREN S35 ....80 B3
High Hazels Golf Club
DARN/MH S9 ....128 B3
High Storrs School
ECC S11 ....138 B4
High Street Cemetery
RAW S62 ....98 A2
High Street Medical Centre
STV/CWN S43 ....182 A4
High View Primary
Learning Centre
WMB/DAR S73 ....49 H2
Highwoods Infant School
MEX/SWTN S64 ....66 C2
Hill House St Marys School
DON DN1 ....7 G2
DONS/BSCR DN4 ....57 H5
Hill Primary School
DEARNE S63 ....37 G1
Hillsborough Barracks
Shopping Mall
ST/HB/BR S6 ....114 B4
Hillsborough Golf Club
ST/HB/BR S6 ....113 E1
Hillsborough Health
Centre
ST/HB/BR S6 ....114 A5
Hillsborough Leisure
Centre
ST/HB/BR S6 ....114 B3

Hillsborough Primary School
ST/HB/BR S6 ....114 A3
Hillstown Business Centre
BSVR S44 ....197 E5
Hilltop Special School
MALT S66 ....110 B2
Hinde House School
SHEFN S5 ....103 E3
HM Prison
BTLY DN5 ....55 H2
Holgate Meadows Community Special School
SHEFN S5 ....102 A4
Holgate School Sports College
BSLY S70 ....2 B5
Holiday Inn
ATT S4 ....11 K1
Hollies Medical Centre
ECC S11 ....139 F3
Hollingwood Primary School
STV/CWN S43 ....181 E5
Hollis Hospital
ECC S11 ....151 E3
Holly House School
CHNE S41 ....179 G3
Hollywood Bowling
DARN/MH S9 ....116 D4
Holme Hall Primary School
CHSW S40 ....186 B4
Holmescarr Junior Mixed School
NROS/TKH DN11 ....91 E2
Holt House Infant School
ABRD S7 ....152 B1
Holy Cross Deanery CE Primary School
BSLYN/ROY S71 ....20 B1
Holy Rood Catholic Primary School
BSLY S70 ....2 C6
Hoober Stand
RAW S62 ....83 H1
Hotel Ibis
CHNE S41 ....5 H5
MALT S66 ....109 F4
SHEF S1 ....11 J2
STV/CWN S43 ....177 E5
Houghton Main Welfare & Sports Club
CUD/GR S72 ....36 A3
Hound Hill
BSLY S70 ....31 F5
Hoyland Cemetery
HOY S74 ....61 G2
Hoyland Common Primary School
HOY S74 ....61 E3
Hoyland St Helens RC Primary School
HOY S74 ....61 H2
Hoyland Sports Centre
HOY S74 ....61 G2
Hoyland Springwood Primary School
HOY S74 ....61 H3
HSBC Sports Club
TOT/DORE S17 ....150 D4
Hucklow Primary School
SHEFN S5 ....115 G2
Hungerhill School
ARMTH DN3 ....29 E5
Hunloke Park Primary School
RCH S42 ....195 G3
Hunningley Primary School
BSLY S70 ....33 E3
Hunters Bar Primary School
ECC S11 ....139 E2
Hutcliffe Wood Cemetery
SHEFS S8 ....152 B3
Hutcliffe Wood Crematorium
SHEFS S8 ....152 B3
Hyde Park Industrial Estate
DONS/BSCR DN4 ....6 E7
Immaculate Conception Catholic Primary School
ECK/KIL S21 ....176 A1
Inkersall Primary School
STV/CWN S43 ....189 G2
Inland Revenue Office
SHEF S1 ....10 E7
Intake Cemetery
HACK/IN S12 ....142 A4
Intake Primary School
HACK/IN S12 ....141 H4
Ireland Industrial Estate
STV/CWN S43 ....182 B5
Ironbridge Industrial Estate
HAN/WDH S13 ....143 G2
Ivanhoe J & I School
CONI DN12 ....88 C2
Jaunty Springs Health Centre
HACK/IN S12 ....154 D1

Jordanthorpe Health Centre
SHEFS S8 ....163 F2
Jump Cemetery
HOY S74 ....62 C1
Junction 34 Industrial Estate
DARN/MH S9 ....117 F3
Kelham Island Museum
OWL S3 ....126 A2
Kendray Hospital
BSLY S70 ....32 C2
Kendray Infant School
BSLY S70 ....32 B3
Kendray Primary School
BSLY S70 ....32 C3
Killamarsh County J & I School
ECK/KIL S21 ....168 C1
Killamarsh Leisure Centre
ECK/KIL S21 ....168 B1
Killamarsh Medical Centre
ECK/KIL S21 ....168 A1
Kilnhurst Business Park
MEX/SWTN S64 ....86 C5
Kilnhurst J & I School
MEX/SWTN S64 ....86 D4
Kimberworth Cemetery
KIMB S61 ....104 D3
Kimberworth Infant School
KIMB S61 ....104 D2
Kimberworth Park Clinic
KIMB S61 ....96 C5
Kimberworth Park Medical Centre
KIMB S61 ....104 C1
King Edward VII Lower School
FUL S10 ....124 C1
King Edward VII School
FUL S10 ....125 F5
King Egbert Secondary School
TOT/DORE S17 ....160 D2
Kingfisher Primary School
WHHL DN2 ....41 E3
Kings Oak Primary Learning Centre
WMB/DAR S73 ....50 C3
The Kingstone School
BSLY S70 ....2 A7
Kirk Balk School
HOY S74 ....61 G2
Kirkby Avenue Primary School
BTLY DN5 ....39 G4
Kirk Sandall Industrial Estate
ARMTH DN3 ....28 D5
Kirk Sandall J & I School
ARMTH DN3 ....29 F4
Kiveton Park Meadows Junior School
AU/AST/KP S26 ....159 G2
Lacewood Primary School
DEARNE S63 ....53 F3
Lakeside First School
DONS/BSCR DN4 ....56 D4
Lakeside Village Shopping Outlet
DONS/BSCR DN4 ....56 D5
Lantern Theatre
ABRD S7 ....139 G2
Laughton J & I School
DIN S25 ....134 B1
Lees Hall Golf Club
SHEFS S8 ....153 G3
Lenthall Infant School
DRON S18 ....163 F5
Library, Art Gallery & Regimental Museum
RHAM/THRY S65 ....9 G3
Limpsfield Junior School
DARN/MH S9 ....116 C2
Listerdale Shopping Centre
RHAM/THRY S65 ....107 G5
Little Theatre
DEARNE S63 ....36 D3
Littleworth Grange Primary Learning Centre
BSLYN/ROY S71 ....20 D5
Lodge Moor Medical Centre
FUL S10 ....137 H1
Longcar Primary School
BSLY S70 ....2 D6
Longley Park Sixth Form College
SHEFN S5 ....115 G1
Longley Primary School
SHEFN S5 ....115 E2
Lound Infant School
CHPT/GREN S35 ....80 D5
Lound Junior School
CHPT/GREN S35 ....81 E5
Lowedges Primary School
SHEFS S8 ....162 D2
Lower Meadows Primary School
SHEFS S8 ....163 E3

Lowfield Primary School
SHEFS S8 ....140 A3
Low Valley Industrial Estate
WMB/DAR S73 ....50 B3
Loxley Primary School
ST/HB/BR S6 ....112 D3
The Lyceum Theatre
SHEF S1 ....11 H4
Lydgate Infants School
FUL S10 ....124 C4
Lydgate Junior School
FUL S10 ....124 C5
Macdonald St Paul's Hotel
SHEF S1 ....11 G4
Magna Science Adventure Centre
RHAM S60 ....105 E5
Malin Bridge Primary School
ST/HB/BR S6 ....113 H4
The Mallard Primary School
DONS/BSCR DN4 ....71 E2
Maltby Cemetery
MALT S66 ....111 F3
Maltby Comprehensive School
MALT S66 ....110 D3
Maltby Crags J & I School
MALT S66 ....111 E4
Maltby Hall Infant School
MALT S66 ....110 C3
Maltby Health Centre
MALT S66 ....110 D3
Maltby Lilly Hall Junior School
MALT S66 ....110 C3
Maltby Manor Primary School
MALT S66 ....110 D3
Maltby Redwood JMI School
MALT S66 ....110 A3
Maltby St Mary's RC Primary School
MALT S66 ....111 F4
Maltby Sports Centre & Swimming Pool
MALT S66 ....110 D3
Manor Clinic
SHEFP/MNR S2 ....141 F4
Manor College
CHSW S40 ....4 D3
Manor Infant School
STV/CWN S43 ....188 D4
Manor Lodge Middle School
SHEFP/MNR S2 ....141 E1
Manor Lodge Primary School
SHEFP/MNR S2 ....141 E1
Manor Park Medical Centre
SHEFP/MNR S2 ....127 G5
Manor Top Medical Centre
SHEFP/MNR S2 ....141 G4
Mansion House
DON DN1 ....6 C3
Maple Industrial Estate
DOD/DAR S75 ....14 B4
Mapplewell Primary School
DOD/DAR S75 ....14 A3
Marcliffe Primary School
ST/HB/BR S6 ....113 H2
Marriott Hotel
ECC S11 ....139 F3
Marsden Industrial Estate
HAN/WDH S13 ....128 D5
Marshgate Industrial Estate
BTLY DN5 ....6 A2
Marsh Lane Primary School
ECK/KIL S21 ....165 G5
Mary Swanick Primary School
CHNE S41 ....179 G3
The McAuley Catholic High School
DONS/BSCR DN4 ....58 C5
Meadow Bank Industrial Estate
KIMB S61 ....104 D3
Meadowbrook Industrial Estate
MOS S20 ....157 G5
Meadowhall Junior School
DARN/MH S9 ....104 C3
Meadowhall Retail Park
DARN/MH S9 ....117 E4
Meadowhall Shopping Centre
DARN/MH S9 ....117 E1
Meadowhead Secondary School
SHEFS S8 ....163 E1
Meadows Community School
CHNE S41 ....179 H3

Meadowview Industrial Estate
ARMTH DN3 ....43 F3
Meersbrook Bank Primary School
SHEFS S8 ....139 H5
Merlin Theatre
ABRD S7 ....139 F3
ST/HB/BR S6 ....113 E3
Metrodome Sports & Leisure Complex
BSLY S70 ....3 J5
Metropolitan Shopping Centre
BSLY S70 ....3 G4
Mexborough Business Centre
MEX/SWTN S64 ....67 F3
Mexborough Bus Station
MEX/SWTN S64 ....67 E4
Mexborough Cemetery
MEX/SWTN S64 ....67 E2
Mexborough Park Road Infant School
MEX/SWTN S64 ....67 E3
Mexborough School
MEX/SWTN S64 ....66 D2
Middlecroft Leisure Centre
STV/CWN S43 ....189 H2
Milefield Primary School
CUD/GR S72 ....17 H5
Millennium Galleries
SHEF S1 ....11 H4
Millfield Industrial Estate
BTLY DN5 ....40 A1
Mill Trading Estate
BSLYN/ROY S71 ....32 B1
Milton Special School
MEX/SWTN S64 ....66 A3
Monk Bretton Cemetery
BSLYN/ROY S71 ....20 C3
Monk Bretton Health Centre
BSLYN/ROY S71 ....20 C3
Monk Bretton Priory
BSLYN/ROY S71 ....21 E5
Monksbridge Trading Estate
DIN S25 ....134 A3
Monkwood Health Centre
RAW S62 ....85 E4
Montagu Hospital
MEX/SWTN S64 ....67 E2
Montagu Junior School
MEX/SWTN S64 ....67 E2
Monteney Primary School
SHEFN S5 ....102 A2
Montgomery Theatre
SHEF S1 ....11 G3
Moorgate Business Centre
RHAM S60 ....9 G5
Moorgate Cemetery
RHAM S60 ....105 H5
Morley Place Junior School
CONI DN12 ....88 D1
Mosborough Medical Centre
MOS S20 ....166 C1
Mosborough Primary School
MOS S20 ....166 D1
Mossbrook First & Middle School
SHEFS S8 ....153 G5
Mount Osborne Industrial Park
BSLYN/ROY S71 ....32 B1
Mount St Marys College
ECK/KIL S21 ....176 A1
Mount Vernon Hospital
BSLY S70 ....31 H4
Myers Grove School
ST/HB/BR S6 ....113 G5
Mylnhurst RC School
ECC S11 ....151 H1
Nether Green Infant School
FUL S10 ....137 H2
Nether Green Junior School
FUL S10 ....138 A2
Netherthorpe Primary School
OWL S3 ....10 D1
Netherthorpe School
STV/CWN S43 ....182 C4
Newbold CE Primary School
CHNE S41 ....187 E2
Newbold Community School
CHSW S40 ....186 D3
New Bolsover Primary School
BSVR S44 ....196 C3
Newfield Secondary School
SHEFS S8 ....153 G2
The New Indoor Market
MALT S66 ....111 E3
Newman Special School
RHAM S60 ....119 G3

New Park Spring
CUD/GR S72 ....23 F3
New Street Health Centre
BSLY S70 ....3 F6
Newton Business Centre
BTLY DN5 ....55 F2
New Whittington Community Primary School
STV/CWN S43 ....180 B3
New Whittington Infant School
STV/CWN S43 ....180 B2
Nine Trees Trading Estate
MALT S66 ....121 H4
Nook Lane Junior School
ST/HB/BR S6 ....112 C5
Norfolk Community Primary School
SHEFP/MNR S2 ....141 E2
Norfolk Park Community Special School
SHEFP/MNR S2 ....140 C1
Norfolk Park Health Centre
SHEFP/MNR S2 ....140 C2
North Anston Business Centre
DIN S25 ....134 A5
North Anston Trading Estate
DIN S25 ....147 H2
Northcliffe School
CONI DN12 ....68 C5
North Derbyshire Tertiary College
BSVR S44 ....196 D3
CHSW S40 ....4 C3
STV/CWN S43 ....185 E2
North Doncaster Technology College
AWS/ASK DN6 ....25 F2
Northern General Hospital
SHEFN S5 ....115 G2
Northfield Junior School
DRON S18 ....163 G5
Northlands Community Health Centre
SHEFN S5 ....101 H5
Northpoint Industrial Estate
DARN/MH S9 ....116 D1
Norton Oakes CC
SHEFS S8 ....153 H4
Norwood Industrial Estate
ECK/KIL S21 ....158 C5
Notre Dame High School
FUL S10 ....138 C1
Novotel
SHEF S1 ....11 G4
Oakes Park School & Talbot Secondary School
SHEFS S8 ....153 G3
Oakhill Primary School
BSLY S70 ....33 G2
Oaks Business Park
BSLYN/ROY S71 ....32 D1
Oakwell Business Centre
BSLYN/ROY S71 ....32 B1
Oakwood Comprehensive School
RHAM S60 ....119 E1
Oakwood Swimming Baths
RHAM S60 ....119 F1
Oakwood Technology College
RHAM S60 ....119 E1
Octagon Centre
FUL S10 ....10 B4
Odeon Cinema
BSLY S70 ....3 G3
DON DN1 ....6 E4
SHEF S1 ....11 H5
Old College of Technology
BSLY S70 ....3 F3
Old Forge Business Park
SHEFP/MNR S2 ....140 A3
The Old Hall Centre
BTLY DN5 ....39 H2
Old Hall Junior School
CHSW S40 ....191 G2
Old Moor Nature Reserve Visitors Centre
WMB/DAR S73 ....51 G4
Open College of the Arts
DOD/DAR S75 ....18 D3
Orchard Infant School
BTLY DN5 ....54 B5
Orchard Square Shopping Centre
SHEF S1 ....11 G3
Our Lady of Mount Carmel RC Primary School
WHHL DN2 ....41 F5
Our Lady of Perpetual Help Catholic Primary School
BTLY DN5 ....39 H1
Our Lady of Sorrows VA RC Primary School
ARMTH DN3 ....42 C3
Oxspring Primary School
STKB/PEN S36 ....45 H5

Parkgate Business Park
RAW S62 ....98 B4
Parkgate Medical Centre
RAW S62 ....98 B2
Park Health Centre
SHEFP/MNR S2 ....11 K4
Park Hill Primary School
SHEFP/MNR S2 ....11 K4
Park Primary School
WHHL DN2 ....40 D4
Parkside Community
School
CHSW S40 ....4 D7
Parkside Shopping Centre
ECK/KIL S21 ....168 B1
Parkwood High School
SHEFN S5 ....114 C2
Parson Cross Primary
School
ST/HB/BR S6 ....101 F5
Pastures Hotel
MEX/SWTN S64 ....68 B3
The Pavement Shopping
Centre
CHSW S40 ....5 F4
Peacock Trading Estate
ST/HB/BR S6 ....114 C4
Pearsons Trading Estate
CHNE S41 ....187 H1
Penistone Cemetery
STKB/PEN S36 ....44 C3
Penistone Grammar
School
STKB/PEN S36 ....44 C1
Penistone CE St John the
Baptist CE Infant School
STKB/PEN S36 ....44 C4
Penistone St John the
Baptist CE Junior School
STKB/PEN S36 ....44 C4
Penistone Sports Centre
STKB/PEN S36 ....44 C4
Penistone Springvale
Primary School
STKB/PEN S36 ....45 F3
Penmore Business Centre
CHNE S41 ....193 E4
The Petersgate Medical
Centre
BTLY DN5 ....39 E2
Pheasant Bank Junior
School
NROS/TKH DN11 ....91 E2
Phillimore Park Primary
School
DARN/MH S9 ....127 H1
Phoenix Golf Club
RHAM S60 ....118 B2
Pipworth Junior School
SHEFP/MNR S2 ....142 A1
Pitt Street Infant School
MEX/SWTN S64 ....67 G4
Platts Common Industrial
Estate
HOY S74 ....61 G1
Plumb Estates
ARMTH DN3 ....28 D5
Pomegranate Theatre
CHNE S41 ....5 H4
Ponds Forge International
Sports Centre
SHEF S1 ....11 J3
Porter Croft CE Primary
School
ECC S11 ....139 G1
Portland Business Park
HAN/WDH S13 ....142 C1
Potteric Carr Nature
Reserve
DONS/BSCR DN4 ....73 E2
Premier Inn
CHNE S41 ....5 G2
DARN/MH S9 ....116 D4
DOD/DAR S75 ....60 A5
DONS/BSCR DN4 ....56 D5
RHAM/THRY S65 ....107 G5
SHEF S1 ....11 H2
WMB/DAR S73 ....51 F4
Prince Edward Primary
School
SHEFP/MNR S2 ....141 G2
Prince of Wales Road
Medical Centre
DARN/MH S9 ....128 A4
Priory School & Sports
College
BSLYN/ROY S71 ....20 D4
Pye Bank Infant School
OWL S3 ....126 B1
Queens Medical Centre
MALT S66 ....111 E3
Queens Park Leisure
Centre
CHSW S40 ....4 E5
Queens Park Sports
Ground
CHSW S40 ....4 E6
Queens Retail Park
SHEFP/MNR S2 ....140 B2
Queens Road Clinic
BSLYN/ROY S71 ....3 H4
Queen Street J & I School
MEX/SWTN S64 ....66 B5

Railwaymens Sports Club
BSLYN/ROY S71 ....13 E5
Railway Staff Social &
Sports Club
STV/CWN S43 ....180 D5
Rands Lane Industrial
Estate
ARMTH DN3 ....43 F3
Ravenside Retail Park
CHSW S40 ....5 G6
Rawmarsh Ashwood
Primary School
RAW S62 ....98 B3
Rawmarsh Community
School & Sports College
RAW S62 ....85 E5
Rawmarsh CC
RAW S62 ....98 C2
Rawmarsh Leisure Centre
RAW S62 ....98 C2
Rawmarsh Monkwood
Infant School
RAW S62 ....85 E4
Rawmarsh Monkwood
Junior School
RAW S62 ....84 D4
Rawmarsh Rosehill Junior
School
RAW S62 ....85 F4
Rawmarsh St Josephs RC
Primary School
RAW S62 ....98 C1
Rawmarsh St Marys CE
Primary School
RAW S62 ....98 B1
Rawmarsh Shopping
Centre
RAW S62 ....98 A1
Rawmarsh Thorogate
J & I School
RAW S62 ....85 F4
RC Cemetery
ST/HB/BR S6 ....124 C2
Redbrook Business Park
DOD/DAR S75 ....18 D2
Red Lion Hotel
AU/AST/KP S26 ....147 F4
Reflex Theatre
SHEFS S8 ....140 A4
Regent Hotel
DON DN1 ....6 E4
Reignhead Primary School
MOS S20 ....157 F2
Renishaw Park Golf Club
ECK/KIL S21 ....175 G1
Renishaw Primary School
ECK/KIL S21 ....175 H5
Restover Lodge Hotel
MALT S66 ....109 G4
Retail World
RHAM S60 ....98 B5
Revolution House
CHNE S41 ....179 G3
Richard Newman Primary
School
BSLYN/ROY S71 ....14 D5
Richmond Hill Primary
School
BTLY DN5 ....55 E2
Richmond Medical Centre
HAN/WDH S13 ....142 A3
Ridgeway Medical Centre
RHAM/THRY S65 ....107 E2
Ridgeway Primary School
HACK/IN S12 ....155 G5
Ridgewood School
BTLY DN5 ....38 C4
Ringwood Hall Hotel
STV/CWN S43 ....189 E1
Rivelin Primary School
ST/HB/BR S6 ....113 H5
The Robert Ogden School
DEARNE S63 ....36 D1
Rockingham Business Park
BSLY S70 ....60 D2
Rockingham J & I School
KIMB S61 ....96 D3
Rosedale Primary School
BTLY DN5 ....38 C3
Rose Hill Cemetery
DONS/BSCR DN4 ....58 A4
Rose Hill Crematorium
DONS/BSCR DN4 ....58 A4
The Rose Hill Crematorium
BSLYN/ROY S71 ....33 G3
Rossington All Saints VA
School
NROS/TKH DN11 ....91 G4
Rossington St Michaels CE
Primary School
NROS/TKH DN11 ....91 H2
Rossington Swimming
Pool
NROS/TKH DN11 ....91 F2
Rotherham Art Gallery
RHAM/THRY S65 ....9 G3
Rotherham Civic Theatre
RHAM/THRY S65 ....9 G4
Rotherham College (Clifton)
RHAM/THRY S65 ....9 F4
Rotherham College
(Howard)
RHAM S60 ....9 F4

Rotherham College of Arts
& Technology
RHAM/THRY S65 ....9 G3
Rotherham College of Art
& Technology
DIN S25 ....134 D3
Rotherham
Crematorium
RHAM/THRY S65 ....107 F3
Rotherham General
Hospital
RHAM S60 ....119 F2
Rotherham Golf Club
RHAM/THRY S65 ....99 H1
Rotherham Road Medical
Centre
BSLYN/ROY S71 ....20 A1
Rotherham RUFC
RHAM S60 ....8 B6
Rotherham Town CC
RHAM/THRY S65 ....9 J6
Rotherham Town Hall
RHAM S60 ....9 F5
Rotherham United FC
(Millmoor Ground)
KIMB S61 ....8 B5
Rother Junior School
CHSW S40 ....192 C4
Rother Valley Country
Park
AU/AST/KP S26 ....158 C4
Rother Valley Golf Club
AU/AST/KP S26 ....158 D4
Rotunda
Business Centre
CHPT/GREN S35 ....80 D3
Roughwood Primary
School
KIMB S61 ....96 C4
Rowan Primary School
TOT/DORE S17 ....161 E2
Rowena Infant School
CONI DN12 ....88 D1
Royal Hallamshire
Hospital
FUL S10 ....10 A5
Royal Hallamshire Hospital,
Jessop Wing
FUL S10 ....10 A5
Royd Infant School
STKB/PEN S36 ....77 F3
Royston Cemetery
BSLYN/ROY S71 ....15 G1
Royston Clinic
BSLYN/ROY S71 ....15 G1
Royston High School
BSLYN/ROY S71 ....12 C5
Royston Meadstead
Primary School
BSLYN/ROY S71 ....15 F1
Royston Parkside Primary
School
BSLYN/ROY S71 ....12 C5
Royston Summerfields
Primary School
BSLYN/ROY S71 ....12 A5
Rudston Preparatory
School
RHAM S60 ....9 K7
Ruskin Gallery
SHEF S1 ....11 G4
Rustlings Road Medical
Centre
ECC S11 ....138 C2
Rutland Business Park
OWL S3 ....125 H1
Ryecroft Infant School
RAW S62 ....85 G5
Sacred Heart Catholic
Primary School
DEARNE S63 ....37 G4
ST/HB/BR S6 ....114 A5
St Albans CE Primary
School
MALT S66 ....108 B5
St Albans RC J & I School
CONI DN12 ....68 C5
St Andrews CE Methodist
Primary School
DRON S18 ....170 B2
St Anns J & I School
RHAM/THRY S65 ....9 J2
St Anns Medical Centre
RHAM S60 ....9 F2
St Anns Primary School
STKB/PEN S36 ....76 D3
St Bedes RC Primary
School
KIMB S61 ....104 C1
St Bernard's Catholic High
School
RHAM/THRY S65 ....107 E4
St Catherines RC Primary
School
SHEFN S5 ....115 E4
St Francis Xavier Catholic
Primary School
DONS/BSCR DN4 ....6 A7
St Georges Church
OWL S3 ....10 D3
St Giles CE Primary
School
ECK/KIL S21 ....168 A2

St Helens Primary School
BSLYN/ROY S71 ....20 D2
St James Swimming Pool
DON DN1 ....6 D5
St John Baptist CE VA Primary
School
BSLYN/ROY S71 ....15 G1
St John Fisher RC Primary
School
HACK/IN S12 ....156 A2
St Johns CE Primary
School
MEX/SWTN S64 ....67 F2
SHEFP/MNR S2 ....126 D4
St Joseph & St Teresas
Catholic Primary School
AWLS/ASK DN6 ....25 G3
St Josephs Convent School
CHSW S40 ....4 C2
St Joseph's RC Primary
School
HAN/WDH S13 ....128 D5
St Josephs RC Primary
School
NROS/TKH DN11 ....91 F2
STV/CWN S43 ....189 H1
St Marie RC Cathedral
SHEF S1 ....11 G3
St Maries Catholic Primary
School
FUL S10 ....138 C1
St Marys Catholic Primary
School
RHAM/THRY S65 ....107 E3
St Mary's CE Primary
School
DOD/DAR S75 ....2 B3
St Mary School
ST/HB/BR S6 ....125 E2
St Marys CE Primary
School
ST/HB/BR S6 ....125 F1
St Marys High Green RC
Primary School
CHPT/GREN S35 ....80 C3
St Marys RC High School
CHNE S41 ....186 C2
St Marys RC Primary
School
CHSW S40 ....4 E2
St Matthews Infant School
DOD/DAR S75 ....2 B1
St Michael & All Angels
Catholic Primary School
WMB/DAR S73 ....50 D1
St Michaels C & CE High
School
BSLYN/ROY S71 ....15 G5
St Oswald's RC Primary
School
CHNE S41 ....127 F1
St Patricks Catholic
Primary School
SHEFN S5 ....102 C5
St Peter & St Paul School
CHNE S41 ....193 E1
St Peters Catholic Primary
School
DONS/BSCR DN4 ....57 E4
St Peters CE Primary
School
DOD/DAR S75 ....60 C3
St Theresas Catholic
Primary School
SHEFP/MNR S2 ....141 H3
St Thomas CE Primary
School
MEX/SWTN S64 ....86 C3
St Thomas More RC
Primary School
CHPT/GREN S35 ....101 F2
St Thomas of Canterbury
RC Primary School
SHEFS S8 ....152 D4
St Thomas's Cemetery
SHEFS S8 ....32 B5
Saint Vincent Medical
Centre
DON DN1 ....7 E2
St Wilfrids Catholic
Primary School
ABRD S7 ....152 A1
St Wilfrids Primary School
SHEFN S5 ....59 F5
Saltergate Health Centre
CHSW S40 ....5 F3
Saltergate Junior School
BTLY DN5 ....39 E4
Sandall Wood School
WHHL DN2 ....41 H5
Sandhill Golf Club
CUD/GR S72 ....35 H2
Sandhill JMI School
RAW S62 ....86 A5
Sandhill Primary School
CUD/GR S72 ....36 A1
Sandpiper Hotel
CHNE S41 ....179 E2
Sandringham Primary
School
WHHL DN2 ....41 F4
Scawthorpe Clinic
BTLY DN5 ....39 F3

Scawthorpe Sunnyfields
Primary School
BTLY DN5 ....39 E3
School of Nursing &
Midwifery (University
of Sheffield)
ST/HB/BR S6 ....10 A2
School of Nursing
(Sheffield University)
WHHL DN2 ....40 D5
Shafton Primary School
CUD/GR S72 ....17 F2
Shardlows Sports Club
CHPT/GREN S35 ....94 B4
Sharrow Infant School
ABRD S7 ....139 H2
Sharrow Junior School
ABRD S7 ....139 H2
Shaw Lane Industrial
Estate
WHHL DN2 ....42 A2
Shaw Wood Primary
School
ARMTH DN3 ....42 C2
Sheaf City Industrial
Estate
SHEFP/MNR S2 ....11 H3
Sheepbridge Business
Centre
CHNE S41 ....179 E4
Sheffield Area Health
Authority Sports &
Social Club
FUL S10 ....137 H3
Sheffield Airport Business
Park
DARN/MH S9 ....116 D1
Sheffield City Airport
DARN/MH S9 ....128 D1
Sheffield College
HACK/IN S12 ....155 E1
SHEF S1 ....11 J3
SHEFN S5 ....101 H2
ST/HB/BR S6 ....113 F5
STKB/PEN S36 ....77 E1
The Sheffield College
(Castle College-
Northside)
SHEFP/MNR S2 ....11 K6
The Sheffield College
(Castle College-
Southside)
SHEFP/MNR S2 ....11 K7
The Sheffield College
(Hillsborough College)
ST/HB/BR S6 ....114 B4
The Sheffield College
(Norton College)
SHEFS S8 ....163 F1
The Sheffield College
DARN/MH S9 ....117 E2
MOS S20 ....157 F5
Sheffield Eagles RLFC
DARN/MH S9 ....116 C5
Sheffield General
Cemetery
ECC S11 ....139 G2
Sheffield Hallam
University
ECC S11 ....138 D3
FUL S10 ....10 A7
SHEF S1 ....11 H5
Sheffield High School
Junior Department
FUL S10 ....125 E5
Sheffield Newspaper
Offices
SHEF S1 ....11 H2
Sheffield Park Hotel
SHEFS S8 ....163 E2
Sheffield Ski Village
OWL S3 ....114 D5
Sheffield Sports
Stadium
ST/HB/BR S6 ....114 B3
Sheffield Technology
Park
DARN/MH S9 ....127 G1
Sheffield United CC
DARN/MH S9 ....117 H3
Sheffield United FC
(Bramall Lane)
SHEFP/MNR S2 ....140 A1
Sheffield Wednesday FC
(Hillsborough)
ST/HB/BR S6 ....114 A2
Shirecliffe Junior School
SHEFN S5 ....114 C2
Shiregreen Cemetery
SHEFN S5 ....103 F5
Shire Green Medical
Centre
SHEFN S5 ....103 E3
Shooters Grove Primary
School
ST/HB/BR S6 ....113 F5
Short Brook Primary
School
MOS S20 ....157 F5
Showroom Cinema
SHEF S1 ....11 H5
Shrewsbury Hospital
SHEFP/MNR S2 ....126 C5

Silverdale School
ECC S11 ....**138** A5
Sir Harold Jackson
Primary School
TOT/DORE S17 ....**161** H3
Sitwell Arms Hotel
ECK/KIL S21 ....**175** G2
Sitwell J & I School
RHAM S60 ....**119** H1
Sitwell Park Golf Club
RHAM S60 ....**120** C1
Skate Central
SHEFP/MNR S2 ....**11** J7
Sothall Leisure Centre
MOS S20 ....**157** F2
Sothall Medical Centre
MOS S20 ....**157** F3
Southey Green Infant
School
SHEFN S5 ....**101** H5
Southey Green Medical
Centre
SHEFN S5 ....**114** D1
South Yorkshire Business
Centre
RAW S62 ....**98** A4
South Yorkshire
(Redbrook) Industrial
Estate
DOD/DAR S75 ....**18** C2
Speedwell Industrial
Estate
STV/CWN S43 ....**182** A5
Speedwell Infant School
STV/CWN S43 ....**182** A5
Spital Cemetery
CHNE S41 ....**5** K5
Springbank Community
Centre
CHSW S40 ....**4** C3
Springfield Primary School
OWL S3 ....**10** D5
Springwell Community
School
STV/CWN S43 ....**189** H2
Sprotbrough Health
Centre
BTLY DN5 ....**55** E3
Stag Medical Centre
RHAM S60 ....**120** A1
Stainborough Castle
DOD/DAR S75 ....**46** B2
Staindrop Lodge Hotel
CHPT/GREN S35 ....**81** E4
Stairfoot Health Centre
BSLY S70 ....**32** D3
Stairfoot Industrial Estate
BSLYN/ROY S71 ....**33** F2
Stannington Health
Centre
ST/HB/BR S6 ....**123** G1
Stannington Infant
School
ST/HB/BR S6 ....**123** G1
Station Lane Industrial
Estate
CHNE S41 ....**179** H4
Station Rd Industrial
Estate
STV/CWN S43 ....**185** E2
Station Road Industrial
Estate
WMB/DAR S73 ....**50** C2
Station Road J & I School
CONI DN12 ....**68** D5
Staveley Cemetery
STV/CWN S43 ....**182** A5
Staveley Health Clinic
STV/CWN S43 ....**182** A5
Staveley Junior School
STV/CWN S43 ....**181** H5
Staveley Norbriggs
County Infants School
STV/CWN S43 ....**183** E3
Stirling Primary School
DON DN1 ....**6** C7
Stocksbridge Cemetery
STKB/PEN S36 ....**77** E2
Stocksbridge & District
Golf Club
STKB/PEN S36 ....**77** F4
Stocksbridge High School
STKB/PEN S36 ....**76** D2
Stocksbridge Infant School
STKB/PEN S36 ....**76** D2
Stocksbridge
Junior School
STKB/PEN S36 ....**76** D3
Stocksbridge Leisure
Centre
STKB/PEN S36 ....**76** C2
Stocksbridge RFC
STKB/PEN S36 ....**76** D1
Stonelow Junior School
DRON S18 ....**171** G1
Storforth Lane Trading
Estate
CHNE S41 ....**192** D4
Stradbroke Primary
School
HAN/WDH S13 ....**142** B3
Strafford Industrial Park
DOD/DAR S75 ....**30** C5

Sues Health Centre
BSLYN/ROY S71 ....**15** E4
Summer Lane Primary
School
DOD/DAR S75 ....**2** B2
Superbowl 2000
KIMB S61 ....**104** C1
Superintendent
Swimming Baths
CHPT/GREN S35 ....**94** A1
Swallownest Health
Centre
AU/AST/KP S26 ....**145** F3
Swallownest Primary
School
AU/AST/KP S26 ....**144** D2
Swinton Brookfield
Primary School
MEX/SWTN S64 ....**86** B1
Swinton Community
School
MEX/SWTN S64 ....**86** A1
Swinton Fitzwilliam J & I
School
MEX/SWTN S64 ....**85** H1
Swinton Meadows
Business Park
MEX/SWTN S64 ....**66** D5
Swinton Meadows
Industrial Estate
MEX/SWTN S64 ....**66** D5
Swinton Swimming Pool
MEX/SWTN S64 ....**66** B5
Sycamore Hall
Preparatory School
DONS/BSCR DN4 ....**71** C1
Talbot School
SHEFS S8 ....**153** C4
Tankersley Manor Hotel
DOD/DAR S75 ....**60** C5
Tankersley Park Golf Club
CHPT/GREN S35 ....**81** E2
Tapton Park Golf Club
CHNE S41 ....**188** A5
Templeborough Business
Centre
RHAM S60 ....**105** C5
Tertiary College
ECK/KIL S21 ....**166** D5
Thomas Rotherham
College
RHAM S60 ....**106** A5
Thornbury Hospital
FUL S10 ....**138** B1
Thornhill Industrial Estate
RHAM S60 ....**8** D1
Thornhill Primary School
RHAM S60 ....**8** C3
Thorpe Hesley Clinic
KIMB S61 ....**95** F2
Thorpe Hesley Infant
School
KIMB S61 ....**95** E2
Thorpe Hesley Junior
School
KIMB S61 ....**95** F2
Thrybergh Comprehensive
School
RHAM/THRY S65 ....**99** H3
Thrybergh Fullerton CE
Primary School
RHAM/THRY S65 ....**99** H3
Thrybergh Medical
Centre
RHAM/THRY S65 ....**99** H4
Thrybergh St Gerards RC
M & I School
RHAM/THRY S65 ....**99** F4
Thurcroft Cemetery
MALT S66 ....**133** E2
Thurcroft Infant School
MALT S66 ....**133** E1
Thurcroft Junior School
MALT S66 ....**133** F1
Thurlstone Primary
School
STKB/PEN S36 ....**44** A2
Thurnscoe Business
Centre
DEARNE S63 ....**37** G2
Thurnscoe Cemetery
DEARNE S63 ....**36** D3
Tickhill Road Hospital
DONS/BSCR DN4 ....**71** H3
Tinsley Industrial Estate
DARN/MH S9 ....**128** A1
Tinsley Infant School
DARN/MH S9 ....**117** G2
Tinsley Junior School
DARN/MH S9 ....**117** G3
Tinsley Park Cemetery
DARN/MH S9 ....**128** B1
Todwick JMI School
AU/AST/KP S26 ....**147** E5
Toll Bar Primary School
BTLY DN5 ....**26** C2
Tornedale Infant School
NROS/TKH DN11 ....**91** F2
Totley All Saints CE
Primary School
TOT/DORE S17 ....**160** C4
Town End Industrial Estate
BTLY DN5 ....**55** G1

Townfield Primary School
DON DN1 ....**7** G2
Trafalgar House Medical
Centre
ST/HB/BR S6 ....**101** F5
Tramways Medical Centre
ST/HB/BR S6 ....**114** A4
Tranmoor Infant & Junior
School
ARMTH DN3 ....**42** D5
Travelodge
BSLY S70 ....**33** E2
CHNE S41 ....**187** G1
SHEFP/MNR S2 ....**128** A5
Treeton CE Primary School
RHAM S60 ....**130** A4
Trinity Croft Primary
School
RHAM/THRY S65 ....**107** F1
Turner Museum of Glass
SHEF S1 ....**10** E3
Turnoaks Business Park
CHSW S40 ....**195** C1
TV Studios
SHEF S1 ....**11** F5
UCI Cinema
MOS S20 ....**157** E2
Ulley Country Park
AU/AST/KP S26 ....**131** F3
University of Sheffield
FUL S10 ....**10** A5
FUL S10 ....**124** D5
FUL S10 ....**138** C1
SHEF S1 ....**10** E3
Unstone Junior School
DRON S18 ....**172** A4
Unstone St Marys Infant
School
DRON S18 ....**172** B3
Upperthorpe Healthy
Living Centre
ST/HB/BR S6 ....**125** G2
Valley Park Community
School
GLV S14 ....**154** A3
Valley Park Industrial
Estate
WMB/DAR S73 ....**51** E4
Vanguard Trading Estate
CHSW S40 ....**192** C5
Verdon Recreation
Centre
OWL S3 ....**126** B2
Victoria Hall
SHEF S1 ....**11** H3
Victoria Quays Shopping
Centre
SHEFP/MNR S2 ....**11** J2
Vue Cinema
DARN/MH S9 ....**117** E2
DONS/BSCR DN4 ....**57** E4
Wales High School
AU/AST/KP S26 ....**159** G2
Wales J & I School
AU/AST/KP S26 ....**159** F3
Walkley Medical Centre
ST/HB/BR S6 ....**125** E1
Walkley Primary School
ST/HB/BR S6 ....**114** B5
Waltheof Secondary
School
SHEFP/MNR S2 ....**127** H5
Walton Holymoorside
Primary School
RCH S42 ....**190** B5
Walton Hospital
CHSW S40 ....**192** A5
Ward Green Primary
School
BSLY S70 ....**31** H4
Wardsend Cemetery
SHEFN S5 ....**114** C3
Warmsworth Halt
Industrial Estate
DONS/BSCR DN4 ....**70** C4
Warmsworth Primary
School
DONS/BSCR DN4 ....**70** C2
Warwick Street Industrial
Estate
CHSW S40 ....**192** D4
Waterdale Centre
DON DN1 ....**6** C4
Water Sports Centre
AU/AST/KP S26 ....**158** B4
Waterthorpe Infant
School
MOS S20 ....**157** E3
Wath Cemetery
DEARNE S63 ....**65** E3
Wath Central Primary
School
DEARNE S63 ....**65** E3
Wath CE Primary School
DEARNE S63 ....**65** E1
Wath Comprehensive
School Language College
DEARNE S63 ....**65** F3
Wath Golf Club
RAW S62 ....**84** D1
Wath Our Lady & St Josephs
RC Primary School
DEARNE S63 ....**65** F2

Wath RUFC
DEARNE S63 ....**65** F1
Wath Victoria Primary
School
DEARNE S63 ....**65** G2
Wath West Industrial
Estate
DEARNE S63 ....**51** G5
Waverley Primary School
DONS/BSCR DN4 ....**71** E2
Wentworth Castle
DOD/DAR S75 ....**46** B2
Wentworth Castle College
of Education
DOD/DAR S75 ....**46** B2
Wentworth CE Primary
School
RAW S62 ....**82** C2
Wentworth Industrial
Park
DOD/DAR S75 ....**60** C4
Westbourne School
FUL S10 ....**125** E5
Westfield Health Centre
MOS S20 ....**157** E5
Westfield Infant School
CHSW S40 ....**191** F2
Westfield Secondary
School
MOS S20 ....**156** D5
West Meadows Primary
School
HOY S74 ....**61** G2
West Melton Primary
School
DEARNE S63 ....**64** C1
Weston Park Hospital
FUL S10 ....**125** F4
Weston Park Museum
FUL S10 ....**10** A3
Westways Primary
School
FUL S10 ....**125** E3
Westwood Country Park
CHPT/GREN S35 ....**80** C2
Westwood Industrial
Estate
ARMTH DN3 ....**43** E5
Wharncliffe Industrial
Complex
STKB/PEN S36 ....**78** A2
Wheatbridge Retail Park
CHSW S40 ....**4** D5
Wheatley Golf Club
WHHL DN2 ....**41** H4
Wheatley Hall Business
Centre
WHHL DN2 ....**41** E3
Whiston Grange School
RHAM S60 ....**119** G3
Whiston Primary School
RHAM S60 ....**119** H2
Whiston Worry Goose JMI
School
RHAM S60 ....**120** B3
Whitecotes Primary
School
CHSW S40 ....**192** B4
Whitelea Grove Trading
Estate
MEX/SWTN S64 ....**66** C4
Whiteley Wood Clinic
FUL S10 ....**138** A3
Whiteways Junior School
ATT S4 ....**115** H4
Whitley Hall CC
CHPT/GREN S35 ....**93** G5
Whitley Hall Hotel
CHPT/GREN S35 ....**93** G4
Whittington Medical
Centre
CHNE S41 ....**179** G3
Whittington Moor
Surgery
CHNE S41 ....**187** H2
Wickersley Health Centre
MALT S66 ....**108** B4
Wickersley School &
Sports College
MALT S66 ....**108** C5
William Levick Infant
School
DRON S18 ....**170** A1
William Levick Primary
School
DRON S18 ....**170** A1
William Rhodes Primary
School
CHSW S40 ....**4** C6
Wilthorpe Infant School
DOD/DAR S75 ....**19** E3
Wilthorpe Junior School
DOD/DAR S75 ....**19** E3
Wincobank Infant School
DARN/MH S9 ....**103** G5
Windhill Primary School
MEX/SWTN S64 ....**67** G2
The Winding Wheel
Theatre
CHNE S41 ....**5** H2
Windmill Hill Primary
School
CHPT/GREN S35 ....**93** H2

Wingfield Comprehensive
School
KIMB S61 ....**97** E4
Winter Garden
SHEF S1 ....**11** G4
Winterhill School
KIMB S61 ....**104** C2
Wisewood Cemetery
ST/HB/BR S6 ....**112** D4
Wisewood Primary School
ST/HB/BR S6 ....**113** F3
Wisewood Secondary
School
ST/HB/BR S6 ....**113** F3
Wombwell Cemetery
WMB/DAR S73 ....**50** A2
Wombwell Clinic
WMB/DAR S73 ....**50** A2
Wombwell CC
WMB/DAR S73 ....**49** H3
Wombwell High School
WMB/DAR S73 ....**50** C4
Wombwell Jump Primary
School
HOY S74 ....**62** B1
Wombwell Park Street
Primary School
WMB/DAR S73 ....**50** C3
Wombwell Public Baths
WMB/DAR S73 ....**50** B3
Woodbourn Athletics
Centre
DARN/MH S9 ....**127** F2
Woodbourn Road
Stadium
DARN/MH S9 ....**127** F2
Woodfield Primary School
DONS/BSCR DN4 ....**71** H2
Woodhouse Clinic
HAN/WDH S13 ....**143** F4
Woodhouse Medical
Centre
HAN/WDH S13 ....**143** F4
Woodlands Primary
School
AWLS/ASK DN6 ....**25** E3
Woodseats Medical
Centre
SHEFS S8 ....**152** D3
Woodseats Primary
School
SHEFS S8 ....**152** D2
Woodthorpe CE Primary
School
STV/CWN S43 ....**183** E5
Woodthorpe Community
Primary School
HAN/WDH S13 ....**142** H3
Woolley Wood J & I School
SHEFN S5 ....**103** E3
Wool Market
DON DN1 ....**6** D3
Worsbrough Bank End
Primary School
BSLY S70 ....**32** C4
Worsbrough Common
Primary School
BSLY S70 ....**31** H4
Worsbrough Health Centre
BSLY S70 ....**32** B5
Worsbrough Mill Country
Park
BSLY S70 ....**47** G2
Worsbrough Mill Museum
BSLY S70 ....**48** A2
Worsbrough St Marys CE
Primary School
BSLY S70 ....**47** H4
Wybourn Primary School
SHEFP/MNR S2 ....**126** D3
Yewlands School
CHPT/GREN S35 ....**101** G2
York & Lancaster
Regimental Museum
RHAM/THRY S65 ....**9** G3
York House Medical
Centre
SHEFP/MNR S2 ....**141** H1
Yorkshire Neurology
Clinic
MALT S66 ....**108** A5
Youth & Community
Centre
MALT S66 ....**110** G2

Schools address data provided by Education Direct.

Petrol station information supplied by Johnsons

Garden centre information provided by

Garden Centre Association Britains best garden centres

Wyevale Garden Centres

The statement on the front cover of this atlas is sourced, selected and quoted
from a reader comment and feedback form received in 2004

How do I find the perfect place?

AA Street by Street   QUESTIONNAIRE

Dear Atlas User
Your comments, opinions and recommendations are very important to us.
So please help us to improve our street atlases by taking a few minutes
to complete this simple questionnaire.

You do not need a stamp (unless posted outside the UK). If you do not want to remove
this page from your street atlas, then photocopy it or write your answers on a plain sheet
of paper.

Send to: Marketing Assistant, AA Publishing, 14th Floor Fanum House,
Freepost SCE 4598, Basingstoke RG21 4GY

ABOUT THE ATLAS...

Please state which city / town / county you bought:

_____

Where did you buy the atlas? (City, Town, County)

_____

For what purpose? (please tick all applicable)

To use in your local area ☐   **To use on business or at work** ☐

Visiting a strange place ☐   **In the car** ☐   **On foot** ☐

Other (please state)

_____

Have you ever used any street atlases other than AA Street by Street?

Yes ☐   **No** ☐

If so, which ones?

_____

Is there any aspect of our street atlases that could be improved?
(Please continue on a separate sheet if necessary)

_____
_____
_____

ML072y

continued overleaf

Please list the features you found most useful:

_____

_____

Please list the features you found least useful:

_____

_____

_____

LOCAL KNOWLEDGE...

Local knowledge is invaluable. Whilst every attempt has been made to make the information contained in this atlas as accurate as possible, should you notice any inaccuracies, please detail them below (if necessary, use a blank piece of paper) or e-mail us at _streetbystreet@theAA.com_

_____

_____

_____

ABOUT YOU...

Name (Mr/Mrs/Ms) _____

Address _____

                                             Postcode _____

Daytime tel no _____

E-mail address _____

Which age group are you in?

Under 25 ☐   **25-34** ☐   **35-44** ☐   **45-54** ☐   **55-64** ☐   **65+** ☐

Are you an AA member?   **YES** ☐   **NO** ☐

Do you have Internet access?   **YES** ☐   **NO** ☐

_____

Thank you for taking the time to complete this questionnaire. Please send it to us as soon as possible, and remember, you do not need a stamp (unless posted outside the UK).

We may use information we hold about you to, telephone or email you about other products and services offered by the AA, we do NOT disclose this information to third parties.

Please tick here if you do not wish to hear about products and services from the AA. ☐

ML072y